NEGOTIATION
Readings, Exercises, and Cases

NEGOTIATION
Readings, Exercises, and Cases

Fourth Edition

Roy J. Lewicki
The Ohio State University

David M. Saunders
University of Calgary

John W. Minton
Havatar Associates, Inc.

Bruce Barry
Vanderbilt University

Boston   Burr Ridge, IL   Dubuque, IA   Madison, WI   New York
San Francisco   St. Louis   Bangkok   Bogotá   Caracas   Kuala Lumpur
Lisbon   London   Madrid   Mexico City   Milan   Montreal   New Delhi
Santiago   Seoul   Singapore   Sydney   Taipei   Toronto

McGraw-Hill Higher Education

A Division of The McGraw-Hill Companies

NEGOTIATION: READINGS, EXERCISES, AND CASES
Published by McGraw-Hill/Irwin, a business unit of The McGraw-Hill Companies, Inc., 1221 Avenue of the Americas, New York, NY, 10020. Copyright © 2003, 1999, 1993, and 1985 by The McGraw-Hill Companies, Inc. All rights reserved. No part of this publication may be reproduced or distributed in any form or by any means, or stored in a database or retrieval system, without the prior written consent of The McGraw-Hill Companies, Inc., including, but not limited to, in any network or other electronic storage or transmission, or broadcast for distance learning.

Some ancillaries, including electronic and print components, may not be available to customers outside the United States.

This book is printed on acid-free paper.

domestic   1 2 3 4 5 6 7 8 9 0 DOC/DOC 0 9 8 7 6 5 4 3 2
international   1 2 3 4 5 6 7 8 9 0 DOC/DOC 0 9 8 7 6 5 4 3 2

ISBN 0-07-242965-8

Publisher: *John E. Biernat*
Senior editor: *John Weimeister*
Editorial coordinator: *Trina Hauger*
Senior marketing manager: *Ellen Cleary*
Senior project manager: *Christine A. Vaughan*
Lead production supervisor: *Heather D. Burbridge*
Coordinator freelance design: *Mary L. Christianson*
Producer, Media technology: *Mark Molsky*
Supplement producer: *Joyce J. Chappetto*
Freelance cover designer: *Sarah Studnicki*
Typeface: *10/12 Times Roman*
Compositor: *Electronic Publishing Services, Inc., TN*
Printer: *R.R. Donnelley & Sons Company*

Library of Congress Cataloging-in-Publication Data

Negotiation.—4th Ed. [edited by] Roy J. Lewicki ... [et al.].
   p. cm.
  Includes index.
  ISBN 0-07-242965-8 (alk. paper) — ISBN 0-07-112316-4 (international : alk. paper)
   1. Negotiation in business. 2. Negotiation. 3. Negotiation—Case studies.
HD58.6 .N45 2003
658.4'052—dc21   2002024635

INTERNATIONAL EDITION ISBN 0-07-112316-4
Copyright © 2003. Exclusive rights by The McGraw-Hill Companies, Inc. for manufacture and export. This book cannot be re-exported from the country to which it is sold by McGraw-Hill. The International Edition is not available in North America.

www.mhhe.com

We dedicate this book to all negotiation, mediation, and dispute resolution professionals who try to make the world a more peaceful and prosperous place.

About the Authors

Roy J. Lewicki is the Dean's Distinguished Teaching Professor and a professor of management and human resources at the Max M. Fisher College of Business, The Ohio State University. He has authored or edited 24 books, as well as numerous research articles. Professor Lewicki has served as the president of the International Association of Conflict Management and received the first David Bradford Outstanding Educator award from the Organizational Behavior Teaching Society for his contributions to the field of teaching in negotiation and dispute resolution.

David M. Saunders is dean of the Faculty of Management at the University of Calgary. He has co-authored several articles on negotiation, conflict resolution, employee voice, and organizational justice. Prior to accepting his current appointment, he was director of the McGill MBA Japan program in Tokyo, and he has traveled extensively throughout Asia, Europe, and South America.

John W. Minton is the president and CEO of Havatar Associates, Inc., a management consultation, development, coaching, and recruiting firm specializing in meeting the needs of small and medium-sized organizations. He has taught in the business schools of Appalachian State and Duke Universities and at Pfeiffer University, where he was the Jefferson-Pilot Professor of Management. He is currently an adjunct professor at Gardner-Webb University and has served as a volunteer mediator and arbitrator.

Bruce Barry is an associate professor of management and sociology at Vanderbilt University and also director of the PhD program at Vanderbilt's Owen Graduate School of Management. His research on negotiation, influence, power, and justice has appeared in numerous scholarly journals and volumes. Professor Barry is serving a term as president of the International Association for Conflict Management (2002–2003), a professional society of researchers, teachers, and practitioners specializing in the fields of conflict, dispute resolution, and negotiation.

Preface

People negotiate every day. During an average day, a person may negotiate with

> The boss, regarding an unexpected work assignment.
>
> Subordinates, regarding unexpected overtime.
>
> A supplier, about a problem with raw materials inventory management.
>
> A banker, over the terms of a business loan.
>
> A government official, regarding the compliance with environmental regulations.
>
> A real estate agent, over the lease on a new warehouse.
>
> His/her spouse, over who will walk the dog.
>
> His/her child, over who will walk the dog (still an issue after losing the previous negotiation).
>
> The dog, once out, as to whether any "business" gets done.

In short, negotiation is a common, everyday activity that most people use to influence others and to achieve personal objectives. In fact, negotiation is not only common but also essential to living an effective and satisfying life. We all need things—resources, information, cooperation, and support from others. Others have those needs as well, sometimes compatible with ours, sometimes not. Negotiation is a process by which we attempt to influence others to help us achieve our needs, while at the same time taking their needs into account. It is a fundamental skill, not only for successful management but also for successful living.

In 1985, Roy Lewicki and Joseph Litterer published the first edition of this book. As they were preparing that volume, it was clear that the basic processes of negotiation had received only selective attention in both the academic and practitioner literature. Scholars of negotiation had generally restricted examination of these processes to basic theory development and laboratory research in social psychology, to a few books written for managers, and to an examination of negotiation in complex settings such as diplomacy and labor–management relations. Efforts to draw from the broader study of techniques for influence and persuasion, to integrate this work into a broader understanding of negotiation, or to apply this work to a broad spectrum of conflict and negotiation settings were only beginning to occur.

In the past 17 years this world has changed significantly. There are several new practitioner organizations, such as the Society for Professionals in Dispute Resolution and the Association for Conflict Resolution, and academic professional associations, such as the Conflict Management Division of the Academy of Management and the International Association for Conflict Management, that have devoted themselves exclusively to facilitating research and teaching in the fields of negotiation and conflict management. There are several new journals (*Negotiation Journal, International Journal of Conflict Management, International Negotiation*) that focus exclusively on research in these fields. Finally, through the generosity of the Hewlett Foundation, there are a number of university centers that have devoted themselves to enhancing the quality of teaching, research, and service in the negotiation and conflict management fields. Many schools now have several courses in negotiation and conflict management—in schools of business, law, public policy, psychology, social work, education, and natural resources. Development has occurred in the practitioner side as well. Books, seminars, and training courses on negotiation and conflict management abound. And, finally, mediation has become an extremely popular process as an alternative to litigation for handling divorce, community disputes, and land-use conflicts. In pragmatic terms, all of this development means that as we assembled this fourth edition, we have had a much richer and more diverse pool of resources from which to sample. The net result for the student and instructor is a highly improved book of readings and exercises that contains many new articles, cases, and exercises, which represent the very best and most recent work on negotiation and the related topics of power, influence, and conflict management.

A brief overview of this book is in order. The Readings portion of the book is ordered into 14 sections: (1) the Nature of Negotiation, (2) Prenegotiation Planning, (3) Strategy and Tactics of Distributive Bargaining, (4) Strategy and Tactics of Integrative Negotiating, (5) Communication and Cognitive Biases, (6) Finding Negotiation Leverage, (7) Ethics in Negotiation, (8) Social Context, (9) Teams and Group Negotiations, (10) Individual Differences, (11) Global Negotiations, (12) Managing Difficult Negotiation Situations: Individual Approaches, (13) Managing Difficult Negotiation Situations: Third-Party Approaches, and (14) Applications of Negotiation.

The next portion of the book presents a collection of role-play exercises, cases, and self-assessment questionnaires that can be used to teach about negotiation processes and subprocesses. **Complete information about the use or adaptation of these materials for several classroom formats is provided in our accompanying Instructor's Manual, which faculty members may obtain from their local McGraw-Hill/Irwin representative, by calling (800) 634–3963 or by visiting the McGraw-Hill website at www.mhhe.com.**

For those readers familiar with the earlier editions of this book, the most visible changes in this edition are to the book's content and organization, as follows:

- The content of this edition is substantially new. Over half of the readings are new to this edition, and the exercises and cases that are not new to this edition have been revised and updated.

- We have reorganized the book slightly. We have organized the Readings portion of the book into the sections described above. We have combined discussion of interdependence with the introduction to negotiation, have included cognitive biases in the communication section, have combined power and persuasion under the heading of leverage, and have better highlighted approaches to take when negotiations go wrong. Section 14, on applications, is entirely new, offering important articles on negotiation applications that do not neatly fit into the 13 core sections.

- The structure of this book parallels that of a completely revised textbook, *Negotiation* by Lewicki, Barry, Saunders, and Minton (4th ed.), also published by McGraw-Hill/Irwin. The text and reader can be used together, or separately. A shorter version of the text, *Essentials of Negotiation* (2d ed.) by Lewicki, Saunders, and Minton, can also be used in conjunction with this readings book; a third edition of *Essentials* should be available in late 2003. We encourage instructors to contact their local McGraw-Hill/Irwin representative for an examination copy—call (800) 634–3963, or visit the website at www.mhhe.com.

- Finally, somewhat less visible but no less important, we are delighted to welcome Bruce Barry of Vanderbilt University to the editorial team! Bruce has an excellent reputation as a teacher and research scholar, and we are delighted to incorporate his ideas and hard work into this revision.

This book could not have been completed without the assistance of numerous people. We especially thank

- The many authors and publishers who granted us permission to use or adapt their work for this book and whom we have recognized in conjunction with specific exercises, cases, or articles.

- The many negotiation instructors and trainers who inspired several of the exercises in this book and who have given us excellent feedback on the previous editions of this book.

- The staff of McGraw-Hill/Irwin, especially our current editor, John Weimeister, and our previous editors, John Biernat, Kurt Strand, and Karen Johnson; Trina Hauger and Tracy Jensen, editorial assistants who can solve almost any problem; and Christine Vaughan, tireless project manager who helped to turn our confusing instructions and tedious prose into eminently readable and usable volumes!

- Our families, who continue to provide us with the time, inspiration, opportunities for continued learning about effective negotiation, and personal support required to finish this project.

Roy J. Lewicki
David M. Saunders
John W. Minton
Bruce Barry

Contents

Exercises   510

Cases   603

Questionnaires   691

SECTION ONE

The Nature of Negotiation

How to Get Them to Show You the Money

Alan M. Webber

It was the phrase of 1997: "Show me the money!" and though the words came from the movie *Jerry Maguire,* they originated in the world of Leigh Steinberg, agent to the sports elite, who was the model for Tom Cruise's character and whose office memorabilia doubled as that of the movie's fictional agent. Steinberg, 49, has been negotiating high-profile, high-stakes contracts for 24 years—ever since he stumbled onto the field of sports law by helping out Steve Bartkowski, a fellow University of California graduate who became the top NFL draft pick in 1975. Bartkowski landed what was then the richest rookie contract ever—$650,000 for four years—and Steinberg began his career as a sports lawyer.

Now Steinberg's firm, Steinberg & Moorad, represents more than 100 athletes and negotiates multimillion-dollar deals for such clients as Troy Aikman, Steve Young, Drew Bledsoe, Warren Moon, and Ryan Leaf. Sensing the growth of the free-agent market in the business world, Steinberg is now exploring ways to expand his practice to include negotiating on behalf of the talent that companies need to attract. As a lawyer and a businessman, Steinberg is involved in several high-tech ventures, including Interplay Productions Inc. (a video-game publisher), Motion Vision Inc. (which sells sports trading cards that show athletes in action via digitized video), and EastSport (which puts sports programming on the Web).

What distinguishes Steinberg's sports-representation practice, however, is his approach to negotiation. To Steinberg, negotiations are a part of everyday life, and they need to be handled with a clear focus and a principled philosophy: "The goal," he says, "is not to destroy the other side. The goal is to find the most profitable way to complete a deal that works for *both* sides." Steinberg insists that his clients look at their negotiations, and at their athletic careers, not just as tests of talent but as tests of character as well. He also encourages them to "give back" part of their huge paychecks to their community—by establishing foundations or by contributing to causes.

In the recently published *Winning with Integrity: Getting What You're Worth without Selling Your Soul* (Random House, 1998, written with Michael D'Orso), Steinberg lays out his philosophy of business, his approach to negotiating, and his techniques for achieving positive results. To find out how you can get people to show *you* the money, Fast Company interviewed Steinberg in his office in Newport Beach, California.

EVERYONE IS A NEGOTIATOR

We're always negotiating, every day of our lives and in every kind of situation—whether it's a boyfriend and girlfriend deciding which movie to see, a husband and wife deciding which city to live in, a customer looking to buy an automobile, or an employee trying to get a raise. We all negotiate. But many of us still have a fundamental fear of negotiation. That fear can make us act meek and obsequious—which means that we're likely to end up with our goals unmet. Or it can make us behave aggressively and angrily—which would break down the discussion altogether. Anybody can learn to negotiate. There is no magic. There are no mirrors. What you need is an understanding of human psychology and an open mind. You need to be able to listen and to have respect for the other person in the negotiation. You don't need to be the stereotypical tough guy. You need to look at negotiations as a process that can be exciting, as an opportunity to improve your condition or to enhance your situation, rather than as a terrifying confrontation.

FIRST, NEGOTIATE WITH YOURSELF

The first key step is introspection. You need the clearest possible view of your goals. And you need to be brutally honest with yourself about your priorities. There are no perfect situations in life, so you will need to make choices. If you don't face that fact, you run the risk of cognitive dissonance: You'll feel increasingly torn between mutually exclusive alternatives, and you'll become more and more confused. That confusion leads to stress, and since the human psyche can withstand only so much stress, you'll be tempted to make a decision—even if it's the wrong decision—just to relieve that stress.

So you start with a comprehensive personal inventory: What do you value most? Is it short-term gain or long-term security? Is it the ability to live or work in a certain geographic area? Is it the culture of your company or the attitudes of the people you work with? Is it a high degree of autonomy or an opportunity to be creative? Is it something as simple as the hours you work, the amount of vacation time you get, or the size and quality of your office? In this constellation of values, each factor may be important. But the question is, What is *most* important? Before you enter a negotiation, you need to establish your priorities.

MOVE FROM YOUR VALUES TO YOUR VALUE

After you've come to terms with your own values, the next step is to understand your value in the world. What are your unique skills and talents? Are you irreplaceable because of those skills and talents, or could anyone fill your slot? To answer these questions, you need to do some research into your own performance—and there are all sorts of tools that you can use. There are internal and external documents that address the issue of employee value, and sometimes you can get actual employee ratings. You can also get important information by talking and listening to other people: What is the market for your services outside your company? What are employees paid at other, comparable companies?

You also need to do research on the person you'll be negotiating with. What is his agenda? How much authority does he have? Is he attempting to impress his boss? What is his track record? Can you find out about previous negotiations that he has been in? What are his negotiating tendencies?

Next, assemble that information into a document that tells your story. Think of it as equivalent to the storybook that I create for sports negotiation: My document details, say, a quarterback's efficiency rating—his completed passes, his touchdowns versus interceptions—as well as his team's overall performance. Your document could include charts that show how productive you've been: This is where sales stood the day I began my job, and this is where they stand today. That's the story of your personal performance. You could also discuss company goals and performance.

But remember: Make sure that this is a confidential document, particularly if it contains head-to-head comparisons and actual rankings. You don't want it to create problems with your coworkers. The important thing is to present a theory about why you merit a certain level of compensation or a certain work situation. Your story should advance that theory.

FIND OUT THE OTHER PERSON'S AGENDA—AND EMBRACE IT

As you do your research, you must put yourself into the mind of the person you'll be negotiating with. You need to ask yourself a set of questions about his point of view: What represents a successful result for him? What will constitute a win for him in a negotiation session? How can you make him look better?

Find out the other person's agenda. And assume that he will be doing the same with you. You must come into a session with your homework done. Otherwise, you'll be showing the other side a fundamental lack of respect.

PRACTICE DEALING WITH FEAR

Most negotiating is tap dancing on the edge of an abyss. The reality is that this may be the best job for you, this may be the most money you will ever make—and yet, if you allow fear to fill you with anxiety, it can paralyze you. So, in any negotiation, part of your mental preparation must be to deal with fear. Remember that walking away from a negotiation is always an option. You've got to ignore the fear that you may find yourself unemployed.

The best analogy is to the fear of death. It's inevitable that we're going to die. That's a fearsome prospect, an inescapable reality. And yet the only way to live well is to come to peace with that fact and not to let it haunt your every moment. Fear comes with the territory of negotiation. But fear needs to be managed, and it needs to be kept in perspective. One way to diffuse your fear is to confront the words that make you afraid, so that they lose some of their sting. Practice saying the words that are hardest for you to hear, or that are hardest for you to say: "If you won't take this proposal, then I guess we have nothing more to talk about." "I'm going to have to start looking for someone to replace you." Or, if you're trying to get up the courage to walk away: "Obviously this is not the place for me. I'm looking for a new job." Rid these words of their power to paralyze.

WHOSE REALITY WILL PREVAIL?

Ultimately, negotiating is all about whose concept of reality is going to prevail. You're facing an amorphous, confusing situation with dozens of variables. Whose vision will prove the most compelling?

In some cases, it's hard to know whom you're dealing with. Is an advertising executive simply one person in a big mass of people? Is he an easily replaceable part of a system that's been in operation for a long time? Or has he pioneered techniques that have opened up new profit centers? Has he changed the company's bottom line? Those questions reflect competing versions of reality.

Here's an example from the NFL. I recently finished a negotiation for Warren Moon, the quarterback of the Seattle Seahawks. Now, is Warren Moon a 41-year-old player who is hanging on by a thread and who is lucky to be employed in the first place? Should he be grateful for *any* money that the team pays him? Or is he a quarterback who was among the league leaders in completions and attempts last year? Is he a team leader who took a previously moribund group of players, united them, helped them have the best record that they've had in recent years? Is he a testament to the fact that talent can come at any age?

In *our* reality, Warren Moon is critical to the resurgence of his team. He makes the players around him better. And off the field, he is instrumental in selling season tickets, in filling the stands, in interacting with advertisers, and in generating ancillary revenue sources for the NFL and for his franchise—in a way that no one else can. That's our version of reality.

IT'S NOT PERSONAL—IT'S STRICTLY BUSINESS

Negotiations can get emotional. But you need to remind yourself that they're about business. It's natural for someone to try to save money, so don't let that attitude be a startling revelation when you walk in to negotiate. And remember, money doesn't reflect your worth as a human being, your value, or whether you live an ethical life.

I know this kind of thing as an employer. When it comes time for me to talk to my employees about compensation, the same thing always happens. After I've rationally figured out a fair salary for someone, and then added a little more for motivational purposes, I sit down with that employee, and inevitably he starts with a figure far above what I've conceptualized. Now, it makes no sense for me to sit there and feel grossly offended. I have to remember that this person's expectations aren't grandiose. From his point of view, what he's asking for probably makes a lot of sense.

That person may not even be saying that he really needs all that money. He may be saying that he needs more recognition. There are all sorts of things that a person may want to say, but those things are usually manifested as demands for more money.

IT'S NOT ABOUT WHAT'S FAIR

There are jobs that are so much fun that you would pay your boss to let you do them! But you can't allow the discussion to turn on your personal circumstances. The real question is, What is the market value of what you do?

I recently negotiated a contract for Ryan Leaf with the San Diego Chargers. As a student last year, Ryan had been living on scholarship money at Washington State University. At a certain point in the negotiation, the Chargers' general manager turned to Ryan and said, "How can you ask for so much? You're going to be rich under any circumstances. All we're talking about is *how* rich you're going to be."

There's some truth in that. But there's also truth in the fact that professional football generates tremendous revenue, and that players take enormous risks. I ended up getting Ryan Leaf $11.25 million as a signing bonus. But I could never have done that if the focus had been on how much he liked to play football or on how little money he had made at college—because the truth is, he might play football for nothing. That is a very important truth, but it's got nothing to do with what's fair in the world.

NEVER SPLIT THE DIFFERENCE

There are many ways to negotiate. The reasonable-person theory says that a reasonable person ought to ask for money or conditions that are very close to what he actually wants and that are close to what is fair. The problem is that those two things are often very different. If the market value for a service is $100,000, and the employee asks for $500,000, and the employer offers $95,000, then splitting the difference makes no sense. In a situation like that, if you simply split the difference, you'd end up with a bizarrely unfair result. At that point, the employer has to assume that he's not dealing with a serious negotiator, because there's no validity to the $500,000 request.

THE SAD TRUTH OF THE INEVITABLE FUDGE FACTOR

In most one-on-one negotiations, in which there are no other parties who might be interested in bidding on your services, my suggestion is that you start by making a proposal that is reasonable—but that has some fudge factor to it. It's a sad aspect of human nature, but it's a fact of life: We don't feel satisfied unless we've gone through a process that involves bargaining back and forth. All human beings like to feel some sense of achievement. They want to feel that they've won something. And they also like to justify the time they spent in the negotiating process. So you've got to play the game: Your first proposal needs to be higher than what you would ultimately take.

HOW TO DEAL WITH DEADLOCK

There is an absolutely predictable point in all negotiations when you appear to be deadlocked. And the question arises: Now what? First, when you're preparing to negotiate, you should assume that this moment will come sooner or later. When it does, don't be surprised, and don't get frustrated. Simply assume that in any negotiation process, a schism, a chasm, a seemingly unsolvable problem will occur. Second, the key to getting through that situation is emotional resilience. You have to face the seemingly impossible deadlock, and then step back—for five minutes, for an hour, or for a couple of days. It could involve simply taking a short break, going for a walk, or moving away from the point that's produced the deadlock, or it could involve shifting to a new setting and changing the context of the negotiation.

When you and the other party get back together, you'll both return with new and creative ways to solve the problem. Both sides can use the break to refocus on the value that they offer each other. They can stop focusing on the specific issue that they're deadlocked over and instead start focusing on the valuable end point of the negotiation: Someone will have a job that he loves, and someone will have an employee whom he will treasure. The goal should be to get back to the original purpose of the negotiation.

IT CAN ALWAYS GET WORSE

There's one last thing to remember about the hard part of negotiating, about that point when the discussion comes to a stop, when you're thinking that you might do better to walk away than to resolve the deadlock—because, you think, things can't get any worse. But let me assure you, they *can* get worse. Unintended consequences occur all the time as a result of botched negotiating sessions. Football players end up being needlessly cut from teams. Careers get cut short before people have really produced their best work.

It is not a victory to play a game of chicken and to let the two cars collide: One car gets totaled, and its driver is lying on the ground in critical condition; the other car has its steering wheel intact, and one of its wheels still works—but let me assure you that its driver is also in critical condition. He did not win. When it comes to negotiating, you can't let the Neanderthal side of your nature dominate. You need to rise above that.

WHEN YOU'RE GOING TO LOSE, GET CREATIVE

Never push a totally losing argument to the end. When you start to face a deadlock and you know that you can't win, it's time to back off. That's when you push yourself to think of a new way to solve the problem.

Here's an example. At one point, the negotiation that I just finished on behalf of Warren Moon was breaking down. The Seahawks' management was concerned that if it paid Warren a signing bonus, and then he retired next year, some portion of that bonus would count against the team's salary cap—which would limit the amount of money that the team could use to sign someone else. So, for instance, if the Seahawks paid Warren a signing bonus of $3 million on a two-year contract, and Warren played for only one year, the team would be held accountable under the salary cap for $1.5 million in the second year. And since they looked at Warren and saw a player who would then be approaching his 43rd birthday, this was a serious issue—so serious that it produced a deadlock that went on for quite a while. Finally, we decided to try something different. We suggested a new provision: If Warren did retire, he would pay back a portion of the signing bonus.

We treated the team's concerns as legitimate and came up with a way to get what we wanted: the signing bonus and the two-year contract. Instead of just speechifying, we thought of something that we could live with—something that was less than perfect but still very desirable. Often, when you get into a deadlock, that's the moment when creativity comes into play.

A NEGOTIATION IS NOT A SEARCH-AND-DESTROY MISSION

In most cases, a negotiation will not be the last time you interact with the other side. And since you will keep interacting with the other side, either in the workplace or in later negotiations, your goal should be to find the most profitable way to complete a deal that works for both sides. The one sure thing that I know about business is that, if you've got your foot on someone else's neck, at some point in the future, that person will have his foot on your neck.

And you never want to treat any one negotiation as the last opportunity to get a fair result. If you come to what seems like a horrendous confrontation, look for a way to take care of the problem that avoids a monumental blowup. You need to look at the whole picture and at the whole relationship—especially at your long-term interests—as opposed to obsessing over the current situation. You can't afford to lose that perspective.

IT'S NOT JUST A CONTRACT—IT'S YOUR REPUTATION

Let's say that you agreed to a deal that gives you $100,000 in salary and two weeks of vacation, but the contract you get calls for $105,000 in salary and three weeks of vacation. Do you sign the contract?

The answer is, no, you don't sign it—because those terms aren't what you agreed to. It's possible that, if you bring the discrepancy to the attention of people on the other side, they may feel indebted enough to do something for you. At a minimum, they will know that you're someone they can trust. I tell the lawyers in our firm, "It's acceptable if we don't get every last client or piece of business that we want. It's *never* acceptable if you lie or mislead someone—that's the one thing that can destroy what we do."

THE ART OF CLOSING A DEAL

There are a few things to keep in mind about closing a deal. Most people—especially on the employer side—will have concessions that they're willing to offer to get the deal done. So the concept of "if it will make the deal" is always worth keeping in mind. One way of doing a deal can be first to agree on a general framework that's still somewhat sketchy, and then to work out the rest of the deal—because at that point, conflict has been replaced by partnership, and both sides have dropped their defenses.

But you can't allow the feeling of exultation, or of relief that the process is almost done, to dull your senses. There are critical points at the end that need to be negotiated and documented. That's when you should draw on your mental discipline: You shouldn't be concerned with what time the last flight leaves. You shouldn't start thinking of what it would be like to surprise your wife by being home half a day early. You must remain focused until the very end.

There is another part of negotiating that you need to anticipate: As a deal comes to a close, there will again be seemingly unsolvable problems. One side or the other is very likely to look at some part of the deal and say, "If that's what you meant, then the whole deal is off." At that point, it's important for you to provide motivation. You may need to buck up people on the other side, to encourage them to stay with the process—"Look, we're almost done. This always happens at this stage"—because at the very last minute, charges of bad faith can surface. You started with wariness, but then you worked through it to achieve what you think is a partnership, and now, as both sides let their guards down, something arises that seems to threaten the whole deal. As hard as it may be, that's the time for you to stay rational.

TAKE TIME TO CELEBRATE

Once the deal is done, remember to have some kind of a ceremonial function. Take a moment to give yourself a sense of emotional completion. Have a celebration with the other side. Have dinner together. Have a drink together. Give each other a present. Do something that commemorates the moment and makes it special. Symbolism is important.

When I finished the deal for Troy Aikman with Jerry Jones, the owner of the Dallas Cowboys, or the one for Drew Bledsoe with Robert Kraft, the owner of the New England Patriots, we all sat down together to sign footballs and jerseys. We made one memento for each of us, so that everyone had a trophy to celebrate the deal.

Did you really graduate from school if you didn't go through your graduation ceremony? Yes. But do you have the *feeling* of completion? Probably not. So when you reach the end of the deal, be sure to celebrate what you've accomplished—and to treat it as something that both sides can feel good about.

Three Approaches to Resolving Disputes: Interests, Rights, and Power

William L. Ury

Jeanne M. Brett

Stephen B. Goldberg

It started with a pair of stolen boots. Miners usually leave their work clothes in baskets that they hoist to the ceiling of the bathhouse between work shifts. One night a miner discovered that his boots were gone.[1] He couldn't work without boots. Angry, he went to the shift boss and complained: "Goddammit, someone stole my boots! It ain't fair! Why should I lose a shift's pay and the price of a pair of boots because the company can't protect the property?"

"Hard luck!" the shift boss responded. "The company isn't responsible for personal property left on company premises. Read the mine regulations!"

The miner grumbled to himself, "I'll show them! If I can't work this shift, neither will anyone else!" He convinced a few buddies to walk out with him and, in union solidarity, all the others followed.

The superintendent of the mine told us later that he had replaced stolen boots for miners and that the shift boss should have done the same. "If the shift boss had said to the miner, 'I'll buy you a new pair and loan you some meanwhile,' we wouldn't have had a strike." The superintendent believed that his way of resolving the dispute was better than the shift boss's or the miner's. Was he right and, if so, why? In what ways are some dispute resolution procedures better than others?

In this chapter, we discuss three ways to resolve a dispute: reconciling the interests of the parties, determining who is right, and determining who is more powerful. We analyze the costs of disputing in terms of transaction costs, satisfaction with outcomes, effect on the relationship, and recurrence of disputes. We argue that, in general, reconciling interests costs less and yields more satisfactory results than determining who is right, which in turn costs less and satisfies more than determining who is more powerful. The goal of dispute systems design, therefore, is a system in which most disputes are resolved by reconciling interests.

THREE WAYS TO RESOLVE DISPUTES

The Boots Dispute Dissected

A dispute begins when one person (or organization) makes a claim or demand on another who rejects it.[2] The claim may arise from a perceived injury or from a need or aspiration.[3] When the miner complained to the shift boss about the stolen boots, he was making a claim that the company should take responsibility and remedy his perceived injury. The shift boss's rejection of the claim turned it into a dispute. To resolve a dispute means to turn opposed positions—the claim and its rejection—into a single outcome.[4] The resolution of the boots dispute might have been a negotiated agreement, an arbitrator's ruling, or a decision by the miner to drop his claim or by the company to grant it.

In a dispute, people have certain interests at stake. Moreover, certain relevant standards or rights exist as guideposts toward a fair outcome. In addition, a certain balance of power exists between the parties. Interests, rights, and power then are three basic elements of any dispute. In resolving a dispute, the parties may choose to focus their attention on one or more of these basic factors. They may seek to (1) reconcile their underlying interests, (2) determine who is right, and/or (3) determine who is more powerful.

When he pressed his claim that the company should do something about his stolen boots, the miner focused on rights—"Why should I lose a shift's pay and the price of a pair of boots because the company can't protect the property?" When the shift boss responded by referring to mine regulations, he followed the miner's lead and continued to focus on who was right. The miner, frustrated in his attempt to win what he saw as justice, provoked a walkout—changing the focus to power. "I'll show them!" In other words, he would show the company how much power he and his fellow coal miners had—how dependent the company was on them for the production of coal.

The mine superintendent thought the focus should have been on interests. The miner had an interest in boots and a shift's pay, and the company had an interest in the miner working his assigned shift. Although rights were involved (there was a question of fairness) and power was involved (the miner had the power to cause a strike), the superintendent's emphasis was on each side's interests. He would have approached the stolen boots situation as a joint problem that the company could help solve.

Reconciling Interests

Interests are needs, desires, concerns, fears—the things one cares about or wants. They underlie people's positions—the tangible items they *say* they want. A husband and wife quarrel about whether to spend money for a new car. The husband's underlying interest may not be the money or the car but the desire to impress his friends; the wife's interest may be transportation. The director of sales for an electronics company gets into a dispute with the director of manufacturing over the number of TV models to produce.

The director of sales wants to produce more models. Her interest is in selling TV sets; more models mean more choice for consumers and hence increased sales. The director of manufacturing wants to produce fewer models. His interest is in decreasing manufacturing costs; more models mean higher costs.

Reconciling such interests is not easy. It involves probing for deep-seated concerns, devising creative solutions, and making trade-offs and concessions where interests are opposed.[5] The most common procedure for doing this is *negotiation,* the act of back-and-forth communication intended to reach agreement. (A procedure is a pattern of interactive behavior directed toward resolving a dispute.) Another interests-based procedure is *mediation,* in which a third party assists the disputants in reaching agreement.

By no means do all negotiations (or mediations) focus on reconciling interests. Some negotiations focus on determining who is right, such as when two lawyers argue about whose case has the greater merit. Other negotiations focus on determining who is more powerful, such as when quarreling neighbors or nations exchange threats and counterthreats. Often negotiations involve a mix of all three—some attempts to satisfy interests, some discussion of rights, and some references to relative power. Negotiations that focus primarily on interests we call "interests-based," in contrast to "rights-based" and "power-based" negotiations. Another term for interests-based negotiation is *problem-solving negotiation,* so called because it involves treating a dispute as a mutual problem to be solved by the parties.

Before disputants can effectively begin the process of reconciling interests, they may need to vent their emotions. Rarely are emotions absent from disputes. Emotions often generate disputes, and disputes, in turn, often generate emotions. Frustration underlay the miner's initial outburst to the shift boss; anger at the shift boss's response spurred him to provoke the strike.

Expressing underlying emotions can be instrumental in negotiating a resolution. Particularly in interpersonal disputes, hostility may diminish significantly if the aggrieved party vents her anger, resentment, and frustration in front of the blamed party, and the blamed party acknowledges the validity of such emotions or, going one step further, offers an apology.[6] With hostility reduced, resolving the dispute on the basis of interests becomes easier. Expressions of emotion have a special place in certain kinds of interests-based negotiation and mediation.

Determining Who Is Right

Another way to resolve disputes is to rely on some independent standard with perceived legitimacy or fairness to determine who is right. As a shorthand for such independent standards, we use the term *rights.* Some rights are formalized in law or contract. Other rights are socially accepted standards of behavior, such as reciprocity, precedent, equality, and seniority.[7] In the boots dispute, for example, while the miner had no contractual right to new boots, he felt that standards of fairness called for the company to replace personal property stolen from its premises.

Rights are rarely clear. There are often different—and sometimes contradictory—standards that apply. Reaching agreement on rights, where the outcome will determine who gets what, can often be exceedingly difficult, frequently leading the parties to turn to a third party to determine who is right. The prototypical rights procedure is adjudication, in which disputants present evidence and arguments to a neutral third party who has the power to hand down a binding decision. (In mediation, by contrast, the third party does not have the power to decide the dispute.) Public adjudication is provided by courts and administrative agencies. Private adjudication is provided by arbitrators.[8]

Determining Who Is More Powerful

A third way to resolve a dispute is on the basis of power. We define power, somewhat narrowly, as the ability to coerce someone to do something he would not otherwise do. Exercising power typically means imposing costs on the other side or threatening to do so. In striking, the miners exercised power by imposing economic costs on the company. The exercise of power takes two common forms: acts of aggression, such as sabotage or physical attack, and withholding the benefits that derive from a relationship, as when employees withhold their labor in a strike.

In relationships of mutual dependence, such as between labor and management or within an organization or a family, the questions of who is more powerful turns on who is less dependent on the other.[9] If a company needs the employees' work more than employees need the company's pay, the company is more dependent and hence less powerful. How dependent one is turns on how satisfactory the alternatives are for satisfying one's interests. The better the alternative, the less dependent one is. If it is easier for the company to replace striking employees than it is for striking employees to find new jobs, the company is less dependent and thereby more powerful. In addition to strikes, power procedures include behaviors that range from insults and ridicule to beatings and warfare. All have in common the intent to coerce the other side to settle on terms more satisfactory to the wielder of power. Power procedures are of two types: power-based negotiation, typified by an exchange of threats, and power contests, in which the parties take actions to determine who will prevail.

Determining who is the more powerful party without a decisive and potentially destructive power contest is difficult because power is ultimately a matter of perceptions. Despite objective indicators of power, such as financial resources, parties' perceptions of their own and each other's power often do not coincide. Moreover, each side's perception of the other's power may fail to take into account the possibility that the other will invest greater resources in the contest than expected out of fear that a change in the perceived distribution of power will affect the outcomes of future disputes.

Interrelationship among Interests, Rights, and Power

The relationship among interests, rights, and power can be pictured as a circle within a circle within a circle (as in Figure 1). The innermost circle represents interests; the middle, rights; and the outer, power. The reconciliation of interests takes place within the context of the parties' rights and power. The likely outcome of a dispute if taken to court or to a strike, for instance, helps define the bargaining range within which a resolution can be found. Similarly, the determination of rights takes place within the context of power. One party, for instance, may win a judgment in court, but unless the judgment can be enforced, the dispute will continue. Thus, in the process of resolving a dispute, the focus may shift from interests to rights to power and back again.

FIGURE 1   Interrelationships among
Interests, Rights, and Power

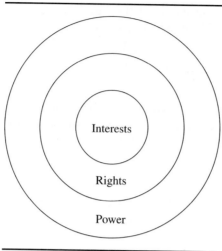

Lumping It and Avoidance

Not all disputes end with a resolution. Often one or more parties simply decide to withdraw from the dispute. Withdrawal takes two forms. One party may decide to "lump it," dropping her claim or giving in to the other's claim because she believes pursuing the dispute is not in her interest, or because she concludes she does not have the power to resolve it to her satisfaction. The miner would have been lumping his claim if he had said to himself, "I strongly disagree with management's decision not to reimburse me for my boots, but I'm not going to do anything about it." A second form of withdrawal is avoidance. One party (or both) may decide to withdraw from the relationship, or at least to curtail it significantly.[10] Examples of avoidance include quitting the organization, divorce, leaving the neighborhood, and staying out of the other person's way.

Both avoidance and lumping it may occur in conjunction with particular dispute resolution procedures. Many power contests involve threatening avoidance—such as threatening divorce—or actually engaging in it temporarily to impose costs on the other side—such as in a strike or breaking off of diplomatic relations. Many power contests end with the loser lumping her claim or her objection to the other's claim. Others end with the loser engaging in avoidance: leaving or keeping her distance from the winner. Similarly, much negotiation ends with one side deciding to lump it instead of pursuing the claim. Or, rather than take a dispute to court or engage in coercive actions, one party (or both) may decide to break off the relationship altogether. This is common in social contexts where the disputant perceives satisfactory alternatives to the relationship.

Lumping it and avoidance may also occur before a claim has been made, thus forestalling a dispute. Faced with the problem of stolen boots, the miner might have decided to lump it and not make a claim for the boots. More drastically, in a fit of exasperation, he might have walked off the job and never returned.

WHICH APPROACH IS "BEST"?

When the miner superintendent described the boots dispute to us, he expressed a preference for how to resolve disputes. In our language, he was saying that on the whole it was better to try to reconcile interests than to focus on who was right or who was more powerful. But what does "better" mean? And in what sense, if any, was he correct in believing that focusing attention on interests is better?

What "Better" Means: Four Possible Criteria

The different approaches to the resolution of disputes—interests, rights, and power—generate different costs and benefits. We focus on four criteria in comparing them: transaction costs, satisfaction with outcomes, effect on the relationship, and recurrence of disputes.[11]

Transaction Costs.   For the mine superintendent, "better" meant resolving disputes without strikes. More generally, he wanted to minimize the costs of disputing—what may be called the transaction costs. The most obvious costs of striking were economic. The management payroll and the overhead costs had to be met while the mine stood idle. Sometimes strikes led to violence and the destruction of company property. The miners, too, incurred costs—lost wages. Then there were the lost opportunities for the company: a series of strikes could lead to the loss of a valuable sales contract. In a family argument, the costs would include the frustrating hours spent disputing, the frayed nerves and tension headaches, and the missed opportunities to do more enjoyable or useful tasks. All dispute resolution procedures carry transaction costs: the time, money, and emotional energy expended in disputing; the resources consumed and destroyed; and the opportunities lost.[12]

Satisfaction with Outcomes.   Another way to evaluate different approaches to dispute resolution is by the parties' mutual satisfaction with the result. The outcome of the strike could not have been wholly satisfactory to the miner—he did not receive new boots—but he did succeed in venting his frustration and taking his revenge. A disputant's satisfaction depends largely on how much the resolution fulfills the interests that led her to make or reject the claim in the first place. Satisfaction may also depend on whether the disputant believes that the resolution is fair. Even if an agreement does not wholly fulfill her interests, a disputant may draw some satisfaction from the resolution's fairness.

Satisfaction depends not only on the perceived fairness of the resolution, but also on the perceived fairness of the dispute resolution procedure. Judgments about fairness turn on several factors: how much opportunity a disputant had to express himself; whether he had control over accepting or rejecting the settlement; how much he was able to participate in shaping the settlement; and whether he believes that the third party, if there was one, acted fairly.[13]

Effect on the Relationship.   A third criterion is the long-term effect on the parties' relationship. The approach taken to resolve a dispute may affect the parties' ability to work together on a day-to-day basis. Constant quarrels with threats of divorce may seriously weaken a marriage. In contrast, marital counseling in which the disputing partners learn to focus on interests in order to resolve disputes may strengthen a marriage.

Recurrence.   The final criterion is whether a particular approach produces durable resolutions. The simplest form of recurrence is when a resolution fails to stick. For example, a dispute between father and teenage son over curfew appears resolved but breaks out again and again. A subtler form of recurrence takes place when a resolution is reached in a particular dispute, but the resolution fails to prevent the same dispute from arising between one of the disputants and someone else, or conceivably between two different parties in the same community. For instance, a man guilty of sexually harassing an employee reaches an agreement with his victim that is satisfactory to her, but he continues to harass other women employees. Or he stops, but other men continue to harass women employees in the same organization.

The Relationship among the Four Criteria.   These four different criteria are interrelated. Dissatisfaction with outcomes may produce strain on the relationship, which contributes to the recurrence of disputes, which in turn increases transaction costs. Because the different costs typically increase and decrease together, it is convenient to refer to all four together as the costs of disputing. When we refer to a particular approach as "high-cost" or "low-cost," we mean not just transaction costs but also dissatisfaction with outcomes, strain on the relationship, and recurrence of disputes.

Sometimes one cost can be reduced only by increasing another, particularly in the short term. If father and son sit down to discuss their conflicting interests concerning curfew, the short-term transaction costs in terms of time and energy may be high. Still, these costs may be more than offset by the benefits of a successful negotiation—an improved relationship and the cessation of curfew violations.

Which Approach Is Least Costly?

Now that we have defined "better" in terms of the four types of costs, the question remains whether the mine superintendent was right in supposing that focusing on interest is better. A second question is also important: when an interests-based approach fails, is it less costly to focus on rights or on power?

Interests versus Rights or Power.   A focus on interests can resolve the problem underlying the dispute more effectively than can a focus on rights or power. An example is a grievance filed against a mine foreman for doing work that contractually only a miner is authorized to do. Often the real problem is something else—a miner who feels unfairly assigned to an unpleasant task may file a grievance only to strike back at his foreman. Clearly, focusing on what the contract says about foremen working will not deal with this underlying problem. Nor will striking to protest foremen working. But if the foreman and miner can negotiate about the miner's future work tasks, the dispute may be resolved to the satisfaction of both.

Just as an interests-based approach can help uncover hidden problems, it can help the parties identify which issues are of greater concern to one than to the other. By trading off issues of lesser concern for those of greater concern, both parties can gain from the resolution of the dispute.[14] Consider, for example, a union and employer negotiating over two issues: additional vacation time and flexibility of work assignments. Although the union does not like the idea of assignment flexibility, its clear priority is additional vacation. Although the employer does not like the idea of additional vacation, he cares more about gaining flexibility in assigning work. An agreement that gives the union the vacation days it seeks and the employer flexibility in making work assignments would likely be satisfactory to both. Such joint gain is more likely to be realized if the parties focus on each side's interests. Focusing on who is right, as in litigation, or on who is more powerful, as in a strike, usually leaves at least one party perceiving itself as the loser.

Reconciling interest thus tends to generate a higher level of mutual satisfaction with outcomes than determining rights or power.[15] If the parties are more satisfied, their relationship benefits, and the dispute is less likely to recur. Determining who is right or who is more powerful, with the emphasis on winning and losing, typically makes the relationship more adversarial and strained. Moreover, the loser frequently does not give up, but appeals to a higher court or plots revenge. To be sure, reconciling interests can sometimes take a long time, especially when there are many parties to the dispute. Generally, however, these costs pale in comparison with the transaction costs of rights and power contests such as trials, hostile corporate takeovers, or wars.

In sum, focusing on interests, compared to focusing on rights or power, tends to produce higher satisfaction with outcomes, better working relationships and less recurrence, and may also incur lower transaction costs. As a rough generalization, then, an interests approach is less costly than a rights or power approach.

Rights versus Power.   Although determining who is right or who is more powerful can strain the relationship, deferring to a fair standard usually takes less of a toll than giving in to a threat. In a dispute between a father and teenager over curfew, a discussion of independent standards such as the curfews of other teenagers is likely to strain the relationship less than an exchange of threats.

Determining rights or power frequently becomes a contest—a competition among the parties to determine who will prevail. They may compete with words to persuade a third-party decision maker of the merits of their case, as in adjudication; or they may compete with actions intended to show the other who is more powerful, as in a proxy fight. Rights contests differ from power contests chiefly in their transaction costs. A power contest typically costs more in resources consumed and opportunities lost. Strikes cost more than arbitration. Violence costs more than litigation. The high transaction costs stem not only from the efforts invested in the fight but also from the destruction of each side's resources. Destroying the opposition may be the very object of a power contest. Moreover, power contests often create new injuries and new disputes along with anger, distrust, and a desire for revenge. Power contests, then, typically damage the relationship more and lead to greater recurrence of disputes than do rights contests. In general, a rights approach is less costly than a power approach.

Proposition

To sum up, we argue that, in general, reconciling interests is less costly than determining who is right, which in turn is less costly than determining who is more powerful. This proposition does not mean that focusing on interests is invariably better than focusing on rights and power, but simply means that it tends to result in lower transaction costs, greater satisfaction with outcomes, less strain on the relationship, and less recurrence of disputes.

FOCUSING ON INTERESTS IS NOT ENOUGH

Despite these general advantages, resolving *all* disputes by reconciling interests alone is neither possible nor desirable. It is useful to consider why.

When Determining Rights or Power Is Necessary

In some instances, interests-based negotiation cannot occur unless rights or power procedures are first employed to bring a recalcitrant party to the negotiating table. An environmental group, for example, may file a lawsuit against a developer to bring about a negotiation. A community group may organize a demonstration on the steps of the town hall to get the mayor to discuss its interests in improving garbage collection service.

In other disputes, the parties cannot reach agreement on the basis of interests because their perceptions of who is right or who is more powerful are so different that they cannot establish a range in which to negotiate. A rights procedure may be needed to clarify the rights boundary within which a negotiated resolution can be sought. If a discharged employee and her employer (as well as their lawyers) have very different estimations about whether a court would award damages to the employee, it will be difficult for them to negotiate a settlement. Nonbinding arbitration may clarify the parties' rights and allow them to negotiate a resolution.

Just as uncertainty about the rights of the parties will sometimes make negotiation difficult, so too will uncertainty about their relative power. When one party in an ongoing relationship wants to demonstrate that the balance of power has shifted in its favor, it may find that only a power contest will adequately make the point. It is a truism among labor relations practitioners that a conflict-ridden union-management relationship often settles down after a lengthy strike. The strike reduces uncertainty about the relative power of the parties that had made each party unwilling to concede. Such long-term benefits sometimes justify the high transaction costs of a power contest.

In some disputes, the interests are so opposed that agreement is not possible. Focusing on interests cannot resolve a dispute between a right-to-life group and an abortion clinic over whether the clinic will continue to exist. Resolution will likely be possible only through a rights contest, such as a trial, or a power contest, such as a demonstration or a legislative battle.

When Are Rights or Power Procedures Desirable?

Although reconciling interests is generally less costly than determining rights, only adjudication can authoritatively resolve questions of public importance. If the 1954 Supreme Court case, *Brown v. Board of Education* (347 U.S. 483), outlawing racial segregation in public schools, had been resolved by negotiation rather than by adjudication, the immediate result might have been the same—the black plaintiff would have attended an all-white Topeka, Kansas, public school. The societal impact, however, would have been far less significant. As it was, *Brown* laid the groundwork for the elimination of racial segregation in all of American public life. In at least some cases, then, rights-based court procedures are preferable, from a societal perspective, to resolution through interests-based negotiation.[16]

Some people assert that a powerful party is ill-advised to focus on interests when dealing regularly with a weaker party. But even if one party is more powerful, the costs of imposing one's will can be high. Threats must be backed up with actions from time to time. The weaker party may fail to fully comply with a resolution based on power, thus requiring the more powerful party to engage in expensive policing. The weaker party may also take revenge—in small ways, perhaps, but nonetheless a nuisance. And revenge may be quite costly to the more powerful if the power balance ever shifts, as it can quite unexpectedly, or if the weaker party's cooperation is ever needed in another domain. Thus, for a more powerful party, a focus on interests, within the bounds set by power, may be more desirable than would appear at first glance.

Low-Cost Ways to Determine Rights and Power

Because focusing on rights and power plays an important role in effective dispute resolution, differentiating rights and power procedures on the basis of costs is useful. We distinguish three types of rights and power procedures: negotiation, low-cost contests, and high-cost contests. Rights-based negotiation is typically less costly than a rights contest such as court or arbitration. Similarly, power-based negotiation, marked by threats, typically costs less than a power contest in which those threats are carried out.

Different kinds of contests incur different costs. If arbitration dispenses with procedures typical of a court trial (extensive discovery, procedural motions, and lengthy briefs), it can be much cheaper than going to court. In a fight, shouting is less costly than physical assault. A strike in which workers refuse only overtime work is less costly than a full strike.

THE GOAL: AN INTERESTS-ORIENTED DISPUTE RESOLUTION SYSTEM

Not all disputes can be—or should be—resolved by reconciling interests. Rights and power procedures can sometimes accomplish what interests-based procedures cannot. The problem is that rights and power procedures are often used where they are not necessary. A procedure that should be the last resort too often becomes the first resort. The goal, then, is a dispute resolution system that looks like the pyramid on the right in Figure 2: most disputes are resolved through reconciling interests, some through determining who is right, and the fewest through determining who is more powerful. By contrast, a distressed dispute resolution system would look like the inverted pyramid on the left in Figure 2. Comparatively few disputes are resolved through reconciling interests, while many are resolved through determining rights and power. The challenge for the systems designer is to turn the pyramid right side up. It is to design a system that promotes the reconciling of interests but that also provides low-cost ways to determine rights or power for those disputes that cannot or should not be resolved by focusing on interests alone.

FIGURE 2   Moving from a Distressed to an Effective Dispute
Resolution System

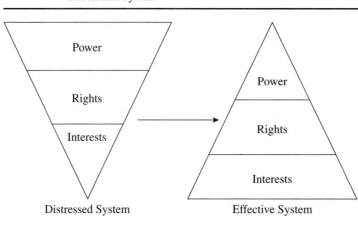

Distressed System   Effective System

ENDNOTES

1. In order to steer between the Scylla of sexist language and the Charybdis of awkward writing, we have chosen to alternate the use of masculine and feminine pronouns.

2. This definition is taken from Felstiner, W. L. F., Abel, R. L., and Sarat, A. "The Emergence and Transformation of Disputes: Naming, Blaming, Claiming." *Law and Society Review,* 1980–81, *15,* 631–54. The article contains an interesting discussion of disputes and how they emerge.

3. See Felstiner, W. L. F., Abel, R. L., and Sarat, A. "The Emergence and Transformation of Disputes: Naming, Blaming, Claiming." *Law and Society Review,* 1980–81, *15,* 631–54.

4. In speaking of resolving disputes, rather than processing, managing, or handling disputes, we do not suggest that resolution will necessarily bring an end to the fundamental conflict underlying the dispute. Nor do we mean that a dispute once resolved will stay resolved. Indeed, one of our criteria for contrasting approaches to dispute resolution is the frequency with which disputes recur after they appear to have been resolved. See Merry, S. E., "Disputing Without Culture." *Harvard Law Review,* 1987, *100,* 2057–73; Sarat, A. "The 'New Formalism' in Disputing and Dispute Processing." *Law and Society Review,* 1988, *21,* 695–715.

5. For an extensive discussion of interests-based negotiation, see Fisher, R., and Ury, W. L. *Getting to Yes.* Boston: Houghton Mifflin, 1981. See also Lax, D. A., and Sebenius, J. K. *The Manager as a Negotiator.* New York: Free Press, 1986.

6. Goldberg, S. B., and Sander, F.E.A. "Saying You're Sorry." *Negotiation Journal,* 1987, *3,* 221–24.

7. We recognize that in defining rights to include both legal entitlements and generally accepted standards of fairness, we are stretching that term beyond its commonly understood meaning. Our reason for doing so is that a procedure that uses either legal entitlements or generally accepted standards of fairness as a basis for dispute resolution will focus on the disputants' entitlements under normative standards, rather than on their underlying interests. This is true of adjudication, which deals with legal rights; it is equally true of rights-based negotiation, which may deal with either legal rights or generally accepted standards. Since, as we shall

show, procedures that focus on normative standards are more costly than those that focus on interests, and since our central concern is with cutting costs as well as realizing benefits, we find it useful to cluster together legal rights and other normative standards, as well as procedures based on either.

8. A court procedure may determine not only who is right but also who is more powerful, since behind a court decision lies the coercive power of the state. Legal rights have power behind them. Still, we consider adjudication a rights procedure, since its overt focus is determining who is right, not who is more powerful. Even though rights, particularly legal rights, do provide power, a procedure that focuses on rights as a means of dispute resolution is less costly than a procedure that focuses on power. A rights-based contest, such as adjudication, which focuses on which disputant ought to prevail under normative standards, will be less costly than a power-based strike, boycott, or war, which focuses on which disputant can hurt the other more. Similarly, a negotiation that focuses on normative criteria for dispute resolution will be less costly than a negotiation that focuses on the disputants' relative capacity to injure each other. Hence, from our cost perspective, it is appropriate to distinguish procedures that focus on rights from those that focus on power.

9. Emerson, R. M. "Power-Dependence Relations." *American Sociological Review,* 1962, *27,* 31–41.

10. Hirschman, A. O. *Exit, Voice, and Loyalty: Responses to Declines in Firms, Organizations, and States.* Cambridge, Mass.: Harvard University Press, 1970. Exit corresponds with avoidance, loyalty with lumping it. Voice, as we shall discuss later, is most likely to be realized in interests-based procedures such as problem-solving negotiation and mediation.

11. A fifth evaluative criterion is procedural justice, which is perceived satisfaction with the fairness of a dispute resolution procedure. Research has shown that disputants prefer third-party procedures that provide opportunities for outcome control and voice. See Lind, E. A., and Tyler, T. R. *The Social Psychology of Procedural Justice.* New York: Plenum, 1988; Brett, J. M. "Commentary on Procedural Justice Papers." In R. J. Lewicki, B. H. Sheppard, and M. H. Bazerman (eds.), *Research on Negotiations in Organizations.* Greenwich, Conn.: JAI Press, 1986, 81–90.

    We do not include procedural justice as a separate evaluation criterion for two reasons. First, unlike transaction costs, satisfaction with outcome, effect on the relationship, and recurrence, procedural justice is meaningful only at the level of a single procedure for a single dispute. It neither generalizes across the multiple procedures that may be used in the resolution of a single dispute nor generalizes across disputes to construct a systems-level cost. The other costs will do both. For example, it is possible to measure the disputants' satisfaction with the outcome of a dispute, regardless of how many different procedures were used to resolve that dispute. Likewise, it is possible to measure satisfaction with outcomes in a system that handles many disputes by asking many disputants about their feelings. Second, while procedural justice and distributive justice (satisfaction with fairness of outcomes) are distinct concepts, they are typically highly correlated. See Lind, E. A., and Tyler, T. R. *The Social Psychology of Procedural Justice.* New York: Plenum, 1988.

12. Williamson, O. E. "Transaction Cost Economics: The Governance of Contractual Relations." *Journal of Law and Economics,* 1979, *22,* 233–61; Brett, J. M., and Rognes, J. K. "Intergroup Relations in Organizations." In P. S. Goodman and Associates, *Designing Effective Work Groups.* San Francisco: Jossey-Bass, 1986, 202–36.

13. For a summary of the evidence of a relationship between procedural and distributive justice— that is, satisfaction with process and with outcome—see Lind, E. A., and Tyler, T. R. *The Social*

Psychology of Procedural Justice. New York: Plenum, 1988. Lind and Tyler also summarize the evidence showing a relationship between voice and satisfaction with the process. For evidence of the effect of participation in shaping the ultimate resolution beyond simply being able to accept or reject a third party's advice, see Brett, J. M., and Shapiro, D. L. "Procedural Justice: A Test of Competing Theories and Implications for Managerial Decision Making," unpublished manuscript.

14. Lax, D. A., and Sebenius, J. K. *The Manager as Negotiator.* New York: Free Press, 1986.

15. The empirical research supporting this statement compares mediation to arbitration or adjudication. Claimants prefer mediation to arbitration in a variety of settings: labor-management (Brett, J. M., and Goldberg, S. B. "Grievance Mediation in the Coal Industry: A Field Experiment." *Industrial and Labor Relations Review,* 1983, *37,* 49–69), small claims disputes (McEwen, C. A., and Maiman, R. J. "Small Claims Mediation in Maine: An Empirical Assessment." *Maine Law Review,* 1981, *33,* 237–68), and divorce (Pearson, J. "An Evaluation of Alternatives to Court Adjudication." *Justice System Journal,* 1982, *7,* 420–44).

16. Some commentators argue that court procedures are always preferable to a negotiated settlement when issues of public importance are involved in a dispute (see, for example, Fiss, O. M. "Against Settlement." *Yale Law Journal,* 1984, *93,* 1073–90), and all agree that disputants should not be pressured into the settlement of such disputes. The extent to which parties should be encouraged to resolve disputes affecting a public interest is, however, not at all clear. See Edwards, H. T. "Alternative Dispute Resolution: Panacea or Anathema?" *Harvard Law Review,* 1986, *99,* 668–84.

Consider Both Relationships and Substance When Negotiating Strategically

Grant T. Savage

John D. Blair

Ritch L. Sorenson

When David Peterson, director of services for Dickerson Machinery, arrives at his office, he notes four appointments on his schedule. With his lengthy experience in negotiating important contracts for this large-equipment repair service, he does not take long to identify the agenda for each appointment.[1]

A steering clutch disk salesman from Roadworks will arrive at 8:30 A.M. Peterson has relied for years on disks supplied by Caterpillar and knows those disks can provide the 8,000 hours of service Dickerson guarantees. Price is an issue in Peterson's selection of a supplier, but more important is a guarantee on the life span of the part.

A meeting is scheduled at 9:30 with a mechanic who has swapped a new company battery for a used battery from his own truck. This "trade" is, of course, against company policy, and the employee has been reprimanded and told his next paycheck will be docked. However, the mechanic wants to discuss the matter.

A representative for Tarco, a large road-building contractor, is scheduled for 10:00 A.M. Peterson has been interested in this service contract for a couple of years. He believes that if he can secure a short-term service contract with Tarco, Dickerson's high-quality mechanical service and guarantees will result in a long-term service relationship with the contractor. The night before, Peterson had dinner with Tarco's representative, and this morning he will provide a tour of service facilities and discuss the short-term contract with him.

A meeting with management representatives for union negotiations is scheduled for 1:00 P.M. That meeting will probably last a couple of hours. Peterson is concerned because the company has lost money on the shop undergoing contract talks, and now the union is demanding higher wages and threatening to strike. The company cannot afford a prolonged strike, but it also cannot afford to increase pay at current service production rates. Negotiating a contract will not be easy.

Reprinted from *Academy of Management Executive* 3, no. 1 (February 1989), pp. 37–47. Used with permission.

CHOOSING NEGOTIATION STRATEGIES

Peterson's appointments are not unique. Researchers and scholars have examined similar situations. What strategic advice does the negotiation literature offer for handling these four situations?

One of the best developed approaches is *game theory*, which focuses on maximizing substantive outcomes in negotiations.[2] Peterson would probably do well by focusing on only the best possible outcome for Dickerson Machinery in his meetings with the salesman and the employee: He already has a good contract for a steering wheel clutch, but if the salesman can offer a better deal, Peterson will take it; and in the case of the employee, Peterson will hear him out but foresees no need to deviate from company policy.

In contrast, an exclusive focus on maximizing the company's substantive outcomes would probably not work in the other two situations: Tarco may continue being serviced elsewhere unless enticed to try Dickerson; and during the union negotiations, strategies to maximize outcomes for management only could force a strike.

Another well-developed strategic approach is *win-win problem solving*. It is designed to maximize outcomes for both parties and maintain positive relationships.[3] This approach could work in the union negotiation, but the outcome would probably be a compromise, not a true win-win solution.

Win-win negotiation probably is not the best strategy in the other three situations. Either Roadwork's salesman meets the guarantee and beats current prices, or he does not; trying to find a win-win solution would probably be a waste of time. Similarly, because the meeting with the employee will occur after company rules have been applied, a win-win solution is probably not in the company's best interest. Lastly, an attempt to maximize the company's substantive outcomes in a short-term service contract with Tarco could hinder long-term contract prospects.

Any one approach to negotiation clearly will not work in all situations. Executives need a framework for determining what strategies are best in different situations. We believe the best strategy depends on desired outcomes. In this article, we characterize the two major outcomes at issue in the previous examples as *substantive* and *relationship* outcomes. Although both types of outcome have been discussed in the literature, relationship outcomes have received much less attention. Our contention is that a systematic model of strategic choice for negotiation must account for both substantive and relationship outcomes. In articulating such a model, we suggest that executives can approach negotiation strategically by assessing the negotiation context; considering unilateral negotiation strategies; transforming unilateral into interactive negotiation strategies; and monitoring tactics and reevaluating negotiation strategies.

ASSESSING THE NEGOTIATION CONTEXT

A crucial context for any negotiation is the manager's current and desired relationship with the other party. Unfortunately, in their rush to secure the best possible substantive outcome, managers often overlook the impact of the negotiation on their relationships. This oversight can hurt a manager's relationship with the other party, thus limiting his or her ability to obtain desired substantive outcomes now or in the future.

Each interaction with another negotiator constitutes an *episode* that draws from current and affects future relationships. Intertwined with pure concerns about relationships are concerns about substantive outcomes. Many times negotiators are motivated to establish or maintain positive relationships and willingly "share the pie" through mutually beneficial collaboration. Other negotiations involve substantive outcomes that can benefit one negotiator only at the expense of the other (a fixed pie). These cases often motivate negotiators to discount the relationship and claim as much of the pie as possible.

Most negotiations, however, are neither clearly win-win nor win-lose situations, but combinations of both (an indeterminate pie). Such mixed-motive situations, in which both collaboration and competition may occur, are particularly difficult for managers to handle strategically.[4] The relationship that exists prior to the negotiation, the relationship that unfolds during negotiations, and the desired relationship often will determine whether either negotiator will be motivated to share the pie, grab it, or give it away.

In any case, managers should keep existing and desired relationships in mind as they bid for substantive outcomes. For example, when negotiators are on the losing end of a win-lose negotiation, they should examine the implications of taking a short-term loss. During his third appointment, Peterson's willingness to make only minimal gains in service contracts for the short term may create a positive relationship that will lead to a lucrative, long-term contract with Tarco. The relative importance of possible substantive and relationship outcomes should help executives decide whether and how to negotiate. To guide their decision process, managers should begin by assessing their relative power and the level of conflict between them and the other party. Both are key determinants of their current relationship with the other party.

Exhibit 1 illustrates the negotiation context, showing those aspects of the situation and negotiation episode that shape relationship and substantive outcomes. Existing levels of power and conflict influence (1) the relationship between the executive and the other party and (2) the negotiation strategies they choose. These strategies are implemented through appropriate tactics during a negotiation episode—a one-on-one encounter, a telephone call, or a meeting with multiple parties—and result in substantive and relationship outcomes.

The multiple arrows linking strategies, tactics, and the negotiation episode in Exhibit 1 show the monitoring process through which both the manager and the other party refine their strategies and tactics during an episode. A complex and lengthy negotiation, such as a union contract negotiation, may include many episodes; a simple negotiation may be completed within one episode. Each episode, nonetheless, influences future negotiations by changing the manager's and the other party's relative power, the level of conflict between them, and their relationship.

Relative Power

The relative power of the negotiators establishes an important aspect of their relationship: the extent of each party's dependence on the other. Researchers have found that individuals assess their power in a relationship and choose whether to compete, accommodate, collaborate, or withdraw when negotiating with others.[5] Managers can assess their power relative to the other party by comparing their respective abilities to

EXHIBIT 1   Assessing the Negotiation Context

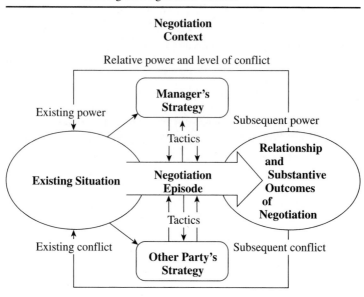

induce compliance through the control of human and material resources. To what extent do they each control key material resources? To what extent do they each control the deployment, arrangement, and advancement of people within the organization?[6]

These questions will help managers determine whether their relationship with the other party is based on independence, dependence, or interdependence. Additionally, these questions should help executives consider how *and* whether their relationship with the other party should be strengthened or weakened. Often managers will find themselves or their organizations in interdependent relationships that have both beneficial and detrimental aspects. These relationships are called mixed-motive situations in the negotiation literature because they provide incentives for both competitive and cooperative actions.

In his relationship with the Roadwork salesman, Peterson has considerable power. He is satisfied with his current vendor and has other vendors wanting to sell him the same product. The numerous choices available allow him to make demands on the salesman. Similarly, Peterson has more relative power than the mechanic. On the other hand, he has relatively little power with Tarco, since the contractor can choose from a number of equipment-service shops. Moreover, Tarco's representative did not make the initial contact and has not actively sought Dickerson's services.

Level of Conflict

The level of conflict underlying a potential negotiation establishes how the negotiators perceive the affective dimension of their relationship—that is, its degree of supportiveness or hostility. Managers can assess the relationship's level of conflict by identifying the differences between each party's interests. On what issues do both parties agree? On what issues do they disagree? How intense and how ingrained are these differences?[7]

EXHIBIT 2   Considering a Unilateral Negotiation Strategy

	Is the substantive outcome very important to the manager?	
	Yes	**No**
Yes — Is the relationship outcome very important to the manager?	*Strategy C1* **Trustingly collaborate** When both types of outcomes are very important *Situation 1*	*Strategy S1* **Openly subordinate** When the priority is on relationship outcomes *Situation 2*
No	*Strategy P1* **Firmly compete** When the priority is on substantive outcomes *Situation 3*	*Strategy A1* **Actively avoid negotiating** When neither type of outcome is very important *Situation 4*

Answers to these questions will reveal whether negotiations will easily resolve differences and whether the relationship is perceived as supportive or hostile. These questions, like the questions about relative power, should also help executives consider how *and* whether the relationship should be strengthened or weakened. Very few negotiations begin with a neutral relationship. Indeed, the affective state of the relationship may be a primary reason for negotiating with a powerful other party, especially if the relationship has deteriorated or been particularly supportive.

In Peterson's case, neutral to positive relationships exist with the Roadwork salesman and the Tarco representative. However, his relationships with the mechanic and the union are potentially hostile. For example, management and union representatives have already had confrontations. Their conflict may escalate if the relationship is not managed and both sides are not willing to make concessions.[8]

Considering a Unilateral Negotiation Strategy

Before selecting a strategy for negotiation, a manager should consider his or her interests and the interests of the organization. These interests will shape the answers to two basic questions: (1) Is the substantive outcome very important to the manager? and (2) Is the relationship outcome very important to the manager?

Four *unilateral* strategies (see Exhibit 2) emerge from the answers: *trusting collaboration, firm competition, open subordination,* and *active avoidance.*[9] We call these unilateral strategies because in using them, managers consider only their own interests or the interests of their organization, ignoring for the time being the interests of the other party.

The unilateral strategies presented in Exhibit 2 are similar to the conflict management styles suggested by the combined works of Blake and Mouton, Hall, and Kilmann and Thomas.[10] However, while we agree that personalities and conflict-management preferences influence a person's ability to negotiate, our selection of terms reflects our focus on strategies instead of styles. For example, Johnston used the term "subordination" to refer to a strategy similar to the conflict-management style variously termed "accommodation" (Kilmann and Thomas), "smoothing" (Blake and Mouton), or "yield-lose" (Hall).[11] We, however, see using the openly subordinative strategy as more than simply "rolling over and playing dead" or "giving away the store." Rather, this strategy is designed to strengthen long-term relational ties, usually at the expense of short-term substantive outcomes. Our discussion below also goes beyond Johnston's conception, showing how a negotiator can focus the openly subordinative strategy according to his or her substantive goals.

Our view is consistent with research that suggests that individuals adopt different strategies in different relational contexts.[12] We anticipate that managers' success with these unilateral strategies depends on their ability to exhibit a variety of conflict styles. To highlight the role of relationship and substantive priorities, we describe these four unilateral strategies in their most extenuated, ideal form, and articulate their underlying assumptions. In many ways our descriptions are classic depictions of each type of strategy. Two of these strategies—competition and collaboration—are frequently discussed in the conflict and negotiation literature.

1. Trusting Collaboration (C1).   In general, if both relationship and substantive outcomes are important to the organization, the manager should consider *trusting collaboration*. The hallmark of this strategy is openness on the part of both parties. By encouraging cooperation as positions are asserted, the executive should be able to achieve important relationship and substantive outcomes. The executive seeks a win-win outcome both to achieve substantive goals *and* maintain a positive relationship.

Trustingly collaborative strategies generally are easiest to use and most effective when the manager's organization and the other party are interdependent and mutually supportive. These circumstances normally create a trusting relationship in which negotiators reciprocally disclose their goals and needs. In this climate, an effective problem-solving process and a win-win settlement typically result.

2. Open Subordination (S1).   If managers are more concerned with establishing a positive relationship with another party than obtaining substantive outcomes, they should openly subordinate. We use the term *subordination* instead of *accommodation* to differentiate this strategic choice from a conflict-management style. An openly subordinative strategy is a yield-win strategy that usually provides desired substantive outcomes to the other party but rarely to the manager. A subordinative strategy may be used regardless of whether the manager exercises more, less, or equal power relative to the other party. Our argument is that subordination can be an explicit strategic negotiation behavior—not simply a reflection of power. If the manager has little to lose by yielding to the substantive interests of the other party, open subordination can be a key way for him or her to dampen hostilities, increase support, and foster more interdependent relationships.

3. Firm Competition (P1).   If substantive interests are important but the relationship is not, the manager should consider *firmly competing.* This situation often occurs when managers have little trust for the other party or the relationship is not good to begin with. In such situations, they may want to exert their power to gain substantive outcomes. To enact this competitive strategy, they may also become highly aggressive, bluffing, threatening the other party, or otherwise misrepresenting their intentions. Such tactics hide the manager's actual goals and needs, preventing the other party from using that knowledge to negotiate its own substantive outcomes. Not surprisingly, the credibility of the executive's aggressive tactics and, thus, the success of the firmly competitive strategy often rests on the organization's power vis-à-vis the other party. When following a firmly competitive strategy, the manager seeks a win-lose substantive outcome and is willing to accept a neutral or even a bad relationship.

4. Active Avoidance (A1).   Managers should consider *actively avoiding negotiation* if neither the relationship nor the substantive outcomes are important to them or the organization. Simply *refusing* to negotiate is the most direct and active form of avoidance. Executives can simply tell the other party they are not interested in or willing to negotiate. Such an action, however, will usually have a negative impact on the organization's relationship with the other party. Moreover, managers must determine which issues are a waste of time to negotiate. We treat avoidance, like subordination, as an explicit, strategic behavior rather than as an option taken by default when the manager is uncertain about what to do.

However, we recognize that these unilateral strategies are most successful only in a limited set of situations. In the next section we include various *interactive* modifications that make these classic, unilateral strategies applicable to a wider set of negotiation situations.

INTERACTIVE NEGOTIATION STRATEGIES

Before using the unilateral strategies suggested by Exhibit 2, the executive should examine the negotiation from each party's perspective. The choice of a negotiation strategy should be based not only on the interests of the executive or organization, but also on the interests of the other party. The manager should anticipate the other party's substantive and relationship priorities, assessing how the negotiation is likely to progress when the parties interact. This step is crucial because the unilateral strategies described above could lead to grave problems if the other party's priorities differ. For example, when using either trusting collaboration or open subordination, the manager is vulnerable to exploitation if the other party is concerned only about substantive outcomes. When anticipating the other party's substantive and relationship priorities, executives should consider the kinds of actions the other party might take. Are those actions likely to be supportive or hostile? Will they represent short-term reactions or long-term approaches to the substantive issues under negotiation? Are those actions likely to change the party's degree of dependence on, or interdependence with, the organization? The answers will depend on (1) the history of the executive's relations with the other party and (2) the influence of key individuals and groups on the manager and the other party.

EXHIBIT 3   Selecting an Interactive Strategy

Manager's priorities		Other party's priorities			
Is the substantive outcome very important to the manager?	Is the relationship outcome very important to the manager?	Is the substantive outcome very important to the other party?	Is the relationship outcome very important to the other party?	Situations	

Unilateral strategies

Interactive strategies

Situations

	Situation
C1	1
C2. P2	2
C1	3
S2	4
C2. P2	5
P1. C2	6
P2. C1	7
C2. P2	8
C1	9
S1	10
C1	11
S1	12
C2. P2	13
A3. P1	14
A2	15
A1	16

Branch labels: C1, P1, S1, A1, and Yes/No decisions.

Suggested Strategies

C1: Trusting collaboration

C2: Principled collaboration

P1: Firm competition

P2: Soft competition

S1: Open subordination

S2: Focused subordination

A1: Active avoidance (refuse to negotiate)

A2: Passive avoidance (delegate negotiation)

A3: Responsive avoidance (apply regulations)

In short, executives should take into account both their own and the other party's substantive and relationship priorities in choosing a negotiating strategy. Exhibit 3 is a decision tree designed to help managers decide which strategy to use. The left side represents, in a different form, the analysis in Exhibit 2; thus, Exhibit 3 also shows how the manager's substantive and relationship priorities lead to *unilateral strategies* based solely on the manager's position. The right side illustrates how these unilateral strategies may be continued, modified, or replaced after the manager considers the other party's potential or apparent priorities.[13]

Managers should examine the appropriateness of a unilateral negotiation strategy by accounting for the other party's priorities before they use it. Sometimes such scrutiny will simply justify its use. For example, when both substantive and relationship outcomes are important to an executive, the appropriate unilateral strategy is trusting collaboration. If the manager anticipates that the other party also values both substantive and relationship outcomes (see Exhibit 3, Situation 1), he or she would continue to favor this strategy. At other times, scrutiny of the other party's priorities may suggest some modifications. We discuss next each of the interactive variations of the classic, unilateral strategies.

1. Principled Collaboration (C2).   The C1 collaborative strategy assumes that the other party will reciprocate whenever the executive discloses information. However, if the manager negotiates openly and the other party is not open or is competitive, the manager could be victimized. Under such circumstances, the manager should use the modified collaborative strategy of principled collaboration.[14] Rather than relying on only trust and reciprocity, the manager persuades the other party to conduct negotiations based on a set of mutually agreed upon principles that will benefit each negotiator.

2. Focused Subordination (S2).   The openly subordinative strategy (S1) assumes that the substantive outcome is of little importance to the organization. Sometimes, however, an organization has both substantive and relationship interests, but the other party has little stake in either interest. By discovering and then acquiescing to those key needs that are of interest only to the other party, the manager can still gain some substantive outcomes for the organization while assuring a relatively positive relationship outcome. Here, managers both create substantive outcomes for the other party and achieve substantive outcomes for themselves or their organization.

3. Soft Competition (P2).   Under some circumstances the directness of the firmly competitive strategy (P1) may need to be softened. For example, even though the manager may place little importance on the relationship outcome, this relationship may be very important to the other party. If the other party is powerful and potentially threatening, the manager would be wise to use a competitive strategy that maintains the relationship. Here the executive would avoid highly aggressive and other "dirty" tactics.

4. Passive Avoidance (A2).   If the manager does not consider either the relationship or the substantive outcome important but the other party views the negotiation as important for a relationship outcome, the manager probably should *delegate* the negotiation. By passively avoiding the negotiation, the manager allows someone else within the organization to explore possible outcomes for the organization and keep the relationship from becoming hostile. Delegating ensures that possible opportunities are not ignored while freeing the executive from what appears to be a low-priority negotiation.

5. Responsive Avoidance (A3).   By contrast, if the manager considers neither the relationship nor the substantive outcome important and the other party considers the substantive outcome important and the relationship unimportant, the manager should *regulate* the issue. Direct interaction with the other party is not necessary; the manager can be responsive but still avoid negotiating by either applying standard operating procedures or developing new policies that address the other party's concern.

Transforming Unilateral Strategies

The model of strategic choice in Exhibit 3 connects unilateral and interactive negotiation strategies. In many instances the interactive strategies are modifications of the unilateral strategies. We base the decision to modify or replace a unilateral strategy almost exclusively on the manager's and other party's differing outcome priorities. Three outcome conditions and three sets of assumptions influence the choice of interactive strategies.

1. Outcome Condition One: The manager may value the relationship, but the other party may not.   For example, a manager who assumes that trust and cooperation will result in a fair outcome may be taken advantage of by another party who is concerned with only substantive outcomes.[15] Hence, we suggest either principled collaboration or soft competition for such cases to ensure that the other party does not take advantage of the manager (see Exhibit 3, Situation 2). On the other hand, the manager may simply want to create a long-term business relationship with someone who currently is interested in neither substantive nor relationship outcomes. In these cases the manager should choose to subordinate in a focused fashion—rather than to trustingly collaborate—to establish a relationship with the other party (see Exhibit 3, Situation 4).

2. Outcome Condition Two: The manager may not value the relationship, but the other party may.   Given only their own substantive priorities, managers would firmly compete or actively avoid negotiation under these circumstances. However, if the other party is interested in the relationship, the manager may not have to compete firmly to obtain desired substantive outcomes. The manager may collaborate or softly compete and still gain substantive goals without alienating the other party (see Exhibit 3, Situations 5–8). Such strategies may also foster a long-term relationship with substantive dividends for the manager.

Similarly, in situations where neither substantive nor relationship outcomes are important to the manager but the relationship is important to the other party, the manager may choose an interactive strategy other than avoidance. The other party is in a position to choose a subordinative strategy and may offer substantive incentives to the manager. If the manager chooses principled collaboration or soft competition, he or she may gain some positive substantive outcomes (see Exhibit 3, Situation 13).

3. Outcome Condition Three.   Both parties may value the relationship, but the manager may not value substantive outcomes. In these cases, whether or not the other party is interested in substantive outcomes, the manager may choose a trustingly collaborative strategy to maintain positive ties with the other party (see Exhibit 3, Situations 9 and 11).

4. Transformation Assumptions.   Underlying these three outcome conditions are three sets of assumptions. First, we assume that most relationships will involve some mixture of dependence and interdependence as well as some degree of supportiveness and hostility. Second, we assume that most negotiators will view the relationship outcome as important under four separate conditions—high interdependence, high dependence, high supportiveness, or high hostility—or possible combinations of those conditions. Third, from a manager's perspective, each of the basic strategies has a different effect with regard to power and conflict: (1) collaborative strategies strengthen the interdependence of the manager and the other party while also enhancing feelings of supportiveness, (2) subordinative strategies increase the other party's dependence on the manager while also deemphasizing feelings of hostility, and (3) competitive strategies decrease the manager's dependence on the other party but may also escalate feelings of hostility.

Thus many of the interactive negotiation strategies in Exhibit 3 seek to enhance interdependent relationships or favorably shift the balance of dependence within a relationship. These same strategies also attempt to dampen feelings of hostility or heighten feelings of supportiveness.

Illustrations of Negotiation-Strategy Transformations

To demonstrate more concretely how Exhibit 3 works, we will examine how Dickerson's Peterson might act if he were to follow the decision tree to choose his negotiation strategies.

1. From Avoidance to Collaboration or Competition.   In planning to meet with the steering clutch salesman, Peterson first considers whether the substantive outcome is very important to Dickerson Machinery. Because the company already has a satisfactory source for clutch disks, the substantive outcome is not very important. Second, Peterson considers the importance of the relationship outcome. Given that Dickerson Machinery currently has no ties with Roadworks and Peterson foresees no need to establish a long-term relationship, the relationship outcome is not very important either. Based on Peterson's priorities only, unilateral avoidance strategy (A1) seems appropriate.

However, Peterson now considers the salesman's priorities. First, is the substantive outcome important to the salesman? Obviously, it is—Roadworks is a struggling, new company and needs new clients. Second, is the relationship outcome important to Roadworks? Because the salesman works on a commission with residuals, he probably desires a long-term sales contract, so the relationship outcome is important. The salesman's priorities suggest that he would probably collaborate trustingly (C1).

After answering the questions forming the decision tree in Exhibit 3 (see Situation 13), Peterson has two options for an interactive strategy. Since he is in a position of power, he does not need to make concessions. Moreover, the salesman may have products worthy of consideration. Thus, Peterson can engage in principled collaboration (C2) or softly compete (P2). In other words, he can collaborate based on principles, taking a strong stand on what he expects in a sales contract; or he can softly compete by making product demands that do not offend the salesman.

2. From Collaboration to Subordination.   For the situation with the contractor, the relationship outcome is very important to Dickerson Machinery but the immediate, substantive outcome is not. Peterson realizes that Dickerson needs Tarco's business for long-term stability but does not need to make a profit in the short term. Therefore, his unilateral strategy would be to subordinate openly (S1). He decides to change his strategy from the trustingly collaborative (C1) approach he has used in past dealings with Tarco.

As Peterson considers the contractor's priorities, he anticipates that the substantive outcome is important to Tarco but the relationship outcome is not. Tarco's representative has made clear the need for reliable service at the lowest possible price; conversely, Tarco has not responded to Peterson's bids to provide service for more than two years. Peterson recognizes, based on Exhibit 2, that Tarco can compete firmly (P1). After assessing both parties' priorities using the decision tree (see Exhibit 3, Situation 10), he decides he should continue with an interactive strategy of open subordination (S1). Such a strategy is more likely to induce Tarco's representative to offer a contract than the trustingly collaborative strategy he has used previously. For example, he is prepared to subordinate by offering a "winter special" to reduce labor costs by 10 percent, cutting competitive parts costs by 15 percent, and providing a new paint job at 50 percent the normal costs or providing a six-month deferment on payment, all in addition to paying for the trip to the plant.

3. From Competition to Collaboration.   Peterson's analysis of the negotiation with the labor union includes an assessment of the recent history of and level of conflict between the union and the company. Previous episodes in this contract negotiation have led both the union and Dickerson Machinery to change their priorities. During the first few episodes, both parties focused on only substantive outcomes and ignored relationship outcomes, using firmly competitive strategies. Also, during these earlier episodes, both sides' demands hardened to the point where the union threatened to strike and management threatened to give no increases in wages or benefits.

Now, however, Peterson believes that both substantive and relationship outcomes are important to Dickerson. The company wants to find a way to increase productivity without giving much of an increase in pay and benefits. It also does not want to lose good mechanics or stimulate a strike. Dickerson's unilateral strategy under these new conditions should be trustingly collaborative (C1).

From analyzing the union's position, Peterson realizes that both the substantive and relationship outcomes should be important to the union. His informal discussions with union representatives have assured him that both sides are now concerned about maintaining the relationship. Nonetheless, the union clearly wants an increase in pay and benefits even though it also does not want a strike. In short, the union now is likely to trustingly collaborate but could easily shift its priorities and choose to firmly compete.

As he enters the negotiation strategy session this afternoon, Peterson plans to recommend to the management negotiation team the use of a principled collaborative (C2) strategy (see Exhibit 3, Situation 2). Because of the current instability in the relationship, he does not want to provide the union with any opportunity to exploit a perceived weakness that a more trustingly collaborative strategy might create.

Monitoring and Reevaluating Strategies

After implementing their interactive strategy, managers should monitor the other party's tactics. How the other party acts will signal its strategy. Based on the other party's tactics, executives can (1) determine if their assumptions and expectations about the other party's strategy are accurate and (2) modify, if needed, their strategies during this and subsequent negotiation episodes. Exhibit 1 provides an overview of this process. The arrows linking strategies to tactics and the negotiation episode represent how tactics (1) are used to implement a strategy (first arrow), (2) provide information to each party (second, reversed arrow), and (3) may affect the choice of alternative strategies during a negotiation episode (third arrow).

Monitoring Tactics

More specifically, we view tactics in two ways: (1) as clusters of specific actions associated with the implementation of one strategy or another, and (2) as actions that derive their strategic impact from the particular phase of the negotiation in which they are used. In Exhibit 4, we combine these two perspectives to provide executives with descriptions of competitive, collaborative, and subordinative tactics across various phases of negotiation. We suggest that most negotiations go through four phases: (1) the search for an arena and agenda formulation, (2) the stating of demands and offers, (3) a narrowing of differences, and (4) final bargaining.[16] Not every negotiation will involve all of these phases. Rather, these phases characterize typical negotiations in mixed-motive situations. Hence, a specific phase may be skipped or never attained.[17]

For example, the search for an arena in which to carry out discussions may be unnecessary for some ongoing negotiations; however, most negotiations will initially involve some Phase 1 interaction about the items to be discussed. During the second phase, both the managers and the other party express their preferences and establish their commitments to specific issues and outcomes. The third phase may be skipped, although it usually occurs if the manager and the other party are far apart in their preferences and commitments. Both sides may add or delete bargaining items or shift preferences to avoid an impasse. The fourth phase completes the negotiation: The manager and the other party reduce their alternatives, making joint decisions about each item until a final agreement is reached.

Exhibit 4 should help managers recognize (1) how using certain tactics during various phases of a negotiation is essential to implementing their strategy and (2) how the tactics of the other party reflect a particular strategic intent. An unanticipated strategy implemented by the other party may indicate that the executive inaccurately assessed the negotiation context or under- or overestimated the strength of the other party's priorities. Hence, once the manager recognizes the other party's actual strategy, he or she should reassess the negotiation, repeating the process discussed in previous sections to check the appropriateness of his or her strategies.

Sometimes, however, the other party's use of an unanticipated strategy does not mean the executive's assessment of the negotiation context was inaccurate. In Exhibit 3, some combinations of the manager's and other party's priorities result in the listing of

EXHIBIT 4   Using Tactics across Negotiation Phases

Negotiation Phases	Negotiation Tactics		
	Competitive	*Collaborative*	*Subordinative*
The search for an arena and agenda formulation	• Seek to conduct negotiations on manager's home ground • Demand discussion of manager's agenda items; curtail discussions of other party's items • Ignore or discount the other party's demands and requests	• Seek to conduct negotiations on neutral ground • Elicit the other party's agenda items and assert manager's items; incorporate both • Consider other party's demands and requests	• Seek to conduct negotiations on the other party's ground • Elicit the other party's agenda items and subvert manager's items • Concede to the other party's demands and requests
The stating of demands and offers	• Insist other party make initial offers or demands on all items • Respond with very low offers or very high demands • Commit to each item; exaggerate manager's position and discredit other party's	• Alternate initial offers and demands on items with other party • Respond with moderate offers or moderate demands • Indicate reasons for manager's commitment to item outcomes; probe the other party's reasons	• Make initial offers or demands on all other party-relevant items • Make high offers or low demands • Accept the other party's commitments to items; explain manager's commitments
A narrowing of differences	• Demand that other party make concession; back up demand with threats • Delete, add, or yield only on low manager-interest items • Magnify degree of manager's concessions; downplay other party's	• Seek equitable exchange of concessions with the other party • Delete, add, or yield items if mutual interests converge • Honestly assess manager's and other party's concessions	• Concede to the other party's demands • Delete, add, or yield to any other party-relevant item • Acknowledge the other party's concessions; downplay manager's concessions
Final bargaining	• Seek large concessions from the other party • Concede only minimally on high manager-interest items • Use concessions on low manager-interest items as bargaining chips	• Seek equitable exchange of concessions from the other party • Seek mutually beneficial outcomes when conceding or accepting concessions on items	• Yield to the other party's relevant preferences by accepting low offers and making low demands

two interactive strategies. Managers should normally use the first (left-hand) strategies in these listings. The secondary (right-hand) strategies are suggested as countermoves the executive should use if the other party uses a strategy different from the one expected, but the executive remains convinced that his or her diagnosis is accurate.

Reevaluating Negotiation Strategies

Take, for example, Peterson's appointment with the mechanic who had swapped a battery from a company truck with his own used battery. Going into the negotiation, Peterson decides that his unilateral strategy should be trusting collaboration: The mechanic is highly skilled and would be hard to replace, yet the infraction is a serious matter. He also anticipates that the employee will be interested primarily in retaining a good relationship with Dickerson's management. Hence, Peterson decides to stick with trusting collaboration as his interactive strategy (see Exhibit 3, Situation 3).

However, during the first five minutes of the meeting, Peterson's efforts to discuss returning the battery to the company and removing the infraction from the mechanic's personnel record are repeatedly rebuffed by the employee. Instead, the mechanic threatens to retire early from Dickerson and collect the benefits due him unless Peterson transfers him. Peterson recognizes that the mechanic is employing competitive tactics to set the agenda, which reflects an interest in substantive outcomes but little concern for relationship outcomes.

As the negotiation enters the next phase, Peterson considers the mechanic's apparent priorities and reevaluates his own priorities. Now neither the substantive nor the relationship outcomes are very important to him. He knows that Dickerson has no opening for the mechanic at any other shop; moreover, if the employee wants to leave, the relationship is of little value. Based on this reassessment (see Exhibit 3, Situation 14), Peterson sees that he has two interactive strategic options: He can regulate the matter (A3) by pressing criminal charges or compete firmly (P1) with the employee.

Rather than withdraw from the interaction, Peterson decides to compete firmly and tells the mechanic that unless the battery is returned, he will do everything he can legally do to prevent the mechanic from receiving optimal severance benefits. If the employee refuses to return the battery, Peterson can still request Dickerson's legal department to file criminal charges against him (A3) as a way to publicize and enforce a legitimate regulatory approach designed to help the company avoid this kind of negotiation.

DISCUSSION

Most of the negotiation literature focuses on substantive outcomes without systematically considering the ways negotiations affect relationships. The approach we have taken underscores how negotiation strategies should address both parties' substantive and relationship priorities. Further, we encourage executives proactively to view negotiation as an indeterminate, reiterative, and often confusing process. It requires them to anticipate and monitor the other party's actions. The other party's tactics will inform managers as to whether their assumptions about the other party's priorities and strategy are correct. Based on this assessment, managers can modify their negotiation strategies as needed during current or future episodes.

Managers should heed, however, a few caveats about our advice:

1. Underlying the strategic choice model in Exhibit 3 is the assumption that most negotiations are of the mixed-motive sort; that is, the manager and other party usually negotiate over several substantive items. Some items have potential outcomes

that can benefit both negotiators; others have potential outcomes that can benefit only one negotiator. Under these conditions, collaborative, competitive, and subordinative strategies may all come into play as the negotiators seek either win-win, win-lose, or yield-win substantive outcomes. Our emphasis in the model is on win-win substantive outcomes brought about through collaborative strategies (C1 and C2).

2. We assume that most relationships will involve some mixture of dependence and interdependence. Furthermore, we posit that most negotiators will view the relationship outcome as important when it is characterized by either high interdependence or high dependence. Collaborative strategies will strengthen the interdependence of the organization and the other party, subordinative strategies will increase the other party's dependence on the organization, and competitive strategies will decrease the organization's dependence on the other party. Our advice about negotiation strategies is directed particularly toward managers who want to enhance relationships of interdependence or favorably shift the balance of dependence within a relationship.

3. We also recognize that the history and level of conflict between an organization and another party strongly influence each negotiator's attitude toward the existing relationship. Feelings of hostility, we assume, will be escalated by a competitive strategy; in contrast, feelings of hostility will be deemphasized by a subordinative strategy. Following this same logic, feelings of supportiveness will be enhanced by a collaborative strategy. Several of the strategies suggested in Figure 3—trusting collaboration, soft competition, open subordination, and passive and responsive avoidance—attempt to dampen hostilities and increase supportiveness between the manager and the other party.

4. Our advice to executives is simultaneously well supported and speculative. On one hand, the classic (unilateral) strategies suggested in Exhibit 3 are fairly well supported within the negotiation literature; the link between these strategies and both relationship and substantive outcomes is the special focus of our approach. On the other hand, the effectiveness of the interactive strategies suggested in Exhibit 3 remains open to continuing empirical investigation. We have developed this interactive model of strategic choice by linking our concerns about relationship outcomes with what is currently known about the basic strategies of negotiation.

Although the three sets of assumptions we make about relationships are usually warranted in most organization-related negotiations, executives should carefully consider whether their situations fit with these constraints before using our strategic choice model (Exhibit 3). However, regardless of the situation, we believe that managers will generally be more effective negotiators when they carefully assess both (1) the relationship and the substantive aspects of any potential negotiation and (2) what is important to the other party and what is important to them.

ENDNOTES

The authors wish to thank the three anonymous Editorial Review Board members who reviewed an earlier draft of this article for their developmental critiques and constructive suggestions for improving the manuscript.

1. The incidents reported in this vignette and throughout the article are based on actual experiences in a multistate machinery servicing company.

2. See H. Raiffa, *The Art and Science of Negotiation* (Cambridge, MA: Harvard University Press, 1982), for a discussion of how game theory can help negotiators maximize their substantive outcomes under a diverse set of situations.

3. Both R. Fisher and W. Ury, *Getting to Yes: Negotiating Agreements without Giving In* (Boston: Houghton-Mifflin, 1981) and A. C. Filley, "Some Normative Issues in Conflict Management," *California Management Review,* 21, no. 2 (1978), pp. 61–65, treat win-win problem solving as a principled, collaborative process.

4. See S. Bacharach and E. J. Lawler, *Power and Politics in Organizations: The Social Psychology of Conflict, Coalitions, and Bargaining* (San Francisco, CA: Jossey-Bass, 1980) for a recent discussion of mixed-motive negotiation situations.

5. See L. Putnam and C. E. Wilson, "Communicative Strategies in Organizational Conflicts: Reliability and Validity of a Measurement Scale," in M. Burgoon, ed., *Communication Yearbook* 6 (Newbury Park, CA: Sage Publications, 1982), pp. 629–52. See also R. A. Cosier and T. L. Ruble, "Research on Conflict Handling Behavior: An Experimental Approach," *Academy of Management Journal* 24 (1981), pp. 816–31.

6. Power as the ability to induce compliance is discussed in J. March and H. Simon, *Organizations* (New York: Wiley, 1958) and in P. Blau, *Exchange and Power in Social Life* (New York: Wiley, 1964). Two recent books discussing power from a material-resource perspective are H. Mintzberg's *Power in and around Organizations* (Englewood Cliffs, NJ: Prentice Hall, 1983), and J. Pfeffer's *Power in Organizations* (Marshfield, MA: Pitman, 1981). A. Giddens, *The Constitution of Society: Outline of the Theory of Structuration* (Berkeley: University of California Press, 1984), discusses power from a critical-theory perspective within the field of sociology, emphasizing how power involves control over human resources.

7. For discussions of conflict intensity and durability, see I. R. Andrews and D. Tjosvold, "Conflict Management under Different Levels of Conflict Intensity," *Journal of Occupational Behaviour* 4 (1983), pp. 223–28, and C. T. Brown, P. Yelsma, and P. W. Keller, "Communication-Conflict Predisposition: Development of a Theory and an Instrument," *Human Relations* 34 (1981), pp. 1103–17.

8. See M. Deutsch, *The Resolution of Conflict* (New Haven: Yale University Press, 1973), for a discussion of how spiraling conflicts can be both inflamed and controlled.

9. For further discussions on these basic strategies, see C. B. Derr, "Managing Organizational Conflict: Collaboration, Bargaining, and Power Approaches," *California Management Review* 21 (1978), pp. 76–82; Filley, "Some Normative Issues in Conflict Management"; Fisher and Ury, *Getting to Yes*; R. Johnston, "Negotiation Strategies: Different Strokes for Different Folks," in R. Lewicki and J. Litterer, eds., *Negotiation: Readings, Exercises, and Cases* (Homewood, IL: Richard D. Irwin, 1985), pp. 156–64; D. A. Lax and J. K. Sebenius, *The Manager as Negotiator: Bargaining for Cooperation and Competitive Gain* (New York: The Free Press, 1986); and D. G. Pruitt, "Strategic Choice in Negotiation," *American Behavioral Scientist* 27 (1983), pp. 167–94.

10. For an overview of the contributions by these and other conflict-management researchers, see the special issue on "Communication and Conflict Styles in Organizations," L. L. Putnam, ed., *Management Communication Quarterly* 1, no. 3 (1988), pp. 291–45. See also R. Blake and J. Mouton's "The Fifth Achievement," *Journal of Applied Behavioral Science* 6 (1970), pp. 413–26; J. Hall's *Conflict Management Survey: A Survey of One's Characteristic Reaction to and Handling of Conflicts Between Himself and Others* (Conroe, TX: Teleometrics, 1986); and R. H. Kilmann and K. W. Thomas, "Interpersonal Conflict-Handling Behavior as Reflections of Jungian Personality Dimensions," *Psychology Reports* 37 (1975), pp. 971–80, and "Developing a Forced-Choice Measure of Conflict-Handling Behavior: The 'Mode' Instrument," *Educational & Psychological Measurement* 37 (1977), pp. 309–25.

11. See notes 9 above; especially see Johnston.

12. M. L. Knapp, L. L. Putnam, and L. J. Davis, "Measuring Interpersonal Conflict in Organizations: Where Do We Go From Here?" *Management Communication Quarterly* 1 (1988), pp. 414–29; Putnam and Wilson, "Communicative Strategies in Organizational Conflicts"; and J. Sullivan, R. B. Peterson, N. Kameda, and J. Shimada, "The Relationship between Conflict Resolution Approaches and Trust—A Cross Cultural Study," *Academy of Management Journal* 24 (1981), pp. 803–15.

13. We call these strategies *interactive* because they take into account the interactive effect of the manager's and the other party's anticipated or actual priorities concerning substantive and relationship outcomes. Interactive strategies based on anticipating the other party's priorities, as we later discuss in some length, may be changed to reflect more closely the actual priorities of the other party, as revealed through the interaction during a negotiation episode.

14. See Fisher and Ury, Endnote 3.

15. See, for example, L. L. Cummings, D. L. Harnett, and O. J. Stevens, "Risk, Fate, Conciliation and Trust: An International Study of Attitudinal Differences among Executives," *Academy of Management Journal* 14 (1971), pp. 285–304.

16. Different researchers offer varying descriptions of negotiation phases. See L. Putnam, "Bargaining as Organizational Communication," in R. D. McPhee and P. K. Tompkins, eds., *Organizational Communication: Traditional Themes and New Directions* (Beverly Hills, CA: Sage, 1985), for a summary of this research. Ann Douglas proposed the first three-step model in "The Peaceful Settlement of Industrial and Intergroup Disputes," *Journal of Conflict Resolution* 1 (1957), pp. 69–81. However, this model and subsequent three-stage models do not consider the search for the arena as a component phase of a negotiation. P. Gulliver, *Disputes and Negotiations: A Cross-Cultural Perspective* (New York: Academic Press, 1979), proposes an eight-stage model of negotiation, remedying that oversight. Our proposed four-phase model condenses and draws extensively from Gulliver's work.

17. Additionally, we view the phases of negotiation as conceptually separate from our notion of negotiation episodes (see Exhibit 1). All four phases may take place during one episode, particularly if the negotiation involves a single issue of low concern to one or another negotiator. On the other hand, during very complex negotiations stretching over a period of months, numerous episodes may constitute each phase.

SECTION TWO
Prenegotiation Planning

Preparing for Negotiations

Bill Scott

It is critically important, when one's strategy is towards cooperation to mutual advantage, to build firm foundations at the start of the negotiation meeting. But before we can lay firm foundations, we must have made a good job of preparing the ground.

Time after time, one finds negotiators having two cries. On the one hand, "We just didn't have time to do our preparation properly before the meeting." On the other hand, after the meeting, "Well, that has certainly taught me that I ought to be more careful about the way I prepare."

There is no substitute for adequate preparation.

We shall deal with the subject in this chapter, making three sets of assumptions:

1. That the negotiator will have done his homework on the content issues for negotiation. That is, the buyer will have researched all specifications, quantities, market competition, market prices, and so on. The banker will be aware of the availability of funds, the appropriate rate of interest, the status of the client, and so on.

2. That the negotiator is familiar with the rules governing the negotiating territory. The company rules for purchasing or for selling, the trade and/or international rules that apply, the essential legal matters.

3. We assume that the deal is one which can be settled within one or two meetings.

This chapter will give suggestions about

- Conducting the preliminaries.
- A general approach to the planning of negotiations.
- The essence of the negotiating plan.
- Physical preparation.

Reprinted from Bill Scott, *The Skills of Negotiating* (Brookfield, VT: Gower, 1981), pp. 77–87. Used with permission of Gower Publishing Co., Old Post Road, Brookfield, VT 05036. British spellings have been changed to American spellings in this book.

CONDUCTING THE PRELIMINARIES

Other Party comes to a meeting bringing with him not only knowledge of the basic facts. He brings also his own way of conducting negotiations, his expectations about the way that our Party will behave, and his counterintentions.

Whether he has done his preparations systematically or not at all, he will bring impressions and opinions which will influence his conduct.

To help him to bring the right attitudes and information, we need to have explored beforehand as far as possible the purpose of the meeting and the agenda of items which we will discuss. This may have been done through correspondence or by telephone or even, for major negotiations, through preliminary meetings between representatives.

A great deal of Other Party's basic values are deeply engrained. We cannot much influence them during the preliminaries, but we can and do influence his opinions of us and his expectations about the way we shall behave, which in turn influence the way he will prepare to behave with us.

In part his expectations will be based on factors outside our control, such as the stories he has heard about us, the sort of relationship he would expect with a different Party in our situation, and the experience he has had with other organizations in our own industry and culture.

He may have more direct evidence about us. Evidence from dealings which he or his colleagues have had with our organization, evidence of the manner in which we negotiate and of the effectiveness with which we have implemented previous deals.

There remain, however, the preliminaries through which we can ourselves influence him. The manner in which we communicate beforehand needs to reflect our interest in dealing with him; our integrity; our cooperativeness. To create the most positive expectations we need to apply the basic ground rules for communication between people distant from one another: to be prompt and polite, clear, concise, and correct.

We need also to be sensitive in the volume of our preliminary work. Sometimes we have to deal with businesses which seem virtually to resist paperwork. Such organizations always appreciate some brief statement on paper, covering issues like purpose, time, and estimated duration; but with them, anything more than one sheet of paper is irritating and counterproductive.

For other organizations, where formality rules strongly, there is a need for meticulous detail in preliminary exchanges. Indeed, the preliminaries can escalate, almost to become the most important part of the negotiating process.

To summarize: it is important in the way we conduct the preliminaries to help the Other Party to prepare himself for the negotiations, and to ensure he enters the negotiating room looking forward to a desirable relationship.

GENERAL APPROACH TO PLANNING

In principle, preparations for negotiation should lead to a plan which is simple and specific, yet flexible.

It must be sufficiently simple for the negotiator himself easily to carry the headlines in his own thinking. He must have these headlines, these principles of his plan, very clear in his mind; so clear, that he can handle the heavy ongoing content of the negotiation with Other Party (making great demands on his conscious energy), yet at the same time subconsciously be able to relate to his plan.

Such simplicity is hard to achieve.

The plan must be specific: it cannot be simple without being very specific. No room for reservations or elaborations.

Yet it must be flexible. The negotiator must be able to listen effectively to Other Party, to see the relationship of Other Party's thinking to his own plans; and to adjust flexibly.

So the aim of our preparation is to produce a plan which is simple and specific, yet flexible.

That is the ideal, but the reality is usually very different. The negotiator hunts out the information, reads through the correspondence in the files, talks to half a dozen colleagues with interest in the negotiation—each putting a different picture—and is under pressure to be on his way to the motorway or the airport with very little time to form this ragged mass of impulses into any coherent pattern.

His need now is for a discipline; for a general approach which he can use quickly and which he can apply to many different types of negotiation.

The general approach we use is in three stages:

Ideas stage

Thesis sentence

Analysis stage

The aim of the *ideas stage* is to make a quick review of the area for negotiation and at the same time to clear one's own mind. . . . Step one is quickly to jot down all one's jumbled ideas about the negotiation. . . . Step two is to jot down our thoughts about Other Party on another sheet of paper. What they do, where they are, what they look like, what we know of the individuals, what we know they want from the negotiation, what we guess they want, and what else we would like to know. Again, random thoughts (Figure 1).

This ideas stage has led us to the production of two sheets of paper. One with random ideas on the subject and one with random ideas on the Other Party. Having been filled in, having got our minds cleared, these sheets have already largely served their purpose. They should now be put away (not necessarily thrown away—they just might serve some useful purpose later in our preparations).

Our conscious energy is now free to prepare our plans, uncluttered by the jumble of thoughts that was previously there; and the first step in this *analytical stage* is to prepare a thesis sentence.

This thesis sentence is a statement in general terms of what we hope to achieve from the negotiation process. It is a statement for our own guidance, and may sometimes differ from the general purpose of the negotiation as defined to/agreed with Other Party.

The thesis sentence needs to be simple, so we should try to specify it within a maximum of 15 to 20 words. If it takes more, the negotiator has not sufficiently simplified his thinking about why he is entering the negotiating process.

FIGURE 1   Random Thoughts about Other Party

Jensen Electric Supply

30 years relationship

Annual golf match

Good customers

Tough but fair

Enjoy dealing

Probably see Alf

Hope not Doug

Are they in trouble?

Maybe need help

Maybe we need to
       protect

Is whole region in
       trouble

Or just them?

Know our
       processes

Keep it friendly

It is critical that his thinking should be so sharp. If he finds it difficult to state his purpose within 20 words, then he needs to spend more time on clearing his mind, drafting his thoughts about the purpose of the meeting, then pruning and modifying until he gets inside the maximum of 20 words (Figure 2).

Continuing the analysis stage the second step is to develop a plan for handling the negotiation meeting.

The need now is to produce an ordered approach to the conduct of the negotiation, together with a statement of one's opening position.

FIGURE 2   Thesis Sentence

Jensen – Generator Contract

Thesis.   _To ensure goodwill, check_
their business strength,
and get best compensation.

THE ESSENCE OF THE PLAN

The control of any meeting hinges on three of the "Four P's" . . . : the *purpose* of the meeting, the *plan* for the meeting and the *pace* of the meeting. (The *personalities* element, the introduction of the people and their roles, should be a routine, not a part of the plan specific to any one meeting.) Our preparation must cover those three Ps:

- The *purpose* spelled out in one sentence which can be offered to Other Party as "our view of the purpose of this meeting." It should be "our declared view" of the purpose, not necessarily the same as the thesis sentence.

- The *plan* or agenda must be kept simple. The human brain has the ability to keep a clear image of only a few agenda topics throughout a negotiation meeting. About four main items. If in the preparation one tries to give equal significance to, say, seven or eight main points—then the brain is overstretched. It cannot later have a sharp recollection of so many main points. It cannot easily, during the negotiation, relate all that is going on to the prepared plan.

So at the analysis stage we are concerned to prepare our plans for the negotiation meeting under about four main headings.

- The *pace*—in terms of "how long"—should also be estimated.

The practical way to go about this preparation is—after going through the brainstorming stage and preparing the thesis sentence—to plan the agenda. Aim for the ideal of *four* main agenda points, subheading each if need be.

- In negotiations "towards agreement," a sequence I regularly find useful is— "Ours—Theirs—Creative possibilities—Practical actions." "Ours" may, in one session, be "what we hope for from the negotiation," with the corresponding "theirs" being what they hope for; then the creative possibilities for the two of us working together; and finally—what we should do before we meet again.

FIGURE 3   Plan for Meeting

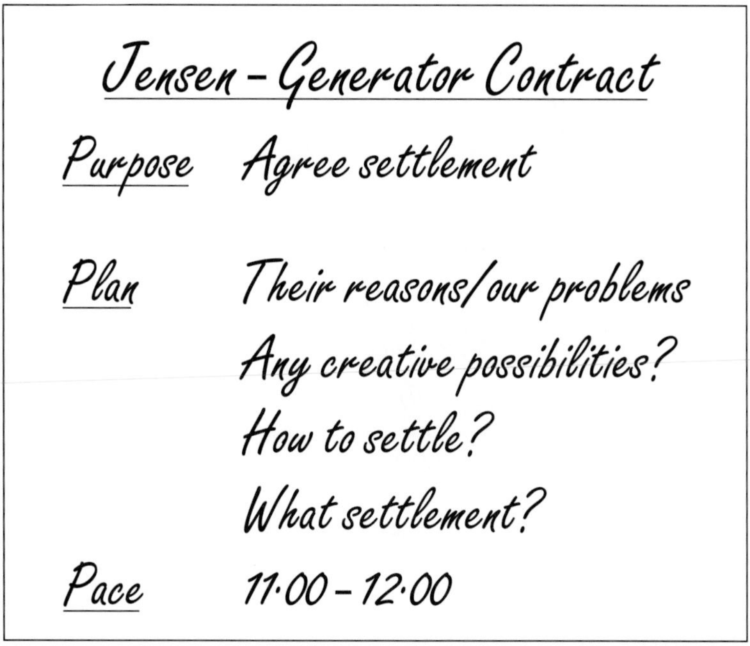

> # Jensen – Generator Contract
>
> <u>Purpose</u>   Agree settlement
>
> <u>Plan</u>   Their reasons/our problems
> Any creative possibilities?
> How to settle?
> What settlement?
>
> <u>Pace</u>   11·00 – 12·00

- In a later session, the same sequence might become—"our offer—their offer—overlaps and problems—action needed to resolve problems."
- And for the next meeting—"Where we'd got to and what we each had to do—our new position—their new position—what is agreed and what remains to be done."

Having got the plan worked out, we should "top" it with a statement of purpose (already considered when building our thesis sentence, though not necessarily to be repeated verbatim); and we should "tail" it with an estimate of the time we shall need (Figure 3).

Finally, the plan needs reducing to key words printed on a postcard.

The purpose of this final stage of planning is to provide a document which the negotiator can have in front of him in the negotiating room. He then needs the key statements prominent and visible at one glance of the eyes. He needs them as prompters for his subconscious, so that he can still control the negotiating process, even when his conscious energy is absorbed in the content of the negotiation (Figure 4).

In addition to this procedural preparation for a negotiation, there is another item to which we have already attached much importance. This is the opening statement to be made at the outset of the negotiating process. It should be systematically prepared. . . .

Following this preliminary work the negotiator goes into the negotiating room properly prepared both to control the process of negotiating, and to present his own position.

What about the room he is going into?

FIGURE 4   Prompter for Control of Negotiation

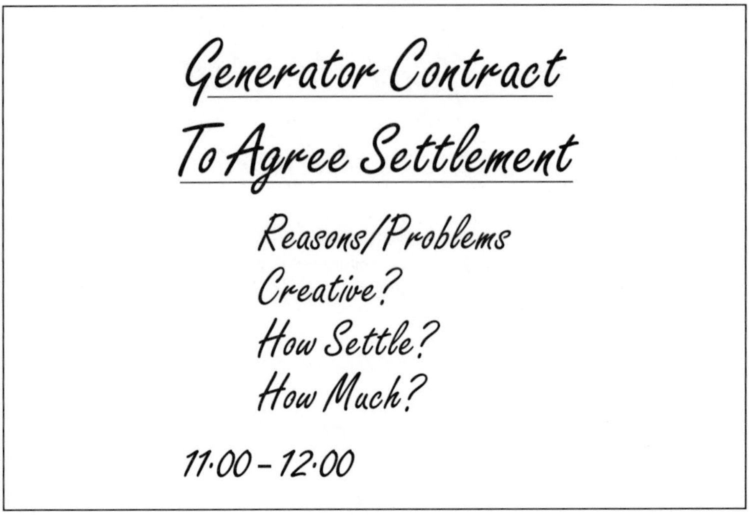

Generator Contract
To Agree Settlement
Reasons/Problems
Creative?
How Settle?
How Much?

11.00 – 12.00

THE PHYSICAL PREPARATION

In this section we shall look briefly at the negotiating room, the layout of the room and the need for services.

The negotiating room itself needs to have the obvious facilities—light, heating, air, noise-proofing.

More contentious are the furnishing and the layout of the room. Negotiators seem to need a table at which to be seated—they seem to feel defenseless without a table between them. But what sort of table? A rectangular table—or the typical business-man's desk—leads to parties being seated opposite to one another. This immediately creates a head-on physical confrontation.

Negotiators recognize that they feel differently on the rare occasions when they sit at round tables. In any poll of negotiators there will be a hefty majority who find it more comfortable and more constructive to use a round table than to use either a rectangular or a square one.

Should negotiators, whether at round or rectangular tables, split into their respective teams or should they intermix? It depends on the mood and style of the negotiations.

Where the parties are relaxed and collaborative, then the relaxation and collaboration are heightened by intermixing. At the extreme this would lead to each negotiator in a team being seated between two negotiators from the Other Party; but that would be contrived only by a formal approach to seating positions. Within an agreement-oriented group, the ice-breaking period leads to informality in the choice of seating positions. It is a purely random matter as to whether one walks up to the table with and sits beside a member of Own or of Other Party.

Where the negotiation process is more conflicting, then it is natural that the parties will gather together, probably on opposite sides of the table. This is both for psychological and for practical reasons. Psychologically, the mood is of "all together against them." Practically, either party may want to refer to papers which they want to keep obscured from Others (impracticable if Others are neighbors) or they may want to sit together so that they can pass notes within their team.

Incidentally neither the regular reference to secret papers nor the passing of notes is a symbol of good negotiators. Energy is needed for the exchanges with Other Party and not for private transactions. It is more skillful to take a recess either to check on the private papers or to handle private communication with colleagues.

It is not only the shape of table that is important—it is also size. There is a comfortable distance at which individuals or groups of individuals may sit from one another. If the parties are sitting a little closer, then the atmosphere becomes warmer. If they are sitting a lot closer, then they become uncomfortable and heated. If the distance apart is, on the other hand, too much, then the parties become remote and the discussion becomes academic.

Apart from the question of the room and the furnishing, the host needs to make suitable provisions for sustenance and for the well-being of Other Party. A special courtesy is in providing Other Party with a room which they can use for recesses, together with such other facilities as typing, telex, and telephone.

SUMMARY

1. The preparation for a negotiation meeting needs discipline. It needs time and the regular use of the same approach.
2. We suggest a disciplined approach of:
   a. brainstorming.
   b. thesis sentence.
   c. planning.
3. The preparation needs to cover purpose, plan, and pace of the meeting.
4. The opening statement should be prepared equally carefully.
5. Physical arrangements influence the form of the subsequent negotiations.

The Negotiation Checklist

Tony Simons

Thomas M. Tripp

Preparation increases your chance of success, whether in combat, sports, or negotiations. The well-prepared negotiator knows the playing field and the players, is seldom surprised, and can promptly capitalize on opportunities. This article offers a tool for use in effectively negotiating important transactions and disputes.

Making deals is a key part of being effective in business. Managers and executives negotiate constantly over issues as varied as hiring decisions and purchases, corporate resource allocations, and labor contracts. One could argue that the American system of government is based on an ongoing process of negotiation, which is sometimes successful and sometimes not.

The "negotiation checklist" that we present in this article is a systematic way to make sure you are well-prepared before you walk into your next negotiation. It is based on proven principles of negotiation that are taught at several of North America's top business schools. The techniques we describe apply whether you are getting ready for a labor negotiation, a negotiation with a supplier, or a negotiation with a customer. This checklist is not a formula for easy success in negotiations. Rather, it is a methodical approach that requires significant work. The amount of time and effort you spend answering the questions should depend on the importance of the negotiation and on the resources you have available. The payoff for your efforts emerges from the confidence and information that you gain from preparation.

THE NEGOTIATION CHECKLIST

The negotiation checklist (in the accompanying box) is a guide for thinking about an important, upcoming negotiation. The pages that follow describe and explain the items on the list.

A. About You

1. What is your overall goal? Start with the big picture. What basic need will an agreement address? Why are you talking to this person or this company? What do you hope to accomplish? Understanding your main goal helps put all the other aspects of the

Negotiation Checklist

A systematic way to ensure you are well-prepared before your next negotiation.

☑ *Item accomplished*

A. About You

❑ 1. What is your overall goal?
❑ 2. What are the issues?
❑ 3. How important is each issue to you?

Develop a scoring system for evaluating offers:

    ❑ (*a*) List all of the issues of importance from step 2.
    ❑ (*b*) Rank order all of the issues.
    ❑ (*c*) Assign points to all the issues (assign weighted values based on a total of 100 points).
    ❑ (*d*) List the range of possible settlements for each issue. Your assessments of realistic, low, and high expectations should be grounded in industry norms and your best-case expectation.
    ❑ (*e*) Assign points to the possible outcomes that you identified for each issue.
    ❑ (*f*) Double-check the accuracy of your scoring system.
    ❑ (*g*) Use the scoring system to evaluate any offer that is on the table.

❑ 4. What is your "best alternative to negotiated agreement" (BATNA)?
❑ 5. What is your resistance point (i.e., the worst agreement you are willing to accept before ending negotiations)? If your BATNA is vague, consider identifying the minimum terms you can possibly accept and beyond which you must recess to gather more information.

B. About the Other Side

❑ 1. How important is each issue to them (plus any new issues they added)?
❑ 2. What is their best alternative to negotiated agreement?
❑ 3. What is their resistance point?
❑ 4. Based on questions B.1, B.2, and B.3, what is your target?

C. The Situation

❑ 1. What deadlines exist? Who is more impatient?
❑ 2. What fairness norms or reference points apply?
❑ 3. What topics or questions do you want to avoid? How will you respond if they ask anyway?

D. The Relationship between the Parties

❑ 1. Will negotiations be repetitive? If so, what are the future consequences of each strategy, tactic, or action you are considering?
❑ 2. ❑ (*a*) Can you trust the other party? What do you know about them?
    ❑ (*b*) Does the other party trust you?
❑ 3. What do you know of the other party's styles and tactics?
❑ 4. What are the limits to the other party's authority?
❑ 5. Consult in advance with the other party about the agenda.

negotiation into perspective. Most people begin and end their negotiation planning by determining their overall goal. We suggest that it is just the beginning.

2. What are the issues? What specific issues must be negotiated for the final outcome or agreement to meet your overall goal? For example, if the overall goal is to book a successful convention, what assurances, services, and constraints will be involved? Price may be an obvious component, but it is worthwhile to consider other items, too— items that might make the agreement much more attractive both to yourself and to the other side. Delivery schedules, duration of contract, product or service upgrades, cancellation clauses, contingency plans, transportation services, complimentary room nights, and many other options all have some value to those negotiating a contract. Such side issues may be researched and introduced as part of a food contract, conference booking, or union contract that you are preparing to negotiate.

Consider also whether any of the issues you have considered might be broken down into multiple components or subissues. For the conference-booking negotiation, for example, you might normally consider the room-block guarantee as a single item (i.e., so many rooms reserved until such-and-such a date). In fact, breaking the room reservations down by percentages and multiple deadlines (e.g., 50 percent by one date, 75 percent by another date) might open avenues for mutually beneficial arrangements.

You should anticipate as many issues as possible for the negotiation. By doing so, you will be better informed and thus feel comfortable and confident when negotiating. Also, the more issues you can introduce, the more likely it becomes that creative solutions will arise, as those are often built by packaging or trading off multiple issues. Creative solutions often make it easier to discover an agreement that both parties like.

By adding items to the negotiations agenda, you increase your chance of discovering some issues that you value more than the other party, and discovering other issues that the other party values more than you. Trading off such differently valued issues dramatically increases the value of the agreement to you without costing the other party. Moreover, if you know what issues the other party highly values that you value less, you can use those issues to get concessions on issues that are important to you.

Imagine that you are a food and beverage director of a hotel seeking a dry-goods supplier and that you have written a request for bids from potential vendors. You have considered your storage capacity and specified every-other-week delivery in your request for bids. Now, suppose you receive a bid from Alpha Dry Goods, which has another customer in town to whom they deliver once every three weeks. Alpha's quote for biweekly delivery might be mediocre, but it turns out that they could save you substantial money on triweekly delivery. They could save you so much money, in fact, that you consider changing your storage arrangement to accommodate their every-three-weeks delivery schedule. If you had been unwilling to negotiate the delivery schedule, you might never have discovered that opportunity. By adding delivery schedule to the agenda, you were able to discover an issue that improved the business potential for both parties. In this example, you are able to secure a lower overall price in return for a concession on delivery schedule.

In general, the more issues you can put on the table (within reason), the better off you are.[1]

Another reason to consider and discuss many issues in a negotiation is that it minimizes the chance of misunderstandings in the final contract. For any issue that is not discussed, the parties risk the possibility of making different assumptions. For example, the "standard frills" that accompany a banquet may not be known by the person purchasing the banquet.

Once you agree that it's a good idea to discuss many issues, how should you determine how many and which ones? For starters, check with your executive committee or association members. Draw also on outside resources. For example, call some friends and colleagues who have conducted similar negotiations and ask them about what issues they put on the table. Library research and obtaining experts' opinions may be helpful, too. Lawyers can be a marvelous source of ideas about which issues to place on the table, especially for a labor negotiation. Be prepared to include all reasonable and relevant issues that are important to you, even if they are not important to the other party.

You can also call the people with whom you plan to negotiate to ask them what issues they expect to discuss and to share your plans. This kind of conversation will begin the negotiation as a cooperative process and should minimize any delays caused by either negotiator's needing to collect additional information, to get authority, or to figure out the value of issues they had not previously considered. As we discuss later, surprise is usually not conducive to effective negotiations.

3. How important is each issue to you? Now that you have listed all the different issues that might be negotiated, you need to develop as precise a picture as possible of their relative importance. Which issues are most important to you and which are not particularly important? Knowing the answer to that question will help you answer the next: On which issues should you stand firm and on which issues can you afford to concede? In other words, what issues might you be willing to trade away?

Setting such priorities can be a complex task. To deal with the complexity of rating the importance of individual issues, we suggest you develop a system to keep track of all the issues without losing sight of the big picture. Many different kinds of systems are possible. The key requirement is that you list and prioritize issues so that no issue is left out when you structure and compare potential agreements. The system you use must allow you to readily determine how well each possible agreement addresses every issue. We offer one such scoring system for your use, as described below.[2]

We suggest developing a table that lists every issue in the negotiation. For each issue the table should list the possible range of settlements.[3] You will then assign points to each issue to reflect its relative priority and to every possible settlement of each issue to reflect the relative desirability of resolving the issue in that way. Such a table allows you to assess the value of any proposed agreement by adding up the points it generates. You can then accurately and quickly determine which of several complex agreements you prefer. Moreover, it can help you keep the big picture in mind as you discuss the details of your agreement. We describe additional benefits in the next few pages.

The first part of Exhibit 1 shows an example of a scoring system that a conference organizer might use to negotiate with a hotel representative. In that example, the issues on the negotiation table are the duration of the room-block reservation, the room rate to be charged, the number of complimentary rooms to be provided, and the late-cancellation policy.[4] The maximum number of points possible here is 100. (If the conference organizer gets 100 percent of what she wants, then she gets 100 points; if she gets none of the issues that are important to her, then she gets 0 points.) The organizer has said that keeping the

EXHIBIT 1 Creating a Scoring System

The example shown is a scoring system such as a conference organizer might use.

Issue 1: *Block Reservation*

Maximum value: *40 points*

Rooms reserved until 7 days before conference	40 pts.
Rooms reserved until 10 days before conference	37 pts.
Rooms reserved until 14 days before conference	35 pts.
Rooms reserved until 21 days before conference	15 pts.
Rooms reserved until 30 days before conference	5 pts.
Rooms reserved until 31 days before conference	0 pts.

Issue 2: *Room Rate*

Maximum value: *25 points*

$95 per person single, $70 per person double	25 pts.
$105 per person single, $80 per person double	20 pts.
$115 per person single, $90 per person double	15 pts.
$125 per person single, $100 per person double	10 pts.
$135 per person single, $100 per person double	5 pts.
$145 per person single, $110 per person double	0 pts.

Issue 3: *Number of Complimentary Room Nights*

Maximum value: *20 points*

3 room nights per 100 booked	20 pts.
2 room nights per 100 booked	15 pts.
1 room night per 75 booked	10 pts.
1 room night per 100 booked	5 pts.
1 room night per 150 booked	0 pts.

Exhibit explanation: *Develop a scoring system for evaluating offers.*

To construct your own scoring system, we recommend that you use the following steps:

(a) List all issues of importance for the negotiation, from step 2 in the checklist.

(b) Rank order all issues according to their value to you. Which is the most important? Next? Last?

(c) Assign points to the issues. The highest ranked issue gets the most points and the lowest ranked issue gets the least points. The sum of maximum points across all issues should be 100. The purpose of this step is to improve upon the simple rank ordering in step b by reflecting the size of the difference between adjacently ranked issues (i.e., how much more important the first issue is than the second, the second issue than the third, and so forth). At 40 points, room-block reservation is worth almost twice as much as the next-most-important issue, room rate. The number of complimentary rooms and room-cancellation policy are slightly less important than room rate.

(d) List the range of possible settlements for each issue. Identify these ranges using industry or local norms or your best assessments of realistic, high, and low expectations. It may be the case that the longest block-reservation policy in the industry is 30 days. This figure establishes a realistic low boundary. Since a seven-day-out guarantee for block reservation is possible but rare, it establishes a challenging high boundary to which one can aspire.

Issue 4: *Late cancellations*

  Maximum value: 15 points

No penalty up to 14 days before conference 15 pts.
No penalty up to 18 days before conference 9 pts.
No penalty up to 22 days before conference 3 pts.
No penalty up to 26 days before conference 0 pts.

(e) Assign points to the possible outcomes that you identified for each issue. Give the maximum number of points to your preferred settlement for that issue, and assign zero points to any settlement that is least acceptable. Now rank and assign points to the possible settlements in between the best and the worst. Consider that the point values might increase dramatically between certain adjacent pairs of settlements in the range, or might just barely increase. The most important thing to remember about assigning points is that the assignment should reflect what is important to you.

(f) Double-check your scoring system. In completing steps *a* through *e* you undoubtedly will make a few capricious choices based on "gut feeling." For example, you may be so focused on the room-block issue that the points assigned to the other issues could be changed by five points either way without affecting your stance. The point is to make sure your scoring system accurately reflects the important issues and highlights the critical plateaus. To check your numbers, compose three to five completely different hypothetical agreements. Each agreement should emphasize different issues. For example, one agreement might offer a cheap room rate but a short no-penalty cancellation period, while another agreement offers high room rates but a long no-penalty cancellation period. Compare the different agreements on the basis of points and intuitive value. The prospective agreement that has the best "gut feel" should also have the most points. If not, you need to tinker with the values you assigned in steps *a* through *e* or reconsider your priorities.

(g) Use the scoring system to assess any offer that is on the table. You should work toward obtaining the highest-scoring agreement that the other party allows.

specially priced block of rooms available to last-minute registrants up until the week before the conference is very important. Room rate is somewhat less critical, she says, but is still important. Complimentary rooms and the cancellation policy are also valued by her, but are less weighty than are the first two. Note that it is not critical for all the increments within an issue to be valued equally. The jump from a 21-day-out block reservation to a 14-day-out reservation, for example, is worth 20 points to the conference organizer, while the four-day jump from 14 days to 10 days is worth only two points. Such a difference in value carries an important message. The organizer is saying that it is *very* important to have at least a 14-day-out block reservation, and that any improvement over that would be nice but is not critical.

Constructing a detailed and accurate scoring system can mean considerable work (see the second column of Exhibit 1). However, the task can be worth the effort for several reasons. First, it allows you to compare any package of settlements that may make up an agreement. With large numbers of issues, it quickly becomes difficult to compare different packages without some kind of scoring system.

Second, having a scoring system can keep you analytically focused while keeping your emotions in check. If you force yourself to evaluate each proposal using a predetermined scoring system, you are less likely to lose sight of your original interest during the heat of the actual negotiations. Resist the temptation to revise your scoring system in mid-negotiation.[5]

Third, a scoring system is a useful communication tool that gives you a format for soliciting detailed information about the priorities and goals of your boss, your company, or your constituency. Building an accurate scoring system can become the topic of prenegotiation meetings that will improve your chances of pleasing the people you represent.

4. What is your BATNA? Before you begin a negotiation, you need to have a backup plan in case you fail to reach an agreement with the other party. Negotiation scholars refer to this backup plan as the Best Alternative to Negotiated Agreement, or BATNA, for short. Are you, for instance, negotiating with the only supplier in town, or do you already have several attractive bids in your pocket? Alternatives make all the difference.

Each side's BATNA is a key factor in determining negotiation power. The better your BATNA, the better an offer the other party must make to interest you in reaching an agreement. Your BATNA—what you get if you leave the table without an agreement—determines your willingness to accept an impasse, which in turn tells you how hard you can press for a favorable agreement. You can negotiate hard for a job if you already have a few offers in your pocket. The better your BATNA, the more you can demand.

Having a clear BATNA helps protect you from accepting a deal that you would be better off not taking. Often people get caught up in the negotiation process and accept a contract they should have rejected. Knowing your BATNA can keep you from accepting an agreement that would make you worse off than you were before you started negotiating.

Having identified your BATNA, calculate its value based on the scoring system you developed for step 3. That is, if the other party were to make an offer that was identical to your BATNA, how many points would that offer achieve under your scoring system? Use that score as a reference point to identify those agreements that are worth less to you than your BATNA.

Even if it is difficult to assign a score to your BATNA because it is qualitatively different from the deal under negotiation or because it involves risk or uncertainty, you should nevertheless assign it a rough score for comparison purposes.

5. What is your resistance point? Your resistance point is the worst agreement you are willing to accept before ending negotiations and resorting to your BATNA. The resistance point is the point at which you decide to walk away from the table for good, and the BATNA is where you're headed when you take that walk.

You should choose your resistance point based primarily on how good your BATNA is. If your BATNA is great, you shouldn't accept anything less than a great offer; if your BATNA is poor, you may have to be willing to accept a meager final offer. Don't forget to factor into your resistance point the switching cost and the risk of the unknown that you would be taking if your BATNA involves changing suppliers.

To illustrate the effect of switching costs, put yourself in the "buying" position of the conference organizer described in Exhibit 1. Suppose the hotel you used last year has already offered to book your conference for $100 a night single occupancy, with a 10-day-out block-reservation clause. If another hotel wants your business, you need to determine your BATNA and decide the margin by which the new hotel must beat the existing agreement—say, five dollars a night—to justify the risk of switching. Conversely, if you are the hotel sales representative in this deal, you have to determine the risks you accept for this new business—namely, that the association might fail to deliver the promised room-nights and the opportunity cost of displacing any existing business. Your BATNA as a hotel sales representative is the probability of your booking the rooms that the conference would otherwise occupy at a given rate, adjusted by the effort (labor and expenses) it will take to book them.

The resistance point is meant to encompass all the issues at the same time rather than each issue independently. If you set a resistance point for each issue under consideration, you sacrifice your strategic flexibility. Your BATNA might include a room rate of, say, $100 a night. If you set a resistance point for room rate, rather than for the agreement as a whole, then you might walk away from what is, in fact, an attractive offer—for example, a $105 per night rate that includes more amenities and a better booking policy than your BATNA. So there should be just one resistance point and not a collection of them. The resistance point should be set just slightly better than your BATNA. Numerically, it will be the sum of the points from your scoring system that represent your minimum requirements for all the issues being negotiated.

Being aware of the resistance point is useful in negotiations. It converts a good BATNA into a powerful negotiating stance. Unless you have previously decided how far you can be pushed, you are vulnerable to being pushed below your BATNA, and thereby may accept an agreement that is worse for you than no agreement at all. The more precise your resistance point, the better.

It may seem awkward to apply a precise resistance point, particularly if your BATNA is vague or not strong. In such circumstances, you might consider setting a "tripwire" or a temporary resistance point. Set it slightly above your actual resistance point; the tripwire then gives you the chance to suspend negotiations for further consultation with your team. For example, imagine that you are booking the conference as discussed earlier. Your members have expressed a slight preference for exploring new places, and so you are negotiating with a new hotel. You are willing to pay more for a new location, but you are not sure exactly how much more your membership will accept. You know that members will balk at an exorbitant room rate. Your BATNA is to stay at the same hotel as last year and face an uncertain amount of members' disappointment. To deal with the uncertainty, you can set a tripwire. If you are comfortable signing a contract that entails a $10-a-night increase, but if you are unable to secure a rate that low or better, the tripwire tells you that you should check with your membership before you make a commitment. You have, in effect, built a "safety zone" around an uncertain BATNA.

B. About the Other Side

Good negotiators seek to understand the other party's needs and limits almost as well as they know their own. Such negotiators might be able to accomplish this understanding before the negotiations begin, or early in the negotiation process. Obviously, the final agreement will reflect not only your own preferences and BATNA, but the other party's as well. Thus, it is useful to ask the same questions about the other party as you ask about yourself.

1. How important is each issue to them (plus any new issues they added)? Consider and attempt to estimate the other party's priorities. What tradeoffs can you offer that enhance the agreement's value for both sides, or that might be neutral for the other side but a boon for you? If your counterpart had a scoring system like yours, what do you think it would look like? Call people who might have information or insight into the other party's priorities. Build a scoring system like your own that estimates their priorities, and use it to design some potential tradeoffs.

As the negotiation proceeds, try to test, correct, and complete your picture of the other party's scoring system. Try to fill out your understanding of what that scoring system might look like if one existed. Gather more information during the negotiations by asking direct questions about priorities, and also by judging the other negotiator's responses to your different offers and proposed tradeoffs.

You might also want to probe whether there are any issues about which the other side will completely refuse to negotiate. Such a refusal might simply be a ploy, or it might be a genuine constraint on the way it does business.

2. What is the other side's BATNA? What are your counterpart's alternatives to doing business with you? How much do you think she or he values those alternatives? How badly does this company want to do business with you? Realize that the other party will probably accept an agreement only if it improves on her or his BATNA.

The other side's BATNA contains key information about how far you can push those negotiators before they walk away. If you are selling, the buyers' BATNA should determine the maximum price they would be willing to pay for your services or product. If you are buying, it should determine the lowest price at which they will sell. If you are booking a hotel conference in Hawaii in December, the hotel representative, who has a waiting list of customers, has a much stronger BATNA than the same representative has in July. If you are absolutely certain of the other side's BATNA, and if you propose an agreement that is just a little more attractive than the other side's BATNA, then those negotiators might accept your proposal.

3. What is the other side's resistance point, if any? Given your assessment of the other party's BATNA, you can estimate the least favorable deal for which the other party might settle. We say "might" because the other party may not have considered his or her resistance point. We have found, though, that it is wise to assume the other party is well prepared. If you know the other party's resistance point, as noted above, you can push for an agreement that barely exceeds it. This kind of low-ball deal is often better for you than an "equitable" deal, though not always.

If you are the type of negotiator who prefers amiable negotiation tactics over low-balling, then you still may want to know the other side's resistance point for two reasons. First, the other party may try to low-ball you. Knowing its resistance point will give you the information and confidence to counter a low-ball tactic. Second, many negotiators consider a fair deal to be one that falls halfway between the two parties' resistance points. To find the halfway point, you need to know both resistance points. Since experienced negotiators consider their true resistance point to be confidential information, you will most likely have to make a best-guess about how far you can push the other party before seriously risking impasse or generating ill will.

Openly asking for the other party's resistance point carries risks. The other party might lie and therefore be forced to take an uncompromising stance to avoid disclosing that misrepresentation. Or, if the other party honestly reveals his or her resistance point to you, that negotiator may expect you to reveal your resistance point, too. At this point, you have two choices. One, you reveal your resistance point and open yourself to being low-balled or, at best, to being offered an agreement that reaches no farther than the halfway point between the two resistance points. Two, if you don't reveal your resistance point, you may violate the norm of reciprocity.

4. What is your target? You set your target based on what you know about the other side. By this point, you should know what is the least favorable agreement that you will accept, and you have estimated the other side's least favorable, acceptable agreement. Now consider the most favorable agreement for you. This is your upper limit—the top of your range. If you focus primarily on your resistance point, which is the bottom of your range, you are unlikely to secure an agreement that is far superior to that resistance point.

To properly set your target, you must consider the bargaining zone, and to do that you have to sum up the other side's situation. The bargaining zone is the range between the two parties' resistance points, comprising the range of mutually acceptable agreements.

C. The Situation

By this point you have drawn up a fairly accurate picture of the issues and the priorities that constitute the negotiations. Here are some additional contextual factors to consider to help you maximize your advantages and minimize your risk of making mistakes.

1. What deadlines exist? Who is more impatient? The negotiator who feels a greater sense of urgency will often make rapid concessions in an effort to secure a deal quickly. Many Western cultures have a quick-paced approach to negotiations. When paired with negotiators from cultures that negotiate deliberately (e.g., Japan, India), quick negotiators risk getting unfavorable agreements. A good way to slow down your pace is to avoid negotiating under a close deadline. Flexibility with regard to time can be a negotiating strength.

2. What fairness norms or reference points apply? Negotiations often involve a discussion of what might constitute a "fair deal." In fact, some experts recommend the approach of always negotiating over the "principle" or standard that you will use to assess fairness before getting down to details and numbers. The abstract discussion may be less threatening or emotionally charged than the details, and may result in a more cooperative tone and outcome for the negotiation.

Recognize, however, that there are many valid ways to determine fairness, and each negotiator will often choose the fairness norm that most favors his or her position. Both parties know that the other is doing this; just the same, each party expects the other to justify an offer as fair by showing how an offer complies with some fairness norm. Because offers that are unaccompanied by a fairness argument will rarely be accepted, you should consider alternative norms of fairness for each negotiation. Ask yourself, Which ones justify your demands and which ones defeat them? Which ones best reflect your conscience?

An associate of one of the authors, for example, faced a salary negotiation upon considering a new job. The potential employer stated an intent to pay "market value" and thought it fair to define market value as the salary that other starting local faculty members were paid. The job seeker, on the other hand, judged that as unfair and argued that market value should be defined as the salary paid to starting management-faculty members at comparable nationally ranked universities. The candidate thereby successfully redefined "market value" by describing the salaries drawn by other graduates of his program who took management-faculty jobs. Since the employer had already agreed to pay market value, the employer found itself making concessions to do the fair thing of acting consistently with its own stated principles.

That example shows how a negotiation often hinges on a discussion of fairness. Prepare for each negotiation by considering alternative norms of fairness.

3. What topics or questions do you want to avoid? How will you respond if the other side asks anyway? You might find yourself in a position where there is something that you do not want the other negotiator to know. Your BATNA may be weak, for instance. Good negotiators plan in advance how to respond to questions they do not want to answer. Prepare an answer that is in no way dishonest but does not expose your weaknesses. Preparation means rehearsing your answer until you can deliver it smoothly, just as if you were practicing for a play. If you do not prepare and practice your answers to dreaded questions, then you risk an awkward pause or gesture that will tip off the other negotiator to a potential weakness. Awkward gestures might even cause the other party to believe you are lying when you are not. We suggest preparation so that you avoid looking like a liar when you tell the truth but choose not to reveal confidential information. If there are things you do not want to discuss, prepare your deflections in advance and polish them until they are seamless.

D. The Relationship between the Parties

1. Are the negotiations part of a continuing series? If so, what are the future consequences of each strategy, tactic, or action you are considering? Consider whether you expect or want to continue a business relationship with the party across the table. If the answer is yes, then you probably want to be careful about using negotiation tactics that the other side might perceive as bullying, insulting, or manipulative. Extracting those last few additional concessions out of the other party is usually not worth the loss of goodwill.

The fact that you plan to do business with the other party in the future offers a few freedoms as well as restrictions. The trust and goodwill that you develop in the current deal may have a payoff for the next time. Also, if you can safely assume that the other party wants a relationship with you, then you can worry less about them negotiating in bad faith. Trust facilitates successful negotiations much more than does paranoia.

2. Can you trust the other party? What do you know about them? Call around to inquire how this company conducts negotiation. How much you trust the other party will influence your negotiation style. To find the tradeoffs and creative solutions that ensure that everyone gets a fair deal, you have to share information about your needs and priorities. Unfortunately, though, sharing your information makes you vulnerable to an unscrupulous negotiator across the table. Untrustworthy opponents can ascertain your priorities before you know theirs and use this knowledge to gain maximum concessions from you. They might also lie about their own priorities.

The extent to which you trust the other party should determine your approach to sharing and collecting information. A series of small information "trades" is a good way to build mutual trust without opening either side to exploitation. A second approach to gathering data when you do not trust or know the other party well is to offer multiple proposals and see which ones the other side prefers. Be careful in this approach, however, as you must be willing to live with all the proposals you offer. It is considered a breach of faith if you propose an offer (for any reason) but have no intention of carrying through with the deal even if the other party says okay.

If you already know and trust the other party, your task is much easier. In such cases negotiations can involve an extensive exchange of information about interests and priorities.

3. What do you know of the other party's styles and tactics? Different negotiators have different personal or cultural preferences. You are likely to secure the best deal and have the most positive interaction if you learn about their style in advance and try to accommodate it.

We have observed three types of negotiators. One type prefers to ease into the issue at hand after some personal contact. Once that negotiator is at ease with you as a person, she or he will be comfortable revealing information afterward.

Another type of negotiator prefers a direct approach and eschews disclosure and creative problem solving. Such a negotiator requires a competitive approach to the interaction.

The third type of negotiator enters the process having carefully computed and decided what is the best deal—and makes that offer upfront and announces that it is non-negotiable. Having already made up his or her mind about what the agreement must be, this negotiator will likely become impatient and annoyed at any attempt at give-and-take. If you know that the person you face prefers to do business this way, recognize that it is probably not a ploy. Simply assess the offer to see if it beats your BATNA. If it does, take it. If it does not, then politely refuse.

Some negotiators use either of two common gambits. One is to return from a break with a request for just one more concession that can seal the deal. This tactic, known as "taking a second bite of the apple," is common among car dealers. The appropriate response is to suggest that if the other party would like to reopen negotiations, you are willing to reopen them, too—but on all the issues, not just one.

"Good cop, bad cop" is a tactic whereby the person with whom you negotiate plays the role of "wanting" to meet all your needs, but "demands" are being made by someone who is higher up and usually absent from the actual negotiation (e.g., the sales manager). One response to this approach is to take a break to reassess the other side's stance compared to your tripwire. Another is to insist on speaking directly with the final decision maker.

4. What are the limits to the other party's authority? Establish early the level of authority held by your counterpart. Most negotiators, unless they are the CEOs of their companies, are authorized to negotiate only certain specified issues and within certain ranges. Determine whether you are negotiating with the right person, or whether far more latitude in generating resolutions might be available if you negotiated with someone else.

5. Consult in advance with the other party about the agenda. As we stated earlier, consider calling the other party beforehand to share what issues you plan to discuss and to ask what issues the other party might raise. In general, holding back information is counter-productive and introducing unexpected issues generally delays the proceedings.

Although good negotiators often get creative in their approach to the issues, this creativity must be well-grounded in an understanding of the issues and of both parties' priorities. A well-prepared negotiator has considered these factors in depth, and has also considered the past and future context of the business relationship between the parties. It has been said that no plan survives contact with the enemy—but it remains true that the shrewd general will have memorized the terrain and analyzed the strengths and weaknesses of both sides before an engagement. Fortune favors the prepared mind.

ENDNOTES

1. There is some risk of overwhelming oneself—and one's negotiation partner—with too many issues. We suggest a combination of moderation in adding issues with an effective system of note-taking and organization.

2. Any method that serves as a mnemonic device to track and evaluate multiple issues and deals may work. The one we describe is one that has received much attention in negotiation courses and research. See D. A. Lax and J. K. Sebenius, *The Manager as Negotiator* (New York: Free Press, 1986).

3. Several negotiation sessions may take place before you can identify all the issues and the range of possible resolutions for those issues. However, we recommend that you list in advance as many issues as you know about and then update the table between negotiation sessions to include additional issues and settlements.

4. Note that we have simplified the issues of such a negotiation for expository purposes. Additional issues might include cancellation clauses, airport transportation, continental breakfasts, function space, additional events or amenities, and so on.

5. In the interest of maintaining your original goals, do not adjust your scoring system while in the middle of discussion with the other party. During negotiations you may hear things that suggest your original preferences and priorities may be in error. Such new information might be valid, or it might simply be the other negotiator's effort to mislead you. There is a bad way and a good way to deal with the uncertainty such rhetoric may cause you. The bad way is to lose confidence in the accuracy of your scoring system, throw it out, and continue to negotiate. The good way is to take a break and verify the information as both true and relevant to your preferences. If it is, during that break adjust your scoring system to reflect the new information and restart negotiations with the new scoring system.

The Right Game: Use Game Theory to Shape Strategy

Adam M. Brandenburger

Barry J. Nalebuff

Business is a high-stakes game. The way we approach this game is reflected in the language we use to describe it. Business language is full of expressions borrowed from the military and from sports. Some of them are dangerously misleading. Unlike war and sports, business is not about winning and losing. Nor is it about how well you play the game. Companies can succeed spectacularly without requiring others to fail. And they can fail miserably no matter how well they play if they make the mistake of playing the wrong game.

The essence of business success lies in making sure you're playing the right game. How do you know if it's the right game? What can you do about it if it's the wrong game? To help managers answer those questions, we've developed a framework that draws on the insights of game theory. After 50 years as a mathematical construct, game theory is about to change the game of business.

Game theory came of age in 1994, when three pioneers in the field were awarded the Nobel Prize. It all began in 1944, when mathematics genius John von Neumann and economist Oskar Morgenstern published their book *Theory of Games and Economic Behavior.* Immediately heralded as one of the greatest scientific achievements of the century, their work provided a systematic way to understand the behavior of players in situations where their fortunes are interdependent. Von Neumann and Morgenstern distinguished two types of games. In the first type, rule-based games, players interact according to specified "rules of engagement." These rules might come from contracts, loan covenants, or trade agreements, for example. In the second type, freewheeling games, players interact without any external constraints. For example, buyers and sellers may create value by transacting in an unstructured fashion. Business is a complex mix of both types of games.

For rule-based games, game theory offers the principle, To every action, there is a reaction. But, unlike Newton's third law of motion, the reaction is not programmed to be equal and opposite. To analyze how other players will react to your move, you need to play out all the reactions (including yours) to their actions as far ahead as possible. You have to look forward far into the game and then reason backward to figure out which of today's actions will lead you to where you want to end up.[1]

For freewheeling games, game theory offers the principle, You cannot take away from the game more than you bring to it. In business, what does a particular player bring to the game? To find the answer, look at the value created when everyone is in the game, and then pluck that player out and see how much value the remaining players can create. The difference is the removed player's "added value." In unstructured interactions, you cannot take away more than your added value.[2]

Underlying both principles is a shift in perspective. Many people view games egocentrically—that is, they focus on their own position. The primary insight of game theory is the importance of focusing on others—namely, allocentrism. To look forward and reason backward, you have to put yourself in the shoes—even in the heads—of other players. To assess your added value, you have to ask not what other players can bring to you but what you can bring to other players.

Managers can profit by using these insights from game theory to design a game that is right for their companies. The rewards that can come from changing a game may be far greater than those from maintaining the status quo. For example, Nintendo succeeded brilliantly in changing the video game business by taking control of software. Sega's subsequent success required changing the game again. Rupert Murdoch's *New York Post* changed the tabloid game by finding a convincing way to demonstrate the cost of a price war without actually launching one. BellSouth made money by changing the takeover game between Craig McCaw and Lin Broadcasting. Successful business strategy is about actively shaping the game you play, not just playing the game you find. We will explore how these examples and others worked in practice, starting with the story of how General Motors changed the game of selling cars.

FROM LOSE-LOSE TO WIN-WIN

In the early 1990s, the U.S. automobile industry was locked into an all-too-familiar mode of destructive competition. End-of-year rebates and dealer discounts were ruining the industry's profitability. As soon as one company used incentives to clear excess inventory at year-end, others had to do the same. Worse still, consumers came to expect the rebates. As a result, they waited for them to be offered before buying a car, forcing manufacturers to offer incentives earlier in the year. Was there a way out? Would someone find an alternative to practices that were hurting all the companies? General Motors may have done just that.

In September 1992, General Motors and Household Bank issued a new credit card that allowed cardholders to apply 5 percent of their charges toward buying or leasing a new GM car, up to $500 per year, with a maximum of $3,500. The GM card has been the most successful credit card launch in history. One month after it was introduced, there were 1.2 million accounts. Two years later, there were 8.7 million accounts—and the program is still growing. Projections suggest that eventually some 30 percent of GM's nonfleet sales in North America will be to cardholders.

As Hank Weed, managing director of GM's card program, explains, the card helps
GM build share through the "conquest" of prospective Ford buyers and others—a traditional win-lose strategy. But the program has engineered another, more subtle change in
the game of selling cars. It replaced other incentives that GM had previously offered. The
net effect has been to raise the price that a noncardholder—someone who intends to buy
a Ford, for example—would have to pay for a GM car. The program thus gives Ford
some breathing room to raise its prices. That allows GM, in turn, to raise its prices without losing customers to Ford. The result is a win-win dynamic between GM and Ford.

If the GM card is as good as it sounds, what's stopping other companies from
copying it? Not much, it seems. First, Ford introduced its version of the program with
Citibank. Then Volkswagen introduced its variation with MBNA Corporation. Doesn't
all this imitation put a dent in the GM program? Not necessarily.

Imitation is the sincerest form of flattery, but in business it is often thought to be a
killer compliment. Textbooks on strategy warn that if others can imitate something you
do, you can't make money at it. Some go even further, asserting that business strategy
cannot be codified. If it could, it would be imitated and any gains would evaporate.

Yet the proponents of this belief are mistaken in assuming that imitation is always
harmful. It's true that once GM's program is widely imitated, the company's ability to
lure customers away from other manufacturers will be diminished. But imitation also
can help GM. Ford and Volkswagen offset the cost of their credit card rebates by scal-
ing back other incentive programs. The result was an effective price increase for GM
customers, the vast majority of whom do not participate in the Ford and Volkswagen
credit card programs. This gives GM the option to firm up its demand or raise its prices
further. All three car companies now have a more loyal customer base, so there is less
incentive to compete on price.

To understand the full impact of the GM card program, you have to use game theory. You can't see all the ramifications of the program without adopting an allocentric
perspective. The key is to anticipate how Ford, Volkswagen, and other automakers will
respond to GM's initiative.

When you change the game, you want to come out ahead. That's pretty clear. But
what about the fact that GM's strategy helped Ford? One common mind-set—seeing
business as war—says that others have to lose in order for you to win. There may indeed
be times when you want to opt for a win-lose strategy. But not always. The GM example shows that there also are times when you want to create a win-win situation.
Although it may sound surprising, sometimes the best way to succeed is to let others,
including your competitors, do well.

Looking for win-win strategies has several advantages. First, because the approach
is relatively unexplored, there is greater potential for finding new opportunities. Second,
because others are not being forced to give up ground, they may offer less resistance to
win-win moves, making them easier to implement. Third, because win-win moves don't
force other players to retaliate, the new game is more sustainable. And finally, imitation
of a win-win move is beneficial, not harmful.

To encourage thinking about both cooperative and competitive ways to change the
game, we suggest the term *coopetition*.[3] It means looking for win-win as well as win-
lose opportunities. Keeping both possibilities in mind is important because win-lose

EXHIBIT 1   Who Are the Players in Your Company's Value Net?

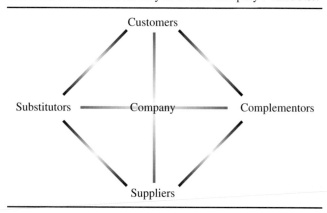

strategies often backfire. Consider, for example, the common—and dangerous—strategy of lowering prices to gain market share. Although it may provide a temporary benefit, the gains will evaporate if others match the cuts to regain their lost share. The result is simply to reestablish the status quo but at lower prices—a lose-lose scenario that leaves all the players worse off. That was the situation in the automobile industry before GM changed the game.

THE GAME OF BUSINESS

Did GM intentionally plan to change the game of selling cars in the way we have described it? Or did the company just get lucky with a loyalty marketing program that turned out better than anyone had expected? Looking back, the one thing we can say with certainty is that the stakes in situations like GM's are too high to be left to chance. That's why we have developed a comprehensive map and a method to help managers find strategies for changing the game.

The game of business is all about value: creating it and capturing it. Who are the participants in this enterprise? To describe them, we introduce the Value Net—a schematic map designed to represent all the players in the game and the interdependencies among them. (See Exhibit 1.)

Interactions take place along two dimensions. Along the vertical dimension are the company's customers and suppliers. Resources such as labor and raw materials flow from the suppliers to the company, and products and services flow from the company to its customers. Money flows in the reverse direction, from customers to the company and from the company to its suppliers. Along the horizontal dimension are the players with whom the company interacts but does not transact. They are its *substitutors* and *complementors*.

Substitutors are alternative players from whom customers may purchase products or to whom suppliers may sell their resources. Coca-Cola and Pepsico are substitutors with respect to consumers because they sell rival colas. A little less obvious is that Coca-Cola and Tyson Foods are substitutors with respect to suppliers. That is because both companies use carbon dioxide. Tyson uses it for freezing chickens, and Coke uses it for carbonation. (As they say in the cola industry, "No fizziness, no bizziness.")

Complementors are players from whom customers buy complementary products or to whom suppliers sell complementary resources. For example, hardware and software companies are classic complementors. Faster hardware, such as a Pentium chip, increases users' willingness to pay for more powerful software. More powerful software such as the latest version of Microsoft Office, increases users' willingness to pay for faster hardware. American Airlines and United Airlines, though substitutors with respect to passengers, are complementors when they decide to update their fleets. That's because Boeing can recoup the cost of a new plane design only if enough airlines buy it. Since each airline effectively subsidizes the other's purchase of planes, the two are complementors in this instance.

We introduce the terms *substitutor* and *complementor* because we find that the traditional business vocabulary inhibits a full understanding of the interdependencies that exist in business. If you call a player a competitor, you tend to focus on competing rather than on finding opportunities for cooperation. *Substitutor* describes the market relationship without that prejudice. Complementors, often overlooked in traditional strategic analysis, are the natural counterparts of substitutors.

The Value Net describes the various roles of the players. It's possible for the same player to occupy more than one role simultaneously. Remember that American and United are both substitutors and complementors. Gary Hamel and C. K. Prahalad make this point in *Competing for the Future* (Harvard Business School Press, 1994): "On any given day, AT&T might find Motorola to be a supplier, a buyer, a competitor, *and* a partner."

The Value Net reveals two fundamental symmetries in the game of business: the first between customers and suppliers and the second between substitutors and complementors. Understanding those symmetries can help managers come up with new strategies for changing the game or new applications of existing strategies.

Managers understand intuitively that along the vertical dimension of the Value Net, there is a mixture of cooperation and competition. It's cooperation when suppliers, companies, and customers come together to create value in the first place. It's competition when the time comes for them to divide the pie.

Along the horizontal dimension, however, managers tend to see only half the picture. Substitutors are seen only as enemies. Complementors, if viewed at all, are seen only as friends. Such a perspective overlooks another symmetry. There can be a cooperative element to interactions with substitutors, as the GM story illustrates, and a competitive element to interactions with complementors, as we will see.

CHANGING THE GAME

The Value Net is a map that prompts you to explore all the interdependencies in the game. Drawing the Value Net for your business is therefore the first step toward changing the game. The second step is identifying all the elements of the game. According to game theory, there are five: players, added values, rules, tactics, and scope—PARTS for short. These five elements fully describe all interactions, both freewheeling and rule-based. To change the game, you have to change one or more of these elements.

Players come first. As we saw in the Value Net, the players are customers, suppliers, substitutors, and complementors. None of the players are fixed. Sometimes it's smart to change who is playing the game. That includes yourself.

Added values are what each player brings to the game. There are ways to make yourself a more valuable player—in other words, to raise your added value. And there are ways to lower the added values of other players.

Rules give structure to the game. In business, there is no universal set of rules; a rule might arise from law, custom, practicality, or contracts. In addition to using existing rules to their advantage, players may be able to revise them or come up with new ones.

Tactics are moves used to shape the way players perceive the game and hence how they play. Sometimes, tactics are designed to reduce misperceptions; at other times, they are designed to create or maintain uncertainty.

Scope describes the boundaries of the game. It's possible for players to expand or shrink those boundaries.

Successful business strategies begin by assessing and then changing one or more of these elements. PARTS does more than exhort you to think out of the box. It provides the tools to enable you to do so. Let's look at each strategic lever in turn.

CHANGING THE PLAYERS

NutraSweet, a low-calorie sweetener used in soft drinks such as Diet Coke and Diet Pepsi, is a household name, and its swirl logo is recognized worldwide. In fact, it's Monsanto's brand name for the chemical aspartame. NutraSweet has been a very profitable business for Monsanto, with 70 percent gross margins. Such profits usually attract others to enter the market, but NutraSweet was protected by patents in Europe until 1987 and in the United States until 1992.

With Coke's blessing, a challenger, the Holland Sweetener Company, built an aspartame plant in Europe in 1985 in anticipation of the patent expiration. Ken Dooley, HSC's vice president of marketing and sales, explained, "Every manufacturer likes to have at least two sources of supply."

As HSC attacked the European market, Monsanto fought back aggressively. It used deep price cuts and contractual relationships with customers to deny HSC a toehold in the market. HSC managed to fend off the initial counterattack by appealing to the courts to enable it to gain access to customers. Dooley considered all this just a preview of things to come: "We are looking forward to moving the war into the United States."

But Dooley's war ended before it began. Just prior to the U.S. patent expiration, both Coke and Pepsi signed new long-term contracts with Monsanto. When at last there was a real potential for competition between suppliers, it appeared that Coke and Pepsi didn't seize the opportunity. Or did they?

Neither Coke nor Pepsi ever had any real desire to switch over to generic aspartame. Remembering the result of the New Coke reformulation of 1985, neither company wanted to be the first to take the NutraSweet logo off the can and create a perception that it was fooling around with the flavor of its drinks. If only one switched over, the other most certainly would have made a selling point of its exclusive use of NutraSweet. After all, NutraSweet had already built a reputation for safety and good taste. Even though generic aspartame would taste the same, consumers would be unfamiliar with the unbranded product and see it as inferior. Another reason not to switch was that Monsanto had spent the previous decade marching down the learning curve for making aspartame—giving it a significant cost advantage—while HSC was still near the top.

In the end, what Coke and Pepsi really wanted was to get the same old NutraSweet at a much better price. That they accomplished. Look at Monsanto's position before and after HSC entered the game. Before, there was no good substitute for NutraSweet. Cyclamates had been banned, and saccharin caused cancer in laboratory rats. NutraSweet's added value was its ability to make a safe, good-tasting low-calorie drink possible. Stir in a patent and things looked very positive for Monsanto. When HSC came along, NutraSweet's added value was greatly reduced. What was left was its brand loyalty and its manufacturing cost advantage.

Where did all this leave HSC? Clearly, its entry into the market was worth a lot to Coke and Pepsi. It would have been quite reasonable for HSC, before entering the market, to demand compensation for its role in the form of either a fixed payment or a guaranteed contract. But, once in, with an unbranded product and higher production costs, it was much more difficult for the company to make money. Dooley was right when he said that all manufacturers want a second source. The problem is, they don't necessarily want to do much business with that source.

Monsanto did well to create a brand identity and a cost advantage. It minimized the negative effects of entry by a generic brand. Coke and Pepsi did well to change the game by encouraging the entry of a new player that would reduce their dependence on NutraSweet. According to HSC, the new contracts led to combined savings of $200 million annually for Coke and Pepsi. As for HSC, perhaps it was too quick to become a player. The question for HSC was not what it could do for Coke and Pepsi; the question was what Coke and Pepsi could do for HSC. Although it was a duopolist in a weak position when it came to selling aspartame, HSC was a monopolist in a strong position when it came to selling its "service" to make the aspartame market competitive. Perhaps Coke and Pepsi would have paid a higher price for this valuable service, but only if HSC had demanded such payment up front.

Pay Me to Play

As the NutraSweet story illustrates, sometimes the most valuable service you can offer is creating competition, so don't give it away for free. People in the takeover game have long understood the art of getting paid to play. The cellular phone business was undergoing rapid consolidation in June 1989, when 39-year-old Craig McCaw made a bid for Lin Broadcasting Corporation. With 50 million POPs (lingo for the population in a coverage area) already under his belt, McCaw saw the acquisition of Lin's 18 million POPs as the best, and possibly the only, way to acquire a national cellular footprint. He bid $120 per share for Lin, which resulted in an immediate jump in Lin's share price from $103.50 to $129.50. Clearly, the market expected more action. But Lin's CEO, Donald Pels, didn't care much for McCaw or his bid. Faced with Lin's hostile reaction, McCaw lowered his offer to $110, and Lin sought other suitors. BellSouth, with 28 million POPs, was the natural alternative, although acquiring Lin wouldn't quite give it a national footprint.

Nevertheless, BellSouth was willing to acquire Lin for the right price. But if it entered the fray, it would create a bidding war and thus make it unlikely that Lin would be sold for a reasonable price. BellSouth knew that only one bidder could win, and it wanted something in case that bidder was McCaw. Thus, as a condition for making a bid, BellSouth got Lin's promise of a $54 million consolation prize and an additional $15 million toward expenses in the event that it was outbid. BellSouth made an offer generally valued at between $105 and $112 per share. As expected, BellSouth was outbid; McCaw responded with an offer valued at $112 to $118 per share. BellSouth then raised its bid to roughly $120 per share. In return, Lin raised BellSouth's expense cap to $25 million. McCaw raised his bid to $130 and then added a few dollars more to close the deal. At the same time, he paid BellSouth $22.5 million to exit the game.[4] At this point in the bidding, Lin's CEO recognized that his stock options were worth $186 million, and the now friendly deal with McCaw was concluded.

So how did the various players make out? Lin got itself an extra billion, which made its $79 million payment to BellSouth look like a bargain. McCaw got the national network he wanted and subsequently sold out to AT&T, making himself a billionaire. And BellSouth, by getting paid first to play and then to go away, turned a weak hand into $76.5 million plus expenses.

BellSouth clearly understood that even if you can't make money in the game the old-fashioned way, you can get paid to change it. Such payments need not be made in cash; you can ask for a guaranteed sales contract, contributions to R&D, bid-preparation expenses, or a last-look provision.

The examples so far show how you can change three of the four players in the Value Net. Lin paid to bring in an extra buyer, or customer. Coke and Pepsi would, no doubt, have been prepared to pay HSC handsomely to become a second supplier. And McCaw paid to take out a rival bidder, or substitutor. That leaves complementors. The next example shows how a company can benefit from bringing players into the complements market.

Cheap Complements

Remember that hardware is the classic complement to software. One can't function without the other. Software writers won't produce programs unless a sufficient hardware base exists. Yet consumers won't purchase the hardware until a critical mass of software exists. 3DO Company, a maker of video games, is attacking this chicken-and-egg problem in the video-game business by bringing players into the complements market. To those who know 3DO's founder, Trip Hawkins, this should come as no surprise. He designed his own major at Harvard in strategy and game theory.

3DO owns a 32-bit CD-ROM hardware-and-software technology for next-generation video games. The company plans to make money by licensing software houses to make 3DO games and collecting a $3 royalty fee (hence the company name). Of course, to sell software, you first need people to buy the hardware. But those early adopters won't find much software. To start the ball rolling, 3DO needs the hardware to be cheap—the cheaper the better.

The company's strategy is to give away the license to produce the hardware technology. This move has induced hardware manufacturers such as Panasonic (Matsushita),

GoldStar, Sanyo, and Toshiba to enter the game. Because all 3DO software will run on all 3DO hardware, the hardware manufacturers are left to compete on cost alone. Making the hardware a commodity is just what 3DO wants: It drives down the price of the complementary product.

But not quite enough. 3DO is discovering that to create momentum in the market, the hardware must be sold below cost, and hardware manufacturers aren't willing to go that far. As an inducement, 3DO now offers them two shares of 3DO stock for each machine sold. The company also has renegotiated its deal with software houses up to $6 royalty, with the extra $3 earmarked to subsidize hardware sales. So Hawkins is actually paying people to play in the complements market. Is he paying enough? Time will tell.

Creating competition in the complements market is the flip side of coopetition. Just as substitutors are usually seen only as enemies, complementors are seen only as friends. Whereas the GM story shows the possibility of win-win opportunities with substitutors, the 3DO example illustrates the possibility of legitimate win-lose opportunities with complementors. Creating competition among its complementors helped 3DO at their expense.

CHANGING THE ADDED VALUES

Just as you shouldn't accept the players of the game as fixed, you shouldn't take what they bring to the game as fixed, either. You can change the players' added values. Common sense tells us that there are two options: raise your own added value or lower that of others.

Good basic business practices are one route to raising added values. You can tailor your product to customers' needs, build a brand, use resources more efficiently, work with your suppliers to lower their costs, and so on. These strategies should not be underestimated. But there are other, less transparent ways to raise your added value. As an example, consider Trans World Airlines' introduction of Comfort Class in 1993.

Robert Cozzi, TWA's senior vice president of marketing, proposed removing 5 to 40 seats per plane to give passengers in coach more legroom. The move raised TWA's added value; according to J.D. Power and Associates, the company soared to first place in customer satisfaction for long-haul flights. This was a win for TWA and a loss for other airlines. But elements of win-win were present as well: With fuller planes, TWA was not about to start a price war.

But what if other carriers copied the strategy? Would that negate TWA's efforts? No, because as others copied TWA's move, excess capacity would be retired from an industry plagued by overcapacity. Passengers get more legroom, and carriers stop flying empty seats around. Everyone wins. Cozzi saw a way to move the industry away from the self-defeating price competition that goes on when airlines try to fill up the coach cabin. This was business strategy at its best.[5]

The idea of raising your own added value is natural. Less intuitive is the approach of lowering the added value of others. To illustrate how the strategy works, let's begin with a simple card game.

Adam and 26 of his M.B.A. students are playing a card game. Adam has 26 black cards, and each of the students has one red card. Any red card coupled with a black card gets a $100 prize (paid by the dean). How do we expect the bargaining between Adam and his students to proceed?

First, calculate the added values. Without Adam and his black cards, there is no game. Thus Adam's added value equals the total value of the game, which is $2,600. Each student has an added value of $100 because without that student's card, one less match can be made and thus $100 is lost. The sum of the added values is therefore $5,200—made up of $2,600 from Adam and $100 from each of the 26 students. Alas, there is only $2,600 to be divided. Given the symmetry of the game, it's most likely that everyone will end up with half of his or her added value: Adam will buy the students' cards for $50 each or sell his for $50 each.

So far, nothing is surprising. Could Adam do any better? Yes, but first he'd have to change the game. In a public display, Adam burns three of his black cards. True, the pie is now smaller, at $2,300, and so is Adam's added value. But the point of this strategic move is to destroy the added values of the other players. Now no student has any added value because 3 students are going to end up without a match, and therefore no one student is essential to the game. The total value with 26 students is $2,300, and the total value with 25 students is still $2,300.

At this point, the division will not be equal. Indeed, because no student has any added value, Adam would be quite generous to offer a 90:10 split. Since 3 students will end up with nothing, anyone who ends up with $10 should consider himself or herself lucky. For Adam, 90 percent of $2,300 is a lot better than half of $2,600. Of course, his getting it depends on the students not being able to get together; if they did, that would be changing the game, too. In fact, it would be changing the players, as in the previous section, and it would be an excellent strategy for the students to adopt.

Just a card trick? No—a strategy employed by the video-game maker Nintendo (which, it so happens, used to produce playing cards). To see how the company lowered everyone else's added value, we take a tour around its Value Net. (See Exhibit 2.)

Nintendo Power

Start with Nintendo's customers. Nintendo sold its games to a highly concentrated market—predominantly megaretailers such as Toys R Us and Wal-Mart. How could Nintendo combat such buyer power? By changing the game. Nintendo did just what Adam did when he burned the cards (although Nintendo made a lot more money): It didn't fill all the retailers' orders. In 1988, Nintendo sold 33 million cartridges, but the market could have absorbed 45 million. Poor planning? No. It's true that the pie shrank a little as some stores sold out of the game. But the important point is that retailers lost added value. Even a giant like Toys R Us was in a weaker position when not every retailer could get supplied. As Nintendo mania took hold, consumers queued up outside stores and retailers clamored for more of the product. With games in short supply, Nintendo had zapped the buyers' power.

The next arena of negotiations concerned the complementors—namely, outside game developers. What was Nintendo's strategy? First, it developed software in-house. The company built a security chip into the hardware and then instituted a licensing program for outside developers. The number of licenses was restricted, and licensees were allowed to develop only a limited number of games. Because there were many Nintendo wanna-be programmers and because the company could develop games in-house, the added value of those that did get the license was lowered. Once again, Nintendo ensured that there were fewer black cards than red. It held all the bargaining chips.

EXHIBIT 2   Nintendo Trumped Every Player in Its Value Net

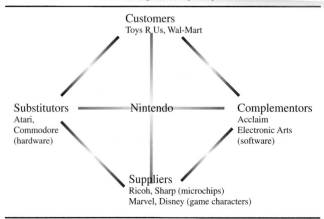

Nintendo's suppliers, too, had little added value. The company used old-generation chip technology, making its chips something of a commodity. Another input was the leading characters in the games. Nintendo hit the jackpot by developing Mario. After he became a hit in his own right, the added value of comic-book heroes licensed from others, such as Spiderman (Marvel), and of cartoon icons, such as Mickey Mouse (Disney), was reduced. In fact, Nintendo turned the tables completely, licensing Mario to appear in comic books and on cartoon shows, cereal boxes, board games, and toys.

Finally, there were Nintendo's substitutors. From a kid's perspective, there were no good alternatives to a video game; the only real threat came from alternative video-game systems. Here Nintendo had the game practically all to itself. Having the largest installed base of systems allowed the company to drive down the manufacturing cost for its hardware. And with developers keen to write for the largest installed base, Nintendo got the best games. This created a positive feedback loop: More people bought Nintendo's systems, leading to a larger base, still lowers costs, and even more games. Nintendo locked in its lead by requiring exclusivity from outside game developers. With few alternatives to Nintendo, that was a small price for them to pay. Potential challengers couldn't simply take successful games over to their platforms; they had to start from scratch. Although large profits might normally invite entry, no challenger could engineer any added value. The installed base, combined with Nintendo's exclusivity agreements, made competing in Nintendo's game hopeless.

What was the bottom line for Nintendo? How much could a manufacturer of a two-bit—well, eight-bit—game about a lugubrious plumber called Mario really be worth? How about more than Sony or Nissan? Between July 1990 and June 1991, Nintendo's average market value was 2.4 trillion yen, Sony's was 2.2 trillion yen, and Nissan's was 2 trillion yen.

The Nintendo example illustrates the importance of added value as opposed to value. There is no doubt that cars, televisions, and VCRs create more value in the world than do Game Boys. But it's not enough simply to create value; profits come from capturing value.

By keeping its added value high and everyone else's low, Nintendo was able to capture a great slice of a largish pie. The name of the enthusiasts' monthly magazine, *Nintendo Power,* summed up the situation quite nicely.

Nintendo's success, however, brought it under scrutiny. In late 1989, Congressman Dennis Eckart (D-Ohio), chairman of the House Subcommittee on Antitrust, Impact of Deregulation and Privatization, requested that the U.S. Justice Department investigate allegations that Nintendo of America unfairly reduced competition. Eckart's letter argued, among other things, that the Christmas shortages in 1988 were "contrived to increase consumer prices and demand and to enhance Nintendo's market leverage" and that software producers had "become almost entirely dependent on Nintendo's acceptance of their games." None of Nintendo's practices were found to be illegal.[6]

Pumping Up Profits

Protecting your added value is as important as establishing it in the first place. Back in the mid-1970s, Robert Taylor, CEO of Minnetonka, had the idea for Softsoap, a liquid soap that would be dispensed by a pump. The problem was that it would be hard to retain any added value once the likes of Procter & Gamble and Lever Brothers muscled in with their brands and distribution clout. Nothing in the product could be patented. But, to his credit, Taylor realized that the hardest part of producing the soap was manufacturing the little plastic pump, for which there were just two suppliers. In a bet-the-company move, he locked up both suppliers' total annual production by ordering 100 million of the pumps. Even at 12 cents apiece, this was a $12 million order—more than Minnetonka's net worth. Ultimately, the major players did enter the market, but capturing the supply of pumps gave Taylor a head start of 12 to 18 months. That advantage preserved Softsoap's added value during this period, allowing the company to build brand loyalty, which continues to provide added value to this day.

As the TWA, Nintendo, and Softsoap examples illustrate, added values can be changed. By reengineering them—raising your added value and lowering others'—you may be able to capture a larger slice of pie.

Game theory holds that in freewheeling interactions, no player can take away more than that player brings to the game, but that's not quite the end of the matter. First, there is no guarantee that any player will get all its added value. Typically, the sum of all the added values exceeds the total value of the game. Remember that in Adam's card game, the total prize was only $2,600 even though the added values of all the players initially totaled $5,200. Second, even if you have no added value, that doesn't prohibit you from making money. Others might be willing to pay you to enter or exit the game (as with BellSouth); similarly, you might be paid to stay out or stay in. Third, rules constrain interactions among players. We will see that in games with rules, some players may be able to capture more than their added values.

CHANGING THE RULES

Rules determine how the game is played by limiting the possible reactions to any action. To analyze the effect of a rule, you have to look forward and reason backward.

The simplest rule is *one price to all.* According to this rule, prices are not negotiated individually with each customer. Consequently, a company can profitably enter a market even when it has no added value. If a new player enters with a price lower than the incumbent's, the incumbent has only two effective responses: match the newcomer's price across the board or stand pat and give up share. By looking forward and reasoning backward, a small newcomer can steer the incumbent toward accommodation rather than retaliation.

Imagine that a new player comes in with a limited capacity—say, 10 percent of the market—and a discounted price. Whether it makes any money depends on how the incumbent responds. The incumbent can recapture its lost market by coming down to match the newcomer's price, or it can give up 10 percent share. For the incumbent, giving up 10 percent share is usually better than sacrificing its profit margin. In such cases, the newcomer will do all right. But it can't get too greedy. If it tries to take away too much of the market, the incumbent will choose to give up its profit margin in order to regain share. Only when the newcomer limits its capacity does the incumbent stand pat and the newcomer make money. For this reason, the strategy is called *judo economics:* By staying small, the newcomer turns the incumbent's larger size to its own benefit.

To pull off a judo strategy, the newcomer's commitment to limit its capacity must be both clear and credible. The newcomer may be tempted to expand, but it must realize that if it does, it will give the incumbent an incentive to retaliate.

Kiwi Is No Dodo

Kiwi International Air Lines understands these ideas perfectly. Named for the flightless bird, Kiwi is a 1992 start-up founded by former Eastern Air Lines pilots who were grounded after Eastern went bankrupt. Kiwi engineered a cost advantage from its employee ownership and its use of leased planes. But it had lower name recognition and a more limited flight schedule than the major carriers—on balance, not much, if any, added value. So what did it do? It went for low prices and limited capacity. According to public statements from its then CEO, Robert Iverson, "We designed our system to stay out of the way of large carriers and to make sure they understand that we pose no threat. . . . Kiwi intends to capture, at most, only 10 percent share of any one market—or no more than four flights per day." Because Kiwi targets business travelers, the major airlines can't use stay-over and advance-purchase restrictions to lower price selectively against it. So Kiwi benefited from the one-price-to-all rule.

Now Kiwi, in turn, became the large player for any newcomer to the same market. That didn't leave much room to be small in relation to Kiwi, so Kiwi had to fight if someone else tried to follow suit. According to Iverson, "[The major airlines] are better off with us than without us." Even though Kiwi was Delta's rival, by staying small and keeping out other potential entrants, it managed to bring an element of coopetition into the game. From Delta's perspective, Kiwi was rather like the devil it knew.

The Kiwi story illustrates how a player can take advantage of existing rules of the marketplace—in this case, the one-price-to-all rule. In addition to practicality, rules arise from custom, law, or contracts. Common contract-based rules are most-favored-nation (most-favored-customer) clauses, take-or-pay agreements, and meet-the-competition clauses. These rules give structure to negotiations between buyers and sellers. Rules are particularly useful for players in commodity-like businesses. As an example, take the carbon dioxide industry.

Solid Profits from Gas

There are three major producers of carbon dioxide: Airco, Liquid Carbonic, and Air Liquide. Carbon dioxide created enormous value (in carbonation and freezing), but it is essentially a commodity, which makes it hard for a producer to capture any of that value. One distinguishing factor, however, is that carbon dioxide is very expensive to transport, which gives some added value to the producer best located to serve a specific customer. Other sources of added value are differentiation through reliability, reputation, service, and technology. Still, a producer's added value is usually small in relation to the total value created. The question is, Can a producer capture more than its added value?

In this case the answer is yes, because of the rules of the game in the carbon dioxide industry. The producers have a meet-the-competition clause (MCC) in their contracts with customers. An MCC gives the incumbent seller the right to make the last bid.

The result of an MCC is that a producer can sustain a higher price and thereby earn more than its added value. Normally, an elevated price would invite other producers to compete on price. In this case, however, a challenger cannot come in and take away business simply by undercutting the existing price. If it tried, the incumbent could then come back with a lower price and keep the business. The back-and-forth could go on until the price fell to variable cost, but at that point stealing the business wouldn't be worth the effort. The only one to benefit would be the buyer, who would end up with a lower price.

Cutting price to go after an incumbent's business is always risky but may be justified by the gain in business. Not so when the incumbent has an MCC: The upside is lost and the downside remains. Lowering price sets a dangerous precedent and increases the likelihood of a tit-for-tat response. The incumbent may retaliate by going after the challenger's business, and even if the challenger doesn't lose customers, it certainly will lose profits. Another downside is that the challenger's customers may end up at a disadvantage. If the challenger supplies Coke and the incumbent supplies Pepsi, the challenger shouldn't help Pepsi get a lower price. Its future is tied to Coke, and it doesn't want to give Pepsi any cost advantage. It might even end up having to lower its own price to Coke without getting Pepsi's business. Finally, the challenger's efforts are misplaced: It would do better to make sure that its existing customers are happy.

Putting in an MCC changes the game in a way that's clearly a win for the incumbent. Perhaps surprisingly, the challenger also ends up better off. True, it may not be able to take away market share, but the incumbent's higher prices set a good precedent: They give the challenger some room to raise prices to its own customers. There also is less danger that the incumbent will go after the challenger's share, because the incumbent, with higher profits, now has more to lose. An MCC is a classic case of coopetition.

As for the customers, why do they go along with this rule? It may be traditional in their industry. Perhaps it's the norm. Perhaps they decide to trade an initial price break in return for the subsequent lock-in. Or maybe they don't thoroughly understand the rule's implications. Whatever the reason, MCCs do offer benefits to customers. The clauses guarantee producers a long-term relationship if they so choose, even in the absence of long-term contracts. Thus producers are more willing to invest in serving their customers. Finally, even if there is no formal MCC, it's generally accepted that you don't leave your current supplier without giving it a last chance to bid.

Using an MCC is a strategy that, far from being undermined by imitation, is enhanced by it. A carbon dioxide producer benefits from unilateral adoption of an MCC, but there is an added kicker when other producers copy it. The MCCs allow them to push prices up further, so they now have even more to lose from starting a share war. As MCCs become more widespread, everyone has less prospect of gaining share. With even more at risk and even less to gain, producers refrain from going after one another's customers. A moral: Players who live in glass houses are unlikely to throw stones. So you should be pleased when others build glass houses.

Both the significance of rules and the opportunity to change the game by changing the rules are often underappreciated. If negotiations in your business take place without rules, consider how bringing in a new rule would change the game. But be careful. Just as you can rewrite rules and make new ones, so, too, can others. Unlike other games, business has no ultimate rule-making authority to settle disputes. History matters. The government can make some rules—through antitrust laws, for example. In the end, however, the power to make rules comes largely from power in the marketplace. While it's true that rules can trump added value, it is added value that confers the power to make rules in the first place. As they said in the old West, "A Smith & Wesson beats a straight flush."

TACTICS: CHANGING PERCEPTIONS

We've changed the players, their added values, and the rules. Is there anything left to change? Yes—perceptions. There is no guarantee that everyone agrees on who the players are, what their added values are, and what the rules are. Nor are the implications of every move and countermove likely to be clear. Business is mired in uncertainty. Tactics influence the way players perceive the uncertainty and thus mold their behavior. Some tactics work by reducing misperceptions—in other words, by lifting the fog. Others work by creating or maintaining uncertainty—by thickening the fog.

Here we offer two examples. The first shows how Rupert Murdoch lifted the fog to influence how the *New York Daily News* perceived the game; the second illustrates how maintaining a fog can help negotiating parties reach an agreement.

The New York Fog

In the beginning of July 1994, the *Daily News* raised its price from 40 cents to 50 cents. This seemed rather remarkable under the circumstances. Its major rival, Rupert Murdoch's *New York Post,* was test-marketing a price cut to 25 cents and had demonstrated its effectiveness on Staten Island. As the *New York Times* saw it (Press Notes, July 4), it was as if the *Daily News* were daring Murdoch to follow through with his price cut.

But, in fact, there was more going on than the *Times* realized. Murdoch had earlier raised the price of the *Post* to 50 cents, and the *Daily News* had held at 40 cents. As a result, the *Post* was losing subscribers and, with them, advertising revenue. Whereas Murdoch viewed the situation as unsustainable, the *Daily News* didn't see any problem—or at least appeared not to. A convenient fog.

Murdoch came up with a tactic to try to lift the fog. Instead of just lowering his price back down to 40 cents, he announced his intention to lower it to 25 cents. The people at the *Daily News* doubted that Murdoch could afford to pull it off. Moreover, they believed that their recent success was due to a superior product and not just to the dime price advantage. They were not particularly threatened by Murdoch's announcement.

Seeing no response, Murdoch tried a second tactic. He started the price reduction on Staten Island as a test run. As a result, sales of the *Post* doubled—and the fog lifted. The *Daily News* learned that its readers were remarkably willing to read the *Post* in order to save 15 cents. The paper's added value was not so large after all. Suddenly, it didn't seem so stupid for Murdoch to have lowered his price to a quarter. It became clear that disastrous consequences would befall the *Daily News* if Murdoch extended his price cut throughout New York City. In London, just such a meltdown scenario was taking place between Murdoch's *Times* and Conrad Black's *Daily Telegraph*. It was in the context of all these events that the *Daily News* raised its price to 50 cents.

Only the *New York Times* remained in a fog. Murdoch had never wanted to lower his price to 25 cents. He never would have expected the *Daily News* to stay at 40 cents had he initiated an across-the-board cut to 25 cents. Murdoch's announcement and the test run on Staten Island were simply tactics designed to get the *Daily News* to raise its price. With price parity, the *Post* no longer would be losing subscribers, and both papers would be more profitable than if they were priced at 25 cents or even at 40 cents. Coopetition strikes again. The *Post* took an initial hit in raising its price to 50 cents, and when the *Daily News* tried to be greedy and not follow suit, Murdoch showed it the light. When the *Daily News* raised its price, it was not daring Murdoch at all. It was saving itself—and Murdoch—from a price war.

In the case of the *Daily News* and the *Post*, the fog was convenient to the former but not to the latter. So Murdoch lifted it.

Disagreeing to Agree

Sometimes, a fog is convenient to all parties. A fee negotiation between an investment bank and its client (a composite of several confidential negotiations) offers a good example. The client is a company whose owners are forced to sell. The investment bank has identified a potential acquirer. So far, the investment bank has been working on good faith, and now it's time to sign a fee letter.

The investment bank suggests a 1 percent fee. The client figures that its company will fetch $500 million and argues that a $5 million fee would be excessive. It proposes a 0.625 percent fee. The investment bankers think that the price will be closer to $250 million and that accepting the client's proposal would cut their expected fee from $2.5 million to about $1.5 million.

One tactic would be to lift the fog. The investment bank could try to convince the client that a $500 million valuation is unrealistic and that its fear of a $5 million fee is therefore unfounded. The problem with this tactic is that the client does not want to hear a low valuation. Faced with such a prospect, it might walk away from the deal and even from the bank altogether—and then there would be no fee.

The client's optimism and the investment bankers' pessimism create an opportunity for an agreement rather than an argument. Both sides should agree to a 0.625 percent fee combined with a $2.5 million guarantee. That way, the client gets the percentage it wants and considers the guarantee a throwaway. With a 0.625 percent fee, the guarantee kicks in only for a sales price below $400 million, and the client expects the price to be $100 million higher. Because the investment bankers expected $2.5 million under their original proposal, now that this fee is guaranteed, they can agree to a lower percentage.

Negotiating over pure percentage fees is inherently win-lose. If the fee falls from 1 percent to 0.625 percent, the client wins and the investment bankers lose. Going from 1 percent to 0.625 percent plus a floor is win-win—but only when the two parties maintain different perceptions. The fog allows for coopetition.

CHANGING THE SCOPE

After players, added values, rules, and tactical possibilities, there is nothing left to change within the existing boundaries of the game. But no game is an island. Games are linked across space and over time. A game in one place can affect games elsewhere, and a game today can influence games tomorrow. You can change the scope of a game. You can expand it by creating linkages to other games, or you can shrink it by severing linkages. Either approach may work to your benefit.

We left Nintendo with a stock market value exceeding both Sony's and Nissan's, and with Mario better known than Mickey Mouse. Sega and other would-be rivals had failed in the 8-bit game. But while the rest fell by the wayside, Sega didn't give up. It introduced a new 16-bit system to the U.S. market. It took two years before Nintendo responded with its own 16-bit machine. By then, with the help of its game hero, Sonic the Hedgehog, Sega had established a secure and significant market position. Today the two companies roughly split the 16-bit market.

Was Sega lucky to get such a long, uncontested period in which to establish itself? Did Nintendo simply blow it? We think not. Nintendo's 8-bit franchise was still very valuable. Sega realized that by expanding the scope, it could turn Nintendo's 8-bit strength into a 16-bit weakness. Put yourself in Nintendo's shoes: Would you jump into the 16-bit game or hold back? Had Nintendo jumped into the game, it would have meant competition and, hence, lower 16-bit prices. Lower prices for 16-bit games, substitutes for 8-bit games, would have reduced the value created by the 8-bit games—a big hit to Nintendo's bottom line. Letting Sega have the 16-bit market all to itself meant that 16-bit prices were higher than they otherwise would have been. Higher 16-bit prices cushioned the effect of the new-generation technology on the old. By staying out of Sega's way, Nintendo made a calculated trade-off: Give up a piece of the 16-bit action in order to extend the life of the 8-bit market. Nintendo's decision to hold back was reasonable, given the link between 8-bit and 16-bit games. Note that the decision not to create competition in a substitutes market is the mirror image of 3DO's strategy of creating competition in a complements market.

THE TRAPS OF STRATEGY

Changing the game is hard. There are many potential traps. Our mind-set, map, and method for changing the game—coopetition, the Value Net, and PARTS—are designed to help managers recognize and avoid these traps.

The first mental trap is to think you have to accept the game you find yourself in. Just realizing that you can change the game is crucial. There's more work to be done, but it's far more rewarding to be a game maker than a game taker.

The next trap is to think that changing the game must come at the expense of others. Such thinking can lead to an embattled mind-set that causes you to miss win-win opportunities. The coopetition mind-set—looking for both win-win and win-lose strategies—is far more rewarding.

Another trap is to believe that you have to find something to do that others can't. When you do come up with a way to change the game, accept that your actions might well be imitated. Being unique is not a prerequisite for success. Imitation can be healthy, as the GM card story and others illustrate.

The fourth trap is failing to see the whole game. What you don't see, you can't change. In particular, many people overlook the role of complementors. The solution is to draw the Value Net for your business; it will double your repertoire of strategies for changing the game. Any strategy toward customers has a counterpart with suppliers (and vice versa), and any strategy with substitutors has a mirror image for complementors (and vice versa).

The fifth trap is failing to think methodically about changing the game. Using PARTS as a comprehensive, theory-based set of levers helps generate strategies, but that is not enough. To understand the effect of any particular strategy, you need to go beyond your own perspective. Be allocentric, not egocentric.

For the Holland Sweetener Company, it would have helped to recognize that Coke and Pepsi would have paid a high price up front to make the aspartame market competitive. BellSouth succeeded with a weak hand only because it understood the incentives of Lin and McCaw. Nintendo's power in the 8-bit game came from lowering everyone else's added value. To craft the right choice of capacity and price, Kiwi had to put itself in the shoes of the major airlines to ensure that they would have a greater incentive to accommodate rather than fight Kiwi's entry. The effect of a meet-the-competition clause becomes clear only after you consider how a challenger thinks you would respond to an attempt it might make to steal one of your customers. To achieve his ends, Murdoch had to recognize that the *Daily News* was in a fog and find a way to lift it. By understanding how different parties perceive the game differently, a negotiator is better able to forge an agreement. Sega's success depended on the dilemma it created for Nintendo by starting a new 16-bit game linked to the existing 8-bit game.

Finally, there is no silver bullet for changing the game of business. It is an ongoing process. Others will be trying to change the game, too. Sometimes their changes will work to your benefit and sometimes not. You may need to change the game again. There is, after all, no end to the game of changing the game.

ENDNOTES

1. In-depth discussion and applications of the principle of looking forward and reasoning backward are provided in *Thinking Strategically: The Competitive Edge in Business, Politics, and Everyday Life,* by Avinash Dixit and Barry Nalebuff (W. W. Norton, 1991).

2. The argument is spelled out in Adam Brandenburger and Harborne Stuart, "Value-based Business Strategy," which will appear in a forthcoming issue of *Journal of Economics & Management Strategy.*

3. This portmanteau word can be traced to Ray Noorda, CEO of Novell, who has used it to describe relationships in the information technology business: "You have to cooperate and compete at the same time" (*Electronic Business Buyer,* December 1993).

4. McCaw paid $26.5 million to Los Angeles RCC—a joint venture between McCaw and Bell-South that was 85 percent owned by BellSouth. Since McCaw did not get any additional equity for his investment, it was in essence a $22.5 million payment to BellSouth and a $4 million payment to himself. Security laws override antitrust laws, so it's legal for one bidder to pay another not to be a player.

5. Unfortunately, the program provided little comfort to Cozzi, who resigned when TWA scaled it back. TWA returned to full-scale Comfort Class in the fall of 1994.

6. On a separate issue, Nintendo made a settlement with the Federal Trade Commission in which it agreed to stop requiring retailers to adhere to a minimum price for the game console. Further, Nintendo would give previous buyers a $5-off coupon toward future purchases of Nintendo game cartridges. Reflecting on the case, *Barron's* suggested that "the legion of trust-busting lawyers would be far more productively occupied playing Super Mario Brothers 3 than bringing cases of this kind" (December 3, 1991).

Strategy and Tactics of Distributive Bargaining

Negotiation Techniques: How to Keep Br'er Rabbit Out of the Brier Patch

Charles B. Craver

Practicing lawyers negotiate constantly—with their partners, associates, legal assistants, and secretaries, with prospective clients and actual clients, and with opposing parties on behalf of clients. Although practitioners tend to use their negotiation skills more often than their other lawyering talents, few have had formal education about the negotiation process.

The process consists of three formal phases:

- the information phase, where each party endeavors to learn as much about the other side's circumstances and objectives as possible.

- the competitive phase, where negotiators try to obtain beneficial terms for their respective clients.

- the cooperative phase, where if multiple-item transactions are involved, parties may often enhance their joint interests.

THE INFORMATION PHASE

The focus of this phase is always on the knowledge and desires of the opposing party. It is initially helpful to employ general, information-seeking questions instead of those that may be answered with a yes or no. Expansive interrogatories are likely to induce the other party to speak. The more that party talks, the more he is likely to divulge.

Where negotiations have effectively used open-ended questions to induce the other party to disclose its opening position and its general legal and factual assumptions, they should not hesitate to resort to specific inquiries to confirm suspected details. They can do this by asking the other side about each element of its perceived position. What exactly does that party hope to obtain, and why? What are the underlying motivational factors influencing that side's articulated demands?

Source: Reprinted with permission of TRIAL (June 1988). Copyright The Association of Trial Lawyers of America.

Negotiators must try to learn as much as possible about the opposing side's range of potential and actual choices, its preferences and their intensity, its planned strategy, and its strengths and weaknesses. Bargainers need to be aware that the opponent's perception of a situation may be more favorable to their own than they anticipated. Even the most proficient negotiators tend to overstate their side's weaknesses and overestimate the opposing party's strengths. Only through patient probing of their adversary's circumstances can they hope to obtain an accurate assessment.

The order in which parties present their initial demands can be informative. Some negotiators begin with their most important topics in an effort to produce an expeditious resolution of those issues. They are anxiety-prone, risk-averse advocates who wish to diminish the tension associated with the uncertainty inherent in the negotiation process. They believe they can significantly decrease their fear of not being able to settle by achieving expeditious progress on their primary topics. Unfortunately they fail to appreciate that this approach may enhance the possibility of a counterproductive impasse. If their principal objectives correspond to those of their adversary, this presentation sequence is likely to cause an immediate clash of wills.

Other negotiators prefer to begin bargaining with the less significant subjects, hoping to make rapid progress on these items. This approach is likely to develop a cooperative atmosphere that will facilitate compromise when the more disputed subjects are explored.

Negotiators must decide ahead of time what information they are willing to disclose and what information they must disclose if the transaction is going to be fruitful. Critical information should not always be directly provided. If negotiators voluntarily apprise the other side of important circumstances, they may appear self-serving and be accorded little weight. If, however, they slowly disclose such information in response to opponent questions, what they divulge will usually be accorded greater credibility.

Where an adversary asks about sensitive matters, blocking techniques may be used to minimize unnecessary disclosure. Such techniques should be planned in advance and should be varied to keep the opposing party off balance. A participant who does not wish to answer a question might ignore it, and the other side might go on to some other area.

Where a compound question is asked, a negotiator may respond to the beneficial part of it. Skilled negotiators may misconstrue a delicate inquiry and then answer the misconstrued formulation; they may respond to a specific question with general information or to a general inquiry with a narrow response. On occasion, negotiators may handle a difficult question with a question of their own. For example, if one party asks whether the other is authorized to offer a certain sum, that side may ask about the first party's willingness to accept such a figure.

Many negotiators make the mistake of focusing entirely on their opponents' stated positions. They assume that such statements accurately reflect the desires of the other side. Making this assumption may preclude the exploration of options that might prove mutually beneficial. It helps to go behind stated positions to try to ascertain the underlying needs and interests generating these positions. If negotiators understand what the other party really wants to achieve, they can often suggest alternatives that can satisfy both sides sufficiently to produce an accord.

THE COMPETITIVE PHASE

Once the information phase ends, the focus usually changes from what the opposing party hopes to achieve to what each negotiator must get for his client. Negotiators no longer ask questions about each other's circumstances; they articulate their own side's demands.

"Principled" Offers and Concessions

Negotiators should develop a rational basis for each item included in their opening positions. This provides the other party with some understanding of the reasons underlying their demands, and it helps to provide the person making those demands with confidence in the positions. Successful negotiators establish high, but rational, objectives and explain their entitlement to these goals.

When negotiators need to change their position, they should use "principled" concessions. They need to provide opponents with a rational explanation for modifications of their position.

For example, a lawyer demanding $100,000 for an injured plaintiff might indicate willingness to accept $90,000 by saying that there is a 10 percent chance that the plaintiff might lose at trial or a good probability that the jury in a comparative-negligence jurisdiction will find that the plaintiff was 10 percent negligent. This lets the other party know why the change is being made, and it helps to keep the person at the $90,000 level until he is ready to use a "principled" concession to further reduce the demand.

Argument

The power-bargaining tactic lawyers use most often involves legal and nonlegal argument. Factual and legal arguments are advanced. Public policy may be invoked in appropriate situations. Emotional appeals may be effective in some circumstances. If an argument is to be persuasive, it must be presented objectively.

Effective arguments should be presented in a comprehensive, rather than a conclusionary, fashion. Factual and legal information should be disclosed with appropriate detail. Influential statements must be insightful and carefully articulated. They must not be fully comprehended, but they must go beyond what is expected.

Contentions that do not surprise the receiving parties will rarely undermine their confidence in their preconceived position. But assertions that raise issues opponents have not previously considered will likely induce them to recognize the need to reassess their perceptions.

Threats and Promises

Almost all legal negotiations involve use of overt or at least implicit threats. Threats show recalcitrant parties that the cost of disagreeing with offers will transcend the cost of acquiescence. Some negotiators try to avoid use of formal "threats," preferring less-challenging "warnings." These negotiators simply caution opponents about the consequences of their unwillingness to accept a mutual resolution.

If threats are to be effective, they must be believable. A credible threat is one that is reasonably proportionate to the action it is intended to deter—seemingly insignificant threats tend to be ignored, while large ones tend to be dismissed. Negotiators should never issue threats unless they are prepared to carry them out, since their failure to do so will undermine their credibility.

Instead of using negative threats that indicate what consequences will result if the opposing party does not alter its position, negotiators should consider affirmative promises that indicate their willingness to change their position simultaneously with the other party. The classic affirmative promise—the "split-the-difference" approach—has been used by most negotiators to conclude a transaction. One side promises to move halfway if only the other side will do the same.

Affirmative promises are more effective than negative threats at inducing position changes, since the first indicates that the requested position change will be reciprocated. A negative threat merely suggests dire consequences if the other side does not alter its position. They are more of an affront to an opponent than affirmative promises, and, as a result, are more disruptive of the negotiation process.

Silence and Patience

Many negotiators fear silence, since they are afraid that they will lose control of the transaction if they stop talking. The more they talk, the more information they disclose and the more concessions they make. When their opponents remain silent, such negotiators often become even more talkative.

When negotiators have something important to say, they should say it and then keep quiet. A short comment accentuates the importance of what they are saying and provides the other party with the chance to absorb what was said. This rule is crucial when an offer or concession is being made. Once such information has been disclosed, it is time for the other side to respond.

Patience can be used effectively with silence. Where the other negotiator does not readily reply to critical representations, he should be given sufficient time to respond. If it is his turn to speak, the first party should wait silently for him to comment. If the first party feels awkward, he should look at his notes. This behavior shows the silent party that a response will be required before further discussion.

Limited Authority

Many advocates like to indicate during the preliminary stages that they do not have final authority from their client about the matter in dispute. They use this technique to reserve the right to check with the client before any tentative agreement can bind their side.

The advantage of a limited-authority approach—whether actual or fabricated—is that is permits the party using it to obtain a psychological commitment to settlement from opponents authorized to make binding commitments. The unbound bargainers can then seek beneficial modifications of the negotiated terms based on "unexpected" client demands. Since their opponents do not want to let such seemingly insignificant items negate the success achieved during the prior negotiations, they often accept the alterations.

Bargainers who meet opponents who initially say they lack the authority to bind their clients may find it advantageous to say that they also lack final authority. This will permit them to "check" with their own absent principal before making any final commitment.

A few unscrupulous negotiators will agree to a final accord with what appears to be complete authority. They later approach their opponent with apparent embarrassment and explain that they did not really have this authority. They say that their principal will require one or two modifications before accepting the other terms of the agreement. Since the unsuspecting opponent and his client are now committed to a final settlement, they agree to the concessions.

Negotiators who suspect that an adversary might use this technique may wish to select—at the apparent conclusion of their transaction—the one or two items they would most like to have modified in their favor. When their opponent requests changes, they can indicate how relieved they are about this, because their own client is dissatisfied. Then they can offer to exchange their items for those their adversary seeks. It is fascinating to see how quickly the opponent will now insist on honoring the initial accord.

The limited-authority situation must be distinguished from the one where an opponent begins a negotiation with no authority. This adversary hopes to get several concessions as a prerequisite to negotiations with a negotiator with real authority.

Negotiators should avoid dealing with a no-authority person, since he is trying to induce them to bargain with themselves. When they give their opening position, the no-authority negotiator will say that it is unacceptable. If they are careless, they will alter their stance to placate the no-authority participant. Before they realize what they have done, they will have made concessions before the other side has entered the process.

Anger

If negotiators become angry, they are likely to offend their opponent and may disclose information that they did not wish to divulge. Negotiators who encounter an adversary who has really lost his temper should look for inadvertent disclosures which that person's anger precipitates.

Negotiators often use feigned anger to convince an opponent of the seriousness of their position. This tactic should be used carefully, since it can offend adversaries and induce them to end the interaction.

Some negotiators may respond with their own retaliatory diatribe to convince their adversary that they cannot be intimidated by such tactics. A quid-pro-quo approach involves obvious risks, since a vituperative exchange may have a deleterious impact on the bargaining.

Negotiators may try to counter an angry outburst with the impression that they have been personally offended. They should say that they cannot understand how their reasonable approach has precipitated such an intemperate challenge. If they are successful, they may be able to make the attacking party feel guilty and embarrassed, shaming the person into a concession.

Aggressive Behavior

Such conduct is usually intended to have an impact similar to that associated with anger. It is supposed to convince an opponent of the seriousness of one's position. It can also be used to maintain control over the agenda.

Those who try to counter an aggressive bargainer with a quid-pro-quo response are likely to fail, due to their inability to be convincing in that role. Negotiators who encounter a particularly abrasive adversary can diminish the impact of his techniques through the use of short, carefully controlled interactions. Telephone discussions might be used to limit each exchange. Face-to-face meetings could be held to less than an hour. These short interactions may prevent the opponent from achieving aggressive momentum.

A few aggressive negotiators try to undermine their opponent's presentation through use of interruptions. Such behavior should not be tolerated. When negotiators are deliberately interrupted, they should either keep talking if they think this will discourage their opponent or they might say that they do not expect their opponent to speak while they are talking.

Uproar

A few negotiators try to obtain an advantage by threatening dire consequences if their opponent does not give them what they want. For example, a school board in negotiations with a teachers' union might say that it will have to lay off one-third of the teachers due to financial constraints. It will then suggest that it could probably retain everyone if the union would accept a salary freeze.

Negotiators confronted with such predictions should ask themselves two crucial questions. What is the likelihood that the consequences will occur? and What would happen to the other party if the consequences actually occurred? In many cases, it will be obvious that the threatened results will not occur. In others, it will be clear that the consequences would be as bad or worse for the other side as for the threatened party.

Bargainers occasionally may have to call an opponent's bluff. If union negotiators were to indicate that they could accept the layoffs if the school board would only raise salaries of the remaining teachers by 30 percent, the board representatives would probably panic. They know the school system could not realistically function with such layoffs. They were merely hoping that the union would not come to the same realization.

Settlement Brochures and Video Presentations

Some lawyers, particularly in the personal injury field, try to enhance their bargaining posture through settlement brochures or video presentations. A brochure states the factual and legal bases for the claim being asserted and describes the full extent of the plaintiff's injuries. Video presentations depict the way in which the defendant's negligent behavior caused the severe injuries the plaintiff has suffered.

Brochures are often accorded greater respect than verbal recitations, due to the aura of legitimacy generally granted to printed documents. Use of brochures may bolster the confidence of the plaintiff's lawyer and may enable him to seize control of the negotiating agenda at the outset. If the plaintiff's lawyer is fortunate, the opponent will begin by suggesting that the plaintiff is seeking too much for pain and suffering. This opening might implicitly concede liability, as well as responsibility for the property damage, medical expenses, and lost earnings requested.

Those presented with settlement brochures or video reenactments should not accord them more respect than they deserve. Lawyers should treat written factual and legal representations just as they would identical verbal assertions.

If lawyers are provided with settlement brochures before the first negotiating session, they should review them and prepare effective counterarguments, which they can state during settlement discussions.

Lawyers should not allow their adversary to use a settlement brochure to seize control of the agenda. Where appropriate, they may wish to prepare their own brochure or video to graphically depict their view of the situation.

Boulwareism

This technique gets its name from Lemuel Boulware, former vice president for labor relations at General Electric. Boulware was not enamored of traditional "auction" bargaining, which involves using extreme initial positions, making time-consuming concessions, and achieving a final agreement like the one the parties knew from the outset they would reach. He decided to determine ahead of time what GE was willing to commit to wage and benefit increases and then formulate a complete "best-offer-first" package. He presented this to union negotiators on a "take-it-or-leave-it" basis unless the union could show that GE had made some miscalculation or that changed circumstances had intervened.

Boulwareism is now associated with best-offer-first or take-it-or-leave-it bargaining. Insurance company adjusters occasionally try to establish reputations as people who will make one firm, fair offer for each case. If the plaintiff does not accept that proposal, they plan to go to trial.

Negotiators should be hesitant to adopt Boulwareism. The offeror effectively tells the other party that he knows what is best for both sides. Few lawyers are willing to accord such respect to the view of opposing counsel.

Boulwareism deprives the opponent of the opportunity to participate meaningfully in the negotiation process. A plaintiff who might have been willing to settle a dispute for $50,000 may not be willing to accept a take-it-or-leave-it offer of $50,000. The plaintiff wants to explore the case through the information phase and to exhibit his negotiating skill during the competitive phase. When the process has been completed, he wants to feel that his ability influenced the final outcome.

Negotiators presented with take-it-or-leave-it offers should not automatically reject them simply because of the paternalistic way in which they have been extended. They must evaluate the amount being proposed. If it is reasonable, they should accept it. Lawyers should not permit their own negative reaction to an approach preclude the consummation of a fair arrangement for their clients.

Br'er Rabbit

In *Uncle Renus, His Songs and His Sayings* (1880), Joel Chandler Harris created the unforgettable Br'er Rabbit. When the fox captured Br'er Rabbit, Br'er Rabbit used reverse psychology to escape. He begged the fox to do anything with him so long as he did not throw him in the brier patch. Since the fox wanted to punish the rabbit, he chose the one alternative the rabbit appeared to fear most and flung him in the brier patch. Br'er Rabbit was thus emancipated.

The Br'er Rabbit technique can occasionally be used against win-lose opponents who do not evaluate their results by how well they have done but by an assessment of how poorly their adversary has done. They are only satisfied if they think the other side has been forced to accept a terrible argument.

The Br'er Rabbit approach has risks. Although adroit negotiators may induce a careless, vindictive opponent to provide them with what is really desired, they must recognize that such a device will generally not work against a normal adversary. A typical win-win bargainer would probably accept their disingenuous representations and provide them with the unintended result they have professed to prefer over the alternative that has been renounced.

Mutt and Jeff

In the Mutt and Jeff routine, a seemingly reasonable negotiator professes sympathy toward the "generous" concessions made by the other, while his partner rejects each new offer as insufficient, castigating opponents for their parsimonious concessions. The reasonable partner will then suggest that some additional concessions will have to be made if there is to be any hope of satisfying his associate.

Single negotiators may even use this tactic. They can claim that their absent client suffers from delusions of grandeur, which must be satisfied if any agreement is to be consummated. Such bargainers repeatedly praise their opponent for the concessions being made, but insist that greater movement is necessary to satisfy the excessive aspirations of their "unreasonable" client when their client may actually be receptive to any fair resolution. The opponent has no way of knowing about this and usually accepts such representations at their face value.

Negotiators who encounter these tactics should not directly challenge the scheme. It is possible that their opponents are not really engaged in a disingenuous exercise. One adversary may actually disagree with his partner's assessment. Little is to be gained from raising a Mutt and Jeff challenge. Allegations about the tactics being used by such negotiators will probably create an unproductive bargaining atmosphere—particularly in situations where the opponents have not deliberately adopted such a strategy.

Those who interact with Mutt and Jeff negotiators tend to make the mistake of directing their arguments and offers to the unreasonable participant to obtain approval when it is often better to seek the acquiescence of the reasonable adversary before trying to satisfy the irrational one. In some instances, the more conciliatory opponent may actually agree to a proposal characterized as unacceptable by his associate. If the unified position of the opponents can be shattered, it may be possible to whipsaw the reasonable partner against the demanding one.

It is always important when dealing with unreasonable opponents to consider what might occur if no mutual accord is achieved. If the overall cost of surrendering to such an adversary's one-sided demands would clearly be greater than the cost associated with not settling, the interaction should not be continued.

Belly-Up

Some negotiators act like wolves in sheepskin. They initially say they lack negotiating ability and legal perspicuity in a disingenuous effort to evoke sympathy and to lure unsuspecting adversaries into a false sense of security. These negotiators "acknowledge" the superior competence of those with whom they interact and say that they will place themselves in the hands of their fair and proficient opponent.

Negotiators who encounter a belly-up bargainer tend to alter their initial position. Instead of opening with the tough "principled" offer they had planned to use, they modify it in favor of their pathetic adversary, who praises them for their reasonableness, but suggests that his client deserves additional assistance. They then endeavor to demonstrate their ability to satisfy those needs. The belly-up participant says the new offer is a substantial improvement, but suggests the need for further accommodation. By the time the transaction is finished, the belly-up bargainer has obtained everything he wants. Not only are his opponents virtually naked, but they feel gratified at having assisted such an inept bargainer.

Belly-up bargainers are the most difficult to deal with, since they effectively refuse to participate in the process. They ask their opponent to permit them to forgo traditional auction bargaining due to their professed inability to negotiate. They want their reasonable adversary to do all the work.

Negotiators who encounter them must force them to participate and never allow them to alter their planned strategy and concede everything in an effort to form a solution acceptable to such pathetic souls. When belly-up negotiators characterize initial offers as unacceptable, opponents should make them respond with definite offers. True belly-up negotiators often find it very painful to state and defend the positions they espouse.

Passive-Aggressive Behavior

Instead of directly challenging opponents' proposals, passive-aggressive negotiators use oblique, but highly aggressive, forms of passive resistance. They show up late for a scheduled session and forget to bring important documents. When they agree to write up the agreed-upon terms, they fail to do so.

Those who deal with a passive-aggressive opponent must recognize the hostility represented by the behavior and try to seize control. They should get extra copies of important documents just in case their opponent forgets to bring them. They should always prepare a draft of any agreement. Once passive-aggressive negotiators are presented with such a fait accompli, they usually execute the proffered agreement.

THE COOPERATIVE PHASE

Once the competitive phase has been completed, most parties consider the process complete. Although this conclusion might be warranted where neither party could possibly obtain more favorable results without a corresponding loss being imposed on the other party, this conclusion is not correct for multi-issue, nonconstant sum controversies.

During the competitive phase, participants rarely completely disclose underlying interests and objectives. Both sides are likely to use power-bargaining techniques aimed at achieving results favorable to their own circumstances.

Because of the anxiety created by such power-bargaining tactics, Pareto optimal arrangements—where neither party may improve its position without worsening the other side's—are usually not generated. The parties are more likely to achieve merely "acceptable" terms rather than Pareto optimal terms due to their lack of negotiation efficiency. If they were to conclude the process at this point, they might well leave a substantial amount of untapped joint satisfaction at the bargaining table.

Once a tentative accord has been achieved, it is generally advantageous for negotiators to explore alternative trade-offs that might simultaneously enhance the interests of both sides. After the competitive phase, one party should suggest transition into the cooperative phase. The parties can initial or even sign their current agreement, and then seek to improve their joint results.

Each should prepare alternative formulations by transferring certain terms from one side to the other while moving other items in the opposite direction. When these options are shown, each negotiator must candidly indicate whether any of the proposals are preferable to the accord already achieved.

Exploring alternatives need not consume much time. Negotiators may substantially increase their clients' satisfaction through this device, and the negotiators lose little if no mutual gains are achieved.

If the cooperative phase is to work effectively, candor is necessary. Each side must be willing to say whether alternatives are more or less beneficial for it.

On the other hand, this phase continues to be somewhat competitive. If one party offers the other an option much more satisfactory than what was agreed upon, he might merely indicate that the proposal is "a little better." Through this technique, he may be able to obtain more during the cooperative phase than would be objectively warranted.

SATISFYING CLIENTS

Lawyers who understand these common negotiating techniques can plan their strategies more effectively. They can enhance their skill in the information phase, increase the likelihood that they will achieve acceptable agreements during the competitive phase, and endeavor to maximize the gains obtained for their clients in the cooperative phase.

Secrets of
Power Negotiating

Roger Dawson

THE MYTH OF "WIN-WIN"

You have probably heard that the objective of negotiation is a win-win solution—a creative way that you and the other person can walk away from the table, both having truly won. Two people have one orange. They assume the best they can do will be to split the orange down the middle—but as they discuss their needs, they find that one wants the orange for juice, and the other wants the rind for a cake. There needn't be a winner and a loser. Both of them can win.

Oh, sure!

That *could* happen in the real world—but not often enough to make the concept meaningful. Let's face it: In a negotiation, chances are that the other side is out for the same thing as you. If they're buying, they want the lowest price, and you want the highest. If they're selling, they want the highest price, and you want the lowest. They want to take money out of your pocket and put it right into theirs.

Power Negotiating takes a different position. It teaches you how to win at the negotiating table but leave the other person *feeling* that he won. And feeling that permanently. He'll be thinking what a great time he had negotiating with you and how he can't wait to see you again.

The ability to make others feel that they won is so important that I would almost give you that as a definition of a Power Negotiator. You come away from the negotiating table knowing that you won and knowing that you have improved your relationship with the other person.

You play Power Negotiating just like the game of chess—by a set of rules. In negotiating, your counterpart doesn't have to know the rules. But in general, he will respond predictably to moves you make.

If you play chess, you know the strategic moves are called Gambits (a word that suggests an element of risk). There are Beginning Gambits to get the game started in your direction. There are Middle Gambits to keep the game moving in your direction. And there are Ending Gambits to use when you get ready to checkmate or, in sales parlance, close the sale. As negotiations progress, you'll find that every advance depends on the atmosphere you created in the early stages.

ASK FOR MORE THAN YOU EXPECT TO GET

This Gambit embodies one of the cardinal rules of Power Negotiating. Henry Kissinger said: "Effectiveness at the negotiating table depends upon overstating demands."

Asking for more than you expect raises the perceived value of what you are offering. And it prevents deadlocking.

Let me give you a contrary example: Before the Persian Gulf War, President Bush presented Saddam Hussein with a very clear and precise opening position. But it was not a true *negotiating* position, because it was also his bottom line. He left no room for any concession to the Iraqi side, to give them a little victory and make it easier for them to withdraw from Kuwait. The President did not overstate his demands at all—he announced that Iraq had to pull out of Kuwait. Therefore, nothing happened at the conference table, which resulted in a deadlock and a military conflict. This was no accident. Bush's position was meant to create a deadlock—to provide a reason to go in and take care of Iraq militarily, since we didn't want them to pull out voluntarily today, only to reappear later. But in your negotiation, you may *inadvertently* create deadlocks because you don't have the courage to *ask for more than you expect to get.*

Sometimes it may be intimidating for you to ask for that much. You simply don't have the courage to make sufficiently way-out proposals. There are many reasons why you should learn to do so anyway.

First of all, you never know: When you ask for more than you expect, you might just get it. You don't know how the universe is aligned that day. Perhaps your patron saint is looking down at you over a cloud thinking, "Look at that nice person, working so hard. . ." The only way to find out is to ask.

Here's a rule of thumb about asking: The less you know about whomever you're up against, the higher your initial position should be. Why? He may be willing to pay more than you think. If he's selling, he may be willing to take far less than you think. In any case, in a new relationship, you will look more cooperative to the other side if you're in a position to make larger concessions.

So, start with your Maximum Plausible Position (MPP)—which is the most you can ask for and still appear credible. Note: Your MPP is probably much higher than you think. We all fear being ridiculed, so you are probably tempted to ask for less than the maximum that the other side would find plausible. You must be on guard against *yourself.*

So, stake out your MPP—and imply flexibility. If you're a salesman, you might say to the buyer, "We may be able to modify this position once we know your needs more precisely, but based on what we know so far about the quantities you'd be ordering, our best price would be in the region of $2.25 per widget." You want him to think, "That's outrageous, but there does seem to be some flexibility there, so I'll invest some time negotiating."

Power Negotiators know that first offers seem extreme but are only the beginning; they know that they will work their way toward a solution both sides can accept. When football players or airline pilots go on strike, initial demands from both sides are outlandish. By making the other side move, eventually, both sides can tell the press that they won in negotiations, and both can be magnanimous in victory.

An attorney friend of mine in Amarillo, Texas, was representing a buyer of a piece of real estate. Even though he had a good deal, he dreamed up 23 paragraphs of requests to make of the seller. Some of them were absolutely ridiculous. He felt sure half of them would get thrown out right away. To his amazement, the seller took strong objection to only one sentence in one of the paragraphs.

Even then, he didn't give in right away. He held out for a couple of days before he reluctantly agreed to strike the sentence. And although my friend gave away only that one sentence in 23 paragraphs of requests, the seller felt he had won.

How much more should you ask than you expect to get?

Get the other side to state a position first. If there is no pressure on you, be bold enough to say, "You approached me. The way things are satisfies me. If you want to do this, you'll have to make a proposal to me."

The car dealer is asking $15,000 for the car. You want it for $13,000. So put the price you want in a bracket between what he is asking and what you will offer up front: Offer $11,000.

One of your employees wants to spend $400 on a new desk. You think $325 is reasonable. Say that it can't be more than $250.

In other words, your proposal should be as far from what you want in your direction as the other guy's proposal is in the other direction. If you end up in the middle, you make your objective. You won't always end up in the middle, but how often it happens will amaze you.

NEVER SAY YES TO THE FIRST OFFER

Why not? If you do, it triggers two negative thoughts in your counterpart's mind:

1. I could have done better.
2. Something must be wrong.

Suppose you are a buyer for a maker of aircraft engines meeting with a salesman for a manufacturer of engine bearings. Bearings are a vital component for you, and your regular supplier has let you down. If you can't make an agreement with this company, your assembly line will shut down within 30 days. And if you can't supply the engines on time, it will invalidate your contract with the aircraft manufacturer who gives you 85 percent of your business.

In these circumstances, the price of the bearings you need is not a high priority. But the thought occurs to you: "I'll be a good negotiator. Just to see what happens, I think I'll make him a super-low offer."

He quotes you $250 each, which surprises you because you have been paying $275. You respond, "We've been paying only $175." He responds, "O.K., we can match that."

In thousands of seminars over the years, I've posed a situation like this to audiences and can't recall getting anything other than the two negative responses listed above. It isn't the price. It's the immediate response to the proposal without a struggle that sends up a warning flag in most people.

I was president of a real estate company in Southern California that had 28 offices. One day, a magazine salesman came in trying to sell me advertising space. I knew it was an excellent opportunity, and he made me a very reasonable offer that required a modest $2,000 investment. Because I love to negotiate, I used Gambits on him and got him down to an incredible price of $800. That made me wonder if I could do even better, and I used the Gambit called Higher Authority and said: "This looks fine. I just have to run it by my board or directors. They're meeting tonight."

A couple of days later, I called him and said: "I felt I wouldn't have any problem selling the board of directors on that $800, but they're so difficult to deal with right now. The budget is giving everyone headaches. They did make a counteroffer, but it is so low, I am frankly embarrassed to tell you what it is."

"How much did they agree to?"

"$500."

"I'll take it."

And I felt cheated. I still felt I could have done better. In other words, if you're too agreeable, it makes the other side uneasy. There are several ways to avoid the mistrust that can develop in your relationship.

1. Flinch

Always react with shock and surprise at the other side's proposals.

The truth of the matter is that when people make a proposal to you, they are watching for your reaction. A concession often follows a Flinch. If you don't Flinch, it makes the other person a tougher negotiator. He may not have thought for a moment you would go along with his request, but if you don't Flinch at something outrageous, he may decide to see how far he can get you to go.

Flinching is critical because most people believe what they see more than what they hear. It's safe to assume that with at least 70 percent of the people with whom you will negotiate, the visual overrides the auditory. Don't dismiss Flinching as childish or too theatrical until you've tried it.

A woman told me that she Flinched when selecting a bottle of wine in one of Boston's finest restaurants, and the wine steward immediately dropped the price by $5. A man told me a simple Flinch took $2,000 off the price of a Corvette.

If you're not negotiating face-to-face, you can gasp in shock and surprise. Phone Fliches can be very effective.

2. Avoid Confrontation

What you say in the first few moments often sets the climate of a negotiation. That's one problem I have with the way lawyers negotiate. Your first communication from them is likely to be a threat. In one workshop I taught that included some lawyers, most of them would start a negotiation exercise with a vicious threat and become more abusive from there. I had to stop the exercise and tell them never to be confrontational early on if they wanted to settle a case without expensive litigation. (I doubted their motives on that score.)

If the other side takes a position with which you disagree, don't argue. That only intensifies their desire to be proven right. Get in the habit of agreeing initially and turning it around. Use the Feel, Felt, Found Formula:

I understand exactly how you Feel about that. Many other people have Felt exactly the same way. But you know what we have always Found? When we took a closer look, we Found. . . (that they changed their minds, of course).

At the very least, this approach gives you time to think. By the time you get around to saying what you found on a closer look, you will have found what you need to say.

PLAY THE RELUCTANT BUYER OR RELUCTANT SELLER

One of my Power Negotiators owns real estate worth probably $50 million, owes $35 million in loans, and therefore has a net worth of about $15 million. Many smaller investors bring him purchase offers, eager to acquire one of his better-known properties. I have seen him make thousands of dollars with the Reluctant Seller Gambit.

He reads the offer quietly and slides it thoughtfully back across the table, scratches above one ear, and says: "I don't know. Of all my properties, I have very special feelings for this one. I was thinking of keeping it and giving it to my daughter for her college graduation present. I really don't think I would part with it for anything less than the full asking price. But it was good of you to make me this offer, and so that you won't have wasted your time, what is the very best price you feel you could give me?"

Many times, I have seen him make thousands of dollars in a few seconds.

Now, put yourself on the other side of the desk for a moment and become the Reluctant Buyer. Let's say you're in charge of buying new computer equipment for your company. How can you get the best possible price? My suggestion is to have the supplier come to your offices and go through the whole presentation. Ask all the questions you can possibly think of, then say: "I really appreciate all the time you've taken. You've obviously put a lot of work into this presentation, but unfortunately, it's not the way we want to go; however, I sure wish you the best of luck."

Pause to examine the crestfallen expression on the salesman's face as he slowly puts away his presentation materials. Then, at the very last moment, as his hand reaches for the doorknob on the way out, come out with the following magic expression. It is one of those expressions in negotiating that, used at the right moment, yields amazingly predictable results. Say: "You know, I really do appreciate the time you took here. Just to be fair to you, what is the very lowest price you would take?"

Would you agree that the first price you were quoted was probably not the bottom? It's a good bet. The first price was probably what I call the "wish number." If you'd signed off on that, the salesman would have shoved the contract into his briefcase, burned rubber all the way back to the office, and run in screaming, "You won't believe what just happened to me!"

When you play the Reluctant Buyer, you'll get a second quote, in which the salesman will probably give away half his negotiating range—between the "wish number" and his lowest possible price, which I call the "walk-away" price. He'll typically respond with: "Well, I tell you what. I like your company. It's the end of our quarter, and we're in a sales contest. If you'll place the order today, I'll give it to you for the unbelievably low price of $200,000. . . ."

It's a game. When someone plays Reluctant Buyer to *you,* the correct response is: "I don't think there's any flexibility in our price, but if you'll tell me what it would take to get your business (getting the other side to commit to a number first), I'll take it to my people (using a Higher Authority as a foil) and see what I can do for you with them (setting up to play Good Guy/Bad Guy)."

THE VISE TECHNIQUE

The Vise is this simple little expression: "You'll have to do better than that."

A veteran negotiator will simply come back at you with: "Just how much better do I have to do?" But it's amazing how often an inexperienced one will give away a big chunk of his range, simply because you did that.

Once you've used that phrase, shut up. Don't say another word. One client called me to say that by using this simple phrase, he got a price $14,000 less than he was prepared to pay.

Are you wondering: "Was that a $50,000 proposal that got knocked down by $14,000, or a multimillion-dollar proposal—in which case, $14,000 is no big deal?" It doesn't matter. The point is that he made $14,000 in those two minutes that it took him to scrawl that phrase on a bid. That would be $420,000 per hour. You'll never make money faster than you do when you're negotiating.

The dollars you save or lose in negotiating are bottom-line dollars, not gross income dollars. I've trained executives at retailers and health maintenance organizations (HMOs) whose profit margin is only 2 percent. They do a billion dollars' worth of business a year, but they bring in only 2 percent in bottom-line profits. In a company like that, a $2,000 concession at the negotiating table has the same effect as a $100,000 sale.

You're probably in an industry that does better than that. In this country, the average profit margin is about 5 percent of gross sales. For such a company, a $2,000 concession at the negotiating table is the equivalent of $40,000 in sales. How long would you be willing to work to get a $40,000 sale?

Perhaps when you read these Gambits you're thinking, "Roger, you've never met the guys I deal with in my business. They make Attila the Hun look like Ann Landers. They'll never fall for that kind of thing." Fair enough. But try these techniques. Time and again, students have told me: "I never thought that would work, but it did. It's amazing." The first time you Flinch or use the Vise on the other person and walk out of negotiations with $1,000 in your pocket that you didn't expect to get, you'll become a believer, too. Negotiating is a game that is played by a set of rules. If you learn the rules well, you can play the game well.

DON'T WORRY ABOUT PRICE

After two decades of sales training, I am convinced that price is a bigger concern to the people selling than it is to those they're selling to. People want to pay more, not less. Customers who may be asking you to cut your price may be secretly wishing they could pay more. Seriously.

I was the merchandising manager at the Montgomery Ward store in Bakersfield, California, which is not a large town. But in a chain of more than 600 stores, ours ranked thirteen in volume. Why? The head office left us alone and allowed us to sell to the needs of the local population. We did a huge business in home air conditioners, because in Bakersfield, it's not unusual for it to be 100 degrees Fahrenheit at midnight. A blue-collar home in that city then cost around $30,000. The air conditioners we sold them cost $10,000 to $12,000. The customers were willing to pay that price, but it was very hard to break in new salesmen because they couldn't believe anybody would pay $12,000 to put an air conditioner in a $30,000 house.

But if I could get these same salesmen to succeed to the point where they made big money and installed air conditioners in their own homes, suddenly they didn't find the price outrageous and would dismiss price objections from customers as if they didn't exist.

Beginning stockbrokers are the same. It's very hard for them to ask a client to invest $100,000 when they don't know where their own lunch money is going to come from. But once they become affluent, their sales snowball.

One of my clients tells me that if three products are on a store shelf—let's say three toasters—and the features of each are described on the carton, customers will most frequently select the highest-priced item. But if a salesman working for minimum wage comes along to assist them, he can't justify spending money on the best and talks the customer down to the low-end or the middle-of-the-line toaster.

The key is the description on the carton. You must give customers a *reason* to spend more money, but if you can do that, they want to spend more money, not less. I think that spending money is what Americans do best. We spend $6 trillion dollars a year in this country. And that's when we're spending our own hard-earned, after-tax dollars. What if you're asking someone at a corporation to spend the company's money? One thing better than spending your own money is spending someone else's money. And corporate expenditures are tax deductible, so Uncle Sam is going to pick up 40 percent of the bill.

Let's face it, does what you pay for something really matter? If you're going to buy a new automobile, does it matter if you spend $20,000 or $21,000? Not really. You'll soon forget what you paid, and the slight increase in payments is not going to affect your lifestyle. What matters is the feeling that you got the best possible deal.

If you're trying to get someone to spend money, all you have to do is give him a reason and convince him there is no way to get a better deal.

Even when dealing with the federal government, price is far from the most important thing. I asked a Pentagon procurement officer point-blank if the government has to buy from the lowest bidder.

"Heavens no," he said. "We'd really be in trouble if that were true. The rules say we should buy from the lowest bidder whom we feel is capable of meeting specifications. We're far more concerned with a company's experience and its ability to get a job done on time."

In a company that doesn't have legal requirements to put out requests for bids, price probably counts for even less. AT&T keeps my telephone business even though it's more expensive than Sprint or MCI and has never pretended otherwise. I stay because the service has been trouble-free and simple to use for many years, and I have more important things concerning me than switching long-distance companies to save a few pennies per call. So don't exacerbate the price problem by assuming that price is uppermost in the other person's mind. Assume that it isn't.

As negotiations proceed, don't narrow the negotiation down to just one issue. If everything is resolved and the only issue left is price, then clearly, somebody has to win, and clearly, somebody does have to lose. But as long as you keep more than one issue on the table, you can work trade-offs so that the other fellow doesn't mind conceding on price because you are able to offer something in return.

Find other ways to make him feel he's winning.

HIGHER AUTHORITY

Once you're in negotiations, it's always good for you to postpone a decision and plead that you have to run the deal by some outside person with Higher Authority. The other side will make more concessions to people they *don't* see or know than they will to you alone.

But by the same token, you will be frustrated over and over if this Gambit is used on you. When I was a real estate broker, I taught our agents that before they put buyers into their cars to show them properties, they must always say: "Just to be sure I understand, if we find exactly the right home for you today, is there any reason you couldn't make a decision today?"

Here's something you can count on when dealing with another person: Any concession you make will lose its value quickly. A material object may appreciate in value over the years, but the value of services declines rapidly after you have performed them. Consequently, when you make a concession, you must ask for a reciprocal concession right away, because two hours later, what you have done will count for little or nothing.

That's one reason why you always have to settle your fee before you perform a service. When a real estate salesman offers to help someone get rid of a property, a 6 percent fee doesn't sound enormous—but the minute the realtor has found the buyer, that 6 percent suddenly starts to sound like a tremendous amount of money.

DON'T SPLIT THE DIFFERENCE

When you are negotiating price, don't offer to split the difference that is keeping you and the person on the other side from agreement. Let him suggest that. You can usually get them to do so if you point out how long you have been negotiating and what a comparatively small sum is keeping you apart.

It makes all the difference psychologically to someone if *he* makes a suggestion and gets you to agree to it, as opposed to unwillingly accepting a proposal from you. It may seem a very subtle thing, but it's a significant factor in determining who feels he has won.

If your counterpart splits the difference with you and moves half the distance toward your price, you can invoke a Higher Authority—maybe it's your partners or your board. After a delay of hours or days, you come back and say that your Higher Authority is not being cooperative and has vetoed the new offer, then point out how it seems too bad that a little difference—between what you're asking and what he just offered—should derail everything. If you keep that up long enough, he will probably offer to split the difference again. So you have that much more bottom-line profit. But even if he won't do it a second time, if you wind up splitting the difference as he first proposed, he will feel he won—because he proposed it.

SET IT ASIDE

In negotiations, you will often find that you are in complete disagreement on one issue. It's easy for an inexperienced negotiator to feel that the whole deal is threatened, but you can handle an impasse on one issue by the Set Aside Gambit: "Let's just set that aside for a moment and talk about some of the other issues, may we?" If you resolve minor issues that you can discuss easily, you'll put momentum into the negotiations again. The other side will be much more flexible after you've reached agreement on the smaller issues.

A stalemate is something different. That's when both sides are still talking but seem unable to make any progress. At this point, you must change the dynamics of the meeting to reestablish momentum.

Change the people in the negotiating team. Remove any member who may have irritated the other side. Change the venue by proposing to continue over lunch or dinner. Ease the tension—tell a funny story, talk about their hobbies or a piece of gossip that's in the news. Explore the possibility of extended credit, a reduced deposit, restructured payments, or a change in specifications, packaging, or delivery method. Remember that the other side may be reluctant to raise these issues for fear of appearing to be in poor financial condition.

Discuss methods of sharing the risk with the other side.

THE ART OF CONCESSION

In negotiations over price, be sure you don't set up a pattern in the way you make concessions. Don't make equal-size concessions. That will certainly make the other side expect that another concession of just the same size is practically his right. And never make the final concession a big one. It never looks final if it's big. To refuse a further, smaller concession after you have just made a big one makes you seem difficult and only creates needless hostility.

MAKE TIME YOUR ALLY

The longer you can keep the other party involved in negotiations, the more likely he is to move around to your point of view. Think of the tugboats in the Hudson River off Manhattan. A tiny tugboat can move a huge ocean liner if it does it a little bit at a time. If the tugboat captain were to back off, rev up the engines, and try to force the ocean liner around, it wouldn't do any good. If you have enough patience, you can change anybody's mind a little bit at a time.

Unfortunately, this works both ways. The longer you spend in a negotiation, the more likely you are to make concessions.

An 80/20 split surfaces repeatedly in apparently unrelated fields. In the nineteenth century, the economist Vilfredo Pareto, who studied the distribution of wealth in Italy, pointed out that 80 percent of the wealth was concentrated in the hands of 20 percent of the people. Sales managers tell me that 80 percent of the business is done by 20 percent of the salespeople. Schoolteachers tell me that 20 percent of the children cause 80 percent of the trouble.

It also seems true that on account of the incredible pressure that time can put on a negotiation, 80 percent of the concessions in a negotiation will occur in the last 20 percent of the time available. If demands are presented early on, neither side may be willing to yield, and the entire transaction can fall apart. But if additional demands or problems surface in the final 20 percent of the time available for the negotiation, both sides will be more flexible.

Think back to the last time you bought a piece of real estate. Probably it took about 10 weeks from signing the initial contract until you actually became the owner of the property. Now think of the concessions that were made in the last 2 weeks. Weren't both sides more yielding at that point?

One rule that obviously follows from this: If you have a deadline pushing you in a negotiation, never reveal that fact to the other side. He'll be sure to squeeze you for concessions at the last minute.

If you have flown to Dallas to resolve a negotiation with a hotel developer, and you have a return flight at 6 o'clock, of course you want to make that flight—but don't let the other people know. If they do know, be sure they know that you have a backup flight at 9 o'clock—and that if you need to, you can stay over until you work out a mutually satisfactory arrangement.

The power that comes from knowing the other side's time limit was shown when President Lyndon Johnson wanted to negotiate with the Vietnamese in time to do his party some good in the election of November 1968. He sent our negotiator, Averell Harriman, to Paris with very clear instructions: Get something done, fast, right now, Texas style.

Harriman rented a suite at the Ritz Hotel in Paris on a week-to-week basis. Vietnamese negotiator Xuan Thuy rented a villa in the countryside for two and a half years. Then the Vietnamese proceeded to spend week after week after week talking to us about the shape of the table.

Did they really care about the shape of the table? Of course not. They were projecting, successfully, that they were not under any time pressure. They were trying to exploit Johnson's November deadline. On November 1, only five days before the election, Johnson called a halt to the bombing of Vietnam.

THE MOST DANGEROUS MOMENT

You are at your most vulnerable at the point when you think the negotiations are over, just after the other party has agreed to go ahead. Making a huge sale has excited you. You're feeling good. At such times, you tend to give away things you otherwise wouldn't. Watch your emotions.

If the other side chooses this moment to Nibble at the deal for some concession now, you're likely to think: "Oh no, I thought we had resolved everything. I don't want to take a chance on going back to the beginning and renegotiating the whole thing. If I do that, I might lose the whole sale. I'm better off just giving in on this little point."

Don't lay yourself open to last-minute Nibbles—some of which could negate the benefit of the deal for you. Your protection is to say *you don't have the authority* to make any concessions now. If the other side persists and wants extra training, installation, extended warranties, or anything else, show them the hard price in writing. Don't let the euphoria of finishing a negotiation cost you the store.

YOUR MOST POWERFUL WEAPON

If there's one thing that I can impress upon you that will make you 10 times more powerful as a negotiator, it's this: Learn to develop walk-away power. Often, there's a point you pass in the heat of negotiation when you will no longer walk away. You start thinking:

"I'm going to buy this car. I'm going to get the best price I can, but I'm not leaving until I get it."

"I'm going to hire this person. For the lowest salary and benefits that I can—but I won't let him get away."

"I have to take this job. I'm going to fight for the best pay and benefits, but I have to take this job."

"I have to make this sale. I can't walk out of here without a commitment."

The minute you're no longer willing to say, "I'm prepared to walk away from this," I guarantee you will lose in the negotiations.

So don't pass that point. There's no such thing as a sale you have to make at any price, or the only car or home for you, or a job or employee you can't do without. The minute you think there is, you've lost.

When people tell me they made a mistake in negotiations, this is always a part of the problem. They passed the point where they were willing to walk away.

Many years ago, my daughter bought her first car. She fell in love with the car, and the dealer knew it. Then she came back from the place and wanted me to go down with her to negotiate a better price. I sat her down and said, "Julia, are you prepared to come home without the car?"

She said, "No, I'm not, I want it, I want it." She was in trouble.

"Julia, you might as well get your checkbook out and give them what they're asking, because you've set yourself up to lose. We've got to be prepared to walk away."

We walked out of the showroom twice in the two hours we spent negotiating over the car and bought it for $2,000 less than she would have paid for it. How much money was she making when she was negotiating? She was making $1,000 an hour. We'd all go to work for $1,000 an hour, wouldn't we? You never make money faster than when you're negotiating.

Defusing the Exploding Offer:
The Farpoint Gambit

Robert J. Robinson

Situations in which offers are made with an expiration date attached are common in negotiation. In a way, all offers are inherently limited by time: One cannot, for example, leave a car dealership, return several years later, and attempt to accept the last offer made by a dealer who may or may not be employed there any longer. Obviously, the validity of an offer is affected by the passage of time. "Exploding offers" in contrast, are deliberate, calculated strategies. They are typically offered together with an extremely short, artificially imposed time limit. Consider, for instance, the following common manifestations of this phenomenon:

- Mary is looking for an apartment in a new city, and finally finds one that suits all her needs. When she asks about the rent, the landlord says: "The rent is $900 per month, but I tell you what—give me a check for the security deposit today, and I'll make it $850. Otherwise it's $900."

- John needs to buy a car. He haggles for several hours with a dealer, getting the price lower and lower. Finally an impasse is reached: John is still not happy with the price, but the dealer is unable to offer a more attractive deal. As John gets up to leave, the dealer says: "Look, it's the end of the month. If we can do this today, I'll make my quota, and that's worth another $500 off the price to me. But if you come back on Monday, we start all over again."

- Pat is an MBA student looking for a summer job between the first and second years of the program. The school has a recognized recruitment "season" when various companies come on campus, interview students and, in many instances, offer summer employment. On the first day of the interviews, Pat interviews with Company X. After about 30 minutes, the Company X spokesperson says, "Well, we'd like to offer you the job," (and names a very generous salary) "but you must say yes or no right now."

Source: Robert J. Robinson "Defusing the Exploding Offer: The Farpoint Gambit," *Negotiation Journal,* July 1995, Kluwer Academic/Plenum Publishers.

Each of these examples illustrates what has become know as an exploding offer. However, each case probably evokes a different affective response in the reader, and has different implications for the protagonists in the vignettes. Mary has the choice of saving $50 per month rent but can still have the apartment if she delays until the following day; John probably will not purchase the car unless he takes advantage of the temporary $500 concession; and Pat has the chance to get an attractive summer job—which disappears if Pat's next response is anything but acceptance of the offer. In this brief article my goal is to further refine the notion of exploding offers (the problem faced by Mary, John, and Pat) and suggest some ideas on how to deal with them, including a tactic that I call the "Farpoint Gambit."

CHARACTERISTICS OF EXPLODING OFFERS

Many negotiation scholars use the notion of an exploding offer in informal discussion, and the concept is directly related to analyses of the role of threats and time in negotiating. [S]pecifically, what makes an offer "exploding"? In my opinion, five characteristics separate "exploding" offers from offers that have naturally decaying life spans. They are:

Power Asymmetry.   Exploding offers generally only exist in situations where there is a considerable asymmetry of power between the offeror and the person receiving the offer. Thus in the cases of Mary and John, one might consider the offers as tactics being used between consenting adults in relatively equal power positions, which might not arouse any sense of discomfort. In Pat's case, the situation is more ambiguous. Faced with a large company offering a choice between a job or possible unemployment for the summer, a student burdened with loans might feel great pressure to accept, as a result of the exploding offer. An even more extreme example is provided by the academic job market which is filled with newly minted PhD recipients who are looking for faculty positions. Colleges routinely make exploding offers which are the equivalent of offering a person dying of thirst a glass of water—if the person accepts right away. This leads to the second condition of concern.

A Pressure-Inducing "Test of Faith."   The exploding offer often places great pressure on the person receiving the offer. This is not in itself unusual or necessarily reprehensible. However, the situation becomes more complex when the pressure is excessive, and is built on power imbalances. Thus in the case of the faculty candidate, I have personally witnessed situations where the person receiving the offer is placed under excessive pressure by the argument that "if you're one of us you'll accept now." This not only applies "normal" negotiation pressure but also raises the threat that accepting later risks making the organization angry with you for "holding out." This makes the act of attempting to negotiate further somehow vaguely (or explicitly, depending on the degree of coercion being applied) treasonable, and leaves the person receiving the offer with no option but to accept, or withdraw completely. In another situation I witnessed, excessive pressure was applied by means of an interesting variation, which consisted of offering the job to the individual, and telling them that they were the person that the company wanted above all others—followed by informing the individual that if they were unable to accept the job *that day,* the offer would be withdrawn, at least until "further candidates have been considered and interviewed for the position."

Restricting Choice.   Another characteristic of the exploding offer is its use as a tool that deliberately restricts the choice of the individual. While there is an element of this factor in the case of Mary (the landlord does not want her looking at other apartments) and John (the salesperson does not want him looking at other cars), it is somewhat peripheral in both of these negotiations, which are aimed at closing a deal. In Pat's case, however, the exploding offer as a means to restrict comparative shopping *is the primary tactic,* and rests on not letting Pat get any other offers or even see representatives of other companies. In fact, it might even emerge that Company X is interviewing particularly early in order to prevent the candidates from seeing anyone else.

Lack of Consideration and Respect.   Exploding offers involve arbitrary deadlines which are unnecessarily rigid. They can create enormous hardship for the individual involved, who may be called from family duties, may be forced to break leases, or may suffer other financial hardships in order to accept the offer. Appeals for flexibility and consideration are routinely ignored by the offeror, displaying an utter lack of regard for the other negotiator.

Lack of Good Faith.   Exploding offers are sometimes because a negotiator is ambivalent about the person or proposal in question, or is using this strategy as a means of resolving internal strife within the negotiator's organization. This is a somewhat cynical viewpoint, and it is not uncommon for one side to make an exceptionally self-advantageous exploding offer. If the offer is accepted, then a fine bargain has been achieved; and if the offer is rejected, the offeror can move on to other options. The problem is that the offer, as made, was not a serious, good faith attempt to reach a settlement. Thus while Pat might be told that he or she is the candidate that Company X wants, the reality is more likely that Company X wants a warm body with Pat's qualifications, and if Pat won't accept, then an interchangeable individual will be substituted.

WHY ARE EXPLODING OFFERS MADE?

It is not difficult to understand the thinking behind the use of exploding offers, in terms of the perceived advantage this affords the offeror. The ability to impose terms and back them up with a tight time limit may force the other side to capitulate or agree before it might otherwise have done so, increasing the value of the deal for the party making the offer. In many ways, the exploding offer is the ultimate hard bargaining tactic: Party A makes a final offer and then threateningly says, "And that's good until noon tomorrow. After that, you can find another partner." In essence, the tactic defines an end to the negotiation process. An exploding offer is not only an offer in the traditional sense but is also the last offer. Rejection will automatically terminate the negotiation, and in some cases, the relationship as well.

In terms of the vignettes mentioned earlier, it is easy to understand how exploding offers can serve the interest of the offeror. In Mary's case, the landlord wants to tie in the new tenant that very day. Perhaps the landlord is going away, and wants to get the apartment filled. Or maybe she just thinks that Mary is the kind of tenant she wants in the building, and is trying to sweeten the deal. Perhaps the rent really is $850, and the landlord is disingenuously offering the $50 discount. Whatever the reason, it is worth $50 per month to the landlord to commit Mary that day, rather than undergoing the opportunity cost of continuing to search for other tenants.

Similarly in John's case, the dealer may in fact be trying to meet the quota for the month, or he may be looking for a way to make a sweeter offer without undercutting the "going" price for that model car. In any event, having John leave the dealership is to be avoided at all costs, and the $500 exploding offer is an incentive for John to stay and make the deal.

In Pat's case, Company X is presumably interviewing several MBA students over the next several days. The company must pay to have the interviewer stay in a hotel until the process is concluded. During that time, the interviewer makes offers and waits for the students to pick among several offers; if rejected, the interviewer might make another offer and so on. How much simpler it is to tie up the first likely-looking individual the interviewer meets, and go home.

There is also another reason why the exploding offer is used. It can be a sign of offeror weakness that might not be at all apparent to the recipient of the offer, but is almost always present.[1] Negotiators who use exploding offers may perceive themselves to be at a disadvantage relative to their competitors in terms of salary, conditions of sale, etc. Or they may have severe time or budget constraints. Once again, the function of the exploding offer can be either to force a quick acceptance by ending the negotiation (and thus avoiding the necessity of sweetening the deal to an unacceptably high level) *or* to restrict the ability of the recipient to comparison-shop, and therefore discover that the market was willing to pay at a significantly higher level.

DEALING WITH EXPLODING OFFERS: TRY BEING REASONABLE FIRST

In the tradition of *Getting to Yes* (Fisher and Ury 1981), and *Getting Past No* (Ury 1991), there are a number of possibilities which exist for the individual faced with an exploding offer. Most of these involve getting away from positional stances, in order to explore underlying interests, and to look to create value via "principled negotiation" (Lax and Sebenius 1986). It is important to realize that exploding offers can be dealt with using these techniques, especially if there is some degree of goodwill in the interaction. An exploding offer is often made by a party who believes it stands to lose out in the negotiation, or is unsure of its power. Building trust and appealing to reason can go a long way toward addressing this underlying concern, resulting in the exploding aspect of the offer being withdrawn.

For example, apartment-hunter Mary might say, "I understand you'd like a check today. Let me be honest. I really like this place, and I want to take it for $850 per month. But I have to see a few other places. How about I call you in the morning, first thing?" This might suffice. Or in the automobile dealership case, John the customer could say, "I really appreciate the $500 reduction. But I need to think this over. What if I call you 9 A.M. Monday? Can we make the offer good until then?" The dealer can accept, in which case the deal is still alive, or reject the counteroffer, in which case John is faced with the same decision as he had before he made the suggestion. If the dealer really wants to make a quota, a sales agreement could be drawn up, dated that day, but requiring John's agreement on Monday before it goes forward (John should probably not pony up any money until Monday).

These are relatively easy situations to resolve. However, the classic exploding offer scenario, replete with elements of hard-bargaining, cynicism, and coercion is the job offer case involving Pat, the student. Here there needs to be a real addressing of interests. My advice to students in Pat's situation is to have them point out to the organization that, since it wants it employees to be happy and productive, it is in the organization's interests to let the student feel that they have freely chosen this position as the most attractive option. The way to achieve this is to make the most attractive offer, not to constrain choice. Also, if the student is really the one that the organization wants, then the employer should be prepared to wait for that individual, rather than treating him or her like an interchangeable part.

The recipient of the exploding offer should also be prepared to make sensible counteroffers. He or she should be able to say when they *would* be in a position to accept, and to explain why this date makes sense (as opposed to choosing an equally arbitrary future time such as a week or 10 days). I usually tell my students about my most enjoyable employment experience, when I was made an offer and told, in effect, "take your time deciding. You're the one we want, and we want you to do the thing that's right for you. We are here to help you make that decision in any way we can." The contrast between this kind of attitude and an exploding offer, both in terms of an individual's feelings and the likelihood of a good future relationship for the parties, should be obvious. I have academic friends who are tortured, years after accepting their jobs, with the question of what would have happened if their employers had allowed them the time to take one more interview, or await the decision of another school.

My first recommendation is, then, to engage in problem solving with respect to uncovering interests, generating and exploring options, moving to creative solutions, and emphasizing relationship issues. However, this can fail if the other party is unsympathetic, or locked into a positional or cynical stance. In such an instance, particularly if one feels that the other side is behaving in an ethically questionable fashion, I recommend the "Farpoint Gambit."

FIGHTING FIRE WITH FIRE: THE FARPOINT GAMBIT

While I always recommend first attempting a "principled" or "integrative solution, I believe that when such tactics prove untenable, more assertive steps need to be taken. Doing this successfully depends on understanding where the power of the exploding offer resides. Exploding offers pivot on a credible, inviolable deadline. If the deadline is violated and the negotiation continues, the credibility of the explosion (the removal of the offer) is destroyed. And if the other side has depended on this threat as a central tactic, their entire position may collapse, putting the recipient of the initial offer in a very advantageous position. The technique I recommend, which I call the "Farpoint Gambit," is from the catalog of "hoist-them-by-their-own-petard" tools, which sometimes makes it particularly satisfying to employ.

The Farpoint Gambit derives from an episode of the science fiction television show, *Star Trek, The Next Generation,* in which the crew of the *Enterprise* (the spaceship from Earth) is put on trial by a powerful alien, "for the crimes of humanity." (The episode is called "Encounter at Farpoint," hence the name of the technique.) The alien creates a kangaroo court with himself as judge, and the captain of the *Enterprise* (Jean-Luc Picard), defends the human race. At a certain point, the alien judge becomes piqued by the captain's spirited defense, and says to the bailiff, "Bailiff, if the next word out of the defendant's mouth is anything but guilty, kill him!" He then turns to Picard and asks, "Defendant, how do you plead?" Picard thinks for a moment as the bailiff menacingly points a weapon at him, them firmly announces: "Guilty." As the courtroom gasps (and after an inevitable television commercial break), he adds, "Provisionally." This is essentially the Farpoint Gambit.

The alien has presented Picard with the ultimate coercive offer: Say you're guilty or I'll kill you. Obviously, Picard doesn't think he's guilty but he doesn't want to die. The power of the threat depends on getting Picard to admit that he's guilty—he does, but in such a way ("provisionally") that the alien judge is compelled to ask, "And what is the provision?" Picard then proceeds to talk his way out of the jam (as always happens with television heroes), and all is well. The point is that the alien is caught in his own trap: He's still arguing with Picard, who is still not guilty or dead. In the same way, an exploding offer can be defused by *embracing it,* using the Farpoint Gambit.

Consider again Pat's situation. Essentially, Company X is the alien, saying to Pat, "either the next words out [of] your mouth are 'I accept', or it's no deal." Pat can attempt to reason with the company's representative, and if that does not work either walk away, accept, or use the Farpoint Gambit, by saying, "I accept. Provisionally." The provision could be anything that takes the negotiation beyond that day, and might be things like: "provided I can meet with the person I would be working for," or "provided my coworkers prove satisfactory," or even "provided I don't get a better offer from the companies I'm still waiting to hear from."

The key is to make requests that are completely reasonable, but which will eventually result in the deadline being violated, due to the need for further clarification, or the lack of authority of the negotiator making the offer. Once the deadline passes, the credibility of the threat is destroyed, and successive attempts to set arbitrary deadlines can be dealt with in exactly the same way. The recipient of the offer can accept at his or her leisure, or reject the offer based on an unsatisfactory resolution of the provisions of the original acceptance.

The Farpoint Gambit also works by leveraging off fractures in the other side, or the imperfections in their informational strategies. Thus in Pat's case, the company's negotiator may not be authorized to offer moving and relocation expenses, or know what the policy is on day care for children. In such situations it is extremely easy to accept "pending satisfactory resolution of these issues," and then to continue to negotiate those and other issues.

The success of the Farpoint Gambit ultimately rests on the notion that the person receiving the exploding offer can eventually withdraw from the situation if no satisfactory resolution is forthcoming, without the offeror being able (or inclined) to sanction them for doing so. While this technique is about helping people get what they want from a coercive negotiating partner, it is *not* about helping people find a way to wriggle out of commitments given in good faith when they change their minds or get a better offer.

Inevitably, some negotiations, even those resuscitated by the Farpoint Gambit, are bound to fail. However, if conditions are attached to the acceptance—and these are not, by a reasonable assessment, met—then there really is not anything the company can do when the student withdraws, or the faculty candidate accepts an offer elsewhere, although possible reputational damage should still not be overlooked. It may be that each side has as much at stake as the other, which will help to keep both reasonable— no organization wants to get the reputation for strong-arming prospective employees with techniques of dubious morality. In other cases, there may be actual legal provisions which allow the individual to withdraw within a specified time limit after accepting, such as in the case of signing an agreement to purchase a car.

The Farpoint Gambit has a further advantage: It is nonescalative (Pruitt and Rubin 1986) and non zero-sum in nature. Like the crew of the *Enterprise* in their endless quest for new frontiers, the Farpoint Gambit may force negotiators toward improved solutions at the "Pareto frontier" (see, e.g., Raiffa 1982). It moves the parties in the "right" direction, that is, toward one another rather than apart. In this sense, the Farpoint Gambit is not as dangerous as techniques that require one side to call the other's bluff, or see who can hold out the longest. In these latter cases, someone frequently wins, and someone loses. The Farpoint Gambit is about both sides being able to take care of underlying interests, and thus able both to "win" and get what they want, with the offeror paying a fair price.

IN CONCLUSION: WHEN TO USE—OR NOT USE—THE GAMBIT

I would strongly caution against using the Farpoint Gambit as a routine technique to gain advantage. Nothing is more frustrating and unacceptable than someone who makes a habit of taking a deal, and who then continues to impose conditions or introduce new issues. Indeed, this is the flip side of the reprehensible lowballing technique employed by shady salespersons. In pondering this, I have come up with some guidelines for situations in which I believe it is legitimate to employ the Farpoint Gambit.

Ideally, I would make sure that all three of these conditions were present before I would feel completely comfortable in using this tactic.

- If the other side is perceived by the recipient of the exploding offer to be behaving unethically, and does not respond to appeals to reason;
- The recipient is truly interested in making a deal but needs more time to make a decision; and/or
- There genuinely are issues that need clarification, which would make the difference between accepting or rejecting the deal.

The Farpoint Gambit is a technique that should not be used lightly, in a spirit of deception, or with a lack of good faith. However, in situations where the individual is trapped by the hardball tactics of an offeror who relies on an exploding offer, the Farpoint Gambit offers a means whereby the pressure applied by the other side can be turned against them, much as a judo expert can use a foe's momentum to provide the energy which leads to the latter's own undoing. To be sure, this is itself a hardball tactic (Schelling1960; Deutsch 1973), and many might not feel comfortable using it. I offer the Farpoint Gambit as someone who has seen many friends, loved ones, and students put under enormous pressure, forced to make critical life decisions under unnecessarily difficult circumstances due to the callous use of power by people and institutions not operating in good faith.

NOTES

The author would like to acknowledge the useful criticism he received on earlier drafts of this work from Professors Roy J. Lewicki of the Ohio State University; the late Jeffrey Z. Rubin of Tufts University; and Michael Wheeler of the Harvard Business School. Also significantly contributing to this work were members of the Program on Negotiation/Fletcher School of Law and Diplomacy "Tuesday Evening Reading Group."

1. Only in the case of a true monopolist, making an offer with many potential buyers, can one argue that the exploding offer is truly an act of self-serving arrogance and convenience on the part of the offeror.

REFERENCES

Deutsch, M. 1973. *The resolution of conflict.* New Haven: Yale University Press.

Fisher, R., and W. L. Ury. 1981. *Getting to yes: Negotiating agreement without giving in.* Boston: Houghton Mifflin.

Lax, D. A., and J. K. Sebenius. 1986. *The manager as negotiator.* New York: Free Press.

Pruitt, D. G., and J. Z. Rubin. 1986. *Social conflict: Escalation, stalemate, and settlement.* New York: Random House.

Raiffa, H. 1982. *The art and science of negotiation.* Cambridge, MA: Harvard University Press.

Schelling, T. 1960. *The strategy of conflict.* Cambridge, MA: Harvard University Press.

Shell, G. R. 1991. When is it legal to lie in negotiations? *Sloan Management Review* 32: 93–101.

Ury, W. 1991. *Getting past no: Negotiating your way from confrontation to cooperation.* New York: Bantam Books.

Strategy and Tactics of Integrative Negotiation

Interest-Based Negotiation: An Engine-Driving Change

John R. Stepp

Kevin M. Sweeney

Robert L. Johnson

Every year, 25,000 to 30,000 managers and union representatives negotiate collective bargaining agreements. These events are the most strategic opportunities they have to produce change, yet they often remain the last bastion of the status quo and old-style labor relations. Most negotiators still engage in old rituals that often result in leaving problems unsolved and potential solutions "on the table."

The inadequacies of traditional negotiations first surface in the preparation phase, which resembles a mobilization for war. Differences are accentuated, villains identified, weapons honed, war paint generously applied. The parties then arrive at the bargaining table in full battle dress. The focus tends to be on separate, or what are assumed to be, competing interests. The negotiations process resembles a strategic retreat from exaggerated positions. Collective bargaining, arguably the parties' most valuable tool, is reduced to an instrument of conflict.

In fairness to traditional bargaining, it works well when the parties control their markets, when they face little competition, when change is proceeding at a digestible pace, and when bargaining structures are centralized, thereby permitting coordinated or pattern bargaining to remove labor costs from the competitive equation.

A NEW BARGAINING TOOL

Interest-based negotiation, on the other hand, has demonstrated its capacity to enhance bargaining outcomes without impairing the parties' relationship. Its essence is information-sharing, creative exploration, and working toward mutually beneficial solutions. There are six basic steps to the process.

1. *The bargainers describe and define the issue,* such as the topic to be discussed and/or the problem to be resolved.

Source: Reprinted with permission of The Association for Quality and Participation from the Sep/Oct 1998 issue of *The Journal for Quality and Participation,* Cincinnati, Ohio. © 1998. All rights reserved. For more information contact AQP at 513-381-1959 or visit www.aqp.org.

2. *An opportunity for each party is provided to identify its interests in regard to the issue—and to explore the interests of the other party.* An interest is a reason why the issue is important to one or both of the parties.

3. *With a shared understanding of all the interests, the parties engage in step three: the creation of options or potential solutions* to satisfy as many of the interests as possible.

4. *The parties agree on the criteria they will use to evaluate the options.* Criteria are the characteristics of an acceptable solution.

5. *The parties select the options that best meet the agreed-upon criteria.*

6. *The parties integrate or craft these options into a comprehensive solution,* concluding the process.

PREPARATION

A decade of experience in assisting managers and union representatives in conducting interest-based negotiations has convinced us that applying certain approaches and techniques to both the preparation and execution phases of the negotiation can make all the difference between success and failure.

Preparation, an essential key, should begin four to six months in advance of bargaining. An early start allows the bargaining committees sufficient time to be trained in the interest-based negotiation process. Interest-based negotiation training is comprised of three key parts:

1. *An introduction to the interest-based negotiation model.*

2. *Skill(s) building.*

3. *Practice through simulations.*

Familiarization with the theoretical constructs of interest-based negotiation is the starting point. Just as traditional bargaining requires a discernible set of skills, so does interest-based negotiation. Active listening, brainstorming, and consensus decision making lead the list. After initial skill-building practice, participants deepen their understanding and hone their skills during a series of increasingly complex and challenging simulations, accompanied by critical feedback from a skilled practitioner.

Following the training, both parties can make an informed decision whether or not to utilize the interest-based negotiation process. If yes, then preparatory work must begin immediately with the constituents of each party. All constituents should be given an explanation of the process to include how it works, why the bargaining committees have elected to utilize it, and how both the preparation and conduct of bargaining will differ from the old rituals witnessed in previous negotiations.

In our experience, the traditional approach thrives on the perception of fervent advocacy. The only means of counteracting this perception is to inform one's constituents of the shortcomings of the traditional bargaining process in today's environment and to explain how interest-based negotiation is less likely to leave problems and potential solutions on the table.

In the end, it is results that matter. Interest-based negotiation yields superior outcomes and undamaged relationships.

HOW TO START OFF

Before formal negotiations begin, the parties should identify the key issues and determine data needs. For complex issues, brainstorming during bargaining may not be an adequate tool. Imagine brainstorming wages, pensions, or a new work system. For these kinds of issues, joint task forces or subcommittees should be specifically chartered—well in advance of bargaining—to gather data, explore options, and/or benchmark best practices.

One large pharmaceutical firm and its union jointly studied a variety of pay-for-performance systems well before bargaining. Their recommendations were then presented to the bargaining committees for consideration and ultimately adopted. Likewise, a Great Lakes utility and one of its largest unions met jointly for nearly a year before bargaining, in an effort to gather information, benchmark best practices, and select the best pension plan for their particular age-mix of employees. Their efforts paid off with a newly negotiated, defined contribution pension plan that better met their needs.

If having the right data is important to expedite negotiations, having the right people present is equally important. The decision to utilize interest-based negotiation requires that careful attention be paid to the composition of the bargaining committees. This is particularly true for management participants in large organizations. In traditional bargaining—utilizing the procedure of proposal, caucus, counterproposal, caucus, and so on—all proposals can be carefully reviewed up and down the organizational hierarchy.

In contrast, interest-based negotiation is a more free-flowing, dynamic, and spontaneous process. Where traditional bargaining emphasizes control, interest-based negotiation accents creativity. Through the synergy resulting from the problem-solving process, unimaginable options are often generated. If every fledgling idea has to be first run up and down the hierarchical flagpole to see who salutes, this synergy and creativity would be stymied.

There are at least three solutions to this dilemma:

1. *Make certain that the key players or decision makers are on the bargaining committee.* In one large (50,000 person) organization, the chief spokesperson for management was five layers down in the organization.

2. *"Empower fully" those at the table to make most, if not all, of the decisions that must be made to reach an agreement.* While most senior managers are not personally inclined to devote the time and attention required to be direct participants in the negotiations, neither are they prepared to delegate such critical issues to subordinates.

3. *Establish wide, but clearly defined, parameters or boundaries around each issue.* So long as the bargainers remain within this predetermined "field of play," they are licensed to do whatever they deem appropriate. Whenever negotiations take them near or perhaps beyond these boundaries, they must be permitted to pursue further guidance from their constituents.

A new set of norms is required for the successful utilization of interest-based negotiation. Reverting to traditional norms and behaviors is commonplace when interest-based negotiation is being attempted for the first time. Only by utilizing an experienced facilitator can this be avoided.

SETTING THE GROUND RULES

Both procedural and behavioral ground rules are critically important to the successful conduct of interest-based negotiation. A mutual understanding should develop around the timetable for bargaining. This timetable would include commencement of bargaining, frequency of meetings, dovetailing local negotiations with master negotiations, discussing any parameters around the field of play, and reviewing the ratification procedure.

A ground rule on information-sharing is needed to encourage free disclosure of information. Ground rules defining the role of spokespersons should be discussed. Participation should not be limited to or funneled through spokespersons. Another key to a successful negotiation is a clear understanding or a ground rule defining consensus decision making. What are the individual's obligations when he or she provides consent?

In addition, parties should adopt a ground rule that holds the solution to any one issue to be a tentative agreement pending the solution of all issues. Solutions reached on issues important to one party have no permanent standing unless all issues are resolved to the satisfaction of both parties.

Ground rules addressing the issue of notes and official records are necessary. Bargaining in the interest-based negotiation format requires engaged participants, not passive stenographers. Flip charts and summary minutes should suffice as a "history" between meetings. There should be a clear understanding (ground rule), that nothing said or done during the interest-based negotiation process can or will be used later, by either party, in an adversarial setting.

The parties should also agree on how communications will be handled. At a minimum, there should be a ground rule prohibiting any revelation of the internal discussions, play-by-play attributions, and options developed during the interest-based negotiation process. It is vital that all participants be confident that they can speak freely and exchange creative, "out-of-the-box" ideas, without political or personal risk.

Caucuses should not be discouraged. A ground rule should permit either side to caucus whenever either side feels a need or experiences discomfort.

Finally, a day of negotiations should not exceed eight hours. Interest-based negotiation is very demanding; therefore, marathon sessions should never be attempted.

GETTING STARTED

We recommend that the first session begin with statements of commitment to the values supporting the interest-based negotiation process. The parties should next examine the issues and determine the relative importance of each to establish a "time budget" for the negotiations.

Knowing which issue to tackle first can have a strong bearing on the success of the negotiations and set the tone. Parties do well to pick an easy, yet meaningful, issue first. It is important that the parties see that the time and energy they have applied to their first issue resulted in a satisfactory solution, one that has brought about meaningful gains for both parties.

Both parties should be encouraged to take risks and to let go of the desire to control the outcome. Exhibiting behaviors aimed at helping the other benefit goes a long way toward creating the positive climate that encourages both parties to find creative solutions.

Finally, alternating between each party's issues may minimize the perception that all of the focus and attention (and possibly the gain) is being given to one party.

TACKLING THE ISSUES

The negotiators must take each issue and work through the six-step interest-based negotiation process.

1. Describe and Define the Issue.   Properly framing the issue is critically important. Issues can be defined too narrowly or too broadly. If defined too narrowly, the issue may allow little opportunity to develop an adequate option pool. Defined too broadly—ballooning an issue, or making a mountain out of a molehill—invariably leads to frustration or exasperation. The rule of thumb is to be as specific as possible in defining the issue, without becoming so specific that only part of the described problem can be resolved.

2. Identifying and Exploring Interests.   This step must be done well. Interest-based negotiation, as the name implies, is an interest-driven process, and well-developed and clearly articulated interests are essential.

The parties must exhibit a genuine desire to understand the other's point of view. Interests, by their very nature, must be accepted as legitimate and not-to-be-debated. To ask clarifying questions and confirm understanding of the interests is desirable.

Next, it is useful to determine which of the interests are mutual. This is not a "marching" process requiring each interest to appear on both lists. It is simply a means of quickly surfacing common or shared interests, which in turn, reveals fertile opportunities for developing viable options. Interests not shared by both parties are referred to as separate interests and remain because they may be required to be satisfied in the final solution.

3. Creating Options.   The key to success in this step is to go for quantity. A technique to encourage brainstorming is to focus on the list of interests. Multiple options should be generated to cover every interest.

4. Agreeing on Criteria.   This is a difficult step. Criteria are the gauges by which we measure, compare, and judge options. There are few "objective criteria." One of the best gauges for evaluating options is the respective interests of the parties. Generally, there are a few interests that must be satisfied for the solution to be viable or acceptable. In effect, these are criteria and should be treated as such. Coming to agreement on these and any other appropriate criteria determines the outcome of step four.

5. Testing the Options against the Criteria.   Evaluating each option in light of the agreed-upon criteria can inhibit dialogue and become overly mechanical and cumbersome, especially when there is a long list of options and a number of criteria. We have discovered several techniques that enable the parties to avoid getting bogged down.

- Review the list of options and focus on those that present broad approaches to solving the problem. Each broad approach is thoroughly discussed and evaluated for its ability to satisfy the interests of the parties.

- Give each participant a marker and ask him or her to place a checkmark next to the five or six options that he or she believes best meet the criteria. One must make clear that this is not a voting process, but a way of testing for initial preferences. The heavily favored options then become the primary focal points. The remaining options are examined to see if they meet the criteria and can be incorporated into the favored options to enhance their utility. Frequently, many ideas are woven together, in ways that meet as many interests as possible.

- In the case of large committees, utilize a "fishbowl." The fishbowl is a table placed within the larger U-shaped table. Chief spokespersons are each asked to designate two or three people who are particularly knowledgeable about the issue being bargained. The designees are seated at the small table (fishbowl) and are tasked with weaving together the promising options identified by the full committees. Two empty chairs are placed at the small table. At any time, other participants observing the deliberations may occupy an empty chair to offer suggestions or make comments. Once made, they must return to the outer table thus making the seat available for others to do likewise.

Process difficulties are not the only obstacles that can arise at this stage. Substantive concerns can also surface. Groups frequently discover that the ultimate solution to the issue being worked is dependent upon what is being done on some closely related issue. When this situation is encountered, "parking" the unfinished solution and working on the related issues is the best course of action. Once the solutions to these related issues are more clearly focused, the parties can resume work on the parked issue.

Interest-based negotiation, however, does not utilize a "tit-for-tat" procedure. No one must give up something on one issue to realize a gain on another. "Horse trading" is discouraged. Each issue must be viewed as a joint problem to be solved.

6. Writing the Contract Language.   The final step can be done by a drafting committee, union-management pair, or an individual. In drafting, confusion or gaps may appear requiring clarification from the full committee. The final written solution comes back to the group to ensure the group's consensus approval.

COMMON CONCERNS

One concern we have experienced regarding interest-based negotiation is the amount of time required. Arriving at the table with problems clearly identified, interests articulated, and a timeline developed expedites the flow of negotiations. As the parties become more experienced with interest-based negotiation, process efficiencies are realized. Some complex issues may be broken into several separate subissues to expedite resolution. An abbreviated process may also be used to resolve an issue where little is in dispute. Jointly developed data will focus the discussion.

Finally, by using subcommittees to explore complex issues well in advance of the beginning of negotiations, it is possible to have agreements in principle or jointly supported recommendations for the bargaining committee's consideration. In dozens of interest-based negotiations—and many more traditional negotiations—the time required for each is essentially the same.

Another concern frequently expressed by traditional negotiators is whether they should reveal their bottom line. Interest-based negotiation neither requires nor encourages disclosing one's bottom line. The process is designed to yield the most elegant or comprehensive solution possible.

There is, on the other hand, a requirement to reveal one's interests. The articulation of interests on a particular issue is an expression of the issue's importance. Interests must be articulated and data shared, but neither party should be expected to reveal the minimum level for satisfying its interests on an issue.

A third and closely related concern is the applicability of interest-based negotiation to economic issues, particularly wages. Applying interest-based negotiation to these issues may be difficult, but helpful. With an agreement on appropriate data, the parties can frequently create a salary or benefit range. Interest-based negotiation is helpful in focusing the parties away from extreme staked-out positions toward substantive discussion on the value associated with job elements, the interest of employees, the needs of the employer in attracting and retaining talent, and competitive requirements or market forces.

COOPERATION IS THE BEST POLICY

On many an occasion, the fledgling efforts of union and management representatives working together have been thwarted by the dynamics of traditional bargaining. Interest-based negotiation, on the other hand, employs the same behaviors, norms, and problem-solving methodologies that are utilized when the parties cooperate during the terms of the agreement. Jekyll and Hyde personas are no longer required.

Interest-based negotiation's subtlety encourages the parties to expand the scope of bargaining. In one automotive-parts plant, the negotiators devoted half of their bargaining time to the issue of how to improve throughput in the operations. Interest-based negotiation fosters problem solving and encourages frank discussions of complex issues. Since strategic issues frequently are not mandatory subjects for bargaining under current labor law, management's willingness to negotiate policy issues is very limited when traditional bargaining prevails.

In arriving at the decision to adopt an interest-based approach to negotiations, the parties need to recognize that interest-based negotiation is an art, not a science, and that flexibility is a must.

Many issues lend themselves to an interest-based approach, but in particular circumstances, the use of a rigid step-by-step interest-based negotiation may not be appropriate. Openness, sharing of information, working to meet each other's interests, exploring new or creative ideas, and employing mutually agreed-upon criteria, rather than power, will be the ingredients of successful negotiations.

Interest-based negotiation is not a magic potion, nor a religion or panacea. It is a tool that can help negotiators be more effective in achieving their aims.

Finally, interest-based negotiation need not be relegated to contract negotiations. Its methods are equally appropriate in resolving day-to-day conflicts in the workplace. Its reliance on a clinical analysis of the underlying interests is more likely to yield lasting solutions than the symptoms-focused, rights-based, litigious techniques employed in traditional grievance handling. The values embedded in interest-based negotiations are consistent with those needed for a high-performance workplace.

Step into My Parlor: A Survey of Strategies and Techniques for Effective Negotiation

Terry Anderson

The idea of active negotiation is intimidating to most people. It conjures up images of smoke-filled rooms, raised voices, dirty tricks, and interminable haggling sessions encompassing a potential win-lose situation that could involve anything from personal relationships to nuclear warfare. Furthermore, most people are generally dubious of their own negotiating skills relative to those of other individuals. They consider encounters with blue-chip negotiators as perilous contests during which they stand a good chance of having the shirt talked right off their backs. Add to this the fact that the most significant negotiation activities are those associated with stressful, life-change events—the compensation package for a new job, custody rights in a divorce, the selling price of a new home—and it is no small wonder that most people have an instinctive aversion to the idea of negotiation. This fear of negotiation has made numerous lawyers, mediators, and professional arbitrators rich.

Like many things in life, negotiation is an aspect of reality that needs to be mastered rather than feared. In fact, skilled negotiators will only deliver a more thorough beating if they smell the fear of an opponent. As a result, it is important to learn effective negotiation techniques as a self-defense mechanism. Putting these techniques into practice and knowing when they are being used by others increase the probability of acquiring greater material rewards. Moreover, the likelihood of sustaining a productive relationship with others can be significantly improved. However, "despite its importance, the negotiation process is often misunderstood and badly carried out. Inferior agreements result, if not endless bickering, needless deadlock, or spiraling conflict" (Lax and Sebenius 1986).

SUBSTANTIVE AND RELATIONSHIP OUTCOMES

Of course, one of the primary incentives for negotiating is the pursuit of material, substantive outcomes: the raise, the promotion, or the rust-proofing option on a new car. However, because a crucial context for any bargaining session is the negotiators' current

---

and desired relationship with each other, the pursuit of these incentives is moderated by the pursuit of a positive relationship between the parties. Before rushing to secure the best possible substantive outcome, the negotiators must assess the impact of their respective negotiation strategies on the relationship that currently exists between them. Obviously, respective levels of power and conflict weigh heavily in this assessment.

The relative power of each negotiator is established by the extent of each party's dependence on the other. Individuals tend to assess the relative levels of power existing in a relationship and then choose whether to compete, accommodate, collaborate, or withdraw when negotiating with others. The level of conflict in a negotiation setting is established by how the negotiators perceive the effective dimension of their relationship—that is, its supportiveness or hostility. Indeed, the pursuit of a positive relationship between negotiating parties may be a primary motivation for continuing negotiation, even at the sacrifice of substantive outcomes, particularly if the relationship has deteriorated and is more highly valued than the issues on the table.

NEGOTIATION STRATEGIES

Only by appraising both their own and the other party's substantive and relationship priorities can negotiators effectively choose a negotiation strategy. To prevent reliance on intuition alone, researchers and academicians have developed formal models, such as simulation programs and decision trees, designed to train and assist individuals in selecting the most appropriate negotiation strategy. "Many people, due to their lack of awareness of any structured approach to the negotiating process, are forced to reuse self-taught methods that have merely appeared to work in the past—methods that were acquired, like diseases, from social contact. There is, however, an important and useful difference between merely knowing a few cunning homemade techniques and understanding the full cooperative human process of negotiation" (Nierenberg 1971).

Although formal approaches serve to add structure to the selection of negotiation strategies, they remain only barely perceptible outlines in a very foggy picture. For this reason, it is important not to be seduced into thinking that the process of negotiation is as simple as some of these models may imply, for the insight and intuition of the negotiator largely provide the musculature necessary to put these strategies into practice. With this in mind, it is useful to survey an entire spectrum of negotiation strategies in a structured yet realistic manner. Generally, negotiators and analysts tend to separate into two groups that are guided by conflicting conceptions of the bargaining process: symbiotic and predatory.

Symbiosis

This negotiation ideology is so named for its predisposition to create value by means of the bargaining process. Symbiotic negotiators tend to believe that mutual agreements are reached by being inventive, collaborative, and persistent in searching for substantial joint gains and the creation of value, relative to no-agreement possibilities. Stressing the importance of open communication and information sharing, symbiotic negotiators are sometimes apt to practice the immoderate strategy of open submission by conceding all but the barest substantive aspects of the negotiation in an attempt to build a productive relationship with the other party. The perception of relationship building as a positive outcome of such a negotiation yields the joint gains necessary for a symbiotic strategy. One side receives primarily substantive gains, while the other side receives the benefits of a strengthened relationship that could come to fruition in the form of future material rewards.

Another symbiotic bargaining strategy is often referred to as "win-win" negotiation, in which both sides win—or at least no one loses. Using this strategy, joint-gains are achieved by avoiding actions that tend to worsen the relationship between the parties while increasing the substantive elements of the negotiation. This is accomplished through the bipartisan efforts of both parties to either make the value of the "pie" larger, or to find elements within it to satisfy both parties.

The Egyptian-Israeli peace treaty formulated at Camp David in 1978 illustrates the ideology behind this negotiation strategy:

> Israel had occupied the Egyptian Sinai Peninsula since the Six Day War of 1967. When Egypt and Israel sat down together in 1978 to negotiate a peace, their positions were incompatible. Israel insisted on keeping some of the Sinai. Egypt, on the other hand, insisted that every inch of the Sinai be returned to Egyptian sovereignty. People continuously drew maps showing possible boundary lines that would divide the Sinai between Egypt and Israel. Compromising in this way was wholly unacceptable to Egypt. To go back to the situation as it was in 1967 was equally unacceptable to Israel.
>
> Looking at their interests instead of their positions made it possible for Israel and Egypt to develop a solution. Israel's interest lay in security; they did not want Egyptian tanks poised on their border ready to roll across at any time. Egypt's interest lay in sovereignty; the Sinai had been part of Egypt since the time of the Pharaohs. After centuries of domination by Greeks, Romans, Turks, French, and British, Egypt had only recently regained full sovereignty and was not about to cede territory to another foreign conqueror.
>
> At Camp David, President Sadat of Egypt and Prime Minister Begin of Israel agreed to a plan that would return the Sinai to complete Egyptian sovereignty and, by demilitarizing large areas, would still assure Israeli security. The Egyptian flag would fly everywhere, but Egyptian tanks would be nowhere near Israel (Fisher and Ury 1981).

Creating Value via the Negotiation Process

In their highly publicized best-seller, *Getting to Yes* (1981), Roger Fisher and William Ury outline four points, each dealing with a basic element of negotiation. These comprise the foundation of a symbiotic negotiation strategy which they call "principled negotiation," or "negotiation on the merits." These four points are as follows:

- *Separate the people from the problem.* The first step in reaching a mutually agreeable solution is to disentangle the substantive elements of the negotiation from the relationship between the parties and deal with each set of elements separately. Negotiators should perceive themselves as working side by side, attacking the problem instead of attacking each other.

- *Focus on interests, not positions.* People's egos tend to become identified with their negotiating positions. Furthermore, focusing on positions often obscures what the participants really need or want. Rather than focusing on the positions taken by each negotiator, a much more effective strategy is to focus on the underlying human needs and interests that had caused them to adopt those positions.

- *Invent options for mutual gain.* Designing optimal solutions under pressure in the presence of an adversary tends to narrow people's vision. Searching for the one right solution inhibits creativity, particularly when the stakes are high. These constraints can be offset by establishing a forum in which a variety of possibilities are generated before deciding which action to take.
- *Insist on using objective criteria.* By discussing the conditions of the negotiation in terms of some fair standards such as market value, expert opinion, custom, or law, the discussion steers away from what the parties are willing or unwilling to do. By using objective criteria, neither party has to give in to the other, and both parties defer to a fair solution.

Symbiotic strategies tend to emphasize open channels of communication, separating the substantive aspects of the negotiation from the people involved in the discussion. By allowing negotiators to deal directly and empathetically with each other as human beings, these strategies increase the probability of reaching an amicable agreement. By focusing on the underlying human interests of each negotiator, they avoid the transactional costs associated with participants locking themselves into positions and then trying to dig their way out. Finally, by focusing on basic interests, mutually satisfying options, and objective standards, these strategies have the potential to produce an agreement that meets the legitimate interests of each side to the extent possible, resolves conflicting interests fairly, and takes into account the interests of associated third parties.

Predation

In direct contrast to their counterparts, predatory negotiators see the notion of a bargaining session characterized by openness, information sharing, clear communication, creativity, and an attitude of cultivating common interests as being naive and weak-minded.

According to the predatory ideology, a pie of fixed size is being divided between negotiators, and each slice that each party receives must be taken away from the other. Hardball is the name of the game as each negotiator tries to claim as much of the value of the pie as possible by giving the other party as little as possible. At the extreme end of the spectrum, predatory negotiators try to devise Machiavellian ways to manipulate individuals in such a manner as to claim the entire pie.

Predation, as a negotiation ideology, is based on the view that negotiation is a hard, tough bargaining process in which neither participant cares about the needs of the other. In all cases, the relationship elements of the negotiation are perceived as subservient to the substantive gains achieved in an adversarial contest.

The object here is to persuade other parties that they want what you have to offer while you are only marginally interested in what they have to offer. Negotiation is a game to be won or lost. The outcome depends on each participant's ability to concede slowly, exaggerate the value of concessions, minimize the benefits of the other's concessions, conceal information, argue forcefully on behalf of principles that imply favorable settlements, wait out the other participant, and make commitments to accept only favorable settlements.

The toughest bargainers will make intransigent demands and threaten to walk away or retaliate aggressively if those demands are not met. Ridiculing, attacking, or intimidating adversaries is perceived simply as part of the game. For example, Lewis Glucksman, once the volatile head of trading activities at Lehman Brothers, utilized a very aggressive predatory strategy to seize control of Lehman from the then-chairman Peter G. Peterson after being promoted to co-CEO status with Peterson. As co-CEO, Glucksman made a thinly veiled threat that unless he were granted full control of Lehman, he would provoke civil war within the firm and take the entire trading department elsewhere. When Peterson and others desperately sought less damaging accommodation, Glucksman refused to budge by indicating that "his feet were wet in cement," even at the cost of destroying the firm. Ultimately, Peterson left with a substantial money settlement and Glucksman presided briefly over the shaken firm until it was sold at a bargain price to American Express.

Claiming Value via the Negotiation Process

In his book *Negotiate Your Way to Financial Success* (1987), Ronald J. Posluns details his "Seven Golden Rules" of negotiating:

- *Negotiate tough.* Negotiators are not necessarily popular individuals, but there is nothing wrong with getting the edge in any deal. However, do not confuse "tough" with arrogant, rude, bullheaded, or ruthless. "Tough" means sticking to your guns, letting the other side know that you mean business, and being unafraid to ask for extra concessions.

- *Scrutinize the details.* The success of a negotiation strategy lies in the details of the final agreement. Go through each of them, point by point, and whenever an item is not settled, try to gain an advantage. Assume nothing, ask for everything, and consider no item insignificant. Negotiate hard on every specific item, especially the smaller ones, in an attempt to wear down your opponents' stamina and weaken their ability to negotiate for the major issues at stake.

- *Focus on the rewards.* Maintain a myopic view of those things you want to take away from the bargaining table, and learn to counter your opponents' negotiating strategies. For example, emotional outbursts should be perceived as merely part of the game, not as personal attacks. The best things to do when your opponents exhibit extreme emotion is to simply let them rant, rave, and pound on the table. Once they play their emotional card to no avail, you will have gained the advantage.

- *Avoid ultimatums.* Give your opponents choices instead of ultimatums. Backing someone into a corner is similar to cornering a wild animal—predicting their reactions becomes impossible. When your opponents give you an ultimatum, the best thing to do is walk away from the deal. A good negotiator will not become committed to a deal that cannot survive another day of indecision.

- *Anything goes.* Negotiation is not a game with established rules. You can stall for time, cloud the issues, or use facial expressions to indicate that the concessions your opponents desire are painful ones (whether or not they actually are). Another strategy is to purposely drop your briefcase, or make a mess with a fountain pen. As you lull your opponents into underestimating you, set them up for the kill.

- *Find your opponents' pressure points.* If you discover that your opponents are facing a deadline, you can stall the negotiations by focusing on details until, as the final hour nears, your opponents are eager to agree on your main goals. Probe your opponents for vulnerabilities, then structure your negotiating stance to take full advantage of them.

- *Control the negotiation.* Get your opponents to follow your game plan, not theirs. For instance, if there is a choice between "your place or mine," consider that you have a turf advantage at home, but when you are "away" you have the option of leaving the table in mock outrage. Another ploy is to let the other party prepare the working document under discussion. Mistakenly believing that this will give them an edge, the other party will happily draft a document that itemizes their substantive priorities and the numbers they attach to those items.

THE NEGOTIATOR'S DILEMMA

In reality, symbiotic negotiation strategies designed to create value through cooperation and collaboration directly conflict with predatory strategies intended to claim value. That is, no matter how creative and collaborative the negotiators are, and no matter how successful they are at creating value by means of the bargaining process, reality dictates that at some point each negotiator must claim part of the pie. Moreover, the use of tactics for claiming value necessarily impedes its creation, and the use of tactics for creating value is vulnerable to predatory negotiation strategies.

First, predatory negotiation strategies intended to claim value tend to impair efforts to satisfy the interests of both parties through symbiotic, value-creating strategies. Exaggerating the value of concessions and minimizing the benefit of others' concessions presents a distorted picture of each negotiator's relative preferences and thereby inhibits the communication process. Making threats or intransigent demands is not conducive to effective listening or understanding the interests of the other party. Concealing information will likely result in leaving joint gains on the table. In fact, excessively using predatory strategies may well sour the relationship between the parties to the point at which conflict escalates and the prospects for arriving at a settlement are virtually eliminated.

Second, openly sharing information required to discover and satisfy joint interests makes symbiotic negotiators more susceptible to being victimized by value-claiming strategies. Revealing information about one's relative preferences is risky, and the willingness to make a new, creative offer can often be taken as a sign that its proponent is able and willing to make further concessions. As a result, these offers, which may satisfy joint interests and provide each negotiator with benefits that could not be attained otherwise, typically remain undisclosed. Even purely shared interests can be held hostage in exchange for concessions on other issues.

A Matrix of Outcomes

Although both negotiators may realize the importance of cooperatively creating value by means of the negotiation process in a symbiotic manner, they must also acknowledge the fact that each must eventually claim value through some degree of predation. The negotiator's dilemma lies in the fact that tactics to claim value tend to repel moves to create it. While an optimal solution normally results when both parties openly discuss the problem, respect each other's substantive and relationship needs, and creatively seek to satisfy each other's human interest, reality dictates that such behavior cannot always be expected to occur.

The legitimate attempts by one negotiator to employ symbiotic strategies will necessarily disclose information that makes that negotiator vulnerable to the predatory strategies of his opponent. As a result, the problem-solving atmosphere created by two symbionts is inevitably replaced by a competitive atmosphere of gamesmanship to the degree that at least one negotiator begins to utilize predatory strategies.

In a negotiation between a predator, who sees the bargaining process as competitive, and a symbiont, who sees the bargaining process as cooperative, the symbiont is highly vulnerable to the value-claiming strategies employed by the predator. For this reason, negotiators develop an inherent apprehension toward the use of symbiotic strategies to the degree that they expect their opponents to use predatory strategies. This mutual suspicion causes negotiators in many settings to leave joint gains on the table. Moreover, after being skewered in several encounters with experienced predators, the pull toward value-claiming tactics becomes insidious and symbionts often "learn" to become predators.

Finally, however, if both negotiators choose to employ predatory strategies, the probability of value being created through the negotiation process is virtually eliminated. This will likely result in both parties receiving only mediocre rewards, in terms of both substantive outcomes and building productive relationships with the other party. If the spectrum of negotiating strategies previously discussed is placed along vertical and horizontal axes, then for negotiating parties A and B, respectively, a matrix of possible outcomes emerging from the bargaining process can be developed to illustrate the negotiator's dilemma (see Figure 1).

Operational Implications

The negotiator's dilemma may enhance the productivity of the bargaining process by providing insight into the mental metabolism of the negotiators. However, regardless of each negotiator's strategy preference, several actions may be taken at the operational level to increase the probability of achieving favorable outcomes while taking the relationship between the parties into account. The bases for these actions are found in the "middle ground" of the strategic spectrum, borrowing concepts from both the predatory and the symbiotic ideologies.

- *Do your homework.* Although it is the least glamorous aspect of the negotiating process, it is the most important. A good negotiator must realize the implications of each item on the table, the consequences associated with making various concessions, and what entails the "bottom line" of the negotiations.

FIGURE 1   A Matrix of Negotiated Outcomes

		Symbiosis	Predation
Strategy of party A	Predation	*Outcome:* Great for party A Terrible for party B	*Outcome:* Mediocre for party A Mediocre for party B
	Symbiosis	*Outcome:* Good for party A Good for party B	*Outcome:* Terrible for party A Great for party B

Symbiosis   Predation

Strategy of party B

- *Go to the top.* Unless you talk directly with individuals who have the authority to make the changes you propose, your success will hinge on someone else's ability to communicate, in minutes, what was discussed over several hours. In addition, dealing with unauthorized subordinates lessens accountability and may hinder the proceedings.
- *Build relationships whenever possible.* Even if you decide to employ a predatory strategy, remember that it is much easier to communicate with a friend than with a stranger, or even worse, an enemy. Relationship gains and losses are as much a part of the negotiated package as the substantive outcomes.
- *Avoid quick concessions.* Making a concession without having fully considered the issues opens you up to the risk of giving up something unnecessarily and compromising your own needs. Use discretion when conceding from your stated position.
- *Accentuate the positive.* By framing negative points in a positive way, you will be more likely to elicit a positive response. Couching controversial issues between positive points increases your chances of getting the other side to listen—and agree—to your demands.
- *Maintain your composure.* In any negotiation, but particularly in protracted ones, emotions may flare up and people may lose their tempers. Under these conditions, it is imperative to maintain composure, sift through emotions, and try to discern the other party's needs and wants.
- *Don't give up.* You may reach a point at which you do not like the proposed agreement, but still you do not see any alternatives. Remember that what seems like a dead end may actually be a corner. With a little perseverance, you can get around it.

At one extreme, the process of negotiation can be called a cooperative pursuit of joint gains and a collaborative effort to create value where none previously existed. At the other extreme, it can be described as a street fight. The negotiator's dilemma lies in determining where the cooperation ends and the street fight begins. Understanding this paradox more fully serves to reduce the anxiety associated with the process of negotiation by giving negotiators a structured approach to tailoring their strategies to both the substantive and relationship elements at stake.

Nevertheless, it is important not to be duped into believing that the bargaining process is as simple as any existing structured model may imply. The experience and intuition of the negotiator must inevitably provide the musculature necessary to put the structure into motion in a pragmatic and practicable manner. By taking a structured yet realistic approach to the negotiating process, and implementing established operational actions, the negotiator substantially increases the probability of acquiring substantive gains, as well as fostering a productive relationship with the other party.

REFERENCES

Deborah Asbrand, "Games B-School Never Taught You," *PC Computing,* April 1989, pp. 153+.

Ellen J. Belzer, "The Negotiator's Art: You Can Always Get What You Want," *Working Woman,* April 1990, pp. 98+.

Paul B. Brown and Michael S. Hopkins, "How to Negotiate Practically Anything," *Inc.,* February 1989, pp. 35+.

Roger Fisher and William Ury, *Getting to Yes* (Boston: Houghton Mifflin, 1981).

John M. Ivancevich and Michael T. Matteson, *Organizational Behavior and Management* (Homewood, IL: Irwin, 1990).

David A. Lax and James K. Sebenius, *The Manager as Negotiator* (New York: Free Press, 1986).

Cynthia Legette, "How to Improve Your Negotiation Skills," *Black Enterprise,* October 1989, pp. 106–10.

Gerald I. Nierenberg, *Creative Business Negotiating* (New York: Hawthorn, 1971).

Ronald J. Posluns, *Negotiate Your Way to Financial Success* (New York: Putnam, 1987).

Michelle Willens, "The Manly Art of Win-Win Negotiating," *Money,* February 1987, pp. 199–202.

Some Wise and Mistaken Assumptions about Conflict and Negotiation

Jeffrey Z. Rubin

CONFLICT SETTLEMENT AND RESOLUTION

For many years the attention of conflict researchers and theorists was directed to the laudable objective of conflict *resolution*. This term denotes as an outcome a state of attitude change that effectively brings an end to the conflict in question. In contrast, conflict *settlement* denotes outcomes in which the overt conflict has been brought to an end, even though the underlying bases may or may not have been addressed. The difference here is akin to Herbert Kelman's (1958) useful distinction among the three consequences of social influence: compliance, identification, and internalization. If conflict settlement implies the consequence of compliance (a change in behavior), then conflict resolution instead implies internalization (a more profound change, of underlying attitudes as well as behavior). The third consequence, *identification,* denotes a change in behavior that is based on the target of influence valuing his or her relationship with the source, and it serves as a bridge between behavior change and attitude change.

In keeping with the flourishing research in the 1950s on attitudes and attitude change, social psychological research on conflict in the 1950s and 1960s focused on conflict *resolution*. Only recently has there been a subtle shift in focus from attitude change to behavior change. Underlying this shift is the view that, while it is necessary that attitudes change if conflict is to be eliminated, such elimination is often simply not possible. Merely getting Iran and Iraq, Turkish and Greek Cypriots, Contras and Sandinistas to lay down their weapons—even temporarily—is a great accomplishment in its own right,

This paper is an expanded version of the presidential address, presented to the Society for the Psychological Study of Social Issues (SPSSI) in Atlanta, Georgia on August 12, 1988. Thanks to Walter Swap and J. William Breslin for helpful comments on an earlier draft of the manuscript.

Source: Reprinted from *Journal of Social Issues* 45, no. 2 (1989), pp. 195–209. Reprinted with permission of Blackwell Publishers.

even if the parties continue to hate each other. And this simple act of cessation, when coupled with other such acts, may eventually generate the momentum necessary to move antagonists out of stalemate toward a settlement of their differences. Just as "stateways" can change "folkways" (Deutsch & Collins, 1951), so too can a string of behavioral changes produce the basis for subsequent attitude change.

The gradual shift over the last years from a focus on resolution to a focus on settlement has had an important implication for the conflict field: It has increased the importance of understanding *negotiation*—which, after all, is a method of settling conflict rather than resolving it. The focus of negotiation is not attitude change per se, but an agreement to change behavior in ways that make settlement possible. Two people with underlying differences of beliefs or values (for example, over the issue of a woman's right to abortion or the existence of a higher deity) may come to change their views through discussion and an exchange of views, but it would be inappropriate and inaccurate to describe such an exchange as "negotiation."

Similarly, the shift from resolution to settlement of conflict has also increased the attention directed to the role of *third parties* in the conflict settlement process—individuals who are in some way external to a dispute and who, through identification of issues and judicious intervention, attempt to make it more likely that a conflict can be moved to settlement.

Finally, the shift in favor of techniques of conflict settlement has piqued the interest and attention of practitioners in a great many fields, ranging from divorce mediators and couples' counselors to negotiators operating in environmental, business, labor, community, or international disputes. Attitude change may not be possible in these settings, but behavior change—as a result of skillful negotiation or third-party intervention—is something else entirely. Witness the effective mediation by the Algerians during the so-called Iranian hostage crisis in the late 1970s; as a result of Algerian intervention, the Iranian government came to dislike the American Satan no less than before, but the basis for a *quid pro quo* had been worked out.

COOPERATION, COMPETITION, AND ENLIGHTENED SELF-INTEREST

Required for effective conflict settlement is neither cooperation nor competition, but what may be referred to as "enlightened self-interest." By this I simply mean a variation on what several conflict theorists have previously described as an "individualistic orientation" (Deutsch, 1960)—an outlook in which the disputant is simply interested in doing well for himself or herself, without regard for anyone else, out neither to help nor hinder the other's efforts to obtain his or her goal. The added word *enlightened* refers to the acknowledgment by each side that the other is also likely to be pursuing a path of self-interest—and that it may be possible for *both* to do well in the exchange. If there are ways in which I can move toward my objective in negotiation, while at the same time making it possible for you to approach your goal, then why not behave in ways that make both possible?

Notice that what I am describing here is neither pure individualism (where one side does not care at all about how the other is doing) nor pure cooperation (where each side cares deeply about helping the other to do well, likes and values the other side, etc.)—but an amalgam of the two.

Trivial though this distinction may seem, it has made it possible in recent years for work to develop that, paradoxically, creates a pattern of *inter*dependence out of the assumption of *in*dependence. Earlier work, focusing as it did on the perils of competition and the virtues of cooperation, made an important contribution to the field of conflict studies. However, in doing so, it also shifted attention away from the path of individualism—a path that is likely to provide a way out of stalemate and toward a settlement of differences. I do not have to like or trust you in order to negotiate wisely with you. Nor do I have to be driven by the passion of a competitive desire to beat you. All that is necessary is for me to find some way of getting what I want—perhaps even *more* than I considered possible—by leaving the door open for you too to do well. "Trust" and "trustworthiness," concepts central to the development of cooperation, are no longer necessary—only the understanding of what the other person may want or need.

A number of anecdotes have emerged to make this point; perhaps the most popular is the tale of two sisters who argue over the division of an orange between them (Fisher & Ury, 1981; Follett, 1940). Each would like the entire orange, and only reluctantly do the sisters move from extreme demands to a 50-50 split. While such a solution is eminently fair, it is not necessarily wise: One sister proceeds to peel the orange, discard the peel, and eat her half of the fruit; the other peels the orange, discards the fruit, and uses her 50 percent of the peel to bake a cake! If only the two sisters had understood what each wanted the orange for—not each side's "position," but rather each side's underlying "interest"—an agreement would have been possible that would have allowed each to get everything that she wanted.

Similarly, Jack Sprat and his wife—one preferring lean, the other fat—can lick the platter clean if they understand their respective interests. The interesting thing about this conjugal pair is that, married though they may be, when it comes to dining preferences they are hardly interdependent at all. For Jack and his wife to "lick the platter clean" requires neither that the two love each other nor care about helping each other in every way possible; nor does it require that each be determined to get more of the platter's contents than the other. Instead, it is enlightened self-interest that makes possible an optimal solution to the problem of resource distribution.

The lesson for international relations is instructive. For the United States and the Soviet Union, Israel and its Arab neighbors, Iran and Iraq, the Soviet Union and Afghanistan, the United States and Nicaragua to do well, neither cooperation nor competition is required, but rather an arrangement that acknowledges the possibility of a more complex mixture of these two motivational states—enlightened individualism. While the United States and Soviet Union will continue to have many arenas of conflict in which their interests are clearly and directly opposed, and will also continue to find new opportunities for cooperation (as in the management of nuclear proliferation, hazardous waste disposal, or international political terrorism), there are also arenas in which each side is not at all as dependent on the other for obtaining what it wants (e.g., the formulation of domestic economic or political policy). The world is a very big place; the pie is big enough for both of us, and for many others, (as my grandmother might have said) to live and be well.[1]

A COMMON PROCESS SUBSTRATE

It has been fashionable for several years now to observe that conflicts are fundamentally alike, whether they take place between individuals, within or between groups, communities, or nations. Nevertheless, conflict analysts in each of these domains have tended not to listen closely to one another, and have largely proceeded as if international conflict, labor disputes, and family spats are distinct and unrelated phenomena.

Within the last decade or so, with the advent of conflict and negotiation programs around the United States, a different point of view has begun to emerge: one that argues for a common set of processes that underlie all forms of conflict and their settlement. Third-party intervention—whether in divorce, international business or trade negotiations, a labor dispute, a conflict over nuclear siting or hazardous waste disposal, or an international border dispute—follows certain principles that dictate its likely effectiveness. Similarly, the principles of negotiation apply with equal vigor to conflicts at all levels of complexity, whether two or more than two parties are involved, negotiating one issue or many issues, with problems varying in difficulty, and so on.

Acceptance of this bit of ideology has had an extremely important effect on the field of conflict studies, for it has made it possible for conversations to take place among theorists and practitioners, at work in an extraordinarily rich and varied set of fields. Anthropologists, sociologists, lawyers, psychologists, economists, business men and women, community activists, labor experts, to name but a few, have not started to come together to exchange ideas, to map areas of overlap and divergence. This, in turn, has made it possible for the development of conflict theory and practice to take shape under a larger umbrella than ever before. In fact, the symbolic location of these conversations is more like a circus tent than an umbrella, with beasts of different stripe, size, and coloring all finding a place under the big top.

Most recently, yet another twist has appeared. Having engaged in fruitful preliminary conversations about the nature of conflict and negotiation in their respective fields and disciplines, scholars and practitioners are now turning to areas of *divergence* rather then *similarity*. Instead of homogenizing theory and practice in the different social sciences, analysts are now beginning to look beyond the areas of process similarity to the distinguishing features that characterize dispute management in different arenas.

At another but related level, conflict analysts are at last beginning to acknowledge that our pet formulations have been devised by, and are directed to, a community that is predominantly white, Western, male, and upper middle class. Now that fruitful conversations have begun to take place among members of out own intellectual community, it is becoming clear that some of our most cherished ideas may be limited in their applicability and generalizability. Other societies—indeed, other people within our own society—may not always "play the conflict game" by the set of rules that scholars and researchers have deduced on the basis of American paradigms.

As one example of what I mean, "face saving" has been an extremely important element of most conflict/negotiation formulations: the idea that people in conflict will go out of their way to avoid being made to look weak or foolish in the eyes of others and themselves. While face saving seems important in the United States and in countries such as Japan or Korea, less obvious is the extent to which this issue is of *universal* significance.

Do Pacific Islanders, Native Americans, or South Asians experience "face," and therefore the possibility of "loss of face?" It is not clear. Do women experience face saving and face loss, or is this a phenomenon that is largely restricted to the XY genetic portions of the population?

Similarly, what does it mean to set a "time limit" in negotiations in different cultures? Do other cultures measure a successful negotiation outcome the same way we tend to in this country? Are coalitions considered equally acceptable, and are they likely to form in much the same way, from one country to the next? Do different countries structure the negotiating environment—everything from the shape of the negotiating table to the presence of observing audiences and various constituencies—in the same way? The answers to questions such as these are not yet in, and we must therefore learn to be cautious in our propensity to advance a set of "universal" principles.

THE IMPORTANCE OF "RELATIONSHIP" IN NEGOTIATION

Much of the negotiation analysis that has taken place over the last 25 years has focused on the "bottom line": who gets how much once an agreement has been reached. The emphasis has thus largely been an *economic* one, and this emphasis has been strengthened by the significant role of game theory and other mathematical or economic formulations.

This economic focus is being supplanted by a richer, and more accurate, portrayal of negotiation in terms not only of economic, but also of relational, considerations. As any visitor to the Turkish Bazaar in Istanbul will tell you, the purchase of an oriental carpet involves a great deal more than the exchange of money for an old rug. The emerging relationship between shopkeeper and customer is far more significant, weaving ever so naturally into the economic aspects of the transaction. An initial conversation about the selling price of some item is quickly transformed into an exchange of a more personal nature: Who one is, where one is from, stories about one's family and friends, impressions of the host country, and lots more. When my wife and I purchased several rugs in Turkey some years ago, we spent three days in conversation with the merchant— not because that is how long it took to "cut the best deal," but because we were clearly having a fine time getting to know one another over Turkish coffee, Turkish delight, and Turkish taffy. When, at the end of our three-day marathon transaction, the shopkeeper invited us to consider opening a carpet store in Boston that could be used to distribute his wares, I was convinced that this invitation was extended primarily to sustain an emerging relationship—rather than to make a financial "killing" in the United States.

Psychologists, sociologists, and anthropologists have long understood the importance of "relationship" in any interpersonal transaction, but only recently have conflict analysts begun to take this as seriously as it deserves. Although it seems convenient to distinguish negotiation in one-time-only exchanges (ones where you have no history of contact with the other party, come together for a "quickie," and then expect never to see the other again) from negotiation in ongoing relationships, this distinction is more illusory than real. Rarely does one negotiate in the absence of future consequences. Even if you and I meet once and once only, our reputations have a way of surviving the exchange, coloring the expectations that others will have of us in the future.

NEGOTIATION IN A TEMPORAL CONTEXT

For too long, analysts have considered only the negotiations proper, rather than the sequence of events preceding negotiation and the events that must transpire if a concluded agreement is to be implemented successfully. Only recently, as analysts have become more confident in their appraisal of the factors that influence effective negotiation, has attention been directed to the past and future, as anchors of the negotiating present.

Analysts of international negotiation (e.g., Saunders, 1985) have observed that some of the most important work takes place *before the parties ever come to the table.* Indeed, once they get to the table, all that typically remains is a matter of crossing the *t*'s and dotting the *i*'s in an agreement hammered out beforehand. It is during *prenegotiation* that the pertinent parties to the conflict are identified and invited to participate, that a listing of issues is developed and prioritized as an agenda, and that the formula by which a general agreement is to be reached is first outlined. Without such a set of preliminary understandings, international negotiators may well refuse to sit down at the same table with one another.

Prenegotiation is important in other contexts as well, something I discovered in conversation with a successful Thai businessman. He observed that Thais are extremely reluctant to confront an adversary in negotiation, or to show any sign whatsoever of disagreement, let alone conflict. Yet many Thais have succeeded admirably in negotiating agreements that are to their advantage. The key to their success is prenegotiation, making sure beforehand that there really *is* an agreement before labeling the process "negotiation," before ever sitting down with that other person. In effect, they use prenegotiation to arrange matters to their advantage, and they do so without ever identifying the relationship with the other party as conflictual, or signaling in any way that concessions or demands are being made.

At the other end of the temporal continuum lies the matter of follow-up and implementation. To reach an agreement through negotiation is not enough. Those parties who are in a position to sabotage this agreement, unless their advice is solicited and incorporated, must be taken into account if a negotiated agreement is to succeed. (Witness the failure of the Michael Dukakis campaign to consult sufficiently with Jesse Jackson and his supporters, prior to the 1988 Democratic Party Convention in Atlanta.) Note the trade-off here: The greater the number of parties to a negotiation, the more difficult it will be to reach any agreement at all. But only if the relevant parties and interests are included in the negotiations is the agreement reached likely to "stick."

As negotiation analysts have broadened the temporal spectrum to include pre- and postnegotiation processes, more work has been done toward devising creative options for improving upon the proceedings. To cite but one example, Howard Raiffa (1985) has proposed a procedure known as "postsettlement settlement," by which parties who have already concluded an agreement are given an opportunity—with the assistance of a third party—to improve upon their agreement. The third party examines the facts and figures that each side has used in reaching a settlement; based on this information, which is kept in strict confidence, the third party proposes a settlement that improves upon the agreement reached. Either side can veto this postsettlement settlement, in which case the *status quo ante* remains in effect. However, if both sides endorse the proposed improvement on the existing contract, then each stands to benefit from this proposal—and the third party, in turn, is guaranteed a percentage of the "added value" of the contract.

NEGOTIATING FROM THE INSIDE OUT

Conventional wisdom regarding effective negotiation calls for the parties to start by making extreme opening offers, then conceding stepwise until an agreement is reached. If you want to sell a used car, purchase a rug, secure a new wage package, or settle a territorial dispute with a neighboring country, you begin by asking for more than you expect to settle for, then gradually move inward until you and the other side overlap; at that point you have got a negotiated settlement.

A large body of negotiation analysis has proceeded in accordance with this conventional wisdom. Moreover, this way of negotiating "from the outside in" makes good sense for several reasons: It allows each negotiator to explore various possible agreements before settling, to obtain as much information as possible about the other negotiator and his or her preferences, before closing off discussion (Kelley, 1966). It also allows each party to give its respective constituency some sense of the degree to which the other side has already been "moved," thereby maintaining constituency support for the positions taken in negotiation.

On the other hand, this "traditional" way of conducting the business of negotiation ignores an important and creative alternative: working "from the inside out." Instead of beginning with extreme opening offers, then moving slowly and inexorably from this stance until agreement is reached, it often makes sense to start with an exchange of views about underlying needs and interests—and on the basis of such an exchange, to build an agreement that both parties find acceptable. The key to such an approach is, as negotiation analysts have observed (e.g., Fisher & Ury, 1981), to work at the level of interests rather than positions—what one really needs and wants (and why), rather than what one states that one would like to have.

This was precisely what happened in October of 1978 at Camp David where, with the mediation of President Jimmy Carter and his subordinates, President Anwar Sadat of Egypt and Prime Minister Menachem Begin of Israel were able to settle the disposition of the Sinai Peninsula. The Sinai had been taken by the Israelis in 1967, and its complete and immediate return had been demanded by the Egyptians ever since. Had the discussions about the fate of the Sinai been conducted solely at the level of positions—with each side demanding total control of the land in question, then making stepwise concessions from these extreme opening offers—*no* agreement would have been possible. Instead, with assistance from President Carter, the Egyptians and Israelis identified their own respective underlying interests—and were able to move to an agreement that allowed the Israelis to obtain the security they required, while the Egyptians obtained the territory they required. "Security in exchange for territory" was the formula used here, and it was a formula devised not by moving from the outside in, but by building up an agreement from the inside out.

A useful variation on this inside-out idea is the "one-text" negotiation procedure (Fisher, 1981), whereby a mediator develops a single negotiating text that is critiqued and improved by each side until a final draft is developed for approval by the interested parties. Instead of starting with demands that are gradually abandoned, the negotiators criticize a single document that is rewritten to take these criticisms into account, and eventually—through this sort of inside-out procedure—a proposal is developed for which both sides have some sense of ownership.

THE ROLE OF "RIPENESS"

Although it is comforting to assume people can start negotiating any time they want, such is not the case. First of all, just as it takes two hands to clap, it takes two to negotiate. *You* may be ready to come to the table for serious discussion, but your counterpart may not. Unless you are both at the table (or connected by a telephone line or cable link), no agreement is possible.

Second, even if both of you are present at the same place, at the same time, one or both of you may not be sufficiently motivated to take the conflict seriously. It is tempting to sit back, do nothing, and hope that the mere passage of time will turn events to your advantage. People typically do not sit down to negotiate unless and until they have reached a point of "stalemate," where each no longer believes it possible to obtain what he or she wants through efforts at domination or coercion (Kriesberg, 1987). It is only at this point, when the two sides grudgingly acknowledge the need for joint work if any agreement is to be reached, that negotiation can take place.

By "ripeness," then, I mean a stage of conflict in which all parties are ready to take their conflict seriously, and are willing to do whatever may be necessary to bring the conflict to a close. To pluck fruit from a tree before it is ripe is as problematic as waiting too long. There is a *right* time to negotiate, and the wise negotiator will attempt to seek out this point.

It is also possible, of course, to help "create" such a right time. One way of doing so entails the use of threat and coercion, as the two sides (either with or without the assistance of an outside intervenor) walk (or are led) to the edge of "lover's leap," stare into the abyss below, and contemplate the consequences of failing to reach agreement. The farther the drop—that is, the more terrible the consequences of failing to settle— the greater the pressure on each side to take the conflict seriously. There are at least two serious problems with such "coercive" means of creating a ripe conflict: First, as can be seen in the history of the arms race between the United States and the Soviet Union, it encourages further conflict escalation, as each side tries to "motivate" the other to settle by upping the ante a little bit at a time. Second, such escalatory moves invite a game of "chicken," in which each hopes that the other will be the first to succumb to coercion.

There is a second—and far *better*—way to create a situation that is ripe for settlement: namely, through the introduction of new opportunities for joint gain. If each side can be persuaded that there is more to gain than to lose through collaboration—that by working jointly, rewards can be harvested that stand to advance each side's respective agenda—then a basis for agreement can be established. In the era of *glasnost,* the United States and Soviet Union are currently learning this lesson—namely, that by working together they can better address problems of joint interest, the solution of which advances their respective self-interest. Arms control stands to save billions of dollars and rubles in the strained budgets of both nations, while advancing the credibility of each country in the eyes of the larger world community. The same is true of joint efforts to slow the consequences of the "greenhouse effect" on the atmosphere, to explore outer space, and to preserve and protect our precious natural resources in the seas.

A "RESIDUE" THAT CHANGES THINGS

It is tempting for parties to a conflict to begin by experimenting with a set of adversarial, confrontational moves in the hope that these will work. Why not give hard bargaining a try at first, since if moves such as threat, bluff, or intimidation work as intended, the other side may give up without much of a fight? Moreover, even if such tactics fail, one can always shift to a more benign stance. The problem with such a sticks-to-carrots approach is that once one has left the path of joint problem solving, it may be very difficult to return again. It takes two people to cooperate, but only one person is usually required to make a mess of a relationship. The two extremes of cooperation and competition, collaboration and confrontation, are thus *not* equally valenced; it is far easier to move from cooperation to competition than the other way around.

In the course of hard bargaining, things are often said and done that change the climate of relations in ways that do not easily allow for a return to a less confrontational stance. A "residue" is left behind (Pruitt & Rubin, 1986), in the form of words spoken or acts committed, which cannot be denied and which may well change the relationship. The words, "I've never really liked or respected you," spoken in the throes of an angry exchange, may linger like a bad taste in the mouth, even when the conflict has apparently been settled. Similarly, a brandished fist or some other threatening gesture may leave scars that long outlive the heat of the moment. Thus, the escalation of conflict often carries with it moves and maneuvers that alter a relationship in ways that the parties do not anticipate.

The implication of this point for conflict and negotiation studies is clear: Insufficient attention has been directed to the lasting consequences of confrontational tactics. Too often scholars, researchers, and practitioners have assumed cooperation and competition are equally weighted, when in fact cooperation is a slippery slope; once left, the path leading to return is difficult indeed. Required for such a return journey is a combination of cooperation and persistence—the willingness to make a unilateral collaborative overture, and then to couple this with the tenacity necessary to persuade the other side that this collaborative overture is to be taken seriously (Axelrod, 1984; Fisher & Brown, 1988).

REFERENCES

Axelrod, R. (1984). *The evolution of cooperation.* New York: Basic Books.

Deutsch, M. (1960). The effect of motivational orientation upon trust and suspicion. *Human Relations,* 13; 123–39.

Deutsch, M., & Collins, M. E. (1951). *Interracial housing: A psychological evaluation of a social experiment.* Minneapolis: University of Minnesota Press.

Fisher, R. (1981). Playing the wrong game? In J. Z. Rubin (Ed.), *Dynamics of third party intervention: Kissinger in the Middle East.* New York: Praeger.

Fisher, R., & Brown S. (1988). *Getting together.* Boston: Houghton Mifflin.

Fisher, R., & Ury, W. L. (1981). *Getting to yes: Negotiating agreement without giving in.* Boston: Houghton Mifflin.

Follett, M. P. (1940). Constructive conflict. In H. C. Metcalf & L. Urwick (Eds.), *Dynamic administration: The collected papers of Mary Parker Follett.* New York: Harper.

Kelley, H. H. (1966). A classroom study of the dilemmas in interpersonal negotiations. In K. Archibald (Ed.), *Strategic interaction and conflict: Original papers and discussion.* Berkeley, CA: Institute of International Studies.

Kelman, H. C. (1958). Compliance, identification, and internalization: Three processes of attitude change. *Journal of Conflict Resolution, 2,* 51–60.

Kriesberg, L. (1987). Timing and the initiation of de-escalation moves. *Negotiation Journal, 3,* 375–84.

Lax, D. A., & Sebenius, J. (1986). *The manager as negotiator.* New York: Free Press.

McGrath, J. E. (1980). What are the social issues? Timeliness and treatment of topics in the Journal of Social Issues: *Journal of Social Issues, 36*(4), 98–108.

Pruitt, D. G., & Rubin, J. Z. (1986). *Social conflict: Escalation, stalemate, and settlement.* New York: Random House.

Raiffa, H. (1985). Post-settlement settlements. *Negotiation Journal, 1,* 9–12.

Russell, R. W. (Ed.). (1961). Psychology and policy in a nuclear age. *Journal of Social Issues, 17,* (3).

Saunders, H. H. (1985). We need a larger theory of negotiation: the importance of prenegotiating phases. *Negotiation Journal, 2,* 249–62.

Susskind, L., & Cruickshank, J. (1987). *Breaking the impasse.* New York: Basic Books.

ENDNOTES

1. Two recent books (Lax & Sebenius, 1986; Susskind & Cruickshank, 1987) treat rather extensively the topic of enlightened self-interest, pointing out ways of expanding the resource pie, or finding uses for it that satisfy the interests of each side.

SECTION FIVE

Communication and Cognitive Biases

Negotiating Rationally: The Power and Impact of the Negotiator's Frame

Margaret A. Neale

Max H. Bazerman

Everyone negotiates. In its various forms, negotiation is a common mechanism for resolving differences and allocating resources. While many people perceive negotiation to be a specific interaction between a buyer and a seller, this process occurs with a wide variety of exchange partners, such as superiors, colleagues, spouses, children, neighbors, strangers, or even corporate entities and nations. Negotiation is a decision-making process among interdependent parties who do not share identical preferences. It is through negotiation that the parties decide what each will give and take in their relationship.

The aspect of negotiation that is most directly controllable by the negotiator is how he or she makes decisions. The parties, the issues, and the negotiation environment are often predetermined. Rather than trying to change the environment surrounding the negotiation or the parties or issues in the dispute, we believe that the greatest opportunity to improve negotiator performance lies in the negotiator's ability to make effective use of the information available about the issues in dispute as well as the likely behavior of an opponent to reach more rational agreements and make more rational decisions within the context of negotiation.

To this end, we offer advice on how a negotiator should make decisions. However, to follow this advice for analyzing negotiations rationally, a negotiator must understand the psychological forces that limit a negotiator's effectiveness. In addition, rational decisions require that we have an optimal way of evaluating behavior of the opponent. This requires a psychological perspective for anticipating the likely decisions and subsequent behavior of the other party. Information such as this cannot only create a framework that predicts how a negotiator structures problems, processes information, frames the situation, and evaluates alternatives but also identifies the limitations of his or her ability to follow rational advice.

Reprinted from *Academy of Management Executive* 6, no. 3 (1992), pp. 42–51. Used with permission of the authors and publisher.

Rationality refers to making the decision that maximizes the negotiator's interests. Since negotiation is a decision-making process that involves other people that do not have the same desires or preferences, the goal of a negotiation is not simply reaching an agreement. The goal of negotiations is to reach a *good* agreement. In some cases, no agreement is better than reaching an agreement that is not in the negotiator's best interests. When negotiated agreements are based on biased decisions, the chances of getting the best possible outcome are significantly reduced and the probabilities of reaching an agreement when an impasse would have left the negotiator relatively better off are significantly enhanced.

A central theme of our work is that our natural decision and negotiation processes contain biases that prevent us from acting rationally and getting as much as we can out of a negotiation. These biases are pervasive, destroying the opportunities available in competitive contexts, and preventing us from negotiating rationally. During the last 10 or so years, the work that we and our colleagues have done suggests that negotiators make the following common cognitive mistakes: (1) negotiators tend to be overly affected by the frame, or form of presentation, of information in a negotiation; (2) negotiators tend to nonrationally escalate commitment to a previously selected course of action when it is no longer the most reasonable alternative; (3) negotiators tend to assume that their gain must come at the expense of the other party and thereby miss opportunities for mutually beneficial trade-offs between the parties; (4) negotiator judgments tend to be anchored upon irrelevant information—such as, an initial offer; (5) negotiators tend to rely on readily available information; (6) negotiators tend to fail to consider information that is available by focusing on the opponent's perspective; and (7) negotiators tend to be overconfident concerning the likelihood of attaining outcomes that favor the individual(s) involved.

Describing the impact of each of these biases on negotiator behavior is obviously beyond the scope of this article. What we will attempt to do, however, is to focus on one particular and important cognitive bias, *framing,* and consider the impact of this bias on the process and outcome of negotiation. The manner in which negotiators frame the options available in a dispute can have a significant impact on their willingness to reach an agreement as well as the value of that agreement. In this article, we will identify factors that influence the choice of frame in a negotiation.

THE FRAMING OF NEGOTIATIONS

Consider the following situation adapted from Russo and Schoemaker:[1]

You are in a store about to buy a new watch which costs $70. As you wait for the sales clerk, a friend of yours comes by and remarks that she has seen an identical watch on sale in another store two blocks away for $40. You know that the service and reliability of the other store are just as good as this one. Will you travel two blocks to save $30?

Now consider this similar situation:

You are in a store about to buy a new video camera that costs $800. As you wait for the sales clerk, a friend of yours comes by and remarks that she has seen an identical camera on sale in another store two blocks away for $770. You know that the service and reliability of the other store are just as good as this one. Will you travel two blocks to save the $30?

In the first scenario, Russo and Shoemaker report that about 90 percent of the managers presented this problem reported that they would travel the two blocks. However, in the second scenario, only about 50 percent of the managers would make the trip. What is the difference between the two situations that makes the $30 so attractive in the first scenario and considerably less attractive in the second scenario? One difference is that a $30 discount on a $70 watch represents a very good deal; the $30 discount on an $800 video camera is not such a good deal. In evaluating our willingness to walk two blocks, we frame the options in terms of the percentage discount. However, the correct comparison is not whether a percentage discount is sufficiently motivating, but whether the savings obtained is greater than the expected value of the additional time we would have to invest to realize those savings. So, if a $30 savings were sufficient to justify walking two blocks for the watch, an opportunity to save $30 on the video camera should also be worth an equivalent investment of time.

Richard Thaler illustrated the influence of frames when he presented the following two versions of another problem to participants of an executive development program.[2]

You are lying on the beach on a hot day. All you have to drink is ice water. For the last hour you have been thinking about how much you would enjoy a nice cold bottle of your favorite brand of beer. A companion gets up to make a phone call and offers to bring back a beer from the only nearby place where beer is sold: a fancy resort hotel. She says that the beer might be expensive and asks how much you are willing to pay for the beer. She will buy the beer if it costs as much as or less than the price you state. But if it costs more than the price you state, she will not buy it. You trust your friend and there is no possibility of bargaining with the bartender. What price do you tell your friend you are willing to pay?

Now consider this version of the same story:

You are lying on the beach on a hot day. All you have to drink is ice water. For the last hour you have been thinking about how much you would enjoy a nice cold bottle of you favorite brand of beer. A companion gets up to make a phone call and offers to bring back a beer from the only nearby place where beer is sold: a small, run-down grocery store. She says that the beer might be expensive and asks how much you are willing to pay for the beer. She will buy the beer if it costs as much as or less than the price you state. But if it costs more than the price you state, she will not buy it. You trust your friend and there is no possibility of bargaining with the store owner. What price do you tell your friend you are willing to pay?

In both versions of the story, the results are the same: you get the same beer and there is no negotiating with the seller. Also you will not be enjoying the resort's amenities since you will be drinking the beer on the beach. Recent responses of executives at a Kellogg executive training program indicated that they were willing to pay significantly more if the beer were purchased at a "fancy resort hotel" ($7.83) than if the beer were purchased at the "small, run-down grocery store" ($4.10). The difference in price the executives were willing to pay for the same beer was based upon the frame they imposed on this transaction. Paying over $5 for a beer is an expected annoyance at a fancy resort hotel; however, paying over $5 for a beer at a run-down grocery store is an obvious "rip-off!" So, even though the same beer is purchased and we enjoy none of the benefits of the fancy resort hotel, we are willing to pay almost a dollar more because of the way in which we frame the purchase. The converse of this situation is probably familiar to many of us. Have you ever purchased an item because "it was too good of a deal to pass up," even though you had no use for it? We seem to assign a greater value to the quality of the transaction over and above the issue of what we get for what we pay.

Both of these examples emphasize the importance of the particular frames we place on problems we have to solve or decisions we have to make. Managers are constantly being exposed to many different frames, some naturally occurring and others that are purposefully proposed. An important task of managers is to identify the appropriate frame by which employees and the organization, in general, should evaluate its performance and direct its effort.

The Framing of Risky Negotiations

The way in which information is framed (in terms of either potential gains or potential losses) to the negotiator can have a significant impact on his or her preference for risk, particularly when uncertainty about future events or outcomes is involved. For example, when offered the choice between gains of equal expected value—one for certain and the other a lottery, we strongly prefer to take the *certain* gain. However, when we are offered the choice between potential losses of equal expected value, we clearly and consistently eschew the loss for certain and prefer the risk inherent in the *lottery*.

There is substantial evidence to suggest that we are not indifferent toward risky situations and we should not necessarily trust our intuitions about risk. Negotiators routinely deviate from rationality because they do not typically appreciate the transient nature of their preference for risk; nor do they take into consideration the ability of a particular decision frame to influence that preference. Influencing our attitudes toward risk through the positive or negative frames associated with the problem is the result of evaluating an alternative from a particular referent point or base line. A referent point is the basis by which we evaluate whether what we are considering is viewed as a gain or a loss. The referent point that we choose determines the frame we impose on our options and, subsequently, our willingness to accept or reject those options.

Consider the high-performing employee who is expecting a significant increase in salary this year. He frames his expectations on the past behavior of the company. As such, he is expecting a raise of approximately $5,000. Because of the recession, he receives a $3,500 salary increase. He immediately confronts his manager, complaining that he has been unfairly treated. He is extremely disappointed in what his surprised manager saw as an exceptional raise because the employee's referent point is $1,500 higher. Had he known that the average salary increase was only $2,000 (and used that as a more realistic referent point), he would have perceived the same raise quite differently and it may have had the motivating force that his manager had hoped to create.

The selection of which relevant frame influences our behavior is a function of our selection of a base line by which we evaluate potential outcomes. The choice of one referent point over another may be the result of a visible anchor, the "status quo," or our expectations. Probably one of the most common referent points is what we perceive to be in our current inventory (our status quo)—what is ours already. We then evaluate offers or options in terms of whether they make us better off (a gain) or worse off (a loss) from what (we perceive to be) our current resource state.

Interestingly, what we include in our current resource state is surprisingly easy to modify. Consider the executive vice president of a large automobile manufacturing concern that has been hit by a number of economic difficulties because of the recession in the United States. It appears as if she will have to close down three plants and the employee rolls will be trimmed by 6,000 individuals. In exploring ways to avoid this alternative, she has identified two plans that might ameliorate the situation. If she selects the first plan, she will be able to save 2,000 jobs and one of the three plants. If she implements the second plan, there is a one-third probability that she can save all three plants and all 6,000 jobs but there is a two-thirds probability that this plan will end up saving none of the plants and none of the jobs. If you were this vice president, which plan would you select (#1 or #2)?

Now consider the same options (Plan 1 or Plan 2) framed as losses: if the vice president implements Plan 1, two of the three plants will be shut down and 4,000 jobs will be lost. If she implements Plan 2, then there is a two-thirds probability of losing all three plants and all 6,000 jobs but there is a one-third probability of losing no plants and no jobs. If you were presented with these two plans, which would be more attractive? Plan 1 or Plan 2?

It is obvious that from a purely economic perspective, there is no difference between the two choices. Yet, managers offered the plans framed in terms of gains select the first plan about 76 percent of the time. However, managers offered the choice between the plans framed in terms of losses only select the first plan about 22 percent of the time. When confronted with potential losses, the lottery represented by Plan 2 becomes relatively much more attractive.

An important point for managers to consider is that the way in which the problem is framed, or presented, can dramatically alter the perceived value or acceptability of alternative courses of action. In negotiation, for example, the more risk-averse course of action is to accept an offered settlement; the more risk-seeking course of action is to hold out for future, potential concessions. In translating the influence of the framing bias to negotiation, we must realize that the selection of a particular referent point or base line determines whether a negotiator will frame his or her decision as positive or negative.

Specifically, consider any recurring contract negotiation. As the representative of Company A, the offer from Company B can be viewed in two ways, depending on the referent point I use. If my referent point were the current contract, Company B's offer can be evaluated in terms of the "gains" Company A can expect relative to the previous contract. However, if the referent point for Company A is an initial offer on the issues under current consideration, then Company A is more likely to evaluate Company B's offers as losses to be incurred if the contract as proposed is accepted. Viewing options as losses or as gains will have considerable impact on the negotiator's willingness to accept side B's position—even though the same options may be offered in both cases.

Likewise, the referent points available to an individual negotiating his salary for a new position in the company include: (1) his current salary; (2) the company's initial offer; (3) the least he is willing to accept; (4) his estimate of the most the company is willing to pay; or (5) his initial salary request. As his referent moves from 1 to 5, he progresses from a positive to a negative frame in the negotiation. What is a modest *gain* compared to his current wage is perceived as a loss when compared to what he would like to receive. Along these same lines, employees currently making $15/hour and demanding an increase of $4/hour can view a proposed increase of $2/hour as a $2/hour gain in comparison to last year's wage (Referent 1) or as a $2/hour loss in comparison to their stated or initial proposal of $19/hour (Referent 5). Consequently, the location of the referent point is critical to whether the decision is positively or negatively framed and affects the resulting risk preference of the decision maker.

In a study of the impact of framing on collective bargaining outcomes, we used a five-issue negotiation with participants playing the roles of management or labor negotiators.[3] Each negotiator's frame was manipulated by adjusting his or her referent point. Half of the negotiators were told that any concessions they make from their initial offers represented losses to their constituencies (i.e., a negative frame). The other half were told that any agreements they were able to reach which were better than the current contract were gains to their constituencies (i.e., the positive frame). In analyzing the results of their negotiations, we found that negatively framed negotiators were less concessionary and reached fewer agreements than positively framed negotiators. In addition, negotiators who had positive frames perceived the negotiated outcomes as more fair than those who had negative frames.

In another study, we posed the following problem to negotiators:

> You are a wholesaler of refrigerators. Corporate policy does not allow any flexibility in pricing. However, flexibility does exist in terms of expenses that you can incur (shipping, financing terms, etc.), which have a direct effect on the profitability of the transaction. These expenses can all be viewed in dollar value terms. You are negotiating an $8,000 sale. The buyer wants you to pay $2,000 in expenses. You want to pay less expenses. When you negotiate the exchange, do you try to minimize your expenses (reduce them from $2,000) or maximize net profit, i.e., price less expenses (increase the net profit from $6,000)?

From an objective standpoint, the choice you make to reduce expenses or maximize profit should be irrelevant. Because the choice objectively is between two identical options, selecting one or the other should have no impact on the outcome of the negotiation. What we did find, in contrast, is that the frame that buyers and sellers take into the negotiation can systematically affect their behavior.[4]

In one study, negotiators were led to view transactions in terms of either (1) net profit or (2) total expenses deducted from gross profits. These two situations were objectively identical. Managers can think about maximizing their profits (i.e., gains) or minimizing their expenses (i.e., losses). These choices are linked; if one starts from the same set of revenues, then one way to maximize profits is to minimize expenses and if one is successful at minimizing expenses, the outcome is that profit may be maximized. That is, there is an obvious relationship between profits and expenses. So, objectively, there is no reason to believe that an individual should behave differently if given the instructions to minimize expenses or to maximize profits. However, those negotiators told to maximize profit (i.e., a positive frame) were more concessionary. In addition, positively framed negotiators completed significantly more transactions than their negatively framed (those told to minimize expenses) counterparts. Because they completed more transactions, their overall profitability in the market was higher, although negatively framed negotiators completed transactions of greater mean profit.[5]

The Endowment Effect

The ease with which we can alter our referent points was illustrated in a series of studies conducted by Daniel Kahneman, Jack Knetsch, and Richard Thaler.[6] In any exchange between a buyer and a seller, the buyer must be willing to pay at least the minimum amount the seller is willing to accept for a trade to take place. In determining the worth of an object, its value to the seller may, on occasion, be determined by some objective third party such as an economic market. However, in a large number of transactions, the seller places a value on the item—a value that may include not only the market value of the item but also a component for an emotional attachment to or unique appreciation of the item. What impact might such an attachment have on the framing of the transaction?

Let's imagine that you have just received a coffee mug.[7] (In the actual demonstration, coffee mugs were placed before one third of the participants, the "sellers," in the study.) After receiving the mug, you are told that in fact you "own the object (coffee mug) in your possession. You have the option of selling it if a price, to be determined later, is acceptable to you." Next, you are given a list (see Exhibit 1) of possible selling prices, ranging from $.50 to $9.50, and are told for each of the possible prices, you should indicate whether you would (a) sell the mug and receive that amount in return, or (b) keep the object and take it home with you. What is your selling price for the mug?

Another third of the group (the "buyers") were told that they would be receiving a sum of money and they could choose to keep the money or use it to buy a mug. They were also asked to indicate their preferences between a mug and sums of money ranging from $.50 to $9.50. Finally, the last third of the participants (the "choosers") were given a questionnaire indicating that they would later be given an option of receiving either a mug or a sum of money to be determined later. They indicated their preferences between the mug and sums of money between $.50 and $9.50. All of the participants were told that their answers would not influence either the predetermined price of the mug or the amount of money to be received in lieu of the mug.

The sellers reported a median value of $7.12 for the mug; the buyers valued the mug at $2.88; and the choosers valued the mug at $3.12. It is interesting that in this exercise, being a buyer or a chooser resulted in very similar evaluations of worth of the mug. However, owning the mug (the sellers) created a much greater sense of the mug's worth. In this case, it was approximately 40 percent greater than the market (or retail) value of the mug.

The explanation for this disparity lies in the fact that different roles (buyer, seller, or chooser) created different referent points. In fact, what seems to happen in such situations is that owning something changes the nature of the owner's relationship to the commodity. Giving up that item is now perceived as loss and in valuing the item, the owner may include a dollar value to offset his or her perceived loss. If we consider this discrepancy in the value of an item common, then the simple act of "owning" an item, however briefly, can increase one's personal attachment to an item—and typically, its perceived value. After such an attachment is formed, the cost of breaking that attachment is greater and is reflected in the higher price the sellers demand to part with their mugs compared to the value the buyers or the choosers place on the exact same commodity. In addition, we would expect that the endowment effect intensifies to the extent that the value of the commodity of interest is ambiguous or subjective, the commodity itself is unique, or not easily substitutable in the marketplace.

EXHIBIT 1   The Coffee Mug Questionnaire

For each price listed below, indicate whether you would be willing to sell the coffee mug for that price or keep the mug.

If the price is $0.50, I will sell _____ ; I will keep the mug _____.
If the price is $1.00, I will sell _____ ; I will keep the mug _____.
If the price is $1.50, I will sell _____ ; I will keep the mug _____.
If the price is $2.00, I will sell _____ ; I will keep the mug _____.
If the price is $2.50, I will sell _____ ; I will keep the mug _____.
If the price is $3.00, I will sell _____ ; I will keep the mug _____.
If the price is $3.50, I will sell _____ ; I will keep the mug _____.
If the price is $4.00, I will sell _____ ; I will keep the mug _____.
If the price is $4.50, I will sell _____ ; I will keep the mug _____.
If the price is $5.00, I will sell _____ ; I will keep the mug _____.
If the price is $5.50, I will sell _____ ; I will keep the mug _____.
If the price is $6.00, I will sell _____ ; I will keep the mug _____.
If the price is $6.50, I will sell _____ ; I will keep the mug _____.
If the price is $7.00, I will sell _____ ; I will keep the mug _____.
If the price is $7.50, I will sell _____ ; I will keep the mug _____.
If the price is $8.00, I will sell _____ ; I will keep the mug _____.
If the price is $8.50, I will sell _____ ; I will keep the mug _____.
If the price is $9.00, I will sell _____ ; I will keep the mug _____.
If the price is $9.50, I will sell _____ ; I will keep the mug _____.

Framing, Negotiator Bias, and Strategic Behavior

In the previous discussion, we described the negotiator behaviors that may arise from positive and negative frames within the context of the interaction. In this section, we identify some of the techniques for strategically manipulating framing to direct negotiator performance.

Framing has important implications for negotiator tactics. Using the framing effect to induce a negotiating opponent to concede requires that the negotiator create referents that lead the opposition to a positive frame by couching the proposal in terms of their potential gain. In addition, the negotiator should emphasize the inherent risk in the negotiation situation and the opportunity for a sure gain. As our research suggests, simply posing problems as choices among potential gains rather than choices among potential losses can significantly influence the negotiator's preferences for specific outcomes.

Framing can also have important implications for how managers choose to intervene in dispute among their peers or subordinates. Managers, of course, have a wide range of options to implement when deciding to intervene in disputes in which they are not active principals. If the manager's goal is to get the parties to reach an agreement rather than having the manager decide what the solution to the dispute will be, he or she may wish to facilitate both parties' viewing the negotiation from a positive frame. This is tricky, however, since the same referent that will lead to a positive frame for one negotiator is likely to lead to a negative frame for the other negotiator if presented simultaneously to the parties. Making use of the effects of framing may be most appropriate when a manager can meet with each side separately. He or she may present different perspectives to each party to create a positive frame (and the subsequent risk-averse behavior associated with such a frame) for parties on both sides of the dispute. Again, if the manager is to effect the frame of the problem in such a way to encourage agreement, he or she may also emphasize the possible losses inherent in continuing the dispute. Combining these two strategies may facilitate both sides' preference for the certainty of a settlement.

Being in the role of buyer or seller can be a naturally occurring frame that can influence negotiator behavior in systematic ways. Consider the curious, consistent, and robust finding in a number of studies that buyers tend to outperform sellers in market settings in which the balance of power is equal.[8] Given the artificial context of the laboratory settings and the symmetry of the design of these field and laboratory markets, there is no logical reason why buyers should do better than sellers. One explanation for this observed difference may be that when the commodity is anonymous (or completely substitutable in a market sense), sellers may think about the transaction in terms of the dollars exchanged. That is, sellers may conceptualize the process of selling as gaining resources (e.g., how many dollars do I gain by selling the commodity); whereas buyers may view transaction in terms of loss of dollars (e.g., how many dollars do I have to give up). If the dollars are the primary focus of the participants' attention, then buyers would tend to be risk seeking and sellers risk averse in the exchange.

When a risk-averse party (i.e., the seller, in this example) negotiates with a risk-seeking party (i.e., the buyer), the buyer is more willing to risk the potential agreement by demanding more or being less concessionary. To reach agreement, the seller must make additional concessions to induce the buyer, because of his or her risk-seeking propensity, to accept the agreement. Thus, in situations where the relative achievements of buyers and seller, can be directly compared, buyers would benefit from their negative frame (and subsequent risk averse behavior). The critical issue is that these naturally occurring frames such as the role demands of being a "buyer" or "seller" can easily influence the way in which the disputed issues are framed—even without the conscious intervention of one or more of the parties.

It is easy to see that the frames of negotiators can result in the difference between impasse and reaching an important agreement. Both sides in negotiations typically talk in terms of a certain wage, price, or outcome that they must get—setting a high referent point against which gains and losses are measured. If this occurs, any compromise below (or above) that point represents a loss. This perceived loss may lead negotiators to adopt a negative frame to all proposals, exhibit risk-seeking behaviors, and be less likely to reach settlement. Thus, negotiators, similar to the early example involving the beach and the beer, may end up with no beer (or no agreement) because of the frame (the amount of money I will pay for a beer from a run-down grocery store) that is placed on the choices rather than an objective assessment of what the beer is worth to the individual.

In addition, framing has important implications for the tactics that negotiators use. The framing effect suggests that to induce concessionary behavior from an opponent, a negotiator should always create anchors or emphasize referents that lead the opposition to a positive frame and couch the negotiation in terms of what the other side has to gain.

In addition, the negotiator should make the inherent risk salient to the opposition while the opponent is in a risky situation. If the sure gain that is being proposed is rejected, there is no certainty about the quality of the next offer. Simultaneously, the negotiator should also not be persuaded by similar arguments from opponents. Maintaining a risk-neutral or risk-seeking perspective in evaluating an opponent's proposals may, in the worst case, reduce the probability of reaching an agreement; however, if agreements are reached, the outcomes are more likely to be of greater value to the negotiator.

An important component in creating good negotiated agreements is to avoid the pitfalls of being framed while, simultaneously, understanding the impact of positively and negatively framing your negotiating opponent. However, framing is just one of a series of cognitive biases that can have a significant negative impact on the performance of negotiators. The purpose of this article was to describe the impact of one of these cognitive biases on negotiator behavior by considering the available research on the topic and to explore ways to reduce the problems associated with framing. By increasing our understanding of the subtle ways in which these cognitive biases can reduce the effectiveness of our negotiations, managers can begin to improve not only the quality of agreements for themselves but also fashion agreements that more efficiently allocate the available resources—leaving both parties and the communities of which they are a part better off.

ENDNOTES

This article is based on the book by Bazerman, M. H., & Neale, M. A., *Negotiating Rationally* (New York: Free Press, 1992).

1. Adapted from J. E. Russo & P. J. Schoemaker, *Decision traps* (New York: Doubleday, 1989).

2. R. Thaler, "Using Mental Accounting in a Theory of Purchasing Behavior," *Marketing Science,* 4, 1985, 12–13.

3. M. A. Neale & M. H. Bazerman, "The Effects of Framing and Negotiator Overconfidence," *Academy of Management Journal,* 28, 1985, 34–49.

4. M. H. Bazerman, T. Magliozzi, & M. A. Neale, "The Acquisition of an Integrative Response in a Competitive Market Simulation," *Organizational Behavior and Human Performance,* 34, 1985, 294–313.

5. See, for example, Bazerman, Magliozzi, & Neale (1985), op. cit.; Neale and Bazerman, (1985), op. cit.; or M. A. Neale & G. B. Northcraft, "Experts, Amateurs and Refrigerators: Comparing Expert and Amateur Decision Making on a Novel Task," *Organizational Behavior and Human Decision Processes,* 38, 1986, 305–17; M. A. Neale, V. L. Huber, & G. B. Northcraft, "The Framing of Negotiations: Context Versus Task Frames," *Organizational Behavior and Human Decision Processes,* 39, 1987, 228–41.

6. D. Kahneman, J. L. Knetsch, & R. Thaler, "Experimental Tests of the Endowment Effect and Coarse Theorem," *Journal of Political Economy,* 1990.

7. The coffee mugs were valued at approximately $5.00.

8. Bazerman et al., (1985), op.cit.; M. A. Neale, V. L. Huber, & G. B. Northcraft, (1987), op. cit.

How to Frame a Message: The Art of Persuasion and Negotiation

Lyle Sussman

If the management mantra of the 1990s was "Do more with less," the mantra for the new millennium will be "Do *even* more with *even* less." Managers must accept the reality that the competition for external customers will be reflected in increasing competition for internal resources. More and more, managers will feel the antagonistic forces of requests from team members for increased resources and pressure from senior staff to curb those requests and conserve those resources.

The major implication of this scenario is that those managers who thrive will both implicitly understand the importance of negotiation and manifest the skills of effective persuasion. They will view the firm as a "marketplace" where ideas are "bought and sold." Rather than bemoaning their fate, they will learn to sell their proposals and overcome any objections others might raise.

The good news for consultants, in-house trainers, and managers is that management literature offers an ever-expanding body of theoretical models and practical strategies that provide a solid foundation for designing in-house training programs and crafting personalized coaching tips. However, scanning this work results in a troubling conclusion. Although most of the literature underscores the importance of *framing the argument* or position one is trying to sell, there is precious little how-to advice.

We are usually instructed to follow two parallel streams of logic. First, we are taught to frame the message based on the other party's needs and the specifics of the situation. Unfortunately, this advice is tantamount to telling an insomniac that the best cure for his problem is a good night's sleep. Exactly, but how does he get it? Yes, a frame should be based on needs and the situation; but how does one construct it?

Second, we are told to construct the message so that the listener/reader perceives it with an overarching theme, either evaluative or descriptive. Depending on the specific proposal, we might want the party to interpret the message through a filter of "good-bad," "profit-loss," or "cost-benefit." Unfortunately, this advice still is not specific enough for the manager looking for the words, phrase, or script most likely to elicit the appropriate impression.

Source: Reprinted with permission from *Business Horizons,* July–August 1999. Copyright 1999 by the Board of Trustees at Indiana University, Kelley School of Business.

We need a new and simple model designed to help managers find those words and write that script. The ability to craft frames may well be the essence of persuasion and negotiation.

THE FRAME: WHAT IT IS AND WHY IT IS IMPORTANT

A frame orients a reader or listener to examine a message with a certain disposition or inclination. Just as framing a picture focuses attention on what is enclosed *within* that frame, framing a message focuses a reader's or listener's attention on data and premises within the frame. The manager selling an idea frames the message to focus attention on what he believes and the most pivotal or salient issues. Frames help decision makers reduce the complexity of issues and make sense of their environments. When they see one problem as more urgent or more costly than another, they necessarily focus their attention and marshal corporate resources to reflect that focus. In short, the frame is neither the specific objective of the message nor the data supporting that objective, but rather a focus for assessing the total message.

The use of a frame will vary depending on the persuader's specific agenda and forum. A frame could be the title of a speech a CEO hopes will rally the troops. The CEO establishes the big picture and the perceptual filter he wants the audience to employ while listening to the message. By entitling the speech "My Vision, Your Gain," he establishes the frame by linking his corporate vision with employees' personal needs.

In a one-on-one negotiation, the frame could be stated a number of times to reinforce both its impact and the validity of the request. A manager trying to negotiate a bigger raise from her boss could present a frame during the initial stages of the "sale" and at those points at which the boss seems resistant. The manager might try to use the frame of "fairness and justice" to make her case and refer to the inequity in her current pay or the injustice of her less skilled coworkers receiving higher pay.

When we frame a message, we achieve three interrelated goals. First, we select an evaluative theme or perspective believed to be the most credible, compelling, and appropriate to our intent. That perspective provides a filter through which we want the other party to assess our position and the supporting evidence. Second, we decide on the specific evidence that best supports that perspective. Finally, we create a structure for organizing that evidence. Thus, the frame provides the *perspective* we want the other party to adopt, a *rationale* for the evidence we present, and the *sequential pattern* for presenting that evidence.

Consider this analogy. Suppose you and a colleague wagered on who could complete the same jigsaw puzzle first. A third party buys two copies of the same 350-piece puzzle, dumping the contents of both boxes on a table in front of each of you. Your opponent has access to the box with a picture of the completed puzzle. You do not. Who will win?

A frame is to a persuasive argument as the picture of a completed puzzle is to the jumbled pieces of the puzzle. Both show the "big picture" and provide implicit rules for putting the pieces together. Without the picture and without the frame, chaos prevails over coherence.

An Example: The Tough Sell

Although hypothetical, the example of Cosmos Electronics illustrates the importance of a frame and key contextual factors in trying to convey a persuasive message under difficult conditions. Cosmos is a major player in the digital communication industry. Founded with the combined genius of an electrical engineer and the savvy of a street-wise entrepreneur, Cosmos developed an international presence in less than five years from its inception. The founders still maintain day-to-day operational responsibilities and continue to take pride in the company's growth and entrepreneurial spirit.

Tanya Edwards has been at Cosmos for three years and is in charge of product development. In a weekly staff meeting, one of her team members convinces her and the other members that his idea for a breakthrough handheld digital communicator will "blow away the competition" and create a huge, long-term revenue stream for the company.

Tanya agrees to champion the cause and to solicit R&D funding from the three-person executive team that signs off on all product development requests. With help from her team, she sets her goal at obtaining $250,000 to develop a working prototype.

Tanya knows she faces a tough sell. Until recently, Cosmos had experienced a meteoric rise in stock price, sales volume, and market penetration, but the last two quarters have sent shock waves through the company. Because of greater competition and new FCC regulations affecting the product line, its stock has dropped 15 percent, sales have plateaued, and large customers are defecting. As a result, the executive committee has taken a stance of maintenance over growth.

To make matters worse, the last R&D project funded by the committee never got off the drawing board and is still referred to at Cosmos as that "$500,000 sink hole." In short, the last thing the committee wants to do is risk capital. Nevertheless, out of respect for Tanya they grudgingly agree to give her 20 minutes to make her best case.

She brings her team together and says, "You guys have to help me plan my sales pitch. We all know that they're geared to say no. We need a hook. How can we get the executive team to at least consider our proposal?" She then turns to a flip chart and says, "OK. Let's brainstorm. How do we hook 'em?" Her team members offer the following hooks:

- $250,000 is an investment, not a cost.
- $250,000 is only a small percentage of our gross margin.
- The last R&D effort was not a sink hole but a learning curve.
- Our mission and values require R&D.

This last statement generated further brainstorming related to the corporate culture, history, and philosophy of Cosmos.

After 15 minutes of bristling, energetic discussion, Tanya says, "That's it. I've got it." She then writes the following statement on the flip chart:

Our paralysis and fear is our competitor's greatest asset.

That hook (frame) quickly generated a 20-minute presentation built around three major points:

FIGURE 1   Four Steps to Framing a Message

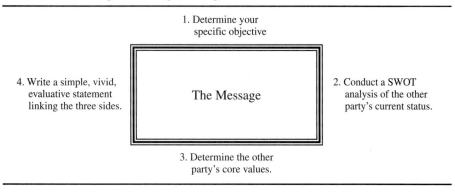

1. Determine your
specific objective

4. Write a simple, vivid,
evaluative statement
linking the three sides.

The Message

2. Conduct a SWOT
analysis of the other
party's current status.

3. Determine the other
party's core values.

1. In our competitive industry, managing for the status quo will guarantee our corporate self-destruction.
2. We created this company to bring innovation to the market. Why back off now?
3. My team's proposal for a handheld digital communicator will return us to our glory and terrify our competitors.

She made the pitch and got the funding.

Tanya's frame was specifically created for a persuasive message to the senior management team. However, it could have been incorporated into a negotiation session. Tanya might have been asked to sit down with the team to craft a negotiated compromise, a position falling somewhere between their reluctance to fund any R&D and her attempt to secure $250,000. But again, she would have tried to focus the negotiation on the belief that failure to fund her prototype would put Cosmos at a competitive disadvantage.

BUILDING A FRAME

In our hypothetical example, Tanya Edwards developed the frame for her proposal through a brainstorming session with her team. However, not all managers have access to brainstorming teams, or the skill to facilitate such a session. Moreover, brainstorming depends on the creative potential and commitment of participants, which is inherently variable. What follows are four sequential steps for building a frame regardless of one's creative potential or access to group brainstorming. These strategies reflect the metaphor presented in Figure 1.

Step 1: Determine Your Specific Objective

This step is reflected at the top of the frame in Figure 1. What specifically do you want the decision maker (person or group) to do? In the example above, the specific objective was to secure $250,000 in R&D funding from the executive committee.

There is a fundamental reason why you must begin here when constructing your frame: *All subsequent decisions about your frame are made on the basis of your specific objective.* In other words, decisions about values, threats, or opportunities are necessarily driven by what you are asking the party to do. Tanya Edwards knew she had a tough sell not only because of Cosmos's declining market position but, more important, because of her specific request relative to that decline.

Sometimes the objective (opening/bid/position) will be stated in financial terms, as demonstrated in the example. Other objectives will reflect the specific agenda of the person or group making the proposal. A manager might try to "sell" upper management on implementing flextime for his staff. Or a marketing manager might try to "sell" senior managers on a new compensation program for the field sales force.

Obviously, your objective could change during the course of the presentation, depending on the "buyer's" counter arguments. For many, if not most, in-house sales calls, the final agreement often represents a compromise between the parties. Nevertheless, without a clear way to measure success or failure, you approach the sale without a vision, direction, or purpose. Moreover, without a clear proposal to accept, negotiate, or reject, buyers will feel that their valuable time is being wasted.

2. Conduct a Focused SWOT Analysis of the Other Party's Current Status

Positioned at the right side of the frame, a SWOT (Strength, Weakness, Opportunity, and Threat) analysis is a fundamental tool in corporate strategic planning. Once planners have conducted a SWOT analysis, they are in a position to articulate the mission, strategy, and objectives of the organization. The logic of SWOT also provides a powerful tool for framing your message. You are trying to persuade a specific person or group at a certain point in time. At the time of your proposal, that party possesses certain strengths and weaknesses while being buffeted by an external environment composed of threats and opportunities.

Strengths are typically defined as abilities, talents, core competencies, and resources. Weaknesses are defined as a deficiency in or lack of same. When you analyze other parties' strengths and weaknesses, you answer a basic question: What makes them strong and what makes them weak?

Opportunities and threats denote the external environment affecting the party. Any force in the environment that enhances the party's ability to perform represents an opportunity. Examples include favorable economic conditions, positive customer relations, and brand loyalty. On the other hand, any force that diminishes the party's ability to perform is a threat. Examples include poor economic conditions, customer defection, and increasing competition. Opportunities represent potential gain, threats potential loss.

The goal of a SWOT analysis is to develop strategies that (*a*) make the most of organizational strengths and external opportunities and/or (*b*) minimize internal weaknesses and external threats. Although Tanya Edwards did not explicitly ask her team to conduct a SWOT analysis, they created a frame that implicitly addressed Cosmos's internal weaknesses and external threats. What her team accomplished implicitly and serendipitously, you can accomplish deliberately and explicitly.

The major guideline for completing step 2 is to focus on *the most significant element* in each of four SWOT dimensions. Thus, rather than searching exhaustively for all strengths, weaknesses, opportunities and threats, focus on the most significant of them. Follow the 80-20 rule: What single issue or factor provides the greatest insight into each of the four SWOT dimensions?

3. Determine the Other Party's Core Values

This step is shown at the bottom of Figure 1. Values reflect character, motives, and behavior. What underlying principles guide the other party's behavior? What values do they cherish? What basic beliefs about themselves and others direct their actions? When you answer these questions, you have determined the values affecting the buyer's decision.

Values may be demonstrated directly (explicitly) or indirectly (implicitly). Examples of the former include personal or corporate mission statements, slogans or posters, and overt comments (written or spoken) expressing values and beliefs. For some individuals and groups, however, the values are implicit and must be inferred. Examples here include unstated norms, attitudes toward working conditions, and personal appearance.

One useful technique for developing a frame based on analyzing core values is to demonstrate any inconsistency between what other parties espouse and how they actually behave. This technique is an application of Festinger's (1957) cognitive dissonance theory. If you are able to frame your message by demonstrating a contradiction between stated values and actual behavior, you have tapped into a powerful persuasive technique. Tanya Edwards and her team crafted a frame that highlighted Cosmos's espoused belief in the importance of entrepreneurship while running daily operations contrary to that belief. The company "talked" competition and entrepreneurship, but "walked" fear and conservatism.

4. Write a Simple, Vivid, Evaluative Statement That Links Steps 1, 2, and 3

This final step is represented at the left side of Figure 1. The statement Tanya Edwards wrote on the flip chart that both summarized and synthesized the team's brainstorming session met the three defining characteristics of step 4.

Simple: The statement was only a single sentence, without adverbial clauses or complex construction. It contained only nine words. If the statement of your frame has more than 15 words, it is probably too complex and too long.

Vivid: Suppose Tanya had written the following statement on the flip chart:

> Our inability to take decisive action and our apparent trepidation are weaknesses that our competitors can use to our disadvantage.

Although this statement is close in meaning to the actual statement, its *psychological impact* is not. (Moreover, it is 20 words long.) Tanya's statement used the words "paralysis," "fear," and "asset," all of which carry an emotional punch. Choose words that are not only heard or read but also *felt*. There is a simple test to determine whether or not your frame is vivid: Can the other party remember the exact wording two hours after you presented it?

Evaluative: The frame must orient a decision maker to assess information from the specific perspective that casts the most favorable light on your proposal.

Depending on your specific objective, the statement of your frame could prepare your reader or listener to judge subsequent arguments and evidence as representing a position on either end of the following value dichotomies: good-bad, right-wrong, smart-stupid, risky-conservative.

In constructing the frame along an evaluative dimension, recognize that the valence of the statement may be implicit rather than explicit. For example, Tanya Edwards did not use the words "good," "bad," "right," "wrong," "smart," or "stupid" in her statement. She used connotation rather than denotation to create the intended valence.

Link steps 1, 2, and 3: Tanya's goal was to obtain R&D funding. Her team implicitly recognized the company's external threats and internal weaknesses. Finally, their statement reflected a mismatch between an espoused value of entrepreneurship and daily actions motivated by fear.

Because the frame must meet the three characteristics of simplicity, vividness, and evaluation, the third characteristic will necessarily produce a statement that intimates and suggests. In other words, the best frames *imply* the specific request, the SWOT analysis, and value assessment, rather than *explicitly* elaborating them. If the frame were to explicitly elaborate the top, right side, and bottom, the statement of the frame might be longer than the message itself. Recall the definition presented earlier. The frame is not a request. Rather, it is the theme, focus, or perceptual set you want the other party to accept or adopt.

Just as there is a test for the frame's vividness, there is also a test for its ability to link steps 1, 2, and 3. If the frame raises thoughtful questions and introspection rather than immediate dismissal, it passes the test.

A popular negotiation skills program builds its promotional materials on the following ad copy: "You don't get what you deserve; you get what you negotiate." We can take this ad copy one step further. Effective negotiators do more than simply ask for what they want; they frame what they ask. The model and four steps presented in this article will not guarantee that all your proposals will be accepted or funded. However, these steps will increase the probability that your proposal will be considered. And without consideration, there can be no acceptance.

REFERENCES

Jay Conger, "The Necessary Art of Persuasion," *Harvard Business Review,* May–June 1998, pp. 85–95.

Jane E. Dutton and Susan E. Ashford, "Selling Issues to Top Management," *Academy of Management Review,* July 1993, pp. 397–410.

S. E Dutton and S. Jackson, "Categorizing Strategic Issues: Links to Organizational Action," *Academy of Management Review,* 12 (1987): 76–90.

K. Eisenhardt, "Making Fast Decisions in High-Velocity Environments," *Academy of Management Journal,* 32 (1989): 543–76.

A. Festinger, *Theory of Cognitive Dissonance* (Stanford, CA: Stanford University Press, 1957).

Terri Fine, "The Impact of Issue Framing on Public Opinion: Toward Affirmative Action Programs," *Social Science Journal,* 29, No. 3 (1992): 323–35.

A. Margaret Neale and Max Bazerman, "The Effects of Framing and Negotiator Overconfidence on Bargaining Behaviors and Outcomes," *Academy of Management Journal,* 28 (1985): 34.

W. K. Schilit and F. J. Paine, "Are Examinations of the Underlying Dynamics of Strategic Decision Subject to Upward Influence Activity?" *Journal of Management Studies,* 24 (1986): 161–87.

Psychological Traps

Jeffrey Z. Rubin

You place a phone call and are put on hold. You wait. And then you wait some more. Should you hang up? Perhaps. After all, why waste another second of your valuable time? On the other hand, if you hang up you'll only have to call again to accomplish whatever business put you on the phone in the first place. Anyway, you've already spent all this time on hold, so why give up now? So you wait some more. At some point you finally resign yourself to the likelihood that you've been left on hold forever. Even as you hang up, though, your ear remains glued to the receiver, hoping to the bitter end that all the time spent waiting was not in vain.

Almost all of us have spent too much time caught in little traps like that. Even when it no longer makes sense, we continue to spend money on a failing automobile or washing machine, on an aging and decrepit house, a risky stock investment, or a doubtful poker hand. We simply to not know when to cut our losses and get out. And the same goes for more serious situations. Some of us remain longer than we should in a marriage or love relationship, a job or career, a therapy that is yielding diminishing returns. On a grander scale, entrapment is part of the dynamic in political controversies—Abscam, Watergate, the war in Vietnam.

A common set of psychological issues and motivations underlies all such situations, a process of entrapment that shares many of the characteristics of animal traps and con games and has been studied in a variety of laboratory and natural settings. As researchers, we are attempting to describe the properties of psychological traps: what they have in common, where they lurk, whom they tend to snare, and how they can be avoided.

When I was growing up in New York City there was a cunning little device that we called the Chinese Finger Trap—a woven straw cylinder about three or four inches long, with an opening at each end just large enough for a child's finger to be inserted. Once you put a finger into each end, the trap was sprung. The harder you tugged in opposite directions in an effort to get free, the more the woven cylinder stretched and pulled tight around each finger. Only by pushing inward, by moving *counter* to the direction in which escape appeared to lie, could you get free. So it is with entrapping situations. The tighter one pulls, the greater the conflict between the lure of the goal and the increasing

Source: Reprinted with permission from *Psychology Today* Magazine, copyright © 1981 Sussex Publishers, Inc.

cost of remaining in pursuit of it. And the tighter one pulls, the greater the trap's bite. Only by letting go at some point can the trap be escaped. Or, as the Chinese philosopher Lao-tzu put it: "Those who would conquer must yield; and those who conquer do so because they yield."

To understand psychological entrapment, we must first understand the simplest traps of all—physical traps for animals. Some time rather early in the evolution of our species, human beings came to understand that the active pursuit of quarry by hunting was often impractical or undesirable. Thus, trapping was invented. A trap allows hunters to outwit their quarry, to offset any advantage that the quarry may have by virtue of its greater power, speed, or the limited destructive capacity of the hunters' weapons. An animal trap accomplishes these ends in a strikingly simple and clever way: it brings the quarry to the hunter rather than the other way around. Instead of continuing to hunt for quarry, often in vain and at considerable cost, trappers get the quarry to catch itself. Once set, the animal trap takes on a life of its own, a surrogate hunter waiting with infinite patience for the quarry to make the unwise choice. The consequence of having this surrogate is that hunters' limited resources can now be devoted to other pursuits, including the construction of additional traps.

Ingenious devices, these animal traps, devilishly clever and efficient—and utterly sinister in their effect on the victims who fall prey to them. What properties, then, make them work?

First of all, an effective trap must be able to lure or distract the quarry into behaving in ways that risk its self-preservation. Often this important first step is accomplished with some form of bait that is so tantalizingly attractive, so well suited to the quarry's particular needs, that the animal is induced to pursue it, oblivious to the trap's jaws.

Second, an effective animal trap permits traffic in one direction only. It is far easier for a lobster to push its way through the cone-shaped net into the lobster trap than, once in, to claw its way out. The bait that motivated the quarry to enter the trap in the first place obscures the irreversibility of that move. Doors that yield easily, inviting the quarry's entry, slam shut with a vengeance.

Third, an effective trap is often engineered so that the quarry's very efforts to escape entrap it all the more. The bear's considerable strength, applied in an effort to pull its paw from a trap, only sinks the trap's teeth deeper into its flesh. A fish's tendency to swim away from anything that constrains its free movement only deepens the bite of the hook. An effective trap thus invites the quarry to become the source of its own entrapment or possible destruction.

Finally, an effective animal trap must be suited to the particular attributes of the quarry it is designed to capture. One cannot catch a guppy with a lobster trap or a mosquito with a butterfly net. Consider the awful and awesomely effective nineteenth century American wolf trap. The simplicity and frightening elegance of this trap is that it depends on the wolf's appetite for the taste of blood. A bloodied knife blade was left to freeze in the winter ice. While licking the knife, the wolf would cut its tongue and begin to bleed. It would then start to lick at the knife all the more, which in turn led to a greater flow of blood—and the wolf's ultimate undoing. The animal's blood attracted other wolves, who then attacked the victim and, eventually, one another. Thus a whole pack of wolves could be destroyed with just one trap.

Confidence games are psychological traps for capturing people and are remarkably similar to self-entrapment. Like animal traps, they rely for their effectiveness on the trapper's (con artist's) ability to lure the quarry (mark) into a course of action that becomes entrapping. The lure is typically based on the mark's cupidity; the fat, wriggling worm is the tempting possibility of getting something for nothing, a big killing that appears to happen at the expense of someone else.

The effective con also depends on the mark's willingness to cheat another person in order to reap large and easy profits. As a result, the mark's progressive pursuit of the lure tends to obscure the fact that the path taken is not easily reversible. With the con artist's kind assistance, the mark is increasingly rendered a coconspirator in a crime against another, a bit like Macbeth: "I am in blood/stepp'd so far that, should I wade no more,/Returning were as tedious as go o'er."

In addition, the mark's very efforts to escape—by making a quick, glorious, and final big killing before quitting once and for all—only lead to deeper entrapment. The more money the mark is persuaded to put up in this effort, the more carefully he or she is apt to guard the investment—and to justify it through the commitment of additional resources.

Finally, just as an animal trap is tailored to its quarry, so must a con be geared to the brand of avarice and dishonesty of the mark. "Different traps for different saps" is the rule.

There are two kinds of cons: so-called short cons, such as Three-Card Monte or the Shell Game, in which the mark is fleeced for a few dollars on the spot; and big cons, in which the mark is directed to a "big store"—a place where the con is played out. Big cons reached their heyday around the turn of the nineteenth century in this country and lined the pockets of skilled con artists with hundreds of thousands of dollars. Big cons included the Rag, the Pay-Off, and the Wire, the last of these made famous by Paul Newman and Robert Redford in *The Sting*. In that con, a mark was persuaded that horse-race results had been delayed long enough for him to place a bet *after* the race had been run, thereby betting on a sure thing. The con took place in a large ground-floor room, rented for a week as the big store. All the roles in the drama, save that of the mark, were played by confederates creating an elaborate and complex ruse.

These steps or stages involved in most big cons are remarkably consistent:

1. "Putting the mark up"—finding the right person to fleece.
2. "Playing the con"—befriending the mark and gaining the mark's confidence.
3. "Roping the mark"—steering the victim to the "inside man," the person who is in charge of running the big store.
4. "Telling the tale"—giving the inside man an opportunity to show the mark how a large sum of money can be made dishonestly.
5. "Giving the convincer"—allowing the mark to make a substantial profit in a test run of the swindle.
6. "Giving the breakdown"—setting the mark up to invest a large sum of money for the final killing.
7. "Putting the mark on the send"—sending the mark home for that amount of money.

8. "The sting"—fleecing the mark in the big store.
9. "Blowing the mark off"—getting the mark out of the way as quickly and quietly as possible.

In psychological entrapment, one person may simultaneously play the role of roper, inside man, and mark. In so doing, we manage to ensnare ourselves. As with physical and psychological devices for capturing others, these traps only work when people are, first and foremost, interested in—and distracted by—the lure of some goal. Final victory in Vietnam, a happy marriage, a big killing at the gambling table, or simply the return of the person who pushed the hold button: all may be viewed as worthy goals—or as bait that conceals a dangerous hook. In entrapping situations, marks initially look in one direction only—forward—as they pursue the mirage of a goal that lies just beyond their grasp.

In their single-minded rush toward the objective, marks neglect the possibility that they are being sucked into a funnel from which escape may prove remarkably difficult. The first stage of entrapment—eager, forward-looking pursuit of one's goal—is thus followed by attention to the costs that have been unwittingly incurred along the way. The compulsive gambler's drive for a killing is inevitably followed by attention to the mounting costs of the pursuit, costs that in turn need to be justified by greater commitment. Similarly, when our personal or professional lives are disappointing—and our efforts to achieve a turnaround do not pay off quickly enough—we may decide to justify the high cost by renewing our commitment and remaining on the treadmill.

But notice that the more resources committed to attaining the goal, the greater the trap's bite. Each additional step toward a rewarding but unattained goal creates new and greater costs, requiring greater justification of the course of action than ever before. With each additional year that a person remains in a dissatisfying job, hoping it will take a turn for the better, he or she feels more compelled to rationalize the time invested by remaining in the job even longer.

In certain entrapping situations, those in which several people are competing with one another, reward pursuit and cost justification are followed by a third stage, in which people try to make sure that their competitors end up losing at least as much—if not more—than they. Like two children in a breath-holding contest or two nations in an arms race, many entrapping situations evolve to the point where each side's focus is no longer on winning or even on minimizing losses, but on getting even with the adversary who engineered the mess.

In the last major stage of entrapment, marks must finally let go, either because their resources are gone, because they are rescued by another person, or because they recognize the desperation of the pursuit. Just as the Chinese Finger Trap can be escaped only by pushing inward, entrapment can be avoided only by letting go.

One devilishly simple and effective example of entrapment is a game known as the Dollar Auction, invented about 10 years ago by Martin Shubik, an economist at Yale. As his proving ground, Shubik allegedly used the Yale University cocktail-party circuit. Anyone can make some money—but perhaps lose some friends—by trying it out at a party.

Take a dollar bill from your pocket and announce that you will auction it off to the highest bidder. People will be invited to call out bids in multiples of five cents until no further bidding occurs, at which point the highest bidder will pay the amount bid and win the dollar. The only feature that distinguishes this auction from traditional auctions, you point out, is the rule that the *second-highest* bidder will also be asked to pay the amount bid, although he or she will obviously not win the dollar. For example, Susan has bid 30 cents and Bill has bid 25 cents; if the bidding stops at this point, you will pay Susan 70 cents ($1 minus the amount she bid), and Bill, the second-highest bidder, will have to pay you 25 cents. The auction ends when one minute has elapsed without any additional bidding.

If my own experience is any indication, the game is likely to follow a general pattern. One person bids a nickel, another bids a dime, someone else jumps the bidding to a quarter or so, and the bidding proceeds at a fast and furious pace until about 50 or 60 cents is reached. At around that point, the number of people calling out bids begins to decrease, and soon there are only three or four people still taking part. The bidding continues, at a somewhat slower pace, until the two highest bids are at about $1 and 95 cents. There is a break in the action at this point, as the two remaining bidders seem to consider what has happened and whether they should continue. Suddenly the person who bid 95 cents calls out $1.05, and the bidding resumes. Soon the two remaining bidders have escalated matters so far that both bids are over $4. Then one of the guests suddenly escalates the bidding by offering $5, the other (who has already bid $4.25 or so) refuses to go any higher, and the game ends. You proceed to collect $4.25 from the loser and $4 from the "winner."

Several researchers have had people play the Dollar Auction game under controlled laboratory conditions and have found that the participants typically end up bidding far in excess of the $1 prize at stake, sometimes paying as much as $5 or $6 for a dollar bill. The interesting question is, of course, why? What motivates people to bid initially and to persist in a self-defeating course of action?

Thanks primarily to the extensive research of Allan Teger, a social psychologist at Boston University, the question has been answered. Teger found that when Dollar Auction participants were asked to give reasons for their bidding, their responses fell into one of two major motivational categories: economic and interpersonal. Economic motives include a desire to win the dollar, a desire to regain losses, and a desire to avoid losing more money. Interpersonal motives include a desire to save face, a desire to prove one is the best player, and a desire to punish the other person.

Economic motives appear to predominate in the early stages of the Dollar Auction. People begin bidding with the hope of winning the dollar bill easily and inexpensively. Their bids increase a little bit at a time, in the expectation that their latest bid will prove to be the winning one. If the other participants reason the same way, however, the bidding escalates. At some subsequent point in the Dollar Auction, the bidders begin to realize that they have been drawn into an increasingly treacherous situation.. Acknowledging that they have already invested a portion of their own resources in the auction, they begin to pay particular attention to the amount they stand to lose if they come in second. As the bidding approaches $1—or when the amount invested equals the objective worth of the prize—the tension rises. At this stage, Teger has found, the participants experience intense inner conflict, as measured by physiological measures of anxiety and nervousness; about half of them then quit the game.

People who remain in the auction past the $1 bid, however, typically stick with it to the bitter end—until they have exhausted their resources or their adversary has quit. Interpersonal motives come to the fore when the bid exceeds the objective value of the prize. Even though both players know they are sure to lose, each may go out of his or her way to punish the other, making sure that the other person loses even more, and each may become increasingly concerned about looking foolish by yielding to the adversary's aggression. Teger found that this mutual concern occasionally leads bidders to a cooperative solution to the problem of how to quit without losing face: a bid of $1 by one player, if followed by a quick final raise to $2 by the second, allows the first person to quit in the knowledge that both have lost equally.

If entrapping situations are as ubiquitous and powerful as I have suggested, how do people ever avoid getting into them? What, if anything, can people do to keep from getting in deeper? Over the past six years or so, I have been working with a research group at Tufts University to find some answers to these questions. We have conducted most of our research in the laboratory, using the Dollar Auction and several other procedures. We have begun to study entrapment in naturalistic settings, by holding contests in which residents of the Boston area, chosen at random, are invited to solve a series of increasingly difficult problems that require more and more of their time.

In one experimental model, people were invited to pay for the ticks of a numerical counter in the hope that they would obtain a jackpot—either by reaching the number that had been randomly generated by computer of by outlasting an adversary. A second laboratory paradigm challenged people to solve a jigsaw puzzle correctly within a limited period; if they succeeded, they received a cash jackpot, but if they failed, they had to pay for the number of pieces they had requested. Finally, in a third type of experiment, undergraduates were instructed to wait for an experimenter or another participant to arrive at the laboratory so that they could receive a research credit; naturally, the experimenter was always late, and the subjects had to continually decide how much longer they would wait.

In one such experiment, Tufts undergraduates were seated in individual rooms, given $2.50 in cash for agreeing to come to our laboratory and invited to win an additional $10 jackpot by solving a crossword puzzle. The puzzle consisted of 10 words of varying difficulty, 8 or more of which had to be correctly solved in order to win the jackpot. Each student was given three "free" minutes to work on the puzzle; after that, 25 cents was deducted from the initial $2.50 stake for each additional minute. People could quit the experiment at any point and leave with their initial stake—minus 25 cents for each minute they remained in the study past the first three. If they remained in the study after 13 minutes had passed, they had to begin paying out of their own pockets, since their initial stake was exhausted at that point. The study was stopped after 15 minutes.

Almost everyone found the puzzle too difficult to solve without the aid of a crossword-puzzle dictionary, which they were told was available on request. Participants were also told that because there were two people working on the puzzle and only one dictionary, it would be available on a first-come, first-served basis. (No such dictionary was actually available.) When students requested the dictionary, they had to turn their puzzles face down, so they were not able to wait for the dictionary and work on the puzzle at the same time. Surprisingly, nearly 20 percent of the students stayed in the experiment the full 15 minutes.

We investigated several important influences on the entrapment process here. First, we created either a competitive or noncompetitive relationship between the participants by telling the students either that the $10 jackpot would be awarded to the first person who solved the puzzle or that it would go to anyone who was able to do so. We found that students who believed they were in a competition became more entrapped—they played the game far longer and spent more of their money—than those not in competition.

We also studied the nature of the investment process by giving participants different instructions about quitting the experiment. Some were told that they could quit at any time. Others were advised that the experimenter would ask them every three minutes if they wished to continue. We expected that the experimenter's intervention would serve as an indirect reminder of the cost of continued participation and that those students who were spoken to would become less entrapped than the others. That is exactly what happened. Students who were not asked if they wished to continue remained in the experiment far longer and, as a group, lost more than twice as much money.

In all of our experiments, as in the one described above, we encourage subjects to move toward some rewarding goal, while we increase the time or money they must invest in it and give them the option to quit at any time. Both our research and Teger's reveal certain repeating themes in the behavior of the participants, which I can summarize in the form of some advice on how to avoid entrapment.

- *Set limits on your involvement and commitment in advance.* We find that people who are not asked to indicate the limits of their participation become more entrapped than those who do indicate a limit, especially publicly. Depending on the entrapping situation you are in, you may wish to set a limit based on your past experience (for example, the average time you've spent waiting on hold); your available resources (the amount of time or money you have left to spend); the importance of reaching your goal on this occasion (you may be able to call later to make a plane reservation); and the possibility of reaching your goal in some other way (using a travel agent to make the reservation).

- *Once you set a limit, stick to it.* We all play little games with ourselves—we flip a coin to make a decision and then when we don't like the result, decide to make the contest two out of three flips. We set limits that are subsequently modified, shaded, and shifted as we get close to the finish. Each new investment, like the addition of an AM/FM radio to a new car that has already been decked out with extras, tends to be evaluated not in relation to zero (the total cost of the investment) but in relation to that inconsequential, minuscule increment above and beyond the amount we've already agreed to spend. If you're the sort of person who has trouble adhering to limits, get some help. Find a friend, tell him or her the limit you wish to set, and have your friend rope you in when you get to the end of your self-appointed tether. Ulysses used that method to resist the deadly temptation of the Sirens' wail.

- *Avoid looking to other people to see what you should do.* It's one thing to use a friend to rope you in, and it's another matter entirely to deal with your uncertainty about what to do by sheepishly following others. Given the uncertainty in entrapping situations, it is tempting to look to others for clues about the appropriateness of one's own behavior. Our research indicates that the presence and continued involvement of another person in an entrapping situation increases one's own entrapment, and that this occurs even when the behavior of each person has no effect on the other's fate. Proprietors of Las Vegas gambling casinos know what they're doing when they use shills to "prime the pump" and get the gambler's competitive juices flowing. Similarly one is far more likely to continue waiting for a bus that has not yet arrived—and even wait for an outrageous, irrationally long time—if other people are also waiting.

- *Beware of your need to impress others.* Other people are not only a source of information about what to do in entrapping situations; they are also a critically important source of praise or disapproval for our behavior. We all want to be liked, loved, and respected by people whose opinions matter to us. This motive is perfectly healthy and often appropriate, but not in entrapping situations. Our research shows that people become more entrapped when they believe their effectiveness is being judged and scrutinized by others. This is particularly powerful when the perceived evaluation occurs early in the game, and diminishes in importance if evaluative observers are introduced later on. We also find that people who are especially anxious about their appearance in the eyes of others and who feel that they have something to prove by toughing things out get more entrapped than their less anxious counterparts.

- *Remind yourself of the costs involved.* Our research indicates that people are less likely to become entrapped when they are made aware early on of the costs associated with continued participation. Even the availability of a chart that depicts investment costs is sufficient to reduce entrapment. The new effect of such information about costs is to offset the distracting, shimmering lure of the goal ahead—especially if the cost information is introduced right away. If you don't start paying attention to the cost of your involvement until fairly late in the game, you may feel compelled to justify those costs by investing even more of your resources.

- *Remain vigilant.* Entrapping situations seem to sneak up on us. People who understand and avoid one brand of trap often manage to get caught in others with surprising frequency and ease. Just because you knew when to bail out of that lousy stock investment doesn't mean that you will have the good sense to give up on an unsatisfactory relationship or a profession in which you feel you have too much invested to quit. Obviously, people who are told about entrapment and its dangers are less likely to become entrapped. Our studies also show that being forewarned about one kind of trap, moreover, can put people on guard against other kinds of traps.

Although very little is known at this point about the kinds of people who tend to get entrapped, we have recently begun to study this issue and can therefore engage in a bit of informed speculation. First, people who go for bait are also likely to end up hooked. Those who are exceptionally ambitious or greedy or unusually self-confident and self-assured about their ability to reach a goal must tread warily. There may be icebergs lurking in those calm and glassy seas ahead. Second, the sort of person who believes that he should—indeed must—profit according to his efforts may also be ripe for the plucking. Those who tend to trust excessively in a just world, who think that people get what they deserve and deserve what they get, may end up caught in a version of the Chinese Finger Trap. They use their belief in justice to rationalize continued investments—and so tighten the noose all the more. Finally, the man or woman who tends to get swept up in macho ideology, who feels that nothing else applies, is also especially vulnerable to entrapment. Such people may be willing to invest more and more in order to avoid some small embarrassment—only to suffer greater humiliation in the final reckoning.

Despite cautionary advice, we all still manage to get ourselves entrapped. When the inevitable happens, when you find yourself asking "What have I done?" remember there are times when the wisest course may be to quit, not fight. There may just not be a way of salvaging the time, effort, money, even the human lives that have gone into a particular sinking ship. Know when to give it up, when to push rather than pull those fingers, and when to yield and wait for victory another day. For there is almost always another day, despite our proclivity for ignoring that fact.

The Behavior of Successful Negotiators

Neil Rackham

BACKGROUND

Almost all publications about negotiating behavior fall into one of three classes:

1. Anecdotal "here's how I do it" accounts by successful negotiators. These have the advantage of being based on real life but the disadvantage that they frequently describe highly personal modes of behavior which are a risky guide for would-be negotiators to follow.

2. Theoretical models of negotiating which are idealized, complex, and seldom translatable into practical action.

3. Laboratory studies, which tend to be short term and contain a degree of artificiality.

Very few studies have investigated what actually goes on face-to-face during a negotiation. Two reasons account for this lack of published research. First, real negotiators are understandably reluctant to let a researcher watch them at work. Such research requires the consent of both negotiating parties and constitutes a constraint on a delicate situation. The second reason for the poverty of research in this area is lack of methodology. Until recently there were few techniques available which allowed an observer to collect data on the behavior of negotiators without the use of cumbersome and unacceptable methods such as questionnaires.

Since 1968 a number of studies have been carried out by Neil Rackham of Huthwaite Research Group, using behavior analysis methods. These have allowed direct observation during real negotiations, so that an objective and quantified record can be collected to show how the skilled negotiator behaves.

THE SUCCESSFUL NEGOTIATOR

The basic methodology for studying negotiating behavior is simple—find some successful negotiators and watch them to discover how they do it. But what is the criterion for a successful negotiator? The Rackham studies used three success criteria:

1. He should be rated as effective by both sides. This criterion enabled the researchers to identify likely candidates for further study. The condition that both sides should agree on a negotiator's effectiveness was a precaution to prevent picking a sample from a single frame of reference.
2. He should have a track record of significant success. The central criterion for choosing effective negotiators was track record over a time period. In such a complex field the researchers were anxious for evidence of consistency. They also wished to avoid the common trap of laboratory studies—looking only at the short-term consequences of a negotiator's behavior and therefore favoring those using tricks or deceptions.
3. He should have a low incidence of implementation failures. The researchers judged that the purpose of a negotiation was not just to reach an agreement but to reach an agreement that would be viable. Therefore, in addition to a track record of agreements, the record of implementation was also studied to ensure that any agreements reached were successfully implemented.

A total of 48 negotiators were picked who met all of these three success criteria. The breakdown of the sample was

Industrial (Labor) Relations Negotiators	
Union representatives	17
Management representatives	12
Contract negotiators	10
Others	9

Altogether the 48 successful negotiators were studied over a total of 102 separate negotiating sessions. For the remainder of this document these people are called the "skilled" group. In comparison, a group of negotiators who either failed to meet the criteria or about whom no criterion data was available were also studied. These were called the "average" group. By comparing the behavior of the two groups, it was possible to isolate the crucial behaviors which made the skilled negotiators different.

THE RESEARCH METHOD

The researchers met the negotiator before the negotiation and encouraged her/him to talk about his/her planning and his/her objectives. For 56 sessions with the skilled negotiators and 37 sessions with the average negotiators this planning session was either tape-recorded or extensive notes were taken.

The negotiator then introduced the researcher into the actual negotiation. The delicacy of this process can be judged from the fact that although most cases had been carefully prehandled, the researchers were not accepted in upward of 20 instances and were asked to withdraw.

During the negotiation the researcher counted the frequency with which certain key behaviors were used by the negotiators, using behavior analysis methods. In all of the 102 sessions interaction data was collected, while in 66 sessions content analysis was also obtained.

HOW THE SKILLED NEGOTIATOR PLANS

Negotiation training emphasizes the importance of planning. How does the skilled negotiator plan?

Amount of Planning Time

No significant difference was found between the total planning time which skilled and average negotiators claimed they spent prior to actual negotiation. This finding must be viewed cautiously because, unlike the other conclusions in this document, it is derived from the negotiator's impressions of themselves, not from their actual observed behavior. Nevertheless, it suggests the conclusion that it is not the amount of planning time which makes for success, but how that time is used.

Exploration of Options

The skilled negotiator considers a wider range of outcomes or options for action than the average negotiator.

Outcomes/Options Considered during Planning (per negotiable issue)	
Skilled negotiator	5.1
Average negotiator	2.6

The skilled negotiator is concerned with the whole spectrum of possibilities, both those which s/he could introduce himself and those which might be introduced by the people s/he negotiates with. In contrast, the average negotiator considers few options. An impression of the researchers, for which, unfortunately, no systematic data was collected, is that the average negotiator is especially less likely to consider options which might be raised by the other party.

Common Ground

Does the skilled negotiator concentrate during his/her planning on the areas which hold most potential for conflict, or does s/he give his/her attention to possible areas of common ground? The research showed that although both groups of negotiators tended to concentrate on the conflict areas, the skilled negotiators gave over three times as much attention to common ground areas as did average negotiators.

Skilled negotiators—38% of comments about areas of anticipated agreement or common ground

Average negotiators—11% of comments about areas of anticipated agreement or common ground

This is a significant finding and it can be interpreted in a variety of ways. It may be, for example, that the skilled negotiator has already built a climate of agreement so that undue concentration on conflict is unnecessary. Equally, concentration on the common-ground areas may be the key to building a satisfactory climate in the first place. A relatively high concentration on common-ground areas is known to be an effective strategy from other Huthwaite Research Group studies of persuasion, notably with "pull" styles of persuasion in selling.

In any event, a potential negotiator wishing to model himself on successful performers would do well to pay special attention to areas of anticipated common ground and not just to areas of conflict.

Long-Term or Short-Term?

It is often suggested that skilled negotiators spend much of their planning time considering the long-term implications of the issues, while unskilled negotiators concentrate on the short term. Is this in practice? The studies found that both groups showed an alarming concentration on the short-term aspects of issues.

Percentage of Planning Comments about Long-Term Considerations of Anticipated Issues	
Skilled negotiators	8.5
Average negotiators	4.0

With the average negotiator, approximately 1 comment in 25 during his/her planning met our criterion of a long-term consideration, namely a comment which involved any factor extending beyond the immediate implementation of the issue under negotiation. The skilled negotiator, while showing twice as many long-term comments, still only averages 8.5 percent of his/her total recorded planning comment. These figures must necessarily be approximate, partly because of the research methods (which may have inadvertently encouraged verbalization of short-term issues) and partly because our ignorance of individual circumstances made some comments hard to classify. Even so, they demonstrate how little thought is given by most negotiators to the long-term implications of what they negotiate.

Setting Limits

The researchers asked negotiators about their objectives and recorded whether their replies referred to single-point objectives (e.g., "we aim to settle at 83p") or to a defined range (e.g., "we hope to get 37p but we would settle for a minimum of 34p"). Skilled negotiators were significantly more likely to set upper and lower limits—to plan in terms of a range. Average negotiators, in contrast, were more likely to plan their objectives around a fixed point. Although one possible explanation is that the skilled negotiator has more freedom, which gives him/her the discretion of upper and lower limits, this seems unlikely from the research. Even where the average negotiator had considerable capacity to vary the terms of an agreement, s/he usually approached the negotiation with a fixed point objective in mind. The conclusion, for would-be negotiators, is that it seems to be preferable to approach a negotiation with objectives specifying a clearly defined range rather than to base planning on an inflexible single-point objective.

Sequence and Issue Planning

The term *planning* frequently refers to a process of sequencing—putting a number of events, points, or potential occurrences into a time sequence. Critical path analysis and other forms of network planning are examples. This concept of planning, called sequence planning, works efficiently with inanimate objects, or in circumstances where the planner has real control which allows him/her to determine the sequence in which events will occur. The researchers found that average negotiators place very heavy reliance on sequence planning. So, for example, they would frequently verbalize a potential negotiation in terms like "First I'll bring up A, then lead to B, and after that I'll cover C, and finally go on to D." In order to succeed, sequence planning always requires the consent and cooperation of the other negotiating party. In many negotiations this cooperation is not forthcoming. The negotiator would begin at point A and the other party would only be interested in point D. This could put the negotiator in difficulty, requiring him/her to either mentally change gear and approach the negotiation in a sequence s/he had not planned for, or to carry through his/her original sequence, risking disinterest from the other party. In many negotiations, sequences were in themselves negotiable and it was ill-advised for the negotiator to plan on a sequence basis.

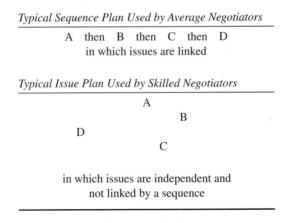

Typical Sequence Plan Used by Average Negotiators

A   then   B   then   C   then   D
in which issues are linked

Typical Issue Plan Used by Skilled Negotiators

A

B

D

C

in which issues are independent and
not linked by a sequence

They would consider issue C, for example, as if issues A, B, and D didn't exist. Compared with the average negotiators, they were careful not to draw sequence links between a series of issues. This was demonstrated by observing the number of occasions during the planning process that each negotiator mentioned sequence of issues.

Number of Mentions Implying Sequence in Planning	
Skilled negotiators	2.1 per session
Average negotiators	4.9 per session

The clear advantage of issue planning over sequence planning is flexibility. In planning a negotiation it is important to remember that the sequence of issues itself (unless a preset agenda is agreed) may be subject to negotiation. Even where an agenda exists, within a particular item, sequence planning may involve some loss of flexibility. So it seems useful for negotiators to plan their face-to-face strategy using issue planning and avoiding sequence planning.

FACE-TO-FACE BEHAVIOR

Skilled negotiators show marked differences in their face-to-face behavior, compared with average negotiators. They use certain types of behavior significantly more frequently while other types they tend to avoid.

Irritators

Certain words and phrases which are commonly used during negotiation have negligible value in persuading the other party but do cause irritation. Probably the most frequent example of these is the term *generous offer* used by a negotiator to describe his/her own proposal. Similarly, words such as *fair* or *reasonable,* and other terms with a high positive value loading, have no persuasive power when used as self-praise, while serving to irritate the other party because of the implication that they are unfair, unreasonable, and so on. Most negotiators avoid the gratuitous use of direct insults or unfavorable value judgments. They know that there is little to gain from saying unfavorable things about the other party during face-to-face exchanges. However, the other side of the coin—saying gratuitously favorable things about themselves—seems harder for them to avoid. The researchers called such words *irritators* and found that although the average negotiator used them fairly regularly, the skilled negotiator tended to avoid them.

Use of Irritators per Hour Face-to-Face Speaking Time	
Skilled negotiators	2.3
Average negotiators	10.8

It is hardly surprising that skilled negotiators use fewer irritators. Any type of verbal behavior which antagonizes without a persuasive effect is unlikely to be productive. More surprising is the heavy use of irritators by average negotiators. The conclusion must be that most people fail to recognize the counterproductive effect of using positive value judgments about themselves and, in doing so, implying negative judgments of the other party.

Counterproposals

During negotiation it frequently happens that one party puts forward a proposal and the other party immediately responds with a counterproposal. The researchers found that skilled negotiators made immediate counterproposals much less frequently than average negotiators.

Frequency of Counterproposals per Hour of Face-to-Face Speaking Time	
Skilled negotiators	1.7
Average negotiators	3.1

This difference suggests that the common strategy of meeting a proposal with a counterproposal may not be particularly effective. The disadvantages of counterproposals are:

- They introduce an additional option, sometimes a whole new issue, which complicates and clouds the clarity of the negotiation.

- They are put forward at a point where the other party has least receptiveness, being concerned with his/her own proposal.

- They are perceived as blocking or disagreeing by the other party, not as proposals. (A study of 87 controlled-pace negotiation exercises by the researchers showed that when one side in a negotiation put forth a proposal there was an 87 percent chance that the other side would perceive it as a proposal. However, if the proposal immediately followed a proposal made by the other side (if in other words it was a counterproposal) the chance of being perceived as a proposal dropped to 61 percent, with a proportionate increase in the chances of being perceived as either disagreeing or blocking.)

These reasons probably explain why the skilled negotiator is less likely to use counterproposing as a tactic than is the average negotiator.

Defend/Attack Spirals

Because negotiation frequently involves conflict, negotiators may become heated and use emotional or value-loaded behaviors. When such behavior was used to attack the other party, or to make an emotional defense, the researchers termed it *defending/attacking*. Once initiated, this behavior tended to form a spiral of increasing intensity: one negotiator would attack, the other would defend himself, usually in a manner which the first negotiator perceived as an attack. In consequence, the first negotiator attacked more vigorously and the spiral commenced. Defending and attacking were often difficult to distinguish from each other. What one negotiator perceived as a legitimate defense, the other party might see as an unwarranted attack. This was the root cause of most defending/attacking spirals observed during the studies. Average negotiators, in particular, were likely to react defensively, using comments such as "You can't blame us for that" or "It's not our fault that the present difficulty has arisen." Such comments frequently provoked a sharp defensive reaction from the other side of the table.

Percentage of Negotiators' Comments *Classified as Defending/Attacking*	
Skilled negotiators	1.9
Average negotiators	6.3

The researchers found that average negotiators used more than three times as much defending/attacking behavior as skilled negotiators. Although no quantitative measure exists, the researchers observed that skilled negotiators, if they did decide to attack, gave no warning and attacked hard. Average negotiators, in contrast, usually began their attacking gently, working their way up to more intense attacks slowly and, in doing so, causing the other party to build up its defensive behavior in the characteristic defending/attacking spiral.

Behavior Labeling

The researchers found that skilled negotiators tended to give an advance indication of the class of behavior they were about to use. So, for example, instead of just asking "How many units are there?" they would say, "Can I ask you a question—how many units are there?" giving warning that a question was coming. Instead of just making a proposal they would say, "If I could make a suggestion . . . " and then follow this advance label with their proposal. With one exception, average negotiators were significantly less likely to label their behavior in this way. The only behavior which the average negotiator was more likely to label in advance was disagreeing.

Percentage of All Negotiators' Behavior
Immediately Preceded by a Behavior Label

	Disagreeing	*All Behavior Except Disagreeing*
Skilled negotiator	0.4	6.4
Average negotiator	1.5	1.2

This is a slightly unusual finding and it may not be immediately evident why these differences should exist. The researcher's interpretation was that, in general, labeling of behavior gives the negotiator the following advantages:

- It draws the attention of the listeners to the behavior that follows. In this way social pressure can be brought to force a response.
- It slows the negotiation down, giving time for the negotiator using labeling to gather his/her thoughts and for the other party to clear his/her mind from the previous statements.
- It introduces a formality which takes away a little of the cut-and-thrust and therefore keeps the negotiation on a rational level.
- It reduces ambiguity and leads to clearer communication.

The skilled negotiator does, however, avoid labeling his or her disagreement. While the average negotiator will characteristically say "I disagree with that because of . . . ," thus labeling that s/he is about to disagree, the skilled negotiator is more likely to begin with the reasons and lead up to the disagreement.

Skilled Negotiators		
Reason/ explanation	Leading to	Statement of disagreement

Average Negotiators		
Statement of disagreement	Leading to	Reason/ explanation

If one of the functions of behavior labeling is to make a negotiator's intentions clear, then it is hardly surprising that the skilled negotiator avoids making it clear that s/he intends to disagree. S/he would normally prefer his/her reasons to be considered more neutrally so that acceptance involved minimal loss of face for the other party. But, if labeling disagreement is likely to be counterproductive, why does the average negotiator label disagreeing behavior more than all the other types of behavior put together? Most probably this tendency reflects the order in which we think. We decide that an argument we hear is unacceptable and only then do we assemble reasons to show why. The average negotiator speaks his/her disagreement in the same order as s/he thinks it—disagreement first, reasons afterward.

Testing Understanding and Summarizing

The researchers found that two behaviors with a similar function, testing understanding and summarizing, were used significantly more by the skilled negotiator. Testing understanding is a behavior which checks to establish whether a previous contribution or statement in the negotiation has been understood. Summarizing is a compact restatement of previous points in the discussion. Both behaviors sort out misunderstandings and reduce misconceptions.

Percent of All Behavior by Negotiator

	Testing Understanding	*Summarizing*	*Testing Understanding and Summarizing*
Skilled negotiators	9.7	7.5	17.2
Average negotiators	4.1	4.2	8.3

The higher level of these behaviors by the skilled negotiator reflects his/her concern with clarity and the prevention of misunderstanding. It may also relate to two less obvious factors.

1. *Reflecting*—Some skilled negotiators tended to use testing understanding as a form of reflecting behavior—turning the other party's words back in order to obtain further responses, for example, "So do I understand that you are saying you don't see any merit in this proposal at all?"

2. *Implementation concern*—The average negotiator, in his/her anxiety to obtain an agreement, would often quite deliberately fail to test understanding or to summarize. S/he would prefer to leave ambiguous points to be cleared later. S/he would fear that making things explicit might cause the other party to disagree. In short, his/her predominant objective was to obtain an agreement and s/he would not probe too deeply into any area of potential misunderstanding which might prejudice immediate agreement, even if it was likely to give rise to difficulties at the implementation stage. The skilled negotiator, on the other hand, tended to have a greater concern with the successful implementation (as would be predicted from the success criteria earlier in this document). S/he would therefore test and summarize in order to check out any ambiguities at the negotiating stage rather than leave them as potential hazards for implementation.

Asking Questions

The skilled negotiator asked significantly more questions during negotiation than did the average negotiator.

Questions as a Percentage of All Negotiators' Behavior	
Skilled negotiator	21.3
Average negotiator	9.6

This is a very significant difference in behavior. Many negotiators and researchers have suggested that questioning techniques are important to negotiating success. Among the reasons frequently given are

1. Questions provide data about the other party's thinking and position.
2. Questions give control over the discussion.
3. Questions are more acceptable alternatives to direct disagreement.
4. Questions keep the other party active and reduce his/her thinking time.
5. Questions can give the negotiator a breathing space to allow him/her to marshal his/her own thoughts.

Feelings Commentary

The skilled negotiator is often thought of as a person who plays his/her cards close to the chest, and who keeps his/her feelings to her/himself. The research studies were unable to measure this directly because feelings are, in themselves, unobservable. However, an indirect measure was possible. The researchers counted the number of times that the negotiator made statements about what was going on inside his/her mind. The behavior category of "Giving Internal Information" was used to record any reference by the negotiator to his/her internal considerations such as feelings and motives.

Giving Internal Information as a Percentage of All Negotiators' Behavior	
Skilled negotiator	12.1
Average negotiator	7.8

The skilled negotiator is more likely to give information about his/her internal events than the average negotiator. This contrasts sharply with the amount of information given about external events, such as facts, clarifications, general expressions of opinion, and so forth. Here the average negotiator gives almost twice as much.

The effect of giving internal information is that the negotiator appears to reveal what is going on in his/her mind. This revelation may or may not be genuine, but it gives the other party a feeling of security because such things as motives appear to be explicit and aboveboard. The most characteristic and noticeable form of giving internal information is a feelings commentary, where the skilled negotiator talks about his/her feelings and the impression the other party has of him/her. For example, the average negotiator, hearing a point from the other party which s/he would like to accept but doubts whether it is true, is likely to receive the point in uncomfortable silence. The skilled negotiator is more likely to comment on his/her own feelings saying something like, "I'm uncertain how to react to what you've just said. If the information you've given me is true, then I would like to accept it; yet I feel some doubts inside me about its accuracy. So part of me feels happy and part feels suspicious. Can you help me resolve this?"

The work of psychologists such as Carl Rogers has shown that the expression of feelings is directly linked to establishing trust in counseling situations. It is probable that the same is true for negotiating.

Argument Dilution

Most people have a model of arguing which looks rather like a balance of a pair of scales. In fact, many of the terms we use about winning arguments reflect this balance model. We speak of "tipping the argument in our favor," of "the weight of the arguments," or how an issue "hangs in the balance." This way of thinking predisposes us to believe that there is some special merit in quantity. If we can find five reasons for doing something, then that should be more persuasive than only being able to think of a single reason. We feel that the more we can put on our scale pan, the more likely we are to tip the balance of an argument in our favor. If this model has any validity, then the skilled negotiator would be likely to use more reasons to back up his/her argument than the average negotiator.

Average Number of Reasons *Given by Negotiator to Back Each* *Argument/Case S/he Advanced*	
Skilled negotiator	1.8
Average negotiator	3.0

The researchers found that the opposite was true. The skilled negotiator used fewer reasons to back up each of his/her arguments. Although the balance-pan model may be very commonly believed, the studies suggest that it is a disadvantage to advance a whole series of reasons to back an argument or case. In doing so, the negotiator exposes a flank and gives the other party a choice of which reason to dispute. It seems self-evident that if a negotiator gives five reasons to back his/her case and the third reason is weak, the other party will exploit this third reason in their response. The most appropriate model seems to be one of dilution. The more reasons advanced, the more a case is potentially diluted. The poorest reason is a lowest common denominator: a weak argument generally dilutes a strong.

Unfortunately, many negotiators who had the disadvantage of higher education put a value on being able to ingeniously devise reasons to back their case. They frequently suffered from this dilution effect and had their point rejected, not on the strength of their principal argument, but on the weakness of the incidental supporting points they introduced. The skilled negotiator tended to advance single reasons insistently, only moving to subsidiary reasons if his/her main reason was clearly losing ground. It is probably no coincidence that an unexpectedly high proportion of the skilled negotiators studied, both in labor relations and in contract negotiation, had relatively little formal education. As a consequence, they had not been trained to value the balance-pan model and more easily avoided the trap of advancing a whole flank of reasons to back their cases.

REVIEWING THE NEGOTIATION

The researchers asked negotiators how likely they were to spend time reviewing the negotiation afterward. Over two-thirds of the skilled negotiators claimed that they always set aside some time after a negotiation to review it and consider what they had learned. Just under half of average negotiators, in contrast, made the same claim. Because the data is self-reported, it may be inaccurate. Even so, it seems that the old principle that more can be learned after a negotiation than during it may be true. An interesting difference between management and union representatives was observed. Management representatives, with other responsibilities and time pressures, were less likely to review a negotiation than were union representatives. This may, in part, account for the observation made by many writers on labor relations that union negotiators seem to learn negotiating skills from taking part in actual negotiations more quickly than management negotiators.

SUMMARY OF THE SUCCESSFUL NEGOTIATOR'S BEHAVIOR

The successful negotiator

- Is rated as effective by both sides.
- Has a track record of significant success.
- Has a low incidence of implementation failure.

Forty-eight negotiators meeting these criteria were studied during 102 negotiations.

Planning

	Negotiators	
	Skilled	*Average*
Overall amount of time spent	No significant difference	
Number of outcomes/options considered per issue	5.1	2.6
Percentage of comments about areas of anticipated common ground	38%	11%
Percentage of comments about long-term considerations of issues	8.5%	4%
Use of sequence during planning (per session)	2.1	4.9

Face-to-Face (Skilled Negotiators)

Avoid	*Use*
Irritators	Behavior labeling (except disagreeing)
Counterproposals	Testing understanding and summarizing
Defend/attack spirals	Lots of questions
Argument dilution	Feelings commentary

Finding Negotiation Leverage

Where Does Power Come From?

Jeffrey Pfeffer

Long-term studies of companies in numerous industries ranging from glass and cement manufacturing to the mini-computer industry "show that the most successful firms maintain a workable equilibrium for several years . . . but are also able to initiate and carry out sharp, widespread changes . . . when their environments shift."[1] These so-called discontinuous or frame-breaking changes always alter the distribution of power. Consequently, organizational innovation often if not inevitably involves obtaining the power and influence necessary to overcome resistance.

To be successful in this process, we need to understand where power comes from. It is critical to be able to diagnose the power of other players, including potential allies and possible opponents. We need to know what we are up against. Knowing where power comes from also helps us to build our own power and thereby increase our capacity to take action. It is useful to know that getting a new product introduced may involve power and politics, and to understand the pattern of interdependence and the points of view of various participants. But, to be effective, we also need to know how to develop sources of power and how to employ that power strategically and tactically.

We all have implicit theories of where power comes from, and we occasionally act on these theories. For instance, we may read and follow the advice of books on "power dressing," pondering issues such as whether yellow ties are in or out and whether suspenders are a signal of power. The cosmetic surgery business is booming, in part, at least, because some executives are worried that the signs of aging may make them appear to be less powerful and dynamic. People attend courses in assertiveness training, go through psychotherapy, and take programs in pubic speaking for numerous reasons, but among them is the desire to be more powerful, dynamic, and effective.

Many of our theories about the origins of power emphasize the importance of personal attributes and characteristics—which are very difficult to alter, at least without herculean efforts. We sometimes overlook the importance of situational factors over which we may have more direct influence. If we are going to be effective in organizations,

---

we need to be skillful in evaluating our theories of the sources of power, as well as sensitive to various cognitive biases. This chapter briefly outlines some issues to think about as we observe the world and try to diagnose the sources of power. It also sets the stage for the consideration of personal characteristics and situational factors as sources of power, which will occur in the later chapters of this section.

PERSONAL ATTRIBUTES AS SOURCES OF POWER

When we walk into an organization, we see people first, not situations. People are talking, moving around, and doing things. People have personalities, idiosyncrasies, and mannerisms that engage our attention and hold our interest. Our preoccupation with the vividness of the people we meet leads to what some psychologists have called "the fundamental attribution error"—our tendency to overemphasize the causal importance of people and their characteristics, and underemphasize the importance of situational factors.[2] The phenomenon is pervasive, and there are many examples. One striking manifestation of the tendency to ignore situational factors in evaluating people is provided in an experimental study done by a colleague.[3] The study entailed assessing the performance of a speaker—a situation not dissimilar to assessing the power of someone we encounter in an organization. In the study, evaluators asked questions that were either positively or negatively biased—and moreover, they were aware of the bias when asked about it later. Nevertheless, evaluators were themselves affected by the answers they elicited through their biased questions. They "underestimated the potential effect of their own behavior (the situation) in drawing conclusions based on potentially constrained answers."[4] Instead of discounting the diagnostic value of the behavior they had affected, evaluators used that information in making assessments both of the performance and (in other studies) of the attitudes of others. In other words, even when we know that the behavior we observe is strongly affected by situational factors, we readily make attributions and evaluations about others based on that behavior.

Not only do we overattribute power to personal characteristics, but often the characteristics we believe to be sources of power are almost as plausibly the consequence of power instead. Interviews with 87 managerial personnel (including 30 chief executive officers, 28 high-level staff managers, and 29 supervisors) in 30 southern California electronics firms assessed beliefs about the personal characteristics of people thought to be most effective in the use of organizational politics and in wielding power.[5] The percentage of all respondents mentioning various characteristics is displayed in Table 1.

Without, for the moment, denying that these characteristics are associated with being powerful and politically effective, consider the possibility that at least some of them result from the experience of being in power. Are we likely to be more articulate and poised when we are more powerful? Are we likely to be more popular? Isn't it plausible that power causes us to be extroverted, as much as extroversion makes us powerful? Aren't more powerful and politically effective people likely to be perceived as more competent? Certainly power and political skill can produce more self-confident and even aggressive behavior. And considering that people usually adjust their ambitions to what is feasible, people who are more powerful are probably going to be more ambitious, and to be viewed as such.

TABLE 1   Personal Traits Characterizing
Effective Political Actors

Personal Characteristic	Percentage Mentioning
Articulate	29.9
Sensitive	29.9
Socially adept	19.5
Competent	17.2
Popular	17.2
Extroverted	16.1
Self-confident	16.1
Aggressive	16.1
Ambitious	16.1

Source: Allen et al., p. 80. Copyright 1979 by The Reagents of the
University of California. Reprinted from the *California Management
Review* 22, no. 1. By permission of The Regents.

Why is the causal ordering of more than academic interest? The answer is that we may try to develop attributes to help us attain power, and if those attributes are ineffective or dysfunctional, we can get into trouble. Most of us can recall people who acted "out the role" and behaved as if they were more powerful and important than they were. This behavior typically only erodes support and makes one ineffective, even if the same behavior, exhibited by someone holding power, is accepted and enhances that person's effectiveness.

A third problem in drawing inferences from personal attributes lies in the fact that people are seldom randomly assigned to their situations. External factors often have a direct bearing on the success or failure of an individual, and yet many studies of power fail to take account of such factors. Consider David Winter's study of the effect of three individual dispositions—the power motive, the need for achievement, and the affiliation-intimacy motive—on various indicators of leader effectiveness, including one measure closely related to a common definition of power: the ability to get one's way in terms of appointments or initiatives.[6]

Winter's sample is the U.S. presidents, a nonrandom sample if ever there was one. Each president's personality traits were assessed by scoring the first inaugural address for imagery that represents the underlying motive. Winter's results are correlations between presidential scores on the three traits and several outcome measures such as being reelected, having court and cabinet appointments approved, and avoiding or entering war.[7] The analysis does not consider the possibility that the type of person elected to office is not independent of the times and conditions that bracket the election, and that perhaps these factors, not just motive profiles, help explain outcomes such as avoiding or entering war.

Errors of this type are made routinely. For instance, in evaluating own-recognizance bail programs, studies often don't account for the fact that the people are not randomly released on their own recognizance; only the less dangerous prisoners are likely to be released.[8] Thus the tendency of those released without bail not to commit crimes does not necessarily mean that if the program were extended to all prisoners the same results would hold. The wider point here is that we need to understand and account for how people wind up in various situations, and to use this information in evaluating their power and their effectiveness. In general, we need to be thoughtful when we analyze personal characteristics as sources of power, particularly if we intend to take action based on those insights.

STRUCTURAL SOURCES OF POWER

Structural perspectives on power argue that power is derived from where each person stands in the division of labor and the communication system of the organization. The division of labor in an organization creates subunits and differentiated roles, and each subunit and position develops specialized interests and responsibilities. Further, each subunit or position makes claims on the organization's resources.[9] In the contest for resources, those who do well succeed on the basis of the resources they possess or control as well as the ties they can form with people who influence allocations.[10] Control over resources, and the importance of the unit in the organization, are derived from the division of labor, which gives some positions or groups more control over critical tasks and more access to resources than others.[11] Power, then, comes from the control over resources, from the ties one has to powerful others, and from the formal authority one obtains because of one's position in the hierarchy.

For instance, in a study of 33 purchase decisions, the most frequently mentioned characteristic of those perceived to have influences over the decision was that the choice would affect them:

> . . . in a company which makes musical instruments, the choice of a tractor truck was said by one informant to have been influenced most by the traffic supervisor. "He lives with the situation, so he must have the choice," he said.[12]

Who is affected by a decision is determined, obviously, by the division of labor. According to those interviewed in the study, people with formal responsibility for the unit where the product was to be used, or with responsibility for the performance or output of the product were also viewed as influential. Although interviewees were asked to judge who had the most influence "regardless of who had the final authority," authority and responsibility were often-mentioned sources of influence in these purchase situations.[13] Authority and responsibility, too, are conveyed by one's position in the formal structure of the organization.

Or consider the power sometimes possessed by purchasing agents.[14] They stand between engineering, production scheduling, and marketing on the one hand, and outside vendors on the other. Some purchasing agents were able to use this intermediary position to obtain substantial influence over other departments that, in may instances, possessed more formal status and authority than they did. By relying on purchasing rules and procedures (which they often had developed themselves), the agents made it necessary for other departments to accede to their power—as is evidenced by the willingness of other departments to provide favors to those in purchasing in exchange for preferential treatment.

The point about situational sources of power is that one possesses power simply by being in the right place—by being in a position of authority, in a place to resolve uncertainty, in a position to broker among various subunits and external vendors—almost regardless of one's individual characteristics. Authority and responsibility are vested in positions, and one's ability to broker is affected significantly by where one sits in the structure of interaction. Of course, not all people in the same situations are able to do equally well. Some purchasing agents, for instance, were much more successful than others in raising the power and status of their departments, in spite of the fact that virtually all wanted to do so, and some of this difference resulted from variations in political skill among the purchasing agents in the various companies. This suggests that while situations are important, one's ability to capitalize on the situation also has decisive implications.

THE FIT BETWEEN SITUATIONAL REQUIREMENTS AND PERSONAL TRAITS

An important source of power is the match between style, skill, and capacities and what is required by the situation. For instance, in a study of influence at a research and development laboratory of 304 professionals, the participants were questioned about influence in their organization. Was influence primarily related to being (1) an internal communication star, someone who had extensive contacts within the laboratory but who was not linked to external sources of information; (2) an external communication star, someone linked primarily to external information and not well connected in his own unit; or (3) a boundary spanner, someone linked both to others within his own unit and to external sources of information?[15] Influence was measured with respect to technical, budgetary, and personnel decisions. The principal finding was that the type of person who was influential depended on the nature of the project: in technical service projects, with less task uncertainty, internal communication stars were most influential, while in applied research units, boundary spanners carried the most weight.

Another illustration of the contingency between situations and the characteristics that provide influence comes from a study of 17 organizations that had recently purchased a piece of offset printing equipment.[16] For some organizations, the purchase was new and therefore totally unfamiliar; for others, it involved the replacement of an existing piece of equipment; and for still others, it involved adding a piece of equipment. Clearly, the amount of uncertainty differed, it being greatest for those buying offset printing equipment for the first time, and posing the smallest problem for those firms that were merely acquiring another piece of the same equipment they already had. Individual experience was most highly related to influence in the case of purchasing an additional piece of equipment. Internal communication and the number of different sources of information consulted were most strongly related to influence in the case of new purchase decisions. Those who were able to affect perceptions of need were most influential in adding a piece of equipment, while those who gathered external information were more influential in the situation in which new equipment was being purchased. These two studies, as well as other research, strongly suggest that

> The influence of a subunit or individual on a decision is a function of (1) the kind of uncertainty faced by an organization, (2) the particular characteristic or capability which enables reducing organizational uncertainty, and (3) the degree to which a particular subunit [or individual] possesses this characteristic. As decision-making contexts vary, so do the sources of organizational uncertainty, and consequently, the bases for influence in organizational decision-making.[17]

The necessity of matching personal characteristics to the situation can be seen in politics as well as in business. Ronald Reagan, the former movie actor and U.S. president, came to office at a time in which mass communication, through the medium of television, was essential. Reagan had no skill in dealing with details, but was a "great communicator." Lyndon Johnson rose to power at a time when television was less important, and party organizations were stronger. The ability to pay attention to small details and the willingness to do favors for colleagues and constituents were critical. Had Reagan and Johnson been able to exchange decades, it is likely that neither one would have been elected president. Johnson's difficulty in responding to the rise of the media in his administration shows his inability to flourish in an era of mass communication. And Reagan would have been unsuited for the continual attention to detail that was required of old-style party politicians. Not only are particular kinds of knowledge and skill differentially critical across time and settings, but personal attributes also become more or less important, depending on the setting.

CAN CHARISMA BE TRANSFERRED?

Charisma is perhaps the best illustration of the fit between situations and personal attributes. The concept of charisma came into social science from theology, where it means "endowment with the gift of divine grace."[18] Charismatic leaders often emerge in times of stress or crisis. They create an emotional (rather than purely instrumental) bond with others; they take on heroic proportions and appeal to the ideological values of followers.[19] President John Kennedy, Martin Luther King, and Gandhi were all charismatic figures.

Some have asserted that charisma is a characteristic of the individual, based on the person's need for power, achievement, and affiliation, as well as on his inhibitions in using power.[20] Moreover, charisma and personality are said to explain the effectiveness of leaders—for instance, that of U.S. presidents.[21] A careful longitudinal study of a school superintendent in Minnesota provides some interesting evidence on the interaction between charismatic properties and situational constraints.[22]

While serving in a large, suburban school district in Minnesota, the superintendent exhibited both charisma and effectiveness. Her work drew attention in the media and the legislature. She "gained wide acclaim for her massive grass roots program to cut $2.4 million from the budget while at the same time successfully avoiding the 'bloodletting' of retrenchment."[23] School personnel described her in interviews as "a mover, a shaker, a visionary . . . who had made a dramatic, unprecedented impact on the district. People believed that she had extraordinary talents."[24] She developed an extremely loyal following, unlike the superintendents who had preceded her. She involved many people in the process of change in the district, forming task forces to investigate district policy and budget problems, hiring consultants to conduct workshops to develop a vision of the future, and redesigning jobs and the administrative structure of the district office. Her effect on the district was striking:

> Budget reductions were scheduled without acrimonious debate. The school board unanimously approved the superintendent's budget reductions after only a brief discussion. Teachers awarded her a standing ovation, despite her recommendations to cut support jobs and program funding. Innovative ideas poured in from district personnel . . . At the end of her two years as superintendent, the district had catalogued over 300 suggestions for innovative ventures.[25]

Then she was appointed by the governor of Minnesota to be the head of the state Department of Education. She brought to this new position the same modus operandi she had used as district superintendent: "Begin with a mission and a vision that outline where one wants to go; generate enthusiasm and support for the vision at the grassroots level; . . . create a structure for change at the Department of Education that will serve to channel the interest and energy into innovative programs."[26] During her first year in her new job, she personally visited almost every one of the 435 school districts in the state. She initiated town meetings held in 388 public school districts, which drew about 15,000 citizens. She sponsored public opinion polls. She replaced the top five assistant commissioners with her own team of nine people, all formerly outsiders to the Department of Education.[27] And what were the results of all of these efforts?

As one might imagine, efforts to restaff and restructure the Department of Education were immediately opposed by those already well served by the existing structure. Five of the new assistants were either fired or resigned from office within the first year.[28] The press soon heard of morale problems, departures of key middle managers, and confusion over routine tasks and job assignments. Instead of being able to focus on long-term change, she now found herself "embroiled in the day-to-day details of established bureaucratic order."[29] Charisma, so evident at the school district level, clearly did not transfer to her new position at the state level, nor could it be created at will.

The administrator had more success in her role as superintendent because it gave her more control and more autonomy over educational matters. She was also able to have closer, more personal relationships with those she wanted to influence when she operated at the local level. As the governor's political appointee, she had to worry about what her actions would mean for him. As head of a large state department, she "was embedded in a much more complex web of relations among the legislature, state executive departments, constituents, interest groups and networks, and state and national educational communities."[30] Her freedom of action was constrained, and her personal contacts were worth much less; in short, she needed to rely more on bureaucratic politics and less on emotional appeal than she had been accustomed to.

As situational factors change, the attributes required to be influential and effective change as well. That is why it is important not only to find positions with the political demands that match our skills and interests, but also to tailor our actions to the circumstances we confront. In any event, we can probably best understand the sources of power as deriving from individual characteristics, from advantages the situation provides, and from the match between ourselves and our settings.

ENDNOTES

1. Michael L. Tushman, William H. Newman, and Elaine Romanelli, "Convergence and Upheaval: Managing the Unsteady Pace of Organizational Evolution," *California Management Review* 29 (1986): 29–44.

2. R. E. Nisbett and L. Ross, *Human Inferences: Strategies and Shortcomings of Social Judgment* (Englewood Cliffs, NJ: Prentice Hall, 1980).

3. Linda E. Ginzel, "The Impact of Biased Feedback Strategies on Performance Judgments," Research Paper #1102 (Palo Alto, CA: Graduate School of Business, Stanford University, 1990).

4. Ibid., 26.

5. Robert W. Allen et al., "Organizational Politics: Tactics and Characteristics of Its Actors," *California Management Review* 22 (1979): 77–83.

6. David G. Winter, "Leader Appeal, Leader Performance, and the Motive Profiles of Leaders and Followers: A Study of American Presidents and Elections," *Journal of Personality and Social Psychology* 52 (1987): 196–202.

7. Ibid., 200.

8. Christopher H. Achen, *The Statistical Analysis of Quasi-Experiments* (Berkeley: University of California Press, 1986).

9. Andrew M. Pettigrew, *Politics of Organizational Decision-Making* (London: Tavistock, 1973), 17.

10. Ibid., 31.

11. D. J. Hickson et al., "A Strategic Contingencies' Theory of Intraorganizational Power," *Administrative Science Quarterly* 16 (1971): 216–29.

12. Martin Patchen, "The Locus and Basis of Influence in Organizational Decisions," *Organizational Behavior and Human Performance* 11 (1974): 209.

13. Ibid., 213.

14. George Strauss, "Tactics of Lateral Relationship: The Purchasing Agent," *Administrative Science Quarterly* 7 (1962): 161–86.

15. Michael L. Tushman and Elaine Romanelli, "Uncertainty, Social Location and Influence in Decision Making: A Sociometric Analysis," *Management Science* 29 (1983): 12–23.

16. Gerald R. Salancik, Jeffrey Pfeffer, and J. Patrick Kelly, "A Contingency Model of Influence in Organizational Decision Making," *Pacific Sociological Review* 21 (1978): 239–56.

17. Ibid., 253.

18. Bernard M. Bass, "Evolving Perspectives on Charismatic Leadership," *Charismatic Leadership,* eds. Jay A. Conger, Rabindra N. Kanungo and Associates (San Francisco: Jossey-Bass, 1988), 40–77.

19. Robert J. House, William D. Spangler, and James Woycke, "Personality and Charisma in the U.S. Presidency: A Psychological Theory of Leadership Effectiveness," unpublished, Wharton School, University of Pennsylvania, 1989.

20. Ibid.; Robert J. House, "A 1976 Theory of Charismatic Leadership," *Leadership: The Cutting Edge,* eds. J. G. Hunt and L. L. Larson (Carbondale: Southern Illinois University Press, 1977).

21. House, Spangler, and Woycke, "Personality and Charisma."

22. Nancy C. Roberts and Raymond Trevor Bradley, "Limits of Charisma," *Charismatic Leadership,* eds. Jay A. Conger, Rabindra N. Kanungo and Associates (San Francisco: Jossey-Bass, 1988), 253–75.

23. Ibid., 254.

24. Ibid., 260.

25. Ibid., 263.

26. Ibid.

27. Ibid., 264.

28. Ibid., 269.

29. Ibid.

30. Ibid., 268.

How to Become an
Influential Manager

Bernard Keys
Thomas Case

A hospital department head attempted in vain to persuade physicians working in a large metropolitan hospital to bring patient medical records up to date. Although doctors consider this an abhorrent chore, hospitals cannot begin the billing process until each record is completed and signed by the physician. After many frustrating attempts, the department head describes how he proved equal to the challenge.

> Every month we served the doctors breakfast and lunch and organized games that would allow them to win prizes. Sometimes we would place balloons on a bulletin board and let them throw darts at the balloons. At other times we would do something ridiculously childlike such as hosting a watermelon seed spitting contest or playing pin the tail on the donkey. The sessions worked beautifully because the doctors knew that when they came in someone would be there to help them and they would even have a little fun. Once when we were really desperate we hired a popular entertainer. The room was full that day and we completed over 1,000 charts.

Influence is simply the process by which people successfully persuade others to follow their advice, suggestion, or order. It can be contrasted with power, which is a personal or positional attribute and enables one to influence others and which can be thought of as "continuing or sustained" influence.[1] A number of popular books have suggested that influence must replace the use of formal authority in relationships with subordinates, peers, outside contacts, and others on whom the job makes one dependent.[2] The writers of these books attribute the need for greater influence to the rapidity of change in organizations, the diversity of people, goals and values, increasing interdependence, and the diminishing acceptability of formal authority.[3] Bennis and Nanus have suggested that leaders must empower themselves by empowering their subordinates. Kouzes and Posner agree with this conclusion, explaining that the more people believe they can influence and control the organization, the greater will be the effectiveness of the organization. Tichy and Devanna extend this thought even further by suggesting that today we need transformational leaders who will allow networks that

Source: Reprinted from *Academy of Management Executive,* 4, no. 4 (1990), pp. 38–51. Used with permission of the authors and publishers.

funnel diverse views upward from the lower level of the organization where a need for change is often first detected. Similarly, John Kotter observes that the increasing diversity and interdependence of organizational role players is creating a "power gap" for managers who often have knowledge and good ideas for organizations but who have inadequate authority to implement their ideas.

For example, effectiveness with subordinates has been found to depend heavily on the ability to develop upward influence with superiors.[4] Influence with the boss often depends on the ability to accomplish things through one's subordinates.[5] Laterally, managers must spend time in group meetings, interorganizational negotiations, and in bids for departmental resources.[6] This is a role replete with power gaps. Most assuredly lateral relationships require the ability to influence without formal authority representatives with unions, customers, and government, or highly autonomous professionals such as the physician in our introductory example.[7]

The concept of "linking groups" seems to drive the middle manager's work while both middle management and executive levels are heavily engaged in "coordinating" independent groups. In this latter role, they must persuade other organizational groups to provide information, products, resources needed, and negotiate working agreements with other groups. Additionally, executive levels of management must frequently maintain relationships with management-level vendors, consultants, and other boundary-spanning agents through outside meetings. Recent research suggests that the "ambassador role" of "representing one's staff" is vitally important to all levels of management. It consists of developing relationships with other work groups and negotiating for information and resources on behalf of the manager's own group.[8]

Building on the previous thoughts and the research of others, we conducted field studies to collect incidents, similar to the one describing the hospital department head, and used these to analyze how managers build and sustain influence. This article explains our research findings and those of related studies for managers who wish to become more influential with subordinates, superiors, peers, and other target groups.

INFLUENCE TACTIC RESEARCH

Only a few writers have identified influence tactics from research investigations. David Kipnis and his colleagues asked evening graduate students to describe an incident in which they actually succeeded in getting either their boss, a coworker, or a subordinate to do something they wanted. Their analysis revealed that the tactics of ingratiation (making the supervisor feel important) and developing rational plans were the most frequently used methods to influence superiors. When attempting to influence subordinates, respondents most often used formal authority, training, and explanations. Only one tactic, that of requesting help, was frequently associated with influencing coworkers. [9]

Our studies were aimed at strengthening the previous research. Since the studies cited above utilized categories of influence tactics derived from research with MBA students, we developed categories from influence incidents collected from practicing managers. Our three studies used trained students from several universities and structured interview forms to collect a wide geographic dispersion of responses.

Attempts were made to collect one successful incident and one unsuccessful incident from managers in a wide variety of both large and small businesses. One study focused on lateral influence processes, another on upward influence processes, and a third study examined downward influence. The primary question asked of each manager was, "Please think of a time when you successfully/unsuccessfully tried to influence a (superior, peer, or subordinate) toward the attainment of a personal, group, or organizational goal. . . . Please tell exactly what happened."

Exhibit 1 presents the summary of findings from these studies.[10] The numbers to the right of each tactic portray the rank order of the frequency with which influence tactics were reported for each target group.

Influencing Superiors

In influence attempts with superiors and peers, rational explanations were the most frequently used tactic. Often these techniques included the presentation of a complete plan, a comparative or quantitative analysis, or documentation of an idea or plan by way of survey, incidents, or interviews. In a few isolated cases, subordinates challenged their superiors' power, tried to manipulate them, bargained for influence, or threatened to quit. When these more assertive techniques were used, the subordinate was successful about 50 percent of the time—not very good odds for the risks which they were taking. In most narratives we found that the subordinate using these methods had discovered a powerless boss, or had developed an unusual position of power themselves by becoming indispensable. In a few cases they had simply become frustrated and thrown caution to the wind.

Upward influence tactics were characterized by numerous supporting tactics such as mustering the support of a variety of other persons (both internal and external to the organization) or by choosing appropriate timing to approach the boss. Only two tactics appeared with significant enough frequency differential to be clearly distinguished as a successful or unsuccessful tactic. Subordinates using the tactic of "talking to or arguing with the boss without support" were more likely to fail. On the other hand, those who continued persistently or repeated an influence attempt continuously were likely to succeed. Caution is in order, however, in interpreting the use of persistence and repetition; this was usually a secondary tactic used in combination with others such as presenting facts and rational plans.

The rational persuasion technique was used by a plant manager to prevent a cutback in his workforce when the army phased out one of its tanks.

> First the plant manager sold a new product line to divisional staff who reported to his boss. In the meantime he developed a presentation in the form of a comparative analysis showing the pros and cons of taking on the new product line. Ideas presented included such things as the reduced burden on other products, risk reward factors, and good community relations from the layoff avoided. The presentation was polished, written on viewgraphs, and presented in person. The plant manager made certain that his technical staff would be at the meeting ready to answer any questions that might damage the strength of the presentation.

Not only did the plant manager succeed with this influence attempt, he felt that his boss and peers were easier to convince on subsequent attempts.

EXHIBIT 1   Rank of Frequency with which Each Influence Tactic Was Reported by Target Groups

	Boss	Peers	Subordinates
Presenting a rational explanation	1	1	3
Telling, arguing, or talking without support	2	0	0
Presenting a complete plan	3	0	0
Using persistence or repetition	4	0	0
Developing and showing support of others (employees, outsiders, etc.)	5	2	12
Using others as a platform to present ideas	6	0	0
Presenting an example of a parallel situation	7	3	5
Threatening	8	4	10
Offering to trade favors or concessions	9	5	0
Using manipulative techniques	10	6	7
Calling on formal authority and policies	0	8	6
Showing confidence and support	0	0	1
Delegating duties, guidelines, or goals	0	0	2
Listening, counseling, or soliciting ideas	0	0	4
Questioning, reviewing, or evaluating	0	0	9
Rewarding with status or salary	0	0	7
Developing friendship or trust	0	7	11

Influencing Subordinates

When dealing with subordinates, of course, the manager may simply tell an employee to do something. But our research suggests that managers who rely on formal authority alone are greatly limiting their options. The power gap noted earlier exists with subordinates as well as with other groups. Today more than ever, it must be filled with methods of influence other than authority. The following incident presents an interesting view of a furniture manufacturer trying to persuade his upholstery foreman to accept the position of plant superintendent.

> The manager met with Foreman Z in the foreman's office for short periods to talk about the promotion. Anticipating resistance, he covered small increments of the superintendent's responsibilities and allowed the foreman time to think about each session. The manager made sure that each session ended on a positive note. He pointed out the many tasks and skills required of the superintendent's job were already inherent in the foreman position. He downplayed the more complex responsibilities, relying on his commitment to future training to resolve these. Several such meetings took place in a five-day period. On one occasion the foreman alluded to resentment from fellow foremen. This prompted the manager to enlist the help of some of the other foremen—several hunting buddies, to talk favorably about Z taking the position. In the last meeting the manager outlined the responsibilities and cited the salary and prestige which accompanied the position.

The senior manager in this incident later commented that he had always had success at using this technique—that is, breaking down a complex influence task into incremental steps and attacking each step separately. While there is some merit to this process, most readers would agree that the major reason for success in this case was the persistence exerted by the senior manager to win in his influence attempt. The mild deception in oversimplifying the open position could merit criticism but must be moderated by the manager's willingness to train and support the foreman. In this case, the influence tactic had positive long-term consequences; the foreman became a very successful plant superintendent and later trained his own successor.

Frequently, subordinates were questioned, reviewed, evaluated, threatened, warned, reprimanded, or embarrassed to change their minds or to solicit compliance with plans of the superior. These more threatening and negative techniques were more frequently associated with failure than success. Occasionally subordinates were transferred or relocated to influence them, but usually with little success. The more assertive tactics were typically used in cases where subordinates were initially reluctant to comply with reasonable requests or had violated policies or procedures.

Influencing Peers

Only one tactic from our lateral influence study was noted significantly more often in successful influence attempts with peers—that of "developing and showing support of others." This tactic was most often used along with others and therefore represented a part of a multiple influence tactic. Often a peer in a staff department or a subordinate is used to support a proposal, as in the influence attempt described by a zone manager with a large tire and rubber company.

> During this time I was managing 25 company-owned stores in which I initiated an effective program to control the handling of defective merchandise. I wanted to see the method utilized by the other store managers throughout the country who were supervised by other zone managers, but I felt that they would consider me to be intruding if I approached them directly. Therefore, I asked my store managers to tell the store managers in other zones about the sizable savings to be had from the use of the method. The other store managers told their zone managers and soon they came to me for information about my program. The new program saved the company $90,000 per year which increased our pay in bonuses at the end of the year.

When dealing with peers, managers made extensive use of rational facts or ideas. They often presented an example of another organization using their idea or proposal. Demonstrating that they had the support of others was a frequently used managerial influence tactic. Occasionally they threatened to go to higher-level management or called on formal authority or policies to support their case. Assertive and manipulative tactics were used more often when attempting to influence the boss or subordinates, but less frequently with peers.

INFLUENCE TACTIC EFFECTIVENESS

Our research on individual influence attempts somewhat simplifies the area of influence effectiveness. In the first place, the methods listed in Exhibit 1 are the ones that are most frequently used and not necessarily the ones which are most successful. In all three studies we found that techniques that succeed in some instances fail in others. The few exceptions to this finding are noted in Exhibit 1 when the ranks of tactics are underlined. These represent tactics that were reported significantly more often, for either successful or unsuccessful influence attempts. For example, unsuccessful influence attempts with the boss often consisted of simply telling the boss something, arguing, or presenting an idea or suggestion without support. While this technique occasionally succeeded, it was more likely to be associated with unsuccessful episodes. Similarly, the use of persistence or repetition was reported more often in successful influence attempts with the boss than with unsuccessful ones.

Judging from the incidents collected, subordinate influence tactics of "threatening or questioning, reviewing, or evaluating" are significantly more likely to lead to failure than to success. Consider the experience of a plant operations manager attempting to introduce quality circles in an area to improve productivity.

> The operations manager requested the assistance of the manager of organizational develop-ment, who warned that such implementation would take time, patience and the building of trust among his employees. Turnover in the operations area was high and negative attitudes tended to prevail. The operations manager became impatient, viewing QC as a quick fix for morale problems. The OD manager made available several persons who had worked suc-cessfully with a QC implementation, but after conversing with them the operations manager elected not to listen. He chose two subordinates to be trained as QC facilitators and imme-diately upon the completion of their training, began to implement QC. The operations man-ager and facilitators subtly coerced employees to join the circles and directed them toward the projects that management wanted attacked. After several months employee interest fell sharply and several complaints were filed with employee relations leading to abandonment of the project.

Contrast this occurrence with a less threatening attempt reported by a manufacturing manager in another part of the country:

> The manager first read numerous articles about QC programs and learned the pitfalls to avoid. QC information handouts were given to the supervisors over a period of a couple of months. The supervisors were never pressured and gradually they approached their manager, asking how they could get quality circles started in their departments. The program was then imple-mented using recognized procedures and is still operating successfully several years later.

The analysis of influence attempts such as the quality circles' incidents demonstrates the need for careful implementation of management processes.

STEPS IN BECOMING AN INFLUENTIAL MANAGER

Power, or sustained influence, may be accumulated and stored by a manager for future use. This allows one to call on existing strength to bolster influence tactics and often affects the future choice of influence tactic. Power may also be provided by the strategic position that one occupies in an organization, but position is often beyond the control of the incumbent. Fortunately, power may also be acquired through the devel-opment and exercise of certain skills by the manager within the organization. It is this skill-based power that we discuss throughout the rest of this article.[11]

Our research, and that of other writers reviewed in this article, indicates that there are five key steps to establishing sustained managerial influence.

- Develop a reputation as a knowledgeable person or an expert.
- Balance the time spent in each critical relationship according to the needs of the work rather than on the basis of habit or social preference.
- Develop a network of resource persons who can be called upon for assistance.
- Choose the correct combination of influence tactics for the objective and for the target to be influenced.
- Implement influence tactics with sensitivity, flexibility, and adequate levels of communication.

These steps in developing influence might be compared to the development of a "web of influence" (no negative implication intended). Unlike the web of a spider, the manager's web of influence can be mutually advantageous to all who interact within it. The web is anchored by a bridgeline of knowledge and expertise. The structure of the web is extended when invested time is coverted into a network of resource persons who may be called upon for information and special assistance or support with an influence attempt. These persons—superiors, peers, subordinates, outside contacts, and others—might be thought of as spokes in the web. Establishing the web, however, does not insure influence attempts will be successful. An effective combination of influence tactics must be selected for each influence target and influence objective sought. Finally, the tactics chosen must be communicated well within the sector of the web targeted.

Our research suggests that the web of influence is continually in a state of construction. It is often broken or weakened by an ill-chosen influence attempt requiring patch-up work for a portion of the web. Some webs are constructed poorly, haphazardly, or incompletely like the tangled web of a common house spider while others are constructed with a beautiful symmetrical pattern like the one of the orb weaver.

Develop a Reputation as an Expert

Of all the influence tactics mentioned by respondents in our interviews, the use of rational facts and explanations was the most commonly reported—although in isolation this method succeeded no more often than it failed. Managers who possess expert knowledge in a field and who continually build that knowledge base are in a position to convert successful attempts into sustained power. In the early stages of a career (or shortly after a move) power from expertise is unusually tentative and fragile like the first strands of a web. Hampton and colleagues explain how expertise is extended to become sustained influence with the following example of Bill, a young staff specialist, hired to provide expertise to a number of production managers:

> Initially, the only influence process available to the specialist is persuasion—gaining the rational agreement of the managers. To be effective he prepares elaborate, clear presentations (even rehearsing with a colleague to anticipate any questions). By data, logic, and argument, he attempts to gain the agreement of his superiors. After a year of this kind of relationship, he goes one day to talk with Barbara, one of the managers. An hour has been reserved for the

presentation. He arrives and begins his pitch. After a couple of minutes, however, the busy manager interrupts: "I'm just too busy to go over this. We'll do whatever you want to do."[12]

But enhancing expert-based power involves publicizing one's expertise as well as acquiring it. For example, Kotter contrasts two 35-year-old vice presidents in a large research and development organization, who are considered equally bright and technically competent.

> Close friends and associates claim the reason that Randley is so much more powerful is related to a number of tactics that he has used more than Kline has. Randley has published more scientific papers and managerial articles than Kline. Randley has been more selective in the assignments he has worked on, choosing those that are visible and that require his strong suits. He has given more speeches and presentations on projects that are his own achievements. And in meetings in general, he is allegedly forceful in areas where he has expertise and silent in those where he does not.[13]

Balance Time with Each Critical Relationship

Managers who desire to become influential must strike a reasonable balance in the investment of their time. In another study using a questionnaire, we surveyed managers from the United States, Korea, Hong Kong, and the Philippines to learn how they spent their time. These managers say that they spend about 10 percent of their time interacting with the boss, approximately 30 percent interacting with subordinates, and about 20 percent interacting with peers. As one might expect, the pattern of outside relations varies with the job (i.e., sales, engineering, etc.), but the managers report, on the average, spending from 15 to 20 percent of their time with external contacts. Time spent alone varies from 15 to 28 percent.[14] Although we cannot argue that this pattern is descriptive of all managers, it is similar to the pattern of communication distribution discovered from a sample of United States managers by Luthans and Larson.[15]

Some popular writers are calling for a heavy rescheduling of time and communications efforts.[16] Peters argues that 75 percent of a middle manager's time must be spent on horizontal relationships to speed up cross-functional communications in the middle of organizations. Johnson and Frostman see this kind of communication as being so critical that it must be mandated by upper-level management. Peters emphasizes the argument that upper-level managers spend too little time visiting with customers or in face-to-face relationships with subordinates (management by walking around). The bottom line is that time should be spent where influence is most needed to accomplish organizational goals.[17]

During our seminars on influence over the years, managers have often told us that they failed to spend enough time with the boss or with peers, or in simply keeping up with organizational happenings. This may be due to the fact that many managers are uncomfortable spending time with those who have more formal power than they (superiors), or with those with whom they must compete (peers). Sayles believes that managers' uneasiness with peers grows out of the difference in values across departments and work groups, the ambiguities which exist in cross-organizational relationships, and the conflict often generated in lateral relationships.[18] Other things being equal, realigning from a narrow focus on subordinates to a bigger picture which includes lateral and upward relationships can often yield a stronger web of sustained influence and should provide the supporting spokes needed to launch influence tactics.

A strong web of influence may even be quite desirable from the boss's viewpoint. Schilit found that managers who had been working for the same upper manager for a long period of time were quite capable of influencing that manager even on strategic issues facing the company. He concludes that, "[Managers] should be encouraged to be assertive in presenting their strategic thoughts because widespread strategic thinking may have a positive impact on their division or organization."[19]

Develop a Network of Resource Persons

Although managers do not use other people in most influence attempts, the more important attempts invariably involve others. For example, in the incident cited earlier about the furniture manufacturer who wanted a foreman to accept the plant manager's job, the assistance of other foremen (fishing buddies) was solicited. Similarly, in the case of the plant manager who tried to avoid a cutback in his workforce after the phaseout of a military contract, the manager sold his idea to division staff and ensured that his own technical staff would be in attendance at the meeting in which he was making a presentation to the boss. The ability to establish and exploit a network is clearly demonstrated by a branch manager of a bank who used the following tactic with his superior, a vice president, when he found his operation in need of additional space.

> My strategy was to convince my immediate superior that the current facilities were too small to not only handle the current volume of business but too small to allow us to increase our share of the market in a rapidly growing area. First, I persuaded my superior to visit the branch more often, especially at times when the branch was particularly busy. I also solicited accounting's help to provide statistical reports on a regular basis that communicated the amount of overall growth in the area as well as the growth of our competitors. These reports showed that our market share was increasing. I then asked my superior to visit with me as I called on several customers and prospects in the area to let him know the type of potential business in the area. During this period of time, I kept pushing to increase all levels of business at the branch. Finally, I encouraged key customers in the bank to say favorable things about my branch when they visited with my senior managers. Eventually my superior got behind my proposal and we were able to build an addition to the building which allowed me to add several new employees.

Such influence attempts clearly illustrate the fact that many managers do not assume that achievement in traditional areas of management—selling, organizing, promoting customers—will inspire sufficient confidence by others. Rather than waiting for good publicity and resources to come to them, they seek them out through influence approaches built on carefully planned networks and persistent effort. The findings of our influence studies are supported by the observations of Luthans and his colleagues who concluded that managers who are both effective (have satisfied and committed subordinates and high performance in their units) and successful (receive relatively rapid promotions) strike a balanced approach between networking, human resource management, communications, and traditional management activities.[20]

To some extent, networking activities may affect the positional strength of managers. The more contacts a manager has with others and the more independent the position relative to others, the more control the manager has over the flow of information. Positions that involve interaction with more influential managers of the organization or control information on which they rely, will typically be ones of power.[21]

Kaplan compares the strengthening of lateral relationships in the organization to the establishment of trade routes in international trade. According to this writer, managers, unlike countries which trade products, often trade power and the ability to get things done. Their goal is to build strong reciprocal relationships with other departments so that when the manager has immediate needs sufficient obligation exists to ensure fast cooperation. Often positions on the boundary of an organization can be especially influential. Consider the example referred to by Kaplan when describing a newly appointed manager of corporate employee relations. "I wanted a base that was different from what the groups reporting to me had and also from what my superiors had, so I established a series of contacts in other American industries until I knew on a first-name basis my counterparts at IBM, TRW, Procter & Gamble, DuPont, and General Electric, and I could get their input—input which the people in my organization didn't have."[22] Kaplan suggests that networks of trading partners can be built by rotating jobs frequently, establishing strong friendships (and maintaining them), and seeking commonality with other managers, such as a shared work history.

Choose the Correct Combination of Influence Tactics

Influence tactics are the threads that complete a web, hold the spokes of the webbed network in place, and in turn are supported by the network. They must be chosen carefully on the basis of influence targets chosen and objectives sought.[23] One of the studies by Kipnis and colleagues found, as did we, that considerably more approaches were used to influence subordinates than were used to influence superiors or peers. Incidents in our studies suggested that most first influence attempts by managers involved soft approaches such as requests reason, but later attempts included stronger tactics when the target of influence was reluctant to comply. This notion was confirmed statistically in the Kipnis study. Both superior and subordinate target groups in the Kipnis sample tended to use reason to sell ideas and friendliness to obtain favors. These authors also emphasize that influence tactics must vary with the target and objective of influence attempts: "only the most inflexible of managers can be expected to rely rigidly on a single strategy, say assertiveness, to achieve both personal and organizational objectives. It may be appropriate to 'insist' that one's boss pay more attention to cost overruns; it is less appropriate to 'insist' on time off for a game of golf."[24]

Taking a cue from the fact that few tactics were found to be associated more frequently with success than failure in any of our studies, we began to examine combinations of influence tactics. In each of the three influence studies (upward, downward, and lateral), managers who use a combination of approaches tended more often to be successful than managers who relied on a single tactic.

We noted that in many incidents short-term success seemed to lead to enhanced influence in the long term; therefore, we sought ways to measure sustained influence over time. Consequently, in our downward influence study, we asked managers about the nature of the subordinate-superior relationship that occurred two months following an influence attempt. As we expected, successful influence attempts led the managers to perceive that their relationships had improved and to believe they had expanded their potential for future influence. For example, the bank branch manager, who was able to enlarge his building reported that because of his success with the influence attempt his profile at the bank was raised, that he was given a promotion and a raise, and that he was transferred to the main office.[25]

Although we cannot be certain that the managers experiencing short-term influence success derived power with their boss from these episodes, the fact that managers believed this to be so caused them, in most cases, to plan additional influence attempts. These findings are supported by a study of Kipnis and his colleagues which found that managers who perceive that they have power are more likely to select assertive influence tactics.[26] Failures at influence attempts may cause managers to plan fewer future attempts and to experience a period of weakened relationships with the boss. Frequently when a subordinate attempts to influence upper-level management in a manner where his or her intention is clearly for the advantage of the organization, failure is not damaging to future influence. When the purpose of an influence attempt is clearly seen as a personal goal, failure may be more serious. Such a case was reported by a supervisor of security services dealing with a vice president of operations:

> I wanted an assistant so that I could have some help in managing my department and would not have to handle petty problems of my employees. I tried to convince my boss that I was overworked since my staff has almost doubled and I was having a lot of people problems. I failed because I was just trying to make it easier on myself and wanted an assistant to do the job that I was supposed to be doing. I was also asking to increase the payroll of the company with no plans to increase revenue or profits. After my boss turned me down, I pouted for a few weeks and later learned that my boss thought I was immature. I then decided to forget about past disappointments and only worry about the future.

Communicate Influence Tactics Effectively

If is very difficult to separate influence tactic choice with the communications process itself. Cohen and Bradford stress the importance of knowing the world of potential allies—the needs, values, and organizational forces working on them. For example, they suggest that setting the stage for an influence attempt by wining and dining influence targets at a fancy restaurant may work well for a public relations director, but may appear to be a buyout attempt when directed toward the head of engineering.[27]

Many of our research participants mentioned the importance of their presentation or their manner of approaching the target. Managers who choose rational ideas based on the needs of the target, wrap them with a blanket of humor or anecdotes, and cast them in the language of the person to be influenced, are much more likely to see their influence objective achieved.

Effective communications become interwoven coils of silk in the web of influence that help ensure the success of tactics. Consider for example the combination of influence tactics and communication used by Iacocca in his turn-a-round strategy of Chrysler. Kotter capsules these as follows:

He developed a bold new vision of what Chrysler should be . . . he (then) attracted, held onto, and elicited cooperation and teamwork from a large network . . . labor leaders, a whole new management team, dealers, suppliers, some key government officials and many others. He did so by articulating his agenda in emotionally powerful ways ("Remember, folks, we have a responsibility to save 600,000 jobs"), by using the credibility and relationships he had developed after a long and highly successful career in the automotive business, by communicating the new strategies in an intellectually, powerful manner and in still other ways.[28]

Upward and lateral communications require more listening and more appreciation of the ideas and thoughts of others than dictated by subordinate relationships. Laborde suggests that a person who would master the communicator part of influence must see more and hear more than most people and must remain flexible to vary their behavior in response to what they see and hear.[29] Kaplan strongly emphasizes the importance of variation in the arsenal of communications skills—knowing when to meet with a person face-to-face, when to call group meetings, and when to use memos.[30]

Implications of Influence Research for Managers

No research is subtle enough to capture all of the relationships present between managers as they work together as peers, subordinates, and superiors. While incident- or questionnaire-type research may be subject to some self-report bias (if possible managers try to make themselves look rational to the researcher), observers, even if they could remain long enough in an area, could never capture and connect all of the thoughts necessary to precisely determine motives, processes, and outcomes of managers attempting to develop long-term influence relationships. We have attempted to capture some of the pieces, reviewed the best of what other experts have said about the subject, and tried to establish some connections. While recognizing these limitations, our influence research over the past 10 years leads us to the following conclusions:

- Managers are continually in a state of building and extending webs of influence and repairing damaged threads. With every career change new webs must be built. In the early part of a career or after a career move, a manager must establish a web of influence by developing a reputation as an expert, balancing this with key influence targets, networking to establish resources, and selecting and communicating appropriate influence tactics.

- No one influence tactic can be isolated as being superior to others. Tactics must be chosen on a basis of the influence target and objective sought. For more important influence objectives, a combination of influence tactics will be necessary.

- Frequency of reported tactic usage suggests that most contemporary managers initially try positive techniques with targets, but will quickly resort to threats or manipulation if necessary, especially if the target is a subordinate.

- The variety of approaches used to influence subordinates is wider than suggested by the traditional leadership models and wider than the variety used in upward and lateral influence attempts.[31] This appears to be due not only to the additional power bases available when dealing with subordinates, but also to the growing difficulty of obtaining subordinate compliance through traditional means.

- Contrary to traditional views that networking outside the hierarchy is disruptive, today's leaders must recognize the value of reciprocal influence relationships and must encourage them as long as they can be fruitfully directed toward organizational goals. Webs of influence may provide advantages for all involved.

- For these reasons, we are quite convinced that influential managers are ones who have developed and maintained a balanced web of relationships with the boss, subordinates, peers, and other key players; influence in each of these directions is banked for leverage to accomplish goals in the other directions. If knowledge alone and positional authority alone will not accomplish the manager's job, those who would be influential must fill power gaps with webs of influence.

ENDNOTES

The authors appreciate the helpful suggestions to an earlier draft of this manuscript by W. J. Heisler, manager, Management Development and Salaries Employee Training, Newport News Shipbuilding, and Fred Luthans, George Holmes professor of management, University of Nebraska. We especially appreciate the work of the anonymous reviewers who assisted us with the paper. Thanks to the professors who participated in original research studies: Robert Bell, Tennessee Tech University; Lloyd Dosier and Gene Murkinson, Georgia Southern University; Tom Miller and Coy Jones, Memphis State University; Kent Curran, University of North Carolina, Charlotte; and Alfred Edge, University of Hawaii.

1. These definitions follow those of D. R. Hampton, C. E. Summer, and R. A. Webber, Chapter 3, *Organizational Behavior and the Practice of Management* (Glenview, IL: Scott Foresman, 1987) fifth ed.

2. See Chapter 1 of A. R. Cohen and D. L. Bradford, *Influence without Authority* (New York: John Wiley, 1990). For a review of these thoughts, see W. Bennis and B. Nanus, *Leaders: The Strategies for Taking Charge* (New York: Harper and Row, 1985) and J. M. Kouzes and B. Z. Posner, *The Leadership Challenge* (San Francisco: Jossey-Bass, 1988). For a book that relates leadership influence to the way in which change is implemented in the American economy, see N. M. Tichy and M. A. Devanna, *The Transformational Leader* (New York: John Wiley & Sons, 1986). See also Chapter 2 of J. P. Kotter, *Power and Influence—Beyond Formal Authority* (New York: Free Press, 1985).

3. For the review of literature and our conceptualization of an influence model, see J. B. Keys and R. Bell, "The Four Faces of the Fully Functioning Middle Manager," *California Management Review,* 24 (4), Summer 1982, 59–66: a condensed version of this article can be found in *World Executive's Digest* 4 (7), 1983, 25–31.

4. For the original research on the importance of upward influence to supervisory success, see D. C. Pelz, "Influence: Keys to Effective Leadership in the First-Level Supervisor," *Personnel,* 29, 1959, 209–17. For a later discussion with case illustrations, see F. Bartolomé and A. Laurent, "The Manager: Master and Servant of Power," *Harvard Business Review,* 64 (6), November–December 1986, 77–81. The ways in which managers, especially middle managers, acquire and sustain upward influence are outlined in D. H. Kreger, "Functions and Problems of Middle Management," *Personnel Journal,* 49 (11), November 1970, 935; P. D. Couch, "Learning to Be a Middle Manager," *Business Horizons,* 22 (1), February 1979, 33–41; R. A. Webber, "Career Problems of Young Managers," *California Management Review,* 18 (4), Summer 1975, 19–33; H. E. R. Uyterhoeven, "General Managers in the Middle," *Harvard Business Review,* 50

(2), March–April 1972, 75–85. For an article that has become a best-selling classic on the subject, see J. J. Gabarro and J. P. Kotter, "Managing Your Boss," *Harvard Business Review,* 58 (1), January–February 1980, 92–100. For a recent article on maintaining loyalty and developing an initial relationship with the boss, see R. Vecchio, "Are You In or Out with the Boss?" *Business Horizons,* 29 (6), November–December 1986, 76–78.

5. For the review of the way in which managers create influence downward, see Uyterhoven, Endnote 4, and S. H. Ruello, "Transferring Managerial Concepts and Techniques to Operating Management," *Advanced Management Journal,* 38 (3), July 1973, 42–48. For a discussion of the importance of defending and supporting subordinates, see Bartolomé and Laurent Endnote 4.

6. For a discussion of how managers develop political skills, see Ruello, Endnote 5, and Uyterhoeven, Endnote 4. To review the integrative role of middle managers, see J. L. Hall and J. K. Leidecker, "Lateral Relations: The Impact on the Modern Managerial Role," *Industrial Management,* June 1974, 3.

7. For a discussion of external relationships, see D. W. Organ, "Linking Pins between Organizations and Environment," *Business Horizons,* 14 (6), December 1972, 73–80.

8. A. I. Kraut, P. R. Pedigo, D. D. McKenna, and M. D. Dunnette, "The Role of the Manager: What's Really Important in Different Management Jobs," *Academy of Management Executive,* 3 (4), 286–93.

9. For other studies on influence tactics, see D. Kipnis S. M. Schmidt, and I. Wilkinson, "Interorganizational Influence Tactics: Explorations in Getting One's Way," *Journal of Applied Psychology,* 65 (4), August 1980, 440–52. This study differed from our field study in that it surveyed evening MBA students and allowed them to describe any successful influence episode in which they had been involved. W. K. Schilit and E. A. Locke, "A Study of Upward Influence in Organizations," *Administrative Science Quarterly,* 1982, 27 (2), 304–16 found that Kipnis and Schmidt's 14 tactic categories were not sufficient to categorize upward influence incident accounts collected from undergraduate and graduate business students and full-time employees or supervisors. They found evidence supporting the use of 20 types of upward influence tactics. Because these previous investigations relied so heavily on unchallenged global categories derived from a relatively small sample of evening MBA students which might not be representative of managers, we began our studies from scratch and collected narrative accounts of incidents from practicing managers. Each study focused on only one type of target and at least 250 influence tactics were collected. Flanagan's critical incident method was used to develop categories and to content analyze the responses. (J. C. Flanagan, "Defining the Requirements of the Executive's Job," *Personnel,* 28, July 1951, 28–35.) Our findings for upward influence were more similar to those of Schilit and Locke than to those of Kipnis et al. Over 46 distinct tactics were observed across the three types of targets. Of course, tactics used to influence some targets are rarely, if ever, used to influence other types of targets. The description of managerial influence tactics which emerges from our three studies is much more detailed and therefore more suited to management applications than that provided by the previous investigations. Of equal importance, unlike the previous studies, our investigations also addressed the use of combinations of tactics vis a vis single tactics, and long-term consequences of the influence attempt for the initiator and the organization.

10. For a more complete description of the research methods and statistical findings of the three studies reported here, see J. B. Keys, T. Miller, T. Case, K. Curran, and C. Jones, "Lateral Influence Tactics," *International Journal of Management,* 4 (3), 1987, 425–31; L. Dosier, T. Case, J. B. Keys, G. Murkinson, "Upward Influence Tactics," *Leadership and Organizational*

Development Journal, 9 (4), 1988, 25–31; T. Case, J. B. Keys, and L. Dosier, "How Managers Influence Subordinates: A Study of Downward Influence Tactics," *Leadership and Organizational Development Journal,* 9 (5), 1988, 22–28.

11. For an interesting theoretical discussion of these and other power producing factors see D. Mechanic, "Source of Power on Lower Participants in Complex Organizations," *Administrative Science Quarterly,* 7 (3), 1962, 349–64. For an excellent case study of how a middle manager combines expertise, networking, and the other techniques noted see D. Izrael: "The Middle Manager and the Tactics of Power Expansion: A Case Study," *Sloan Management Review,* 16 (2), 1975, 57–69.

12. See Endnote 1. p. 35

13. See Kotter in Endnote 2, p 35.

14. B. Keys, T. Case, and A. Edge, "A Cross-National Study of Differences between Leadership Relationships of Managers in Hong Kong with those in the Philippines, Korea, and the United States," *International Journal of Management,* 6 (4), 1989, 390–404.

15. For a look at the pattern of managerial communications and time investment, see F. Luthans and J. K. Larson, "How Managers Really Communicate," *Human Relations,* 39 (2), 1986, 161–78.

16. For a discussion of the need for middle managers to spend time in lateral and external relationships, see T. Peters, *Thriving on Chaos: Handbook for a Management Revolution* (New York: Harper & Row. 1987); T. Peters and N. Austin, *Passion for Excellence,* (New York: Random House, 1985); and L. Johnson and A. L. Frohman, "Identifying and Closing the Gap in the Middle of Organizations," *Academy of Management Executive,* 3 (2), 107–14.

17. R. E. Kaplan, "Trade Routes: The Manager's Network of Relationships," *Organizational Dynamics,* 12 (4), 1984, 37–52, and J. Kotter, *The General Managers* (New York: Free Press 1983).

18. For an excellent guide to handling lateral relations complete with case illustrations, see Chapter 5 of L. Sayles, *Leadership: Managing in Real Organizations* (New York: McGraw Hill), second ed.

19. For a discussion of why managers should encourage their subordinates to influence them see W. K. Schilit, "An Examination of Individual Differences as Moderators of Upward Influence Activity in Strategic Decisions," *Human Relations,* 30 (10), 1986, 948. The author's findings from this empirical study lend support to the suggestions about transformational leaders by Tichy and Devana and Kotter in Endnote 2.

20. For a further discussion of the activities of successful and effective managers, see F. Luthans, R. M. Hodgetts, and S. A. Rosenkrantz, *Real Managers* (Cambridge: Ballenger Publishing Company, 1988).

21. For a review of network theory, see J. Blau and R. Alba, "Empowering Nets of Participation," *Administrative Science Quarterly,* 27, 1982, 363–79. See also Endnote 18.

22. See Kaplan, Endnote 17 above.

23. For an excellent treatment of the objectives and targets of influence, see D. Kipnis, S. Schmidt, C. Swaffin-Smith, and I. Wilkinson, "Patterns of Managerial Influence: Shotgun Managers, Tacticians, and By-Standers," *Organizational Dynamics,* 12 (3), 1984, 58–67, and Kipnis et al., 1980, Endnote 9 above. These studies and the Erez et al. study noted below also used a common questionnaire and a similar factor analysis to find broader categories of influence in which individual influence tactics (similar to those in Exhibit 1) fall. The categories derived include:

Reason: The use of facts and data to support logical arguments.

Manipulation: The use of impression management, flattery, or ingratiation.

Coalitions: Obtaining the support of other people in the organization.

Bargaining: The use of negotiation and exchange of benefits or favors.

Assertiveness: Demanding or acting in a forceful manner.

Upward appeal: Making an appeal to higher levels of management in the organization to back up requests.

Sanctions: Threatening to withhold pay, advancement or to impose organizational discipline.

M. Erez, R. Rim and I. Keider, "The Two Sides of the Tactics of Influence: Agent vs. Target," *Journal of Occupational Psychology,* 59, 1986, 25–39.

24. See D. Kipnis et al., Endnote 23 above, p. 32.

25. For a discussion of the use of manipulation as an influence, and/or managerial approach, see Erez, Endnote 23 above, and A. Zalesnik, "The Leadership Gap," *Academy of Management Executive,* 4 (1), 1990, 7–22.

26. See D. Kipnis et al. in Endnote 23, p. 32.

27. A. R. Cohen and D. L. Bradford, "Influence Without Authority: The Use of Alliances, Reciprocity, and Exchange to Accomplish Work," *Organizational Dynamics,* 17 (3), 1989, 5–17.

28. J. P. Kotter, *The Leadership Factor,* (New York: Free Press, 1988), 18.

29. G. Laborde, *Influencing Integrity: Management Skills for Communication and Negotiation* (Palo Alto: Syntony Publishing, 1987).

30. See Endnote 17 above, p. 32.

31. For a discussion of power and influence as a leadership approach, see G. Yukl, "Managerial Leadership: A Review of Theory and Research," *Journal of Management,* 15 (2), 1989, 251–89.

Breakthrough Bargaining

Deborah M. Kolb
Judith Williams

Negotiation was once considered an art practiced by the naturally gifted. To some extent it still is, but increasingly we in the business world have come to regard negotiation as a science—built on creative approaches to deal making that allow everyone to walk away winners of sorts. Executives have become experts in "getting to yes," as the now-familiar terminology goes.

Nevertheless, some negotiations stall or, worse, never get off the ground. Why? Our recent research suggests that the answers lie in a dynamic we have come to call the "shadow negotiation"—the complex and subtle game people play before they get to the table and continue to play after they arrive. The shadow negotiation doesn't determine the "what" of the discussion, but the "how." Which interests will hold sway? Will the conversation's tone be adversarial or cooperative? Whose opinions will be heard? In short, how will bargainers deal with each other?

The shadow negotiation is most obvious when the participants hold unequal power—say subordinates asking bosses for more resources or new employees engaging with veterans about well-established company policies. Similarly, managers who, because of their rage, age, or gender, are in the minority in their companies may be at a disadvantage in the shadow negotiation. Excluded from important networks, they may not have the personal clout, experience, or organizational standing to influence other parties. Even when the bargainers are peers, a negotiation can be blocked or stalled— undermined by hidden assumptions, unrealistic expectations, or personal histories. An unexamined shadow negotiation can lead to silence, not satisfaction.

In doesn't have to be that way. Our research identified strategic levers—we call them power moves, process moves, and appreciative moves—that executives can use to guide the shadow negotiation. In situations in which the other person sees no compelling need

Source: Reprinted by permission of Harvard Business Review. From "Breakthrough Bargaining" by Deborah M. Kolb and Judith Williams, February 2001. Copyright © 2001 by the Harvard Business School Publishing Corporation; all rights reserved.

Most of the negotiating stories used in this article have been adapted from The Shadow Negotiation: How Women Can Master the Hidden Agendas that Determine Bargaining Success (Simon & Schuster, 2000) and the authors' interviews with businesspeople. To respect interviewees' candor and to protect their privacy, their identities and situations have been disguised, sometimes radically.

to negotiate, *power moves* can help bring him or her to the table. When the dynamics of decision making threaten to overpower a negotiator's voice, *process moves* can reshape the negotiation's structure. And when talks stall because the other party feels pushed or misunderstandings cloud the real issues, *appreciative moves* can alter the tone or atmosphere so that a more collaborative exchange is possible. These strategic moves don't guarantee that bargainers will walk away winners, but they help to get stalled negotiations out of the dark of unspoken power plays and into the light of true dialogue.

POWER MOVES

In the informal negotiations common in the workplace, one of the parties can be operating from a one-down position. The other bargainer, seeing no apparent advantage in negotiating, stalls. Phone calls go unanswered. The meeting keeps being postponed or, if it does take place, a two-way conversation never gets going. Ideas are ignored or overruled, demands dismissed. Such resistance is a natural part of the informal negotiation process. A concern will generally be accorded a fair hearing only when someone believes two things: the other party has something desirable, and one's own objectives will not be met without giving something in return. Willingness to negotiate is, therefore, a confession of mutual need. As a result, a primary objective in the shadow negotiation is fostering the perception of mutual need.

Power moves can bring reluctant bargainers to the realization that they must negotiate: they will be better off if they do and worse off if they don't. Bargainers can use three kinds of power moves. Incentives emphasize the proposed value to the other person and the advantage to be gained from negotiating. Pressure levers underscore the consequences to the other side if stalling continues. And the third power move, enlisting allies, turns up the volume of the incentives or on the pressure. Here's how these strategies work.

Offer Incentives

In any negotiation, the other party controls something the bargainer needs: money, time, cooperation, communication, and so on. But the bargainer's needs alone aren't enough to bring anyone else to the table. The other side must recognize that benefits will accrue from the negotiation. These benefits must not only be visible—that is, right there on the table—but they must also resonate with the other side's needs. High-tech executive Fiona Sweeney quickly recognized this dynamic when she tried to initiate informal talks about a mission-critical organizational change.

Shortly after being promoted to head operations at an international systems company, Sweeney realized that the organization's decision-making processes required a fundamental revamping. The company operated through a collection of fiefdoms, with little coordination even on major accounts. Sales managers, whose bonuses were tied to gross sales, pursued any opportunity with minimal regard for the company's ability to deliver. Production scrambled to meet unrealistic schedules; budgets and quality suffered. Sweeney had neither the authority nor the inclination to order sales and production to cooperate. And as a newcomer to corporate headquarters, her visibility and credibility were low.

Sweeney needed a sweetner to bring sales and production together. First, she made adjustments to the billing process, reducing errors from 7.1 percent to 2.4 percent over a three-month period, thereby cutting back on customer complaints. Almost immediately, her stock shot up with both of the divisions. Second, realizing that sales would be more reluctant than production to negotiate any changes in the organization's decision-making processes, she worked with billing to speed up processing the expense account checks so that salespeople were reimbursed more quickly, a move that immediately got the attention of everyone in sales. By demonstrating her value to sales and production, Sweeney encouraged the two division managers to work with her on improving their joint decision-making process.

Creating value and making it visible are key power moves in the shadow negotiation. A bargainer can't leave it up to the other party to puzzle through the possibilities. The benefits must be made explicit if they are to have any impact on the shadow negotiation. When value disappears, so do influence and bargaining power.

Put a Price on the Status Quo

Abba Eban, Israel's former foreign minister, once observed that diplomats have "a passionate love affair with the status quo" that blocks any forward movement. The same love affair carries over into ordinary negotiations in the workplace. When people believe that a negotiation has the potential to produce bad results for them, they are naturally reluctant to engage on the issues. Until the costs of *not* negotiating are made explicit, ducking the problem will be the easier or safer course.

To unlock the situation, the status quo must be perceived as less attractive. By exerting pressure, the bargainer can raise the cost of business-as-usual until the other side begins to see that things will get worse unless both sides get down to talking.

That is exactly what Karen Hartig, one of the women in our study, did when her boss dragged his heels about giving her a raise. Not only had she been promoted without additional pay but she was now doing two jobs because the first position had never been filled. Although her boss continued to assure her of his support, nothing changed. Finally, Hartig was so exasperated that she returned a headhunter's call. The resulting job offer provided her with enough leverage to unfreeze the talks with her boss. No longer could he afford to maintain the status quo. By demonstrating that she had another alternative, she gave him a push—and the justification—he needed to argue forcefully on her behalf with his boss and with human resources.

Enlist Support

Solo power moves won't always do the job. Another party may not see sufficient benefits to negotiating, or the potential costs may not be high enough to compel a change of mind. When incentives and pressure levers fail to move the negotiation forward, a bargainer can enlist the help of allies.

Allies are important resources in shadow negotiations. They can be crucial in establishing credibility, and they lend tangible support to incentives already proposed. By providing guidance or running interference, they can favorably position a bargainer's proposals before talks even begin. At a minimum, their confidence primes the other party to listen and raises the cost of not negotiating seriously.

When a member of Dan Riley's squadron faced a prolonged family emergency, the air force captain needed to renegotiate his squadron's flight-rotation orders. The matter was particularly sensitive, however, because it required the consent of the wing commander, two levels up the chain of command. If Riley approached the commander directly, he risked making his immediate superior look bad since his responsibilities covered readiness planning. To bridge that difficulty, Riley presented a draft proposal to his immediate supervisor. Once aware of the problem, Riley and his superior anticipated some of the objections the commander might raise and then alerted the wing commander to the general difficulties posed by such situations. When Riley finally presented his proposal to the commander, it carried his immediate superior's blessing, and so his credibility was never questioned; only the merits of his solution were discussed.

PROCESS MOVES

Rather than attempt to influence the shadow negotiation directly through power moves, a bargainer can exercise another kind of strategic move, the process move. Designed to influence the negotiation process itself, such moves can be particularly effective when bargainers are caught in a dynamic of silencing—when decisions are being made without their input or when colleagues interrupt them during meetings, dismiss their comments, or appropriate their ideas.

While process moves do not address the substantive issues in a negotiation, they directly affect the hearing those issues receive. The agenda, the prenegotiation groundwork, and the sequence in which ideas and people are heard—all these structural elements influence others' receptivity to opinions and demands. Working behind the scenes, a bargainer can plant the seeds of ideas or can marshal support before a position becomes fixed in anyone's mind. Consensus can even be engineered so that the bargainer's agenda frames the subsequent discussion.

Seed Ideas Early

Sometimes parties to a negotiation simply shut down and don't listen; for whatever reason, they screen out particular comments or people. Being ignored in a negotiation doesn't necessarily result from saying too little or saying it too hesitantly. When ideas catch people off guard, they can produce negative, defensive reactions, as can ideas presented too forcefully. Negotiators also screen out the familiar: if they've already heard the speech, or a close variant, they stop paying attention.

Joe Lopez faced this dilemma. Lopez, a fast-track engineer who tended to promote his ideas vigorously in planning meetings, began to notice that his peers were tuning him out—a serious problem since departmental resources were allocated in these sessions. To remedy the situation, Lopez scheduled one-on-one lunch meetings with his colleagues. On each occasion, he mentioned how a particular project would benefit the other manager's department and how they could work together to ensure its completion. As a result of this informal lobbying, Lopez found he no longer needed to oversell his case in the meetings. He could make his ideas heard with fewer words and at a lower decibel level.

Preliminary work like this allows a bargainer to build receptivity where a direct or aggressive approach might encounter resistance. Once the seeds of an idea have been planted, they will influence how others view a situation, regardless of how firmly attached they are to their own beliefs and ideas.

Reframe the Process

Negotiators are not equally adept in all settings. Highly competitive approaches to problem solving favor participants who can bluff and play the game, talk the loudest, hold out the longest, and think fastest on their feet. Bargainers who are uncomfortable with this kind of gamesmanship can reframe the process, shifting the dynamic away from personal competition. That's what Marcia Philbin decided to do about the way in which space was allocated in her company. Extra room and equipment typically went to those who pushed the hardest, and Philbin never fared well in the negotiations. She also believed that significant organizational costs always accompanied the process since group leaders routinely presented the building administrator with inflated figures, making it impossible to assess the company's actual requirements.

Positioning herself as an advocate not only for her department but also for the company, Philbin proposed changing the process. Rather than allocating space in a series of discrete negotiations with the space administrator, she suggested, why not collaborate as a group in developing objective criteria for assessing need? Management agreed, and Philbin soon found herself chairing the committee created to produce the new guidelines. Heated arguments took place over the criteria, but Philbin was now positioned to direct the discussions away from vested and parochial interests toward a greater focus on organizational needs.

Within organizations or groups, negotiations can fall into patterns. If a bargainer's voice is consistently shut out of discussions, something about the way negotiations are structured is working against his or her active participation. A process move may provide a remedy because it will influence how the discussion unfolds and how issues emerge.

Build Consensus

Regardless of how high a bargainer is on the organizational ladder, it is not always possible—or wise—to impose change on a group by fiat. By lobbying behind the scenes, a bargainer can start to build consensus before formal decision making begins. Unlike the first process move, which aims at gaining a hearing for ideas, building consensus creates momentum behind an agenda by bringing others on board. The growing support isolates the blockers, making continued opposition harder and harder. Moreover, once agreement has been secured privately, it becomes difficult (although never impossible) for a supporter to defect publicly.

As CEO of a rapidly growing biotechnology company, Mark Chapin gradually built consensus for his ideas on integrating a newly acquired research boutique into the existing company. Chapin had two goals: to retain the acquired firm's scientific talent and to rationalize the research funding process. The second goal was at odds with the first and threatened to alienate the new scientists. To mitigate this potential conflict, Chapin focused his attention on the shadow negotiation. First, he met one-on-one with key leaders of the board and the research staffs of both companies. These private talks provided him with a strategic map that showed where he would find support and where he was likely to meet challenges. Second, in another round of talks, Chapin paid particular attention to the order in which he approached people. Beginning with the most supportive person, he got the key players to commit, one by one, to his agenda before opposing factions could coalesce. These preliminary meetings positioned him as a collaborator—and, equally important, as a source of expanding research budgets. Having privately built commitment, Chapin found that he didn't need to use his position to dictate terms when the principal players finally sat down to negotiate the integration plan.

APPRECIATIVE MOVES

Power moves exert influence on the other party so that talks get off the ground. Process moves seek to change the ground rules under which negotiations play out. But still, talks may stall. Two strong advocates may have backed themselves into respective corners. Or one side, put on the defensive, even inadvertently, may continue to resist or raise obstacles. Communication may deteriorate, turn acrimonious, or simply stop as participants focus solely on their own demands. Wariness stifles any candid exchange. And without candor, the two sides cannot address the issues together or uncover the real conflict.

Appreciative moves break these cycles. They explicitly build trust and encourage the other side to participate in a dialogue. Not only do appreciative moves shift the dynamics of the shadow negotiation away from the adversarial, but they also hold out a hidden promise. When bargainers demonstrate appreciation for another's concerns, situation, or "face," they open the negotiation to the different perspectives held by that person and to the opinions, ideas, and feelings shaping those perspectives. Appreciative moves foster open communication so that differences in needs and views can come to the surface without personal discord. Frequently the participants then discover that the problem they were worrying about is not the root conflict, but a symptom of it. And at times, before a negotiation can move toward a common solution, the participants must first experience mutuality, recognizing where their interests and needs intersect. A shared problem can then become the basis for creative problem solving.

Help Others Save Face

Image is a concern for everyone. How negotiators look to themselves and to others who matter to them often counts as much as the particulars of an agreement. In fact, these are seldom separate. "Face" captures what people value in themselves and the qualities they want others to see in them. Negotiators go to great lengths to preserve face. They stick to their guns against poor odds simply to avoid losing face with those who are counting on them. If a bargainer treads on another's self-image—in front of a boss or colleague, or even privately—his or her demands are likely to be rejected.

Sensitivity to the other side's face does more than head off resistance: it lays the groundwork for trust. It conveys that the bargainer respects what the other is trying to accomplish and will not do anything to embarrass or undermine that person. This appreciation concedes nothing, yet as Sam Newton discovered, it can turn out to be the only way to break a stalemate.

Newton's new boss, transferred from finance, lacked experience on the operations side of the business. During department meetings to negotiate project schedules and funding, he always rejected Newton's ideas. Soon it was routine: Newton would make a suggestion and before he got the last sentence out, his boss was issuing a categorical veto.

Frustrated, Newton pushed harder, only to meet increased resistance. Finally, he took a step back and looked at the situation from his boss's perspective. Rubberstamping Newton's proposals could have appeared as a sign of weakness at a time when his boss was still establishing his credentials. From then on, Newton took a different tack. Rather than present a single idea, he offered an array of options and acknowledged that the final decision rested with his boss. Gradually, his boss felt less need to assert his authority and could respond positively in their dealings.

Bosses aren't the only ones who need to save face; colleagues and subordinates do, too. Team members avoid peers who bump a problem upstairs at the first sign of trouble, making everyone appear incapable of producing a solution. Subordinates muzzle their real opinions once they have been belittled or treated dismissively by superiors. In the workplace, attention to face is a show of respect for another person, whatever one's corporate role. That respect carries over to the shadow negotiation.

Keep the Dialogue Going

Sometimes, talks don't get off the ground because the timing is not right for a participant to make a decision; information may be insufficient, or he or she is simply not ready. People have good reasons—at least, reasons that make sense to them—for thinking it's not yet time to negotiate. Appreciating this disposition doesn't mean abandoning or postponing a negotiation. Instead, it requires that a bargainer keep the dialogue going without pushing for immediate agreement. This appreciative move allows an opportunity for additional information to come to the surface and affords the other side more time to rethink ideas and adjust initial predilections.

Francesca Rossi knew instinctively that unless she kept the communication lines open, discussions would derail about the best way for her software firm to grow. The company had recently decided to expand by acquiring promising applications rather than developing them in-house from scratch. As head of strategic development, Rossi targeted a small start-up that designed state-of-the-art software for office computers to control home appliances. The director of research, however, was less than enthusiastic about acquiring the firm. He questioned the product's commercial viability and argued that its market would never justify the acquisition cost.

Needing his cooperation, Rossi pulled back. Instead of actively promoting the acquisition, she began to work behind the scenes with the start-up's software designers and industry analysts. As Rossi gathered more data in support of the application's potential, she gradually drew the director of research back into the discussions. He dropped his opposition once the analysis convinced him that the acquisition, far from shrinking his department's authority, would actually enlarge it. Rossi's appreciative move had given him the additional information and time he needed to reevaluate his original position.

Not everyone makes decisions quickly. Sometimes people can't see beyond their initial ideas or biases. Given time to mull over the issues, they may eventually reverse course and be more amenable to negotiating. As long as the issue isn't forced or brought to a preemptive conclusion—as long as the participants keep talking—there's a chance that the resistance will fade. What seems unreasonable at one point in a negotiation can become more acceptable at another. Appreciative moves that keep the dialogue going allow the other side to progress at a comfortable speed.

Solicit New Perspectives

One of the biggest barriers to effective negotiation and a major cause of stalemate is the tendency for bargainers to get trapped in their own perspectives. It's simply too easy for people to become overly enamored of their opinions. Operating in a closed world of their making, they tell themselves they are right and the other person is wrong. They consider the merits of their own positions but neglect the other party's valid objections. They push their agendas, merely reiterating the same argument, and may not pick up on cues that their words aren't being heard.

It's safe to assume that the other party is just as convinced that his or her own demands are justified. Moreover, bargainers can only speculate what another's agenda might be—hidden or otherwise. Appreciative moves to draw out another's perspectives help negotiators understand why the other party feels a certain way. But these moves serve more than an instrumental purpose, doing more than add information to a bargainer's arsenal. They signal to the other side that differing opinions and perspectives are important. By creating opportunities to discover something new and unexpected, appreciative moves can break a stalemate. As understanding deepens on both sides of the table, reaching a mutual resolution becomes increasingly possible.

Everyone agreed that a joint venture negotiated by HMO executive Donna Hitchcock between her organization and an insurance company dovetailed with corporate objectives on both sides. The HMO could expand its patient base and the insurance carrier its enrollment.

Although the deal looked good on paper, implementation stalled. Hitchcock couldn't understand where the resistance was coming from or why. In an attempt to unfreeze the situation, she arranged a meeting with her counterpart from the insurance company. After a brief update, Hitchcock asked about any unexpected effects the joint venture was exerting on the insurance carrier's organization and on her counterpart's work life. That appreciative move ultimately broke the logjam. From the carrier's perspective, she learned, the new arrangement stretched already overworked departments and had not yet produced additional revenues to hire more staff. Even more important, her counterpart was personally bearing the burden of the increased work.

Hitchcock was genuinely sympathetic to these concerns. The extra work was a legitimate obstacle to the joint venture's successful implementation. Once she understood the reason behind her counterpart's resistance, the two were able to strategize on ways to alleviate the overload until the additional revenues kicked in.

Through these appreciative moves—actively soliciting the other side's ideas and perspectives, acknowledging their importance, and demonstrating that they are taken seriously—negotiators can encourage the other person to work with them rather than against them.

There's more to negotiation than haggling over issues and working out solutions. The shadow negotiation, though often overlooked, is a critical component. Whether a bargainer uses power, process, or appreciative moves in the shadow negotiation depends on the demands of the situation. Power moves encourage another party to recognize the need to negotiate in the first place. They help bring a reluctant bargainer to the table. Process moves create a context in which a bargainer can shape the negotiation's agenda and dynamic so that he or she can be a more effective advocate. Appreciative moves engage the other party in a collaborative exchange by fostering trust and candor in the shadow negotiation. While power and process moves can ensure that a negotiation gets started on the right foot, appreciative moves can break a stalemate once a negotiation is under way. By broadening the discourse, appreciative moves can also lead to creative solutions. Used alone or in combination, strategic moves in the shadow negotiation can determine the outcome of the negotiation on the issues.

The Good Guy's*
Guide to Office Politics

Michael Warshaw

When Cindy Casselman took a communications job at Xerox headquarters in Stamford, Connecticut, the company's communications weren't so good. If Xerox made a big acquisition or had a disappointing quarter, many of its 85,000 people read the news in the papers before they got the scoop from the company. Casselman was determined to change things. "I was manager of employee communications," she says. "I took my job seriously."

But Casselman, now 50, didn't have much formal authority. She was, to use an out-of-favor phrase, a middle manager: someone whose boss had a boss who had a boss. So she assembled a makeshift budget and mustered a volunteer team that she called the Sanctioned Covert Operation (SCO)—"sanctioned," because her direct boss tolerated what looked like a modest project; "covert," because her actual goals were more ambitious than she let on.

Today, thanks to the SCO, any Xerox employee can visit the WebBoard, the company's spirited intranet site, and talk to other employees, read up-to-the-minute news about internal developments—and in general get more connected to what's happening inside this vast enterprise. How did Casselman have such a big impact with so few resources? She had a knack for playing politics.

Chris Newell, 47, is founder and executive director of Lotus Institute, a 20-member unit of Lotus Development Corp. (based in Cambridge, Massachusetts) that develops solutions using Lotus Notes software. It's a fun and interesting job—but hardly a position of power. "We generate new ideas about how software interacts with culture," he says. "We're the shrinks of shrinkwrap."

Last year, Newell became convinced that the emerging field of "knowledge management" represented a big market opportunity for Lotus and its parent company, IBM. So he became a major catalyst behind a series of knowledge-management products that Lotus and IBM began to roll out by the end of the year. Newell didn't have the authority to order such initiatives. But he did know how to play politics.

---

*and Gal's

About three and a half years ago, when the Discovery Channel wanted to extend its high-profile brand beyond cable TV, CEO John Hendricks assembled a committee to explore interactive television. Tom Hicks, now 44, thought the company should focus on the Internet. But this was 1994, when pundits were heralding interactive TV and the Net was still an unproven medium. Worse, Hicks ran the division that produced Discovery's magazines. Today the Discovery Channel Online is a much-celebrated presence on the Web. And when was the last time you watched interactive TV? Pushing for this mid-course correction wasn't easy. It meant playing politics.

Office politics. Just say the words, and you sense the disdain. Isn't "playing politics" a tool for people who can't get ahead on merit—who pursue their own agenda regardless of what's good for their colleagues or the company? That's the downside of office politics. But what about the upside? Office politics is a lot like "real" politics. Plenty of politicians launch campaigns simply because they relish the privileges of power. But at least some politicians campaign for things that matter to people other than themselves. Dismissing all political campaigns as cynical and self-aggrandizing becomes a self-fulfilling prophecy. The same goes for office politics.

"When people talk about office politics, they usually mean something dirty or underhanded," says management professor Allan Cohen, dean of faculty at Babson College and coauthor of *Influence without Authority* (John Wiley & Sons, 1991). "But nobody exists in an atmosphere where everybody agrees. Politics is the art of trying to accomplish things within organizations."

Marilyn Moats Kennedy, a career coach based in Wilmette, Illinois, claims that the underlying logic of office politics is changing—and opening the door to campaigners who want to get things done rather than do other people in. "Workers today," she says, "compete for schedules and projects, for money and training. But they rarely compete for power—especially when that means power over others. Instead of power, people want assignments that build skills valued by the market. Learning experiences are what's really important."

Herminia Ibarra, an associate professor at the Harvard Business School who teaches a popular course called "Power and Influence," offers yet another perspective on office politics: You don't have to be a jerk to make things happen. "Integrity," she says, "can be a source of power."

So throw your hat in the ring! If you've got an idea worth fighting for, don't hire a campaign consultant. Consult Fast Company's five-step manual for waging a successful campaign. To paraphrase Plato, that well-known consultant: Those who think they're too smart to engage in politics will be governed by those who are dumber.

RULE 1. NOBODY WINS UNLESS EVERYBODY WINS

Office politics is no different from other aspects of life at the office—or of life in general. Appearances matter. It's usually the best-packaged idea that wins, not the best idea. And the first step toward victory is to position your idea so that your victory is everyone's victory.

"Real political skill isn't about campaign tactics," says Lou DiNatale, a senior fellow at the McCormack Institute of Public Affairs at the University of Massachusetts/

Boston and a veteran political consultant. "It's about pulling people toward your ideas and then pushing those ideas through to other people. In electoral politics, people overestimate the importance of polls and direct mail. What really matters is, Can you make people want to vote for you? The questions in business are, Can you get people to move? Do people trust your instincts? It comes down to personality and positioning."

RULE 2. DON'T JUST ASK FOR OPINIONS—CHANGE THEM

Opinion polls have a bad name, but no serious candidate runs for office without them. Politicians don't use polls just to identify their supporters. They also try to find out who opposes them, how deep the opposition is, and how people's views evolve over time. What goes for electoral politics goes for office politics. You can't change people's minds if you don't know what they're thinking.

John Gorman, a veteran pollster based in Cambridge, Massachusetts, got his start in the field when, as a Harvard undergraduate, he conducted surveys for George McGovern's 1972 presidential campaign. His firm, Opinion Dynamics Corp., now conducts polls for the Fox News Channel as well as for a wide range of companies and associations. "Go after basic questions," he advises: "Do people really believe that what you're proposing will benefit the company. Do they believe that what the company says it's about—its mission statement—is what it really is about? Whose help do you need? Whose permission do you need?"

Gorman makes a second point: The process of exploring people's opinions gives you an opportunity to shape them as well. You can ask questions in ways that build support for the outcome you want. The political pros call it "push polling." Chris Newell of Lotus calls it common sense. He was forever selling his ideas to colleagues even as he was testing out those ideas. "I tried to create an internal groundswell," he says.

Jim Krzywicki, 36, Lotus's vice president of worldwide customer support and education, says that Newell never wasted an encounter with him—or with anyone else in the organization. "He had his 'elevator speech' ready at all times," Krzywicki reports. "If he met the president of the company on the elevator, he would have made his point by the time they got off. Chris is continually checking with people. That gives him very sensitive antennae—and it helps him develop broad-based support and understanding."

How persistent was Newell? "Let me put it this way," Krzywicki says with a smile. "My wife's the only one with the number to my car phone. But I remember picking it up once and saying, 'Hi, honey.' It turned out to be Chris. He wanted to bounce an idea off me."

Over time, Kryzwicki became a key ally in Newell's campaign. "I would call Jim to test out strategies," Newell says. "But he always gave me more than just information. He became a cheerleader, a champion. He started bringing my ideas to people or into meetings that I couldn't reach."

Gorman also offers a word of warning that many people overlook: If you solicit feedback from the wrong people, he says, you're likely to reach the wrong conclusions. "You always have a bias to go to the easy people first, the people you already know or can get to fast," he says. "You have to overcome that bias. You have to reach out to the hard-to-get people."

Tom Hicks approached the hard-to-get crowd right from the start. He knew his campaign to redirect the Discovery Channel's commitment to interactive TV faced long odds. So he did some polling on how strong the opposition would be. His approach? Go to the toughest constituency of all—the interactive-TV committee. He and two colleagues made a presentation and asked for feedback: "They patted us on the head, said our plan was nice, and asked how we could make money. They didn't see a business model."

Hicks gained some useful insights from that reaction. For one thing, the committee didn't take his ideas seriously enough to fight them. For another he realized that his proposal had a genuine weakness: the lack of a convincing business model. "We then did what all good groups do," Hicks says. "A bunch of us got together after work, had some beers, and dreamed about how this thing was going to happen and how we could tap the enthusiasm that [CEO] John Hendricks had about interactivity."

Gorman makes one final point about polling your colleagues: Don't let the process of testing the waters sink your ship before it sails. "For the truly creative, brilliant, once-in-a-lifetime idea, opinion research is a deadly thing," he says. "Research is a conservative process. I always remind people that the personal computer didn't research very well in the 1970s."

RULE 3: EVERYONE EXPECTS TO BE PAID BACK

Here's the good news about office politics: You don't have to spend late nights at fund-raisers or badger high rollers for big checks. Sure, you need resources. But most people have most of what they need—even if they work out of a small office or hold a modest title. "People tend to underestimate their potential power," says Allan Cohen. "Because they don't know how to get power, they assume they don't have power. Don't think you have nothing to offer people just because you don't have the budget to buy them. Even the 'poorest' people in an office have currencies they can work with."

So what is the most precious currency of organizational life? On this question, all the experts agree: personal relationships. "All favors are personal," says Marilyn Moats Kennedy. "If your boss works hard to get you an assignment, that's between you and your boss. You should understand that the boss is acting personally, not institutionally. Nothing done in the name of the organization earns credit for the organization. Only the individual who did the good deed earns the credit." Cohen has a name for this phenomenon—the Law of Reciprocity. "The secret of the universe," he says, "lies in six words: *Everyone expects to be paid back.*"

How do you turn the Law of Reciprocity into support for your campaign? First you should never underestimate the power of a good idea. Most people in most companies want to do the right thing. Give them an opportunity to make a positive contribution, and chances are that they will. Second, you should never underestimate the desire to leave a mark. Most new-idea champions aren't in a position to order people to participate in their projects. But people will often volunteer when they see that their work will make a difference—and perhaps earn them recognition in the process. Finally, never underestimate the value of a simple "thank you." Keep expressing appreciation for what your supporters do, and they'll keep doing it. Share the credit, and they may do more.

"You're always working on two fronts: your specific goal, and the relationships you have," says Cohen. "And people always send off messages about what matters to them. It's good politics to make people feel good."

RULE 4: SUCCESS CAN CREATE OPPOSITIONS

You've positioned your idea for broad appeal. You've tested the waters with informal polling. You've evaluated your currencies. Now it's time for the real work of the campaign: cutting the deals, big and small, that turn your goal into a reality—and reckoning with the resistance that any campaign generates.

"A campaign is really a series of exchanges," argues Herminia Ibarra. "You swap influence and inspiration for support from all kinds of people. You also have to deal with adversaries. Opposition often comes quickly—and from unexpected places. You need to be smart about taking in information and about dealing with misinformation."

Xerox's Cindy Casselman had a ready-made information network in the form of her SCO team. But she needed both money and programming talent. So she launched a deal-making spree across the company. "I met with our CIO, Pat Wallington," she says. "I met with the head of education and learning, Carolyn McZinc. I identified reasons why they would want to help. I said to Pat, 'You spend all this money on a new infrastructure. If you give me a little money, I'll put content there.' I said to Carolyn, 'You enable learning at Xerox. I'm going to provide you with a place to make that happen.'"

Casselman also cut a deal with her boss, Joe Cahalan, Xerox's director of communications: He would allow her to work on the project, but only if she raised $250,000 for the WebBoard on her own. Piece by piece, Casselman got the funds. "I was shocked," Cahalan admits. "I still don't understand how she did it."

But Casselman's very success began to ruffle feathers. An opposition (or at least healthy skepticism) started in an unlikely place—with Joe Cahalan. The closer the WebBoard got to becoming a reality, the more he appreciated the stakes involved in the project. "Up to that point," he says, "I had given Cindy free reign. But I became dictatorial about one thing: I didn't want the site to have a false start or to get a bad name. I didn't want people to visit and be disappointed."

Then came more opposition—this time from Casselman's own department. She'd been so busy selling her idea to other parts of Xerox that she'd overlooked the people closest to her. A few of her colleagues resented Casselman's high profile. And many of them worried about the extra work. "I had this vision," Casselman says. "I saw this as the North Star. But other people asked, 'Does this mean we're doing news? Are we going to have to write for this every day?'"

A compromise emerged. Casselman would conduct a 30-day trial before the WebBoard's public debut. Cahalan could then assure himself of the WebBoard's quality, and the communications department could get a feel for the work. It was a nerve-wracking month for Casselman, but the trial was a huge success.

That success was no accident. "The more open you are," argues Allan Cohen, "the better prepared you'll be when opposition shows up. Always work to build a climate in which everybody can put information on the table. The most creative solutions to conflict come from being completely open."

RULE 5. DON'T IGNORE THE AFTERMATH OF SUCCESS

Election day for Cindy Casselman was November 15, 1995. Chairman and CEO Paul Allaire traveled to Dallas to deliver the keynote address for Xerox Teamwork Day. Allaire celebrated the spirit of cooperation at the company. He spoke honestly about a recent round of job cuts. He talked about the future. And he described Xerox's newest internal communications tool—the WebBoard.

"We want this site to become a place where Xerox people come to do work," Allaire said. "A place where you'll find the information you need to do your job and learn new things; a place where there's a community of Xerox people with whom to share information and best practices."

It was a huge win for the SCO team. It was also the beginning of the end for its campaign. The team had never developed a strategy for the aftermath of success. Everyone shared the unspoken assumption that after the WebBoard's creation, Xerox would create a stand-alone team to maintain and improve the site. Bad assumption. The WebBoard never became a formally independent unit. Tight budgets limited its expansion. Rick Beach returned to his regular duties. Malcolm Kirby left the company. The SCO disbanded. "I was so focused on creating the WebBoard," Casselman explains. "Nothing was going to stop me. But once it was up, I couldn't maintain that energy. It's very successful, but I had a much bigger vision."

That said, there's no denying that Casselman herself has benefited from the Web-Board's creation—even if things did not turn out exactly as she expected. In February, she became executive assistant to Mark Myers, the head of corporate research and technology at Xerox. She travels the world as a liaison between the company's senior staff and its research operations. "The WebBoard raised my profile and proved that I could follow through on an ambitious project and form the relationships needed to support the project," Casselman says. "It definitely helped me win my new job."

Tom Hicks of Discovery skillfully navigated the aftermath of his success. When he began his campaign, Hicks was running the company's magazine division. Today Discovery has only one magazine left in its stable. But Hicks is thriving as publisher of Discovery Channel Online, a respected website that gets 75,000 visits a day.

"The key to winning a campaign like this," Hick says, "is to consider your personal ambitions separately from your strategic goals for the company. You'll be validated personally at some point. Meanwhile, you will have moved the company to a place where it might not have gone without you. We helped take the Discovery Channel to another dimension."

SECTION SEVEN

Ethics in Negotiation

The Ethics and Profitability of Bluffing in Business

Richard E. Wokutch
Thomas L. Carson

Consider a standard case of bluffing in an economic transaction. I am selling a used car and say that $1,500 is my final offer, even though I know that I would accept considerably less. Or, suppose that I am a union representative in a labor negotiation. Although I have been instructed to accept $10 an hour if that is the highest offer I receive, I say that we will not accept a wage of $10 an hour under any circumstances. This sort of bluffing is widely practiced and almost universally condoned. It is thought to be morally acceptable. It is our contention, however, that bluffing raises serious ethical questions. For bluffing is clearly an act of deception; the bluffer's intent is to deceive the other parties about the nature of his bargaining position. Furthermore, bluffing often involves lying. The two examples of bluffing presented here both fit the standard definition of lying: they are deliberate false statements made with the intent of deceiving others.[1]

Common sense holds that lying and deception are prima facie wrong. One could also put this by saying that there is a presumption against lying and deception: that they require some special justification in order to be permissible.[2] Almost no one would agree with Kant's view that it is wrong to lie even if doing so is necessary to protect the lives of innocent people. According to Kant it would be wrong to lie to a potential murderer concerning the whereabouts of his intended victim.[3]

Assuming the correctness of the view that there is a moral presumption against lying and deception, and assuming that we are correct in saying that bluffing often involves lying, it follows that bluffing and other deceptive business practices require some sort of special justification in order to be considered permissible. Businesspeople frequently defend bluffing and other deceptive practices on the grounds that they are profitable or economically necessary. Such acts are also defended on the grounds that they are standard practice in economic transactions. We will argue that these standard justifications of bluffing are unacceptable. Then we will propose an alternative justification for lying and deception about one's bargaining position.

Reprinted from *Westminster Institute Review* 1, no. 2 (May 1981), pp. 77–83. Used with permission of the publisher and the authors.

There are those who hold that lying and deception are never profitable or economically necessary. In their view, honesty is always the best policy. One incentive for telling the truth is the law, but here we are referring to lying or bluffing which is not illegal, or for which the penalty or risk of being caught is not great enough to discourage the action.

Those who hold that honesty is always in one's economic self-interest argue that economic transactions are built on trust and that a violation of that trust discourages an individual or organization from entering into further transactions with the lying party for fear of being lied to again. Thus, some mutually beneficial transactions may be foregone for lack of trust. Moreover, word of deceitful practices spreads through the marketplace and others also avoid doing business with the liar. Thus, while some short-run profit might accrue from lying, in the long run it is unprofitable. If this argument were sound, we would have a nonissue. Lying, like inefficiency, would be a question of bad management that would be in one's own best interest to eliminate.

Unfortunately, there are some anomalies in the marketplace which prevent the system from operating in a perfectly smooth manner. The very existence of bluffing and lying in the first place suggests that the economists' assumption of perfect (or near perfect) market information is incorrect. Some transactions, such as buying or selling a house, are one-shot deals with little or no chance of repeat business. Thus, there is no experience on which to base an assessment of the seller's honesty, and no incentive to build trust for future transactions. Even when a business is involved in an ongoing operation, information flows are such that a large number of people can be duped before others hear about it (e.g., selling Florida swampland or Arizona desertland sight unseen). Other bluffs and lies are difficult or even impossible to prove. If a union negotiator wins a concession from management on the grounds that the union would not ratify the contract without it—even though he has reason to believe that this is untrue—it would be extremely difficult for management to prove later that ratification could have been achieved without the provision. By the same token, some product claims, such as the salesman's contention that "this is the best X on the market," are inherently subjective. When the competing products are of similar quality, it is difficult to prove such statements untrue, even if the person making the statement believes them to be untrue. Another exception to the assumption of perfect information flows is the confusion brought on by the increasing technological complexity of goods and services. In fact, a product information industry in the form of publications like *Consumer Reports, Canadian Consumer, Consumer Union Reports, Money,* and *Changing Times* has arisen to provide, for a price, the kind of product information that economic theory assumes consumers have to begin with.

These arguments suggest not only that the commonly cited disincentives to bluffing and lying are often ineffective, but that there are some distinct financial incentives for these activities. If you can convince consumers that your product is better than it really is, you will have a better chance of selling them that product and you may be able to charge them a higher price than they would otherwise be willing to pay. It is also obvious that in a negotiating setting there are financial rewards for successful lies and bluffs. If you can conceal your actual minimal acceptable position, you may be able to achieve a more desirable settlement. By the same token, learning your negotiating opponent's true position will enable you to press toward his minimal acceptable position. This is, of course, why such intrigues as hiding microphones in the opposing negotiating team's private quarters or hiring informants are undertaken in negotiations—they produce valuable information.

An individual cannot, however, justify lying simply on the grounds that it is in his own self-interest to lie, for it is not always morally permissible to do what is in one's own self-interest. I would not be justified in killing you or falsely accusing you of a crime in order to get your job, even if doing so would be to my advantage. Similarly, a businessman cannot justify lying and deception simply on the grounds that they are advantageous, that is, profitable, to his company. This point can be strengthened if we remember that any advantages that one gains as a result of bluffing are usually counterbalanced by corresponding disadvantages on the part of others. If I succeed in getting a higher price by bluffing when I sell my house, there must be someone else who is paying more than he would have otherwise.

Economic necessity is a stronger justification for lying than mere profitability. Suppose that it is necessary for a businessman to engage in lying or deception in order to insure the survival of his firm. Many would not object to a person stealing food to prevent himself or his children from starving to death. Perhaps lying in an extreme situation to get money to buy food or to continue employing workers so that *they* can buy food would be equally justifiable. This case would best be described as a conflict of duties—a conflict between the duty to be honest and the duty to promote the welfare of those for/to whom one is responsible (one's children, one's employees, or the stockholders whose money one manages). However, it is extremely unlikely that bankruptcy would result in the death or starvation of anyone in a society which has unemployment compensation, welfare payments, food stamps, charitable organizations, and even opportunities for begging. The consequences of refraining from lying in transactions might still be very unfavorable indeed, involving, for example, the bankruptcy of a firm, loss of investment, unemployment, and the personal suffering associated with this. But a firm which needs to practice lying or deception in order to continue in existence is of doubtful value to society. Perhaps the labor, capital, and raw materials which it uses could be put to better use elsewhere. At least in a free market situation, the interests of economic efficiency would be best served if such firms were to go out of business. An apparent exception to this argument about economic efficiency would be a situation in which a firm was pushed to the edge of bankruptcy by the lies of competitors or others. It seems probable that the long-term consequences of the bankruptcy of a firm which needs to lie in order to continue in existence would be better, or no worse, than those of its continuing to exist.

Suppose, however, that the immediate bad consequences of bankruptcy would not be offset by any long-term benefits. In that case it is not clear that it would be wrong for a company to resort to lying and deception out of economic necessity. One can, after all, be justified in lying or deceiving to save individuals from harms far less serious than death. I can be justified in lying about the gender of my friend's roommate to a nosy relative or boss in order to protect him from embarrassment or from being fired. If the degree of harm prevented by lying or deception were the only relevant factor, and if bankruptcy would not have any significant long-term benefits, then it would seem that a businessman could easily justify lying and deceiving in order to protect those associated with his business from the harm which would result from the bankruptcy of the firm. There is, however, another relevant factor which clouds the issue. In the case of lying about the private affairs of one's friends, one is lying to others about matters about which they have no right to know. Our present analogy warrants lying and deception for the sake of economic survival only in cases in which the persons being lied to or deceived have no right to the information in question. Among other things, this rules out deceiving customers about dangerous defects in one's products, because customers have a right to this information; but it does not rule out lying to someone or deceiving them about one's minimal bargaining position.

We have argued that personal or corporate profit is no justification for lying in business transactions, and that lying for reasons of economic necessity is also morally objectionable in many cases. But what about lying in order to benefit the party being lied to? There are certainly many self-serving claims to this effect. Some have argued that individuals derive greater satisfaction from a product or service if they can be convinced that it is better than is actually the case. On the other hand, an advertising executive made the argument in the recent Federal Trade Commission hearings on children's advertising that the disappointment children experience when a product fails to meet their commercial-inflated expectations is beneficial because it helps them develop a healthy skepticism. These arguments are not convincing. In fact, they appear to be smoke screens for actions taken out of self-interest. It is conceivable that consumers might benefit from it. For example, deceptive advertising claims may cause one to purchase a product which is of genuine benefit. While lying and deception can sometimes be justified by reference to the interests of those being lied to or deceived, such cases are very atypical in business situations. As was argued earlier, successful bluffing almost always harms the other party in business negotiations. The net effect of a successful bluff is paying more or receiving less than would otherwise have been the case.

A further ground on which lying or deception in bargaining situations is sometimes held to be justifiable is the claim that the other parties do not have a right to know one's true bargaining position. It is true that the other parties do not have a right to know one's position, that is, it would not be wrong to refuse to reveal it to them. But this is not to say that it is permissible to lie or deceive them. You have no right to know where I was born, but it would be prima facie wrong for me to lie to you about the place of my birth. So, lying and deception in bargaining situations cannot be justified simply on the grounds that the other parties have no right to know one's true position. However, other things being equal, it is much worse to lie or deceive about a matter concerning which the other parties have a right to know than one about which they have no right to know.

But what of the justification that lying and deception are standard practice in economic transactions? Certainly, lying and deception are very common, if not generally accepted or condoned. Bluffing and other deceptive practices are especially common in economic negotiations, and bluffing, at least, is generally thought to be an acceptable practice.[4] Does this fact in any way justify bluffing? We think not. The mere fact that something is standard practice or generally accepted is not enough to justify it. Standard practice and popular opinion can be in error. Such things as slavery were once standard practice and generally accepted. But they are and were morally wrong. Bluffing cannot be justified simply *because* it is a common and generally accepted practice. However, we shall now use the prevalence of bluffing involving lying and deception as a premise of an argument to show that there is a presumption for thinking that bluffing of this sort is morally permissible. If one is involved in a negotiation, it is very probable that the other parties with whom one is dealing are themselves bluffing. The presumption against lying and deception does not hold when the other parties with whom one is dealing are themselves lying to or otherwise attempting to deceive one. Given this, there is no presumption against lying or deceiving others about one's bargaining position in the course of an ordinary business negotiation, since the parties with whom one is dealing may be presumed to be doing the same themselves.

It is prima facie wrong to use violence against another person, but when one is a victim of violence oneself, it is permissible to use violence if doing so is necessary in order to prevent or limit harm to oneself. One is not morally required to refrain from self-defense. Similarly, other things being equal, if X is being harmed by the lies or deception of Y and if X can avoid or mitigate that harm only by lying to or deceiving Y, then it is permissible for X to lie to or deceive Y. These intuitions are captured by the following principle:

> (P) Other things being equal, it is permissible for X to do a to Y, even if a is a prima facie wrong, provided that X's doing a to Y is necessary in order to prevent or mitigate harm to X caused by Y's doing a to X.[5]

In business negotiations an individual can typically gain some benefit (balanced by corresponding harm to the other party) if he is willing to lie or deceive the other person about his own negotiating position. The other party can avoid or mitigate this harm only by being willing to do the same. In our society most people routinely practice this sort of lying and/or deception in business negotiations. Given this, (P) implies that one may presume that one is justified in bluffing (by means of lying and deception about one's negotiating position) in ordinary circumstances, unless either (1) one has special reasons to suppose that the other party will not do the same (e.g., one might know that the individual with whom one is dealing is unusually scrupulous or naive), or (2) one has special reasons for thinking that one will not be harmed by the bluffing of the other party, even if one does not bluff oneself.

Space does not permit an extended discussion or defense of (P). We would, however, like to forestall two possible objections: (1) (P) does not constitute a blanket endorsement of retaliation or the policy of "an eye for an eye and a tooth for a tooth." (P) would not justify my killing your child in retaliation for your having killed mine. (P) would justify my killing another person X only if my killing X is necessary in order to prevent X from killing me. (2) It is standard practice for people involved in negotiations to misrepresent the terms they are willing to accept. In ordinary circumstances (P) will justify such actions. However, there are types of lying and deception which are not generally practiced in negotiations. For example, while meeting with a prospective buyer a person selling a house might have a friend pretend to make an offer to buy the house in order to pressure the prospective buyer. (P) does not imply that there is any presumption for thinking that such a ruse would be morally permissible.

NOTES

We are indebted to Thomas Beauchamp for comments on a previous version of this paper. Earlier versions of this paper were presented to a conference on Business and Professional Ethics at Kalamazoo College and Western Michigan University, November 1979, and to the Philosophy Department at Denison University.

1. For a much more thorough defense of the claim that bluffing involves lying, with an appeal to a somewhat different definition of lying, see our paper "The Moral Status of Bluffing and Deception in Business" in *Business and Professional Ethics,* ed., Wade L. Robison and Michael S. Pritchard (New York: Humana Press). Also see our paper "Bluffing in Labor Negotiations: Legal and Ethical Issues," with Kent F. Mursmann, *Journal of Business Ethics,* vol. 1, no. 1, January 1982.

2. The classic statement of this view is included in Chapter 11 of Sir David Ross's *The Right and the Good* (Oxford: Oxford University Press, 1930).

3. Immanual Kant, "On the Supposed Right to Tell Lies from Benevolent Motives," (1797), in *Moral Rules and Particular Circumstances,* ed. Baruch Brody (Englewood Cliffs, New Jersey: Prentice Hall, 1970), pp. 32 and 33.

4. In a well-known defense of bluffing, Albert Carr claims that it is permissible to make false statements in the course of business negotiations because doing so is "normal business practice," and part of what is involved in "playing the business game." See "Is Business Bluffing Ethical?" *Harvard Business Review,* January–February 1968.

5. It seems plausible to say that it would be permissible to do an act that is prima facie wrong to another person (X) if doing so were necessary in order to prevent X from harming a third party by doing the same act. For example, one would be justified in killing another person if doing so were necessary in order to prevent him from killing a third party. We accept the following stronger version of P:

   (P') Other things being equal, it is permissible for X to do *a* to Y, even if *a* is prima facie wrong, provided that X's doing *a* to Y is necessary in order to prevent or mitigate harm to *someone* caused by Y's doing *a* to that person.

   The weaker principle (P) is sufficient for the purposes of our argument.

Ethics in Negotiation: Oil and Water or Good Lubrication?

H. Joseph Reitz

James A. Wall, Jr.

Mary Sue Love

In his 1996 year-end column for *Forbes,* merchant banker and economist John Rutledge describes two weeks of negotiations over an acquisition for a private equity fund. The hours of bargaining were tense, long, hard, and far more complicated than he had envisioned. Nevertheless, he reports:

> Despite all the haggling, we ended on a friendly note. All of us—buyer, seller, lender—shook hands and clinked champagne glasses. As we were leaving, the seller said he would like to discuss teaming up with us in a joint venture. I beamed. Some buyers wouldn't have liked this. They think if the seller doesn't hate them at the end of the deal, they haven't squeezed out every last drop of money. I disagree. We believe that when someone wants to do repeat business with us, it is the highest form of praise. Allowing your opponent in a transaction to walk away with his dignity, his humor, and his bearing intact, and with a pretty good deal in his pocket, is the right way to do business.

Rutledge then lists a set of principles learned from his first business partner and admonishes his readers to

> walk away from a deal, any deal, rather than violate your principles to win it . . . The twist, of course, is that business organizations organized around principles are often more successful and make more money that those organized around the idea that greed is good. Nice guys often finish first.

Rutledge's thesis that ethical negotiating is not only the right thing to do but frequently is also more profitable represents an argument more common today than in the so-called decade of greed in the 1980s—and one that finds more receptive audiences.

Should businesspeople take this as an article of faith? Or can reason bring us to similar conclusions? In probing that question, we shall list a number of questionable

---

negotiation tactics or behaviors and evaluate them according to four commonly used ethical criteria. This will help us assess the costs and benefits of ethical versus unethical negotiation tactics.

QUESTIONABLE NEGOTIATION TACTICS AND ETHICAL CRITERIA

We all have a general idea of what negotiation is: two parties attempting to work out a trade of items or services that is acceptable to both sides. Each side has an array of tactics to employ in achieving this trade. Below are 10 popular tactics, the ethics of which have been challenged over the years:

1. *Lies*—Statements made in contradiction to the negotiator's knowledge or belief about something material to the negotiation.
2. *Puffery*—Exaggerating the value of something in the negotiation.
3. *Deception*—An act or statement intended to mislead the opponent about the negotiator's own intent or future actions relevant to the negotiations.
4. *Weakening the opponent*—Actions or statements designed to improve the negotiator's own relative strength by directly undermining that of the opponent.
5. *Strengthening one's own position*—Actions or statements designed to improve the negotiator's own position without directly weakening that of the opponent.
6. *Nondisclosure*—Keeping to oneself knowledge that would benefit the opponent.
7. *Information exploitation*—Using information provided by the opponent to weaken him, either in the direct exchange or by sharing it with others.
8. *Change of mind*—Engaging in behaviors contrary to previous statements or positions.
9. *Distraction*—Acts or statements that lure the opponent into ignoring information or alternatives that might benefit him.
10. *Maximization*—The negotiator's single-minded pursuit of payoffs at the cost of the opponent's payoffs.

How do negotiators decide if such tactics—laid out in greater detail in Figure 1—are ethical? Our interviews with businesspeople have yielded such comments as

- A lie is not a lie when a lie is expected.
- When someone tells the truth, that's good: when someone lies, that's wrong. It's that simple.
- What's right or wrong really depends on the situation.

The variety in comments vis-à-vis the first tactic indicates that opinions can vary as to what is ethical. Fortunately, moral reasoning can help negotiators assess the ethical nature of lies and other tactics. Summarized in Figure 2, the four criteria most widely used in business ethics today are the *Golden Rule, utilitarianism, universalism,* and *distributive justice.*

FIGURE 1   Questionable Tactics

Tactic	Description / Clarification / Range
Lies	Subject matter for lies can include limits, alternatives, the negotiator's intent, authority to bargain, other commitments, acceptability of the opponent's offer, time pressures, and available resources.
Puffery	Among the items that can be puffed up are the value of one's payoffs to the opponent, the negotiator's own alternatives, the cost of what one is giving up or is prepared to yield, importance of issues, and attributes of the products or services.
Deception	Acts and statements may include promises or threats, excessive initial demands, careless misstatements of facts, or asking for concessions not wanted.
Weakening the opponent	The negotiator here may cut off or eliminate some of the opponent's alternatives, blame the opponent for his own actions, use personally abrasive statements to or about the opponent, or undermine the opponent's alliances.
Strengthening one's own position	This tactic includes building one's own resources, including expertise, finances, and alliances. It also includes presentations of persuasive rationales to the opponent or third parties (e.g., the public, the media) or getting mandates for one's position.
Nondisclosure	Includes partial disclosure of facts, failure to disclose a hidden fact, failure to correct the opponents' misperceptions or ignorance, and concealment of the negotiator's own position or circumstances.
Information exploitation	Information provided by the opponent can be used to exploit his weaknesses, close off his alternatives, generate demands against him, or weaken his alliances.
Change of mind	Includes accepting offers one had claimed one would not accept, changing demands, withdrawing promised offers, and making threats one promised would not be made. Also includes the failure to behave as predicted.
Distraction	These acts or statements can be as simple as providing excessive information to the opponent, asking many questions, evading questions, or burying the issue. Or they can be more complex, such as feigning weakness in one area so that the opponent concentrates on it and ignores another.
Maximization	Includes demanding the opponent make concessions that result in the negotiator's gain and the opponent's equal or greater loss. Also entails converting a win-win situation to win-lose.

The Golden Rule

Most managers tend to explain ethical behavior as a function of personal values. One of the most frequently cited values is the Golden Rule: Do unto others as you would have them do unto you. A relatively popular principle, perhaps its most famous and vocal advocate in the industry was J. C. Penney, who used it in building and running his business from his youth until his nineties. In practice, it requires decision makers to apply the same standards of fairness and equity to their own actions that they would demand of others.

FIGURE 2   Ethical Criteria

Criteria	Explanation / Interpretation
Golden Rule	Do unto others as you would have them do unto you.
Universalism	People are not to be used as a means to an end.
Utilitarianism	Do the greatest good for the greatest number of people.
Distributive justice	Everyone is better off because of this act.

Universalism

A more complex ethical base is universalism, which argues that the rightness or wrongness of actions can be determined a priori, or before the actual outcomes of those actions can be realized. Based on a system of individual rights and obligations founded by philosopher Immaneul Kant, it argues that human beings are incapable of foreseeing all the outcomes of their decisions and actions, and thus should be held morally accountable for the *way* they made them.

For an act or decision to be moral, it must meet several criteria:

1. It must respect the inherent worth and dignity of those involved or affected; people must never be used primarily as a means to an end.
2. It must be universally applicable to all human beings facing similar situations—there are no special treatments.
3. It must be consistent with all other universal moral principles.

Consider the dilemma of downsizing. Universalism would permit downsizing for sound economic reasons, but it would require informing all those being laid off of that decision when it is made. Withholding such information from employees to keep them working with the same level of dedication and effort would be unethical because it would be using them primarily as a means to an end. Unaware of their impending doom, they might make family, career, or financial decisions they would not have made with valid information about their employer's plans.

Utilitarianism

In contrast to universalism, utilitarianism judges the rightness or wrongness of actions and decisions by their consequences. It argues that human beings ought to seek those alternatives that produce the greatest amount of good for the greatest number of people, or to maximize the total good produced. When seeking the greatest net good, one must consider all people likely to be affected by a set of alternatives and the array of outcomes (both good and bad) each alternative might generate for each person.

Distributive Justice

John Rawls's ethical concept of justice implies that individuals have an obligation to exercise their own rights in a way that permits others to enjoy theirs. Justice occurs when all individuals get what they deserve; injustice, when people are deprived of that to which they have a right. In brief, this ethical norm asks, Is everyone (the group) better off because of this act? And for each person, it asks, Would you be willing to trade places with any of the other parties after this act takes place?

Rawls's concept of justice, like universalism, focuses on the *process* by which outcomes are distributed rather than on the outcomes themselves. Like Kant's universalist perspective, Rawls's attempts to derive a set of principles that would be acceptable to all rational people.

In considering the justice of any process, we are asked to assume a *veil of ignorance*. That is, we act as if we are ignorant of our *own* roles in the situation, and assume we could be assigned *any* role. Would we be willing to abide by our decision if we might be any of the players affected by it? According to Rawls, the veil of ignorance leads us to construct processes in which

1. All members of the process could agree to be part of it, regardless of the position they might happen to occupy in the process.
2. Each person would have an equal right to the most extensive liberty that can accommodate similar liberties for others.
3. Inequalities work to the benefit of all.
4. These inequalities are attached to positions that are accessible to all.

Using Multiple Criteria

Evaluating bargaining tactics raises the question of which of these four criteria takes precedence. If a tactic is condoned by one criterion and condemned by another, what is a negotiator to do?

In the first place, if applied correctly, these criteria ought to yield similar results. They are not designed to bring about different answers; rather they are different ways of looking for the same answer. Which criterion one uses can be a matter of personal preference or may be dictated by the nature of the dilemma. Utilitarianism is useful when the number of affected parties is relatively small and known and the outcomes are relatively predictable. However, when the number of affected parties is large, knowledge of their preferences is unreliable, or outcomes are unpredictable, then other criteria are more useful. When dealing with unfamiliar situations (new technology), unfamiliar parties (new markets), or complex issues (mergers and acquisitions), principle-based criteria such as universalism are going to be more reliable than those, such as utilitarianism, that require predictions about very uncertain future events.

ETHICAL NEGOTIATIONS

Having delineated these four standards, we shall now apply them to the ten questionable negotiation tactics, from lying to maximizing.

Lies

A lie is a statement made by a negotiator that contradicts his knowledge or beliefs about something material to the negotiations. In negotiating, lies are intended to deceive the opponent about values, intents, objectives, alternatives, constraints, and beliefs. Examples include

- "Why should I buy it from you for $10,000 when I've got another seller willing to let me have one just as good for $8,500"—when the buyer has no such alternative.
- "I can't possibly pay $10,000. I have only $8,500 to spend"; or "My client has directed me to pay no more than $9,000"—when the negotiator has no such constraints.

Lying and the Golden Rule.   Most religions, including Christianity, Judaism, and Islam, contain strict injunctions against lying. Some religions, however, permit lying when it is the only possible way to prevent a greater harm. For example, you may lie to someone in a murderous rage in order to prevent a homicide, or to a drunken, abusive person in search of his usual victims. These exceptions are really not inconsistent with the Golden Rule. The question would be, Would you prefer to be lied to if that were the only way to keep you from committing a terrible deed? The rational answer is yes.

The examples of lying in negotiations, however, do not prevent a greater harm. They are simply examples of immediate self-interest, of doing harm by deceit to further your own interest. The question would be, Would you prefer that others deceive you to enrich themselves at your expense? The rational answer is no.

Lying and Universalism.   In his late years, Kant argued that honesty was so important to the concept of intrinsic human worth and dignity that *no* lie could be justified. The argument is that human beings rely on information to make decisions for themselves. And to make the best decisions, they must have the truth. When others deprive them of the truth through lies, the victims of those lies may be led to make faulty decisions.

Some will propose that lying is permissible when you believe your opponent is lying. They argue, in fact, that lying is the only defense against an opponent who lies. But this argument is flawed. First, there are other options, one of which is to terminate the negotiation. Second, you can try to discover the truth that will expose the lie, thus turning a disadvantage into an advantage. If you cannot possibly ascertain the truth, then you must admit that you only believe your opponent to be lying; you don't know it as fact. Such a belief is not sufficient to justify a lie.

Lying and Utilitarianism.   At first blush, it might seem that utilitarianism could make a case for lying under certain circumstances. A negotiator might think, This lie helps my company a lot and doesn't harm my opponent very much. However, utilitarianism requires us to consider all the possible consequences to all the people potentially affected by the action—and to consider all the people so affected as equals. We cannot weight the interests of some, such as ourselves, as greater than the interests of others.

A further problem with attempting to justify lying through utilitarianism is that one must consider the effects of the lying itself. Beyond the direct effects of a lie are the indirect effects of harm done to society in general by increasing cynicism and decreasing trust. The liar also suffers some loss of self-esteem by admitting that his success, however noteworthy, was achieved by dishonorable means. Cynicism and lack of trust entail significant costs for any society, which requires more laws, surveillance, and sanctions—none of which add value to a transaction—to be in place before enacting agreements.

Lying and Distributive Justice.   Distributive justice requires us to be willing to take the role of either party in the situation. Would we willingly trade places with the party being lied to? No, because being lied to increases our chances of making a decision that is not in our best interests.

Second, does a lie decrease the freedom to act of any of the parties? Yes; consistent with the maxim that the truth frees us to make the best decisions, a lie reduces that freedom. One can also argue that a lie decreases the freedom of the liar, whose subsequent statements and actions are now constrained to be (or appear to be) consistent with the lie. Suppose a buyer lies about her reservation price, claiming she could never pay more than $8,000 for an object for which she is willing to pay $9,000, and for which the seller is asking $11,000. If the seller reduced his price to $10,000, the buyer cannot reinforce that concession by raising her offer above $8,000, lest her lie be exposed. Lies constrain the freedom of both the victim and the liar.

None of the four ethical models can justify lying in negotiations. Lying is seen to be what it is—an act of self-interest usually taken as a convenient alternative to (*a*) the hard work of preparing for negotiations, including improving one's knowledge about an opponent, or (*b*) walking away from a negotiation when one comes to believe the opponent is lying. Only when a lie is the only possible means of preventing a greater harm to another could it possibly be justified. Such an exceptional circumstance is extremely rare in most negotiations, and those circumstances, such as hostage negotiation, would be dramatic enough to be relatively obvious.

Puffery

Puffery is exaggerating the value of something, such as its cost, condition, or worth. Negotiators will often exaggerate the value of alternatives, what they are giving up or are prepared to give up, the importance of issues, product or service attributes, or the value of their case. Examples:

- "I have a six-figure offer from another company"—when no such offer has actually been made, or the offer is less than six figures.
- "This union will never give up the right to strike"—when job security is actually more important.
- "I consistently get up to 33 miles per gallon"—when in fact that happened only once in the car's lifetime.
- "We have enough evidence right now to put your client away for 20 years"—when the real evidence at hand is less than convincing.

Clearly, puffery is simply a euphemism for lying. Every one of these statements contradicts the negotiator's knowledge or beliefs. Exaggeration may be considered by some as a milder form of lying in that there is a shred of truth in it; nevertheless, a statement that contradicts the truth is a lie. Like lies, exaggerations are intended to deceive and gain advantage at another's expense.

Deception

A deception is an act or statement intended to mislead another about one's own intent or future actions relevant to the negotiations. These include false promises or empty threats, excessive initial demands, careless statements of fact, and asking for things not wanted. Examples include

- "If you give us the contract, we'll begin shipments in 30 days"—when such a delivery date is known to be impossible (false promise).
- "If we don't settle this right now, the whole deal is off and we'll just find somebody else"—when the negotiator has no intention of losing this deal (empty threat).
- "In order to accept a position on your board, I would expect to receive 20,000 shares of stock, luxury class travel and lodging, and to be named chair of the personnel committee"—when what the negotiator really wants is 10,000 shares and a seat on the personnel committee (excessive demands, asking for things not wanted).
- "We need at least a $50,000 contribution from loyal supporters like you because our people tell us that the opposition plans to eliminate Medicare for people like you if they are elected"—when the negotiator knows that the opponents will only seek to halt increases in Medicare spending (careless statement of facts).

Some of these deceptive tactics clearly fall into the first category of lies. False promises and empty threats are statements made in contradiction to the negotiator's knowledge or beliefs. We have already determined that lies are unethical. But what about excessive demands, careless statements of fact, asking for things not wanted, or distracting statements?

Deception as a category of acts is clearly designed to profit at others' expense—to lead others into acts that are not in their self-interest, or away from an act that is. In this light, deceptive acts can be seen to be unethical.

None of us wants to be deceived, so deception fails the Golden Rule. It does not treat the deceived parties with respect, but takes advantage of their trust or vulnerability, so it fails the test of universalism. It does not create the greatest good for the greatest number of people, but only allows the deceiver to profit at the expense of the deceived, violating the standards of utilitarianism. And it limits the deceived person's choices, failing the test of distributive justice. In the end, then, deception fails all four tests of ethical behavior.

Weakening the Opponent

A tactic for improving your relative position is to weaken that of your opponent, either psychologically or economically. Direct attacks are generally aimed at lowering another's self-esteem, often through guilt or embarrassment. Indirect attacks include closing off another's alternatives or undermining his support or alliances.

Frequently, the means for weakening one's opponent involve lying, deception, or exaggeration. You could blame your opponent for damage caused by others or of unknown origin, or create the impression that he was the author of harm done to you or others when no real harm had been done. We have already demonstrated that such tactics are unethical.

But what about those cases in which the negotiator can weaken an opponent by telling the truth? The morality of the tactic depends on a number of factors. Information about your own position ("Our company will be bankrupt if we increase wages by that much") would meet ethical criteria. Such admissions are usually painful, and you should be permitted to make personal sacrifices under any of the frameworks we have studied. They typically involve uncertainty and risk for the discloser; the opponent may ignore or even exploit such knowledge.

However, when the information concerns the opponent, the situation becomes murkier. Can you ethically publicize personal information about an opponent that would undermine his support or embarrass him in some way? If you obtained that information in confidence during the negotiations, you may not use it to do your opponent harm for your benefit. It would be permissible only if revealing the information would prevent a greater harm to others, such as disclosing evidence of criminal activity. If you did not obtain the information in confidence, the moral question would shift to one of intent: Would you be morally required to reveal the information if you and your opponent were not negotiating? In other words, your benefit in the revelation should not influence your decision.

The difference between taking risks for oneself and doing direct harm to another is best understood in the context of distributive justice. A key maxim is whether an action would increase or decrease the other's freedom. Risk-taking and self-disclosure increase an opponent's options, so they are permissible. Harming him reduces his options, and thus requires other justification.

Strengthening One's Own Position

A host of tactics are designed to improve one's own position without doing direct harm to the opponent. Instead of involving lying, deception, or exaggeration, they entail ability, effort, and intelligence. Moreover, conceptually at least, they are available to all parties in a negotiation.

Again, distributive justice tells us inequalities are permitted as long as all parties have the opportunity to pursue them. If you work harder, train better, prepare more effectively, or create and follow a more successful strategy than your opponents, you have done them no direct harm. You are willing to permit them to do their best in preparation and execution. We are all permitted to improve ourselves; none of the four ethical frameworks deny self-improvement.

Under the Golden Rule, we are willing to permit others to strengthen themselves. According to utilitarianism, the net benefits of strengthening go to those who have done the best job—a "survival of the fittest" outcome. Under universalism, one can argue that preparation and discipline in execution actually enhance the dignity of one's opponent. To be well prepared is to show respect for the other; shoddy preparation is actually demeaning to the opponent.

Nondisclosure

We have determined that negotiators are ethically required to tell the truth—lying, deception, and exaggeration are wrong. But are they required to tell the *whole* truth? May a negotiator withhold factual information that could be of use to an opponent? The answer depends on the nature of the hidden truth.

If failure to disclose the truth would harm one's opponent, it would be unethical. Hiding a product or service defect or flaw that would mislead the other about the value of the item being bargained for would be wrong. If, to induce a potential buyer into paying a higher price, you fail to disclose a lien on property or a mechanical problem with an automobile you are attempting to sell, you are wrong. Just so, potential buyers who fail to disclose information revealing that they are, in fact, unlikely to be able to make payments on a purchase are acting unethically.

However, you are not required to disclose personal information that could be harmful to your case. You need not reveal that you are able and/or willing to pay far more for an item than the asking price. And you are not required to disclose your reservation price, although you are not permitted to lie about it.

Likewise, if you—as a buyer—suspect that the value of an offered item is greater than the asking price, you are not required to disclose that fact to the seller, presuming the seller has the competence to assess the value of the object. It would be wrong to take advantage of someone incapable of evaluating the worth of an object.

From a different perspective, are you permitted to disclose the true value of an object to a misinformed seller? Yes; there is nothing wrong with being more generous in a negotiation than you are morally required to be, as long as you are negotiating for yourself. However, if you are acting as an agent for another, you are required to obtain the best deal that is legally and ethically permissible, so you cannot disclose the true value.

Exploiting Information

Effective negotiators uncover information about themselves, their opponents, and the object of a negotiation during both the preparation phase and the negotiation itself. If that information is gained by legal and ethical means, no ethical proscription forbids a negotiator from using it. If you learn that your opponent *really* wants what you have to offer—in fact, values it more than he is disclosing—you are permitted to raise your asking price. If you learn that your opponent has fewer options than he suggests, thereby raising his valuation of what you have to offer, you may do likewise. As long as that information is legally and ethically accessible to both parties, you are permitted to use it to strengthen your position.

Are you permitted to use information obtained by illegal or unethical means? Certainly not if you had a hand in the unethical or illegal act—committed it yourself or induced someone else to commit it. But what if information so gained became public knowledge, and you had nothing to do with either the discovery or the publication of that information? Then you would be permitted to exploit it. Earlier, we concluded that one is not permitted to do direct harm to an opponent; however, if the harm has already been done by another, one may take advantage of it. If a police report of a burglary reveals that your opponent has a greater need or ability to pay for an item over which you are negotiating, you are *permitted* to use the information to your advantage. May you use it to defame your opponent, thereby decreasing his options or weakening his alliances? No, because that would be doing direct harm to him that would not be done without your action.

Change of Mind

Sometimes in the course of negotiations, something happens to alter the attraction of the object for one of the parties. The need is diminished or increased; an attractive alternative appears or vanishes; one's ability to pay is changed. May you abruptly change your negotiating position in light of these new circumstances? As long as you are not breaking a commitment or agreement, you are permitted to change your mind. You may decide to accept an offer you said you would never accept, or to pay a higher price than your original reservation price. If you intentionally lied about your reservation price, the act of lying was wrong. However, paying more than you said you would pay or accepting less than you said you would accept is not wrong—your act is doing no harm to your opponent; in fact, it benefits him.

May you withdraw an offer you have made? Yes, providing your withdrawal meets the legal requirements and the opponent has not accepted the offer. However, once the opponent has *accepted* an offer or commitment in any way, you may not ethically withdraw it even if it is legal to do so. Reneging on agreements is wrong from all standpoints. You would not wish others to do so to you. It does more harm than good, not only to your opponent but to the general level of trust among negotiators. And you certainly would not be willing to trade places with the person who accepted your offer.

Of course, you are permitted to ask an opponent to withdraw his acceptance of your offer or release you from your commitment because of changed circumstances. However, if he refuses to do so, then you are morally bound to your agreement.

Distraction

Negotiators are sometimes tempted to protect a weakness or conceal their interest in a particular issue by distracting their opponents. As long as the distractive tactic did not involve lying, puffery, or outright deception, is one ethically permitted to distract an opponent?

We concluded earlier that you need not disclose harmful information about yourself if the nondisclosure would do no harm to another. We can assume that the other is entitled to a fair outcome in the negotiation; however, he is not *entitled* to maximize his outcomes at your expense. He may attain them through his skill, your ineptitude, or other factors; you are not depriving him of his rights by limiting his outcomes to something between fair and maximization.

Distraction as a tactic does not reduce an opponent's options, according to distributive justice. It also provides him with information—if he is skilled enough to uncover it—about your perceptions of what *you* believe to be important and what you believe *he* considers to be important. If you evade answering certain questions, your opponent may learn that you do so to protect a weakness. Burying issues that you see as important or surrounding critical questions with questions you consider trivial reflect your own judgments. They may not be correct; they do not limit the opponent's options; they provide an opponent with opportunities to learn from them; they certainly involve risk on your part. Neither the Gold Rule nor universalism would prohibit distraction.

Maximization

Is it ethical to pursue your own payoffs at another's expense? Yes, but it depends on the manner in which the gain is pursued. Keep in mind that a negotiation has two facets. First, one side usually does not have the same goals as the other, yet both share a goal in that they want to have an exchange with the other side. A machine shop operator buying bolts from a manufacturer has a goal that differs from the manufacturer's. The operator wants a low price and the manufacturer seeks a high one. Yet they both want an exchange, because the machine shop operator needs bolts to produce machines and the manufacturer prefers money to an inventory of bolts.

In the negotiation exchange, the two sides usually bargain over a number of items. And the value of each item differs for each side. In the bolt negotiation, there might be four issues: antirust coating, bolt strength, delivery schedule, and method of payment. For the machine shop operator, the first two items would be very important. He needs antirust coating so that the bolts don't rust in inventory, and he must have strong bolts in order to produce high-quality machines. Because these two characteristics are important, he is willing to pay handsomely for them.

By contrast, the bolt manufacturer knows he can put an antirust coating on the bolts rather inexpensively, and, with some minor modifications of his production process, produce very strong bolts. Consequently, the bolts are of low cost to him. However, the delivery schedule is important to the manufacturer, as is the method of payment. Specifically, he would prefer to make deliveries when he is sending bolts to other customers in the city, and he wants the shop owner to use a standard invoicing system that cuts the amount of paperwork.

In this setting, it would be unethical for the manufacturer to maximize his own goals—at the machine shop owner's expense—on every item. To do so would violate the Golden Rule; he probably would not want the operator to behave in this manner. It violates the universalism criterion because it exploits the opponent; that is, it uses the opponent for the benefit of the negotiator rather than permitting the opponent, as well as the negotiator, to share adequately in the negotiation benefits. It also violates the utilitarianism criterion because this approach does not provide the greatest good to the greatest number. Rather, it forces the negotiation into a win-lose result and does not allow the two sides to improve their total joint benefit. Likewise, it violates the distributive justice criterion because everyone is not better off from this act.

How, then, should the negotiator bargain if all items are fixed sum ("My loss is your gain") and of equal value to the negotiator and opponent? The utilitarian criterion proffers no guidance here because there is no variation in the total value; rather, all points have equal total value. Moreover, distributive justice provides modest instruction because everyone will not be better off in the various agreement points.

However, the universalism and Golden Rule criteria do assist us. The former dictates that the negotiator must consider the well-being of the opponent. Therefore, it posits that the negotiator can press his own interests up to the point at which the well-being of the opponent is endangered. The Golden Rule's dictate is consistent with this idea; the negotiator should pursue his own interests only as far as he would want the opponent to do so.

APPLYING ETHICS TO NEGOTIATIONS: OIL ON WATER?

A cynic's retort to these evaluations might be "Ethics are fine in theory. I can negotiate ethically and sleep well at night, but I'll be hungry tomorrow, and next week." In other words, some might expect that ethical bargaining would lead to low payoffs, or no agreement, or one that costs them their job. How do we respond to that?

True, ethical bargaining does entail risks and sometimes seems to place a negotiator in a vulnerable position. Yet the ethical route, for operational as well as moral reasons, is the preferable one, because unethical negotiation has four major costs that are often overlooked:

- Rigidity in future negotiations.
- A damaged relationship with the opponent.
- A sullied reputation.
- Lost opportunities.

Rigid Negotiating

Even when it is successful, unethical behavior has a personal cost for negotiators. If their lies, deceptions, and puffery yield high-outcome agreements, they will repeat those behaviors in subsequent negotiations, because such actions have paid off. In addition, they will tend to attribute their success to such acts. Consequently, unethical negotiators will sacrifice some of their flexibility, creativity, and openness to others' ideas, thereby trapping themselves into a rigid bargaining approach that will eventually be matched by their opponents.

Keep in mind that unethical negotiating is not as advantageous as it may seem. One may lie about an alternative; but doesn't silence about an alternative prove as valuable as the lie? Wouldn't the comment "I'd better find another buyer" be just as potent as the statement "I've got another buyer"? Moreover, it is a wiser strategy to interrupt the negotiation, find another buyer, and let the original opponent know about it than to lie about already having another buyer.

Damaged Relationships

Unethical negotiation also mars the relationship between the two sides, causing emotional fallout (such as anger) as well as higher operational costs. When the negotiation is a single event—such as the sale of building materials—a negotiator who has been the victim of unethical behavior is less likely to implement the deal fully, perhaps not delivering all the materials. Or he will be less than cooperative when postagreement problems arise, such as if some of the building materials are defective or do not meet construction specifications.

When negotiations are of a repeated nature, the costs of unethical behavior mount. Today's bargainer becomes an embittered enemy rather than tomorrow's customer. Such an enemy might refuse to bargain with an unethical opponent, could return to the table with some open Machiavellian tactics of his own, or, more devastatingly, could voice no complaints but secretly seek revenge in the next round.

Sullied Reputation

Seldom do victims of unethical behavior hold their tongue, in public or across the bargaining table. At times, they are even apt to embellish. Thus, an unethical reputation often permeates the business environment and precedes or accompanies its owner to the bargaining arena. Consequently, the opposing negotiator expects unethical behavior. A building contractor once commented about a subcontractor, "He'll lie to you, cheat you, steal from you, and then brag about it, if you give him a chance."

Once an opponent has experienced unethical behavior, he will prepare to counteract your unethical tactics in the future. Moreover, he will suspect that they are present, even if they are not. And often he will use them as excuses for his own obstinate behavior.

Lost Opportunities

The most detrimental effect of unethical behavior comes in the negotiation itself. The explanation for this is somewhat complex, but with assistance from a simple example it can be quickly understood: The essence of a productive negotiation is trading a *package* of issues in which each idea concedes heavily on issues that are of low cost (or value) to it in return for major concessions on issues that are of high cost (or value) to it.

A company supplying tractor seats to John Deere probably finds that the cost of painting them green and packing them 10 to a carton for shipment is not very difficult. If Deere places high value on green seats packed 10 to a carton, it would be wise for the supplier to agree (or concede) on these issues. In turn, the firm could have John Deere—with its large storage facilities—accept the supplier's entire production run and store it until used. This concession would cost Deere quite little and would be a major benefit to a small company with limited storage facilities.

Most negotiations have manifold issues like these—namely, they are of low cost to one side and high value to the other. For the negotiators, the key is to find as many of these issues as possible and arrange trades among packages of them. In such trades, the first step is to determine which issues—of those currently under negotiation—have differential value to the two sides. To locate these, the parties must exchange valid information. If either side lies, deceives, or engages in puffery or distracts the other, it is very difficult, if not impossible, to determine the win-win trades, because the opponent does not receive accurate information. Moreover, the unethical behavior, if detected, motivates the opponent to withhold information (that he feels will be used against him) about the cost and values of the issues.

Not only does unethical behavior undermine the first step toward package trading, it also precludes the second: discovery of new issues. Productive negotiations are those that grow beyond the issues on the table. A simple expansion is one in which both sides agree on a two-year contract, even though the negotiation began with a one-year frame. A more complex expansion, taken from our earlier example, might be that Deere and its seat supplier jointly discover that Deere has vibration-reduction expertise that the supplier could use in its production machines. And the supplier has discovered a method for mixing and applying paint that makes it highly chip-resistant—which Deere would no doubt find useful. With an open, trusting negotiation, the two sides probably would be able to ferret out the two new issues and, through some creative discussions, arrange a trade on these or explore the prices for each technology transfer.

Here the impact of unethical bargaining is clear. Not only does it undermine the negotiators' capabilities to reach win-win agreements on the current issues, it also interferes with discussions that would bring new, mutually profitable issues to the table.

Coming full circle, then, we agree with John Rutledge that ethical negotiation is not only morally right, it is frequently more profitable. Business men and women often feel they move into a different environment when they negotiate—one in which anything goes and the rules are understood by all players.

Yet negotiations today are not a separate function; they are an integral part of all business environments. Joint ventures, purchasing options, labor contracts, leasing agreements, salaries and benefits, day-to-day disputes, mergers, and spinoffs are all negotiated. And in such bargaining, ethical rules must apply. The four we have touched on—the Golden Rule, universalism, utilitarianism, and distributive justice—rule out several negotiation tactics, guide the use of some, and permit the use of others.

This guidance does not make negotiating easy. With their high stakes, complexity, deadlines, uncertainty, emotions, and stress, negotiations will always remain tough going. But those who take care to negotiate ethically should find the process better for them—personally, interpersonally, and economically.

REFERENCES

Richard T. DeGeorge, *Business Ethics*, 4th ed. (New York: Prentice Hall, 1994).

Larue Tone Hosmer, *Moral Leadership in Business* (Burr Ridge, IL; Richard D. Irwin, 1994): Ch. 4.

J. C. Penney, *View from the Ninth Decade* (New York: Thomas Nelson & Sons, 1985).

John Rawls, *A Theory of Justice* (Cambridge, MA: Harvard University Press, 1971).

John Rutledge, "The Portrait on My Office Wall," *Forbes*, December 30, 1996, p. 78.

Deception and Mutual Gains Bargaining: Are They Mutually Exclusive?

Raymond A. Friedman

Debra L. Shapiro

In the interest of being fair, a prospective car buyer goes to a car dealership with price-related information obtained from objectively valid sources, such as the American Automobile Association, *Consumer Reports*, and the "book" value (which reflects the car's model, year, and mileage). The car salesperson expresses an interest in reducing inventory *today* and the prospective buyer indicates that is possible, if they can agree on a price that is fair. The two parties share information regarding price-related criteria and their respective priorities with regard to car features, payment terms, and service-related concerns. In so doing, they learn that they have complementary needs, and only the issue of price seems competing (since the seller and buyer want a higher and lower price, respectively). Differences regarding price, however, seem resolvable when the parties focus their conversation on their mutual interests, these being a fair price and a long-term car service-based relationship. Two hours later, the parties have reached an agreement—at a price both deem fair.

The above scenario describes two parties engaged in problem-solving behaviors, such as focusing on being fair, basing proposals on objective (neutral) criteria, sharing information regarding priorities, discussing more than one issue as a means for determining possible concessionary tradeoffs, and focusing on their shared interests, which results in a mutually satisfying agreement. This is a description of what has become commonly known as "integrative," "win-win," or "mutual gains" bargaining, or MGB (see, e.g. Walton and McKersie 1965; Fisher and Ury 1981; Susskind and Cruikshank 1987).

How would we characterize this scenario if the buyer was deceptive during the exchange—for example, by referring to a lower price obtainable from another, phantom dealership? Would such a tactic be considered distributive (win-lose) negotiation? No, because even in light of the deception created by referring to a nonexistent alternative, the

Source: Raymond A. Friedman and Debra L. Shapiro, "Deception and Mutual Gains Bargaining: Are They Mutually Exclusive?" *Negotiation Journal*, July 1995, Kluwer Academic/Plenum Publishers.

car buyer and the salesperson have engaged in an exchange that is predominantly mutual gains bargaining. The modifier "predominantly" highlights the fact that the bargaining situation in *not* purely integrative. Indeed, many theorists have argued that no bargaining situation is purely integrative nor purely distributive, and thus all are "mixed-motive" (Lax and Sebenius 1986; Stevens 1963; Raiffa 1982; Walton and McKersie 1965).

Because of this duality, we believe negotiators can practice integrative bargaining effectively, even when this strategy includes deception (for example, the car buyer's phantom dealership). Yet negotiation scholars and trainers may leave the impression instead that anyone who wishes to be deceptive cannot engage in integrative bargaining, or MGB—that is, MGB and deception are presented as mutually exclusive. We arrived at this conclusion after a discussion among negotiation scholars at a recent national academic conference regarding what is ethical and unethical behavior in negotiations and what we should be teaching students in our courses on negotiations. About an hour into the discussion, someone suggested that, in pursuit of being ethical teachers and promoting ethical behavior on the part of students, we should teach students integrative bargaining tactics only, and not traditional distributive bargaining tactics. This proposal created quite a debate among those attending, and an ensuing vote among the scholars showed that an overwhelming majority favored the proposal.

The turn of events was, for us, a great cause for concern. Should integrative bargaining really be promoted based on ethical arguments? Should we automatically label distributive bargaining as unethical? We were concerned because this equating of ethics and integrative, or mutual gains, bargaining had a familiar ring to it. In both training sessions and classrooms, it is not uncommon for MGB to be confused with being good, ethical, or nice. Moreover, confounding ethics and MGB can have negative effects—on our ability to understand ethical conventions in traditional negotiations, and on our ability to teach and implement MGB.

In this article, our goal is to clarify the *distinction* between ethics and MGB. In particular, our focus is on the one bargaining strategy—deception—that triggers many ethical discussions (Blodgett 1968; Lewicki 1983). We believe that negotiation teachers and trainers should be careful to keep ethics and integrative bargaining separate. It is obviously important to teach about ethics in bargaining, including the issue of deception, and to teach about integrative bargaining, but these are separate issues—both in theory and practice.

ETHICALLY AMBIGUOUS TACTICS

Many commonly used or taught negotiation tactics are fraught with ethical concerns. The types of tactics that are most often cited as being ethically ambiguous are ones involving deception (Dees and Cramton 1993; Carr 1968; Lewicki 1983; Shapiro and Bies 1994). For example, when a manufacturer is negotiating the price of a part, and no other supplier is available at the time, she or he would refrain from sharing that fact during negotiations. In addition to hiding this information, the manufacturer would probably try to lead the other side to believe that there were many suppliers to choose from, either by saying so explicitly or making statements that imply this. Negotiators commonly hide their true level of dependency, and commonly exaggerate the value of their options in the event of no agreement, their willingness and ability to choose other options, and the likelihood that their constituents (whose supposed demands may even be fabricated) will disapprove of concessions under discussion.

In such situations, the negotiator's goal is to shift the opponent's perception of the zone of possible agreement in one's favor. When this is done well, the opponent is left to decide whether s/he would rather risk having no agreement, or give in to the demands that have been made. Since the opponent has the same goal, if one listens to what is said early in the negotiations one might believe that there is no zone of possible agreement at all when in fact there may be. The process of negotiating is at its core a process of shaping perceptions of reality (Berger and Luckman 1967). Deceptive tactics like hiding or exaggerating information often shape the perception of negotiators' power, which some have identified to be the most critical perception of all (Bacharach and Lawler 1988).[1]

Whether these behaviors are ethical is a great source of debate. People with absolutist moral positions might argue that misleading others is unethical in general and therefore should not be used in the context of bargaining. A more tolerant approach is to say that we should not do things that are acknowledged to be socially unacceptable. Using the test of whether people would want their actions told to their mother (Murnighan 1993) or described in a newspaper (Lax and Sebenius 1986), many would find it embarrassing for others to know that they acted deceptively. Others might counter that whether deception is considered ethical or not depends on the context, not the act of deceiving. For example, if one is negotiating with terrorists for the release of hostages and lives could be saved through deception, many would say the use of deception was ethical. Or, if one is acting as a negotiator for a relatively powerless community group trying to block the construction of a toxic waste dump, deception may be one of the few ways to create a balance of power in the negotiations, especially if the dump's owner has a history of misrepresenting data about the effects of toxins on drinking water. The ethically good "end" thus justifies the use of deception in some negotiation situations.

These are complex issues that are difficult to resolve on a philosophical level. It is not our goal in this article to make a definitive statement about the ethics of deceptive negotiating tactics. Rather, we shall examine the relationship between ethically ambiguous behaviors in negotiations and the use of MGB in negotiations. Our contention is that it is easy to confuse MGB with behaviors that are ethically pure, and that doing so may actually make it harder to teach MGB or get people to use it.

MUTUAL GAINS BARGAINING AND ETHICAL CLAIMS

MGB is an approach that helps negotiators produce the greatest joint gains possible. As noted earlier, it is also called "integrative bargaining," "win-win" or "principled" negotiation, and is often contrasted with "distributive" bargaining, that is, bargaining that is zero-sum or focused on getting more for oneself by forcing the opponent to take less. As explained by Fisher and Ury (1981), MGB is based on four principles: separating the people from the problem; focusing on interests, not positions; inventing options for mutual gain; and insisting on objective criteria.

There is nothing in these principles that directly addresses the issue of ethical behavior or deceptive tactics. However, there are several ways in which these principles can be inadvertently related to ethical behavior and trainees may come to believe that the primary reason for MGB is that it is more "honest" than traditional negotiations. It is possible that some trainers do frame MGB as the more ethical way to bargain, or that the "principled" and "mutual gains" labels themselves convey that message to trainees. More importantly, the connection between MGB and ethics may come from more deep-seated and fundamental misunderstandings of the ideas of MGB, especially the difference between interests and positions.

MGB suggests that negotiators explain to their opponent what their *interests* are, so that the opponent can propose actions that meet one's real needs at least cost. It does not, however, say anything about revealing one's alternatives to a negotiated agreement, what one's true reservation price is, or how much money is in the bargaining budget—all of which influence what final *position* will be acceptable. The problem is that the distinction is difficult for many negotiators to understand; even for trainers, the line between the two is frequently not completely clear. In fact, the distinction represents more of a continuum than an absolute difference. For example, a "5 percent pay raise" is a position in that it is one way to achieve the interest of "a better quality of life." From another perspective, it is an interest that may be achieved in various ways (such as 3 percent base wage increase and a 2 percent lump sum or via other "positions"). Therefore, some will tend to hear the MGB prescriptions as saying "reveal everything about oneself." MGB says only that you should not deceive the other party about your core, underlying interests. And—this is worth emphasizing—the reason for this prescription is not that being honest about interests is inherently ethical. Rather, it is that being honest about one's interests can help you get more. If others do not know what really matters to you, they cannot help search for ways to meet your needs that are feasible for them.

Confusion is also likely to the degree that MGB is framed as an alternative to distributive bargaining. For pedagogical reasons it may be necessary at some stage of training to present MGB as a completely different model for negotiations, but few scholars would presume that many negotiations are wholly integrative. Rather, most negotiations are "mixed motive" (Stevens 1963); they include both opportunities for joint gain, and opportunities for grabbing more from the other side. Walton and McKersie (1965) call this the integrative and distributive dimensions of negotiation, while Lax and Sebenius (1986) write of the distinction between creating and claiming value in negotiation. There is indeed a tension between the two: strategies that are wise for creating are often opposite from those that are wise for claiming (e.g., deception about positions and power is necessary for claiming, while deception about interests is disruptive for creating). But all negotiations include both elements, and few negotiations occur where a wise negotiator would not employ at least some of each set of behaviors. Indeed, one of the more interesting challenges faced by negotiators is how to balance both of these elements.

Pruitt and Lewis (1977) have argued that the two approaches appear in the same negotiation by means of separating creating and claiming into distinct phases of the process, or by having different individuals on bargaining teams engage in creating or claiming. More recently, Friedman (1994) has argued that the two approaches coexist by having separate "stages" for each. While distributive tactics and deception occur front stage, integrative tactics and honest communication about interests occur backstage. In public, labor negotiators engage in a great deal of bravado, exaggeration, hiding, and, in general, attempts to deceive the other about what they want, what they are willing to accept, and what they are willing to fight over. But out of public view, negotiators engage in a well-understood process of signaling to opponents, discounting information, and engaging in private sidebar meetings to clarify interests.

In sum, MGB does teach negotiators not to deceive the opponent—about their interests. But it makes this suggestion based on effectiveness, not ethics. And it does not presume that all parts of negotiations are integrative—there is a domain for distributive bargaining in most negotiations. This distinction can be easily lost if the interest-position distinction is not made clear, or if teachers express a preference for MGB because of its higher ethical status.

If, in these ways, ethics and MGB become conflated, several problems can occur. First, negotiators may miss the distinctions between ethical and unethical behavior that exist in traditional negotiation. Second, they may misunderstand the true benefits that MGB provides. And third, they may perceive MGB as naive and therefore avoid using it.

ETHICAL CONVENTIONS IN LABOR NEGOTIATIONS

Equating MGB with ethics overlooks the fact that there are ethical constraints on deception in traditional negotiations. We can see this by looking at the example of labor negotiations. During a study of labor negotiations (Friedman 1994), the first author studied 13 negotiations, including direct observations of eight cases and over 150 interviews, and in addition interviewed 19 experienced labor negotiators. The negotiators in that study talked extensively about their relationships with opponents and the kinds of tactics that they used and expected others to use. From these interviews and observations, it became clear that professional labor negotiators have a definite sense, in practice, of what is appropriate and inappropriate behavior. Experienced labor negotiators expect that opponents will hide information and try to build up false perceptions about their limits and determination. Negotiators on both sides expect their opponents to have "laundry lists" of demands, put exaggerated financial offers on the table, declare that constituents will not accept less, say that they and their constituents could and would weather a strike, and even put on displays of anger and resolve to show how tough they will be in defense of these demands.

Nonetheless, some types of deception are beyond the pale. The same negotiators who expressed tolerance for some levels of deception also reported that there was a limit to what was acceptable. Overtly inaccurate statements are considered unethical (and unprofessional) by lead bargainers. It is acceptable and expected for the company to say "we cannot pay a penny more for health care," while it is unacceptable to say "adding physical therapy to the benefit package will cost us an additional $100 a year per employee" when it is known that it would only add $20 a year. The first statement is a general claim that can be readily interpreted as a bargaining stance; the latter is a factual claim that is either true or false. The first type of statement would be considered "bargaining" by experienced labor negotiators, and those who do it with cleverness and gusto are respected as savvy and skilled. The latter type of statement would be considered a lie, and the bargainer who was caught in such a lie would be deemed unprofessional and untrustworthy. In addition, for these negotiators it makes a difference if either statement is made in private between lead bargainers or in public across the main table. What is said across the table is expected to be exaggerated and not fully accurate; what is said in private is expected to be accurate.

To claim inaccurately that the company cannot spend one penny more on health care across the table is expected and not deemed unethical; to make that same false claim in private would produce outrage if the lie was discovered.

Underlying this distinction is an understanding that some statements are *expected* to be untrue, while others are not. When negotiators make statements that are expected to be untrue, the other negotiators are able to make appropriate adjustments, calculations, and predictions. These statements are interpreted, discounted, and treated with caution (Friedman 1994). Negotiators anticipate that these statements are made as bargaining stances, open to change, or that they are positions that need to be stated to look good to constituents and teammates. By contrast, when one negotiator makes statements that are expected to be true, the other party proceeds to act on them; this information is often represented to constituents as true, and major decisions are made based on it. The consequences of deception in those situations can be great: there might be an unnecessary strike, the negotiators could be hurt professionally if constituents find out that they were duped, and negotiators' ability to count on some truthful communication between the two sides is eliminated and their ability to manage the negotiations wisely is greatly diminished.

The ethical conventions that are common among labor negotiators ensure that both deception and honesty can occur, and that there is a common understanding of when and how deception is limited. These conventions are based not on some abstract moralism, but a very practical concern for enabling the negotiators to do their jobs, negotiate well for their side, and avoid an unnecessary strike. Negotiators still try to indicate that their side will stand tough against the opponent, and they still try to deceive (as one labor lawyer put it, even in sidebar meetings "I don't put all my cards on the table"). But there is also much trust and communication between opponents, particularly the lead bargainers. This lessens the personal nature of the conflict and makes the integrative bargaining possible. While these negotiators would never want to be completely honest with their opponents, they do place limits on deception and will withdraw cooperation from those who cross the line.

The example from labor relations shows that there are ethical constraints on negotiations, regardless of whether one mentions mutual gains bargaining. And it shows that these ethical constraints operate despite the acknowledged presence of deception during much of negotiations. What might appear logically as mutually exclusive behaviors—being honest and deceiving—are not so in practice.

Thus, there are reasons to engage both in deception *and* honesty in negotiations, and there are enormous risks associated with either a purely honest or purely deceptive strategy. And negotiators have developed mechanisms to engage in both strategies. This mixture of tactics works exactly because negotiators recognize the need for both tactics, because the divide between them is well understood, and because an ethical system exists that ensures that negotiators act honestly when expected to and which keeps deception within some practical limit.

PUTTING THE MGB MESSAGE IN CONTEXT

If the message of mutual gains bargaining is not that integrative tactics alone should be used or that deception should be completely precluded, and if integrative tactics (including prohibitions against deception during integrative phases of negotiations) already exist in most negotiations, why have MGB training? We can identify three primary benefits to teaching MGB that do not depend on the "do-not-ever-be-deceptive" message. First, MGB training can help inexperienced trainees to discover that there is an integrative— and not only a distributive—side to bargaining. This discovery is especially likely among negotiators who may have been exposed only to the more public, high conflict aspects of bargaining.

Second, MGB can help negotiators anticipate times when their emotions make them forget what they know about integrative bargaining, and focus only on distributive bargaining. In this way, emotionally triggered escalation traps are made less likely (Pruitt and Rubin 1986). Although professional bargainers usually know how to keep their emotions under control and "focus on the problem not the person," less experienced bargainers may not be as well prepared for the pressures of bargaining. And there may be times when relations between the two sides have become so difficult that even experienced bargainers have a difficult time sustaining the integrative side to bargaining that they know should exist. Third, MGB can encourage negotiators to be integrative bargainers somewhat more than they traditionally are. More specifically, MGB training may help negotiators lengthen the phase of negotiations that is more integrative, or to include more people in the backstage arena where integrative bargaining is done. While not eliminating hard bargaining, or telling negotiators to give up the deceptive tactics that are central to hard bargaining, MGB training may be able to shift the balance somewhat towards integrative bargaining.

THE DANGERS OF NAIVE MGB TRAINING

Not only is the "do-not-ever-deceive" message unnecessary in MGB training, it may also reduce the effectiveness of the training. The message "do-not-ever-deceive" does not recognize the fact that, even when integrative bargaining works well, there is still a need to engage in distributive tactics, nor the fact that being completely honest about one's fallback positions can diminish one's power. For these distributive elements of negotiations, tactics such as hiding information and shaping impressions are often necessary and do work. To teach that negotiators should abandon all impression management tactics would be unwise from an analytic perspective, would make the teacher appear naive, and ensure that the MGB approach would be seen as damaging to one's negotiating goals.

Moreover, these costs are not necessary; practicing mutual gains bargaining does not require that negotiators make themselves vulnerable through comprehensive revelations about their situation. It says only that it makes no sense to deceive the opponent about one's *interests*. Finally, to the degree that trainers signal an ethical priority (or allow trainees to read that into the training), trainees have a more difficult time seeing that MGB helps people to negotiate *smarter* and get better results. While some may believe that MGB helps make negotiations more ethical, that is unlikely to generate among trainees a true commitment to understand and use the MGB lessons.

That is not to say, however, that there are no ethical constraints. MGB does not free negotiators to be deceptive in ways that are traditionally unacceptable. If one is found to have lied, that would be a source of distrust during negotiations, it would engender uncooperative behavior by the opponent, and make him or her less likely to engage in integrative bargaining—with or without MGB training. To the degree that we might encourage people to use MGB techniques, or at least not to do less of it, negotiators should stay within commonly understood norms of acceptable behavior. Misrepresentations that cross the line have been found to interfere with negotiators' willingness to use MGB (Friedman 1993), just as those that cross the line make backstage interactions more difficult in traditional negotiations.

RECOMMENDATIONS FOR TEACHING MGB

From this analysis we suggest that those who teach mutual gains bargaining make clear that the benefits of MGB are practical, not ethical. Operationally, this means that MGB trainers may wish to consider the following three suggestions:

1. Given the degree to which it is easy for students to read into MGB training the message that they should "do MBG because it seems 'nicer' or more 'ethical'," special care must be taken to highlight the practical benefits of MGB, and to avoid moralistic statements that enhance this misreading.

2. Since MGB does encourage disclosure of one's interests, special care must be taken to clarify the distinction between interests and positions. Only then will it be possible for students to see that revealing one aspect of what a bargainer knows (i.e., his or her interests) does not imply that all information about one's strategies and fallback positions must be revealed.

3. MGB teachers and trainers should also teach their students about tough bargaining tactics, including deception, and acknowledge that there are benefits to hard bargaining. Moreover, students need to understand the "mixed motives" of negotiations and the need to be prepared for both integrative and distributive aspects of bargaining.

This advice does not mean that teachers should not teach ethics in bargaining. It is extremely valuable for students to evaluate both the ethical and practical costs of crossing the line. They need to understand what actions constitute fraud from a legal point of view (see, e.g., Shell 1991) and what actions are considered among negotiators to be excessive misrepresentation or lying. They also need to consider the effects that unethical behaviors can have on trust, and the effects that lack of trust can have on one's ability to negotiate effectively and one's ability to maintain a relationship with the opponent after negotiations are over. Teaching the effects of unethical behavior in negotiation does not require negotiation trainers to confuse MGB (and an understanding of the techniques and logic of integrative bargaining) with ethical concerns, nor does it require efforts to preclude all types of deception in negotiations. Indeed, we believe confusing ethics and MGB threatens a teacher's ability to teach effectively, and obtain a commitment to using MGB principles in practice. Such confusion diminishes the positive impact that MGB can otherwise have.

CONCLUSION

We have made great strides in recent years teaching more people—in classrooms, corporate training sessions, and actual negotiations—about negotiations, including how to be more ethical and how to ensure that integrative joint gains are not left on the table. The fact that we even need to write an article like this is an indication of the advances that have been made.

Yet exactly because of these advances, more care needs to be taken to ensure that the subtle distinction between what is ethical and what is integrative is maintained. Being ethical in negotiations is more complicated than producing greater joint utility, and the techniques that are helpful for producing greater joint utility should not be made more complicated by the addition of ethical concerns. Each issue—ethics and mutual gains bargaining—can stand on its own, and benefits by being considered on its own. By maintaining this distinction, we believe each will have greater clarity and greater impact, and our teaching and training will be both better received and more valuable to those we teach.

NOTES

1. Negotiators can actually reshape reality itself, not just perceptions of it. This is done by taking actions which really do tie one's hands so that compromise is impossible. Such commitment tactics are discussed by Schelling (1960) and Raiffa (1982). These tactics are not considered in this article since they are not instances of deception.

REFERENCES

Bacharach, S. B., and E. J. Lawler. 1988. *Bargaining: Power, tactics, and outcomes.* San Francisco: Jossey-Bass.

Berger, P. I., and T. Luckman. 1967. *The social construction of reality.* Garden City, NY: Anchor Books.

Carr, A. Z. 1968. Is business bluffing ethical? *Harvard Business Review.* January–February, 143–50.

Dees, J. Gregory, and P. Cramton. 1993. Promoting honesty in negotiations: An exercise in practical ethics. *Business Ethics Quarterly* 3(4): 44–61.

Fisher, R., and W. L. Ury. 1981. *Getting to yes. Negotiating agreement without giving in.* Boston: Houghton Mifflin.

Friedman, R. A. 1994. *Front stage, backstage: The dramatic structure of labor negotiations.* Cambridge, MA: MIT Press.

_____. 1993. Bringing mutual gains bargaining to labor negotiations: The role of trust, understanding, and control. *Human Resource Management Journal* 32(4): 435–59.

Lax, D. A., and J. K. Sebenius. 1986. *The manager as negotiator.* New York: Free Press.

Lewicki, R. 1993. Comments presented as part of the symposium "Ethical dilemmas in negotiating and getting people to 'yes'." Conflict Management Division, National Academy of Management meeting. Atlanta.

_____. 1983. Lying and deception. In *Negotiating in organizations*, edited by M. H. Bazerman and R. J. Lewicki. Beverly Hills, CA: Sage.

Murninghan, K. 1993. Comments presented as part of the preconference workshop "Ethical dilemmas in negotiating and getting people to 'yes'." Conflict Management Division. National Academy of Management meeting, Atlanta.

Pruitt, D. G. and S. A. Lewis. 1977. The psychology of integrative bargaining. In *Negotiations: Social psychological perspectives*, edited by D. Druckman. London: Sage.

Pruitt, D. G., and J. Z. Rubin. 1986. *Social conflict: Escalation, stalemate, and settlement.* New York: Random House.

Raiffa, H., 1982. *The art and science of negotiation.* Cambridge, MA: Harvard University Press.

Shapiro, D. I., and R. J. Bies. 1994. Threats, bluffs, and disclaimers in negotiation. *Organization Behavior and Human Decision Processes* 60: 14–35.

Shell, R. 1991. When is it legal to lie in negotiations? *Sloan Management Review* 32(3): 78–94.

Schelling, T. C. 1960. *The strategy of conflict.* Cambridge, MA: Harvard University Press.

Stevens, C. 1963. *Strategy and collective bargaining negotiations.* New York: McGraw Hill.

Susskind, I., and J. Cruikshank. 1987. *Breaking the impasse.* New York: Basic Books.

Walton, R. E., and R. B. McKersie. 1965. *A behavioral theory of labor negotiations: An analysis of a social interaction system.* New York: McGraw Hill.

SECTION EIGHT

Social Context

When Should We Use Agents?
Direct versus Representative
Negotiation

Jeffrey Z. Rubin
Frank E. A. Sander

Although we typically conceive of negotiations occurring directly between two or more principals, often neglected in a thoughtful analysis are the many situations where negotiations take place indirectly, through the use of representatives or surrogates of the principals. A father who speaks to his child's teacher (at the child's request), two lawyers meeting on behalf of their respective clients, the foreign service officers of different nations meeting to negotiate the settlement of a border dispute, a real estate agent informing would-be buyers of the seller's latest offer—each is an instance of negotiation through representatives.

In this brief essay, we wish to build on previous analyses of representative negotiation[1] to consider several key distinctions between direct and representative negotiations, and to indicate the circumstances under which we believe negotiators should go out of their way either to choose *or* to avoid negotiation through agents.

The most obvious effect of using agents—an effect that must be kept in mind in any analysis of representative negotiation—is complication of the transaction. As indicated in Figure 1, if we begin with a straightforward negotiation between two individuals, then the addition of two agents transforms this simple one-on-one deal into a complex matrix involving at least four primary negotiators, as well as two subsidiary ones (represented by the dotted lines in Figure 1). In addition, either of the agents may readily serve as a mediator between the client and the other agent or principal. Or the two agents might act as co-mediators between the principals. At a minimum, such a complex structure necessitates effective coordination. Beyond that, this structural complexity has implications—both positive and negative—for representative negotiation in general. Let us now review these respective benefits and liabilities.

Source: Jeffrey Z. Rubin and Frank E. A. Sander, "When Should We Use Agents? Direct vs. Representative Negotiation" from *Negotiation Journal,* October 1988, Copyright Kluwer Academic/Plenum Publishers.

FIGURE 1   Possible Relations among Two Principals (P1 and P2) and Their Respective
Agents (A1 and A2) (A solid line denotes an actual relation, a dotted line a
potential one.)

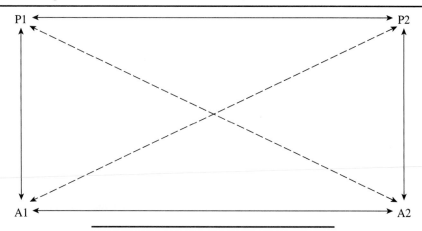

EXPERTISE

One of the primary reasons that principals choose to negotiate through agents is that
the latter possess expertise that makes agreement—particularly favorable agreement—
more likely. This expertise is likely to be of three different stripes.

Substantive Knowledge.   A tax attorney or accountant knows things about the
current tax code that make it more likely that negotiations with an IRS auditor will benefit the client as much as possible. Similarly, a divorce lawyer, an engineering consultant,
and a real estate agent may have substantive knowledge in a rather narrow domain of
expertise, and this expertise may redound to the client's benefit.

Process Expertise.   Quite apart from the specific expertise they may have in particular content areas, agents may have skill at the negotiation *process,* per se, thereby
enhancing the prospects of a favorable agreement. A skillful negotiator—someone who
understands how to obtain and reveal information about preferences, who is inventive,
resourceful, firm on goals but flexible on means, etc.—is a valuable resource. Wise
principals would do well to utilize the services of such skilled negotiators, unless they
can find ways of developing such process skills themselves.

Special Influence.   A Washington lobbyist is paid to know the "right" people, to
have access to the "corridors of power" that the principals themselves are unlikely to
possess. Such "pull" can certainly help immensely, and is yet another form of expertise
that agents may possess, although the lure of this "access" often outweighs in promise
the special benefits that are confirmed in reality.

Note that the line separating these three forms of expertise is often a thin one, as in
the case of a supplier who wishes to negotiate a sales contract with a prospective purchaser,

and employs a former employee of the purchaser to handle the transaction; the former employee, as agent, may be a source of both substantive expertise *and* influence.

Note also that principals may not always know what expertise they need. Thus, a person who has a dispute that seems headed for the courts may automatically seek out a litigator, not realizing that the vast preponderance of cases are settled by negotiation, requiring very different skills that the litigator may not possess. So, although agents do indeed possess different forms of expertise that may enhance the prospects of a favorable settlement, clients do not necessarily know what they need; it's a bit like the problem of looking up the proper spelling of a word in the dictionary when you haven't got a clue about how to spell the word in question.

DETACHMENT

Another important reason for using an agent to do the actual negotiation is that the principals may be too emotionally entangled in the subject of the dispute. A classic example is divorce. A husband and wife, caught in the throes of a bitter fight over the end of their marriage, may benefit from the "buffering" that agents can provide. Rather than confront each other with the depth of their anger and bitterness, the principals (P1 and P2 in Figure 1) may do far better by communicating only *indirectly,* via their respective representatives, A1 and A2. Stated most generally, when the negotiating climate is adversarial—when the disputants are confrontational rather than collaborative—it may be wiser to manage the conflict through intermediaries than run the risk of an impasse or explosion resulting from direct exchange.

Sometimes, however, it is the *agents* who are too intensely entangled. What is needed then is the detachment and rationality that only the principals can bring to the exchange. For example, lawyers may get too caught up in the adversary game and lose sight of the underlying problem that is dividing the principals (e.g., how to resolve a dispute about the quality of goods delivered as part of a long-term supply contract). The lawyers may be more concerned about who would win in court, while the clients simply want to get their derailed relationship back on track. Hence the thrust of some modern dispute resolution mechanisms (such as the minitrial) is precisely to take the dispute *out* of the hands of the technicians and give it back to the primary parties.[2]

Note, however, that the very "detachment" we are touting as a virtue of negotiation through agents can also be a liability. For example, in some interpersonal negotiations, apology and reconciliation may be an important ingredient of any resolution (see, e.g., Goldberg, Green, and Sander, 1987). Surrogates who are primarily technicians may not be able to bring to bear these empathic qualities.

TACTICAL FLEXIBILITY

The use of agents allows various gambits to be played out by the principals, in an effort to ratchet as much as possible from the other side. For example, if a seller asserts that the bottom line is $100,000, the buyer can try to haggle, albeit at the risk of losing the deal. If the buyer employs an agent, however, the agent can profess willingness to pay that sum but plead lack of authority, thereby gaining valuable time and opportunity for fuller consideration of the situation together with the principal. Or an agent for the seller who senses that the buyer may be especially eager to buy the property can claim that it is necessary to go back to the seller for ratification of the deal, only to return and up the price, profusely apologizing all the while for the behavior of an "unreasonable" client. The client and agent can thus together play the hard-hearted partner game.

Conversely, an agent may be used in order to push the other side in tough, even obnoxious, fashion, making it possible—in the best tradition of the "good cop/bad cop" ploy—for the client to intercede at last, and seem the essence of sweet reason in comparison with the agent. Or the agent may be used as a "stalking horse," to gather as much information about the adversary as possible, opening the way to proposals by the client that exploit the intelligence gathered.

Note that the tactical flexibility conferred by representative negotiations presupposes a competitive negotiating climate, a zero-sum contest in which each negotiator wishes to outsmart the other. It is the stuff of traditional statecraft, and the interested reader can do no better than study the writings of Schelling (1960) and Potter (1948), as well as Lax and Sebenius (1986). To repeat, the assumption behind this line of analysis is that effective negotiation requires some measure of artifice and duplicity, and that this is often best accomplished through the use of some sort of foil or alter ego—in the form of the agent. But the converse is not necessarily true: Where the negotiation is conducted in a problem-solving manner (cf. Fisher and Ury, 1981), agents may still be helpful, not because they resort to strategic ruses, but because they can help articulate interests, options, and alternatives. Four heads are clearly better than two, for example, when it comes to brainstorming about possible ways of reconciling the parties' interests.

Offsetting—indeed, typically *more* than offsetting—the three above apparent virtues of representative negotiation are several sources of difficulty. Each is sufficiently important and potentially problematic that we believe caution is necessary before entering into negotiation through agents.

EXTRA "MOVING PARTS"

As indicated in Figure 1, representative negotiations entail greater structural complexity, additional moving parts in the negotiation machinery that—given a need for expertise, detachment, or tactical flexibility—can help move parties toward a favorable agreement. Additional moving parts, however, can also mean additional expense, in the form of the time required in the finding, evaluating, and engaging of agents, as well as the financial cost of retaining their services. And it can mean additional problems, more things that can go wrong. For instance, a message intended by a client may not be the message transmitted by that client's agent to the other party. Or the message received by that agent from the other party may be very different from the one that that agent (either deliberately or inadvertently) manages to convey to his or her client.

At one level, then, the introduction of additional links in the communication system increases the risk of distortion in the information conveyed back and forth between the principals. Beyond that lies a second difficulty: the possibility that eventually the principals will come to rely so extensively on their respective agents that they no longer communicate directly—even though they could, and even though they might well benefit from doing so.

In effect (see Figure 1), P1, in order to reach P2, now invariably goes through the A1–A2 chain, even though such maneuvering is no longer warranted. Consider, for example, the case of a divorcing couple who, in explicit compliance with the advice of their adversary lawyers, have avoided any direct contact with each other during the divorce proceedings. Once the divorce has been obtained, will the parties' ability to communicate effectively with each other (e.g., over support and custody issues) be adversely affected by their excessive prior reliance on their attorneys?

Yet another potentially problematic implication of this increasingly complex social machinery is that unwanted conditions may arise that apply undue pressure on individual negotiators. Thus A2, in performing a mediatory function between P2 and the other side (P1 and A1) may be prone to become allied with the opposing team—or at least to be so viewed by P2. Greater number does not necessarily mean greater wisdom, however, and the pressures toward uniformity of opinion that result from coalition formation may adversely affect the quality of the decisions reached.

In sum, the introduction of agents increases the complexity of the social apparatus of negotiation, and in so doing increases the chances of unwanted side effects. A related problem should be briefly noted here: the difficulty of asymmetry, as when an agent negotiates not with another agent but directly with the other principal. In effect, this was the case in 1978 when Egypt's Sadat negotiated with Israel's Begin at Camp David. Sadat considered himself empowered to make binding decisions for Egypt, while—at least partly for tactical purposes—Begin represented himself as ultimately accountable to his cabinet and to the Israeli parliament. While this "mismatched" negotiation between a principal (Sadat) and an agent (Begin) *did* result in agreement (thanks in good measure to President Carter's intercession as a mediator), it was not easy. The asymmetry of role meant that the two sides differed in their readiness to move forward toward an agreement, their ability to be shielded by a representative, and their willingness/ability to guarantee that any agreement reached would "stick."[3]

Different dynamics will characterize the negotiation depending on whether it is between clients, between lawyers, or with both present. If just the clients are there, the dealings will be more direct and forthright, and issues of authority and ratification disappear. With just the lawyers present, there may be less direct factual information but concomitantly more candor about delicate topics. Suppose, for example, that an aging soprano seeks to persuade an opera company to sign her for the lead role in an upcoming opera. If she is not present, the opera's agent may try to lower the price, contending that the singer is past her prime. Such candor is not recommended if the singer is present at the negotiation!

PROBLEMS OF "OWNERSHIP" AND CONFLICTING INTERESTS

In theory, it is clear that the principal calls the shots. Imagine, however, an agent who is intent on applying the *Getting to Yes* (Fisher and Ury, 1981) approach by searching for objective criteria and a fair outcome. Suppose the client simply wants the best possible outcome, perhaps because it is a one-shot deal not involving a future relationship with the other party. What if the agent (a lawyer, perhaps) *does* care about his future relationship with the other *agent,* and wants to be remembered as a fair and scrupulous bargainer?

How *should* this conflict get resolved and how, in the absence of explicit discussion, *will* it be resolved, if at all? Conversely, the client, because of a valuable long-term relationship, may want to maintain good relations with the other side. But if the client simply looks for an agent who is renowned for an ability to pull out all the stops, the client's overall objectives may suffer as the result of an overzealous advocate.

This issue may arise in a number of contexts. Suppose that, in the course of a dispute settlement negotiation,[4] a lawyer who is intent on getting the best possible deal for a client turns down an offer that was within the client's acceptable range. Is this proper behavior by the agent? The Model Rules of Professional Conduct for attorneys explicitly require (see Rules 1.2(a), 1.4) that every offer must be communicated to the principal, and perhaps a failure to do so might lead to a successful malpractice action against the attorney if the deal finally fell through.

Another illustration involves the situation where the agent and principal have divergent ethical norms. Suppose that a seller of a house has just learned that the dwelling is infested with termites, but instructs the agent not to reveal this fact, even in response to specific inquiry from the buyer. How should these tensions be fairly resolved, keeping in mind the fact that the agent may be subject to a professional code of conduct that gives directions that may conflict with the ethical values of the client?[5] There may, of course, be artful ways of dealing with such dilemmas, as, for example, slyly deflecting any relevant inquiry by the buyer. But preferably these problems should be explicitly addressed in the course of the initial discussion between agent and principal. To some extent, the problem may be resolved by the principal's tendency to pick an agent who is congenial and compatible. But, as we pointed out before, principals are not always aware of and knowledgeable about the relevant considerations that go into the choice of an agent. Hence, if these issues are not addressed explicitly at the outset, termination of the relationship midstream in egregious cases may be the only alternative.

Differing goals and standards of agent and principal may create conflicting pulls. For example, the buyer's agent may be compensated as a percentage of the purchase price, thus creating an incentive to have the price as high as possible. The buyer, of course, wants the lowest possible price. Similarly, where a lawyer is paid by the hour, there may be an incentive to draw out the negotiation, whereas the client prefers an expeditious negotiation at the lowest possible cost.

While these are not insoluble problems, to be sure, they do constitute yet another example of the difficulties that may arise as one moves to representative negotiations. Although in theory the principals are in command, once agents have been introduced the chemistry changes, and new actors—with agenda, incentives, and constraints of their own—are part of the picture. Short of an abrupt firing of the agents, principals may find themselves less in control of the situation once agents have come on the scene.

ENCOURAGEMENT OF ARTIFICE AND DUPLICITY

Finally, as already noted, the introduction of agents often seems to invite clients to devise stratagems (with or without these agents) to outwit the other side. Admittedly, there is nothing intrinsic to the presence of representatives that dictates a move in this direction; still, perhaps because of the additional expense incurred, the seductive lure of a "killing" with the help of one's "hired gun," or the introduction of new, sometimes perverse incentives, representative negotiations often seem to instill (or reflect) a more adversarial climate.

CONCLUSION

It follows from the preceding analysis that, ordinarily, negotiations conducted directly between the principals are preferable to negotiation through representatives. When the principals' relationship is fundamentally cooperative or informed by enlightened self-interest, agents may often be unnecessary; since there is little or no antagonism in the relationship, there is no need for the buffering detachment afforded by agents. Moreover, by negotiating directly, there is reduced risk of miscoordination, misrepresentation, and miscommunication.

On the other hand, representative negotiation *does* have an important and necessary place. When special expertise is required, when tactical flexibility is deemed important and—most important—when direct contact is likely to produce confrontation rather than collaboration, agents *can* render an important service.

Above all, the choice of whether to negotiate directly or through surrogates is an important one, with significant ramifications. It therefore should be addressed explicitly by weighing some of the considerations advanced above. And if an agent *is* selected, careful advance canvassing of issues such as those discussed here (e.g., authority and ethical standards) is essential.

NOTES

We thank Michael Wheeler for the many constructive comments, suggestions, and conversations that preceded this article; and we gratefully acknowledge the helpful comments of Stephen B. Goldberg on an earlier draft of this manuscript.

1. See, in particular, the concise and insightful discussion by Lax and Sebenius (1986) in Chapter 15 of their *The Manager as Negotiator.*

2. Compare in this connection the unfortunate recent decision of the United States Court of Appeals for the Seventh Circuit to the effect that a federal district court judge has no power to compel principals with settlement authority to attend a settlement conference. *G. Heileman Brewing Co.* v. *Joseph Oat Corp.,* 848 F. 2d 1415 (7th Circuit 1988).

3. Compare in this connection Rule 4.2 of the American Bar Association's Model Rules of Professional Conduct, which prohibits a lawyer from dealing directly with the opposing principal, if that principal is represented by an attorney.

4. See Sander and Rubin (1988) for a discussion of the differences between dealmaking and dispute settlement negotiation.

5. See, for example, Rule 4.1 of the ABA's Model Rules of Professional Conduct, prohibiting attorneys from making materially false statements.

REFERENCES

Fisher, R., and Ury, W. L. (1981). *Getting to yes: Negotiating agreement without giving in.* Boston: Houghton Mifflin.

Goldberg, S., Green, E., and Sander, F. E. A. (1987). "Saying you're sorry." *Negotiation Journal* 3: 221–24.

Lax, D. A., and Sebenius, J. K. (1986). *The manager as negotiator.* New York: Free Press.

Potter, S. (1948). *The theory and practice of gamesmanship: The art of winning games without actually cheating.* New York: Holt.

Sander, F. E. A., and Rubin, J. Z. (1988). "The Janus quality of negotiation: Dealmaking and dispute settlement." *Negotiation Journal* 4: 109–13.

Schelling, T. (1960). *The strategy of conflict.* Cambridge, MA: Harvard University Press.

Negotiating in Long-Term Mutually Interdependent Relationships among Relative Equals

Blair H. Sheppard

For somehow this is tyranny's disease, to trust no friends.

Aeschylus, 525–456 B.C., *Prometheus Bound*, 1. 224

INTRODUCTION

In U.S. business theory and practice, market and hierarchy have dominated as mechanisms for organizing economic activity (Arrow, 1974; Barnard, 1938; Ouchi, 1980). Consider the decision about how to source a part or service. The sourcing decision has typically been thought of as a make-or-buy decision in which a firm has the choice between building or servicing internally to the firm using traditional hierarchical controls, such as budgeting, accounting, and performance appraisals processes, so that the production of a part or service can be planned and integrated into other aspects of a firm's performance, or buying that part or service on the open market and depending on competition to ensure good value and innovation. Until recently, alternatives to making it internally or buying in a market have gone largely unheeded in modern thought and practice. However, many firms are now experimenting with a plethora of alternative means for better sourcing a part or service, such as developing long-term relationships with a given set of suppliers rather than buying on the spot market, building alliances with competitors to produce the part or service, or building peer-based organizations within a firm to codesign and manufacture the part. Each of these models represents a radical departure from market or hierarchy as a way of organizing economic activity. The central argument of this chapter is that such alternative means of organizing work are evolving rapidly and that our models of management are being outstripped by these changes in the marketplace.

Abridged version, originally appearing in *Research on Negotiation in Organizations,* Vol 5, 1995, pp. 3–44. Reprinted with permission of JAI Press and author.

In particular, it will be argued that market and hierarchy have been assumed as the backdrop against which our models of Micro-organizational Behavior have been developed. Thus, much management research has been about the exercise of power or control within a hierarchical organization or managing exchanges in the marketplace (see Sheppard and Tuchinsky, in press). Nowhere is the purity of our view of economic activity better expressed than in the dominant model of negotiation in academic research. Most negotiation research is concerned with how to engage in transactional, one-time negotiations in a relatively pure market (compare Lewicki, Litterer, Minton, and Saunders, 1994). The premise of this chapter is that unless we can develop models of negotiation that incorporate alternative models of economic exchange we are, in the extreme, doomed to irrelevancy . . . .

NEGOTIATING IN A RELATIONSHIP

For some, negotiation is considered a key skill for effectively managing within these emerging forms of business relationship (see Greenhalgh, 1987; Sheppard and Tuchinsky, in press). It follows that long-standing relationships among relative equals require bargaining, as formal controls and sanctions do not exist as a means of getting others to do what we wish. In relationships it is necessary to discuss, quibble, exchange, and engage in quid pro quo as a way to get someone over whom one does not have power to do what is desired. Partially based on this observation, research on negotiation has been conducted to help fill in the void. This research has taken as its model either the bargaining model developed in labor relations (see for example, Lewicki, Litterer, Minton, and Saunders, 1994); game theory (see for example, Murnighan, 1991); or decision theoretic models of negotiation (for example, see Bazerman and Neale, 1992). Each of these points of view is primarily transactional. They have as their model maximizing return to self in each negotiation. They do not address, as their primary focus, negotiation as a means of establishing and growing long-term relationships nor how the context of a given relationship changes the nature of a negotiation.

Recent research methodologies are also limited. For example, a fairly typical study involves two relative strangers engaging in a simulated negotiation over a few dimensions where each has been given a set of information outlining the returns to them for a set of settlement points on each dimension. The most frequently used simulation is a variant on the two-person, three-issue negotiation developed by Dean Pruitt for the study of integrative bargaining (Pruitt, 1972). These are poor proxies for at least three reasons: (1) the negotiation is not in the context of a relationship, (2) the simulation entails a predefined, highly stylized problem, and (3) there is no past and no future. Negotiations among long-term cross-functional team members, strategic allies, and parties to a long-term customer–supplier relationship have a past and a future, occur in the context of a very elaborate relationship, and involve messy problems. Therefore, the field has attempted to address a very important question: how negotiations occur within the context of an ongoing relationship among relative equals. But given the limiting set of perspectives and methodologies, it really has not. Research has concentrated on transactional exchanges, not relationships. It has ignored the temporal element that colors ongoing bargaining. Up to this point, research has inadequately addressed issues unique to relational negotiations. To make this case, however, it is necessary to illustrate how negotiations in the context of ongoing relationships differ significantly from transactional negotiations. Let us turn to that question now.

The Relational Context for Negotiation

Sustaining effective ongoing relationships in which there is an investment in mutual development is a very difficult enterprise. Some marriages end in divorce. Some strategic alliances fail. Some teams splinter. Some friendships break up. With even greater frequency we find ourselves in unsatisfying relationships from which there is no obvious escape. The challenge of maintaining a cooperative relationship is illustrated no place better than in the consideration of negotiations within marriages. They entail greater emotion. They are more complicated. They frequently do not end. They cannot be easily separated from other ongoing discussions. It is with good reason that transactional, decontextualized negotiations have been the primary topic of study. At least it is possible to understand them. But for all their trouble, negotiations within a partnership, marriage, alliance, or team are fun, interesting, important, and a defining aspect of what it means to be human. The challenges of distributive and integrative negotiation in an ongoing relationship are somewhat different. Thus, we will take them one at a time.

Distributive Negotiation in a Relationship

A recently married couple are discussing whose parents they will be spending Christmas vacation with. Procter & Gamble and Wal-Mart are discussing who will own the inventory in their new relationship. Pricewaterhouse is discussing a cost overrun with an extremely important audit client. Members of a new task force are determining their new roles only to discover that the two wish to serve the same function. Each of these discussions could be modeled quite well as a single-issue, distributive-negotiation problem. There are two parties—a single critical dimension and opposing positions. A great portion of each of these discussions will entail a search for the other's walkaway point and hiding of one's own. But the discussions are also more complicated than the simple distributive problem.

Transforming Distributive to Integrative Bargains.   Most obviously, because a history and a future exist in each of these discussions, there exist ways of identifying integrative potential not likely to be found in a simple transaction. A one-time distributive problem does not permit introducing other issues into a discussion. However, because within relationships there exists a past and a future, it is possible to transform a single-issue distributive discussion into a multiple-issue integrative discussion. One spouse cares a great deal about where to spend their first married Christmas, while the other harbors strong preferences about where to spend their summer vacation time. Procter & Gamble wishes Wal-Mart to own any inventory, Wal-Mart wishes to establish a mechanism to ensure a quick response on any future issues arising in the relationship. The customer is very concerned about paying additional costs, while the accountant is concerned about changing client procedures and practices during future audits. Existing procedures result in a slow, unprofitable audit. One member of the task force truly wishes to be the initial point of contact with a critical group, the other may really wish to be central in the final presentation to that group. In each of these examples, a difficult distributive negotiation problem becomes less difficult as the parties are allowed to logroll over time. Consider a husband and wife, one of whom wishes to vacation in the mountains and the other at the beach. If all else fails, it is possible to go to the mountains one year and the beach the next. To do so, however, there needs to be a next year. In transactional negotiation, a future does not exist, or it exists very tentatively and with no assurances. Thus, a bird in the hand is worth two in the bush. In an ongoing relationship, however, birds in the bush are much less likely to get away.

Not only is there an incentive to shift from distributive to integrative solutions without relationships, there is also an incentive to shift away from distributive processes. Because partners see future interaction, they are unlikely to wish to use the most problematic of distributive tactics. Knowing that the other can get them back and that cooperation is undermined by the tone created with the sorts of tactics typical of distributive negotiations, marital negotiators are less likely to use them. Similarly, revealing critical information is more likely as we come to believe that our partners are less likely to use that information unfairly. The abused partner has many chances to get the other partner back.

Distributive Negotiations within a Relationship Are Hot.   But the future is a two-edged sword. While integrative potential is raised by the possibility of introducing a second issue into the discussion there is also potential for the discussion to become very heated and focused on the single issue at hand. Frequently, distributive discussions in ongoing relationships are precedent establishing. Discussions over precedent are very important discussions, as the stakes entail all future such problems. The couple may not only be determining where to go at Christmas, but where to go for all future Christmases, whose family matters more and the relative priority of parents and in-laws versus the members of the couple themselves. Thus, a simple little distributive problem takes on great new importance. Who owns the inventory for one P&G product line has clear implications for who owns the inventory for all product lines and all future products. Thus, the discussion is not over just toothpaste for this year, but potentially the allocation of profits across all brands. A solution for determining payment in overruns frequently becomes the baseline for all future discussions. Simple allocation questions become questions of precedent and thus more important and more heated. A clear implication of this point is that negotiators within relationships need to be able to handle well emotion-laden or very important issues.

Emotion is likely to arise for several other reasons as well. The most important, although not the most obvious, reason that negotiations within relationships are likely to be more emotional and conflict filled than transactional negotiation is that distributive negotiations within relationships frequently serve to define the partners. We know from social psychology that a central means through which people develop an identity is through the people they interact with most intimately (Linville and Carlston, 1994). I, for example, define my sense of self very much through my relationship with my wife, children, mother, father, siblings, and close friends and colleagues. Who I am is to a large degree who I am for them. Distributive negotiation issues within these relationships are self-defining in two ways. First, the roles the other assumes are not me. Second, the things I do and the roles I assume are me. Of course, it is also true that identity emerges from considering ourselves in light of our competitors (see, for example, Sherif et al., 1961). In the terminology of social psychologists, our sense of self derives both from those we consider members of our in-group and our out-group. The difference is that elements of self and long-term capacity are negotiated with in-group members. With competitors, direct conversation about who one is and what one will do are not frequent; instead, the market is the field through which identity and comparative competencies are established.

Teams are a setting in which the negotiation of self occurs frequently. The roles each member of a team assumes influences the skills each will become better at, the roles others see them fulfilling, and how they come to think of themselves. I recently spoke to a member of a design team who recounted that she started out thinking of herself as a design engineer, but now considers herself the quality guru in the company. Others have come to think of her the same way as well. Interestingly, at the time it happened she was upset that another team member drove the design components of the project she was working on, while she was left with quality. But, since the emerging importance of quality in her firm, she is glad she lost the initial battle. Another business example can be found in strategic alliances. Two companies come together in the development of a long-term joint design and production relationship. The discussion at hand concerns who is to perform what function. Writing on strategic alliances suggests that it is important to retain control over and delivery of those things which are a firm's core competencies. Those things a firm does better than the competition should be done by that firm. Good alliances entail firms with complementary core competencies. In such instances the allocation of work between allies has the character of an integrative discussion. But there always exist gray areas in which both sides wish control or primary responsibility. The outcome of those instances matters a great deal. Who performs which roles has implications for the competencies each firm is going to develop or accentuate over the course of the alliance. Even sticking to one's core competence is not all that desirable if an objective of a strategic alliance is to learn how to do other things well (cf. Sitkin and Stickel, in press).

The methods and vocabulary presently used in the study of negotiation do not lend themselves well to the study of emotion in negotiations. First, the use of simulated negotiations with relative strangers does not evoke deep conflicts, critical future dependencies, or threats to one's sense of self. Second, the absence of a past does not permit the study of patterns of emotion management that naturally emerged between related others over time. Finally, the fields from which we borrow our theoretical models may need to expand. Marital research (e.g., Gottman, 1979), research on friendship and social relationships (e.g., Putallaz and Sheppard, 1992), and even facets of organizational development have much to offer us (for example, Brown, 1985). The predominant models entail a view that is somewhat too calculative, too cold, and too abstracted from relational contexts to help with the study of emotion in negotiation. I do not mean to argue that laboratory or rigorous theory be abandoned. John Gottman (1979), for example, has studied extremely well in the laboratory the negotiation patterns that serve as precursors to divorce. One very interesting device he has used is to ask married couples to begin describing a frequent conflict they have. Inevitably, that conflict reemerges in the discussion and can be studied. Another is to create proxies for negotiations parties are presently engaged in. In any instance, precedent, deeply interdependent outcomes, and implications for future competence need to be parameters incorporated into our research designs and theory.

Distributive Negotiations in Relationships May Never End.   All negotiations are performed with incomplete information. Parties' preferences are not entirely known. Critical uncertainties are not entirely understood. How others important to the negotiators will behave is not entirely known. For example, the newlyweds do not know how their families will react to the decision they reach. The audit partner and controller do not know how senior management or the audit committee will react to their decision. Procter & Gamble and Wal-Mart do not know how their method for establishing inventory levels will work, nor do they know if the new delivery arrangements are truly feasible. Task force members do not know if the anticipated work reflects what really needs to be done. Because a decision must be reached, however, settlements are reached on incomplete information. In a transactional environment settlements must attempt to anticipate all important contingencies and have specified the method for dealing with those. Stewart MacAulay (1963) outlined the type of planning typical of a buyer/seller negotiation in a transaction:

> (1) They can plan what each is to do or refrain from doing, e.g., S might agree to deliver ten 1963 Studebaker four-door sedan automobiles to B on a certain date in exchange for a specified amount of money. (2) They can plan what effect certain contingencies are to have on their duties; e.g., what is to happen to S and B's obligation if S cannot deliver the cars because of a strike at the Studebaker factory? (3) They can plan what is to happen if either of them fails to perform; e.g., what is to happen if S delivers nine of the cars two weeks late? (4) They can plan their agreement so that it is a legally enforceable contract—that is, so that a legal sanction would be available to provide compensation for injury suffered by B as a result of S's failure to deliver the cars on time (p.57).

Sometimes such planning entails mutual negotiation between the parties. Sometimes it is done unilaterally in the form of fine-print boilerplate prepared by the house counsel of the seller or the buyer. Sometimes boilerplate is found on forms as they come from the printer. Sometimes typical industry practice is applied. In any instance, transactional negotiations often entail elaborate plans. However, in ongoing relationships these plans are frequently unnecessary and sometimes harmful. They are unnecessary because parties prefer to rely on a person's word, a handshake, or common honesty and decency. MacAulay (1963) quotes one purchasing agent who expresses this view:

> If something comes up, you get the other man on the telephone and deal with the problem. You don't read legalistic contract clauses at each other if you ever want to do business again. One doesn't run to lawyers if he wants to stay in business because one must behave decently (p.61).

In the instance of this purchasing agent, the term *decently* means be open for further negotiation. Oliver Williamson (1975) best articulated the major reason for not depending on well-specified contracts: people are not infinitely smart. If we could anticipate and plan for all possible contingencies, then a contract could serve our needs. However, people have limited capacity, an especially important complication in today's increasingly complex, ambiguous world. For most interesting negotiations, neither all important contingencies, nor all important aspects of performance can be identified in advance. This is especially true as changes in products and services occur with increasing rapidity and the focus on customization increases. Moreover, even if we could anticipate all important contingencies, a contract covering them would be too cumbersome. Thus, more open-ended vehicles permit ongoing discussion as a method for responding to changes as they arise.

A second reason for leaving negotiations open is that binding, planful discussions can create antagonistic relations. The tactics and tone associated with a fine-tooth comb negotiation process tend to create a legalistic environment. Such an environment does not serve as a good basis for developing stronger ongoing relations.

Of course, there are times that extreme planning is called for in a relationship. When relations are faltering, a frequent tactic of behavioral therapists is to get parties to develop explicit contracts about things on which they can agree. Frequently, incomplete discussions or inaccurate implicit assumptions served as the basis for the relationship failing in the first place. To raise to discussion important little issues and create agreements on these can set the parties on the track to building a more solid base of understanding. Said differently, parties may act as if their relationship is more of a marriage than it is. In such cases, returning to market conditions for a while may be a good idea. A second instance is when coordination of activities is essential and communication either difficult or very disruptive. A large building project is one example. The client, engineers, architect, contractor, and subcontractors often cannot meet frequently enough to work through the details of a project. Moreover, detailed planning permits a level of coordination that ad hoc communication cannot. Thus, planning should take place. Even in such instances, however, it is wise to leave open the possibility of ongoing negotiation as all contingencies cannot be foreseen and it builds stronger relationships.

Enforcement of Distributive Settlements within a Relationship.   In a related vein, the mechanisms for the enforcement of an agreement tend to be much more informal for negotiations within a relationship than for transactional negotiations. One source of informal sanctions are those that come directly from the relationships between involved members. In interfirm relationships, personal relationships can be extensive. Again, refer to MacAulay (1963):

> At all levels of the two business units personal relationships across the boundaries of the two organizations exert pressures for conformity to expectations. Salesmen know purchasing agents well. The same two individuals occupying these roles may have dealt with each other from 5 to 25 years. Each has something to give the other. Salesmen have gossip about competitors, shortages, and price increases to give purchasing agents who treat them well. Salesmen take purchasing agents to dinner, and they give purchasing agents Christmas gifts hoping to improve chances of making sales. The buyer's engineering staff may work with the seller's engineering staff to solve problems jointly. The seller's engineers may render great assistance, and the buyer's engineers may desire to return the favor by drafting specifications which only the seller can meet. The top executives of the two firms may know each other. They may sit

together on government or trade committees. They may know each other socially and even belong to the same country club. The interrelationships may be more formal. Sellers may hold stock in corporations which are important customers; buyers may hold stock in important suppliers. Both buyer and seller may share common directors on their boards. They may share a common financial institution which has financed both units (p. 63).

Executives, salespeople, and engineers do not like to hear that an important customer or supplier has been treated badly, or that an agreement with that customer or supplier has not been followed. To do so too often has clear career implications.

Other forms of enforcement hold as well. Most typically people who interact frequently with each other also interact with others important to one another. For example, an audit client probably knows many of the accounting firm's other clients. Wal-Mart personnel know people in similar positions at other retailers. Spouses know each other's parents, children, aunts, uncles, cousins, friends, and colleagues. The threat of lost reputation with important others is a very potent stimulus to following through on an agreement.

The dependence on the partner in a relationship is also a strong incentive to follow through on agreements. As indicated earlier, each member of a relationship comes to be dependent on the other for important services, advice, and help. The risk of losing those services is usually sufficient threat to follow through on an agreement.

Integrative Negotiation in a Relationship

In transactional negotiation, discussions are about the exchange of goods, services, or money. While these issues are central to discussions within ongoing business relationships, they take on a very different cast, one relating directly to the reasons why one would develop a close business relationship in the first place. Investment in an ongoing relationship permits the parties in that relationship to accrue real increases in efficiency, quality, and other forms of effectiveness. However, this is only true if investment occurs. Each side of the relationship should be learning about the other. Each side of the relationship should be working to improve their value to the other. Each side of the relationship should be developing plans that incorporate the other's interests into those plans. Without doing so, a long-term relationship entails the disadvantage of closing off options, without accruing the benefits of the longer-term commitment. Without mutual development, long-term relationships have no value. It is this quality of relationships that influences the meaning and form of integrative bargaining within them. Integrative bargaining within a relationship is where the seeds of mutual development are planted. Therefore, integrative bargaining within a relationship is directly about the people, or functions or firms, not about concepts that can be isolated from the parties to the relationship. Given the notion of mutual development as the cornerstone of effective relationship, how is integrative bargaining different within such a context?

Integrative Bargaining Entails Opportunities for Mutual Development.   As I just argued, within ongoing, interdependent relationships most discussions entail opportunities to discuss improving the relationship or each other in the context of the relationship. I do not mean to imply that pure exchange-based discussions never happen within a relationship. Clearly, they do. For example, a husband and wife in discussing house cleaning discover that one likes cleaning with water, while the other likes dusting, vacuuming, and tidying. The integrative deal entails giving the washrooms and kitchen to one spouse and the rest of the cleaning to the other. In a buyer–seller relationship the buyer may care about inventory levels, while the seller cares about delivery date. However, I do mean to imply that such pure exchanges are rare and to ignore the importance of mutual development is to miss opportunities for improving the value of each partner to the other. They have a static quality to them that minimizes growth. The couple may wish to talk about means for making cleaning easier. Sponging stains that have been allowed to dry is much harder than cleaning as spills occur. Tidying throughout the house is harder than tidying in a concentrated area. In other words, to separate the discussion of cleaning from the rest of their interchanges loses the real efficiencies that can accrue. If the buyer and seller restrict their discussion only to issues within the confines of existing business practice, they miss opportunities to think about whole new ways of doing ordering, methods for integrating information systems across partners, means for mutually reducing costs, identification of new strategic opportunities, product development possibilities, or identification of competitive threats.

I recently had a conversation with the chief operating officer (COO) of a large electronics firm (call it Firm X) who was very concerned about his company's efforts to improve relations with suppliers as a step in improving overall product quality. Like most of its competition, this firm reduced the number of suppliers of each part to manage better those that remain, increased the number of parts each supplier provided the firm to better tie the interests of the supplier to the firm, put suppliers through a rigorous supplier qualification program, trained suppliers in manufacturing quality processes, and raised dramatically the expected quality of supplied parts. This COO had just returned from a visit to his key supplier where he discovered that his company's program, while having some positive effect, was so poorly implemented that much of the potential benefit was lost. For example, the supplier ran a continuous improvement program in its plants. When a suggested improvement in process or product was made that had implications for Firm X, the supplier was required to submit a large set of drawings at its own expense and wait while its suggested changes underwent a lengthy review process. Often, the supplier did not hear back for six months, sometimes not at all. As a result of the cost and difficulty associated with this review process, the supplier just did not make many small but important improvements. This was in contrast to one of the Firm X's chief competitors, who for most suggestions required no drawings be submitted, and who provided an answer within a few days on all but the most complicated suggestions. Frequently, this competitor would fly someone down at its own expense to the supplier's plant site to clarify any questions. The supplier clearly admitted that this second firm received better and lower cost materials than did Firm X. In fact, the COO estimated that his parts were 30 percent more expensive and had far greater quality problems than his competitor. He was extremely concerned about his firm's ability to effectively manage adjustments in supplier relationships and within his own firm to meet the challenges this visit suggested.

In Many Relational Negotiations the Person Is the Problem.   A corollary of the notion of mutual development and negotiations in relationship is that in such negotiations, the person is the problem. Consider the husband and wife just discussed above. In many instances it behooves the couple to discuss messes throughout the house in a very depersonalized manner. In doing so, offense is not taken and the problem of multiple messes to tidy can be discussed without resulting in a long debate about character or personality. In other words, in relationships it is often important to separate the person from the problem. However, this is impossible or bad advice to follow in two particular instances. First, the problem of distributed mess may simply be part of a larger set of behaviors endemic to the other. The husband may not just leave trails of mess throughout the house, but also not turn his socks right side out before putting them in the laundry, leave paper, money and other assorted mess in his shirt pocket, bring the dog and children in all muddy and have them traipse throughout the house without concern for the new oriental rug, and leave coffee cups in every nook and cranny in the house. In sum, he may just be messy. Discussing his messiness, provided it is done with care for his feelings, permits a kind of conversation not permitted by separating the person from the problem. Discussing messiness provides an opportunity to diagnose why he is messy and thus potentially take action on the root cause. Discussing his messiness permits a broad-based discussion of the aspects of messy that cause his wife real concern and those that are not a problem or are even endearing. Discussing his messiness permits him and his wife to learn something about themselves and about each other. None of these could be easily done if a list of depersonalized local messes was brought up for discussion. Moreover, if the list is too long or different messes are discussed over frequent exchanges, the person has become the problem and in a much less direct passive-aggressive manner.

The example just given is clearly a limited one, not illustrating the full potential of making the person the problem. More important discussions may occur over issues such as self and career, orientation to family, personal values, or the role of one's childhood experiences in their present relationship. Consider an extreme example. Parents who were abused as children are much more likely to abuse their own children than are parents who were not abused as children. It appears that a critical determinant of whether or not abuse will be transferred from generation to generation is the ability for people who were abused as children to be able to confront their views and feelings about relationships with a trusted other. Good relationships are a context in which a person may be able to deal with her/his feelings about relationships and tendencies to abuse. Without recognizing that they are the problem, it is difficult for such abused people to develop truly effective relationships.

Equivalent business examples abound. Two people are going to be working together for a long time and one does not trust the other. A key supplier has adopted a long-term strategy inconsistent with a critical customer's needs. A colleague has become too arrogant to work with. A task force chair is lacking in confidence and is crippling performance. It is essential to have direct conversations about the other party as the problem in this situation.

Integrative Negotiations Have Implications for Power and Future Dependence.
A related aspect of integrative negotiations is that they entail implications for future power and dependence. In long-term relationships the members are and should be quite concerned about the nature of the dependency between them. Mutual development entails mutual dependence. Long-term commitment entails dependence. Dependence

on others means that they wield power over you and they can take advantage of you. Consider the example of the supplier to the electronics company described above. One electronics company committed to the supplier over a very long term. In doing so, they shared critical information about their processes, strategy, and upcoming product design. They invested heavily in developing capabilities in that supplier so that the supplier could meet better and better the electronics company's material needs. They got to learn the processes of the supplier and incorporated their unique abilities into product development efforts. As a result, the electronics company has better, less expensive, and better integrated parts than their competitor described in the same example who did none of these things. However, they are also more dependent on the supplier. Because of information and abilities unique to their two-party relationship the supplier provides better, less expensive, and more integrated parts. As a result, the electronics company needs that supplier to sustain existing quality, cost, and integration. Williamson (1985) refers to this phenomenon as the development of firm-specific skills, that is, skills that only have value in relation to a particular company. The other electronics company has no such advantages, but they also are not as dependent. In the argot of 1950s teenagers, one firm is "going steady," while the other is "playing the field." The consequence is that both the supplier and the customer are at risk in this relationship. Negotiations when such potential for abuse exist are likely to be quite different from transactional discussions among relative strangers in a spot. They will likely be more tacit, focused on determining the appropriate level of involvement, and concerned with identifying protections against abuse. Negotiations when one side has taken advantage are especially likely to be quite different from one-off discussions.

Dependence can take many forms (Pfeffer and Salancik, 1978; Tichy, 1973). We can depend on others for information, goods, services, money, clout, personal support, or counsel. We can become dependent because of relationship-specific abilities. We can become dependent because of the development of a sense of attachment or identity. In each instance, dependence implies power. Where there exists power there is potential for abuse. This argument is a variant of Williamson's concern for opportunistic behavior. A solution is to develop mechanisms and relational qualities that permit trust.

Context Matters.   One mechanism that creates trust in an interdependent relationship is the social context in which the relationship is embedded. This point was alluded to earlier (see section on enforcement), but it deserves repeating and elaboration. Investment in another firm, or another function within the same firm is not just a relationship between people. It is a relationship between sets of people, systems, procedures, capital, and strategies. It is also a relationship that occurs in the context of a broader set of related economic relations of which this is just one. As such, a negotiation takes on a very new cast. For example, separating the dimensions of a problem from its broader context to permit effective problem solving must be done with great care. It is necessary to understand that any negotiated decision has implications for many other related decisions. I knew a dean once who made extremely sensible decisions, but without consideration of the interdependence among those decisions. The resulting chaos from inconsistencies, undermining of precedents, unanticipated consequences, and confusion of recipients of the decisions would have been amusing if some people I knew well were not affected by such local rationality.

But more important for the previous point, this context entails a set of social actors engaged in a set of exchanges entailing some obligation to monitor each other. This set of interdependent actors is engaged in a network of relationships having what Alan Fiske would call jural qualities, meaning they "have intrinsic imperative force and are the source of moral, . . . customary, and traditional rules and practices" (Fiske, 1991, p.172). The primary moral and social rules guiding an exchange derive from an interdependent network of relationships. For Fiske, "every social relationship entails moral obligations, and every moral obligation derives from the imputation of a social relationship." The potency of this notion of jural forms is clear when one considers the responsibilities of a person observing the violation of the obligation entailed in one of the social forms. Consider Ellen, who notices that her sister Mary is not satisfying the essential needs of Mary's newborn child (a violation of the need principle in a communal sharing relationship). Ellen would be found quite at fault by the broader community, such as her mother, husband, or children, if she did not speak to Mary about Mary's not meeting her obligations as a parent. It is the force on Mary by interested others that gives their network of relationships such jural status. In fact, being engaged in a network of interdependent relationships entails a moral obligation at three distinct levels:

> First, the parties immediately and directly participating in the primary relationship have a duty to conform to the model (Mary should care for the needs of her child). Second, people with social links to the primary parties have a duty to react when the primary parties fail to meet their obligations—they must modify their social relationships with the primary parties in suitable ways (Ellen should speak to Mary about not caring for the needs of her child). Third, it is the duty of others with social links to the secondary parties to appropriately modulate their social relationships with the secondary parties if the latter fail to react to the primary parties' breach of duty (the community should remove support for Ellen if she does not deal with Mary's neglect of her child). In other words, people get sanctioned for failing to sanction (p.171; items in parentheses my addition).

From this discussion it should be obvious that much of the discourse of relational negotiations will be about parties' respective obligations as determined by the broader network of which they are members and that negotiations frequently are not just the business of the parties to that negotiation. Often, the broader community will consider it their business to know and influence the discussions of network members. This is in sharp contrast to the relatively isolated dyadic discussions implied by the methods and theory of most present negotiation research . . . .

Hostile Context

Lastly, a given relationship will often have to learn to exist in a relatively hostile environment and often with conflicting motives. This problem exists in shifts from hierarchy and transactional exchanges. A cross-functional team will need to learn to live within a bigger hierarchy. Parties to a relationship between Ford and a critical supplier will need to learn to ignore others engaged in more predatory practices. However, the problem of a hostile environment and conflicting motives is most prevalent and perhaps most interesting in the context of alliances among competitors.

We cannot do it alone and frequently find that only a competitor has what we need to succeed. IBM and Apple shocked the world when they announced that they needed to join forces, at least temporarily, to achieve their business needs. General Motors is perhaps the most striking example. The independent, vertically integrated giant of business now finds itself in alliances of some form or another with nearly every other competitor in the automobile business. The reasons for creating alliances of convenience between hostile parties are many. Access to capital, access to new markets, access to critical technology or processes, completion of a product line, and assistance in the management of difficult international regulatory issues are among the many examples given for firms joining with the enemy. This need also arises inside firms among warring factions. The gurus of continuous improvement and the gurus of radical re-engineering occasionally discover they have a shared roadblock in driving effective organizational change. Egoists in competition for the same position recognize the need for an integrated corporate decision on an important issue likely to influence the existence of the job for which they are vying. Again, enemies discover that they need to cooperate in a local instance to succeed. Such discussions are very different from transactions between parties in a market exchange and very different from negotiations between partners. The motives are truly more mixed. I need you now, but will do what I can to undermine your long-term competitive posture in the process. As such, negotiations between competitors differ from other long-term negotiations in three critical ways: (1) the negative prior history has potential to undermine effective negotiations; (2) the exchange provides a dual opportunity: cut a good deal now, but use the situation to improve your own or undermine their long-term competitive posture; and (3) control over the implementation of the negotiated settlement is a critical consideration. Consider each briefly.

Negative Prior History.   It is long understood that a history of past competition makes collaboration difficult. Expectations entering a negotiation have a great deal of impact upon the negotiation. If one expects a negotiation partner to be competitive she or he will act so as to cause that partner to be competitive (Kelley and Stahelski, 1970). Parties with a history of hostile relations tend to make negative attributions about the other's behavior. A history of competition is often supported by an escalatory dance that is well programmed. For these reasons, it is especially likely that negotiations between competitors will be hot and negatively valent. Great care must be taken to build a sense of commonality, break stereotypes, and engage in the establishment of effective forms of communication. Mitigation of strong statements, explanation of difficult or easily misinterpreted issues, recognition of the need for deescalatory behavior, and efforts at consolidation all need be practiced in such circumstances. In addition to these points of negotiation process is the simple observation that it is most often necessary to separate the alliance from the two parents. Feuding parents have a way of spoiling children; so do feuding companies. This argument is supported by the number of allied efforts between competitors that take the form of independent joint ventures (Harrigan, 1988).

Negative Underside.   At the same time that the parties are learning to speak politely with one another, there is a negative underside to negotiations with competitors. Each side of the partnership is simultaneously attempting to maximize the value of the alliance and learn as much about the other party as possible so as to gain advantage in future competitive arenas. IBM is not just attempting to build a better chip with Apple and Motorola, they are also attempting to learn software skills from Apple, management practices from Motorola, and points of weakness of both. This learning is to be used in the broader competitive arena, including in direct competition with Apple and Motorola. Thus, the alliance is truly mixed motive and thus even more confusing to those engaged in efforts to make the local negotiation work well. This observation has obvious implications for how to conduct such negotiations and what the substance of the negotiation should be. For example, it is easier to steal hard knowledge, such as a type of technology, or manufacturing process, than it is to steal soft knowledge, such as manufacturing culture or management practices. Similarly, it is important to construct the deal so that there exists possibilities to observe that which a firm wishes to learn about an ally. However, less obvious but equally important are the implications for the capacities that need reside in the allying firms. Firms that have mechanisms for studying the partner and transferring that knowledge throughout the parent organization will benefit more than those that do not.[1]

Fight for Control.   A by-product of the two previous points is that alliances often become battles for control by the two parent companies. Like divorcing parents it is important whom the child is more loved by, who has more influence. This is not just an emotionally driven event, but has important value. Control means capacity to observe. Control means one's strategic objectives will be met. Control means one is more likely to end up with the child in the case of a divorce. Each of these is an important considera-tion. However, in such considerations of control, ownership is mistaken for control. For example, Ford and Volkswagen have been engaged in a long-term alliance in Brazil. Ford has majority ownership in this venture. However, managers from Ford have historically done two-year stints in Brazil, while managers from Volkswagen have moved to Brazil for at least five years. Ford recently discovered that although they owned controlling interest in the venture, it was their German partners who knew the language, local cus-toms, regulations, market conditions, employees, and systems of the subsidiary venture. Ford owned the firm but did not have control.

This last point illustrates the subtlety of negotiation in relationships. Things are not always what they seem at first blush, and the application of traditional models of relation-ships be they the logic of contract, logic of ownership, or logic of competition will not do one well. I recently met a scientist from Japan who is responsible for helping transfer technology from Japanese companies to their U.S. subsidiaries. He made the observation that his experience with Japanese partners and American partners differed in many ways, but two struck him as especially interesting. One was that U.S. partners were generally not willing to admit that they could not do something and that a partner should look elsewhere for a particular type of assistance. The other was that in Japan it was not unusual for sup-pliers and customers to exchange equal amounts of stock (often the stock in question is of small quantities), while in the United States such stock exchanges were quite uncommon

---

[1]For a more complete discussion of this issue, see Hamel et al., 1989, Ohmae in James, 1993.

and if they occurred the customer invariably bought stock in the supplier, but not the reverse. He was puzzled why a partner did not recognize the need to honestly admit limitations with the security that such admission would strengthen the relationship, and why partners did not recognize the symbolic value of the exchange of stock, much like the exchange of rings among newlyweds. He questioned if we knew how to get married.

REFERENCES

Agnew, J. (1986). *Worlds apart: The market and the theater in Anglo-American thought, 1550–1750.* New York: Cambridge University Press.

Aoki, M. (1988). *Information, incentives and bargaining in the Japanese economy.* New York: Cambridge University Press.

Arrow, K. (1974). *The limits of organization.* New York: Norton.

Barnard, C. I. (1938). *The function of the executive.* Cambridge, MA: Harvard University Press.

Bazerman, M. H., and Neale, M. A. (1992). *Negotiating rationally.* New York: Free Press.

Bazerman, M. H., and Samuelson, W.F. (1983). I won the auction but don't want the prize. *Journal of Conflict Resolution,* 27, 618–34.

Brown, L. D. (1985). *Managing conflict at organizational interfaces.* Reading, MA: Addison-Wesley.

Finley, M. (1973). *The ancient economy.* Berkeley: University of California Press.

Fiske, A. P. (1991). *Structures of social life.* New York: Free Press.

Gottman, J. M. (1979). *Marital interaction: Experimental investigation.* New York: Academic Press.

Greenhalgh, L. (1987). The case against winning in negotiations. *Negotiation Journal,* 3(2), 167–73.

Hamel, G., Doz, Y. L., and Prahalad, C. K. (1989). Collaborate with your competitor—and win. *Harvard Business Review,* 67, 133–39.

Harrigan, K. R. (1988). *Managing maturing businesses: Restructuring declining industries and revitalizing troubled operations.* Lexington, MA: Lexington Books.

Hergert, M., and Morris, D. (1988). Trends in international collaborative agreements. In F. J. Contractor & P. Lorange (eds.), *Cooperative strategies in international business.* Lexington, MA: Lexington Books.

James, H. S. (1993). *When businesses cross international borders: Strategic alliances and their alternatives.* Westport, CT: Praeger.

Kelley, H. H., and Stahelski, A. J. (1970). The inference of intentions from moves in the prisoner's dilemma game. *Journal of Experimental Social Psychology,* 6, 401–19.

Landes, D. S. (1966). *The rise of capitalism.* New York: Macmillan.

Larson, A. (1988). *Cooperative alliances: A study of entrepreneurship.* Unpublished doctoral dissertation, Harvard Business School.

Lewicki, R. J., Litterer, J. A., Minton, J. W., and Saunders, D. M. (1994). *Negotiation* (2nd ed). Burr Ridge, IL: Richard D. Irwin.

Lincoln, J. R. (1990). Japanese organization and organization theory. In *Research on Organizational Behavior* (vol. 12). Greenwich, CT: JAI Press.

Linville, P. W., and Carlston, D. (1994). Social cognition of the self. In P. G. Devine, D. L. Hamilton, and T. M. Ostrom (eds.), *Social cognition: Its impact on social psychology.* New York: Academic Press.

MacAulay, S. (1963). Noncontractual relations in business: A preliminary study. *American Sociology Review,* 28, 55–67.

Murnighan, J. K. (1991). *The dynamics of bargaining games.* Englewood Cliffs, NJ: Prentice Hall.

Ouchi, W. G. (1980). Markets, bureaucracies and clans. *Administrative Science Quarterly,* 25, 129–41.

Parsons, T. (1960). *Structure and process in modern society.* New York: Free Press.

Pfeffer, J., and Salancik, G. (1978). *The extended control of organizations.* New York: Harper & Row.

Polanyi, K. (1957). *The great transformation.* Boston: Beacon.

Porter, M. E. (1980). *Competitive strategy: Techniques for analyzing industries and competitors.* New York: Free Press.

Powell, W. W. (1990). Neither market nor hierarchy: Network forms of organization. In B. M. Staw and L. L. Cummings (eds.), *Research in organizational behavior* (vol. 12, 295–336). Greenwich, CT: JAI Press.

Pruitt, D. (1972). Methods for resolving differences of interest: A theoretical analysis. *Journal of Social Issues,* 28, 133–54.

Putallaz, M., and Sheppard, B. (1992). Conflict management and social competence. In C. U. Shantz and W. W. Hartup (eds.), *Conflict in child and adolescent development.* New York: Cambridge University Press.

Sheppard, B. H., and Tuchinsky, M. (in press). Micro OB and the network organization. In R. Kramer and T. Tyler (eds.), *Trust in organizations.* Beverly Hills, CA: Sage.

Sherif, M., Harvey, D. J., White, B. J., Hood, W. R., and Sherif, C. W. (1961). *Intergroup conflict and cooperation: The robbers cave experiment.* Norman, OK: Institute of Group Relations.

Sitkin, S. B., and Stickel, D. (in press). The road to hell . . . The dynamics of distrust in an era of quality management. In R. Kramer and T. Tyler (eds.), *Trust in organizations.* Beverly Hills, CA: Sage.

Smith, Adam. ([1776] 1976). *An inquiry into the nature and causes of the wealth of nations.* Oxford: Clarendon Press.

Smitka, M. (1991). *Competitive ties: Subcontracting in the Japanese automotive industry.* New York: Columbia University Press.

Teece, D. (1986). Profiting from technological innovation: Implications for integration, collaboration, licensing, and public policy. *Research Policy,* 15(6), 785–805.

Thompson, J. D. (1967). *Organizations in action.* New York: McGraw-Hill.

Tichy, N. (1973). An analysis of clique formation and structure in organizations. *Administrative Science Quarterly,* 18, 194–208.

Wheelwright, S. C., and Clark, K. B. (1992). *Revolutionizing product development.* New York: Free Press.

Williamson, O. E. (1975). *Markets and hierarchies.* New York: Free Press.

_____. (1985). *The economic institution of capitalism.* New York: Free Press.

Womack, J. P., Jones, D. T., and Roos, D. (1991). *The machine that changed the world.* New York: Harper Perennial.

Can We Negotiate and Still Be Friends?

Terri Kurtzberg

Victoria Husted Medvec

You have finally decided to indulge your midlife fantasy and buy yourself a sportscar. Knowing that this car is not all that practical, you're considering buying a secondhand one. You have been scouting the car lots and scouring the want ads when you hear that one of your colleagues from work is selling a cherry-red, five-year-old sportscar. Red isn't your top choice for color (it seems a little splashy) but you could live with it, and other than the color, this could be perfect: You know that your colleague is the type of person who would have taken care of the car. Before discussing the idea of buying this car, however, you hesitate; somehow, it seems like it might be uncomfortable to negotiate the price of the car with your friend. You don't exactly know why, but your instincts are telling you to call the used car salesman. Why would you rather negotiate with a used car salesman—who you don't trust—than negotiate with someone with whom you share a trusting relationship?

In this essay we want to explore why people may prefer to negotiate with a stranger rather than risk harming a relationship by negotiating with a friend. Do people want to separate their negotiations from their social relationships? This paper summarizes a discussion on these topics at the January 1999 Hewlett Conference, held at Northwestern University's Kellogg Graduate School of Management. We propose a two-pronged approach to analyzing the interplay between negotiations and relationships: namely, that relationships can be affected by the negotiation process, and that the negotiation process itself (i.e., the fundamental dynamics and assumption in a negotiation) can be altered by the relationship between the parties involved.

RELATIONSHIPS AFFECT NEGOTIATIONS

Social relationships are an integral part of every human interaction. When the parties know each other outside of the negotiation context, the negotiation takes on an emotional overtone that can, depending on how it is dealt with, either help or hurt the process. Previous research has looked at the cost of having a bad relationship on the negotiation

Source: Terri Kurtzberg and Victoria Medvec, "Can We Negotiate and Still be Friends?" *Negotiation Journal*, October 1999, Kluwer Academic/Plenum Publishers.

process by examining what happens when trust is broken and conflict spirals out of control (Ross and LaCroix 1996); Bies and Tripp 1996; Lewicki and Bunker 1995 and 1996; Pruitt 1981). While discussion at this conference generally focused on the positive effects of relationships on negotiation, we in our session focused on the limits of these benefits and asked the question: When is it a problem to negotiate with a friend?

Negotiators may pay more attention to their behaviors, and may monitor their words and actions for standards of trust and fairness when negotiating with a friend rather than a stranger. Even unconsciously, speech, gesture, and tone can all signal relationship cues that can affect the negotiation process. Generally, as described in the scenario that opens this brief report, our intuition often warns us to steer clear of these situations, since the potential risk to the friendship seems to far outweigh the potential gain to be had through negotiating in a trusting manner.

People in any society carry around "scripts" for every context as to what constitutes appropriate behavior. When we go to a restaurant, we know to wait to be seated, to look at a menu, to select a meal. Similarly, we know how to act with friends, including which behaviors are acceptable and which are not. We have yet another script for how to act in a negotiation situation: don't tell the other side too much about your other offers, but do look for ways to trade off issues to the benefit of both sides. Try to grow the pie, while also trying to claim as much of the pie as possible for oneself.

Negotiating within a pre-existing relationship can cause these scripts to clash; friendship dictates that we should be concerned with fairness and the other person's welfare, while negotiations dictate that we should get a good deal for ourselves. For example, when you're selling a car to a friend, are you really "selling a car *to a friend*" or are you *"selling a car* to a friend"? Which script takes priority? These conflicting scripts point us to a key issue: It can be difficult to assess appropriate behavior when negotiating with a friend.

Friendship scripts may lead to a new set of "appropriate" negotiation behaviors. For example, people who feel like they received too good a deal from a friend may insist on giving gifts in return to "even the score." Here, the conflicting priority is between friendship and money. In the "friendship world," money is only important in that it can help promote caring. Thus, when we do sell a car to a friend, we sell it at a lower price and assume a contract of responsibility instead of creating the highest value deal. Relationship norms and scripts may limit the amount of surplus we can create in a negotiated agreement.

One way around this potential pitfall is for negotiators to change the dialogue and labels associated with negotiation when in a friendship context. For example, it is not uncommon in a negotiation context to hear someone say that what they are doing and asking for is "just business," meaning that nobody should interpret the behaviors in a personal way, or one which relates to the relationship of the parties involved. Yet successful people constantly remind us that good business sense is rooted in good relationship sense, and that the best businesspeople always return their phone calls first, signaling their priority on maintaining positive relationships.

Relationships are not always on equal footing, however. Some types of relationships, such as mentoring and parenting, are designed around teaching and caring, instead of reciprocity. This may create an entirely new dynamic when it comes to negotiations, because the scripts for appropriate behavior are unique to this context. For example, the Teaching Assistant strikes that occurred recently at some U.S. universities came with a lot of very bad feelings because the mentoring relationship does not include an easy forum for the student to make demands on the mentor. This, like a discussion of sacred values, establishes the bonds of a relationship and demonstrates how negotiations in these situations can sometimes create discord and break down.

Clearly, relationships play many important psychological roles in the minds of negotiators. Even when focusing on the larger-scale relationships between and among countries, organizations, or other large groups of the population, the dynamics which motivate us to consider and maintain a relationship as an important goal in a negotiation process will alter how we approach and proceed with a negotiation.

MEASURING THE EFFECTS OF FRIENDSHIP ON THE NEGOTIATION

How can we even tell what the outcome effects are in these friendship-negotiation instances? In terms of newly formed relationships, there are many approaches to measuring these effects on negotiated outcomes. For example, one way to assess the success and quality of a newly formed relationship on the negotiation outcomes is by examining the salesperson-customer interaction. Future sales from a particular salesperson to a particular customer can be an indication of the quality of the relationship that has been established initially in this dyad. Another example involves the judgments made by people in terms of discounting future events for the sake of current events. This could be a measure of relationship strength by showing that the more connected a negotiator feels with someone who has a future stake in the deal on the table, the more they might take that future state into account in their own actions, decisions, and concessions. In this way, researchers can measure the value that a negotiator places on the future based on present relationships.

In the case of longer-term relationships that exist prior to negotiations, there are both benefits and risks associated with negotiating with a friend to the value of the negotiated agreement. It is possible that the trust associated with a pre-existing relationship will promote more sharing of information and more cooperation and therefore increase the likelihood of creating good deals. Friendship may, in this way, eliminate the asymmetries of information and value typically associated with negotiation situations. Relationships may also cloud the negotiation process, though, by providing expectations of over-concessionary behavior or too much sharing of information.

WHAT HAPPENS WHEN THINGS GO WRONG?

Things can go wrong for the relationship and for the negotiation when scripts are broken. The effects of negotiation on any relationship depend, of course, on the power of the negotiation and the strength of the relationship. Sometimes, negotiators will bow to the relationship and forgo their negotiating position. In this case, a friend might say, "I paid too much for this lamp because fighting with my friend wasn't worth the extra $30." Sometimes, though, the relationship is severed by the necessities of the negotiation process. A vivid example of this is when students face a professor after they get their midterm grades with a disappointed expression that reads: "I thought we were friends." In this case, the hard negotiating power of the professor based on exam scores overrides the good feelings that the professor and students have toward each other in class.

An interesting repercussion of script-breaking is in the attributions that people expect and make toward one another. For example, when negotiating with a friend, one party might take a hard line in an effort to be a "good" negotiator, not realizing that the other party may well take this behavior as a personal affront, resulting in a damaged friendship. In addition, we know from previous research that when faced with someone else's behavior, people tend to perceive actions as characteristics of the individual person, while when faced with their own behavior, people tend to attribute actions to situational influences. Clearly, this difference leaves room for some misinterpretations of actions among friends engaged in negotiations with each other. So, in summary, though negotiators may not actually behave any differently when facing a friend than they would have otherwise, the perception of behavior can be entirely changed when it is coming from a friend. Though negotiation behaviors may not have been intended on a personal level, the presence of a relationship encourages us to make attributions that we would not normally develop.

MEASURING THE IMPACT OF A NEGOTIATION ON FRIENDSHIP

Professional athletes refuse to engage in negotiations directly with their team owners, so that the hard stances and bargaining tactics used will not affect the future of the relationship, and instead employ an agent to take the heat off of the principal negotiators. Clearly, people understand that negotiations require elements that may not be conducive to positive relationships. The task is left to researchers to isolate and analyze the critical elements of this interplay and be able to quantify in some way the potential benefits and damage that can be done to the relationship.

For starters, it is crucial that researchers be able to define and measure both the relationship and the negotiation occurring. In some cases, this is an easy task: if people are all asked to participate in the same negotiation exercise, the parameters of the negotiation are fixed. But in more natural settings, it can be more difficult to define what constitutes a negotiation, the issues, and the time frame. For instance, a married couple may regularly trade off on issues across time without clearly defining that a "negotiation" has taken place. Inefficiency on a one-term deal may actually be an indication of intertemporal logrolling. Similarly, in terms of relationships, it can be difficult to define exactly what a relationship consists of and how it changes over time.

It is important to distinguish what types of relationships are being discussed. Again, one major criterion for distinction is the amount of time that the relationship has existed. Clearly, the longer the relationship, the more that is at stake when engaging in a potentially damaging negotiation. Short-term relationships (or newly formed relationships) may be easier to observe and measure than pre-existing long-term relationships. One approach to look at newly formed relationships is to pair strangers together in a negotiation task, and then ask them afterward how likely each party would be to acknowledge the other in a chance meeting (Morris and Drolet 1997), or to ask them how likely they would be to want to negotiate with each other again (Moore, Kurtzberg, Thompson, and Morris 1999).

Another mechanism might be to have people negotiate together, then report the outcomes to a researcher, and then measure how far apart the pair stands from each other after the negotiation (e.g., see Byrne and Griffith 1973; Byrne, Baskett, and Hodges 1971). These types of behaviors might reflect the degree of relationship established between the negotiators. Furthermore, for researchers to study more clearly the dynamics of a negotiation's effect on relationships, people most likely need to engage in real-world negotiations, as opposed to being assigned into a role-play exercise. There is an argument to be made as well that the most effective way to assess someone's feelings about a relationship is to ask them—have people rate their degree of liking and trust both before and after a negotiation has occurred. Since relationships are subjective by nature, this might be a worthwhile tool for researchers.

Yet these kinds of tools, used primarily to assess the effects of negotiations on *developing* relationships, often miss the "romance" of interpersonal relationships that have a longer-term past and future to them. Also, the more that each person cares about the other, the stronger the concern will be about potentially damaging the relationship through negotiation. It is possible to become friends with someone with whom you are negotiating, as a salesperson-customer interaction would demonstrate. Other real-world examples of this situation include people who become friends while maintaining ongoing negotiations, such as labor-management negotiators who continually work out deals over the years and create a warm relationship with each other. Yet this is distinctly different from negotiating with someone with whom you have a pre-existing relationship.

In order for a negotiation situation to affect an ongoing relationship, the negotiation clearly has to be one of some importance to the negotiators. This can be either because the negotiation takes place over a long period of time or because the issues involved are ones that are meaningful to the participants. The risks are great, though. While newly formed couples are still engaged in pushing the boundaries of their relationship, couples already settled in long-term relationships have their own mechanisms for dealing with each other to keep negotiations from damaging their relationship. This can be viewed by observing the differences between the arguments and negotiation strategies of young married couples and older couples ("There goes Harry being Harry again!") who have much more experience with their partner.

Generally speaking, it seems that there are many elements of a relationship which can be impacted by a negotiation, such as the affect between the parties, the parties' communication, and their level of trust. Negotiators must remain aware of the potential effects that their interchange can have on their relationship.

CONCLUSION

In summary, we have addressed why it is that people may not feel comfortable negotiating with friends. We have hypothesized what the effects of friendship could be on the negotiation process and outcome, and have proposed also how a negotiation could impact a friendship. Finally, we have suggested means for measuring this impact. The discussion at the conference did not provide the answers, but instead proposed the questions, with the hope that these questions will provoke future research into these areas.

REFERENCES

Bies, R. J., and T. M. Tripp. 1996. Beyond revenge, "Getting even" and the need for revenge. In *Trust in organizations: Frontiers of theory and research*, edited by R. M. Kramer, T. R. Tyler et al. Thousand Oaks, CA: Sage.

Byrne, D., G. D. Baskett, and L. Hodges. 1971. Behavioral indicators of interpersonal attraction. *Journal of Applied Social Psychology* 1: 137–49.

Byrne, D., and W. Griffith. 1973. Interpersonal attraction. *Annual Review of Psychology 1973:* 317–36.

Lewicki, R. J., and B. B. Bunker. 1995. Trust in relationships: A model of trust development and decline. In *Conflict, cooperation, and justice*, edited by B. B. Bunker and J. Z. Rubin. San Francisco: Jossey-Bass.

_____. 1996. Developing and maintaining trust in work relationships. *Trust in organizations: Frontiers of theory and research*, edited by R. M. Kramer, T. R. Tyler et al. Thousand Oaks, CA: Sage

Moore, D. A., T, R. Kurtzberg, L. L. Thompson, and M. W. Morris. 1999. Long and short routes to success in electronically mediated negotiations: Group affiliations ad good vibrations. *Organizational Behavior and Human Decision Processes* 77: 22–43.

Morris, M. W., and A. Drolet. 1997. *Rapport and dominance: Nonverbally mediated dyadic dynamics that affect value creation and value claiming in negotiation*. Unpublished manuscript. Graduate School of Business. Stanford University.

Pruitt, D. G. 1981. *Negotiation behavior*. Orlando, FL: Academic Press.

Ross, W., and J. LaCroix. 1996. Multiple meanings of trust in negotiation theory and research: A literature review and integrative model. *The International Journal of Conflict Management* 7: 314–60.

Whom Can You Trust?
It's Not So Easy to Tell

Thomas A. Stewart

April 21, 1994, was one of those mornings when Southern California lives up to its hype: The sky was clear over Santa Monica, the air pleasantly cool; a breeze that barely ruffled the blue Pacific was enough to toss the hair of the blondes gliding by on Rollerblades. Warren Bennis arrived for breakfast, perpetually youthful, preternaturally suntanned. I was doing a story about how e-mail networks were changing the style and content of management, and wanted to talk to Warren, a professor at the University of Southern California and an expert on the style and substance of leadership.

I had eggs. Warren had fruit and, I think, toast. He began by saying he might not be the best person to talk on the subject—he himself wasn't all that familiar with electronic networks. He didn't say it, but I guessed he'd never sent an e-mail. No shame if so: April 1994 was the month Marc Andreessen filed the papers incorporating Netscape, the company that made the World Wide Web navigable and popular; that same month America Online, which has more than 21 million subscribers today, had just 712,000. Warren, then 69, might reasonably have figured he'd never have to worry about e-mail.

Having warned me of his ignorance, Warren went on to offer a set of observations more expert than any others I'd heard while reporting that story. Here's what he said: Networks, by definition, connect everyone to everyone. Hierarchies, by definition, don't; they create formal channels of communication, which you're expected to follow. Hierarchies are concrete-lined irrigation ditches, where water flows along prescribed lines. Networks are flat, rich, mysterious Okefenokees of every-which-way communication.

A hierarchy—this was his key point—acts as a "prosthesis for trust." It is a trellis on which trust's fragile vine twines and blooms. Warren said, "That organizational armature reinforces or replaces interpersonal trust." You can count on me because you're my boss; I can count on you for the same reason.

When a network becomes the main means by which information is conveyed and work gets done in a corporation, those hierarchical crutches are knocked away. Rank is unclear. We work in teams, which are often interdepartmental—so hierarchical power can't guarantee that work gets done. Networks encourage people to operate informally, with few rules. They depend on trust.

Few businesspeople I meet are mystified by power. Trust, on the other hand, baffles them—yet it is more important, Warren argues. In his new book, *Douglas McGregor, Revisited*, he and co-authors Gary Heil and Deborah C. Stephens write, "Gathering information, and above all developing trust, have become the key source of sustainable competitive advantage."

How do we create a climate of trust? How much can we trust our suppliers? How can I make sure that people will do what they say they will do, when they don't report to me? These are hard questions in life as in business. I can't answer them, but I can begin to sketch the answer to another question: What are the prostheses for trust—its helpers and stand-ins—in a posthierarchical company?

Trust's first truss is competence: I can trust you if I know you're good at what you do. Trouble is, it's harder to judge competence today. Traditionally work was handed from one department to another—design to manufacturing to shipping. Each department head vouched for the competence of his staff, and the boss himself was boss because he was the most skilled of the bunch—at least, that was the idea.

The boss today isn't the most talented functional specialist; she is Peter Drucker's conductor-CEO, a coordinator of knowledge work. She knows the score, but the trumpeter blows his own horn. When musicians have trouble with a passage, conductors say, "Take it to your teacher." Specialists are led, not supervised.

Five Supports for Trust in a Networked World
No hierarchy left to guide you? Try these.
1. **Competence**—People are good at what they do.
2. **Community**—Competent people come together.
3. **Commitment**—Everyone has the same mission.
4. **Communication**—Leaders tell the truth.
5. **Cupidity**—Trust must pay.

Smarter than My Boss, says a button I keep in my office. I won't say if I think it's true in fact (power not being mysterious), but it's true in theory. The leader of a team consisting of a butcher, a baker, and a candlestick maker can't evaluate them like a functional boss. "I leave it in your hands," she tells the butcher, being all thumbs.

So trust needs a second crutch: community. Networks naturally spawn informal groups of like-minded souls. When these emerge around a common discipline or problem—a work-related subject like graphic design or the behavior of derivative financial instruments—they become "communities of practice," a term coined in 1987 by Etienne Wenger and Jean Lave of the Institute for Research on Learning. I have elsewhere described these communities as "the shop floor of human capital, the place where the stuff gets made." Communities of practice create and validate competence. The boss may not know which butcher is best, but the other butchers do.

General Electric demonstrates how the process works. Leadership development is GE's most important business process. Its well-known formal aspects are so rigorous they would amount to hazing were it not for GE's communities of practice. The place is riddled with them—manufacturing councils, finance councils, technology councils—literally hundreds of interdisciplinary and interbusiness affinity groups. Here GE's young leaders form the networks of friendships they will use during the rest of their careers. They're expected to bring ideas to share at these meetings, where their friends and equals test them, improve them, and take them home to be implemented in their own businesses. Here people get noticed, and from these groups managers learn which bright kids are really good. Reviews and training, however searching the tests or superb the school, can't create, show, or anneal skill the way communities can. Without them, GE's leadership development process would be much less reliable.

Commitment, a third prosthesis for trust, is an adjunct to both competence and community, neither of which necessarily implies loyalty. Indeed, communities of practice create a rival allegiance if a group's passion (for example, research in cardiology) conflicts with the goals of an employer (such as a managed-care company).

Trust obviously needs people who root for the home team. As we flatten hierarchies and empower knowledge workers, it's vital that there be a shared commitment to the same mission. Unfortunately, the randomized bromides and buzzwords that pass for vision in most companies breed cynicism, not trust. Consultant George Bailey of Pricewaterhouse-Coopers once printed up half a dozen companies' vision statements, then challenged their CEOs to identify theirs. Half failed. And who wouldn't? Most companies could get better mission statements if they used Mad-Libs.

What's needed is a clear understanding of and commitment to behavior that makes the difference between success and failure. No more hiding the business model behind high-sounding nonsense. It's crucial, too, that personal success come to people who act right. The company that asks for innovation and rewards obedience should not be surprised if its creative people seem diffident.

Beyond competence, community, and commitment, trust needs communication, which can be its best friend or its worst enemy. That morning in Santa Monica, Warren said communication "will take a hell of a lot more time than it used to. And it will take a lot of emotional labor on the part of the leader." He understated the case.

Hierarchies lie and get away with it pretty well. Naked emperors go unchallenged. Incoming CEOs rewrite history with an Orwellian avidity. The newest trick: Take a big restructuring charge right away, thus reducing current earnings; a year later, you can boast how results have improved, while polishing your résumé.

A revolutionary way to build trust: Tell the truth. "If you can't say something nice, don't say anything at all" might be good etiquette, but it's bad management. Rick Levine, Christopher Locke, Doc Searls, and David Weinberger, the rabble-rousing authors of *The Cluetrain Manifesto*, exaggerate only slightly when they say, "There are no secrets . . . We are immune to advertising. Just forget it."

One of trust's important, little-noticed allies—and the last I'll mention—is cupidity. (I'd have preferred another word—reward, perhaps—but after competence, community, etc., I need one that begins with *C*.) The point here is simple and obvious: If trust is a source of competitive advantage, it should pay. Failure always breeds mistrust—backbiting, toxic politics. Trust needs to be seen to be good business. Bosses should display it in stormy times as well as in balmy, palmy ones. Instead, when the going gets tough, managers dust off their old command-and-control hats, destroying the comity that's their best chance of getting out of the mess.

That's got to change. Managers need to use the tools of trust as deftly as they do the tools of power. Business begins with trust. It begins with a deal: If you pay me *X*, I will give you *Y*. As companies abandon bureaucratic mechanisms, their leaders need to understand that trust is as important to management as it is to relationships with customers.

Coalitions, Multiple Parties, and Teams

A Core Model of Negotiation

Thomas Colosi

THE CONVENTIONAL PERCEPTION OF BILATERAL NEGOTIATION

Negotiations are typically depicted as involving one group sitting across a bargaining table from a second. One side presents its demands or proposals to the other, and a discussion or debate follows. Counterproposals and compromises are offered. When the offers are eventually accepted on both sides, the dispute is settled and an agreement is signed.

Within this model, all the interesting and relevant action is presumed to occur back and forth between the two sides. The model assumes that each party is monolithic, even if represented by bargaining teams. The way in which the participants are billed—labor versus management, prisoners versus guards, environmentalists versus industry—reflects the same monolithic assumption; that is, that all team members share the same set of demands, agree on a strategy for handling the opposition, and have come to the table with equal enthusiasm for the negotiating process.

Unfortunately, the conventional model of negotiation obscures much of the richness and complexity of the bargaining process. In practice, bargaining teams are seldom monolithic. Team members often have conflicting goals and values; some sort of consensus must develop internally before agreement can be reached with the other side. While some students of negotiation have recognized the importance of this internal bargaining, conventional models do not explain their relationship to the functioning of the larger process. By contrast, the model developed in this article attempts to incorporate this dimension and thus to present a richer and more realistic view of negotiation.

For the sake of simplicity, the model presented below assumes—at this point—just two bargaining teams. Later in the article it is expanded to incorporate multiparty situations; conceivably it might also be applied to cases involving just two individuals. In any event, the model is intended to describe the structure or core of negotiation, regardless of the particular issues at stake, the identity of the parties, or the sector (public or private) in which the dispute takes place.

Reprinted from *American Behavioral Scientist* (Newbury Park, CA; Sage, 1983). Copyright © 1983 Sage Publications, Inc. Reprinted by permission of Sage Publications, Inc.

STABILIZERS, NONSTABILIZERS, AND QUASI MEDIATORS

Within each team, negotiators usually hold quite different attitudes. Some negotiators tend to settle at any cost. They may be called *stabilizers*. They seek agreement with the other side to avoid the disruptive consequences of nonsettlement, particularly such lengthy, expensive, or disruptive alternatives as litigation, strikes, demonstrations, riots, and wars. A second general type, the *nonstabilizers,* do not particularly like the negotiation process. Nonstabilizers tend to disagree with most of the proposals of their own team and all of the counterproposals of the other side. They would rather see disruption through raw contests of will and power than compromise on a given position. The terms nonstabilizers would accept are far more stringent than those to which the stabilizers would agree.

Finally, in the middle is a third type, the *quasi mediator,* who plays several roles. He or she is usually the spokesperson charged with the success of the effort. To those sitting across the table, the quasi mediator may simply look like another negotiator, but within a team he or she often acts as a kind of mediator between the stabilizers and the nonstabilizers. As will be shown later, the quasi mediator can also be a mediator between the team and its own constituents or clients.

HORIZONTAL, INTERNAL, AND VERTICAL NEGOTIATIONS

Although most conventional models limit their analysis to the bargaining that goes on across the table, relatively little true negotiating goes on horizontally. Instead, speeches are made, symbols and platitudes are thrown out, and emotions are displayed. If the communication is healthy, the two teams use this time constructively to educate each other: They explain proposals and counterproposals, compare data, show videotapes, share printouts, and present experts. Except for this opportunity to educate and to learn, however, all of this may be less important than the real activity going on internally.

The standard model also misses another important dimension of negotiation: the interchanges that occur between a bargaining team and its vertical hierarchy. A team is rarely independent of a larger constituency. It is at the bargaining table because it has been sent to accomplish something. In the context of private-sector labor negotiation, for example, management's vertical hierarchy is the company's leadership; for the union's bargaining committee, it is the international union and, most times, ultimately the membership who must vote on a proposed contract. Almost always, important negotiations must take place between a team and its vertical hierarchy at one point or another in the bargaining.

Since negotiators are continually being reeducated through the horizontal negotiations occurring at or near the bargaining table, they are frequently far more advanced in their thinking than are their constituents back home. The resulting gap can be a dangerous trap for all concerned. Part of the art and skill of being a negotiator is recognizing how far from the constituents the bargaining team has moved. The negotiator must also know when and how to go back and educate his or her own constituents.

Sometimes the vertical hierarchy will tell a negotiator what should be achieved at the bargaining table, but after several sessions with the other side, the negotiator may come to believe that these goals cannot be reached. It is within this context that negotiation between the team and its own vertical hierarchy takes place. The quasi mediator is often responsible for negotiating with the hierarchy of the team's parent organization. In labor–management negotiations, for instance, the spokesperson or quasi mediator on the union team may wind up intellectually positioned between the local's viewpoint on an issue and management's last known position. In such a case, the union spokesperson not only tries to get management to go along with labor's point of view but may also have to try to get the rest of the union team to accept management's view on some points.

INTERNAL TEAM NEGOTIATIONS

Resolving differences between the stabilizers and nonstabilizers may be a prerequisite for effective negotiation with the other side, as well as one for reaching accommodation with the team's own vertical hierarchy if settlement is the objective. Unless some means exist for coordinating positions and goals over time, there will be serious problems. When a team is considering making an offer, for example, the stabilizers likely will want to present a generous package, while the nonstabilizers will not want to offer anything. The quasi mediator must begin to explore with the stabilizers why the concessions might be excessive. At the same time, of course, the quasi mediator must discuss with the nonstabilizers why the proposal may be good and why the team should not be so rigid. In the same way, when a team receives an offer from the other side, the quasi mediator must show the nonstabilizers why the team should not hold out for more while checking the stabilizers' tendency to grab the offer too quickly. Much like a neutral mediator, the quasi mediator may meet jointly and separately with the stabilizers and nonstabilizers. If the team is not well disciplined, these discussions unfortunately may take place at the table. Ideally, they should take place in a separate caucus, away from the other side.

RAISING AND MAINTAINING DOUBTS TO FOSTER SETTLEMENT

In a sense, this internal team negotiation process is a microcosm of the larger negotiations that occur across the table. Similar aspects of bargaining positions come into play; the same kinds of negotiation skills are required. As in across-the-table bargaining, the most important effects are those directed at changing the minds of parties who do not want to settle.

It is reasonable to ask why the focus should be on those who oppose settlement: Perhaps those who are anxious to settle—to sell the farm—should be challenged with at least as much force. The answer lies in the true essence of negotiation. Negotiations are not squabbles or battles between two sides. The goal of the process is not for one team to extract huge concessions from the other. Instead, the essence of negotiation is to provide an opportunity for parties to exchange promises through which they will resolve their differences with one another. A settlement thus is no more—and no less—than an expression of an exchange of promises. Because the emphasis in negotiations is on the resolution of differences through the exchange of promises, the process is oriented in favor of settlement. Attention is naturally focused on parties who seem to stand in settlement's way.

Settlement is fostered through the raising and maintaining of doubts. In all negotiations, parties that want to reach some settlement (e.g., the stabilizers and quasi mediators) work to raise or maintain doubts in the minds of others as to the viability of their particular positions, as well as doubts about the consequences of nonagreement. This effort is focused on nonstabilizers and the team across the table. The nonstabilizers are asked to consider the implications of nonsettlement, what it would mean to them personally, or to their organization, objectives, ideals, and reputations. Thus, the same techniques and strategies teams may use to raise and maintain doubts in the minds of parties across the table are also appropriate internally with the nonstabilizers. By the same token, of course, the nonstabilizers engage in a parallel effort to raise doubts in the minds of stabilizers and the quasi mediator about the consequences of settlement.

Because a particular settlement may not be in the interests of the nonstabilizer, he or she frequently must be convinced to accept a settlement through some method other than fostering doubts. Negotiators have an additional tool when dealing with a nonstabilizing teammate: the discipline of the parent organization. This discipline, which might rely upon power, title, prestige, or majority rule, operates within the team. The decision-making process is normally carried over from the parent organization through the chief spokesperson or team leader, which reinforces the roles and relationships of the vertical hierarchy. For instance, an organization that makes most of its important decisions by a majority vote will probably be represented in negotiations by a team that also makes its decisions by majority vote.

According to most practitioners, negotiation is a consensual process. The negotiators come to agreement precisely because they find settlement preferable to nonagreement. But it is erroneous to conclude, as some have, that everyone wins or gains from a negotiated agreement. The notion of "win-win" outcomes is another reflection of the limits of the conventional model of negotiation. Both sides across a table may appear to win, but within each team—where so much more bargaining goes on—there are often nonstabilizers who may view themselves as definite losers in the process.

TARGETING UNDERLYING CONCERNS

The creation and maintenance of doubts about the consequences of nonagreement (or one decision versus another) is central to inducing skeptics to settle. This is true whether they are nonstabilizers within a team or nonstabilizers across the table. But where should this effort be directed?

Fisher and Ury (1981) observe that a negotiator can move the opposite side closer to settlement by convincing it to participate in joint problem solving. This may be accomplished by separating the opposing side's *position* from its underlying *interests*.

Although positions are usually explicit, the interests that underlie them often are left unstated. For example, a community coalition might oppose the establishment of a home for mentally retarded adults in its neighborhood. Yet what is its true interest? Frequently, the community feels that the retarded adults would make the neighborhood less safe. Preserving safe streets may be the real interest at stake. A sophisticated advocate of the home would try to raise doubts about whether the community's stated position will actually satisfy its interests: "Might not additional numbers of sincere, capable adults contribute to community safety? Look at their abilities as well as their problems." An educational process showing that the retarded adults would pose no danger to neighborhood residents—and in fact might improve their security—could foster doubts in the minds of the neighbors about their flat refusal to consider the proposal. Even if opponents are not convinced on this particular score, identifying safety as their prime interest allows the parties to explore mitigating measures.

Education can be the most effective way to raise doubts. It is used, therefore, in every phase of negotiation: across the table, within a team, and between a team and its constituents. The plan of attack is to move the opponent to a more agreeable position.

As Fisher and Ury observe, the effective negotiator aims for the underlying interests that form the foundation of the adversary's position. What happens, however, if a negotiator cannot identify the opponent's interests? Where else can doubts be targeted to get others to adopt a more flexible stance? An answer requires a closer look at the different levels of concern that are often negotiated: issues, proposals, problem definitions, and assumptions.

ISSUES, PROPOSALS, PROBLEMS, AND ASSUMPTIONS

The negotiator's job is to raise and maintain doubts on all four levels of concern. Consider, for example, a proposal to site a hazardous waste management facility that requires the approval of a community board. If there is local opposition, it probably will be based on the assumption that such facilities are inherently dangerous. If that assumption cannot be questioned, no basis exists for negotiations between the community and the developer. As a consequence, the facility will be blocked.

Moreover, even if the project sponsors can convince the community that such facilities are not necessarily dangerous, they may encounter a different obstacle—that of problem definition. For example, the community might contend that its opposition is not to treatment facilities in general but to the proposed location of this particular plant. (It might be near a flood plain.) Casting the problem in these terms obviously would affect proposed solutions. The range of proposals could include the following: having no facility at all, putting the facility at another site, using control technologies to make the facility fit the site, or making the site more acceptable for the proposed use. The issues to be discussed in negotiation would be tied to such proposals. For example, discussion might focus on the need for such a facility, the reasons for (and against) this particular location, and the cost-effectiveness of various mitigating measures.

The task of the facility sponsor would be to raise doubts about the viability of any unacceptable proposals or issues. As assumptions and problem definitions are revealed—which is much more likely than the disclosure of an opponent's real interests—the sponsor would also question them. Since the issues and proposals are derived from the problems and assumptions, the sponsor would probably try to move the negotiations into discussions of the latter before considering specific issues and proposals. In short, the sponsor would focus on the underlying concerns.

EXPANDING THE CORE MODEL

Multilateral Negotiations

The core model that has been described above includes five axes of negotiation: one horizontal, two internal, and two with vertical hierarchies. This model was based on the simplifying assumption that only two teams are at the table. While there are many instances of two-party negotiation, in other cases—particularly those that arise in the public sector—many more parties may be involved. How must the core model be expanded to accommodate additional parties?

The most important difference between two-party and multiparty negotiation is that the latter opens up the possibility of coalition. For example, three parties—A, B, and C—may come to full agreement or no agreement, but they also may be able to forge alternative side deals. Any two parties may strike a deal that leaves the third out. Were A negotiating with just one other party, he could simply weigh any proposed settlement against the consequences of nonagreement. Here, however, he must also compare a possible settlement with both B and C with the advantages of different agreements with B alone or C alone. The addition of each new party at the bargaining table greatly increases the number of theoretical alliances. The introduction of additional parties, necessary as they might be, greatly complicates the negotiation process. Some coalitions may hold for the entire negotiation, but often alliances shift with various issues. Moreover, the lineup of coalitions may shift over time as events, personalities, and loyalties change. Consensus building is always a delicate balancing act.

Finally, the presence of so many parties at the table usually will mean that much more business must be transacted. The important education process usually requires much more time, as the negotiators at the table have the burden of carrying far more information back through their vertical hierarchy. Perhaps we should not be surprised that so many public disputes seem to take months—even years—to negotiate.

The Solitary Negotiator

When only two individuals are negotiating, each acting on his or her own behalf, the conventional model with its emphasis on two independent units bargaining across the table may afford understanding. Yet perhaps even here it is an oversimplification if we do not look at the negotiation that occurs within each of us. Individuals often have mixed feelings and competing priorities. People must admit (to themselves at least) that they sometimes vacillate between accepting a settlement and holding out for more.

Speculation as to whether stabilizing, nonstabilizing, and mediating impulses may exist in one mind is best left to psychiatrists, psychologists, behaviorists, neurologists, and theologians. It does seem true, however, that even in one-on-one bargaining, there can be distinct and contradictory attitudes toward a particular settlement. One strength of the model developed here is that it recognizes the stabilizing and nonstabilizing forces within each bargaining unit (be it a team or an individual), and attempts to understand the means by which they may be integrated.

Quasi Mediators and Mediators

Outside mediators enter disputes for a very specific reason: to fill a trust vacuum that exists at an impasse among and within the parties. The quasi mediator and mediator play separate, yet related, roles: Both use the creation and maintenance of doubts to move other negotiators closer to settlement. The quasi mediator, like the other negotiators, has personal, organizational, and institutional stakes in the outcome of the negotiation process. The truly neutral mediator does not. The quasi mediator also has some power to make decisions about substantive and procedural issues. Whatever power the mediator might enjoy is procedural.

Reengineering Negotiations

Susan Doctoroff

With reengineering has come a shift in the way managers and their staff negotiate both inside and outside their organizations. Managers must now devise new ways for employees to interact with each other, with suppliers, and with customers and clients more efficiently, more responsively, and more profitably.

Several years ago, Roger Fisher examined the impact of a government's or nation's internal negotiations on its external negotiations.[1] Fisher asserted that "internal" discussions frequently compromise the effectiveness of external negotiations and consequently undermine the ability of designated negotiators to satisfy national interests. In this article, I extend Fisher's analysis from the world of international diplomacy to the corporate world.

By examining the unique dynamics of multiparty negotiations inside and outside organizations, I hope to (1) help managers think about the impact of their internal communication and negotiation procedures on their own and their staff's external negotiations, and (2) identify ways to reengineer systems of coordinated discourse between internal and external parties in order to improve the efficiency and results of their organizations' externally negotiated agreements.

INTERNAL AND EXTERNAL NEGOTIATIONS AT ALTA SYSTEMS

To differentiate between internal and external negotiations, consider the case of an information technology consulting services company, Alta Systems, that works with clients to develop specialized applications and integrated system solutions. The client manager's world might look something like that shown in Figure 1.

Every time an Alta client manager interacts with a client (whether trying to contain a project's scope, muster project resources, or navigate the politics of a client's organization), he or she must reconcile the competing interests of and "mini-negotiations" among a myriad of constituencies: within Alta—senior and junior employees; within the client organization—project coordinators, line-of-business sponsors, and IT resources; within a third-party vendor, contractor, solution provider, or partner organization—sales reps, consultants, programmers, and so on.

Source: Reprinted from "Reengineering Negotiations" by Susan Doctoroff, *Sloan Management Review*, Spring 1998, pp. 63–71, by permission of publisher. Copyright 1998 by Sloan Management Review Association. All rights reserved.

FIGURE 1   The World of a Client Manager

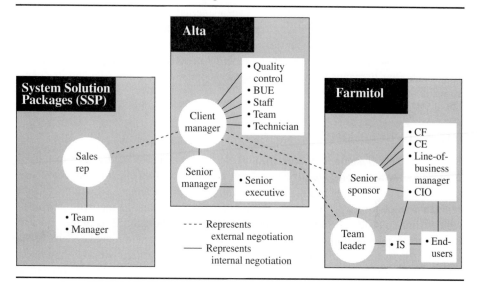

While this diagram represents a complex multiparty negotiation, let us first focus on a relatively simple negotiation in which a senior executive at Alta asks a senior manager to contract with a subcontractor, System Solution Packages (SSP), to help deliver special, high-visibility projects for significant clients like the new pharmaceutical company, Farmitol. If we break the negotiation down, we find at least six smaller negotiations within that single interaction:

- External—between Alta manager and SSP sales representative.
- Internal—between Alta manager and senior executive.
- Internal—between Alta senior executive and CEO.
- Internal—between SSP sales representative and manager.
- External—between Alta manager and Farmitol sponsor.
- Internal—between Farmitol sponsor and CIO.

As Alta's senior manager and the SSP sales representative negotiate the project and contract to work together, both companies invest considerable time exploring the services needed and the best way to provide them. In doing so, they engage in something of a dance, discussing an array of issues, including time frames, scope of services, assessment of risk, how they will work together and interact with Alta's significant clients, and so forth. All the while, each conducts frequent internal meetings about the deal each hopes to strike and the services each wants to receive or provide at an acceptable price or cost. Rather than a single, discrete "at the table" negotiation, there is a series of conversations that occur over time; each is a negotiation within the context of a bigger negotiation.

Partly due to the increased number of small negotiations and partly due to changing organizational structures, the dynamic between internal and external negotiations has also changed. Unfortunately, managers' reengineering of communication and negotiation procedures is not keeping pace with their structural transformation efforts. To understand the problems that arise when internal and external negotiations among multiple parties are not consciously managed, let's examine the negotiation between Alta and its client, Farmitol.

THE ALTA SCENARIO

As the Alta Systems scenario unfolds, the senior manager and senior executive seem pleased with their deal with SSP and ready for the Farmitol client manager to share the news with the client, Farmitol. The client manager specifies that SSP will be doing a significant amount of work with Alta during the next five years, so the two companies will be working hand-in-hand on a number of projects. Although SSP is in the midst of some internal organizational change and needs to get up to speed on new systems technologies, Alta is certain it is the right partner to work with Farmitol over the long term. SSP's team is very "hands on"—terrific when dealing with clients (like Farmitol) with a limited understanding of computer technology and limited resources.

The Alta senior manager had charged the client manager with the role of negotiator. The client manager calls Farmitol's project manager and explains that SSP is now the subcontractor working on the Farmitol account. The two get into a heated debate. The client feels a lack of respect and argues that Farmitol is paying top dollar for what he feels are second-class resources; he insists he want Alta staff people only and claims that Farmitol will walk away from the deal if Alta hands the work over to SSP. Alta's client manager, threatened by this attack and fearful of losing this opportunity to a competitor, caves in. Due to what has transpired internally, the client manager doubts that Alta will be able to work as well for Farmitol without SSP's involvement but is unwilling to risk blowing the whole deal. The senior manager had clearly said, "Close the Farmitol deal."

Inherent in this scenario are several obstacles that can undermine the value derived in negotiations. The obstacles that emerge here typically surface when organizations are balancing internal and external negotiations:

1. Negotiators may walk away from good deals because the deals do not match the organization's articulated position.
2. Negotiators may agree to suboptimal deals because the organization perceives any agreement as better than no agreement.
3. Making demands and arguing over positions inhibit useful discussions about the many parties' underlying interests.
4. Negotiators' roles are defined and understood as advocates rather than as joint problem solvers.
5. Internal and external negotiations are compartmentalized.
6. The parties do not discuss the process explicitly, apart from the substance of the negotiation.

Given these obstacles, how can managers improve their processes so that their external negotiators can systematically achieve more profitable agreements? To answer this question, we must first understand the nature of the obstacles.

OBSTACLES 1 AND 2: WALKING AWAY FROM A DEAL

The possibility of an optimal outcome for both Alta and Farmitol is threatened by tactical games (threats and concessions) between the two external negotiators. Farmitol risks walking away from an excellent vendor and months of investment because Alta's proposed agreement does not match its stated position. At the same time, Alta risks accepting a deal that would undermine its ability to serve Farmitol and other clients in the best way possible.

One internal norm that promotes these games and inhibits parties from jointly discussing their mutual concerns is people's tendency to engage in a series of informal, one-on-one conversations that are independent and discrete. While it is important for a range of parties to be consulted in a decision-making process, managers often neglect to systematically survey each constituency's interests and priorities. Without clear discussions about underlying interests, what emerges from these seemingly innocuous conversations among internal groups is a single "lowest common denominator" position—a deal to which all parties who were consulted can agree.

At Farmitol, a series of independent discussions may have caused the negotiator to insist that all work *must* be done by Alta. For instance, the IT manager may have warned, "We need to minimize the number of contacts we have," and the CFO may have said, "As soon as third parties are brought in, the price increases enormously. I can guarantee we'll pay a surcharge." Then the line-of-business manager may have insisted, "Be careful about getting hooked into a third party. I've had bad experiences in the past. And, if this project runs amok because of subcontractors, don't come crying to me. It's on your shoulders." With those internal conversations in the background, the Farmitol negotiator is certainly going to insist that Alta do all the work.

While Alta's performance of all work may be the appropriate outcome, the decision on whether Farmitol's negotiator or any other external negotiator walks away from a deal is best based on an in-depth understanding of the company's and constituencies' interests and ability to satisfy those needs through some alternative to the negotiated agreement. Neither negotiator deeply explored underlying interests, and neither used that understanding to evaluate the option on the table compared to the "best alternative to a negotiated agreement." This internal shortcoming pushes external negotiators to form hasty, ill-informed conclusions.

Choose Wisely between Options and Alternatives

Any agreement that a negotiator makes should be better than the company's walkaway alternative. Without understanding their organization's best alternative, negotiators cannot make wise choices about when to walk away. Negotiators should have as much information as possible about the strengths and weaknesses of their best alternative in order to effectively use it as a benchmark to evaluate options (possible solutions requiring both parties' agreement). An important goal of internal negotiations is, therefore, to agree on what the organization will do if forced to break a deal. Furthermore, managers should ensure that the internal team continues to explore ways to improve the organization's best alternative so the negotiator's benchmark is as high as possible. In that way, the organization will eventually choose the best option or alternative possible. Such conversations promote internal alignment, so that if and when the other side tries to go over one negotiator's head to solicit a preferred response from someone more senior, the negotiator will have some backup.

When reengineering the internal negotiation process, managers should use internal prenegotiation conversations to gain alignment on the best alternatives and to clarify the negotiator's role and authority with respect to gathering information, sharing interests and alternatives, and quitting the deal or committing. As managers attempt to define the negotiator's role in committing or walking away, they should consider the tension between a negotiator's power to commit to a deal on the table and his or her ability to generate creative options. The more authority that negotiators have to commit to an option or position, the less practical ability they have to constructively brainstorm options—the key to optimizing value in negotiation. Conservative managers tightly confine the exercise of individuals' power in order to protect themselves against poor judgment calls. The following guidelines can help managers avoid this pitfall:

- Give negotiators full authority to explore and discuss interests, options, decision criteria, relationships, communication processes, and alternatives, as they see fit (based on understanding of internal interests).
- Limit negotiators' authority to commit to a position (at least early in the negotiation).
- Encourage negotiators to determine whether to walk away solely on the basis of comparison to the organization's alternative.

By limiting the authority of Alta's and Farmitol's negotiators to commit to an option early in the negotiation, the managers will, in effect, enhance their negotiators' abilities to explore interests and generate optimal agreements later. The two will surely commit in the future, after exploring many options.

OBSTACLES 3 AND 4: POORLY DEFINED MISSION AND ROLE

In the Alta case, the client manager is in the midst of negotiations with Farmitol. Alta has caved in and agreed to staff the project with Alta resources only. Had Alta insisted it would do the work only in conjunction with SSP, the two parties might have deadlocked, each waiting to see who would flinch or make the first move. Each party's failure to examine interests internally undermined each one's ability to decide wisely when to walk away from or commit to the deal. Another mistake is Alta's failure to discuss interests externally. By sticking to positions and staking claims (i.e., Alta insisted on using SSP, Farmitol insisted Alta must do all the work), the two parties became locked into positions. They lost the capacity to see the other's perspective and the ability to examine other creative ways to satisfy their range of similar, compatible, and differing interests.

Frequently, negotiators fall into this situation because managers create internal processes in which they conduct a lot of research and analysis early on and arrive at a solution they know is reasonable, workable, and safe. The problem rests in the inherent difficulty to create an optimal solution with only half a picture. That is, without full knowledge or understanding of both sides' interests, negotiators cannot be relied on to achieve extraordinary, or even consistent, results.

Managers and negotiators tend to stake out an opening position so that they can (1) structure plenty of negotiating room (that is, state an extreme opening position that can be adjusted as negotiations proceed through each party's trading of concessions), and (2) know that their representatives are clearly advocates of the organization's best interest. While these tendencies are understandable, they can be counterproductive in enabling a manager to achieve the goal. Trading concessions, for instance, causes an already fixed pie to quickly get eaten away, minimizing the amount of value that negotiators are able to derive from the deal. Also, advocates, skilled in not budging from what may be a reasonable position, may never discover a key solution. A key solution for Alta's and Farmitol's advocates would be one that gives the client a feeling of security, top resources, and instant access to help. However, in arguing for their positions and advocating their single perspectives, the two negotiators would never uncover a solution. Furthermore, the negotiators' focus on their own interests and concerns would likely undermine their attention to the interests of the other parties they represent—a common mistake in multiparty negotiations.

Change Negotiator's Role

What can a manager do differently to enable negotiators to find creative solutions? Managers need to treat negotiators as "handymen," asking them to undertake different tasks at different times. This takes a transformation of internal and external negotiation processes.

When reengineering the internal process, managers and negotiators must recognize all the parties involved and engage in broad prenegotiation discussions to clarify the negotiator's role and the types of information sharing, exchange, or commitment to strive for at different junctures during external interactions. In addition to articulating individual and shared goals, interests, and fears, a prenegotiation meeting should produce a negotiation strategy. Alta's strategy statement might specify, for example,

- Building a relationship by establishing the ground rules and a timeline for negotiations.
- Defining all constituencies' interests.
- Brainstorming a range of options to meet all parties' objectives.
- Narrowing the range of options.
- Formulating a final commitment.

Because the internal and external processes are integrally linked, the internal process redesign should be followed by an adjustment in the negotiator's role vis-à-vis the external world. If a manager believes he or she has all the answers and charges negotiators with defending that position, their efforts will be ones of persuasion and coercion. Alternatively, if the manager engages negotiators at meeting facilitators or joint problem solvers, then they should conduct external conversations according to the strategy defined during the internal prenegotiation strategy discussions (see Figure 2).

FIGURE 2 Two Approaches to Negotiations

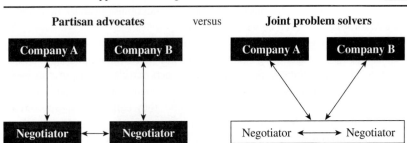

Negotiators can act as partisan advocates, pushing their side's position, or act as joint problem solvers, working with the other side to develop a solution that is better for both organizations than either one could develop independently.

Arguing in favor of one set of interests is less than half the task. Two negotiators acting on behalf of their respective companies have the joint responsibility of efficiently producing a workable agreement that reconciles, as well as possible, the interests of the two groups in a manner acceptable to both. If one side's interests are not well served by an agreement, that side might have an incentive to break the agreement or comply with it only halfheartedly. Sharing interests, however, does not necessitate an organization's full disclosure of its most well-kept secrets to the other side. In fact, managers may consciously choose not to disclose the exact nature of their organization's interests and preferences. Still, managers must work with negotiators to make wise decisions about whether, and how, to disclose interests by balancing the risk with the possibility of improving the deal. Each negotiator is both joint problem solver and advocate.

OBSTACLE 5: GAP BETWEEN INTERNAL AND EXTERNAL NEGOTIATIONS

To understand the risk of compartmentalizing internal and external negotiations, consider the Alta situation. After the Alta manager commits to using only Alta resources, during the course of the project, the work team has difficulty involving Farmitol in the day-to-day management of the project. The senior sponsor is, by now, somewhat detached from the project and leaves the work to a team leader and the small team he designated well before the work began. Each time the Alta manager approaches Farmitol about the need for support and resources, the team leader says:

> Listen, I don't have the time to help you. I am trying to do my job and the jobs of two other people in my department who are on leave. I cannot take another job on, nor can anyone else on this "appointed" team. Besides, you're the one getting paid for this, not me.

In addition, when the manager approaches the team leader to ask about talking with the information services department and some end-users, the team leader says:

> We are paying Alta top dollar to figure things out and do the job, so do it and come back with results. If you need more people to work on the project, bring them in from Alta. If you can't do the work and don't have the expertise to make this project a success, we'll call it quits and find help elsewhere.

Alta's client manager understands how the team leader feels but also knows that without Farmitol's cooperation and active participation, the project will take much longer and its chances of success will be limited. Alta's client manager and Farmitol's team leader have neglected to discuss their constituencies' underlying interests. A variety of internal conversations might have transpired at the two corporate headquarters. Perhaps Alta's engineers discussed internally their need to talk with IS and end-users in order to finalize system specs and create useful reports and interfaces. Perhaps Farmitol's internal discussions centered around the organization's internal reorganization and turmoil or the IS group's attempts to claim ownership of the project. Fearful that Alta will take Farmitol for all it's worth because of internal difficulties, a corporate mission to reevaluate all new technology initiatives, and an inability to rely on IS, Farmitol instead does nothing. And, because none of these discussions has surfaced between client manager and team leader, the two companies will likely never address the underlying problems.

Consequently, Alta's client manager may perceive Farmitol's resistance to putting its own resources on the project as a lack of commitment. Both parties should be faulted for the miscommunication; the team leader is not aware of the message he is inadvertently sending; the client manager is attributing intent to incomplete communication. Together, their failure to share interests and concerns across the organizations—for example, the compartmentalization of internal and external conversations—has created poor feelings and set them off on the wrong foot.

Organizations frequently keep private negotiations wholly distinct from their external conversations with clients, vendors, or partners because (1) they don't want to expose their lack of knowledge; (2) they don't want to expose their shortcomings or dirty laundry; (3) managers fear that sharing their concerns about the risk of a certain project or endeavor will jeopardize it; (4) multiple parties need to work out differing perspectives before external parties are brought into the mix; and (5) internal teams are unable to come to agreement. Each rationale may be warranted and appropriate in certain circumstances.

Still, managers should know that compartmentalizing internal and external conversations can also exacerbate confusion, waste time, and send mixed messages to the other side. Outsiders, wholly unaware of internal negotiations and rationales, may attribute wrong intent or motives to actions or statements they don't understand and don't like, thereby causing both parties to mistrust one another and sadly sabotage their working agreements and relationships.

Integrate Internal and External Negotiations

Highly structured divisions between internal and external negotiations tend to restrict the negotiators' ability to create synergistic solutions. To produce optimal outcomes, managers should institute more flexible processes that:

- Permit people to build on each other's knowledge, skills, and interests, and take into account their constraints.
- Use prenegotiation sessions to survey the interests of all parties.
- Continually facilitate communication among affected parties in ongoing discussions (bring together large groups or create joint subcommittees, joint fact-finding teams, brainstorming sessions, or small working groups of specialists).

In the case of Alta and Farmitol, the companies might have an explicit conversation about the advantages and disadvantages of including IS on the project team, the nature of Farmitol's reevaluation of technology projects, and so on. The Alta manager and Farmitol team leader might jointly invite a member of Farmitol's redesign task force to a meeting so they can discuss the repercussions of the organizational initiative on the project. These actions, in addition to improving the trust and the relationship between the manager and the team leader, might yield a creative solution in which Alta managers discuss the project with higher level executives, adjust the project specs to employ technological solutions to eliminate the inefficiencies, and so forth.

In the reengineered model, managers plan and encourage contact among internal and external groups. Negotiators, in turn, continually promote ongoing interaction within their internal and external teams. In doing so, they more effectively generate solutions that optimize value.

OBSTACLE 6: LACK OF PROCESS DISCUSSIONS

Just as Alta's manager approaches the negotiation with Farmitol with a preconceived understanding about which underlying substantive interests are appropriate for discussion, negotiators frequently come to negotiations with set notions about the process protocols to abide by (who leads the discussion, what roles people have, what topics to discuss, and so forth). For instance, when Alta insisted on bringing in SSP and Farmitol threatened to walk out on the deal, the two negotiators didn't discuss their process of negotiation. They never articulated, even to themselves, the ramifications of their negotiation styles—that is, haggling, threats, agreeing too easily—on their substantive outcome. It makes sense, then, that neither negotiator recommended an alternative way to resolve the issue. Instead, each waited to react to the other's behavior, hoping not to have to act first.

Two problems arise here that are typical in corporate negotiations. First, individuals tend to react to the other party's tone or process, rather than proactively establish their own tone and agenda. In this case, the rationale might be that Alta respects the Farmitol project manager's experience and seniority, or Farmitol assumes this is the way to deal with vendors. The result is that, with little systematic thinking, the two fall into familiar patterns of interaction. Second, individuals seldom articulate, to themselves or each other, the process they are engaged in, or explicitly negotiate over alternative processes or agendas. For Alta's and Farmitol's representatives, this may simply be unfamiliar territory, or it may be considered rude to engage in such discussions because that would overstep established bounds. Whatever the reason, the two negotiators are left with suboptimal outcomes because of their inability to change the dynamics of the process by which they are interacting.

Introduce and Explicitly Discuss the Process

While the tendency not to discuss process issues primarily affects external negotiations, an internal preparation procedure that encourages and rewards negotiators for jointly taking control of the negotiation process could achieve improved negotiation results. Managers working with negotiators to proactively plan a process for moving negotiations forward might encourage them to:

- Set meeting agendas that focus on meeting goals and purposes.
- Set long-term meeting plans.
- Plan long-term relationship goals.
- Anticipate challenges from the other party.

For Alta's and Farmitol's negotiators, just raising process discussions is difficult. But what if Alta's manager proactively says, "The way we're going about these negotiations isn't working. I'm afraid we will both leave the table with a compromised agreement," and Farmitol's team leader defensively responds, "Well, I'm going to get what I want, or else." Such challenges to a negotiator's attempts to raise new and sensitive topics are to be expected. Managers can't make those challenges go away, but they can work with negotiators to improve their ability to deal with them productively. A manager reengineering internal negotiation procedures might carve out some time to act out difficult conversations with a negotiator, so the two can anticipate some of the challenges and strategize how to deal with them.

As managers consider how they can support their negotiators and enable them to do better, they must recognize that process preparation is as critical to the outcome as substantive preparation.

CONCLUSION

Too often organizations' informal internal communication systems inhibit success in external negotiations. In a complete reengineering effort, managers should conduct a comprehensive internal audit that explores everything that might have an impact on negotiations—underlying assumptions, stated and unstated goals and values, people management skills, negotiation styles, methods for preparation and review, and so on—in order to identify other ways that organizational systems and procedures might disempower negotiators. Even without those exhaustive efforts, managers' awareness of the need to align internal and external negotiations to better prepare negotiators representing the company's multiple constituencies and interests will improve results. As coaches, mentors, and evaluators, managers are in a unique position to influence the amount of value their negotiators derive in any agreement.

ENDNOTE

1. See R. Fisher, "Negotiating Inside Out: What Are the Best Ways to Relate Internal Negotiations to External Ones?" *Negotiation Journal: On the Process of Dispute Settlement*, vol. 5 (New York: Plenum Press, January 1989), pp. 33–42.

Get Things Done through Coalitions

Margo Vanover

What do the American Paper Institute, National Coffee Association, Milk Industry Foundation, and American Council on Education have in common?

It may seem unlikely, but the answer is "an interest in sewer user charges."

These four associations and 11 others formed the Coalition for ICR Repeal to protect their members' interests in sewer user charges. Coalition members term industrial cost recovery (ICR) as "an unfair, unnecessary, and costly provision of the 1972 Federal Water Pollution Control Act."

This particular example of a coalition illustrates two very important points that you, a leader of your association, should be aware of. First of all, the coalition was successful. The industrial cost recovery provision was repealed on October 1, 1980, and coalition members frankly admit that they could never have done it alone. It took the efforts and— even more important—the clout of all 15 members to accomplish their goal.

The second point is this: Coalition members seemed like unlikely allies. Who would have thought they had anything in common?

"It's an interesting conglomeration of business groups with one similar interest," acknowledges Sheldon E. Steinbach, general counsel for the American Council on Education, Washington. "We all had one common problem—a proposed increase in sewer user charges."

"I remember the stunned look on the faces of the people at the first coalition meeting," he says with a chuckle. "They found out quickly that my association had the exact concern theirs did."

WHO ARE YOUR ALLIES?

Right now, your association is probably a member of a coalition. But do you know what the coalition's purpose is? If you don't, ask your association's chief paid officer. He or she usually represents an association's interests in a coalition effort.

And while you are talking to your chief paid officer, ask what other associations comprise the coalition. You could be surprised. Like the Coalition for ICR Repeal, their names might not suggest a tie-in with your association's cause. In fact, they may be the names of associations that have been adversaries or competitors in the past.

It's not all that unusual, says Mr. Steinbach. "We look for common cause with other groups. We may be allies on one cause and enemies on another. It's happened time after time."

It's important to overlook past differences and concentrate on the present goal of the coalition, agrees Dr. Paul A. Kerschner, associate director for legislation, research, and programs at the National Retired Teachers Association/American Association of Retired Persons, Washington. "Two organizations can be in deep dissent on some issues," he says. "On those issues, we know we disagree. But on the issues where we do agree, it's much more powerful to speak in a unified voice."

Of course, sometimes your association's allies are obvious. Such was the case when the Distributive Services Committee was formed 17 years ago. Eighteen Ohio associations whose members were involved in distributing formed the coalition to reduce property tax on retail inventory. At the time, the tax was 70 percent of the value of the inventory. The coalition has successfully obtained several reductions since its formation, and the coalition's goal of a 35 percent inventory tax will go into effect in two years.

In this case, both the allies and the enemy were obvious. The allies: trade associations with retail merchant members. The enemy: the state legislature.

SO MANY SUCCESS STORIES

Case after case of association coalitions that have been successful in their pursuits can be cited. William T. Robinson, CAE, senior vice president of the American Hospital Association, Chicago, relates one coalition success story.

Several years ago, he says, the annual rate of increase in the level of expenditures for health care was out of control. Predictions were that if health care costs continued at the same rate it would be necessary to spend the entire gross national product on health care alone by the year 2010. In fact, the government's outlay for health care—Medicare and Medicaid—was beginning to compete with the defense budget.

Government officials, concerned, issued a challenge to the health care field to voluntarily control the rate of increase. A coalition called Voluntary Effort was created. It represented the interests of trade associations, commercial insurance companies, and others. Now, three years after the start of the coalition, "the rate of increase has been sufficiently retarded," Mr. Robinson says.

Edie Fraser, president of Fraser/Associates, Washington, has been involved in enough similar success stories to become a firm believer in their power. "Coalitions are the new trend in business relations on policy issues," she says. "I believe they are the most effective means of achieving results."

WHAT'S THEIR PURPOSE?

She explains that the basic purpose of a coalition is "to join forces together behind a mutual interest—generally a policy issue—and work together for common effectiveness and results."

"More and more associations are recognizing the power of coalitions," Ms. Fraser continues, "because they can achieve far more by integrating their resources and dividing the effort behind a common cause."

Paul Korody, director of public affairs for the National Meat Association, Washington, says coalitions are growing in numbers in response to a changing Congress. "Within the past 10 years, we have seen a decentralization of power on Capitol Hill. Today, every congressman is almost as important as another. They all have to be talked to."

That means, he says, that only the really large associations with members in every congressional district can tackle an issue alone.

> The rest of us have to pool our memberships to be effective in Congress. Whereas we have a lot of meatpackers in the Northwest and Southwest, there are many congressional districts where we have no members at all. We would be less effective in those states [without a coalition]. By combining resources with a number of associations with different memberships but the same goals, you can cover the country.

He adds that, in most cases, congressional staffs appreciate a coalition's efforts. Why? Because it makes their jobs that much easier. They can get one document or have one conversation with a coalition leader and know who and how many are for or against an issue. That's in lieu of speaking with 50,000—a number that five association executives involved in a coalition can easily represent.

CHOOSING A LEADER

In order for any coalition to be successful, it has to have a leader or coordinator with a commitment to the cause and time to devote to it, says Sheldon Steinbach, American Council on Education.

> The effectiveness of the ICR repeal was solely due to the continuous scrutiny and daily monitoring of one person.
>
> A coalition functions only when one person is given responsibility to make that issue move. Someone must call the shots. A leader must have ample time to spend on the issue, almost to the point of making it his or her primary preoccupation.

Because of the considerable time requirement, choosing a coalition coordinator is often simply a process of elimination. Who has the time to spend on it? Who was the expertise on the issue?

When these questions are answered, only a few eligibles are likely to remain. Usually it's the executive of the association which the outcome of the issue most affects.

Or as Ms. Fraser puts it, "The leader usually represents the one association that has the most to gain . . . or lose."

GUIDELINES FOR EFFECTIVENESS

Obviously, the selection of the leader can either make or break a coalition. But other factors also enter into the outcome of your association's coalition.

Here are just a few elements common to successful coalition efforts:

- A commitment by members to work, not in their own self-interest, but in the interest of the group.
- Expertise on the part of all members on the subject matter and its ramifications.
- Knowledge of how the legislature—either state or federal—works.
- Ability to plan a strategy and allow enough lead time to develop it detail by detail so nothing slips through the cracks and is left undone.
- Communication with members of the coalition—whether it's through meetings, newsletters, memos, or telephone calls.
- Keeping on the offensive, rather than the defensive. "Use facts, data, and public opinion to build on your important points," Ms. Fraser says. "It's not necessary to attack your opposition." She ticks off campaign after campaign that was lost because one side began to react defensively to the opposition.
- Member involvement. "If the issue is important to your members—and it should be or you shouldn't be part of the coalition—get them involved," Ms. Fraser urges. "The grassroots campaign is important. The work should really come from members; your association should serve as the catalyst."
- Latitude from you and your board of directors. "Our board sets broad policy," says John C. Mahaney, Jr., president of the Ohio Council of Retail Merchants in Columbus. "After that, my board leaves me alone. It doesn't tie the staff's hands."

A COMMITMENT TO GO

The last point, the latitude you give to your chief paid executive, can be a crucial item to your association's contribution to the coalition. "The board gives us a broad delegation of authority," Sheldon Steinbach says. "We are paid to exercise good judgment and proceed. If you are hamstrung, it will slow you down, if not completely cripple your coalition."

He explains that if he had to go back to his board of directors every time a decision was made in a coalition, he would lose valuable time—not to mention the confidence of other coalition members.

SURVEY OF MEMBERSHIP

To make sure his board of directors will agree with his decisions, Mr. Steinbach surveys his membership on major issues that concern the association. "If they think it is important, they tell us to go," he says. "But they don't tell us how to go."

Dr. Kerschner explains that the only time he goes back to his board for a coalition decision is when the issue is controversial and the association's stance involves a change in previous policy.

What do you do with dissent among coalition members?" asks Dr. Kerschner. "How do you handle it? Do you avoid the issue? Do you go with the majority?"

He explains that chief paid officers must answer these questions, and answer them adequately, for a coalition to work. He has found one possible answer for the coalitions he has been involved with: If there is a disagreement on one particular point of an issue, the dissenting party removes his or her name and endorsement from that specific letter but continues to endorse the remainder of the issue.

"Trade-offs are important because one small issue can divide the coalition," he says. "Before you say 'I will not sign that,' look at all sides. You might have to make a compromise. Internal negotiations are necessary to present a united front to those you are dealing with."

GOODWILL A KEY INGREDIENT

William Robinson advises associations to go into a coalition with the idea that there might have to be a trade-off. "Your pet ideas are going to be examined by others," he says.

> You might have to accept the fact that the publicity will be given to the coalition and not to your association. A coalition takes goodwill by the participants. Sometimes the goodwill is there in the beginning; sometimes it takes time for it to grow.

Speaking realistically, Edie Fraser says it almost never happens that members of a coalition agree on every item, every detail of a coalition.

> That's where the art of negotiation is important. The common end of the allies is more important than the priority of any one association.

SHARING IN THE GLORY

You may wonder why your association's past efforts in coalitions have not been more heavily publicized . . . why your association didn't take more credit for the outcome.

"A coalition, to be effective, is without limelight or glory for the association involved," says Paul Korody.

> The purpose is to get a particular job done. We're there to serve our members, and coalitions are the more effective means of doing that. Any glory is in the fact that we satisfactorily served our members.

Sheldon Steinbach admits that sharing the spotlight is a problem for some associations. Sometimes, they are so greedy for the recognition that they won't participate in a coalition—and risk losing the fight. Other times, they might participate in a coalition, but afterward they will attempt to garner all of the credit for their association alone.

When William Robinson was working on Voluntary Effort, he says that the businesses and associations involved had no qualms about giving complete credit to the coalition, not to themselves. "It would have been counterproductive to publish under any one member's name," Mr. Robinson says. "We wanted the coalition to become a familiar name . . . to have its own identity."

POTENTIAL PROBLEMS

Powerful though they may be, coalitions are not perfect. Problems arise, and they have to be alleviated before the cause can be won. Here are some snags that can occur. With negotiation, respect, and planning, all can be overcome.

1. *One member dominates.* Sometimes, when a coalition is composed of one or two large, domineering associations and a variety of small ones, representatives from the smaller associations are not given the chance to express their opinions. Or, if they are given the opportunity, they are not given priority. All members must listen to one another.

2. *Jealousy between members.* This usually occurs at the outset, Ms. Fraser points out, until coalition members realize that "they can achieve far more by integrating their resources and dividing the effort behind a common cause."

3. *Conflicting goals.* "You've got to go for the greatest good for the greatest number," Mr. Steinbach says.

4. *Conflicting strategy.* This occurs most often when two or more coalition members have considerable legislative experience. Because of their backgrounds, each thinks his own plan of attack is best.

5. *Minor disagreements.* Even though the association executives agree on the major issue, they sometimes bicker about a minor part of it. "You can't let a specific point divide and conquer the group," Dr. Kerschner says.

6. *Too formal.* Dr. Kerschner differentiates between organization, which you can never have enough of, and formalization, which you can. He says it's important to remember that each member of the coalition has an association to which he is responsible and that the coalition should not become a substitute for it.

7. *Too many meetings.* Some coalitions are permanent. Others are temporary—disbanded as soon as their cause is settled. Dr. Kerschner warns that members of permanent coalitions have to be careful not to call a meeting just to be calling a meeting. Unless a crisis has occurred or a new development has come up, he recommends meeting about once a month. Between meetings, he uses the phone for exchanges of information.

8. *Lack of follow-through.* Sometimes a coalition member will slip up, and the work assigned to him or her will not get done. If that happens, and it is not caught in time, all of the coalition efforts will be wasted.

EVERYONE'S DOING IT

Coalitions are not limited to associations. Business groups, consumer groups—just about any group you can think of is involved in some type of coalition. "On any side of any issue, you can find a coalition that has formed, is being formed, or will be formed," Mr. Korody says.

Whatever type of coalition your association may now be involved in, your chances of victory are better through unity. Mr. Mahaney firmly believes Ohio merchants would not have received inventory tax relief without the Distributive Service Committee. "We could not have done it alone," he states. "It took everyone in the coalition to do it."

"Sometimes a coalition is the only way to do something," he continues. "Especially now, as the problems become more complex. It seems like they are too big for any one—or even two—associations to handle."

Paul Korody couldn't agree more. "A smart association executive seeks his peers and works through a coalition. The days of trying to do it all yourself are long gone."

Twenty Tips for Making a Coalition Work

If you aren't convinced of the value of coalitions, talk to Edie Fraser, president of Fraser/Associates, Washington, D.C. She's a firm believer in the effectiveness of coalitions and presents a persuasive argument on their behalf.

She asserts that coalitions are the wave of the future. "On most policy issues, a coalition is the only way to go—if you have a common interest," she says.

In her opinion, more and more association executives are recognizing the potential—and power—of coalitions, but they aren't sure how to proceed. "Carrying out the program is where they often fall down."

Here are her 20 rules for participating in an effective coalition:

1. Clearly define issues and strategy.
2. Determine a timetable and needs.
3. Identify both allies and opposition.
4. Build constituency and recruit allies.
5. Select leadership from within allies.
6. Devise a clear plan of action.
7. Determine resources, budget, and meet those needs.
8. Divide up tasks within the coalition.
9. Establish a working task force or executive committee.
10. Keep coalition members informed and involved.
11. Establish a communication program plan; clearly distribute tasks.
12. Build supportive case materials.
13. Develop an internal communication program with each association involving its members.
14. Enlist experts to support the coalition's case.
15. Explain the issue in economic impact terms when possible; use appropriate public opinion.
16. Utilize all pertinent media for greatest impact.
17. Remember to keep all coalition constituents informed and involved.
18. If it's a legislative issue, review the congressional strategy on a regular basis.
19. Determine if the coalition leadership is serving as a catalyst for communication.
20. Prove the results and communicate them to the member constituencies.

Individual Differences

The Power of Talk: Who Gets Heard and Why

Deborah Tannen

The head of a large division of a multinational corporation was running a meeting devoted to performance assessment. Each senior manager stood up, reviewed the individuals in his group, and evaluated them for promotion. Although there were women in every group, not one of them made the cut. One after another, each manager declared, in effect, that every woman in his group didn't have the self-confidence needed to be promoted. The division head began to doubt his ears. How could it be that all the talented women in the division suffered from a lack of self-confidence?

In all likelihood, they didn't. Consider the many women who have left large corporations to start their own businesses, obviously exhibiting enough confidence to succeed on their own. Judgments about confidence can be inferred only from the way people present themselves, and much of that presentation is in the form of talk.

The CEO of a major corporation told me that he often has to make decisions in five minutes about matters on which others may have worked five months. He said he uses this rule: If the person making the proposal seems confident, the CEO approves it. If not, he says no. This might seem like a reasonable approach. But my field of research, sociolinguistics, suggests otherwise. The CEO obviously thinks he knows what a confident person sounds like. But his judgment, which may be dead right for some people, may be dead wrong for others.

Communication isn't as simple as saying what you mean. How you say what you mean is crucial, and differs from one person to the next, because using language is learned social behavior: How we talk and listen are deeply influenced by cultural experience. Although we might think that our ways of saying what we mean are natural, we can run into trouble if we interpret and evaluate others as if they necessarily felt the same way we'd feel if we spoke the way they did.

Since 1974, I have been researching the influence of linguistic style on conversations and human relationships. In the past four years, I have extended that research to the workplace, where I have observed how ways of speaking learned in childhood affect judgments of competence and confidence, as well as who gets heard, who gets credit, and what gets done.

The division head who was dumbfounded to hear that all the talented women in his organization lacked confidence was probably right to be skeptical. The senior managers were judging the women in their groups by their own linguistic norms, but women—like people who have grown up in a different culture—have often learned different styles of speaking than men, which can make them seem less competent and self-assured than they are.

WHAT IS LINGUISTIC STYLE?

Everything that is said must be said in a certain way—in a certain tone of voice, at a certain rate of speed, and with a certain degree of loudness. Whereas often we consciously consider what to say before speaking, we rarely think about how to say it, unless the situation is obviously loaded—for example, a job interview or a tricky performance review. Linguistic style refers to a person's characteristic speaking pattern. It includes such features as directness or indirectness, pacing and pausing, word choice, and the use of such elements as jokes, figures of speech, stories, questions, and apologies. In other words, linguistic style is a set of culturally learned signals by which we not only communicate what we mean but also interpret others' meaning and evaluate one another as people.

Consider turn taking, one element of linguistic style. Conversation is an enterprise in which people take turns: One person speaks, then the other responds. However, this apparently simple exchange requires a subtle negotiation of signals so that you know when the other person is finished and it's your turn to begin. Cultural factors such as country or region of origin and ethnic background influence how long a pause seems natural. When Bob, who is from Detroit, has a conversation with his colleague Joe, from New York City, it's hard for him to get a word in edgewise because he expects a slightly longer pause between turns than Joe does. A pause of that length never comes because, before it has a chance to, Joe senses an uncomfortable silence, which he fills with more talk of his own.

Both men fail to realize that differences in conversational style are getting in their way. Bob thinks that Joe is pushy and uninterested in what he has to say, and Joe thinks that Bob doesn't have much to contribute. Similarly, when Sally relocated from Texas to Washington, D.C., she kept searching for the right time to break in during staff meetings—and never found it. Although in Texas she was considered outgoing and confident, in Washington she was perceived as shy and retiring. Her boss even suggested she take an assertiveness training course. Thus slight differences in conversational style—in these cases, a few seconds of pause—can have a surprising impact on who gets heard and on the judgments, including psychological ones, that are made about people and their abilities.

Every utterance functions on two levels. We're all familiar with the first one: Language communicates ideas. The second level is mostly invisible to us, but it plays a powerful role in communication. As a form of social behavior, language also negotiates relationships. Through ways of speaking, we signal—and create—the relative status of speakers and their level of rapport. If you say, "Sit down!" you are signaling that you have higher status than the person you are addressing, that you are so close to each other that you can drop all pleasantries, or that you are angry. If you say, "I would be honored if you would sit down," you are signaling great respect—or great sarcasm, depending on your tone of voice, the situation, and what you both know about how close you really are. If you say, "You must be so tired—why don't you sit down," you are communicating either closeness and concern or condescension. Each of these ways of saying "the same thing"—telling someone to sit down—can have a vastly different meaning.

In every community known to linguists, the patterns that constitute linguistic style are relatively different for men and women. What's "natural" for most men speaking a given language is, in some cases, different from what's "natural" for most women. That is because we learn ways of speaking as children growing up, especially from peers, and children tend to play with other children of the same sex. The research of sociologists, anthropologists, and psychologists observing American children at play has shown that, although both girls and boys find ways of creating rapport and negotiating status, girls tend to learn conversational rituals that focus on the rapport dimension of relationships whereas boys tend to learn rituals that focus on the status dimension.

Girls tend to play with a single best friend or in small groups, and they spend a lot of time talking. They use language to negotiate how close they are; for example, the girl you tell your secrets to becomes your best friend. Girls learn to downplay ways in which one is better than the others and to emphasize ways in which they are all the same. From childhood, most girls learn that sounding too sure of themselves will make them unpopular with their peers—although nobody really takes such modesty literally. A group of girls will ostracize a girl who calls attention to her own superiority and criticize her by saying, "She thinks she's something"; and a girl who tells others what to do is called "bossy." Thus girls learn to talk in ways that balance their own needs with those of others—to save face for one another in the broadest sense of the term.

Boys tend to play very differently. They usually play in larger groups in which more boys can be included, but not everyone is treated as an equal. Boys with high status in their group are expected to emphasize rather than downplay their status, and usually one or several boys will be seen as the leader or leaders. Boys generally don't accuse one another of being bossy, because the leader is expected to tell lower-status boys what to do. Boys learn to use language to negotiate their status in the group by displaying their abilities and knowledge, and by challenging others and resisting challenges. Giving orders is one way of getting and keeping the high-status role. Another is taking center stage by telling stories or jokes.

This is not to say that all boys and girls grow up this way or feel comfortable in these groups or are equally successful at negotiating within these norms. But, for the most part, these childhood play groups are where boys and girls learn their conversational styles. In this sense, they grow up in different worlds. The result is that women and men tend to have different habitual ways of saying what they mean, and conversations between them can be like cross-cultural communication: You can't assume that the other person means what you would mean if you said the same thing in the same way.

My research in companies across the United States shows that the lessons learned in childhood carry over into the workplace. Consider the following example: A focus group was organized at a major multinational company to evaluate a recently implemented flextime policy. The participants sat in a circle and discussed the new system. The group concluded that it was excellent, but they also agreed on ways to improve it. The meeting went well and was deemed a success by all, according to my own observations and everyone's comments to me. But the next day, I was in for a surprise.

I had left the meeting with the impression that Phil had been responsible for most of the suggestions adopted by the group. But as I typed up my notes, I noticed that Cheryl had made almost all those suggestions. I had thought that the key ideas came from Phil because he had picked up Cheryl's points and supported them, speaking at greater length in doing so than she had in raising them.

It would be easy to regard Phil as having stolen Cheryl's ideas—and her thunder. But that would be inaccurate. Phil never claimed Cheryl's ideas as his own. Cheryl herself told me later that she left the meeting confident that she had contributed significantly, and that she appreciated Phil's support. She volunteered, with a laugh, "It was not one of those times when a woman says something and it's ignored, then a man says it and it's picked up." In other words, Cheryl and Phil worked well as a team, the group fulfilled its charge, and the company got what it needed. So what was the problem?

I went back and asked all the participants who they thought had been the most influential group member, the one most responsible for the ideas that had been adopted. The pattern of answers was revealing. The two other women in the group named Cheryl. Two of the three men named Phil. Of the men, only Phil named Cheryl. In other words, in this instance, the women evaluated the contribution of another woman more accurately than the men did.

Meetings like this take place daily in companies around the country. Unless managers are unusually good at listening closely to how people say what they mean, the talents of someone like Cheryl may well be undervalued and underutilized.

ONE UP, ONE DOWN

Individual speakers vary in how sensitive they are to the social dynamics of language—in other words, to the subtle nuances of what others say to them. Men tend to be sensitive to the power dynamics of interaction, speaking in ways that position themselves as one up and resisting being put in a one-down position by others. Women tend to react more strongly to the rapport dynamic, speaking in ways that save face for others and buffering statements that could be seen as putting others in a one-down position. These linguistic patterns are pervasive; you can hear them in hundreds of exchanges in the workplace every day. And, as in the case of Cheryl and Phil, they affect who gets heard and who gets credit.

Getting Credit

Even so small a linguistic strategy as the choice of pronoun can affect who gets credit. In my research in the workplace, I heard men say "I" in situations where I heard women say "we." For example, one publishing company executive said, "I'm hiring a new manager. I'm going to put him in charge of my marketing division," as if he owned the corporation. In stark contrast, I recorded women saying "we" when referring to work they alone had done. One woman explained that it would sound too self-promoting to claim credit in an obvious way by saying "I did this." Yet she expected—sometimes vainly—that others would know it was her work and would give her the credit she did not claim for herself.

Managers might leap to the conclusion that women who do not take credit for what they've done should be taught to do so. But that solution is problematic because we associate ways of speaking with moral qualities: The way we speak is who we are and who we want to be.

Veronica, a senior researcher in a high-tech company, had an observant boss. He noticed that many of the ideas coming out of the group were hers but that often someone else trumpeted them around the office and got credit for them. He advised her to "own" her ideas and make sure she got the credit. But Veronica found she simply didn't enjoy her work if she had to approach it as what seemed to her an unattractive and unappealing "grabbing game." It was her dislike of such behavior that had led her to avoid it in the first place.

Whatever the motivation, women are less likely than men to have learned to blow their own horn. And they are more likely than men to believe that if they do so, they won't be liked.

Many have argued that the growing trend of assigning work to teams may be especially congenial to women, but it may also create complications for performance evaluation. When ideas are generated and work is accomplished in the privacy of the team, the outcome of the team's effort may become associated with the person most vocal about reporting results. There are many women and men—but probably relatively more women—who are reluctant to put themselves forward in this way and who consequently risk not getting credit for their contributions.

Confidence and Boasting

The CEO who based his decisions on the confidence level of speakers was articulating a value that is widely shared in U.S. businesses: One way to judge confidence is by an individual's behavior, especially verbal behavior. Here again, many women are at a disadvantage.

Studies show that women are more likely to downplay their certainty and men are most likely to minimize their doubts. Psychologist Laurie Heatherington and her colleagues devised an ingenious experiment, which they reported in the journal *Sex Roles* (Volume 29, 1993). They asked hundreds of incoming college students to predict what grades they would get in their first year. Some subjects were asked to make their predictions privately by writing them down and placing them in an envelope; others were asked to make their predictions publicly, in the presence of a researcher. The results showed that more women than men predicted lower grades for themselves if they made their predictions publicly. If they made their predictions privately, the predictions were the same as those of the men—and the same as their actual grades. This study provides evidence that what comes across as lack of confidence—predicting lower grades for oneself—may reflect not one's actual level of confidence but the desire not to seem boastful.

These habits with regard to appearing humble or confident result from the socialization of boys and girls by their peers in childhood play. As adults, both women and men find these behaviors reinforced by the positive response they get from friends and relatives who share the same norms. But the norms of behavior in the U.S. business world are based on the style of interaction that is more common among men—at least, among American men.

Asking Questions

Although asking the right questions is one of the hallmarks of a good manager, how and when questions are asked can send unintended signals about competence and power. In a group, if only one person asks questions, he or she risks being seen as the only ignorant one. Furthermore, we judge others not only by how they speak but also by how they are spoken to. The person who asks questions may end up being lectured to and looking like a novice under a schoolmaster's tutelage. The way boys are socialized makes them more likely to be aware of the underlying power dynamic by which a questions asker can be seen in a one-down position.

One practicing physician learned the hard way that any exchange of information can become the basis for judgments—or misjudgments—about competence. During her training, she received a negative evaluation that she thought was unfair, so she asked her supervising physician for an explanation. He said that she knew less than her peers. Amazed at his answer, she asked how he had reached that conclusion. He said, "You ask more questions."

Along with cultural influences and individual personality, gender seems to play a role in whether and when people ask questions. For example, of all the observations I've made in lectures and books, the one that sparks the most enthusiastic flash of recognition is that men are less likely than women to stop and ask for directions when they are lost. I explain that men often resist asking for directions because they are aware that it puts them in a one-down position and because they value the independence that comes with finding their way by themselves. Asking for directions while driving is only one instance—along with many others that researchers have examined—in which men seem less likely than women to ask questions. I believe this is because they are more attuned than women to the potential face-losing aspect of asking questions. And men who believe that asking questions might reflect negatively on them may, in turn, be likely to form a negative opinion of others who ask questions in situations where they would not.

CONVERSATIONAL RITUALS

Conversation is fundamentally ritual in the sense that we speak in ways our culture has conventionalized and expect certain types of responses. Take greetings, for example. I have heard visitors to the United States complain that Americans are hypocritical because they ask how you are but aren't interested in the answer. To Americans, How are you? is obviously a ritualized way to start a conversation rather than a literal request for information. In other parts of the world, including the Philippines, people ask each other, "Where are you going?" when they meet. The question seems intrusive to Americans, who do not realize that it, too, is a ritual query to which the only expected reply is a vague "Over there."

It's easy and entertaining to observe different rituals in foreign countries. But we don't expect differences, and are far less likely to recognize the ritualized nature of our conversations, when we are with our compatriots at work. Our differing rituals can be even more problematic when we think we're all speaking the same language.

Apologies

Consider the simple phrase *I'm sorry.*

Catherine: How did that big presentation go?

Bob: Oh, not very well, I got a lot of flak from the VP for finance, and I didn't have the numbers at my fingertips.

Catherine: Oh, I'm sorry. I know how hard you worked on that.

In this case, *I'm sorry* probably means "I'm sorry that happened," not "I apologize," unless it was Catherine's responsibility to supply Bob with the numbers for the presentation. Women tend to say *I'm sorry* more frequently than men, and often they intend it in this way—as a ritualized means of expressing concern. It's one of many learned elements of conversational style that girls often use to establish rapport. Ritual apologies—like other conversational rituals—work well when both parties share the same assumptions about their use. But people who utter frequent ritual apologies may end up appearing weaker, less confident, and literally more blameworthy than people who don't.

Apologies tend to be regarded differently by men, who are more likely to focus on the status implications of exchanges. Many men avoid apologies because they see them as putting the speaker in a one-down position. I observed with some amazement an encounter among several lawyers engaged in a negotiation over a speakerphone. At one point, the lawyer in whose office I was sitting accidentally elbowed the telephone and cut off the call. When his secretary got the parties back on again, I expected him to say what I would have said: "Sorry about that. I knocked the phone with my elbow." Instead, he said, "Hey, what happened? One minute you were there; the next minute you were gone!" This lawyer seemed to have an automatic impulse not to admit fault if he didn't have to. For me, it was one of those pivotal moments when you realize that the world you live in is not the one everyone lives in and that the way you assume is the way to talk is really only one of many.

Those who caution managers not to undermine their authority by apologizing are approaching interaction from the perspective of the power dynamic. In many cases, this strategy is effective. On the other hand, when I asked people what frustrated them in their jobs, one frequently voiced complaint was working with or for someone who refuses to apologize or admit fault. In other words, accepting responsibility for errors and admitting mistakes may be an equally effective or superior strategy in some settings.

Feedback

Styles of giving feedback contain a ritual element that often is the cause for misunderstanding. Consider the following exchange: A manager had to tell her marketing director to rewrite a report. She began this potentially awkward task by citing the report's strengths and then moved to the main point: the weaknesses that needed to be remedied. The marketing director seemed to understand and accept his supervisor's comments, but his revision contained only minor changes and failed to address the major weaknesses. When the manager told him of her dissatisfaction, he accused her of misleading him: "You told me it was fine."

The impasse resulted from different linguistic styles. To the manager, it was natural to buffer the criticism by beginning with praise. Telling her subordinate that this report is inadequate and has to be rewritten puts him in a one-down position. Praising him for the parts that are good is a ritualized way of saving face for him. But the marketing director did not share his supervisor's assumption about how feedback should be given. Instead, he assumed that what she mentioned first was the main point and that what she brought up later was an afterthought.

Those who expect feedback to come in the way the manager presented it would appreciate her tact and would regard a more blunt approach as unnecessarily callous. But those who share the marketing director's assumptions would regard the blunt approach as honest and no-nonsense, and the manager's as obfuscating. Because each one's assumptions seemed self-evident, each blamed the other: The manager thought the marketing director was not listening, and he thought she had not communicated clearly or had changed her mind. This is significant because it illustrates that incidents labeled vaguely as "poor communication" may be the result of differing linguistic styles.

Compliments

Exchanging compliments is a common ritual, especially among women. A mismatch in expectations about this ritual left Susan, a manager in the human resources field, in a one-down position. She and her colleague Bill had both given presentations at a national conference. On the airplane home, Susan told Bill, "That was a great talk!" "Thank you," he said. Then she asked, "What did you think of mine?" He responded with a lengthy and detailed critique, as she listened uncomfortably. An unpleasant feeling of having been put down came over her. Somehow she had been positioned as the novice in need of his expert advice. Even worse, she had only herself to blame, since she had, after all, asked Bill what he thought of her talk.

But had Susan asked for the response she received? When she asked Bill what he thought about her talk, she expected to hear not a critique but a compliment. In fact, her question had been an attempt to repair a ritual gone awry. Susan's initial compliment to Bill was the kind of automatic recognition she felt was more or less required after a colleague gives a presentation, and she expected Bill to respond with a matching compliment. She was just talking automatically, but he either sincerely misunderstood the ritual or simply took the opportunity to bask in the one-up position of critic. Whatever his motivation, it was Susan's attempt to spark an exchange of compliments that gave him the opening.

Although this exchange could have occurred between two men, it does not seem coincidental that it happened between a man and a woman. Linguist Janet Holmes discovered that women pay more compliments than men (*Anthropological Linguistics,* Volume 28, 1986). And, as I have observed, fewer men are likely to ask, "What did you think of my talk?" precisely because the question might invite an unwanted critique.

In the social structure of the peer groups in which they grow up, boys are indeed looking for opportunities to put others down and take the one-up position for themselves. In contrast, one of the rituals girls learn is taking the one-down position but assuming that the other person will recognize the ritual nature of the self-denigration and pull them back up.

The exchange between Susan and Bill also suggests how women's and men's characteristic styles may put women at a disadvantage in the workplace. If one person is trying to minimize status differences, maintain an appearance that everyone is equal, and save face for the other, while another person is trying to maintain the one-up position and avoid being positioned as one down, the person seeking the one-up position is likely to get it. At the same time, the person who has not been expending any effort to avoid the one-down position is likely to end up in it. Because women are more likely to take (or accept) the role of advice seeker, men are more inclined to interpret a ritual question from a woman as a request for advice.

Ritual Opposition

Apologizing, mitigating criticism with praise, and exchanging compliments are rituals common among women that men often take literally. A ritual common among men that women often take literally is ritual opposition.

A woman in communications told me she watched with distaste and distress as her office mate argued heatedly with another colleague about whose division should suffer budget cuts. She was even more surprised, however, that a short time later they were as friendly as ever. "How can you pretend that fight never happened?" she asked. "Who's pretending it never happened?" he responded, as puzzled by her question as she had been by his behavior. "It happened," he said, "and it's over." What she took as literal fighting to him was a routine part of daily negotiation: a ritual fight.

Many Americans expect the discussion of ideas to be a ritual fight—that is, an exploration through verbal opposition. They present their own ideas in the most certain and absolute form they can, and wait to see if they are challenged. Being forced to defend an idea provides an opportunity to test it. In the same spirit, they may play devil's advocate in challenging their colleagues' ideas—trying to poke holes and find weaknesses—as a way of helping them explore and test their ideas.

This style can work well if everyone shares it, but those unaccustomed to it are likely to miss its ritual nature. They may give up an idea that is challenged, taking the objections as an indication that the idea was a poor one. Worse, they may take the opposition as a personal attack and may find it impossible to do their best in a contentious environment. People unaccustomed to this style may hedge when stating their ideas in order to fend off potential attacks. Ironically, this posture makes their arguments appear weak and is more likely to invite attack from pugnacious colleagues than to fend it off.

Ritual opposition can even play a role in who gets hired. Some consulting firms that recruit graduates from the top business schools use a confrontational interviewing technique. They challenge the candidate to "crack a case" in real time. A partner at one firm told me,

> Women tend to do less well in this kind of interaction, and it certainly affects who gets hired. But, in fact, many women who don't "test well" turn out to be good consultants. They're often smarter than some of the men who looked like analytic powerhouses under pressure.

The level of verbal opposition varies from one company's culture to the next, but I saw instances of it in all the organizations I studied. Anyone who is uncomfortable with this linguistic style—and that includes some men as well as many women—risks appearing insecure about his or her ideas.

NEGOTIATING AUTHORITY

In organizations, formal authority comes from the position one holds. But actual authority has to be negotiated day to day. The effectiveness of individual managers depends in part on their skill in negotiating authority and on whether others reinforce or undercut their efforts. The way linguistic style reflects status plays a subtle role in placing individuals within a hierarchy.

Managing Up and Down

In all the companies I researched, I heard from women who knew they were doing a superior job and knew that their co-workers (and sometimes their immediate bosses) knew it as well, but believed that the higher-ups did not. They frequently told me that something outside themselves was holding them back and found it frustrating because they thought that all that should be necessary for success was to do a great job, that superior performance should be recognized and rewarded. In contrast, men often told me that if women weren't promoted, it was because they simply weren't up to snuff. Looking around, however, I saw evidence that men more often than women behaved in ways likely to get them recognized by those with the power to determine their advancement.

In all the companies I visited, I observed what happened at lunchtime. I saw young men who regularly ate lunch with their boss, and senior men who ate with the big boss. I noticed far fewer women who sought out the highest-level person they could eat with. But one is more likely to get recognition for work done if one talks about it to those higher up, and it is easier to do so if the lines of communication are already open. Furthermore, given the opportunity for a conversation with superiors, men and women are likely to have different ways of talking about their accomplishments because of the different ways in which they were socialized as children. Boys are rewarded by their peers if they talk up their achievements, whereas girls are rewarded if they play theirs down. Linguistic styles common among men may tend to give them some advantages when it comes to managing up.

All speakers are aware of the status of the person they are talking to and adjust accordingly. Everyone speaks differently when talking to a boss than when talking to a subordinate. But, surprisingly, the ways in which they adjust their talk may be different and thus may project different images of themselves.

Communications researchers Karen Tracy and Eric Eisenberg studied how relative status affects the way people give criticism. They devised a business letter that contained some errors and asked 13 male and 11 female college students to role-play delivering criticism under two scenarios. In the first, the speaker was a boss talking to a subordinate; in the second, the speaker was a subordinate talking to his or her boss. The researchers measured how hard the speakers tried to avoid hurting the feelings of the person they were criticizing.

One might expect people to be more careful about how they deliver criticism when they are in a subordinate position. Tracy and Eisenberg found that hypothesis to be true for the men in their study but not for the women. As they reported in *Research on Language and Social Interaction* (Volume 24, 1990/1991), the women showed more concern about the other person's feeling when they were playing the role of superior. In other words, the women were more careful to save face for the other person when they were managing down than when they were managing up. This pattern recalls the way girls are socialized: Those who are in some way superior are expected to downplay rather than flaunt their superiority.

In my own recordings of workplace communication, I observed women talking in similar ways. For example, when a manager had to correct a mistake made by her secretary, she did so by acknowledging that there were mitigating circumstances. She said, laughing, "You know, it's hard to do things around here, isn't it, with all these people coming in!" The manager was saving face for her subordinate, just like the female students role-playing in the Tracy and Eisenberg study.

Is this an effective way to communicate? One must ask, effective for what? The manager in question established a positive environment in her group, and the work was done effectively. On the other hand, numerous women in many different fields told me that their bosses say they don't project the proper authority.

Indirectness

Another linguistic signal that varies with power and status is indirectness—the tendency to say what we mean without spelling it out in so many words. Despite the widespread belief in the United States that it's always best to say exactly what we mean, indirectness is a fundamental and pervasive element in human communication. It also is one of the elements that vary most from one culture to another, and it can cause enormous misunderstanding when speakers have different habits and expectations about how it is used. It's often said that American women are more indirect than American men, but in fact everyone tends to be indirect in some situations and in different ways. Allowing for cultural, ethnic, regional, and individual differences, women are especially likely to be indirect when it comes to telling others what to do, which is not surprising, considering girls' readiness to brand other girls as bossy. On the other hand, men are especially likely to be indirect when it comes to admitting fault or weakness, which also is not surprising considering boys' readiness to push around boys who assume the one-down position.

At first glance, it would seem that only the powerful can get away with bold commands such as "Have that report on my desk by noon." But power in an organization also can lead to requests so indirect that they don't sound like requests at all. A boss who says, "Do we have the sales data by product line for each region?" would be surprised and frustrated if a subordinate responded, "We probably do" rather than "I'll get it for you."

Examples such as these notwithstanding, many researchers have claimed that those in subordinate positions are more likely to speak indirectly, and that is surely accurate in some situations. For example, linguist Charlotte Linde, in a study published in *Language in Society* (Volume 17, 1988), examined the black-box conversations that took place between pilots and copilots before airplane crashes. In one particularly tragic instance, an Air Florida plane crashed into the Potomac River immediately after attempting takeoff from National Airport in Washington, D.C., killing all but 5 of the 74 people on board. The pilot, it turned out, had little experience flying in icy weather. The copilot had a bit more, and it became heartbreakingly clear on analysis that he had tried to warn the pilot but had done so indirectly. Alerted by Linde's observation, I examined the transcript of the conversations and found evidence of her hypothesis. The copilot repeatedly called attention to the bad weather and to ice buildup on other planes:

> *Copilot:* Look how the ice is just hanging on his, ah, back, back there, see that? See all those icicles on the back there and everything?
>
> *Pilot:* Yeah.
>
> (The copilot also expressed concern about the long waiting time since deicing.)
>
> *Copilot:* Boy, this is a, this is a losing battle here on trying to deice those things; it [gives] you a false feeling of security, that's all that does.
>
> (Just before they took off, the copilot expressed another concern—about abnormal instrument readings—but again he didn't press the matter when it wasn't picked up by the pilot.)
>
> *Copilot:* That don't seem right, does it? (3-second pause). Ah, that's not right. Well—
>
> *Pilot:* Yes it is, there's 80.
>
> *Copilot:* Naw, I don't think that's right (7-second pause) Ah, maybe it is.

Shortly thereafter, the plane took off, with tragic results. In other instances as well as this one, Linde observed that copilots, who are second in command, are more likely to express themselves indirectly or otherwise mitigate, or soften, their communication when they are suggesting courses of action to the pilot. In an effort to avert similar disasters, some airlines now offer training for copilots to express themselves in more assertive ways.

This solution seems self-evidently appropriate to most Americans. But when I assigned Linde's article in a graduate seminar I taught, a Japanese student pointed out that it would be just as effective to train pilots to pick up on hints. This approach reflects assumptions about communication that typify Japanese culture, which places great value on the ability of people to understand one another without putting everything into words. Either directness or indirectness can be a successful means of communication as long as the linguistic style is understood by the participants.

In the world of work, however, there is more at stake than whether the communication is understood. People in powerful positions are likely to reward styles similar to their own, because we all tend to take as self-evident the logic of our own styles. Accordingly, there is evidence that in the U.S. workplace, where instructions from a superior are expected to be voiced in a relatively direct manner, those who tend to be indirect when telling subordinates what to do may be perceived as lacking in confidence.

Consider the case of the manager at a national magazine who was responsible for giving assignments to reporters. She tended to phrase her assignments as questions. For example, she asked, "How would you like to do the X project with Y?" or said, "I was thinking of putting you on the X project. Is that okay?" This worked extremely well with her staff; they liked working for her, and the work got done in an efficient and orderly manner. But when she had her midyear evaluation with her own boss, he criticized her for not assuming the proper demeanor with her staff.

In any work environment, the higher-ranking person has the power to enforce his or her view of appropriate demeanor, created in part by linguistic style. In most U.S. contexts, that view is likely to assume that the person in authority has the right to be relatively direct rather than to mitigate orders. There also are cases, however, in which the higher-ranking person assumes a more indirect style. The owner of a retail operation told her subordinate, a store manager, to do something. He said he would do it, but a week later he still hadn't. They were able to trace the difficulty to the following conversation: She had said, "The bookkeeper needs help with the billing. How would you feel about helping her out?" He had said, "Fine." This conversation had seemed to be clear and flawless at the time, but it turned out that they had interpreted this simple exchange in very different ways. She thought he meant, "Fine, I'll help the bookkeeper out." He thought he meant, "Fine, I'll think about how I would feel about helping the bookkeeper out." He did think about it and came to the conclusion that he had more important things to do and couldn't spare the time.

To the owner, "How would you feel about helping the bookkeeper out?" was an obviously appropriate way to give the order "Help the bookkeeper out with the billing." Those who expect orders to be given as bold imperatives may find such locutions annoying or even misleading. But those for whom this style is natural do not think they are being indirect. They believe they are being clear in a polite or respectful way.

What is atypical in this example is that the person with the more indirect style was the boss, so the store manager was motivated to adapt to her style. She still gives orders the same way, but the store manager now understands how she means what she says. It's more common in U.S. business contexts for the highest-ranking people to take a more direct style, with the result that many women in authority risk being judged by their superiors as lacking the appropriate demeanor—and, consequently, lacking confidence.

WHAT TO DO?

I am often asked, What is the best way to give criticism? or What is the best way to give orders?—in other words, What is the best way to communicate? The answer is that there is no one best way. The results of a given way of speaking will vary depending on the situation, the culture of the company, the relative rank of speakers, their linguistic styles, and how those styles interact with one another. Because of all those influences, any way of speaking could be perfect for communicating with one person in one situation and disastrous with someone else in another. The critical skill for managers is to become aware of the workings and power of linguistic style, to make sure that people with something valuable to contribute get heard.

It may seem, for example, that running a meeting in an unstructured way gives equal opportunity to all. But awareness of the differences in conversational style makes it easy to see the potential for unequal access. Those who are comfortable speaking up in groups, who need little or no silence before raising their hands, or who speak out easily without waiting to be recognized are far more likely to get heard at meetings. Those who refrain from talking until it's clear that the previous speaker is finished, who wait to be recognized, and who are inclined to link their comments to those of others will do fine at a meeting where everyone else is following the same rules but will have a hard time getting heard in a meeting with people whose styles are more like the first pattern. Given the socialization typical of boys and girls, men are more likely to have learned the first style and women the second, making meetings more congenial for men than for women. It's common to observe women who participate actively in one-on-one discussions or in all female groups but who are seldom heard in meetings with a large proportion of men. On the other hand, there are women who share the style more common among men, and they run a different risk of being seen as too aggressive.

A manager aware of those dynamics might devise any number of ways of ensuring that everyone's ideas are heard and credited. Although no single solution will fit all contexts, managers who understand the dynamics of linguistic style can develop more adaptive and flexible approaches to running or participating in meetings, mentoring or advancing the careers of others, evaluating performance, and so on. Talk is the lifeblood of managerial work, and understanding that different people have different ways of saying what they mean will make it possible to take advantage of the talents of people with a broad range of linguistic styles. As the workplace becomes more culturally diverse and business becomes more global, managers will need to become even better at reading interactions and more flexible in adjusting their own styles to the people with whom they interact.

Are You Smart Enough to Keep Your Job?

Alan Farnham

When I graduated from Harvard College as an ostensibly smart guy, I discovered that I did not know how to make change. This was brought to my attention when I got a job selling cigars and pipes in a tobacconist's shop. I understood subtraction and addition okay . . . in the abstract. But when confronted with a cash register (a nonintelligent one; this was 1977) and a testy, foot-tapping customer, sapience fled. My boss did not fire me; he pitied me. The Angel of Duh passed over, and I lived to make change another day.

A smartness deficit of this kind, while embarrassing, is seldom fatal, since it arises from a lack of skill. And skills can be learned. Innumerate? Scott Flansburg, the Human Calculator, has people making change and doing logarithms in a jiffy. Inarticulate? An hour with Verbal Advantage, and you may be mistaken for Dick Cavett. Memory bad? Haven't read the Fifty Greatest Books? Illiterate? All these deficits and more can be put right, for a price.

Failures of perception, however, are tougher, attacking otherwise smart, highly successful people. Seldom do they explode in a single career-killing solar flare of foolishness. Instead they gnaw away, year by year, quietly undermining accomplishment, until one day someone finally says, "You know, I don't care if O'Reilly *is* making twice his quota. He's a jerk. I want him out of here."

This, allowing for poetic license, is what happened to Dick Snyder, former head of publishing giant Simon & Schuster. For years he seemed unable to stop himself from degrading and humiliating subordinates, even as he pushed S&S to ever higher earnings. Viacom eventually bought S&S, and Frank Biondi, Viacom's CEO, fired Snyder. Explaining why he had done so to writer Roger Rosenblatt in a *New York Times Magazine* article, Biondi said Snyder had "not been a team player." Yes, said Rosenblatt, but what if Snyder had been able to double S&S's business? Would Biondi still have fired him? "Probably," replied the axman coolly.

Snyder displayed a deficit of what author Daniel Goleman calls "emotional intelligence," or, as it is sometimes known, EQ. This he defines as the power not only to control emotions but also to perceive them. Failing to perceive can be costly.

George McCown, co-founder of McCown De Leeuw, a buyout partnership in Menlo Park, California, hired a "very data-driven individual" with such a deficit, though he didn't know it at first. She was smart—very smart—and from the finest schools. When Jane crunched numbers, they stayed crunched. So pleased was McCown with her ability that he entrusted her with the job of checking out a company he hoped to buy. She visited it and returned with her recommendation: Buy. Why? The numbers said so.

McCown then visited, and what he saw shocked him. "I could tell in the first two minutes of talking to the CEO that he was experiencing serious burnout. The guy was being overwhelmed by problems. On paper, things looked great. But he knew what was coming down the line. Jane had missed those cues completely." She no longer works for the firm.

Goleman's book *Emotional Intelligence,* used science to confirm what common sense has long observed: There's more to success than having a high IQ. Knowing when to laugh at the boss's jokes, when to trust a coworker with a confidence, and when someone is on the verge of a nervous breakdown are, collectively, a form of smarts every bit as vital to workplace survival as understanding the electoral college or knowing how to do cube roots.

Goleman doesn't denigrate IQ. He merely notes that in a group of people with identical IQs, some will outperform the others. Something more than IQ is at work. The mental component of "something more" is EQ.

It has, he says, five dimensions: knowing one's own emotions and controlling them; recognizing emotions in others (empathy) and controlling them; and self-motivation. Empathy—the ability to see life as somebody else sees it—he considers the fundamental skill of management.

Moreover, Goleman asserts, emotional intelligence is handmaiden to IQ. When the emotions are at peace IQ functions static-free. When they are engaged positively, they can enhance intellectual performance. Proof? Dr. Robert Rosenthal, a professor of psychology at Harvard and an expert on empathy, has shown that when people giving IQ tests treat their subjects warmly, the subjects score higher.

Goleman's book has struck a nerve, I think, because it plays off a couple of deeply held folk beliefs:

- Smart people can be "too smart for their own good," falling prey to their own special stupidities. The dim, by contrast, possess a mystic wisdom.

- Smartness isn't, by itself, especially attractive (which may account for the poor newsstand sales of *Playboy*'s November 1985 cover—"The Women of Mensa"). Dumbness, however, is forever amiable. If the long march of 20th-century film comedians (Ed Wynn, Stan Laurel, Shemp Howard, Lou Costello, Huntz Hall, Red Skelton, Jerry Lewis, Jim Carrey) proves anything at all, it is that three generations of imbeciles are not enough.

We digress.

Goleman's book holds valuable insights for navigating the reefs and shoals of a contemporary career. The skills he describes are exactly those required of people struggling to lead (or work within) a group. Thanks to the weakening of corporate hierarchies, ours is the age of the group.

Ellen Hart, a vice president of Gemini Consulting and a specialist in group dynamics, thinks the advent of group structure has wrought subtle changes to the Peter Principle: Men and women still may rise to the level of their incompetence; but incompetence now manifests itself, most often, as a want of EQ. A star—a technician with a specialty—rises to a height at which, if he is to advance any further, he must solicit help from others. To get it, he must learn how to persuade, listen, exercise patience and restraint, offer sympathy, feel empathy, and recover from the emotional assaults common to group give-and-take.

At Chemical Bank, Ernest Pelli's bosses suggested he polish these very skills. So, late on a Thursday night in Manhattan, Pelli, 32, attends a Dale Carnegie class, explaining to classmates that he is there "to practice showing interest in other people." Trained as an accountant, he rates his technical skills as very good. But Chemical wanted him to work on "the intangibles"—the people skills required of managers. "Especially in accounting," he explains, "you see a lot of people who are interested only in the technical aspect." When, for example, the bank values an asset one way and the client another, a lack of EQ skills can make discussions "more contentious than they need to be."

The emotionally illiterate can degrade what Yale psychologist Robert Sternberg calls "group IQ." The term doesn't refer to the numerical average of team members' individual IQs, but to how harmoniously players work together. Though the group may never work smarter than its members' strengths would suggest, it certainly can work dumber by allowing friction and infighting to frustrate its efforts.

At Bell Labs, researchers for the *Harvard Business Review* studied e-mail patterns to determine why certain scientists underperformed their equally distinguished colleagues. What they found was that scientists who were disliked had been frozen out of the informal e-chat circles that distributed advice, gossip, and other useful information. When these pariahs asked for help from netmates in times of crisis, what they got was the cold e-shoulder.

Computers, so successful at modeling other aspects of human intelligence, haven't yet mastered EQ, which may explain why companies are starting to value it more highly.

At Forte Hotels, a computer does what a smart person might once have done, noting and recording each guest's preferences. No human need recall that Mrs. Dunbar likes white roses on her nightstand. That information is recalled automatically the next time she books a reservation. What form of human intelligence does Sir Rocco Forte, CEO, most prize?

"I know the most amazing waitress," he says. "She can look at a counterful of people eating breakfast and tell immediately who wants chatting up, who wants to be left alone. Uncanny. Just uncanny."

Employers have begun to screen for EQ attributes. Jonathan Grayer, CEO of Kaplan Educational Centers in New York City, sees a new type of test aborning. "We've had, in just the past three months, companies approach us asking us to create such a test," he says.

He thinks the Scholastic Assessment Test (formerly the Scholastic Aptitude Test), to a degree, already captures EQ.

People taking the SAT have to have mastered the content—the ability to reason, add, subtract. But if they have confidence in their ability, that plays into the score. Their ability to guess effectively under stress, the frequency with which they change their answers, their ability to go on when they've missed a question—all those things that we might call confidence or optimism are part of EQ.

The challenge for Kaplan and other testing companies is to come up with adult analogues to the "marshmallow test" made famous in Goleman's book. A child is given a marshmallow and told that if he can put off eating it until later, he can have two. Writes Goleman: "The diagnostic power of how this moment of impulse was handled became clear some 12 years to 14 years later, when the same children were tracked down as adolescents." The plucky holdouts for two marshmallows were socially more adept by any definition. At age 4, the test was twice as powerful a predicator of how the kids would do on the SAT as was IQ.

A few employers have already tried to measure aspects of EQ deemed important for certain jobs. Met Life, for example, tested salesmen for optimism. Martin Seligman, a professor of psychology at the University of Pennsylvania, had found that optimism was predictive of academic performance. Success in Seligman's words, came down to a "combination of reasonable talent [with] the ability to keep going in the face of defeat." Might the same be true for insurance salesmen, who must constantly rebound from having doors slammed in their face? Met Life said: Go find out.

Seligman discovered that in the first two years on the job, salesmen who scored high for optimism sold 37 percent more insurance than their more pessimistic brethren. Seligman then tried another experiment: Applicants who were optimists, but who failed to meet Met Life's other standard test criteria, were hired anyway. This group outsold its pessimistic counterparts by 21 percent its first year and by 57 percent the next.

Seligman now believes optimism can be taught and has devoted a book to that subject (*Learned Optimism*). What about the other competencies subsumed in EQ? Can they be learned?

There's no question that the observational skills supporting empathy can be sharpened. Jim Brosnahan, a star litigator with the San Francisco law firm of Morrison & Foerster, has devoted a professional lifetime to reading the cues and clues that signal, often unconsciously, what people are thinking and feeling. "Most of us don't use our powers of observation," he says. "The way people gesture, the look in their eyes, their tone of voice—it all discloses how they feel."

The most accomplished observers, thinks Brosnahan, can further refine their powers. "I see it all the time in trial work and in poker." Poker? An entire school of poker playing holds that the best way to beat an opponent is to watch his "tells"—pokerese for body language. Does the player, for example, look away from his cards in a way that suggests lack of interest? It likely means he's got a killer hand. Whole books have been devoted to cataloguing and diagnosing tells.

On a deeper level, EQ can be cultivated to assist problem solving and decision making. Traditional, analytical approaches to decision making, as taught in business school and the military, are described succinctly in *The Thinker's Toolkit: Fourteen Skills for Making Smarter Decisions in Business and Life,* by Morgan Jones, a former teacher of analytic skills for the CIA. In most, the decision maker assigns weight or rank to variables, based on his estimation of their significance. For example: For your big interview on Tuesday, should you wear your blue suit or your brown plaid plus fours? Easy: the blue suit. Experience tells you so. Says Jones: "We would be in serious trouble making decisions without this built-in software for ranking."

How serious trouble? Goleman gives an extreme (but real) example: A corporate lawyer underwent brain surgery for removal of a tumor. All his cognitive functions emerged intact, including logic and memory, but he somehow lost his emotional capacity to form preferences. He no longer knew whether he preferred to sleep with the window open or shut or if he preferred coffee to tea.

He found it virtually impossible to make even simple decisions quickly, since, faced with a choice of several equally logical choices, his gut feeling for each was neutral. Goleman's point: "While strong feelings can create havoc in reasoning, the lack of an awareness of them can be ruinous."

Since gut instinct, bidden or not, enters into rational decision-making, experts have begun to wonder if the gut might not be harnessed to the decision-maker's advantage. The most interesting research, so far, comes from the military, where battlefield exigencies discourage use of neat decision trees.

John Schmitt, a major in the U.S. Marine Corps Reserves, has studied the way officers actually make decisions on the battlefield. Most of the time they don't use analytical constructs. They size up a situation and do what gut instinct tells them. That process Schmitt calls intuitive decision making. "It's a sensing activity," he says, "essentially artistic."

Gary Klein, Ph.D., owner and chief scientist of Klein Associates, which does R&D in applied cognitive psychology for the military, explains how intuitive decision making works: "People call it 'intuitive,' and I guess that's accurate; but the word conjures up an image of Luke Skywalker summoning the Force." The approach, he says, is anything but mysterious.

People with years of experience to draw upon quickly recognize a pattern of information that might mean nothing to a novice. While the novice would have to attack the problem by considering, analytically, many possible solutions, the experienced person sees a possible solution immediately—not the best solution, maybe, but one that works.

Says Klein: "This is different from the kind of advice you get in management books, which say look at all the options and identify the evaluation criteria and weigh the options numerically, and see which option has the highest score. Everybody talks about that approach. The fact is, hardly anybody ever uses it."

Decisions reached via gut get attributed to "intuition," says Klein, because people lack a vocabulary to explain what they're really doing: using a sophisticated form of pattern recognition. "Because we don't have a vocabulary," he says, "a lot of organizations don't trust it."

The Marine Corps wants to trust it more. To that end, it tried a novel experiment in December. For two days, 11 senior officers, including several generals, were remanded to the care of traders at the New York Mercantile Exchange. Why? Generals in time of war must analyze complex information quickly under high-stress conditions, making split-second decisions. Traders do that all the time, as they buy and sell and shout and scream at each other in the pits. Perhaps these most uncivil civilians could teach the generals a thing or two. So, after a little coaching (and after the exchange had closed for the evening), the generals began to trade.

It wasn't pretty. Real traders winced as their pretend counterparts yelled things to one another like, "Ten at $290, sir!" One general said to another condescendingly, "No, no. I'm the seller; you're the buyer." Slowly, however, they improved, and by session's end the guys with diamond studs in their ears were patting their charges on their olive-drab backs. Said Lieutenant General Paul K. Van Riper: "Analytical problem solving is fine, if you've got all the time in the world. With these guys, it's all ingrained. If they have to stop to think about it, they lose millions of dollars."

Shoshana Zuboff, a professor of business administration at Harvard, says organizations that don't trust intuition are making a mistake. "So many people go awry because they use sterile analytic tools," she says. She uses the example of a shoe company deciding what new style of women's shoe to make. The company could reach one sort of decision by studying market analysis. It could reach an entirely different—and perhaps superior—one by going to shoe stores, listening to customers' comments, and using a little empathy to put itself into the shopper's shoes.

If the gut is the practical site of decision-making, how can one make it smarter?

Says Klein: "We've not found a strategy we can teach people to make them better decision-makers, because what distinguishes the better ones is their body of experience." Smartness, then, lies in gaining more experience—as much relevant experience as you can get your hands on. That may not always be easy, says Klein. "Somebody can sit in a fire department that's not very busy and, 10 years later, emerge not very skilled. In a busy one, they build up experience more quickly."

An employee who wants to sharpen her decision-making should ask, for example, to be rotated through a variety of jobs within her specialty and to serve on task forces, and should try to soak up as much secondhand experience as she can from old-timers in the office. Prospectively, she should try to anticipate the types of experience that will be needed tomorrow: Is the corporation expanding to Mexico? Taking a vacation south of the border to get a better feeling for Mexican culture might not be dumb.

Ellen Hart of Gemini Consulting thinks one of the smartest things an employee can do is to assume full management of his own career. Keeping a job—any job—is not, after all, the test of smartness. Smartness is making sure your intellectual and emotional abilities are matched to a job that promotes their growth. If EQ and IQ are telling you your job no longer fits, it may be time to ask yourself: Is your job smart enough to keep you?

Should You Be a Negotiator?

Ray Friedman

Bruce Barry

For decades, researchers have tried to find if there were any connections between individual characteristics and bargaining outcomes. These researchers studied an array of personality measures—including "Machiavellianism," "authoritarianism," and "interpersonal orientation"—but the results were contradictory and inconclusive. We decided to conduct a more comprehensive and careful study of individual differences and negotiations. The results were surprising.

We began by building upon recent advances in the study of personality. Instead of hundreds of idiosyncratic personality types, psychologists have identified five overarching elements of personality and developed better ways to measure these elements. Three of them, we thought, might relate to negotiations. A person who is "extraverted" is sociable, talkative, and excitable. An "agreeable" person tends to be generous, cooperative and flexible. And a "conscientious" person is organized, persevering, and planful. In addition to these three personality factors or traits, we examined how general intelligence affects the outcome of negotiating situations.

For win-lose negotiations, such as haggling over a used car, we thought those who were agreeable would tend to be more easily influenced by their opponent and more uncomfortable with the conflict. They would be less aggressive in opening offers, more easily anchored by their opponent's opening offer, and more likely to give in to the other side. We thought those who were extraverted would be more likely to reveal secret information and more influenced by opponent opening offers, since they were more socially engaged with the opponent. Those who were conscientious would plan better for negotiations, we thought, and be better able to counter opponent tactics. Similarly, we assumed general intelligence helps negotiators, making it easier to understand what tactics make sense.

To test these predictions, we put hundreds of students through a simulated business negotiation involving a simple win-lose premise: a supplier and a manufacturer negotiating over the price of a single component. We had these same students fill out personality tests, and we consulted their standardized academic test scores as a measure of intelligence. (Tests like the SAT and the GMAT are well accepted as pretty good measures of what psychologists call "general cognitive ability," or general intelligence.)

Reprinted from *Owen Manager* (Summer, 1999) pp. 8–9. Used with permission.

To our surprise, conscientiousness and intelligence had no effects. (In other studies of employee accomplishments these were usually the most important factors predicting success.) Agreeableness and extraversion, however, did impact bargaining outcomes and in the ways we predicted.

Those who were extraverted tended more than others to raise their opening offers when their opponent started high. In other words, extraverts were likely to be swayed by an opponent's extreme first offer (for example, thinking "hmm, she's asking a very high price—perhaps those widgets are worth more than I thought"). Those who were agreeable had the same problem and in the end came away with lower results for themselves.

Thus, for this type of win-lose negotiation, how you tend to engage socially with the opponent makes a difference, but intelligence and planning does not. The implication: If you are extraverted or agreeable, be aware that your personality may undermine your ability to do well in this kind of bargaining encounter. You may be easily influenced by an opponent's tactics in win-lose bargaining. Perhaps you should not be the one to negotiate these types of deals.

We did, however, find one silver lining that may help people high in extraversion or agreeableness overcome these risks. The effects of these traits were less pronounced among those who entered our simulated negotiations with high expectations for themselves. A robust principle, confirmed by many research studies, is that negotiators who come to the bargaining table with high aspirations generally do better for themselves. People with high aspirations seem to pay more attention to the dynamics of the situation and bargain more aggressively.

So, if you are high in these traits of extraversion or agreeableness, and have to or want to be at the bargaining table, make sure you set high aspirations for yourself. Although this may seem like good common-sense advice, the fact is many negotiators, especially inexperienced ones, don't take the time to think seriously in advance about what they hope to gain from an encounter. And those who do may have relatively little confidence in their ability to do well, and as a result carry into the encounter rather modest expectations. The research tells us that high expectations often translate into better outcomes, and this may be particularly true for individuals whose personalities otherwise work against them.

We also studied a very different type of negotiation—one that allows for the creation of mutual gain through creative problem solving. There are many situations like the previous one in this article, where negotiating is just a pure haggle over a single issue, like the price of an object for sale. But other situations are far more complex, with negotiators trying to sort their way through several issues—some of which involve shared interests and some of which involve divergent interests. The challenge in these situations is to figure out where agreements can benefit both parties and where compromises have to be made—all while juggling a variety of concerns and issues. These types of encounters, sometimes called "mixed motive" situations, are more likely to be found in complex business negotiations, political disputes, and the like. To the extent that bargainers can successfully find common ground and produce a settlement that pleases both parties, these situations are also sometimes referred to as "win-win" bargaining encounters.

For these negotiations we had different predictions. We expected those who were agreeable and extraverted to do better, since information sharing and cooperation help problem solving. We also expected intelligence to be a plus, since cognitive ability helps negotiators develop creative solutions to complex problems. We tested these predictions by, again, having students participate in a bargaining simulation. But this time, the simulation was more complex—a negotiation between a shopping mall developer and a potential retail tenant. Price was not the issue; rather, bargainers had to hammer out a contractual agreement regarding several issues related to the use, potential subletting, and assignment of the leased property. We evaluated and coded these agreements in order to test our predictions about how personality and intelligence would affect who does well and whether both parties can benefit from the individual characteristics of bargainers.

To our surprise, agreeableness and extraversion had no effects. How one interacts socially with the other side did not affect the results of this type of "win-win" negotiation. Intelligence, however, did yield the results we expected. The smarter negotiators were, the more they were able to produce creative, well-structured solutions to difficult bargaining problems. The smarter the negotiators were, the bigger the pie that was split between the two sides.

In one twist to this story, we examined whether one side or the other captured for themselves a bigger share of the increased value from joint gains. In other words, if bargaining pairs featuring at least one "smarter" person were able to generate a bigger pie to split, who got how much of the pie? You might assume that the smarter of the two individuals would grab the bigger share of whatever is at stake. But surprisingly, it turned out that those who bargained with a smarter opponent did better for themselves. The moral of the story: In negotiations where there is a need for creative problem solving, try to negotiate with the smartest opponent you can. In these kinds of complex situations, the real gains come not necessarily from crushing the other person with aggressiveness, but from finding creative ways to solve problems that add value for both parties. Our study suggests that more smarts at the bargaining table—whether yours or the other person's—increases the chances that creative solutions benefiting both parties can be discovered.

Stepping back to look at both of our studies, the results were intriguing. For win-lose negotiations, personality matters but intelligence does not matter. For win-win negotiations, personality does not matter, but intelligence does matter. There is no one overall best person to do all negotiations; rather, who is best for negotiation depends on the type of negotiation. Whether you are the right person to negotiate depends on the situation.

The challenge is to know yourself and what type of negotiation you are facing. Many people assume that success in bargaining is a simple matter of nerve and tactical aggressiveness. Our research tells a different and more complicated story. Different types of bargaining situations call for different types of tactics and quite possibly different types of negotiators. Personality traits that help you in one kind of situation may undermine your success in another. Much of our teaching covers exactly these points—what are your tendencies when you negotiate, and how can you tell if a negotiation has the potential for mutual gains? Effective negotiators are apt to have a thoughtful response to both of these questions.

SECTION ELEVEN

Global Negotiations

International Negotiations: An Entirely Different Animal

Drew Martin

Jackie Mayfield

Milton Mayfield

Paul Herbig

INTRODUCTION

The impact of international business to American companies has been considerably understated. With two-way trade in goods and services mounting to well over $1 trillion dollars and over 20 percent of the U.S. GDP in 1994, no part of the economy is sacrosanct and can avoid the international dimension. Over 70 percent of American firms are actively competing against foreign firms. If an American firm is not competing against a foreign firm, chances are it is either being supplied by or selling to foreign-based firms. Foreign direct investment in the United States has reached over $400 billion and continues to increase year by year. Foreign direct investment by U.S. multinationals exceeds even that tremendous amount, and continues to increase. In the decade of the nineties, the only firms that will be exempt from dealing with foreign entities, either U.S.-based affiliates or foreign customers, suppliers, or competitors, will be those firms that are out of business or are going out of business. The playing field for business is now the globe. Businesses of all sizes must search the entire world for customers and suppliers.

As the proportion of foreign to domestic trade increases, so does the frequency of business negotiations between people from different countries and cultures. Experts estimate that over 50 percent of an international manager's time is spent negotiating. At the forefront of international business opportunities are the agreements between firms. Agreements are the most important international documents that must be negotiated between firms of different nationalities. Since implementation has become increasingly difficult and complex, cross-cultural negotiations has begun to take on an increasing importance to the globalizing firm. Every sale or purchase has its negotiation aspect and

Reprinted from *Journal of Professional Services Marketing* 17, no. 1 (1998), pp. 43–61. Copyright 1998, The Haworth Press, Inc., Binghamton, NY.

every negotiation presents opportunities and dangers for both parties. International negotiations are fast becoming a fact of life for a growing number of U.S.-based firms. Failure to negotiate effectively can undo careful prior planning; operating across national cultures often magnifies negotiation problems.

DIFFERENCES BETWEEN INTERNATIONAL AND DOMESTIC NEGOTIATIONS

Points important in international (cross-cultural) negotiations which are normally unimportant in domestic negotiations and which could become barriers to global deal include (Salacuse, 1991): (1) negotiating environment, (2) cultural and subcultural differences (it is important to know whether you are negotiating with a Hindu or a Moslem in India, with an Moslem or Coptic in Egypt, or with a Kongo or Muluba in Zaire), (3) ideological differences, (4) foreign bureaucracy, (5) foreign laws and governments, (6) financial insecurity due to international monetary factors, and (7) political instability and sudden political and economic changes. Barriers increase the risk of failure and lengthen the time it takes to arrive at a deal. Many foreign governments must be convinced that a deal is consistent with their country's overall economic priorities before they will enter into discussions.

An important dimension to cross-cultural negotiations is culture shock. Culture shock occurs when a person finds himself in a place where all his prior norms are challenged and no longer correct; entire sets of values, rules, and attitudes are different. Culture shock can incapacitate a visitor, causing him to withdraw from contact with other persons, feel confused, become excessively concerned about his health, or refuse to eat any local food. If seriously disoriented, visitors can actually fall physically ill. Familiar psychological clues that help an individual to function in society (as provided by his or her host culture) are suddenly withdrawn and replaced by new ones that are strange or incomprehensible. The effects of culture shock vary from individual to individual. It is common for people to suffer from anxiety, confusion, and apathy when they are first immersed in an unfamiliar environment. The emotional stress of the situation can easily lead to emotional and intellectual withdrawal. Culture shock has been known to cause violent aggressive behavior in previously docile personalities.

CULTURAL INFLUENCES IN NEGOTIATIONS

All human interactions are, by definition, intercultural. When two individuals meet, it is an intercultural encounter since they both have different (sometimes drastically different, if not opposite) ways to perceive, discover, and create reality. All negotiations are therefore intercultural. Negotiations with a boss, spouse, child, friend, fellow employee, union representative, official from a foreign country, and so on are all interculturally loaded. In some countries, negotiating is seen in practically every transaction, from settling a taxi fare to buying bread. Intercultural negotiations do not only exist because people who think, feel, and behave differently have to reach agreements on practical matters such as how to produce, consume, organize, and distribute power and grant rewards, but because of the very nature of the challenging, unpredictable, and contradictory world we live in. We are forced to negotiate. In every negotiation (domestic or international), the participants have different points of view and different objectives.

When you are negotiating with someone from your own country, it is often possible to expedite communications by making reasonable cultural assumptions. The situation reverses itself when two cultures are involved. Making assumptions about another culture is often counterproductive since it can lead to misunderstandings and miscommunications. The international negotiator must be careful not to allow cultural stereotypes to determine his or her relations with local businesspersons. Needs, values, interests, and expectations may differ dramatically. Many have little if any shared experience. It is like the proverbial fish out of water: When in water, a fish is unaware of any possible alternate environments; the water surrounding the fish is all it knows of the universe; hence, the whole universe must be made of water. Only when the fish is removed from the water does it perceive a different environment.

What gives a person his or her identity no matter where he or she was born is his or her culture—the total communication framework. Culture is a set of shared and enduring meanings, values, and beliefs that characterize national, ethnic, or other groups and orient their behavior. Culture directs judgment and opinion, describes the criteria for what is good or bad. Language structures reality and orders experience. Culture is the property of a society, it is acquired through acculturation or socialization by the individual from the society, and it subsumes every area of social life. The language of an individual significantly influences his or her perceptions and thoughts. Culture may be an obstacle to the extent that cultural stereotypes and differences distort signals and cause misunderstandings. National negotiating styles combine culture, history, political system, and economic status. Some cultures are likely to search for compromise while others will strive for consensus and still others will fight until surrender is achieved. Some cultures prefer a deductive approach: first agree on principles and later these principles can be applied to particular issues. Other cultures think inductively: deal with problems at hand and principles will develop.

Culture impacts negotiation in four ways: by conditioning one's perception of reality, by blocking out information inconsistent or unfamiliar with culturally grounded assumptions, by projecting meaning onto the other party's words and actions, and impelling the ethnocentric observer to an incorrect attribution of motive. Culture affects the range of strategies that negotiators develop as well as the many ways they are tactically implemented. Israeli preference for direct forms of communication and the Egyptian preference for indirect forms exacerbate relations between the two countries. The Egyptians interpreted Israeli directness as aggression and were insulted; the Israelis viewed Egyptian indirectness with impatience and viewed it as insincere. Negotiators are likely to assess foreign cultures through their own cultural lenses, to interpret and judge other cultures by their own standards.

Nations tend to have a national character that influences the types of goals and process the society pursues in negotiations. This character is called culture: "the collective programming of the mind which distinguishes the members of one human group from another." A cultural dimension exists in the way negotiators view the negotiation process. In international negotiations, you bring to the negotiating table the values, beliefs, and background interference of your culture and normally will unconsciously use those elements in both the presentation and interpretation of the data. Culture influences members' negotiations—through their conceptualizations of the process, the ends they target, the means they use, and the expectations they hold of counterparts' behavior. Ample evidence exists that such negotiation rules and practices vary across cultures. Thus cross-cultural negotiators bring into contact unfamiliar and potentially conflicting sets of categories, rules, plans, and behaviors. The cross-cultural negotiator cannot take common knowledge and practices for granted. Difficulties sometimes arise from the different expectations negotiators have regarding the social setting of the negotiation. These patterns can extend to styles of decision making (the way officials and executives structure their negotiation communication systems and reach institutional decisions) and logical reasoning (the way issues are conceptualized, the way evidence and new information are used, or the way one point seems to lead to the next, paying more attention to some arguments than others, different weight to legal, technical, or personal relations). Culture influences negotiation through its effects on communications. Intercultural differences may cause misperceptions and misunderstandings.

DIMENSIONS OF CULTURE

Beliefs and behaviors differ between cultures because each develops its own means for coping with life. Culture has been defined as "the collective programming of the mind which distinguishes members of one human group from another" (Hofstede, 1984:21). Hofstede devised four cultural dimensions which could explain much of the differences between cultures. These four dimensions are masculinity, uncertainty avoidance, power distance, and individualism.

Masculine cultures value assertiveness, independence, task orientation, and self achievement (traditional "masculine" characteristics) while feminine cultures value cooperation, nurturing, relationships, solidarity with the less fortunate, modesty, and quality of life (traditional "feminine" characteristics). Masculine societies tend to have more rigid division of sex roles. Masculine cultures subscribe to "live-to-work" while feminine societies subscribe to "work-to-live." The competitiveness and assertiveness embedded in masculinity may result in individuals perceiving the negotiation situation in win-lose terms. Masculinity is related to assertiveness and competitiveness while femininity is related to empathy and social relations; a more distributive process is expected in masculine societies where the party with the most competitive behavior is likely to gain more. The most masculine country is Japan, followed by Latin American countries. The most feminine societies are Nordic countries.

Uncertainty avoidance refers to the degree to which one feels uncomfortable in risky and ambiguous (uncertain, unpredictable) situations, favors conformity and safe behavior, and tolerates deviant ideas. In high uncertainty avoidance cultures, people tend to avoid uncertain situations while in low uncertainty avoidance cultures, people are generally more comfortable with ambiguous uncertain situations and are more accepting of risk. Low risk-avoiders require much less information, have fewer people involved in the decision making, and can act quickly. High risk avoidance cultures tend to have lots of formal bureaucratic rules, rely on rituals, standards, and formulas, and trust only family and friends. People in low uncertainty avoidance societies dislike hierarchy and typically find it inefficient and destructive. In weak uncertainty avoidance cultures, deviance and new ideas are more highly tolerated. Uncertainty avoidance may lead to focus on the obvious competitive and positional aspects of negotiation and may hinder the exchange of information on interests and development of creative proposals. A problem-solving orientation is likely to be found in cultures characterized by low uncertainty avoidance and low power distance. The United States, the Nordic nations, Hong Kong, and Singapore all have low uncertainty avoidance.

Power distance refers to the acceptance of authority differences between people; the difference between those who hold power and those affected by power. In low power distance one strives for power equalization and justice while high power distance cultures are status conscious respectful of age and seniority. In high power cultures, outward forms of status such as protocol, formality, and hierarchy are considered important. Decisions regarding reward and redress of grievances are usually based on personal judgments made by powerholders. Power distance implies a willingness to accept that the party which comes out most forcefully gets a larger share of the benefit than the other party. A low power distance culture values competence over seniority with resulting consultative management style. Low power distance cultures include the Anglo-American, Nordic, and Germanic cultures. High power distance cultures are Latin America, South Asia, and Arabic cultures. Low masculinity and low power distance may be related to the sharing of information and the offering of multiple proposals as well as more cooperative and creative behavior. High masculinity and high power distance may result in competitive behavior, threats, and negative reactions.

In individualistic cultures, a tendency exists to put task before relationship and to value independence highly. Individuals in individualistic cultures are expected to take care of themselves, to value the needs of the individual over that of the collective, the group, community, or society. These individuals are self-actualized, self-motivated and any relationships are defined by self-interest. Collectivism implies ingroup solidarity, loyalty, and strong perceived interdependence among individuals. Relationships are based on mutual self-interest and dependent on the success of the group. Collectivistic cultures emphasize face, protecting others' self-image while individualistic cultures emphasize protecting one's own self-image and freedom from imposition. Collectivist cultures define themselves in terms of their membership within groups, sharply distinguishing ingroups from outgroups. Maintaining the integrity of ingroups is stressed so that cooperation, conflict avoidance, solidarity, and conformity dominate. Individualistic cultures tend to value open conflict while collectivist societies tend to minimize conflict. Individualistic cultures tend to have linear logic while collectivist societies tend to stress abstract, general agreements over concrete, specific issues. Collectivist arguments tend to contain appeals to the emotional and imagery.

Collectivistic negotiators tend to assume that details can be worked out in the future if two negotiators can agree on generalities. Collectivist societies tend to use more solution oriented strategies than do individualist societies, who are prone to use more controlling strategies. Collectivist societies show more concern for the needs of the other party and focus more on group goals than do individualist societies. Members from individualist societies expect the other side's negotiators to have the ability to make decisions unilaterally, something difficult or impossible in collectivist societies.

Members from collectivist societies are annoyed to find individualist culture negotiating members promoting their own positions, decisions, and ideas, sometimes even openly contradicting one another. The United States, United Kingdom, Netherlands, France, and the Nordic countries are highly individualistic. Latin American and Asian countries tend to be highly collectivist.

VARIABLES INFLUENCING CROSS-CULTURAL NEGOTIATIONS

The process of international business negotiation is considered to be influenced by two groups of variables (Ghauri):

1. Background factors, which includes the parties' objectives, often categorized as being common, conflicting, or complementary. Other aspects include third parties involved, such as consultants, agents, and the respective government. The position of the market (seller's versus buyer's) and finally, the skills and experience of the negotiators.

2. Atmosphere is the perceived "milieu." It can include: perceived cooperation/conflict— that the parties have something to negotiate for and something to negotiate about; power and dependence—that one of the parties gains more power in the relationship; and perceived distance—that the parties are unable to understand each other. Finally, the expectations, long-term expectations of the true deals or benefits and short-term expectations, concerning the prospects of the present deal.

Weiss (1983) identified 12 variables in the negotiations process which will lead to understand negotiating styles better include the following:

Basic Concept.   Different groups view the purpose and process of negotiation differently. Negotiation may be seen as a conflict in which one side wins and another loses, as a competition to identify who is best or as a collaborative process to formulate some undertaking. The winner of a negotiation in some countries is the one who gains the most concessions regardless of the value of the concessions. Americans tend to see negotiations as a competitive process; the Japanese see it as collaborative.

Criteria for Selecting Negotiators.   Different groups choose negotiators on the basis of a variety of factors. Negotiators may be selected on the basis of their previous experience, their status, knowledge of a particular subject, or personal attributes such as trustworthiness. Americans tend to select negotiators on the basis of ability and experience; the Japanese look for high-status negotiators.

Issues Stressed.   Different groups stress different aspects of the negotiations. Some groups stress substantive issues directly related to the agreement while others stress relationships. Americans tend to stress substantive issues (price, delivery, quality) while the Japanese are more concerned with building relationships.

Protocol.   Different groups have their own particular etiquette associated with the negotiation process and their adherence to protocol varies according to its perceived importance. Protocol factors that should be considered are gift giving, entertainment, dress codes, seating arrangements, numbers of negotiators, timing of breaks, planned duration of the process of negotiations. Degree of formality or informality is an important component of protocol that should be assessed. Americans tend to be informal; the Japanese are conservative and formal.

Communications.   Different groups communicate in different ways and are more comfortable with one or another form of communications. Some groups rely on verbal communications, others on nonverbal such as gestures, space, and silence. Some groups rely on one method, others mixed. The more varied the methods of communications, the more complex is the communications context and the more care must be given to understand this context. Americans tend to be verbal; Japanese often use periods of silence.

Nature of Persuasive Arguments.   Different groups attempt to persuade others and are persuaded by the use of a variety of different types of arguments. Some rely on facts and logical arguments, others on tradition and the way things were done in the past, still others on intuition or emotion, and others on the beliefs associated with a particular religion or philosophy. Americans emphasize empirical information and rational arguments; the Japanese rely more on sensitivity and intuition.

Role of the Individual.   Individuals play different roles in different societies. In some groups, the individual is seen as very important and a particular individual's success or failure can depend on the outcome of the negotiation process. In other groups, individuals are subordinate to the home negotiating party and personal ambitions are contained. Still others may view the entire group as consisting of all negotiation parties, both home and host, and are most concerned with achieving overall success. Americans are individualistic; the Japanese are collectivist and rely on the group as a whole in the negotiations process.

Basis for Trust.   Trust is a necessity if groups are going to work together to their mutual benefit and all groups seek to establish trust with the other parties in the negotiation process. Each group may, however, establish trust on a different basis. Some groups look to past experience and past records, others rely on intuition and emotion, and still others are most comfortable when sanctions exist to guarantee performance. Americans look to the past record of those with whom they are negotiating and trust in sanctions; the Japanese are more concerned with the relationships that have been built with their counterparts.

Risk-Taking Propensity.   Negotiations involve a degree of risk because the final outcome is unknown when the negotiations begin. Different groups view uncertainty and risk as relatively desirable or undesirable. Some groups are therefore open to new ideas and unexpected suggestions whereas others prefer to remain within the expected boundaries and accustomed agreements. Americans tend to take risks and accept uncertainty; the Japanese are more risk averse.

View of Time.   The value of time differs from one group to another. Some people view time as limited and something to be used wisely. Punctuality, agenda, and specified timeframes are important to them. Others view time as plentiful and always available; therefore, they are more likely to expect negotiations to progress slowly and to be flexible about schedules. Americans view time as a scarce commodity that must be maximized so as not to be wasted; the Japanese view time in the long term.

Decision-Making Systems.   Decisions are made differently in different groups. They may be made by individuals or by the group as a whole. Within a group, participants may defer to the person of highest status or to the most senior group member; alternatively, some groups accept the decision of the majority of the group members; other groups seek consensus among group members and will not make a decision until all members have agreed.

Form of Agreement.   In some cultures, written agreements are expected; in others verbal agreements or a handshake is accepted. In some cultures, agreements are detailed and set out as many points as possible, discussing contingencies and potential events; in others, broad general agreements are preferred with details to be worked out as they arise. In some cultures, agreements are expected to be legally binding; in others, there is little faith in legal contracts and much more emphasis is placed on a person's obligation to keep his or her word.

Fisher (1980) identified five considerations that should be addressed before negotiating with persons from another culture: the players and the situation (find out how negotiators and negotiating teams are selected and the background of the players), decision-making styles (the way members of the other negotiating team reach a decision), national character (differences in culture), cultural noise (anything that would distract or interfere with the message being communicated), and the use of interpreters and translators (positively gives one more time to think about statements, but it may not convey the full intended message). Moran and Stripp (1991, pg. 92) indicate four components affect the outcome of intercultural negotiations: policy (basic concept of negotiation, selection of negotiators, role of individuals, concern with protocol, and type of issue), interaction (complexity of language, nature of persuasion, value of time), deliberation (bases of trust, risk-taking propensity, internal decision-making function), and outcome (form of satisfactory agreement).

Casse and Deol (1991) provide the list of factors that must be considered when negotiating internationally: appreciation of cultural differences, conscious endeavor to manage cultural differences, communicate clearly and effectively, ascertain expectations and work for their achievement, narrow down difference and emphasize commonalities, both written and unwritten aspects of negotiations are important, give and take, familiarize yourself with management styles and assumptions of other side, establish your credibility, reduce differences to reach an agreement, appreciate problems and limitations of the other side, be systematic and simple, manage conflicting interests, and create the need first.

Harris and Moran (1991) propose four communicative negotiating styles. They argue that negotiators around the globe differ in terms of cultural conditioning regarding the nature of negotiation, trust, problem solving, importance of protocol selection of negotiation team, and view of the decision-making process.

Normative: Concentrates on creating a harmonious relationship between bargainers. This style requires attention to self and other emotions and values. Appeal to emotions to reach a fair deal.

Intuitive: Imagination solves problems. Intuitive negotiators look to the future, offer creative solutions, draw attention to prospective opportunities being created in present agreements, and follow their inspirations of the moment.

Analytic: Logical analysis leads to universally true conclusions. Forming reasons, drawing conclusions, identifying cause and effect, and weighing the pros and cons.

Factual: Facts speak for themselves. Points out facts and details in a neutral way, keeps track of what has been said, and clarifies the issues.

THE PROCESS OF INTERCULTURAL NEGOTIATIONS

According to Graham (1984, 1986, 1987, 1989) intercultural negotiations consist of four major processes:

- Non-task sounding (rapport).
- Task-related exchange of information.
- Persuasion, compromise.
- Concessions and agreement.

Although all negotiations include these four aspects, strategies, tactics, content duration and sequence spent in each phase, emphasis and importance of phase differ between cultures. Non-task sounding focuses on establishing a relationship among the negotiating parties. During this stage, information specific to the issue under negotiation is not considered; rather, the parties seek to get to know each other. Task-related exchange of information focuses on providing information directly connected to the issue under negotiation. During this stage, each party explains its needs and preferences. Persuasion focuses on efforts to modify the views of the other parties and sway them to "our" way of thinking. This stage of negotiations is often intertwined with other stages (i.e., persuasion goes on while exchanging information and making concessions). Concessions and agreement are the culmination of the negotiation process at which an agreement is reached. To reach an agreement that is mutually acceptable, each side frequently must give up some things; concessions by both sides are usually necessary to reach an agreement.

FAILURE AND SUCCESS IN CROSS-CULTURAL NEGOTIATIONS

Bargaining means many different things to different people from different cultures. If one does not bargain aggressively with Arabs, one is considered naive. In traditional Arab culture, the bargaining, the haggling, the give-and-take, serves many functions, not the least being the opportunity for both sides to get to know each other as individuals. The process of bargaining is meant to establish personal relationships built on a mutual perception of virtue, honesty, and personal merit. The process of extended bargaining is a vehicle for developing the critical personal relationship. For the Japanese, bargaining too soon can be a sign of untrustworthiness. Yet the Scandinavians are uncomfortable with much bargaining at all. Basic differences in the expectations of the negotiations process must be understood and accepted prior to entering into serious negotiations with another individual or group from a different cultural background.

The American business negotiator who arrives in China hoping to establish rapport by presenting his host with the gift of a fine clock creates a problem before negotiations begin. Clocks are inappropriate gifts in China. They are associated with death in China. A U.S. businessman who presented a clock to the female child of his Chinese counterpart on the occasion of her marriage not only failed to establish a rapport, his insult led to the termination of the business relationship. The Arab businessman who insists on giving his Japanese counterpart gifts of greater value than those he receives harms the alliance before it even begins to form.

A 10-year license agreement was signed between U.S.-based Cummins Engine Company Ltd. and China National Technical Import Corporation. Much of the success of the early negotiations was attributed to careful selection of the negotiation team. Cummins insisted that its people have the ability to reach across cultural lines and close intercultural gaps. It also looked for at least one member who could understand the language and thinking of its Chinese counterparts. One member of the Cummins team understood Chinese and the Chinese culture. This expertise, along with his ability to listen carefully, saved the negotiations from an early demise.When misunderstandings occurred because of poor translation, this team member assisted in resolving conflicts. For example, when one Chinese negotiator used the word "strategy," the Cummins side assumed that far-reaching strategic decisions had been made by the Chinese, when in fact the term was being used more loosely than interpreted. Throughout the negotiations, misunderstandings of mannerisms, habits, and word choices were resolved by attending to cultural differences (Schnepp et al. 1990).

MANAGEMENT IMPLICATIONS

The road to success in cross-cultural negotiations is recognizing that a foreign negotiator is different from you—in perceptions, motivation, beliefs, and outlook. Identify, understand, accept, and respect the other side's culture. One must be prepared to communicate and operate on two separate and different cultural wavelengths. One must also be culturally neutral. Being different does not denote being better or inferior. One should not cast judgment on the other party's cultural mores any more than you would want them to judge your values. It may be true that from a detached objective moral point of view some foreign customs may appear senseless, capricious, even cruel and insane to you. But remember you are visiting the country as a businessman—not as a missionary; you plan to do business there—not convert the natives to the American customs and practices. Recognize that they probably feel the same way about your culture as you do theirs. It may not be necessary to adopt their values as part of your own personal value system. All that is necessary is that you accept and respect their norms as part of their culture.

One should be sensitive to their cultural norms, try to understand what they are and how your behavior may impact them even if it causes you discomfort or emotional stress. Yet it is necessary to accept, and to proceed with the business without showing distress if one wishes to come home with an agreement beneficial to both parties and the start of a long-term healthy relationship between two companies from two cultures. Negotiations can easily break down because of a lack of understanding of the cultural component of the negotiations process. Negotiators who take the time to understand the approach that the other parties are likely to use and to adapt their own styles to that one are likely to be more effective negotiators. It is worth the time to investigate those differences prior to entering into a negotiation situation.

A knowledge of the other side's culture allows a negotiator to communicate, to understand, to plan, and to anticipate more effectively. In addition to the conventional preparation for any negotiation, the need for extensive study of the culture(s) cannot be overstressed. This should include reading about the history and customs of the country in question and discussion with others who have had experience dealing with citizens of the foreign country. The focus of these preparations should be on the culture, not the language. However, cultural stereotypes should be avoided. Although a particular approach to negotiations to a culture should be followed, sufficient flexibility should be available. Planning is crucial. We should know sufficiently, if not intimately about the cultures of the people we are going to negotiate with. Some things that are going to be irritants should be avoided. Other items are likely to facilitate the process and should be utilized effectively.

To augment his or her own capabilities, a business negotiator can employ cultural experts, translators, outside attorneys, financial advisors, or technical experts who have at least moderate and preferably high familiarity with both the counterpart's and the negotiator's cultures. These experts serve two distinguishable roles, as "agents" who replace the negotiator at the negotiating table or as "advisors" who provide information and recommend sources of action to the negotiator. The use of go-betweens, middle-men, brokers, and other intermediaries is a common practice within many cultures and represents a potentially effective approach to cross-cultural negotiation as well.

Effective international negotiators understand that negotiation, first and foremost, is not about numbers or terms or dates but personal relationships. It is about developing relationships of trust and mutual respect. He or she must become relationship oriented rather than deal oriented. The problem with deal orientation is that the difficulty of creating and entering a legal agreement across multiple legal and government jurisdictions can be insurmountable. A deal orientation is essentially static in nature while the world is dynamic. Negotiators who have an effective ongoing relationship will be able to agree to disagree and not have the disagreement negatively affect their relationship. Therefore, working on developing solid mutually beneficial relationships is the first step to traveling the road to success.

The effective international negotiator knows how to probe, how to ask questions, and how to listen. He or she seeks areas where needs are mutual and hence, easiest to satisfy, as well as being the first step toward establishing trust and relationships. Once mutual needs are established, meeting individual needs can begin to be accomplished. Sharing of information is crucial toward success. Effective international negotiators have staying power. They recognize that things take longer to communicate across cultures, that relationship building can be a time-consuming process, that the long-term perspective must be pursued. They must remain calm, not lose sight of the ultimate objectives of the negotiation, be flexible and willing to accept new conditions, remain on the creative lookout for needs, and communicate a commitment to the negotiation and the satisfaction of mutual needs. Experienced international negotiators create agendas in advance and try to get buy-in from the other side on the agenda before the actual start of the negotiation.

REFERENCES

Adler, Nancy J., and John L. Graham (1989), "Cross-Cultural Interaction: The International Comparison Fallacy," *Journal of International Business Studies,* vol. 20 (3), Fall, 515–37.

———, Theodore Swartz Gehrke, and John L. Graham (1987), "Business Negotiations in Canada, Mexico, and the United States," *Journal of Business Research,* vol. 15, October, 411–30.

Altany, David (1988), "Culture Clash: International Negotiation Etiquette," *Industry Week,* vol. 238 (October 2), 13–18.

Anand, R. P. (ed.) (1986), *Cultural Factors in International Relations,* New York: Abhinav Publications.

Banks, John C. (1987), "Negotiating International Mining Agreements: Win-Win versus Win-Lose Bargaining," *Columbia Journal of World Business* (Winter), 67–75.

Barnum, Cynthia, and Natasha Wolniansky (1989), "Why Americans Fail at Overseas Negotiations," *Management Review*, 78/10, October, 55–57.

Beliaev, Edward, Thomas Mullen, and Betty Jane Punnett (1985), "Understanding the Cultural Environment: US-USSR Trade Negotiations," *California Management Review,* vol. XXVII, no.2 (Winter), 100–10.

Binnendijk, Hans (ed.) (1987), *National Negotiating Styles*, Washington DC: Center for the Study of Foreign Affairs, Foreign Service Institute, U.S. Dept. of State.

Burt, David N. (1989), "Nuances of Negotiating Overseas," *Journal of Purchasing and Materials Management,* vol. 25, 56–64.

Campbell, Nigel C. G., John L. Graham, Alain Jilbert, and Hans Gunther Meissner (1988), "Marketing Negotiations in France, Germany, the United Kingdom and the United States," *Journal of Marketing*, vol. 52, no. 2 (April) 49–62.

Casse, Pierre, and Surinden Deal (1985), *Managing Intercultural Negotiations*, Washington DC: Sietar International.

Druckman, Daniel, Alan A. Benton, Faizunisa Ali, and J. Susana Bagur (1976), "Cultural Differences in Bargaining Behavior," *Journal of Conflict Resolution*, vol. 20, no. 3, 413–49.

Dreyfus, Patricia A., and Amy Roberts (1988), "Negotiating the Kremlin Maze," *Business Month*, vol. 132 (November), 55–62.

Elishberg, Jehoshua, Stephane Gauvin, Gary Lilien, and Arvind Rangaswamy (1991), "An Experimental Study of Alternative Preparation Aids for International Negotiations," Institute of the Study of Business Markets working paper 9, 1991.

Fayerweather, J., and Ashok Kapoor (1976), *Strategy and Negotiation for the International Corporation*, Ballinger Publishers.

deFerrer, Robert J. (1989), "Playing the Away Game," *Marketing*, February 16, 24–26.

Fisher, Glen (1980), *International Negotiations: A Cross-Cultural Perspective*, Chicago: Intercultural Press, Inc.

Fisher, Roger, and William Ury (1983), *Getting to Yes: Negotiating Agreement without Giving In*, New York: Penguin Books.

Foster, Dean Allen (1992), *Bargaining across Borders*, New York: McGraw-Hill.

Frances, June N. P. (1991), "When in Rome? The Effects of Cultural Adaptation on Intercultural Business Negotiations," *Journal of International Business Studies*, vol. 22, no. 3 (third quarter), 403–28.

Frank, Sergy (1992), "Global Negotiating," *Sales & Marketing Management*, May, 64–70

Ghauri, Perdez N. (1988), "Negotiating with Firms in Developing Countries: Two Case Studies," *Industrial Marketing Management*, volume 17, 49–53.

——, (1986), "Guidelines for International Business Negotiations," *International Marketing Review*, Autumn, 72–82.

Graham, John L., Dong Ki Kim, Chi-Yuan Lin, and Michael Robinson (1988), "Buyer Seller Negotiations around the Pacific Rim: Differences in Fundamental Exchange Processes," *Journal of Consumer Research*, vol. 15 (June) 48–54.

—— and J. Douglas Andrews (1987), "A Holistic Analysis of Japanese and American Business Negotiations," *Journal of Business Communications*, vol. 24, no. 4 (Fall), 63–73.

——(1985a), "The Influence of Culture on the Process of Business Negotiations, an Exploratory Study," *Journal of International Business Studies*, Spring, 81–96.

——(1981), "A Hidden Cause of America's Trade Deficit with Japan," *Columbia Journal of World Business,* Fall, 5–15.

—— (1985b), "Cross-Cultural Marketing Negotiations: a laboratory experiment," *Marketing Science*, Spring, 130–46.

—— and R. A. Herberger, "Negotiators Abroad: Don't Shoot from the Hip," *Harvard Business Review*, July–August, 160–68.

——(1984), "A Comparison of Japanese and American Business Negotiations," *International Journal of Research in Marketing*, vol. 1, 51–68.

——(1983), "Business Negotiations in Japan, Brazil, and the United States," *Journal of International Business Studies*, vol. 14 (Spring–Summer), 47–62.

—— and Yoshihiro Sano (1989), *Smart Bargaining: Doing Business with the Japanese*, New York: Harper Business.

—— (1986), "Across the Negotiating Table from the Japanese," *International Marketing Review*, Autumn, 58–70.

——, Leonid I. Evenko, and Mahesh N. Rajan (1992), "An Empirical Comparison of Soviet and American Business," *Journal of International Business Studies*, 23/3, third quarter, 387–418.

Griffin, Trenholme J., and W. Russell Daggatt (1990), *The Global Negotiator*, NY: Harper.

Gulbro and Herbig (1996), "Differences between Success and Failure in Cross-Cultural Negotiations," *Industrial Marketing Management*, forthcoming.

Gulbro and Herbig (1995), "Differences in Cross-Cultural Negotiating Behavior between Industrial Product and Consumer Product Firms," *Journal of Business and Industrial Marketing*.

Gulbro and Herbig (1995), "Differences in Cross-Cultural Negotiating Behavior between International and Domestic-Oriented Firms," *Cross-Cultural Management*.

Gulbro & Herbig (1994), "External Effects of Cross-Cultural Negotiations," *Journal of Strategic Change*, 3/158: 1–12.

Gulbro and Herbig (1995), "Differences in Cross-Cultural Negotiating Behavior between Small and Large Businesses," *Journal of Business and Entrepreneurship*.

Hawrysh, Brian M., and Judith Lynne Zaichkowsky (1990), "Cultural Approaches to Negotiations: Understanding the Japanese," *International Marketing Review*, 7(2).

Heiba, Farouk I. (1984), "International Business Negotiations: A Strategic Planning Model," *International Marketing Review*, 1/4 (Autumn/Winter), 5–16.

Hendon, Donald W., and Rebecca Angeles Hendon (1990), *World-Class Negotiating*, New York: John Wiley & Sons Inc.

Herbig, Paul A., and Hugh E. Kramer (1992), "The Dos and Donts of Cross-Cultural Negotiations," *Industrial Marketing Management*.

—— (1991), "Cross-Cultural Negotiations: Success through Understanding." *Management Decisions*, vol. 29, no. 1, 19–31.

—— (1992), "The Role of Cross-Cultural Negotiations in International Marketing," *Marketing Intelligence and Planning*, 10/2, 10–13.

Ikle, Fred Charles (1982), *How Nations Negotiate*, New York: Harper and Row.

Jastram, Roy W. (1974), "The Nakodo Negotiator," *California Management Review*, vol. XVII, no. 2 (Winter), 88–92.

Kapoor, Ashok (1974), "MNC Negotiations: Characteristics and Planning Implications," *Columbia Journal of World Business*, Winter, 121—32.

Kramer, Hugh E. (1989), "Cross-Cultural Negotiations: The Western Japanese Interface," *Singapore Marketing Review*, vol. IV.

March, Robert M. (1983), *Japanese Negotiations*, New York: Kodansha Int.

—— (1985), "NoNos in Negotiating with the Japanese," *Across the Board*, April, 44–50.

McCall, J. B., and M. B. Warrington (1987), *Marketing by Agreement: A Cross-Cultural Approach to Business Negotiations*, 2nd ed., New York: John Wiley and Sons.

Moran, Robert T., and William G. Stripp (1991), *Successful International Business Negotiations,* Houston: Gulf Publishing Company.

Nite, Mikhail (1985), "Business Negotiation with the Soviet Union," *Global Trade Executive*, 104 (June), 27–38.

Oikawa, Naoko, and John Tanner Jr. (1992), "Influences of Japanese Culture on Business Relations and Negotiations," *Journal of Services Marketing*, 6/3 Summer.

Pascale, Richard Tanner (1978), "Communications and Decision Making across Cultures: Japanese and American Comparisons," *Administrative Science Quarterly*, vol. 23 (March), 91–110.

Peak, Herschel (1985), "Conquering Cross-Cultural Challenges," *Business Marketing*, October, 138–46.

Pye, Lucian (1982), *Chinese Commercial Negotiating Style*, Cambridge, MA: Oelgeschlager, Gunn and Hain Publishers Inc.

Rangaswany, Arvind, Jehoshua Eliashberg, Raymond R. Burke, and Jerry Wind (1989), "Developing Marketing Expert Systems: An Application to International Negotiations," *Journal of Marketing*, vol. 53 no. 4 (October), 24–38.

Salacuse, Jeswalk W. (1991), *Making Global Deals: Negotiating in the International Marketplace*, Boston: Houghton Mifflin.

Samuelson, Louis (1984), *Soviet and Chinese Negotiating Behavior*, London: Sage Pub.

Schoonmaker, Alan (1989), *Negotiate to Win*, Englewood Cliffs, NJ: Prentice Hall.

Smith, Raymond E. (1989), *Negotiating with Soviets*, Washington DC: Institute for Study of Diplomacy, Georgetown University.

Swierczek, Fredric William (1990), "Culture and Negotiation in the Asian Context," *Journal of Managerial Psychology*, 5/5, 17–25.

Tung, Rosalie L., "Handshakes across the Sea: Cross-Cultural Negotiating for Business Success," *Organizational Dynamics*, 30–40.

——*Business Negotiations with the Japanese,* Lexington Books, 1982.

—— (1989), "A Longitudinal Study of United States–China Business Negotiations," *China Economic Review*, vol. 1, no. 1, 57–71.

—— (1982), "US–China Trade Negotiations: Practices, Procedures and Outcomes," *Journal of International Business Studies*, Fall, 25–37.

—— (1983), "How to Negotiate with the Japanese," *California Management Review*, vol. 26 no. 4, 52–77.

Van Zandt, Howard F. (1970), "How to Negotiate in Japan," *Harvard Business Review*, November/December, 45–56.

Weiss, Stephen E. (1987), "Creating the GM-Toyota Joint Venture: A Case in Complex Negotiation," *Columbia Journal of World Business*, vol. 22, no. 2, 23–37.

Wells, Louis T., Jr (1977), "Negotiating with Third-World Governments," *Harvard Business Review*, 55 (January–February), 72–80.

Wright, P. (1981), "Doing Business in Islamic Markets," *Harvard Business Review*, vol. 59, no. 1, 34ff.

Intercultural Negotiation in International Business

Jeswald W. Salacuse

INTRODUCTION

Although negotiating a purely domestic business deal and negotiating an international transaction have much in common, the factor that is almost always present in an international negotiation and generally absent from a domestic negotiation is a difference in culture among the parties. In international business, transactions not only cross borders, they also cross cultures. Culture profoundly influences how people think, communicate, and behave, and it also affects the kinds of deals they make and the way they make them. Differences in culture among business executives, for example, between a Chinese public sector plant manager in Shanghai and an American division head of a family company in Cleveland, can therefore create barriers that impede or completely stymie the negotiating process. The purpose of this article is to examine the effect of differences in culture on international business negotiations and to suggest ways to overcome problems encountered in intercultural dealings.

THE NATURE OF CULTURE

Definitions of culture are as numerous and often as vague as definitions of negotiation itself (Moran and Stripp 1991, pp. 43–56; Zartman 1993, p. 19). Some scholars would confine the concept of culture to the realm of ideas, feeling, and thoughts. For example, one working definition offered by two negotiation experts is that "Culture is a set of shared and enduring meanings, values, and beliefs that characterize national, ethnic, and other groups and orient their behavior" (Faure and Sjostedt 1993, p. 3). Others would have culture also encompass behavior patterns and institutions common to a given group or community. E. Adamson Hoebel, a noted anthropologist, defined culture as "the integrated system of learned behavior patterns which are characteristic of the members of a society and which are not the result of biological inheritance" (Hoebel 1972, p. 7). While the essence of culture may reside in the mind, it must be pointed out that persons

Reprinted from Jeswald W. Salacuse, "Intercultural Negotiation in International Business," *Group Decision and Negotiation,* vol. 8, pp. 217-36, © 1999 Kluwer Academic/Plenum Publishers.

gain their understanding of their and others' cultures primarily, if not exclusively, from observing the behavior and institutions of a particular group.

For purposes of this paper, culture is defined as the socially transmitted behavior patterns, norms, beliefs, and values of a given community (Salacuse 1991, p. 45). Persons from that community use the elements of their culture to interpret their surroundings and guide their interactions with other persons. So when an executive from a corporation in Dallas, Texas, sits down to negotiate a business deal with a manager from a Houston company, the two negotiators rely on their common culture to interpret each other's statements and actions. But when persons from two different cultures—for example an executive from Texas and a manager from Japan—meet for the first time, they usually do not share a common pool of information and assumptions to interpret each others' statements, actions, and intentions. Culture can therefore be seen as a language, a "silent language" which the parties need in addition to the language they are speaking if they are truly to communicate and arrive at a genuine understanding (Hall 1959). Like any language, the elements of culture form a system, which has been variously characterized as a "system for creating, sending, storing, and processing information" (Hall and Hall 1990, p. 179) and "group problem-solving tool that enables individuals to survive in a particular environment" (Moran and Stripp 1991, p. 43). Culture serves as a kind of glue—a social adhesive—that binds a group of people together and gives them a distinct identity as a community. It may also give them a sense that they are a community different and separate from other communities.

This article is concerned primarily with national cultures, cultures identified with a particular country. But culture and nationality are not always the same thing. Within Nigeria, for example, the culture of the Ibos of the largely Christian southeastern part of the country and the Hausas of the mainly Moslem north are different and distinct. Similarly, individual corporations and professions may have their own distinct organizational or professional cultures whose norms and behavior patterns may predominate in certain respects over the ethnic or national cultures of their profession's members. For example, a continuing concern in the current wave of mergers and acquisitions in the United States is the problem of blending the cultures of two organizations, such as Morgan Stanley and Dean Witter, after the deal has been signed (Lublin and O'Brian, 1997). But while cultural values, attitudes, and behavior patterns may appear permanently embedded in a group, particularly in the context of an encounter between two different cultures, in fact culture is dynamic. It is constantly changing (Bohannan 1995).

And finally, in considering the role of culture in international business negotiation and relationships, it is important to remember that the world has a staggering diversity of cultures. For example, while certain observers speak of "Asian culture" as if it were a homogeneous set of values, beliefs, and behavior patterns followed by all Asians (Mahbubani 1995), in reality Asia has many different and distinct cultures from India to Laos, from Korea to Indonesia. Each has its own values and practices that may differ markedly from those prevailing in another country—or indeed in another part of the same country. The negotiating style of Koreans, for example, is not the same as that of the Lao. And even within countries that from outward appearances seem to have a fairly uniform cultural identity, like the French and the Germans, significant differences may nonetheless exist between regions, for example the difference between the business community in Paris and that of the *midi* in southern France.

FIGURE 1   Culture as an Onion

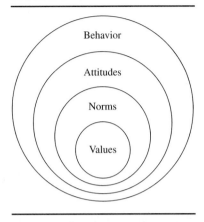

THE ELEMENTS OF CULTURE

One may conceive of the four cultural elements mentioned in the definition above—behavior, attitudes, norms, and values—as forming a series of concentric circles, like the layers of an onion, illustrated by Figure 1.

The process of understanding the culture of a counterpart in a negotiation is similar to peeling an onion. The outermost layer of the onion is behavior, the words and actions of one's counterpart. It is this layer which a negotiator first perceives in an intercultural negotiation. A second inner layer consists of attitudes of persons from that culture toward specific events and phenomena, for example, attitudes about beginning meetings punctually or the appropriate format of presentations. Attitudes may become evident to a counterpart in an intercultural negotiation only after protracted discussions. Next are norms, the rules to be followed in specific situations. Here, for example, a negotiator may come to realize that his or her counterpart's seemly rigid insistence on punctuality is not merely a personal idiosyncrasy but is based on a firm rule derived from his or her culture.

The innermost layer—the core—consists of values. Norms about the way meetings are conducted, representatives chosen, or persons rewarded are usually based on certain values that are important to that culture. Such differences in values are often the most difficult for negotiators to detect and understand. Indeed, the parties to an international negotiation may discover their value differences only after they have signed the contract and begun to work together. Such differences in cultural values between partners in an international joint venture, for example, may lead to severe conflict and ultimately the failure of their enterprise, a factor which may explain why many international ventures have a short life.

In their valuable book *The Seven Cultures of Capitalism*, based on extensive survey research among thousands of executives from throughout the world, Hampden-Turner and Trompenaars (1993) found sharp differences that could only be explained by different cultural values to such basic management tasks as group decision making, hiring, rewarding employees, and making and applying rules. For example, with respect to group decision making, wide variations among cultural groups existed in answering the following question:

What is the better way to choose a person to represent a group?

A. All members of the group should meet and discuss candidates until almost everybody agrees on the same person; or

B. The group members should meet, nominate persons, vote, and choose the person with a majority of the votes even if several people are against the person.

In this question, according to the authors, the values of adversarial democracy and consensual democracy were in tension. While 84.4 percent of the Japanese opted for Answer A (consensual democracy), only 37.7 percent of the Americans did so. It is interesting to note that there were differences among Asians on this question. For example, unlike the Japanese, only 39.4 percent of the Singaporeans chose Answer A, exhibiting an aversion to consensual democracy that is perhaps reflected in Singapore's authoritarian political system. One can imagine that this difference in cultural values about decision making between Japanese and American Executives in a joint venture might lead to serious conflict between the joint venture partners. Other kinds of value conflicts may arise, for example, between individualism prized by Americans and communitarianism embodied in many Asian cultures, about whether in hiring an employee it is more important to consider individual talent or the ability to fit into the organization, about whether to reward persons on the basis of group performance or by individual achievement only.

Differences in cultural values can present themselves in international business transactions and relationships time after time and day after day, and they may ultimately turn what appeared to be harmonious negotiation or business relationship into a continuing source of conflict between the parties. Once the conflict surfaces, it may be exacerbated by the way the parties try to cope with it. One unfortunate tendency is for each of the parties to extol their own cultural values but to denigrate those of their business or negotiating partner. For example, Americans, with their high store on individualism, will tend to see their value system positively: as for individual rights and human freedom, as putting the individual above the tyranny of the group, as knowing that a group prospers only when individuals prosper, and as efficient. Persons coming from cultures where communitarian values are prized will see themselves as unselfish, humane, for group interests and rights, and knowing that individuals prosper only when the group prospers. Yet, Americans, when confronted with a communitarian culture, may tend to ascribe to it only negative characteristics. So Americans, reacting to Japanese values in a decision to retain a 15-year employee whose performance has declined, might consider their Japanese counterparts as: tolerant of free loaders, giving in to the tyranny of the group, weak and inefficient. On the other hand, the Japanese would probably characterize the Americans as ignoring the contributions and needs of the group, lacking in loyalty, inhumane, and selfish.

It is important therefore for business executives in a negotiation to understand the values inherent in the culture of their counterparts and not to characterize those values in a negative way.

THE EFFECT OF CULTURAL DIFFERENCES ON NEGOTIATION

Differences in culture between deal makers can obstruct negotiations in many ways. First, they can create misunderstandings in communication. If one American executive responds to another American's proposal by saying, "That's difficult," the response, interpreted against American culture and business practice, probably means that the door is still open for further discussion, that perhaps the other side should sweeten its offer. In some other cultures, for example in Asia, persons may be reluctant to say a direct and emphatic "no," even when that is their intent. So when a Japanese negotiator, in response to a proposal says, "That is difficult," he is clearly indicating that the proposal is unacceptable. "It is difficult," means "no" to the Japanese, but to the American it means "maybe."

Second, cultural differences create difficulties not only in understanding words, but also in interpreting actions. For example, most Westerners expect a prompt answer when they make a statement or ask a question. Japanese, on the other hand, tend to take longer to respond. As a result, negotiations with Japanese are sometimes punctuated with periods of silence that seem excruciating to an American. For the Japanese, the period of silence is normal, an appropriate time to reflect on what has been said. The fact that they may not be speaking in their native language lengthens even more the time needed to respond.

From their own cultural perspective, Americans may interpret Japanese silence as rudeness, lack of understanding, or a cunning tactic to get the Americans to reveal themselves. Rather than wait for a response, the American tendency is to fill the void with words by asking questions, offering further explanations, or merely repeating what they have already said. This response to silence may confuse the Japanese, who are made to feel that they are being bombarded by questions and proposals without being given adequate time to respond to any of them.

On the other hand, Latin Americans, who place a high value on verbal agility, have a tendency to respond quickly. Indeed, they may answer a point once they have understood it even though the other side has not finished speaking. While inexperienced American negotiators are sometimes confused by Japanese delays in responding, they can become equally agitated in negotiations with Brazilians by what Americans consider constant interruptions..

Third, cultural considerations also influence the form and substance of the deal you are trying to make. For example, in many parts of the Moslem world, where Islamic law prohibits the taking of interest on loans, one may need to restructure or relabel finance charges in a deal as "administrative fees" in order to gain acceptance at the negotiating table. More substantively, differences in culture will invariably require changes in products, management systems, and personnel practices. For example, in Thailand, the relationship between manager and employee is more hierarchical than it is in the United States. Workers are motivated by a desire to please the manager, but they in turn expect and want their managers to sense their personal problems and be ready to help with them. In other cultures, for example, in Australia, employees neither expect nor want managers to become involved with employees' personal problems. Thus an Australian project in Thailand would need to change its concept of employee relations because of the local culture (Hughes and Sheehan 1993).

And finally, culture can influence "negotiating style," the way persons from different cultures conduct themselves in negotiating sessions. Research indicates fairly clearly that negotiation practices differ from culture to culture (Weiss 1994, p. 51). Indeed, culture may influence how persons conceive of the very nature and function of negotiation itself. Studies of negotiating styles are abundant (e.g., Binnendijk 1987; Fisher 1980; Graham et al. 1988; Campbell et al. 1988). Some seek to focus on describing and analyzing the negotiating styles of particular groups. Indeed, the practitioner's fascination with cultural negotiating styles seems to have spawned a distinct literary genre: the "Negotiating with . . ." literature. Numerous books and articles bearing such titles as "Negotiating with the Japanese," "Negotiating with the Arabs," and "Negotiating with the Chinese" seek to lead the novice through the intricacies of negotiating in specific cultures (for a bibliography of such literature, see Salacuse 1991, pp. 174–83). Another approach to studying negotiating style is cross-cultural and comparative. It seeks to identify certain basic elements in negotiating style and to determine how they are reflected in various cultures. It is this approach which the next part of this article will adopt.

CULTURE AND NEGOTIATING STYLES:
TEN FACTORS IN DEAL MAKING

The great diversity of the world's cultures makes it impossible for any negotiator, no matter how skilled and experienced, to understand fully all the cultures that he or she may encounter. How then should an executive prepare to cope with culture in making deals in Singapore this week and Seoul the next? One approach is to identify important areas where cultural differences may arise during the negotiation process. A knowledge of those factors may help an international business negotiator to understand a counterpart and to anticipate possible misunderstandings. Toward this end, scholars have developed a variety of frameworks and checklists which may be applied cross-culturally (e.g., Weiss 1985; Moran and Stripp 1991; Salacuse 1991). Based on a review of the literature as well as interviews with practitioners, the author, in an earlier work (Salacuse 1991) identified 10 factors which seemed to be the most problematical. These 10 factors, each of which consisted of two poles, were (1) negotiating goals (contract or relationship?); (2) attitudes to the negotiating process (win/win or win/lose?); (3) personal styles (formal or informal?); (4) styles of communication (direct or indirect?); (5) time sensitivity (high or low?); (6) emotionalism (high or low?); (7) agreement form (specific or general?); (8) agreement-building process (bottom up or top down?); (9) negotiating team organization (one leader or consensus?); and (10) risk taking (high or low?). Negotiating styles, like personalities display a wide range of variation. The 10 negotiating traits listed above can be placed on a spectrum or continuum as is illustrated in Figure 2.

The purpose of the matrix in Figure 2 is to identify specific negotiating traits affected by culture and to show the possible variation that each trait or factor may take. With this knowledge, an international business negotiator may be able to understand better the negotiating styles and approaches of his counterparts from other cultures. Equally important, it may help negotiators determine how their own styles appear to those same counterparts on the other side of the bargaining table.

In order to test this approach to understanding negotiating style, the above matrix was translated into a survey questionnaire and administered to 310 business executives, lawyers, and graduate business students (many of whom had substantial work experience) from all continents at various sites in North America, Latin America, and Europe. The respondents came from 12 countries: the United States, the United Kingdom, France, Germany, Spain, Mexico, Argentina, Brazil, Nigeria, India, China, and Japan. After receiving an explanation of the matrix and questionnaire, respondents were asked

FIGURE 2   The Impact of Culture on Negotiation

Trait		
Goal	Contract ↔	Relationship
Attitudes	Win/lose ↔	Win/win
Personal styles	Informal ↔	Formal
Communications	Direct ↔	Indirect
Time sensitivity	High ↔	Low
Emotionalism	High ↔	Low
Agreement form	Specific ↔	General
Agreement building	Bottom up ↔	Top down
Team organization	One leader ↔	Consensus
Risk taking	High ↔	Low

to rate their own attitudes anonymously toward each of these negotiating traits on a five-point scale. In general, as will be seen below, the survey revealed significant corelations between the respondents' assessment of certain traits of their negotiating styles and the national cultures from which they came.

The results of the survey must be read with several caveats. First, the answers that the respondents gave reflected only how they saw themselves (or would like others to see them) rather than their negotiating styles and behavior in actual negotiations. The results can only be read as indicating a certain predisposition of individual cultures toward certain factors affecting the negotiation process. Second, negotiating style in a given negotiation may be influenced by numerous factors besides culture, including personality, bureaucracy, business experience, and the nature of the transactions under negotiation. For example, an executive who is predisposed to approach a business negotiation as a problem-solving, integrative process (win/win) may behave in a distributive, confrontational way (win/lose) when confronted by a hostile counterpart at the negotiating table. Third, all the respondents spoke English, completed the survey in English, had substantial international experience, and were participating in graduate university education or advanced executive seminars, also conducted in the English language. As a result, they may not be representative of most business executives in their cultures. On the other hand, they are fairly representative of the kinds of persons who conduct international negotiations on behalf of companies. Fourth, the meaning of key terms in the survey, such as *direct, indirect, risk, general,* and *specific* were not strictly defined but instead were interpreted by each respondent according to his or her own subjective interpretation, a factor obviously influenced by culture. Fifth, both the size of the sample and the number of cultures surveyed were limited.

Negotiating Goal: Contract or Relationship?

Different cultures may view the very purpose of a business negotiation differently. For many American executives, the goal of a business negotiation, first and foremost, is often to arrive at a signed contract between the parties. Americans consider a signed contract as a definitive set of rights and duties that strictly binds the two sides, an attitude succinctly summed up in the statement "a deal is a deal."

TABLE 1   Goal: Contract or Relationship?

Contract:	Spn.	Fr.	Braz.	Jpn.	USA	Ger.	UK	Nig.	Arg.	Chi.	Mex.	Ind.
Percent:	73.7	70	66.7	54.5	53.7	54.5	47.1	46.7	46.2	45.5	41.7	33.3

Japanese, Chinese, and other cultural groups in Asia, it is said, often consider that the goal of a negotiation is not a signed contract, but the creation of a relationship between the two sides (e.g., Pye 1982). Although the written contract describes the relationship, the essence of the deal is the relationship itself. For Americans, signing a contract is closing a deal; for many Asians, signing a contract might more appropriately be called opening a relationship. This difference in view may explain why Asians tend to give more time and effort to prenegotiation, while Americans want to rush through this first phase in deal making. The activities of prenegotiation, whereby the parties seek to get to know one another thoroughly, are a crucial foundation for a good business relationship. They may seem less important when the goal is merely a contract.

The results of the survey showed significant differences among the cultures surveyed with respect to the negotiating goals of contract and relationship. Thus, only 26 percent of the Spanish respondents claimed that their primary goal in a negotiation was a relationship compared to 66 percent of the Indians. On the other hand, the preference for a relationship was not as pronounced among the Chinese (54.5 percent) as one might have expected from the literature, and the Japanese appeared almost evenly divided on the question, with a slight preference for contract as a negotiating goal. Table 1 summarizes the survey results on this issue.

Negotiating Attitude: Win/Lose or Win/Win?

Because of differences in culture or personality, or both, businesspersons appear to approach deal making with one of two basic attitudes: that a negotiation is either a process in which both can gain (win/win) or a struggle in which of necessity, one side wins and the other side loses (win/lose). Win/win negotiators see deal making as a collaborative and problem-solving process; win/lose negotiators see it as confrontational. In a reflection of this dichotomy, negotiation scholars have concluded that these approaches represented two basic paradigms of the negotiation process: (1) distributive bargaining (i.e., win/lose) and (2) integrative bargaining or problem-solving (i.e., win/win) (e.g., Hoppman 1995; Lewicki et al. 1993). In the former situation , the parties see their goals as incompatible, while in the latter they consider themselves to have compatible goals.

For example, developing-country officials often view negotiations with multinational corporations as win/lose competitions. In negotiating investment contracts, they often consider profits earned by the investor as automatic losses to the host country. As a result, they may focus their efforts in the negotiation fixedly on limiting investor profit in contrast to discovering how to maximize benefits from the project for both the investor and the country. It is interesting to note that those same officials might approach negotiations in their home villages with members of their ethnic group or clans on a win/win basis.

TABLE 2 Negotiating Attitude: Win/Win or Win/Lose?

Win/Win:	Jpn.	Chi.	Arg.	Fr.	Ind.	USA	UK	Mex.	Ger.	Nig.	Braz.	Sp.
Percent:	100	81.8	80.8	80	77.8	70.7	58.8	50	54.5	46.7	44.4	36.8

The survey conducted by the author found wide differences among the cultures represented in the survey on this question. Whereas 100 percent of the Japanese viewed business negotiation as a win/win process, only 36.8 percent of the Spanish were so inclined. The Chinese and Indians, the other two Asian cultures represented in the survey, also claimed that negotiation was for them win/win, and the French, alone among Europeans, took a similarly pronounced position on the question. Table 2 summarizes the results of all groups surveyed with respect to this attitude toward negotiation.

Personal Style: Informal or Formal?

Personal style concerns the way a negotiator talks to others, uses titles, dresses, speaks, and interacts with other persons. Culture strongly influences the personal style of negotiators. It has been observed, for example, that Germans have a more formal style than Americans (Hall and Hall 1990, p. 48). A negotiator with a formal style insists on addressing counterparts by their titles, avoids personal anecdotes, and refrains from questions touching on the private or family life of members of the other negotiating team. An informal style negotiator tries to start the discussion on a first-name basis, quickly seeks to develop a personal, friendly relationship with the other team, and may take off his jacket and roll up his sleeves when deal making begins in earnest. Each culture has its own formalities, which have special meaning within that culture. They are another means of communication among the persons sharing that culture, another form of adhesive that binds them together as a community. Negotiators in foreign cultures must respect appropriate formalities. As a general rule, it is always safer to adopt a formal posture and move to an informal stance, if the situation warrants it, than to assume an informal style too quickly.

On the other hand, an encounter between negotiators having different personal styles can sometimes lead to conflict that impedes a negotiation. For an American or an Australian, calling someone by his or her first name is an act of friendship and therefore a good thing. For a Japanese or an Egyptian, the use of the first name at a first meeting is an act of disrespect and therefore a bad thing.

Except for the Nigerians, a majority of the respondents within each of the 12 groups surveyed claimed to have an informal negotiating style; however, the strength of this view varied considerably. While nearly 83 percent of the Americans considered themselves to have an informal negotiating style, only 54 percent of the Chinese, 52 percent of the Spanish, and 58 percent of the Mexicans were similarly inclined. Among the four European national cultures surveyed, the French were the strongest in claiming an informal style. Although both the Germans and Japanese have a reputation for formality, only slightly more than one quarter of the respondents in these two groups believed they had a formal negotiating style. Differences in cultures with respect to the meaning of the terms *formal* and *informal* may have influenced this result. The survey's findings on this negotiating trait are summarized in Table 3.

TABLE 3   Personal Style: Formal or Informal?

Formal:	Nig.	Spn.	Chi.	Mex.	UK	Arg.	Ger.	Jpn.	Ind.	Braz.	Fr.	USA
Percent:	53	47.4	45.5	41.7	35.3	34.6	27.3	27.3	22.2	22.2	20	17.1

Communication: Direct or Indirect?

Methods of communication vary among cultures. Some place emphasis on direct and simple methods of communication; others rely heavily on indirect and complex methods. It has been observed, for example, that whereas Germans and Americans are direct, the French and the Japanese are indirect (Hall and Hall 1990, p. 102). Persons with an indirect style of communication often make assumptions about the level of knowledge possessed by their counterparts and to a significant extent communicate with oblique references, circumlocutions, vague allusions, figurative forms of speech, facial expressions, gestures, and other kinds of body language. In a culture that values directness such as the American or the Israeli, one can expect to receive a clear and definite response to proposals and questions. In cultures that rely on indirect communication, such as the Japanese, reaction to proposals may be gained by interpreting seemingly indefinite comments, gestures, and other signs.

The confrontation of these styles of communication in the same negotiation can lead to friction. For example, the indirect ways Japanese negotiators express disapproval have often led foreign business executives to believe that their proposals were still under consideration when they had in fact been rejected by the Japanese side. In the Camp David negotiations, the Israeli preference for direct forms of communication and the Egyptian tendency to favor indirect forms sometimes exacerbated relations between the two sides. The Egyptians interpreted Israeli directness as aggressiveness and, therefore, an insult. The Israelis viewed Egyptian indirectness with impatience and suspected them of insincerity, of not saying what they meant.

In the survey, respondents in all cultural groups by a high margin claimed to have a direct form of communication. Here too the organizational culture of the participants and their international experience may have strongly influenced their responses to the questionnaire. It is worth noting, however, that the two cultural groups with the largest percentage of persons claiming an indirect style were the Japanese and the French. Table 4 summarizes the results on this issue.

Sensitivity to Time: High or Low?

Discussions of national negotiating styles invariably treat a particular culture's attitudes toward time. So it is said that Germans are always punctual, Latins are habitually late, Japanese negotiate slowly, and Americans are quick to make a deal. Commentators sometimes claim that some cultures "value" time more than others, but this may not be an accurate characterization of the situation. Rather they may value differently the amount of time devoted to and measured against the goal pursued. For Americans, the deal is a signed contract and "time is money," so they want to make a deal quickly.

TABLE 4   Communication: Direct or Indirect?

Indirect:	Jpn.	Fr.	Chi.	UK	Braz.	Ind.	Ger.	USA	Arg.	Spn.	Mex.	Nig.
Percent:	27.3	20	18.2	11.8	11.1	11.1	9.1	4.9	3.8	0	0	0

Americans therefore try to reduce formalities to a minimum and get down to business quickly. Japanese and other Asians, whose goal is to create a relationship rather than simply sign a contract, will need to invest time in the negotiating process so that the parties can get to know one another well and determine whether they wish to embark on a long-term relationship. They may view aggressive attempts to shorten the negotiating time with suspicion as efforts to hide something.

As a general rule, Asians tend to devote more time and attention to the prenegotiation phase of deal making than do Americans. Whereas American executives and lawyers generally want to "dispense with the preliminaries" and "to get down to cases," most Asians view prenegotiation as an essential foundation to any business relationship; consequently, they recognize the need to conduct prenegotiation with care before actually making a decision to undertake substantive negotiations of a deal. One of the consequences of this difference in approach is that Americans sometimes assume that discussions with Asian counterparts have passed from prenegotiation to a subsequent stage when in fact they have not because the Asians have not yet decided to undertake substantive negotiations. This type of misunderstanding can lead to suspicions of bad faith, resulting ultimately in total failure of the talks. Negotiators need to be sure that they and their counterparts are always in the same phase of the deal-making process. One way of making sure is by using written agendas, memoranda, and letters of intent to mark the various phases.

The survey did not reveal significant divergences with respect to time. A majority of the respondents from all cultural groups surveyed claimed to have a high sensitivity to time; however, the strength of the minority view on this question varied considerably among the groups. The Indians, French, and Germans included a substantial percentage of respondents asserting a low sensitivity to time. Table 5 summarizes the results.

These survey results on this question could have been affected by the organizational cultures of the respondents, as well as by variations in the way that respondents interpreted the term "time sensitivity." Cultural discussions about time in negotiations often refer to two elements: promptness is meeting deadlines and the amount of time devoted to a negotiation. Thus Germans, it has been observed, are highly time-sensitive with regard to promptness but less so with respect to their willingness to devote large amounts of time to a negotiation (Hall and Hall 1990, p. 37). Thus they are punctual (high time sensitivity) but slow to negotiate and make decisions (low time sensitivity).

TABLE 5   Sensitivity to Time: High or Low?

Low:	Ind.	Fr.	Ger.	Mex.	Spn.	Arg.	US	Jpn.	Chi.	Nig.	UK	Braz.
Percent:	44.4	40	36.4	33.3	21.1	15.4	14.6	9.1	9.1	6.7	5.9	0

TABLE 6   Emotionalism: High or Low?

Low:	Ger.	UK	Jpn.	Ind.	Fr.	Nig.	USA	Chi.	Spn.	Mex.	Arg.	Braz.
Percent:	63.6	52.9	45.5	44.4	40	40	36.6	27.3	21.1	16.7	15.4	11.1

Emotionalism: High or Low?

Accounts of negotiating behavior in other cultures almost always point to a particular group's tendency or lack thereof to act emotionally. According to the stereotype, Latin Americans show their emotions at the negotiating table, while Japanese and many other Asians hide their feelings. Obviously, individual personality plays a role here. There are passive Latins and hotheaded Japanese. Nonetheless, various cultures have different rules as to the appropriateness and form of displaying emotions, and these rules are brought to the negotiating table as well.

In the survey conducted by the author, Latin Americans and the Spanish were the cultural groups that ranked themselves highest with respect to emotionalism in a clearly statistically significant fashion. Among Europeans, the Germans and English ranked as least emotional, while among Asians the Japanese held that position, but to a lesser degree than the two European groups. Table 6 summarizes the results with regard to emotionalism.

Form of Agreement: General or Specific?

Cultural factors also influence the form of the written agreement that parties try to make. Generally, Americans prefer very detailed contracts that attempt to anticipate all possible circumstances and eventualities, no matter how unlikely. Why? Because the "deal" is the contract itself, and one must refer to the contract to handle new situations that may arise in the future. Other cultures, such as the Chinese, prefer a contract in the form of general principles rather than detailed rules. Why? Because it is claimed that the essence of the deal is the relationship between the parties. If unexpected circumstances arise, the parties should look to their relationship, not the contract, to solve the problem. So in some cases, a Chinese may interpret the American drive to stipulate all contingencies as evidence of lack of confidence in the stability of the underlying relationship.

Some practitioners argue that differences over the form of an agreement are caused more by unequal bargaining power than by culture. In a situation of unequal bargaining power, the stronger party usually seeks a detailed agreement to "lock up the deal" in all its possible dimensions, while the weaker party prefers a general agreement to give it room to "wiggle out" of adverse circumstances that are bound to occur. So a Chinese commune as the weaker party in a negotiation with a multinational corporation will seek a general agreement as a way of protecting itself against an uncertain future. According to this view, it is context, not culture, that determines this negotiating trait.

The survey showed that a majority of respondents in each cultural group preferred specific agreements over general agreements. This result may be attributed in part to the relatively large number of lawyers among the respondents, as well as to the fact that multinational corporate practice favors specific agreements and many of the respondents,

TABLE 7   Agreement Form: General or Specific?

General:	Jpn.	Ger.	Ind.	Fr.	Chi.	Arg.	Braz.	USA	Nig.	Mex.	Spn.	UK
Percent:	45.5	45.4	44.4	30	27.3	26.9	22.2	22	20	16.7	15.8	11.8

regardless of nationality, had experience with such firms. The survey responses on this point may have been a case where professional or organizational culture dominated over national cultural traits. On the other hand, the degree of intensity of responses on the question varied considerably among cultural groups. While only 11 percent of the British favored general agreements, 45.5 percent of the Japanese and of the Germans claimed to do so. Table 7 sets out the survey results with respect to agreement form.

Building an Agreement: Bottom Up or Top Down?

Related to the form of the agreement is the question of whether negotiating a business deal is an inductive or a deductive process. Does it start from agreement on general principles and proceed to specific items, or does it begin with agreement on specifics, such as price, delivery date, and product quality, the sum total of which becomes the contract? Different cultures tend to emphasize one approach over the other.

Some observers believe that the French prefer to begin with agreement on general principles, while Americans tend to seek agreement first on specifics. For Americans, negotiating a deal is basically making a series of compromises and trade-offs on a long list of particulars. For the French, the essence is to agree on basic principles that will guide and indeed determine the negotiation process afterward. The agreed-upon general principles become the framework, the skeleton, upon which the contract is built.

A further difference in negotiating style is seen in the dichotomy between "the building-down approach" and the "building-up approach." In the building-down approach, the negotiator begins by presenting the maximum deal if the other side accepts all the stated conditions. In the building-up approach, one side begins by proposing a minimum deal that can be broadened and increased as the other party accepts additional conditions. According to many observers, Americans tend to favor the building-down approach, while the Japanese tend to prefer the building-up style of negotiating a contract.

The survey did not reveal significant cultural trends on this issue among Americans, Germans, and Nigerians, since the respondents from these three groups were relatively evenly divided on the question. On the other hand, the French, Argentineans, and Indians tended to view deal making as a top-down (deductive) process, while Japanese, Mexicans, and Brazilians tended to see it as a bottom-up (inductive) process. Table 8 summarizes the results on the question.

TABLE 8   Building an Agreement: Bottom Up or Top Down?

Top down:	Ind.	Arg.	Fr.	UK	Chi.	Ger.	USA	Nig.	Spn.	Jpn.	Braz.	Mex.
Percent:	66.7	61.5	60	58.8	54.5	54.5	53.7	53.3	52.6	36.4	33.3	33.3

Team Organization: One Leader or Group Consensus?

In any international business negotiation, it is important to know how the other side is organized, who has the authority to make commitments, and how decisions are made. Culture is one important factor that affects how executives and lawyers organize themselves to negotiate a deal. Some cultures emphasize the individual while others stress the group. These values may influence the organization of each side to a negotiation. One extreme is the negotiating team with a supreme leader who has complete authority to decide all matters. Many American teams tend to follow this approach, which has been labeled the "John Wayne style of negotiations" (Graham and Herberger 1983, p.160). Other cultures, notably the Japanese, stress team negotiation and consensus decision making. When you negotiate with such a team, it may not be apparent who is the leader and who has authority to commit the side. In the first type, the negotiating team is usually small; in the second it is often large. For example, in negotiations in China on a major deal, it would not be uncommon for the Americans to arrive at the table with three persons and for the Chinese to show up with ten. Similarly, the one-leader team is usually prepared to make commitments and decisions more quickly than a negotiating team organized on the basis of consensus. As a result, the consensus type of organization usually takes more time to negotiate a deal.

The survey on negotiating styles revealed differences in preference among respondents, depending on culture. The group with the strongest preference for a consensus organization were the French. French individualism has been noted in many studies (Hall and Hall 1990), and perhaps a consensus arrangement in French eyes is the best way to protect that individualism. Despite the Japanese reputation for consensus arrangements, only 45 percent of the Japanese respondents claimed to prefer a negotiating team based on consensus. The Brazilians, the Chinese, and Mexicans, to a far greater degree than any other groups, preferred one-person leadership, a reflection perhaps of the political traditions in those countries. The results of the survey on this point are summarized in Table 9.

Risk Taking: High or Low?

Research supports the conclusion that certain cultures are more risk averse than others (Hofstede 1980). In deal making, the culture of the negotiators can affect the willingness of one side to take "risks" in the negotiation—to divulge information, try new approaches, tolerate uncertainties in a proposed course of action. A negotiator who senses that the other side is risk averse needs to focus efforts on proposing rules and mechanisms that will reduce the apparent risks in the deal for them.

The Japanese, with their emphasis on requiring large amounts of information and their intricate group decision-making process, tend to be risk averse, a fact affirmed by the author's survey which found Japanese respondents to be the most risk averse of all

TABLE 9   Team Organization: One Leader or Concensus?

One leader:	Braz.	Chi.	Mex.	UK	USA	Spn.	Arg.	Ger.	Jpn.	Ind.	Nig.	Fr.
Percent:	100	90.9	90.9	64.7	63.4	57.7	57.7	54.5	54.5	44.4	40	40

TABLE 10   Risk Taking: High or Low?

Low:	Fr.	Ind.	UK	Chi.	USA	Nig.	Arg.	Ger.	Braz.	Mex.	Spn.	Jpn.
Percent:	90	88.9	88.2	81.8	78	73.3	73.1	72	55.6	50	47.4	18.2

countries covered in the survey. Americans in the survey, by comparison, considered themselves to be risk takers, but an even higher percentage of French, British, and Indians claimed to be risk takers. Table 10 summarizes the survey results with respect to risk.

COPING WITH CULTURE

In view of the importance of cultural differences in international business negotiations, how should negotiators seek to cope with them? The following are a few simple rules:

Rule No. 1: Learn the Other Side's Culture

In any international business dealing, it is important for a negotiator to learn something about the other side's culture. The degree to which such learning takes place depends on a number of factors, including the nature and importance of the transaction, the experience of the negotiators, the time available for learning, and the similarities or lack thereof between the cultures represented in the negotiation. For example, the negotiation of a simple, one-time export sale may demand less cultural knowledge than the negotiation of a long-term strategic alliance, which may require the parties to audit each other's culture as well as their financial assets.

Ideally, learning another's culture can require several years of study, mastery of a foreign language, and prolonged residence in the country of that culture. An American faced with the task of negotiating a strategic alliance with a Thai company in Bangkok in two weeks' time cannot, of course, master Thai culture that fast. At best, he or she can learn enough to cope with some of the principal effects that Thai culture may have on making the deal. Important sources of information on Thai culture would include histories of the country, consultation with persons having business experience in the country, local lawyers and consultants, anthropological and ethnographic studies, reports on the current political situation, and accounts, if any, on negotiating with the Thais. As Weiss quite correctly points out, the degree of a negotiator's cultural knowledge will influence strategies and tactics during the negotiation (Weiss 1994, p. 53). For example, a person with strong familiarity with the counterpart's language and culture may use the negotiation style and approach of his counterpart's culture, while a person with less familiarity may choose, as a strategy, to employ an agent or mediator from that culture to assist in the negotiations.

As international business transactions increasingly take the form of long-term relationships, what Gomes-Casseres (1996) has termed the "alliance revolution," it is equally important to recognize that cultural learning continues long after the contract is signed. In effect, the dynamics of such long-term relationships between the parties is very much a continuing negotiation as the alliance partners shape the rules and practices of their business relationship.

Rule No. 2: Don't Stereotype

If rule number one in international negotiation is "know the other side's culture," rule number two is "avoid overreliance on that knowledge." As the survey indicates, not all Japanese evade giving a direct negative answer. Not all Germans will tell a counterpart specifically what they think of a proposal. In short, the negotiator who enters a foreign culture should be careful not to allow cultural stereotypes to determine his or her relations with local businesspersons. Foreign business executives and lawyers will be offended if they feel their counterparts are not treating them as individuals, but rather as cultural robots. In addition to giving offense, cultural stereotypes can be misleading. Many times the other side simply does not run true to the negotiating form suggested by books, articles, and consultants. The reason, of course, is that other forces besides culture may influence a person's negotiating behavior. Specifically, these forces may include the negotiator's personality, the organization he or she represents, and the context of the particular negotiation in question.

Rule No. 3: Find Ways to Bridge the Culture Gap

Generally, executives and lawyers who confront a culture different from their own in a negotiation tend to view it in one of three ways: as an obstacle, a weapon, or a fortress (Salacuse 1993). At the operational level, cultural differences are hardly ever seen as positive.

The conventional view among most American executives is that cultural differences are an obstacle to agreement and effective joint action. They therefore search for ways to overcome the obstacle. But a different culture in a business setting can become more than an obstacle; it can be seen as a weapon, particularly when a dominant party tries to impose its culture on the other side. For example, American lawyers' insistence on structuring a transaction "the way we do it in the United States" may be considered by their foreign counterparts as the use of American culture as a weapon.

Faced with a culture that it perceives as a weapon, a party to a business deal may become defensive and try to use its own culture as a fortress to protect itself from what it perceives as a cultural onslaught. The Japanese have often adopted this approach when confronted with American demands to open their markets. France's drive to limit the use of English in advertising is a defensive response to what it considered to be the weapon of "Anglo-Saxon" culture.

It may be helpful to try to think of cultural differences in yet another way. Differences in cultures tend to isolate individuals and groups from each other. In short, cultural differences create a gap between persons and organizations. Often the action that people take when confronted with cultural differences serves only to widen the gap, as, for example, when one side denigrate's the other side's cultural practices.

Remembering the words of the English poet Philip Larkin, "Always it is by bridges that we live," effective international business negotiators should seek to find ways to bridge the gap caused by cultural difference. One way to build that bridge is by using culture itself. If culture is indeed the glue that binds together a particular group of people, the creative use of culture between persons of different cultures is often a way to link those on opposite sides of the culture gap. Basically, there are four types of cultural bridge building that one may consider when confronted with a culture gap in a negotiation:

1. *Bridge the gap using the other side's culture.* One technique for bridging the gap is for a negotiator or manager to try to assume some or all of the cultural values and characteristics of the foreign persons with whom he or she is dealing. In international business, negotiators often try to use or identify with the other side's culture in order to build a relationship. For example, when President Sadat of Egypt negotiated with Sudanese officials, he always made a point of telling them that his mother had been born in the Sudan. He was thus using a common cultural thread to build a relationship with his counterparts. In effect, he was saying: "Like you, I am Sudanese, so we have common cultural ties. I understand you and I value your culture. Therefore you can trust me." Similarly, an African-American managing a joint venture in Nigeria stressed his African heritage to build relationships with Nigerian counterparts. And an Italian-American negotiating a sales contract in Rome emphasized his Italian background as of way of bridging the cultural gap that he perceived.

2. *Bridge the gap using your own culture.* A second general approach to bridging the culture gap is to persuade or induce the other side to adopt elements of your culture. To implement this approach successfully requires time and education. For example, in order to give a common culture to a joint venture, an American partner incurred significant cost by sending executives of its foreign partner to schools and executive training programs in the United States and then assigning them for short periods to the U.S. partner's own operations.

3. *Bridge with some combination of both cultures.* A third approach to dealing with the culture gap is to build a bridge using elements from cultures of both sides. In effect, cultural bridging takes place on both sides of the gap and hopefully results in the construction of a solid integrated structure. The challenge in this approach is to identify the most important elements of each culture and to find ways of blending them into a consistent, harmonious whole that will allow business to be done effectively. Sometimes a third person in the form of mediator or consultant can help in the process.

4. *Bridge with a third culture.* A final method of dealing with the culture gap is to build a bridge to rely on a third culture that belongs to neither of the parties. Thus, for example, in a difficult negotiation between an American executive and a Chinese manager, both discovered that they had a great appreciation of French culture since they had both studied in France in their youth. They began to converse in French, and their common love of France enabled them to build a strong personal relationship. They used a third culture to bridge the cultural gap between China and America. Similarly, negotiators from two different national cultures may use elements of their common professional cultures, as lawyers or as engineers, to bridge the gap between them.

CONCLUSION

Cultural bridging, like bridge construction, requires the cooperation of the parties at both ends of the divide. No negotiator will permit a bridge to be built if he or she feels threatened or sees the bridge as a long-term danger to security. Consequently, negotiators who want to build a bridge across the cultural divide to their counterpart must be concerned to strengthen the other side's sense of security, not weaken it as happens all too often in international business relationships.

REFERENCES

Binnendijk, H. (ed.), (1987). *National Negotiating Styles*. Washington, DC: US Department of State.

Bohannan, P. (1995). *How Culture Works*. New York: Free Press.

Campbell, N. C. G. et al. (1998). "Marketing Negotiations in France, Germany, the United Kingdom, and the United States," *Journal of Marketing* 52, 49–62.

Faure, G. O., and G. Sjostedt. (1993). "Culture and Negotiation: An Introduction," in G.O. Faure and J. Z. Rubin (eds.), *Culture and Negotiation*. Newbury Park: Sage Publications.

Fisher, G. (1980). *International Negotiation: Across-Cultural Perspective*. Yarmouth, ME: Intercultural Press.

Gomes-Casserea, B. (1996). *The Alliance Revolution*. Cambridge, MA: Harvard University Press.

Graham, J. L. et al. (1988). "Buyer-Seller Negotiations around the Pacific Rim: Differences in Fundamental Exchange Processes," *Journal of Consumer Research* 15, 48–54.

Graham J. L., and R. A. Herberger. (1983). "Negotiators Abroad—Don't Shoot from the Hip: Cross-Cultural Business Negotiations," *Harvard Business Review* 61, 160–83.

Hall, E. T. (1959). *The Silent Language*. New York: Doubleday.

Hall, E. T., and M. Reed Hall. (1990). *Understanding Cultural Differences*. Yarmouth, ME: Intercultural Press.

Hampden-Turner, C., and A. Trompenaars. (1993). *The Seven Cultures of Capitalism*. New York: Doubleday.

Hoebel, E. A. (1972). *Anthropology: The Study of Man* (4th ed.) New York: McGraw-Hill.

Hofstede, G. (1980). *Culture's Consequences: International Differences in Work-Related Values*. Newbury Park, CA: Sage Publications.

Hoppman, T. (1995). "Two Paradigms of Negotiation: Bargaining and Problem Solving," *Annals, AAPSS* 542, 24–47.

Hughes, P., and B. Sheehan. (1993). "Business Cultures: The Transfer of Managerial Policies and Practices from One Culture to Another," *Business and the Contemporary World* 5, 153–70.

Lewicki, R. et al. (1993). *Negotiation—Readings, Exercises, and Cases*. Burr Ridge, IL: Richard D. Irwin, Inc.

Lublin, J. S., and B. O'Brian. (1997). "Merged Firms Often Face Culture Clash," *The Wall Street Journal*, February 14, 1997, A9A.

Mahbubani, K. (1995). "The Pacific Way," *Foreign Affairs* 74, 100–11.

Moran, R. T., and W. G. Stripp. (1991). *Successful International Business Negotiations*. Houston: Gulf Publishing Company.

Pye, L. (1982). *Chinese Negotiating Style*. Cambridge, MA: Oelgeschlager, Gunn and Hain.

Salacuse, J. W. (1991). *Making Global Deal—Negotiating in the International Market Place*. Boston: Houghton Mifflin.

Salacuse, J. W. (1993). "Implications for Practitioners," in G. O. Faure and J. Z. Rubin (eds.), *Culture and Negotiation*. Newbury Park: Sage Publications.

Weiss, S. E. (1994). "Negotiating with Romans," (parts 1 and 2), *Sloan Management Review* 35, 51 and 85.

Zartman, I. W. (1993). "A Skeptics View," in G. O. Faure and J. Z. Rubin (eds.), *Culture and Negotiation*. Newbury Park: Sage Publications.

American Strengths and Weaknesses

Tommy T. B. Koh

AMERICAN STRENGTHS AND QUALITIES

Two caveats are appropriate for any discussion of national negotiating styles. First, there may not necessarily be a definable negotiating style for each country or people. Good and effective negotiators, irrespective of their national or cultural background, have certain common skills. Second, although it is probably possible to say impressionistically that the American people possess certain character and personality traits, there are many exceptions to the rule, and a person's negotiating style is inevitably affected by his character, temperament, and attitude toward people.

American negotiators have many strengths and qualities. If distance makes the heart grow fonder, my perception of Americans may be unrealistically favorable and idealized, since Singapore is located 12,000 miles away from the United States.

First, U.S. negotiators are usually well prepared. They arrive at negotiations with their homework completed, and they are armed with facts, figures, maps, and charts. They usually know what their national interests are and what their negotiating objectives are. This is not always the case among Third World negotiators.

Second, American negotiators tend to speak clearly and plainly. As someone who was educated in the Anglo-Saxon legal tradition, I regard this as a virtue, not a liability. However, the American preference for plain speaking can sometimes cause unintended offense to other negotiators whose national culture prefers indirectness, subtlety, and avoidance of confrontation. There are, of course, exceptions to this rule.

Third, U.S. negotiators tend to be more pragmatic than doctrinaire. They focus on advancing their country's interests rather than principles which they cherish. The Reagan administration, however, was a clear exception to this rule, and at the Third U.N. Conference on the Law of the Sea, decided, for rational and arguable reasons, that principles were more important than interests.

Fourth, American negotiators generally do not regard negotiations as a zero-sum game. A good U.S. negotiator is even prepared to put himself in the place of his negotiating adversary. A good U.S. negotiator is prepared to admit that his adversary, like himself, has certain irreducible, minimum national interests. A good U.S. negotiator is prepared to

Reprinted from *International Negotiation,* 1 (1996), pp. 313–17. Used with permission.

engage in a process of give and take, and he believes that the successful outcome of a negotiation is not one in which he wins everything and his adversary loses everything, but rather one in which there is a mutuality of benefits and losses, in which each side has a stake in honoring and maintaining the agreement.

Fifth, a U.S. negotiator's opening position is never his final position. He expects his opponent to make a counterproposal or a counteroffer. He is anxious to reach an agreement and will, therefore, make concessions to his opponent, expecting—not unreasonably—that his adversary will behave in like manner. Americans are sometimes completely exasperated at international forums when their adversaries do not behave as they do.

Sixth, the American people are very candid and straightforward, and this is reflected in their negotiating style. Americans are not usually perceived as cunning or devious. In only one incident have I found American negotiators to be devious, and that was shocking. This incident occurred in July 1981 when the United Nations sponsored an international conference on Cambodia. The conference was initiated by the ASEAN (Association of Southeast Asian Nations) countries, which proposed a framework for the resolution of the Cambodian situation. All Cambodian factions were invited to participate in the conference, including, of course, the Khmer Rouge. Vietnam was invited, but boycotted the meeting. At the conference, General Alexander Haig, then U.S. Secretary of State staged a dramatic walk-out, accompanied by the entire U.S. delegation, when the Khmer Rouge leader approached the rostrum to speak. The picture of this walk-out appeared on the front page of the *New York Times*.

On a subsequent day, the ASEAN countries and the People's Republic of China (PRC) were locked in a ferocious confrontation over the future role of the Khmer Rouge in any post-settlement Cambodia. The ASEAN countries argued that in light of the massacres and atrocities that the Khmer Rouge had committed, it would be morally and legally impermissible to allow them to return to power. We demanded a public election to be organized and supervised by the United Nations. To ensure free elections, we insisted that all armed elements be disarmed or sequestered in camp. The Chinese fought against all these points. The negotiating group was composed of 25 delegations, but the dynamics of the discussions revolved around the PRC, the ASEAN countries, and Pakistan as a middleman. Pakistan, however, was not an honest broker and basically submitted a series of amendments to dilute the ASEAN position. I assumed that Pakistan, because of its proximity to the PRC, was "fronting" for the Chinese, and was shocked to learn later that they were actually fronting for the Americans. Although the American delegation had publicly walked out of the negotiations, they were privately supporting China for geostrategic reasons. This is the only example of devious behavior by American negotiators of which I am aware, but I will remember it.

WEAKNESSES AND IDIOSYNCRASIES

One problem in negotiating with Americans is that American delegations usually suffer from serious interagency rivalries. During the U.N. Law of the Sea Conference, the American delegation met every morning and sometimes their internal meetings lasted longer than the other meetings in the conference.

A second problem in negotiating with the United States is the separation of power between the administration and the Congress. One has to be very careful if one is negotiating an agreement that is subject to ratification by the U.S. Senate. It is important to always keep in touch with U.S. senators as the negotiating process continues in order to obtain their independent inputs, be aware of their sensitivities, and recognize vested domestic interests and blocking constituencies.

A third special characteristic is the influence of the U.S. private sector and private interest groups on negotiations. During the Law of the Sea Conference I made it a point to meet not only with the official U.S. delegation and members of the Congress, but also to meet with representatives from the seabed mining industry, the petroleum industry, fishing industry, the marine scientific community, the environmental lobby, and individuals who have an affection for marine mammals. The reality of political life in America is that even one of these many lobbies can block ratification of a treaty. Foreign negotiators must understand the domestic political process in the United States and must, in some way, interfere in American internal affairs to ensure the success of their mission.

A fourth problem—the role of U.S. media—is a problem more for U.S. negotiators than for their counterparts. This is a problem because somehow the good nature of Americans and their propensity to candor makes it very difficult even for negotiators to keep confidences. And, in the midst of a sensitive negotiation it is sometimes very counterproductive for the media to report on issues that are under negotiation. In a speech to the House Foreign Affairs Committee, Secretary of State George Shultz recounted with great frustration an occasion when the U.S. and U.S.S.R. were engaged in bilateral negotiations. The negotiation had reached a critical point and he had that day drafted a cable giving his final instructions. He said he found to his horror at breakfast the next morning that the *New York Times* had reported the content of his cable. Members of the U.S. media should be asked whether they should exercise more discretion and self-restraint. Do they not feel an allegiance as American citizens to the advancement and protection of American national interests? Should not the right of the public to know and the freedom of the press sometimes be modulated by competing and larger interests? The extent to which the U.S. exposes its flank makes it easier for others to win at the negotiating table.

A fifth weakness is impatience. Americans suffer from an "instant-coffee complex." They do not have time, as Europeans and Asians do, to buy coffee beans, grind them every day, brew the coffee, enjoy the aroma, and savor every sip. Americans are always in a rush and are extremely frustrated when there is a lack of progress. Americans are result-oriented. Jeane Kirkpatrick had a shock several years ago when she visited the ASEAN capitals and met the foreign ministers of the six ASEAN countries. To each she asked, "Do you think there are prospects for settling the Cambodian conflict?" All six ASEAN foreign ministers said yes. She said, "Do you think it will be soon?" They all said, "Oh yes, very soon." She said, "Well, how soon?" They said, "Oh, about five years' time." She was shocked because to an American five years' time is certainly not soon.

A sixth weakness is cultural insensitivity. Everyone is guilty of this, not only Americans. Everyone assumes that others have similar cultures, customs, and manners. Singaporeans are "the barbarians of Southeast Asia." We are "the least sensitive and least subtle people in the region." But, if one is a professional negotiator, then part of the preparation for an effective negotiation is to learn enough about the culture of one's adversary to at least avoid simple errors of behavior, attribution, and body language.

Finally, it is surprising that in many recent multilateral forums the United States has been represented by amateur rather than professional negotiators. Given that the United States is so rich in human resources and has a foreign service studded by superstars, it is amazing how inadequately the United States is represented at important international negotiations.

CONCLUSION

In conclusion, a good negotiator, whether an Indian, an American, a Canadian, English, Ghanian, or whoever, is a person with certain definable skills, aptitudes, and temperaments. His character and personality have an impact on his effectiveness. Some American negotiators put people off; others readily win people's confidence. In choosing a negotiator, select someone who does not bristle like a porcupine but who can win the trust and confidence of his negotiating partners. What are these qualities that attract people's confidence and trust? These are moral qualities, qualities of leadership. If a negotiator is a leader, a person who acquires a reputation for competence, reliability, and trustworthiness, then others will trust him with leadership roles. The word *charisma* is not useful because it does not accurately portray the quality that bestows leadership on certain negotiators and not others. Henry Kissinger is not charismatic; he is dominating and impassive and has an exceptional intellect and a monotonous voice. In 1976, when the Law of Sea Conference was deadlocked between industrialized and developing countries, Kissinger, who was then secretary of state and had no background in the law of the sea and knew nothing about seabed mining, spent one morning in New York meeting with the U.S. delegation. In the afternoon he met with other leaders of the Group of 77, and by the end of the day presented an innovative scheme for reconciling the competing ambitions and claims of the different countries.

There probably is an American negotiating style, and this partakes of the qualities, attitudes, customs, conventions, and reflexes that have come down through U.S. history, culture, and political institutions. On the whole, American negotiators have very positive qualities, being well prepared, reasonable, competent, and honorable. Even more than this, some, like Elliott Richardson, will take it upon themselves to be an honest broker and help to settle a conflict between two other groups in which they are a totally disinterested party. This graciousness and willingness to help is a positive attribute as well.

Negotiating with "Romans"—Part 1

Stephen E. Weiss

"Smith," an American, arrived at the French attorney's Paris office for their first meeting. Their phone conversations had been in French, and Smith, whose experience with the language included 10 years of education in the United States, a year of residence in France with a French family, and annual trips to Paris for the previous seven years, expected to use French at this meeting. "Dupont," the Frenchman, introduced himself in French. His demeanor was poised and dignified; his language, deliberate and precise. Smith followed Dupont's lead and they went on to talk about a mutual acquaintance. After 10 minutes, Dupont shifted the topic by inquiring about Smith's previous work in international negotiations. One of Dupont's words—"operations"—surprised Smith, and he hesitated to respond. In a split second, Dupont, in fluent English, asked: "Would you like to speak in English?"[1]

Smith used the approach to cross-cultural interaction most widely advocated in the West, with a history dating back to St. Augustine: "When in Rome, do as the Romans do." It had seemed to be a reasonable way to convey cooperativeness, sensitivity to French culture, and respect for Dupont as an individual. But Smith overlooked important considerations, as have many other people who continue to recommend or follow this approach.[2]

The need for guidance for cross-cultural negotiators is clear. Every negotiator belongs to a group or society with its own system of knowledge about social interaction—its own "script" for behavior.[3] Whether the boundaries of the group are ethnic, organizational, ideological, or national, its culture influences members' negotiations—through their conceptualizations of the process, the ends they target, the means they use, and the expectations they hold of counterparts' behavior. There is ample evidence that such negotiation rules and practices vary across cultures.[4] Thus cross-cultural negotiators bring into contact unfamiliar and potentially conflicting sets of categories, rules, plans, and behaviors.

Doing as "Romans" do has not usually resolved this conflict effectively. (Throughout this article, the terms "Romans" and "non-Romans" are used as shorthand for "other-culture negotiators" and "own-culture negotiators," respectively.) "Fitting in" requires capabilities that relatively few non-Romans possess; most cultures involve much more than greeting protocols.[5] The approach takes for granted that Romans accept a non-Roman's behaving like a Roman when, actually, many Romans believe in at least some limits for outsiders.[6] Also, the approach presumes, misleadingly, that a Roman will always act Roman with a non-Roman in Rome.

Today's challenges should motivate a cross cultural negotiator to search for additional approaches or strategies. An American negotiator may meet on Tuesday with a group of Japanese who speak through an interpreter and meet on Thursday one-on-one with a Japanese who is fluent in English and a long-time personal friend. In addition, geographical referents are blurring: just off of Paris's Boulevard St. Germain, an American can go to a Japanese restaurant in search of Japanese food and customs, yet find there Chinese waiters who speak Chinese to each other and French to their customers. Indeed, Americans negotiate with Japanese not only in Tokyo and Los Angeles but at third sites such as London. They may forgo face-to-face meetings to communicate by fax, e-mail, telephone, or video conference. Some of the negotiators have one day to finalize a sale; others have 14 months to formulate a joint venture agreement. This variety of people and circumstances calls for more than one strategic approach.

What are the options for conducting negotiations in culturally sensitive ways? What should non-Roman negotiators do, especially when they lack the time and skills available to long-time expatriates?[7] How should the non-Roman businessperson prepare to use a culturally responsive strategy for negotiation with a particular Roman individual or group in a particular set of circumstances?

This article presents a range of eight culturally responsive strategies for Americans and other groups involved in cross-cultural negotiations at home and abroad. The corresponding framework takes into account the varying capabilities of different negotiators across different circumstances and thus provides options for *every* cross-cultural negotiator. Among other benefits, it enables a negotiator to move beyond the popular, one-size-fits-all lists of "dos and don'ts" for negotiating in a particular culture to see that what is appropriate really depends on the negotiating strategy. In short, this article offers the manager a broadened, realistic view of strategies for effective cross-cultural negotiation.

EIGHT CULTURALLY RESPONSIVE STRATEGIES

Stories of cross-cultural conflict—faux pas and "blunders"—abound.[8] They highlight feelings of anxiety, disorientation, misunderstanding, and frustration, and they tempt negotiators to try to minimize apparent behavioral differences by "matching" or "imitating" their counterparts' ways. But there are more fundamental goals for a cross-cultural negotiator.

Consider what often happens when Americans negotiate with Japanese. Viewing negotiation as a process of exchange involving several proposal-counterproposal iterations, Americans inflate their demands in initial proposals and expect later to give and receive concessions. Their Japanese counterparts often do not promptly reciprocate with a counterproposal. Thus the Americans offer concessions, hoping that they will kick the exchange model—"the negotiations"—into gear. The Japanese, however, ask many questions. By the end of the talks, the Americans feel frustrated with the extent of their concessions and conclude that Japanese do not negotiate. Although the Americans may believe that the Japanese are shrewdly trying to determine how much their American counterparts will concede, it is quite likely that these Japanese are operating from a different model of negotiation: negotiation as a process of gathering information, which, when consistent and complete, will reveal a "correct, proper, and reasonable" solution.[9]

FIGURE 1   Cultural Characteristics of Negotiation

General Model

1. Basic concept of process

   Distributive bargaining / Joint problem solving / Debate / Contingency bargaining / Nondirective discussion

2. Most significant type of issue

   Substantive / Relationship-based / Procedural / Personal-internal

Role of the Individual

3. Selection of negotiators

   Knowledge / Negotiating experience / Personal attributes / Status

4. Individuals' aspirations

   Individual ◄─────────────────────► Community

5. Decision making in groups

   Authoritative ◄─────────────────────► Consensual

Interaction: Dispositions

6. Orientation toward time

   Monochronic ◄─────────────────────► Polychronic

7. Risk-taking propensity

   High ◄─────────────────────► Low

8. Bases of trust

   External sanctions / Others' reputation / Intuition / Shared experiences

Interaction: Process

9. Concern with protocol

   Informal ◄─────────────────────► Formal

10. Communication complexity

    Low ◄─────────────────────► High

11. Nature of persuasion

    Direct experience / Logic / Tradition / Dogma / Emotion / Intuition

Outcome

12. Form of Agreement

    Contractual ◄─────────────────────► Implicit

Source: Adapted from S. E. Weiss with W. Stripp, *Negotiating with Foreign Business Persons* (New York: New York University Graduate School of Business Administration, Working Paper #85-6, 1985), p. 10.

Research on communication suggests that the minimal, fundamental goal for non-Romans is to ensure that both sides perceive that the pattern of interaction makes sense.[10] For negotiation to occur, non-Romans must at least recognize those ideas and behaviors that Romans intentionally put forward as part of the negotiation process (and Romans must do the same for non-Romans). Parties must also be able to interpret these behaviors well enough to distinguish common from conflicting positions, to detect movement from positions, and to respond in ways that maintain communication. Yet a non-Roman's own script for negotiation rarely entails the knowledge or skills to make such interpretations and responses.

Figure 1 shows the range of negotiation characteristics that may vary across cultures. The basic concept of the process, for instance, may be one of distributive bargaining, joint problem solving, debate, contingency bargaining, or nondirective discussion. Groups and organizations may select their negotiators for their knowledge, experience, personal attributes, or status. Protocol may range from informal to formal; the desired outcome may range from a contract to an implicit understanding.

A culturally responsive strategy, therefore, should be designed to align the parties' negotiating scripts or otherwise bring about a mutually coherent form of negotiator interaction. This definition does *not* assume that the course of action is entirely premeditated; it can emerge over time. But a culturally responsive strategy does involve a clear goal and does consist of means by which to attain it. Effectively implemented, such a strategy enables the negotiators to convey their respective concerns and to respond to each other's concerns as they attempt to reach agreement.

By contrast, strategies that do not consider cultural factors are naive or misconceived. They may sometimes be successful for non-Romans, but they are hardly a reliable course of action. One such strategy is to deliberately ignore ethnic or other group-based differences and operate as if "business is business anywhere in the world." A "business is business" approach does not avoid culture; it actually represents a culture, one usually associated with U.S. businesspeople or a cosmopolitan elite. Negotiators cannot blithely assume the predominance of this particular business culture amid the multiple cultures represented in their negotiations.

The framework shown in Figure 2 organizes eight culturally responsive strategies according to the negotiator's level of familiarity with the counterpart's culture; the counterpart's familiarity with the negotiator's culture; and the possibility for explicit coordination of approaches.[11] For the sake of clarity, it focuses on negotiations between two parties, each belonging to one predominant culture.

"Familiarity" is a gauge of a party's current knowledge of a culture (in particular, its negotiation scripts) *and* ability to use that knowledge competently in social interactions.[12] Operationally, high familiarity denotes fluency in a predominant Roman language, extensive prior exposure to the culture, and a good track record in previous social interactions with Romans (which includes making correct attributes of their behavior).[13] This is no mean accomplishment; it takes some 24 to 36 months of gradual adaptation and learning for expatriates to "master" how to behave appropriately.[14] Note that negotiators can consider using the strategies feasible at their level of familiarity and *any* strategies corresponding to lower levels of familiarity.

The strategies in brackets in the figure are those that require coordination between parties. Although all negotiators must ultimately coordinate their approaches with counterparts during the talks, if only tacitly, sometimes parties can explicitly address coordination and coherence issues.

FIGURE 2   Culturally Responsive Strategies and Their Feasibility

High	Induce counterpart to follow one's own script	Improvise an approach [effect symphony]	
Counterpart's familiarity with negotiator's culture	Adapt to the counterpart's script [coordinate adjustment of both parties]		Brackets indicate a joint strategy, which requires deliberate consultation with counterpart. At each level of familiarity, a negotiator can consider feasible the strategies designated at that level and any lower level.
Low	Employ agent or adviser [involve mediator]	Embrace the counterpart's script	
	Low **Negotiator's familiarity with counterpart's culture** High		

Low Familiarity with Counterpart's Culture

The negotiator who has had little experience with a counterpart's culture has a choice of two culturally responsive strategies and, depending on the counterpart's familiarity with the negotiator's culture, a possible third. If the counterpart's familiarity level is low, neither party is well equipped cross-culturally; their interaction can be facilitated by changing the people involved.[15] That is, the negotiator can employ an agent or adviser or involve a mediator. If the counterpart's familiarity level is high, a third strategy becomes feasible: inducing the Roman to follow the negotiating script of one's own cultural group.

Employ Agent or Adviser.   To augment his or her own capabilities, a business negotiator can employ cultural experts, translators, outside attorneys, financial advisers, or technical experts who have at least moderate and preferably high familiarity with both the counterpart's and the negotiator's cultures. These experts serve two distinguishable roles, as "agents" who replace the negotiator at the negotiating table or as "advisers" who provide information and recommend courses of action to the negotiator.

> In 1986, a U.S. chemical company that had bartered chemicals for tobacco from Zimbabwe hired an American commodities trader in London to negotiate the sale of the tobacco and some chemicals to Egyptian officials and executives. The Egyptians were offering payment in commodities; the U.S. company sought $20 million cash. As an agent, the American trader engaged in lengthy meetings, rounds of thick coffee, and late-night talks with the Egyptians and succeeded in arranging cash sales of the Egyptian commodities to the United Kingdom, Bangladesh, and other countries.[16]

The value of this strategy depends on the agent's attributes. Skilled, reputable agents can interact very effectively with a negotiator's counterpart. However, their employment may give rise to issues of increased structural complexity, trust, and ownership of the process, not to mention possible cultural tensions between principal and agent.[17] Clearly decipherable by a counterpart, this strategy works well when the counterpart accepts it and the particular agent involved.

Employing an adviser involves other actions and effects.

> Between 1983 and 1986, IBM prepared proposals for a personal computer plant for approval by Mexico's National Commission on Foreign Investment. The company hired Mexican attorneys, consulted local experts such as the American Chamber of Commerce and U.S. embassy staff, and met with high-level Mexican government officials. These advisers provided information about political and social cultures and the foreign investments review process, access to influential individuals, and assessments of the leanings of key decision makers on the commission.[18]

A negotiator can select this strategy unilaterally and completely control its implementation. Of all eight strategies, this one is the least decipherable, sometimes even undetectable, by the counterpart. It is also uniquely incomplete in that it does not directly provide a script for negotiating. The negotiator must go on to select, with or without the adviser's assistance, a complementary strategy.

Involve a Mediator. The use of go-betweens, middlemen, brokers, and other intermediaries is a common practice within many cultures and represents a potentially effective approach to cross-cultural negotiation as well. It is a joint strategy; both negotiator and counterpart rely on a mutually acceptable third party to facilitate their interaction. In its most obvious form, the strategy involves contacting a mediator prior to negotiations and deliberately bringing him or her into the talks. A mediator may also emerge, as happens when the "introducer" (*shokai-sha* in Japanese[19]) who first brought the negotiator to the counterpart continues to play a role or, in team-on-team negotiations, when an individual involved in the talks who does not initially have authority as a mediator, such as an interpreter, becomes a de facto mediator in the course of the negotiation. Such cross-cultural mediators should be at least moderately and preferably highly familiar with the cultures of both parties.

> In the 1950s, an American truck manufacturer negotiated a deal to sell trucks to a Saudi contractor because of the intermediation of Adnan Khashoggi. Khashoggi, the son of the personal physician of the founder of Saudi Arabia, had met the manufacturer while in college in the United States and learned about the contractor's needs upon returning to Saudi Arabia. This was his first "deal," long before his involvement with Lockheed and Northrop. By the 1970s, each of his private jets reportedly contained two wardrobes: "one of three-piece suits, shirts, and ties; . . . the other of white cotton thobes [and] headdresses, . . . the full traditional Arabian regalia."[20]

With this strategy, a negotiator faces some uncertainty about the negotiation process: Will the mediator use one side's negotiation script at the expense of the other's? If the mediator is from a third culture, will he or she use that culture's ways—or introduce something else?[21] In relying on a mediator, the negotiator relinquishes some control of the negotiation. Then again, the mediator can educate the negotiator about the counterpart's culture and bring out ideas and behavior from each side that make the interaction coherent. It is important to find an individual who is not only appropriately skilled but who will also maintain the respect and trust of both parties.[22]

Induce the Counterpart to Follow One's Own Script.   Deliberately inducing the counterpart to negotiate according to the model common in one's own culture is feasible when the counterpart is highly familiar with one's culture. Possibilities for inducement range from verbal persuasion to simply acting as if the counterpart will "come along"—as happens when Americans speak English to non-American counterparts known to speak English as a second language.

> When U.S. based ITT and CGE of France conducted merger talks in the mid-1980s, negotiators used "an American business—American M&A [merger and acquisition]" approach, according to French participants. The French went along with it (despite their unfavorable impressions that it consisted of a "vague" general concept of the deal, emphasis on speed, and formulation of long contracts), because only U.S. law and investment firms had the capacity to carry out this highly complex negotiation. Although their motivations are not exactly known, ITT lawyers have stated that their chief negotiator followed their own methodical style, one developed within ITT."[23]

The pros and cons of this strategy hinge on the counterpart's perception of the negotiator's motivations for pursuing it. The counterpart may conclude that the negotiator is naïve or deliberately ignorant of cultural differences; arrogant; culturally proud but not antagonistic; or merely using an expedient strategy.[24] It is reported that IBM's Thomas Watson, Sr., once said: "It's easier to teach IBM to a Netherlander than to teach Holland to an American."[25] Using one's own ways could also be the result of mistakenly concluding that the two parties share one culture (e.g., Americans and English-speaking Canadians).

For this strategy to work most effectively, the negotiator should convey that it is not based on a lack of respect for the counterpart or for the counterpart's culture. It is the counterpart, after all, who is being called on to make an extra effort; even with a high level of familiarity with the negotiator's culture, a counterpart usually feels more skilled and at ease with his or her own ways. (Were the counterpart to *offer* to follow the negotiator's script, we would be talking about an embrace strategy by the counterpart, which is described below.)

Moderate Familiarity with Counterpart's Culture

The negotiator who already has had some successful experience with a counterpart's culture gains two more strategic options, provided that the counterpart is at least moderately familiar with the negotiator's culture. The unilateral strategy is to adapt one's usual approach to the counterpart's. The joint version is to coordinate adjustment between the two cultures.

Adapt to the Counterpart's Script.   Negotiators often modify their customary behavior by not expressing it to its usual degree, omitting some actions altogether, and following some of the counterpart's ways. The adapt strategy refers to more than this behavior, however; it refers to a broad course of action usually prompted by a deliberate decision to make these modifications.[26]

> In the early 1980s, American negotiators in the Toyota-Ford and GM-Toyota talks over car assembly joint ventures prepared by reading books such as James Clavell's *Shogun* and Edwin Reischauer's *The Japanese*, watching classic Japanese films (e.g. *Kagemusha*), and

frequenting Japanese restaurants. Then they modified their usual negotiating behavior by (1) paying extra attention to comportment and protocol, (2) reducing their expectations about substantive progress in the first few meetings, (3) providing Japanese counterparts with extensive, upfront information about their company and the U.S. business environment, and (4) trying "not to change positions too much once they had been voiced."[27]

A major challenge for the negotiator considering this strategy is to decide which aspects of his or her customary negotiating script to alter or set aside. The aspects most seriously in conflict with the counterpart's may not be easily changed or even readily apparent, and those most obviously in conflict or easily changed may not, once changed, markedly enhance the interaction. Marketing specialists have distinguished between customs to which non-Romans must conform, those to which non-Romans may but need not conform, and those from which non-Romans are excluded.[28] Although a marketing specialist has a fixed, one-sided target in seeking entry into the counterpart's arena, these distinctions may also guide some of the cross-cultural negotiator's deliberations.

A counterpart usually notices at least some evidence of a negotiator's use of the adapt strategy. Deciphering all of the modifications is difficult. It may also be difficult for a counterpart to distinguish an adapt strategy from a badly implemented embrace strategy (described below). Further, if both the negotiator and the counterpart pursue this strategy on their own initiative, their modifications may confuse rather than smooth the interaction. Still, a negotiator can independently make the choice to adapt and usually finds at least some areas within his or her capacity to do so.

Coordinate Adjustment of Both Parties.   The parties may develop, subtly or overtly, a joint approach for their discussions; they may negotiate the process of negotiation. The jointly developed script is usually a blend of elements from the two parties' cultures; it is not totally distinct from them yet not wholly of one or the other. It may take various forms.

> At the outset of a 1988 meeting to discuss the telecommunications policies of France's Ministry of Industry and Tourism, the minister's chief of staff and his American visitor each voiced concern about speaking in the other's native language. They expressed confidence in their listening capabilities and lacked immediate access to an interpreter, so they agreed to proceed by each speaking in his own language. Their discussion went on for an hour that way, the American speaking in English to the Frenchman, and the Frenchman speaking in French to the American.

In a special case of this strategy, the parties "bypass" their respective home cultures' practices to follow the negotiating script of an already existing, third culture with which both have at least moderate familiarity. The parties know enough about the other's culture to recognize the limits of their capabilities in it and the desirability of additional guidance for their interaction.

> Negotiations over MCA's acquisition by Matsushita Electric Industrial Company in 1990 were conducted largely via interpreters. At one dinner, MCA's senior American investment banker and Matsushita's Japanese head of international affairs were stymied in their effort to communicate with each other until they discovered their fluency in the same second language. They conversed in French for the rest of the evening.[29]

Professional societies, trade groups, educational programs and institutions, and various other associations can similarly provide members with third scripts for conduct. This phenomenon is dramatically illustrated, within and between teams, when people who do not share a language play volleyball or soccer socially. The sport provides a script for behavior.

Overall, the strategy has the benefits of the adapt strategy while minimizing the likelihood of incompatible "adjustments." For some Roman counterparts (e.g., Arabs and Chinese), verbally explicit implementation of this strategy for interaction will be awkward—even unacceptable.[30] Other groups' members will appreciate its decipherability and the shared burden of effort that it implies. Since both parties must go along with it, the negotiator's opportunity to "veto" also preserves some control over its implementation.

High Familiarity with Counterpart's Culture

Finally, the negotiator highly familiar with a counterpart's culture can realistically contemplate, not only the five aforementioned strategies, but at least one and possibly two more. If the counterpart is not familiar with the negotiator's culture, the negotiator can unilaterally embrace the other's negotiating script (i.e. "do as the Romans do"). If both parties are highly familiar with each other's cultures, they can jointly or unilaterally search for or formulate a negotiating script that focuses more on the individuals and circumstances involved than on the broader cultures. Such strategies may radically change the process.

Embrace the Counterpart's Script.   The embrace strategy calls for the negotiator to use the negotiation approach typical of the counterpart's culture.

In the 1970s, Coca-Cola undertook negotiations with a state-run, foreign trade organization in the People's Republic of China in order to produce and sell cola drinks there. The company sent one of its research chemists, a China-born man with no business background, to Cambridge University to study Chinese language and culture studies for a full year. Later acclaimed to be highly knowledgeable about China, this chemist was the most active negotiator for Coca-Cola in what became a ten-year endeavor.[31]

Relatively few individuals should attempt this strategy. It demands a great deal of the negotiator, especially when the cultures involved differ greatly. In general, it requires bilingual, bicultural individuals—those who have generally enjoyed long-term overseas residence.

When implemented well, especially when very different cultures are involved, this strategy is clearly decipherable by a counterpart. (When it is not, a counterpart may confuse it with an adapt strategy.) Furthermore, the embrace strategy can make the interaction relatively easy and comfortable for the counterpart. The strategy requires considerable effort by the negotiator, and its implementation remains largely—but not completely—within the negotiator's control.

Improvise an Approach.   To improvise is to create a negotiation script as one negotiates, focusing foremost on the counterpart's particular attributes and capabilities and on the circumstances. Although all negotiators should pay some attention to the Roman counterpart as an individual, not all can or should improvise. The term is used here as it is used in music, not in the colloquial sense of "winging it" or of anyone being able to do it. Musical improvisation requires some preconception or point of departure and a model (e.g., a melody, basic chord structure) that sets the scope for performance. Similarly, the negotiator who improvises know the parties' home cultures and is fully prepared for their influence but can put them in the background or highlight them as negotiation proceeds.

> In the early 1990s, Northern Telecom, a Canadian-owned telecommunications equipment supplier with many Americans in its executive ranks and headquarters in both Mississauga, Ontario, and McLean, Virginia, maintained a "dual identity." Its personnel dealt with each other on either an American or a Canadian basis. On the outside, the company played up its Canadian identity with some governments (those unenthusiastic about big American firms, or perhaps not highly familiar with American ways), and played up its American identity with others.[32]

This strategy is feasible only when both parties are highly familiar with the other's culture. Without that level of familiarity, the negotiator would not know what the counterpart is accustomed to or how he or she is affected, and would not be able to invoke or create ways to relate to the counterpart effectively; nor would the counterpart recognize or respond to these efforts appropriately. At the same time, since the counterpart is highly skilled in at least two cultures and may introduce practices from both or either one of them, it is extremely important to consider the counterpart as an individual, not just as a member of a culture. High familiarity enables the negotiator to do just that, because he or she does not need to devote as much effort to learning about the counterpart's culture as other negotiators do.

> During the Camp David "peace" talks between Egypt, Israel, and the United States in the late 1970s, then President Jimmy Carter set up a one-on-one meeting with Prime Minister Menachem Begin to try to break an impasse. Carter took along photos of Begin's eight grandchildren, on the backs of which he had handwritten their names. Showing these photos to Begin led the two leaders into talking about their families and personal expectations and revitalized the intergovernmental negotiations.[33]

This strategy is often used at high levels, especially at critical junctures, but it need not be limited to that. It can counteract the treatment of a counterpart as an abstraction (e.g., stereotype) and can facilitate the development of empathy. It also seems particularly efficacious with counterparts from cultures that emphasize affective, relationship factors over task accomplishment and creativity or presence over convention.

On the down side, the cultural responsiveness of the improvise strategy is not always decipherable by the counterpart. When a top-level negotiator is involved, the counterpart may assume that the negotiator's strategy is to appeal to status or authority rather than to recognize cultural issues. If the strategy overly "personalizes" negotiation, its implementation can lead to the kinds of problems once pointed out in former U.S. Secretary of State Henry Kissinger's "personal diplomacy": becoming too emotionally involved, failing to delegate, undercutting the status of other possible representatives, and ignoring those one does not meet or know.[34] The strategy may not be appropriate for all cultures and may be difficult to orchestrate by a team of negotiators. It also offers fewer concrete prescriptions for action and greater uncertainty than the four other unilateral strategies. Nevertheless, its malleability should continue to be regarded as a major attribute.

Effect Symphony.   This strategy represents an effort by the negotiator to get both parties to transcend exclusive use of either home culture by exploiting their high familiarity capabilities. They may improvise an approach, create and use a new script, or follow some other approach not typical of their home cultures. One form of coordination feasible at this level of familiarity draws on both home cultures.

> For their negotiations over construction of the tunnel under the English Channel, British and French representatives agreed to partition talks and alternate the site between Paris and London. At each site, the negotiators were to use established, local ways, including the language. The two approaches were thus clearly punctuated by time and space. Although each side was able to use its customary approach some of the time, it used the scripts of the other culture the rest of the time.[35]

Effecting symphony differs from coordinating adjustment, which implies some modification of a culture's script, in that both cultures' scripts may be used in their entirety. It is also one resolution of a situation where both parties start out independently pursuing induce or embrace strategies. Perhaps the most common form of effecting symphony is using a third culture, such as a negotiator subculture.

> Many United Nations ambassadors, who tend to be multilingual and world-traveled, interact more comfortably with each other than with their compatriots.[36] Similarly, a distinct culture can be observed in the café and recreation area at INSEAD, the European Institute of Business Administration, which attracts students from 30 countries for 10 intensive months.

Overall, the effect symphony strategy allows parties to draw on special capabilities that may be accessible only by going outside the full-time use of their home cultures' conventions. Venturing into these uncharted areas introduces some risk. Furthermore, this strategy, like other joint strategies, requires the counterpart's cooperation; it cannot be unilaterally effected. But then, as former U.S. ambassador to Japan Edwin Reischauer suggested about diplomatic protocol, a jointly established culture—the "score" of a symphony—makes behavior predictable.[37] It can also make it comprehensible and coherent.

IMPLICATIONS

A cross-cultural negotiator is thus not limited to doing as the Romans do or even doing it "our way" or "their way." There are eight culturally responsive strategies. They differ in their degree of reliance on existing scripts and conventions, in the amount of extra effort required of each party, and in their decipherability by the counterpart. As a range of options, these strategies offer the negotiator flexibility and a greater opportunity to act effectively.

Because the strategies entail different scripts and approaches, they also allow the negotiator to move beyond the simplistic lists of behavioral tips favored to date in American writings. For example, an American working with Japanese counterparts is usually advised to behave in a reserved manner, learn some Japanese words, and exercise patience.[38] Such behavior applies primarily to an adapt strategy, however, and different strategies call for different concepts and behaviors. Table 1 gives some examples of how an American might behave with Japanese counterparts, depending on the unilateral strategy employed.

TABLE 1   Recommended Behavior for Americans Negotiating with the Japanese* (by type of culturally responsive strategy)

Employ

- Use "introducer" for initial contacts (e.g., general trading company).
- Employ an agent the counterpart knows and respects.
- Ensure that the agent/adviser speaks fluent Japanese.

Induce

- Be open to social interaction and communicate directly.
- Make an extreme initial proposal, expecting to make concessions later.
- Work efficiently to "get the job done."

Adapt

- Follow some Japanese protocol (reserved behavior, name cards, gifts).
- Provide a lot of information (by American standards) up front to influence the counterpart's decision making early.
- Slow down your usual timetable.
- Make informed interpretations (e.g., the meaning of "it is difficult").
- Present positions later in the process, more firmly and more consistently.

Embrace

- Proceed according to an information-gathering, *nemawashi* (not exchange) model.
- "Know your stuff" cold.
- Assemble a team (group) for formal negotiations.
- Speak in Japanese.
- Develop personal relationships; respond to obligations within them.

Improvise

- Do homework on the individual counterpart(s) and circumstances.
- Be attentive and nimble (improvising entails different behaviors for different Japanese).
- Invite the counterpart to participate in mutually enjoyed activities or interests (e.g., golf).

---

*These are examples, not a complete listing, of attitudes and behaviors implied by a negotiator's use of each strategy.

Similarly, for his meeting with Dupont in Paris, Smith could have considered strategies other than "embrace" and its associated script. An adapt strategy may not have necessitated speaking exclusively in French. Table 2 suggests some ways he might have behaved, given each unilateral strategy. Smith might also have contemplated using strategies in combination (e.g., "adapt," then "embrace"), especially if meetings had been scheduled to take place over a number of months.

At the same time, only the negotiator highly familiar with the counterpart's culture can realistically consider using all eight strategies. The value of high familiarity, as a current capability or as an aspiration to achieve, should be clear. The value of the cultural focus should also be clear, notwithstanding the importance of also focusing on the

TABLE 2   Recommended Behavior for Americans Negotiating with the French* (by type of culturally responsive strategy)

Employ

- Employ an agent well-connected in business and government circles.
- Ensure that the agent/adviser speaks fluent French.

Induce

- Be open to social interaction and communicate directly.
- Make an extreme initial proposal, expecting to make concessions later.
- Work efficiently to "get the job done."

Adapt

- Follow some French protocol (greetings and leave-takings, formal speech).
- Demonstrate an awareness of French culture and business environment.
- Be consistent between actual and stated goals and between attitudes and behavior.
- Defend views vigorously.

Embrace

- Approach negotiation as a debate involving reasoned argument.
- Know the subject of negotiation *and* broad environmental issues (economic, political, social).
- Make intellectually elegant, persuasive yet creative presentations (logically sound, verbally precise).
- Speak in French.
- Show interest in the counterpart as an individual but remain aware of the structures of social and organizational hierarchies.

Improvise

- Do homework on the individual counterpart(s) and circumstances.
- Be attentive and nimble (improvising entails different behaviors for different French individuals).
- Invite counterpart to participate in mutually enjoyed activities or interests (e.g., dining out, tennis).

---

*These are examples, not a complete listing, of attitudes and behaviors implied by a negotiator's use of each strategy.

individual counterpart (Part 2 of this article will expand on this point). Culture provides a broad context for understanding the ideas and behavior of new counterparts as well as established acquaintances. It also enables the negotiator to notice commonalities in the expectations and behavior of individual members of a team of counterparts, to appreciate how the team works as a whole, and to anticipate what representatives and constituents will do when they meet away from the cross-cultural negotiation. As long as the negotiator intends to go on negotiating with other Romans, it behooves him or her to pay attention to commonalities across negotiation experiences with individual Romans—to focus on cultural aspects—in order to draw lessons that enhance effectiveness in future negotiations.

As presented here, the eight culturally responsive negotiation strategies reflect one perspective: feasibility in light of the negotiator's and counterpart's familiarity with each other's cultures. That is a major basis for selecting a strategy, but it is not sufficient. This framework maps what is doable; it should not be interpreted as recommending that the best strategies for every negotiation are those at the highest levels of familiarity— that improvising is always better than employing advisers. The best strategy depends on additional factors that will be discussed in Part 2. In its own right, the framework represents a marked shift from prevailing wisdom and a good point of departure for today's cross-cultural negotiators.

ENDNOTES

1. All examples that are not referenced come from personal communication or the author's experiences.

2. Contemporary academic advocates of this approach for negotiators include S. T. Cavusgil and P. N. Ghauri, *Doing Business in Developing Countries* (London: Routledge, 1990), pp. 123–124; J. L. Graham and R. A. Herberger, Jr., "Negotiators Abroad—Don't Shoot from the Hip," *Harvard Business Review*, July–August 1983, p. 166; and F. Posses, *The Art of International Negotiation* (London: Business Books, 1978), p. 27.

3. The concept of a script has been applied by W. B. Gudykunst and S. Ting-Toomey, *Culture and Interpersonal Communication* (Newbury Park, CA: Sage, 1988), p. 30.

4. See, for example, N. C. G. Campbell et al., "Marketing Negotiations in France, Germany, the United Kingdom, and the United States," *Journal of Marketing* 52 (1988): 49–62; and J. L. Graham et al., "Buyer-Seller Negotiations around the Pacific Rim: Differences in Fundamental Exchange Processes," *Journal of Consumer Research* 15 (1988): 48–54. For evidence from diplomacy, see R. Cohen, *Negotiating across Cultures* (Washington, DC): U.S. Institute of Peace Press, 1991); and G. Fisher, *International Negotiation: A Cross-Cultural Perspective* (Yarmouth, ME: Intercultural Press, 1980).

5. See J. L. Graham and N. J. Adler, "Cross-Cultural Interaction: The International Comparison Fallacy," *Journal of International Business Studies* 20 (1989): 515–37. The authors conclude that their subjects adapted to some extent, but a lack of adaptability could also be convincingly argued from their data.

6. For an experimental study showing that moderate adaptation by Asians in the United States was more effective than substantial adaptation, see J. N. P. Francis, "When in Rome: The Effects of Cultural Adaptation of Intercultural Business Negotiations," *Journal of International Business Studies* 22 (1991): 403–28.

7. The majority of leaders of North American firms still lack any expatriate experience and foreign language ability, according to N. J. Adler and S. Bartholomew, "Managing Globally Competent People," *The Executive* 6 (1992): 58.

8. See, for example, D. Ricks and V. Mahajan, "Blunders in International Marketing: Fact or Fiction?" *Long Range Planning* 17 (1984): 78–83. Note that the impact of faux pas may vary in magnitude across cultures. In some cultures, inappropriate behavior constitutes an unforgivable transgression, not a "slip-up."

9. M. Blaker, *Japanese International Negotiating Style* (New York: Columbia University Press, 1977), p. 50.

10. See V. E. Cronen and R. Shuter, "Forming Intercultural Bonds," *Intercultural Communication Theory: Current Perspectives*, ed. W. B. Gudykunst (Beverly Hills, CA: Sage, 1983), p. 99. Their concept of "coherence" neither presumes that the interactants make the same sense of the interaction nor depends always on mutual understanding.

11. Although similar in form, this plot differs in theme from the "model of conflict-handling responses" developed by K. W. Thomas and R. H. Kilmann, *Thomas-Kilmann Conflict Mode Instrument* (Tuxedo, NY: Xicom, Inc., 1974). It also differs in key variables from the "Dual Concerns" model of D. G. Pruitt and J. Z. Rubin, *Social Conflict: Escalation, Stalemate, and Settlement* (New York: Random House, 1986), p. 35ff. Moreover, neither of these models appears to have yet been applied cross-culturally.

12. This notion of familiarity draws on Dell Hymes's concept of communicative competence. See R. E. Cooley and D. A. Roach, "A Conceptual Framework," *Competence in Communication*, ed. R. N. Bostrom (Beverly Hills, CA: Sage, 1984), pp. 11–32.

13. See, for example, R. W. Brislin et al., *Intercultural Interactions* (Beverly Hills, CA: Sage, 1986); A. T. Church, "Sojourner Adjustments," *Psychological Bulletin* 91 (1982): 545–49; P. C. Earley, "Intercultural Training for Managers," *Academy of Management Review* 30 (1987): 685–98; and J. S. Black and M. Mendenhall, "Cross-Cultural Training Effectiveness: A Review and Theoretical Framework for Future Research," *Academy of Management Review* 15 (1990): 113–36.

14. J. S. Black and M. Mendenhall, "The U-Curve Adjustment Hypothesis Revisited: A Review and Theoretical Framework," *Journal of International Business Studies* 22 (1991): 225–47.

15. Changing the parties involved is commonly mentioned in dispute resolution literature. See, for example, R. Fisher and W. Ury, *Getting to Yes* (Boston: Houghton Mifflin, 1981), pp. 71–72.

16. S. Lohr, "Barter Is His Stock in Trade," *New York Times Business World*, September 25, 1988, pp. 32–36.

17. For empirical research on negotiating representatives and their boundary role, constituents, and accountability within a culture, see D. G. Pruitt *Negotiation Behavior* (New York: Academic Press, 1981), pp. 41–44, 195–97. With respect to agents, see J. Z. Rubin and F. E. A. Sander, "When Should We Use Agents? Direct vs. Representative Negotiation," *Negotiation Journal*, October 1988, pp. 395–401.

18. S. E. Weiss, "The Long Path to the IBM-Mexico Agreement: An Analysis of the Microcomputer Investment Negotiations, 1983–1986." *Journal of International Business Studies* 21 (1990): 565–96.

19. J. L. Graham and Y. Sano, *Smart Bargaining: Doing Business with the Japanese* (New York: Ballinger, 1989), p. 30.

20. R. Lacey, *The Kingdom: Arabia and the House of Sa'ud* (New York: Avon Books, 1981), pp. 464–66. See also P. E. Tyler, "Double Exposure: Saudi Arabia's Middleman in Washington," *New York Times Magazine*, June 7, 1992, pp. 34ff.

21. For additional ideas about what a mediator may do, see P. J. D. Carnevale, "Strategic Choice in Mediation," *Negotiation Journal* 2 (1986): 41–56.

22. See J. Z. Rubin, "Introduction," *Dynamics of Third Party Intervention*, ed. J. Z. Rubin (New York: Praeger, 1981), pp. 3–43; and S. Touval and I. W. Zartman, "Mediation in International Conflicts" *Mediation Research*, eds. K. Kressel and D. G. Pruitt (San Francisco: Jossey-Bass, 1989), pp. 115–37.

23. S. E. Weiss, "Negotiating the CGE-ITT Telecommunications Merger, 1985–1986: A Framework-then-Details Process," paper presented at the Academy of International Business annual meeting, November 1991.

24. Such positions have been associated with people in nations with long-established cultures, such as China, France, and India. For instance, some Mexican high officials who speak English fluently have insisted on speaking Spanish in their meetings with Americans. While this position could be influenced by the historical antipathy in the U.S.-Mexico relationship and the officials' concern for the status of their office, it also evinces cultural pride.

25. "IBM World Trade Corporation," Harvard Business School, reprinted in S. M. Davis, *Managing and Organizing Multinational Corporations* (New York: Pergamon Press, 1979), p. 53.

26. Adapting has been widely discussed in the literature. See, for example, S. Bochner, "The Social Psychology of Cross-Cultural Relations," *Cultures in Contact,* ed. S. Bochner (Oxford: Pergamon, 1982), pp. 5–44.

27. S. E. Weiss, "Creating the GM-Toyota Joint Venture: A Case in Complex Negotiation," *Columbia Journal of World Business*, Summer 1987, pp. 23–37; and S. E. Weiss, "One Impasse, One Agreement: Explaining the Outcomes of Toyota's Negotiations with Ford and GM," paper presented at the Academy of International Business annual meeting, 1988.

28. P. R. Cateora and J. M. Hess, *International Marketing* (Homewood, IL: Irwin, 1971), p. 407.

29. C. Bruck, "Leap of Faith," *New Yorker*, September 9, 1991, pp. 38–74.

30. See C. Thubron, *Behind the Wall* (London: Penguin, 1987), pp. 158, 186–87.

31. L. Sloane, "Lee, Coke's Man in China," *New York Times*, February 5, 1979, p. D2.

32. W. C. Symonds et al., "High-Tech Star," *Business Week*, July 27, 1992, pp. 55–56.

33. Found among the exhibits at the Carter Center Library and Museum, Atlanta, Georgia.

34. R. Fisher, "Playing the Wrong Game?" *Dynamics of Third Party Intervention*, ed. J. Z. Rubin (New York: Praeger, 1981) pp. 98–99, 105–6. On the additional problem of losing touch with constituencies, see the 1989–1991 Bush-Gorbachev talks described in M. R. Beschloss and S. Talbott, *At the Highest Levels* (Boston: Little, Brown, 1993).

35. See C. Dupont, "The Channel Tunnel Negotiations, 1984–1986: Some Aspects of the Process and Its Outcome," *Negotiation Journal* 6 (1990): 71–80.

36. See, for example, C. F. Alger, "United Nations Participation as a Learning Experience," *Public Opinion Quarterly*, Summer 1983, pp. 411–26.

37. E. O. Reischauer, *My Life between Japan and America* (New York: Harper and Row, 1986), p. 183.

38. N. B. Thayer and S. E. Weiss, "Japan: The Changing Logic of a Former Minor Power," *National Negotiating Styles*, ed. H. Binnendijk (Washington, DC: Foreign Service Institute, U.S. Department of State, 1987), pp. 69–72.

Negotiating with "Romans"—Part 2

Stephen E. Weiss

Managers are increasingly called on to negotiate with people from other cultures. Cross-cultural negotiation need not be as frustrating nor as costly as it is often made out to be; it can be a productive and satisfying experience. Which of these outcomes a manager achieves depends in part on the negotiation strategies taken in response to—or better, in anticipation of—the counterpart's plans and behavior. There are eight culturally responsive strategies for a manager to consider (see Figure 1).[1] Clearly, the quality of a negotiation outcome and a manager's satisfaction with it also depend on how well he or she chooses and implements one of these approaches.

This article presents five steps for selecting a culturally responsive strategy and then offers various tips for implementation, such as making the first move, monitoring feedback, and modifying the approach. These guidelines reflect four basic, ongoing considerations for a strategy: its *feasibility* for the manager, its fit with the counterpart's likely approach and therefore its capacity to lead to *coherent interaction*, its *appropriateness* to the relationship and circumstances at hand, and its *acceptability* in light of the manager's values. There are challenges involved in all of these efforts, and they are pointed out below rather than ignored or belittled, as happens in much cross-cultural negotiation literature. Thus, from this article, managers stand to gain both an operational plan and the heightened awareness necessary to use a culturally responsive negotiation strategy effectively.

SELECTING A STRATEGY

Every negotiator is advised to "know yourself, the counterpart, and the situation."[2] This advice is useful but incomplete, for it omits the relationship—the connection—between the negotiator and the counterpart.[3] (For clarity, the negotiator from the "other" culture will be called the "counterpart" in this article.) Different types of relationships with counterparts and even different phases of a relationship with a particular counterpart call for different strategies.

For the cross-cultural negotiator, the very presence of more than one culture complicates the process of understanding the relationship and "knowing" the counterpart. In contrast to the "within-culture" negotiator, the cross-cultural negotiator cannot take

FIGURE 1   Culturally Responsive Strategies and Their Feasibility

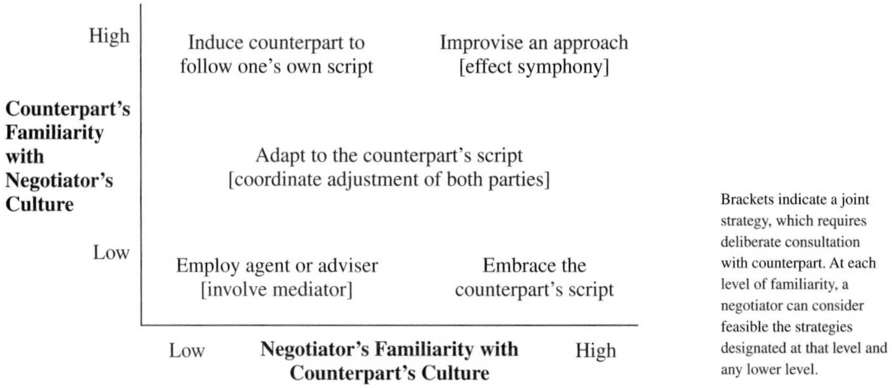

common knowledge and practices for granted and thereby simply concentrate on the individual. It becomes important to actively consider the counterpart in two respects: as a member of a group and as an individual.

The right balance in these considerations is not easily struck. An exclusive emphasis on the group's culture will probably lead the negotiator off the mark because individuals often differ from the group average. Members of the same group may even differ very widely on certain dimensions. At the same time, the degree of variation tolerated between group members is itself an aspect of culture. For example, Americans have traditionally upheld the expression, "He's his own man," while Japanese believed that "the protruding nail is hammered down." The cross-cultural negotiator should thus consider both the counterpart's cultural background and individual attributes, perhaps weighting them differently according to the culture involved, but mindful always that every negotiation involves developing a relationship with a particular individual or team.[4]

> For years, Japanese managers have come to one of my classes each term to negotiate with graduate students so the students can experience negotiating first-hand and test the often stereotypical descriptions they have read about Japanese negotiating behavior. I deliberately invite many Japanese, not just one or two. The students invariably express surprise when the Japanese teams "deviate" from the Japanese negotiating script, as the students understand it, and when differences appear in the behavior of various Japanese teams.

The five steps for selecting a culturally responsive negotiation strategy take into account these complexities:

1. Reflect on your culture's negotiation script.
2. Learn the negotiation script of the counterpart's culture.
3. Consider the relationship and circumstances.
4. Predict or influence the counterpart's approach.
5. Choose your strategy.

These steps take minutes or months, depending on the parties and circumstances involved. Each step will probably not require the same amount of time or effort. Furthermore, the sequencing of the steps is intended to have an intuitive, pragmatic appeal for an American negotiator, but it should not be treated rigidly. Some steps will be more effective if they are coupled or treated iteratively. Nor should these efforts start at the negotiation table when time, energy, resources, and introspection tend to be severely limited. Every one of these steps merits *some* attention by every cross-cultural negotiator before the first round of negotiation.

It is important to remember that the procedure represented by these five steps is itself culturally embedded, influenced by the author's cultural background and by that of the intended audience (American negotiators).[5] Not all counterparts will find the pragmatic logic herein equally compelling. As two Chinese professionals have observed, "In the West, you are used to speaking out your problems. . . . But that is not our tradition," and "In our country, there are so many taboos. We're not used to analytic thinking in your Western way. We don't dissect ourselves and our relationships."[6] Even with this procedure, culture continues to influence what we do and how we do it.

One way to deal with this inescapable cultural bias is to acknowledge it and remain aware of the continual challenges of effectively choosing and implementing a strategy. Often these challenges do not stand out—books on international negotiation have not addressed them—yet they can hamper, even ruin, a negotiator's best efforts. Each step below thus includes a list of cautions for cross-cultural negotiating.

1. Reflect on Your Culture's Negotiation Script

Among members of our "home" group, we behave almost automatically.[7] We usually have no impetus to consider the culture of the group because we repeatedly engage in activities with each other without incident or question. It is easy to use these "natural," taken-for-granted ways in a cross-cultural situation—too easy.

> A book on international negotiation published by the U.S. State Department displays the flags of six nations on its front cover. On initial copies of the book, the French flag appeared in three bands of red, white, and blue. The actual French flag is blue, white, and red.[8]

A cross-cultural negotiator should construct a thoughtful, systematic profile of his or her culture's negotiation practices, using personal knowledge and other resources. Let's say you want to develop an "American negotiator profile." There is a vast amount of research and popular literature on negotiation in the United States.[9] For insights about American culture more broadly, consider both Americans' self-examinations and outsiders' observations.[10] Then organize this information into the profile represented in Figure 2.[11] The profile consists of four topic areas: the general model of the negotiation process, the individual's role, aspects of interaction, and the form of a satisfactory agreement. The left side of the ranges in Figure 2 generally fit the American negotiator profile (e.g., the basic concept is distributive bargaining, the most significant issues are substantive ones, negotiators are chosen for their knowledge, individual aspirations predominate over community needs, and so forth).

This profile should also uncover the values that support these tendencies. For instance, distributive bargaining implies certain attitudes toward conflict and its handling

FIGURE 2   Negotiator Profile

General Model

1. Basic concept of process

 Distributive bargaining / Joint problem solving / Debate / Contingency
 bargaining / Nondirective discussion

2. Most significant type of issue

 Substantive / Relationship-based / Procedural / Personal-internal

Role of the Individual

3. Selection of negotiators

 Knowledge / Negotiating experience / Personal attributes / Status

4. Individuals' aspirations

 Individual ◄——————————————————► Community

5. Decision making in groups

 Authoritative ◄——————————————► Consensual

Interaction: Dispositions

6. Orientation toward time

 Monochronic ◄——————————————► Polychronic

7. Risk-taking propensity

 High ◄——————————————————► Low

8. Bases of trust

 External sanctions / Other's reputation / Intuition / Shared experiences

Interaction: Process

9. Concern with protocol

 Informal ◄——————————————————► Formal

10. Communication complexity

 Low ◄——————————————————► High

11. Nature of persuasion

 Direct experience / Logic / Tradition / Dogma / Emotion / Intuition

Outcome

12. Form of agreement

 Contractual ◄——————————————► Implicit

Source: Adapted from S. E. Weiss with W. Stripp, *Negotiating with Foreign Business
Persons* (New York: New York University Graduate School of Business Administration,
Working Paper #85-6, 1985), p. 10.

(direct), toward business relationships (competitive), and toward the purpose of negotiation (to maximize individual gains). Since some of your group's tendencies and values
may not align with your own, develop a personal profile as well. Doing so does not require
probing deeply into your unconscious. Simply ask yourself, "What do I usually do at times

like this? Why? What do I gain from doing it this way?" These kinds of questions resemble those used in basic negotiation training to distinguish an underlying interest from a bargaining position, namely, "What does this bargaining position do for me? Why?"

> In the mid-1980s, a white American banker planned to include an African-American analyst on his team for a forthcoming visit to white clients in South Africa. When they learned about this, the clients intimated their preference that she not attend. While the banker wanted to serve his clients, he also had strong feelings about including the analyst and about basing qualifications on merit. She was the best analyst on his staff. The banker's values swayed his decision: he told his clients that he would not make the trip without this analyst on his team.[12]

Developing cultural and personal profiles is an ongoing task. Instead of writing them up once and moving on, return to them and refine them as you gain experience and understanding. The value of such a process is considerable. It increases your self-awareness; it helps you explain your expectations and behavior to a counterpart; it prepares you to make decisions under pressure; it allows you to compare your culture to another on a holistic rather than fragmented basis; it helps you determine a counterpart's level of familiarity with your culture; its products—profiles—can be used in future negotiations with other cultural groups; it motivates interest in other cultures; and it enables you to act consistently and conscientiously.

This process demands a good deal of effort, especially at the outset (note the cautions in Table 1). But as a negotiator, you will find such reflection to be a good basis for developing a cross-cultural negotiation strategy.

2. Learn the Negotiation Script of the Counterpart's Culture

This step applies to both the negotiator highly familiar with a counterpart's culture and the one who knows next to nothing about it.[13] The highly familiar negotiator should review what he or she knows and gather additional information to stay current. The uninitiated negotiator should begin to construct a negotiator profile from the ground up. Ideally, this process involves learning in the active sense: developing the ability to use the counterpart's cultural and personal negotiation scripts, as well as "knowing" the scripts and related values.

Learning these scripts enhances the negotiator's ability to anticipate and interpret the counterpart's behavior. Even a negotiator with low familiarity who is likely to employ an agent needs some information in order to interact effectively with the agent to assess the agent's performance. Although few negotiators learn everything about a counterpart before negotiation, advance work allows for assimilation and practice, provides a general degree of confidence that helps the negotiator to cope with the unexpected, and frees up time and attention during the negotiation to learn finer points.

Again, the negotiator profile framework is a good place to start. Try especially to glean and appreciate the basic concept of negotiation because it anchors and connects the other dimensions. Without it, a negotiator, as an outsider, cannot comprehend a counterpart's actions; they appear bizarre or whimsical. Moreover, if you focus merely on tactics or simple "do and don't"-type tips and reach a point in a transaction for which

TABLE 1   Cautions: Understanding Your Own Culture's Script

- Beware of psychological and group biases, such as denial and "groupthink."
- Probe for assumptions and values; they are seldom identified explicitly in day-to-day life.
- Don't become rigidly wedded to your own ways.
- Take time during negotiations to step out of the action and reflect on your behavior.

you have no tip, you have no base—no sense of the "spirit of the interaction"—to guide you through this juncture. For instance, the "spirit" of French management has been described like this:

> French managers see their work as an intellectual challenge requiring the remorseless application of individual brainpower. They do not share the Anglo-Saxon view of management as an interpersonally demanding exercise, where plans have to be constantly "sold" upward and downward using personal skills. The bias is for intellect rather than for action.[14]

Continuing with this example, let's say you are preparing to negotiate with a French counterpart. You may find information about French negotiation concepts and practices in studies by French and American researchers and in natives' and outsiders' popular writings.[15] In addition to general nonfiction works on French culture, novels and films can convey an extraordinary sense of interactions among individuals and groups.[16] Other sources include intensive culture briefings by experts and interviews with French acquaintances, colleagues, and compatriots familiar with French culture, and, in some cases, even the counterpart.

Here, as in reflections on your own culture, make sure to consider core beliefs and values of the culture. Keep an eye on the degree of adherence to them as well as their substantive content.

> A Frenchman involved in the mid-1980s negotiations between AT&T and CGE over a cross-marketing deal revealed his own culture's concern for consistency in thought and behavior as he discussed AT&T's conduct. He described the AT&T representatives' style as "very strange" because they made assurances about "fair" implementation while pushing a very "tough" contract.

Moving from information gathering to assimilation and greater familiarity with a culture usually requires intensive training on site or in seminars.[17] Some Japanese managers, for example, have been sent overseas by their companies for three to five years to absorb a country's culture before initiating any business ventures. When the time comes, familiarity may be assessed through tests of language fluency, responses to "critical incidents" in "cultural assimilator" exercises, and performance in social interactions in the field.[18]

Whether of not you have prior experience working with a particular counterpart or other inside information, try to explore the counterpart's own negotiation concepts, practices, and values. They can be mapped in a negotiator profile just as you mapped your own values.

This entire undertaking poses challenges for every negotiator, regardless of the strategy ultimately chosen. One of the highest hurdles may be the overall nature of the

TABLE 2   Cautions: Learning about the Counterpart's Culture

- Don't be too quick to identify the counterpart's home culture. Common cues (name, physical appearance, language, accent, and location) may be unreliable. The counterpart probably belongs to more than one culture.
- Beware of the Western bias toward "doing." In Arab, Asian, and Latin groups, ways of being (e.g., comportment, smell), feeling, thinking, and talking can more powerfully shape relationships than doing.
- Try to counteract the tendency to formulate simple, consistent, stable images. Not many cultures are simple, consistent, or stable.
- Don't assume that all aspects of the culture are equally significant. In Japan, consulting all relevant parties to a decision (*nemawashi*) is more important than presenting a gift (*omiyage*).
- Recognize that norms for interactions involving outsiders may differ from those for interactions between compatriots.
- Don't overestimate your familiarity with your counterpart's culture. An American studying Japanese wrote New Year's wishes to Japanese contacts in basic Japanese characters but omitted one character. As a result, the message became "Dead Man, congratulations."

learning itself. Learning about another culture's concepts, ways, and values seems to hinge on the similarity between that culture and one's own. Learning is inhibited when one is isolated from members of that culture (even if one is living in their country) and "may fail to occur when attitudes to be learned contradict deep-seated personality orientations (e.g., authoritarianism), when defensive stereotypes exist, or at points where home and host cultures differ widely in values or in conceptual frame of reference.[19] Other significant challenges can be seen in Table 2. Remember that, ultimately, you have access to different strategies for whatever amount of learning and level of familiarity you attain.

3. Consider the Relationship and Circumstances

Negotiators and counterparts tend to behave differently in different relationships and contexts.[20] One does not, for instance, act the same way as a seller as one does as a buyer. So a negotiator should not count on the same strategy to work equally well with every counterpart from a given cultural group (even if the counterparts have the same level of familiarity with the negotiator's culture) or, for that matter, with the same counterpart all the time. The peaks and valleys that most relationships traverse require different strategies and approaches. In the same vein, circumstances suggest varying constraints and opportunities.

To continue your preparations for a negotiation, consider particular facets of your relationship with the counterpart and the circumstances. The most important facets on which to base strategic choices have not yet been identified in research and may actually depend on the cultures involved. Furthermore, laying out a complete list of possibilities goes beyond the scope of this article.[21] But the following considerations (four for relationships, four for circumstances) seem significant.

TABLE 3   Cautions: Considering the Relationship and Circumstances

---

- Pay attention to the similarities *and* differences, in kind and in magnitude, between your negotiator profiles and those of the counterpart.
- Be careful about judging certain relationship aspects as major (big picture issues) and minor (fine details). This dichotomy, let alone the particular contents of the two categories, is not used in all cultures.
- Consider the relationship from the counterpart's perspective.
- Identify the relationship factors and circumstances most significant to you *and* the counterpart.
- Beware of the use and abuse of power.
- Discover the "wild cards" either party may have.
- Remember that the relationship will not remain static during negotiation.

Life of the Relationship.   The existence and nature of a prior relationship with the counterpart will influence the negotiation and should figure into a negotiator's deliberations. With no prior contact, one faces a not-yet personal situation; general information and expectations based on cultural scripts will have to do until talks are under way. Parties who have had previous contact, however, have experienced some form of interaction. Their expectations concerning the future of the relationship will also tend to influence negotiation behavior.[22] In sum, the negotiator should acknowledge any already established form of interaction, assess its attributes (e.g., coherence) and the parties' expectations of the future, and decide whether to continue, modify, or break from the established form. These decisions will indicate different culturally responsive strategies.

Fit of Respective Scripts.   Having completed steps 1 and 2, you can easily compare your negotiator profiles, both cultural and individual, with those of the counterpart. Some culture comparisons based on the negotiator profile in Figure 2 have already been published.[23] Noting similarities as well as differences will enable you to identify those aspects of your usual behavior that do not need to change (similarities) and those aspects that do (major differences) if you choose a strategy that involves elements of both your negotiation script and the counterpart's (e.g., the adapt strategy). The number and kinds of differences will also suggest how difficult it would be to increase your level of familiarity with the counterpart's culture or to use certain combinations of strategies.

Do not allow such a comparison to mislead you. Some people overemphasize differences. Others, focusing on superficial features, overestimate similarities and their understanding of another culture (e.g., when Americans compare American and Canadian cultures). The cautions in Table 3 can help you stay on track.

Of course a negotiator highly familiar with the counterpart's culture who plans to adopt an embrace strategy, operating wholly within that culture, has less need for these comparisons.

Balance of Power.   It may seem that power would have a lot to do with the choice of strategy. A more powerful party could induce the other to follow his or her cultural script. A less powerful party would have to embrace the other's script. A balance of power might suggest an adapt or improvise strategy.

But the issue is not so simple. The tilt of the "balance" is not easily or clearly determined; parties often measure power using different scales.[24] Indeed, forms of power, their significance, and appropriate responses are all culturally embedded phenomena.[25] Furthermore, it makes little sense to rely on power and disregard a counterpart's familiarity with one's culture when one's goal is coherent interaction. This is not to say that one could not benefit from an imbalance of power *after* choosing a culturally responsive strategy or in other areas of negotiation. Still, since power is culturally based and Americans have a general reputation for using it insensitively, American negotiators should be extremely careful about basing the strategy decision on power.

Gender.   Consider the possible gender combinations in one-on-one cross-cultural relationships: female negotiator with female counterpart, male negotiator with male counterpart, male negotiator with female counterpart, and female negotiator with male counterpart. Within most cultures, same-gender and mixed relationships entail different negotiating scripts. There are few books on negotiation designated for American women, but communication research has shown that men tend to use talk to negotiate status, women tend to use it to maintain intimacy, and they are often at cross-purposes when they talk to each other.[26] The debates over how American women should act in male-dominated workplaces further substantiate the existence of different scripts. In a sense, gender groups have their own cultures, and mixed interaction within a national culture is already cross-cultural.

Mixed interaction across national and other cultures holds even greater challenges. One of the primary determinations for a woman should be whether a male counterpart sees her first as a foreigner and second as a woman, or vice versa. According to some survey research, Asian counterparts see North American businesswomen as foreigners first.[27] The opposite may be true in parts of France. Edith Cresson, former French prime minister, once said, "Anglo-Saxons are not interested in women as women. For a [French] woman arriving in an Anglo-Saxon country, it is astonishing. She says to herself, "What is the matter?"[28] Thus, although current information about negotiating scripts for other countries tends to be based on male-male interactions, complete culturally based negotiator profiles should include gender-based scripts.

Whether your negotiation involves mixed or same-gender interaction, try to anticipate the counterpart's perception of the gender issue and review your core beliefs. Gender-based roles in France, for instance, may appear so antithetical (or laudable) that you will not entertain (or will favor) the embrace strategy.

With regard to circumstances, the second part of step 3, there are at least four relevant considerations.

Opportunity for Advance Coordination.   Do you have—or can you create—an opportunity beforehand to coordinate strategy with your counterpart? If so, consider the joint strategies. If not, concentrate at the outset on feasible, unilateral strategies.

Time Schedule.   Time may also shape a negotiator's choice in that different strategies require different levels of effort and time. For the negotiator with moderate familiarity of the counterpart's culture but an inside track on a good agent, employing an agent may take less time than adapting to the counterpart's script. The time required to implement a strategy also depends on the counterpart's culture (e.g., negotiations based on the French script generally take longer than the American script). And time constrains the learning one can do to increase familiarity. Imagine the possibilities that open up for a diligent negotiator when discussions are scheduled as a series of weekly meetings over a 12-month period instead of as one two-hour session.

Audiences.   Consider whether you or the counterpart will be accompanied by other parties, such as interpreters, advisers, constituents, and mass media. Their presence or absence can affect the viability and effectiveness of a strategy. If no one else will attend the meeting, for instance, you have no one to defer to or involve as a mediator at critical junctures.

> During the early months of the ITT-CGE telecommunications negotiations in 1985 and 1986, fewer than 10 individuals were aware of the talks. That permitted the parties to conduct discussions in ways not possible later, when over a 100 attorneys, not to mention other personnel, became involved. At the same time, that choice may have ruled out the initial use of some culturally responsive strategies.

Wild Cards.   Finally, you should assess your own and the counterpart's capacities to alter some relationship factors and circumstances. Parties may have extra-cultural capabilities such as financial resources, professional knowledge, or technical skills that expand their set of feasible options, bases for choice, or means of implementation.

> During the GM-Toyota joint venture negotiations in the early 1980s, Toyota could afford to and did hire three U.S. law firms simultaneously for a trial period in order to compare their advice and assess their compatibility with the company. After three months, the company retained one of the firms for the duration of the negotiations.

4. Predict or Influence the Counterpart's Approach

The last step before choosing a strategy is to attempt to determine the counterpart's approach to the negotiation, either by predicting it or by influencing its selection. For the effectiveness of a culturally responsive strategy in bringing about coherent interaction depends not only on the negotiator's ability to implement it but also on its complementarity with the counterpart's strategy. Embracing the counterpart's script makes little sense if the counterpart is embracing your script. Further, reliable prediction and successful influence narrow the scope of a negotiator's deliberations and reduce uncertainty. And the sooner the prediction, the greater the time available for preparation. While these concerns relate to the parties' relationship (step 3), they have a direct impact on interaction that merits a separate step.

Assuming that your counterpart will not ignore cultural backgrounds and that each of you would adopt only a unilateral strategy, you can use Figure 3 to preview all possible intersections of these strategies.[29] They fall into three categories: complementary, potentially but not inherently complementary, and conflicting. Thus the figure shows the coherence of each strategy pair.

FIGURE 3   The Inherent Coherence of Parties' Culturally Responsive Strategies

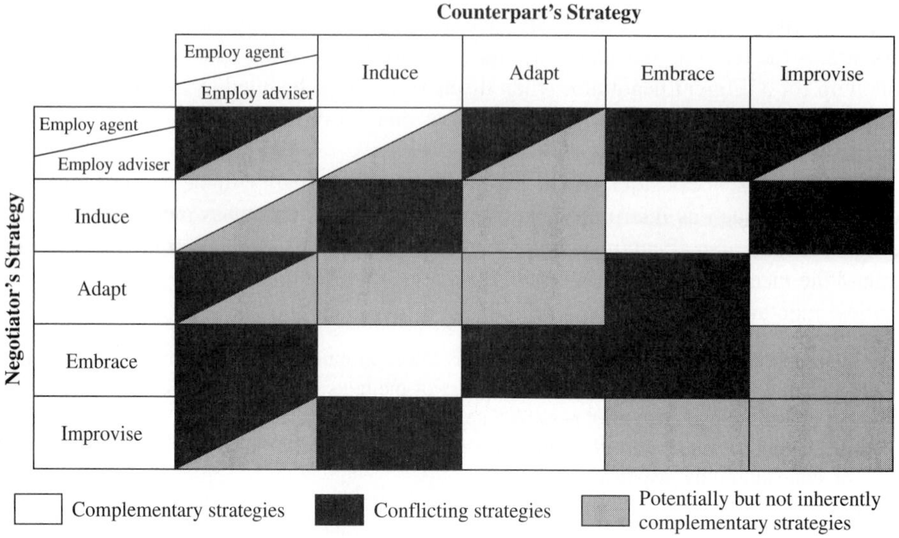

Among these pairs, adapt-adapt and improvise-improvise might seem inherently complementary. The catch is that parties can adapt or improvise in conflicting ways. Of all the potentially complementary cells, the improvise-improvise interaction may, however, be the most likely to become coherent, given the nature of the improvise strategy and the capabilities it entails.

Not all of the strategies in Figure 3 will be available to you in every situation. Remember that in addition to potential coherence, your choice will be based on your familiarity with the counterpart's culture, the counterpart's familiarity with yours, appropriateness, and acceptability.

Prediction.   Sometimes a counterpart will make this step easy by explicitly notifying you of his or her strategy in advance of your talks. If the counterpart does not do that, there may be telling clues in the counterpart's prenegotiation behavior, or other insiders (associates or subordinates) may disclose information.

Without direct and reliable information, you are left to predict the counterpart's strategy choice on the basis of his or her traits and motivations. Some counterparts will have a rational, task-directed orientation. Strategy research based on this perspective shows that counterparts seeking to coordinate their actions with a negotiator often select the course of action most prominent or salient to both parties (e.g., choosing a river as a property boundary).[30] Other counterparts will focus on what is socially proper. Indeed, whether a counterpart even responds to the cross-cultural nature of the interaction may vary with his or her cosmopolitanism. A cosmopolitan counterpart may lean toward adapt and improvise strategies, whereas a counterpart having little experience with other cultures may be motivated primarily by internal, cultural norms, In the latter case,

TABLE 4   Cautions: Predicting or Influencing the Counterpart's Approach

- Try to discern whether the counterpart's culture categorically favors or disfavors certain strategies.
- Don't fixate on "what's typical" for someone from the counterpart's cultural group.
- Recognize the difficulty in accurately assessing the counterpart's familiarity with your culture's negotiating script.
- Heed the line, however fuzzy, between influencing and "meddling"—a U.S. diplomat was detained in Singapore in 1988 for interfering in internal affairs.*
- Track changes in the counterpart's strategic choices over time.
- Don't focus so obsessively on parties' strategies that you ignore the richness of the relationship or the context.

*F. Deyo *Dependent Development and Industrial Order* (New York: Praeger, 1981), p. 89.

the counterpart's negotiator profile may be used to predict some behavior. For example, the internally focused individual from a culture with high communication complexity (reliance on nonverbal and other contextual cues for meaning), which often correlates with low risk-taking propensity, would be more likely to involve a mediator than to coordinate adjustment (which is too explicit) or to embrace or improvise (which are too uncertain).[31]

Influence.   Whether or not you can predict a counterpart's strategy choice, why not try to influence it? If you predict a strategy favorable to you, perhaps you can reinforce it; if unfavorable, change it; and if predicted without certainty, ensure it. Even if prediction proves elusive, it behooves you to try to influence the counterpart.

The first task in this process is to determine your own preferred strategy based on the criteria in step 5. This may appear to be jumping ahead, but choosing and influencing go hand in hand. They will go on throughout negotiation, for new information will come to light and necessitate reassessments.

Once you have chosen a strategy, use the matrix in Figure 3 to locate interaction targets. Your prime targets should be the coherent (complementary) combinations, followed by the potentially coherent ones. For example, if you intend to employ an agent, influence the counterpart to use the induce strategy.

Some negotiators may also contemplate targeting conflicting strategies. In this line of thinking, a conflict could bring out the parties' differences so dramatically as to provide valuable lessons and "working" material for both the negotiator and counterpart. Influencing the counterpart to pursue a strategy that conflicts with one's own (or selecting one by oneself if the counterpart has already set a strategy) might establish that one is not a negotiator who can be exploited. However, these effects lie outside of our main purposes of demonstrating responsiveness to cultural factors and establishing a coherent form of interaction. Furthermore, such conflict often confuses, causes delays, and provokes resentment. (Note also the other cautions in Table 4.)

With respect to means of influence, Americans sometimes preemptively take action, such as using English in conversation without inquiring about a non-American counterpart's wishes or capabilities, but there are other, often more mutually satisfactory, ways to influence a counterpart. They range from direct means, such as explicitly requesting a counterpart to choose a particular strategy, to tacit means, such as disclosing one's level of familiarity with the counterpart's culture, revealing one's own strategy choice, or designating a meeting site likely to elicit certain types of conduct. For example, in 1989, then U.S. Secretary of State James Baker hosted his Soviet counterpart Eduard Shevardnadze in Jackson Hole, Wyoming, instead of Washington, D.C. Prenegotiation communications may also be carried out by advance staff or through back channels. As you evaluate these options, bear in mind that their effectiveness will probably differ according to the counterpart's culture and personal attraction to you.[32]

5. Choose Your Strategy

When you have completed the previous steps, it is time to choose a strategy or a combination of strategies. Four selection criteria emerge from these steps. The strategy must be feasible given the counterpart and cultures involved; able to produce a coherent pattern of interaction, given the counterpart's likely approach; appropriate to the relationship and circumstances; and acceptable, ideally but not necessarily, to both parties. These criteria apply to the prenegotiation choice of strategy, but you may also use them to assess your strategy during negotiation.

A possible fifth criterion would be your degree of comfort with a strategy. Even negotiators highly familiar with two cultures' scripts favor one script over another in certain circumstances. So if the four criteria above do not direct you to only one right strategy, consider, at the end, which of the remaining strategies you would be most comfortable implementing.

Apply the four criteria in order, for their sequence is deliberate and designed for negotiators with a pragmatic orientation (e.g., Americans). Feasibility, after all, appears first. Acceptability appears later because the value judgment it involves impedes deliberation in cross-cultural situations when used too early.[33] (Note that counterparts from other cultural groups may prefer to use a list that begins with appropriateness or acceptability.)

Each criterion deserves attention. Feasibility and coherence considerations may narrow your choices down to one unilateral strategy, yet you should still check that choice for its appropriateness, given the relationship and circumstances, and its consonance with core beliefs and values. For a negotiation scheduled to take place over many years, for example, the negotiator might look at a strategy that is potentially but not inherently complementary to the counterpart's (see Figure 3) or at combinations or progressions of strategies. For a negotiation where the negotiator cannot narrow strategy options by reliably predicting the counterpart's strategy, the negotiator may actually have to rely on the last two criteria. And when a negotiator wishes to consider joint strategies, relationship factors and circumstances are essential to consult. In sum, the support of all four criteria for a particular strategy choice should give you confidence in it.

Occasionally, criteria may conflict. Feasibility and coherence point to an embrace strategy for a counterpart's induce strategy, but the negotiator may find aspects of the counterpart culture's script unacceptable (e.g., *fatwa*, Iran's death threat). Or the embrace-induce strategy pairing may have worked well in a cross-cultural relationship for years, but now you expect your counterpart to be at least moderately familiar with

TABLE 5   Cautions: Choosing a Strategy

- Don't assume the counterpart will use the same criteria or order you do (e.g., efficiency is not a universal concern).
- Watch out for parties' miscalculations and conflicting impressions (e.g., the counterpart's assessments of your respective levels of cultural familiarity may differ from yours).
- Proceed carefully when criteria conflict; further research may help.
- Don't treat an embrace strategy, by mere definition, as costly or a concession.

---

your culture. The resolution of such conflicts begs for further research. In the meantime, you may want to defer to your core beliefs and values. Values define the very existence of your home group and your membership in it; by ignoring or violating them you risk forfeiting your membership.[34]

As an example of strategy selection based on all four criteria, consider an American, Smith, who is preparing for a confidential, one-on-one meeting with a Frenchman he has never met before, Dupont.

> Smith once lived in France and, as the meeting is being held in Dupont's Paris office, his gut feeling is to speak in French and behave according to Dupont's culture—that is, to use an embrace strategy. However, he takes the time to evaluate his options. Smith realizes that he is no longer familiar enough with French language and culture to use an embrace strategy, and the short lead time prevents him from increasing his familiarity. With a moderate level of familiarity, he has five feasible strategies: employ an agent or adviser, involve a mediator, induce Dupont to follow his script, adapt to Dupont's script, or coordinate adjustment by both parties. Smith does some research and learns that Dupont has only a moderate level of familiarity with American negotiation practices. That rules out the induce strategy. The relationship and circumstances make an agent or mediator inappropriate. An adapt strategy would be hit-or-miss because Smith has no cues from previous face-to-face interaction and only one meeting is planned. Overall, the best strategy choice is to coordinate adjustment.

A complicated situation will require more complex considerations. (See also the cautions on choosing a strategy in Table 5.) But the five steps above—reflect, learn, consider, predict, and choose—constitute a sound and useful guide for strategy selection.

IMPLEMENTING YOUR STRATEGY

The full value of the most carefully selected strategy rests on effective implementation, a formidable task in the general fluidity of negotiations and especially in the multifaceted process of most cross-cultural negotiations. It is here, in a negotiation's twists and turns, that a negotiator deals head on with distinctions between the counterpart's attributes as an individual and as a member of a cultural group. Simply adhering to one's own plan of action is difficult—and may become undesirable. For the negotiator must ensure that the strategy complements the counterpart's approach and enables the two of them to establish and maintain a coherent form of interaction.

Whatever the chosen culturally responsive strategy, a negotiator may enhance the effectiveness of first moves and ongoing efforts by generally respecting the counterpart and his or her group's culture and by demonstrating empathy (both of which may take different forms for different cultures). These qualities, among others, have been recommended in the literature on cross-cultural competence and are consistent with cultural responsiveness.[35] They do not necessitate lowering one's substantive negotiation goals.[36]

First Moves

The strategies of employ agent, embrace, and induce entail complete, existing scripts for negotiation. Pursuing one of these strategies essentially involves following the script associated with it. The adapt strategy involves modifications of your own script, at least some of which should be determined beforehand. With the improvise strategy, you ought to give some advance thought to a basic structure even if much of the path will emerge as you travel on it. Thus you have a starting point for each of the five unilateral strategies.

These strategies assume that when a counterpart recognizes your strategy, he or she will gravitate toward its corresponding script.[37] The counterpart wants to understand you and to be understood; that is what occurs in *coherent* interaction. If you have accurately assessed the counterpart's level of familiarity with your culture and ability to use a particular script, and if the counterpart recognizes the strategy you are using, you stand a better chance of achieving coherence.

Should you make the first strategic move or wait until the counterpart does? This decision affects the transition from preliminary "warm-up" discussions to negotiation of business matters. It depends, in part, on whether you need to gather more information about the counterpart's strategic intentions and abilities. This would matter when both parties have at least moderate familiarity with each other's cultures and have more than one unilateral strategy they can realistically choose, and when you have chosen a strategy (e.g., adapt, improvise) that relies on cues from the counterpart. The decision over timing also depends on whether you need to make the strategy you have chosen distinguishable from another one (e.g., improvise from adapt) and want to clearly establish this strategy at the outset. (Note that if a negotiator has chosen to employ an agent or has successfully influenced the counterpart, then timing should not be an issue.) In sum, to decide on timing, you should weigh the benefits of additional information against the costs of losing an opportunity to take leadership and set the tone of the interaction, a loss that includes being limited in your strategy options by the counterpart's strategy choice.

The three joint strategies are explicit and coordinated by definition. Once parties have decided to use a joint strategy, first moves consist of fleshing out particulars. Which mediator? What kinds of adjustments? What basic structure will underlie improvisation? These discussions may require the intermediate use of one of the five unilateral strategies.

Parties coordinating adjustment might consider trading off their respective priorities among the 12 cultural aspects in the negotiator profiles. If your counterpart values certain interpersonal conduct (protocol) more than the form of the agreement, for example, and you value the latter more than the former, the two of you could agree to adhere to a certain protocol and, on agreement, to draw up a comprehensive legal document. This pragmatic approach will probably appeal more to Western counterparts than to Asian ones, however, particularly if the Asian counterparts have only low or moderate cultural familiarity. So take this approach with caution rather than presuming that it will always work.

Whichever joint strategy you adopt, pursue it visibly in your first moves. Espe-cially in first-time encounters, a counterpart reads these moves as indications of one's integrity ("sincerity," in Japan) and commitment to coordination.

Ongoing Efforts

A cross-cultural negotiator has myriad concerns and tasks, including vigilant attention to the cautions in the tables presented thus far. Still, as negotiation proceeds, one's most important task is concentrating on interaction with the counterpart. Parties' actions and reac-tions evidence adherence to and departures from a given negotiation script, fill out the incomplete scripts associated with some strategies (i.e., adapt, improvise, effect symphony), and determine the ultimate effectiveness of every one of the eight culturally responsive strategies. These interactions occur so quickly that analyzing them makes them seem frag-mented and in "slow motion." Nevertheless, some analysis can have tremendous value.

As you negotiate, shift most of your attention from the counterpart's culture to the counterpart as an individual. Specifically, monitor feedback from him or her, be pre-pared to modify, shift, or change your strategy, and develop *this* relationship.

Monitor Counterpart's Feedback.   A counterpart's reactions to your ideas and conduct provide critical information about the counterpart personally and about the effectiveness of your chosen strategy with this particular individual. As you use that information to make continual adjustments and to evaluate your strategy, you may want to return to the four criteria of feasibility, coherence, appropriateness, and acceptability.

Some verbal and nonverbal cues transcend cultures in signaling positive or nega-tive reception to a negotiator's use of a certain script. They range from a counterpart's statements ("Things are going well," "We don't do things that way") to a tightening of the corner of the mouth and cocked head, which convey contempt.[38]

> In one film of the "Going International" series, an American manager urges his Saudi coun-terpart to expedite delivery of supplies from the docks to the hospital building site. He points out that the supplies have already sat at the dock for a week just because of paperwork, he personally is "in a crisis," "nobody works here" on Thursday and Friday (it is now Tuesday), and during the upcoming Ramadan observance "things really slow down." At various points during theses remarks, the Saudi does not respond at all to a direct question, perfunctorily sets aside a written schedule he receives, and looks disparagingly at the American's shoes. In the end, the Saudi states, "Mr. Wilson, my people have been living for many years without a hospital. We can wait two more weeks."[39]

Admittedly, a counterpart's statements can be more or less honest or truthful, and the gradations are often fuzzy to an outsider. A number of cultures distinguish between saying what is socially acceptable (*tatemae* in Japanese) and saying what is truly on one's mind (*honne*). Other standards may also differ across cultures.

Many cues (e.g., silence) do not carry consistent meaning from culture to culture. Generally, individuals learn the culturally specific meanings as they become familiar with a culture. Negotiator profiles include some cues and imply others under dimensions such as "communication complexity" and "nature of persuasion." A negotiator can use these cues when he or she embraces the counterpart's culture.

TABLE 6   Cautions: Implementing Your Strategy

- Remember that cross-cultural interaction can be creative and satisfying, not always taxing.
- Stay motivated.
- Separate your observations of the counterpart's behavior from your interpretations and conclusions about his or her intentions.
- Notice the changes as well as the constants in the counterpart's behavior over time.
- Try to pick up even the subtle cues.
- Give some thought to whether the counterpart might be feigning low familiarity with your culture and language.
- Don't get in too deep; don't unwittingly lead the counterpart to think your familiarity with his or her culture is higher than it actually is.
- Accept some of the limitations that the counterpart's culture may impose on outsiders; not all limitations can be surmounted no matter how well or long you try.
- Balance your responsiveness to cultural factors with your other aspirations and needs as a negotiator.

Then again, some singularly powerful cues are very subtle. (See other cautions for strategy implementation in Table 6.)

> In the 1950s, an American couple—the lone foreigners—at a Japanese wedding banquet in Tokyo were socializing and dining like everyone else. All of a sudden, everyone else finished eating and left the reception. Residents of Japan for many years, the Americans concluded later that a signal had been sent at some point, and they had not even detected it.

In cross-cultural interactions that do not involve embracing or inducing, or when a negotiator cannot clearly decipher the counterpart's strategy, nonuniversal cues are disconcertingly difficult to detect and interpret correctly. You can handle ambiguous cues (e.g., the hesitation of a counterpart who has so far been loquacious) by keeping them in mind until additional cues and information convey and reinforce one message. Other ambiguous cues may be decoded only by asking the counterpart; alternatively, they remain unclear. Dealing with these cues is a very real and ongoing challenge.

Be Prepared to Modify, Shift, or Change.   Even the well-prepared negotiator faces some surprises and some negative feedback in a negotiation. You want to be nimble enough to respond effectively. "Modifying" refers to refining implementation of a strategy without abandoning it; "shifting" refers to moving from one strategy to another within a previously planned combination of strategies; and "changing" refers to abandoning the strategy for another, unplanned one.

Making alterations is relatively easy with some counterparts.

> For the first round of the 1980–1981 Ford-Toyota talks, Ford negotiators employed a bilingual Japanese staffer from their Japan office. The Toyota team, apparently confident in their English language abilities, suggested that Ford not bring the interpreter to subsequent meetings, so that the negotiators could "talk directly." Ford negotiators obliged and changed their approach.

On other occasions, one may have to explain modifications, shifts, and changes before they are made in order to minimize the odds of being perceived as unpredictable or deliberately disruptive. One may also deflect criticism by directly or indirectly associating these actions with changes in circumstances, the subject on the agenda, phase of the discussion, or, when negotiating as part of a team, personnel. For ideas about specific modifications to make, other than those prompted by your counterpart, review the counterpart's negotiator profile. Changes in strategy should be shaped by both a negotiator's culturally relevant capabilities and the strategy being abandoned. You may go relatively smoothly from an adapt to a coordinate adjustment strategy, for example, but not from inducing to embracing or from involving a mediator to employing an agent.

Over time, some movement between strategies may occur naturally (e.g., adapt to coordinate adjustment), but a *shift* as defined here involves a preconceived combination, or sequence of strategies (e.g., coordinate adjustment, then effect symphony). A negotiator could plot a shift in strategies for certain types of counterpart feedback, variation in circumstances or relationship factors, or, especially during a long negotiation, for a jump in his or her level of cultural familiarity.

Develop *This* Relationship.   Pragmatic Americans may view the cultivation of a relationship with the counterpart primarily as an instrument for strategy implementation. Concentrating on coherent interaction and a satisfactory relationship usually does enhance a culturally responsive strategy's effectiveness. But the strategy should also— even primarily—be seen as serving the relationship.

> Riding describes the views of Mexican negotiators when they returned home from Washington after the negotiations over Mexico's insolvency in 1982: "'We flew home relieved but strangely ungrateful,' one Mexican official recalled later. 'Washington had saved us from chaos, yet it did so in an uncharitable manner.' Even at such a critical moment, the substance and style of the relationship seemed inseparable."[40]

Many of your non-American counterparts will be accustomed to an emphasis on relationships. Indeed, greater attention to relationship quality may be the most common distinction between negotiators from American and non-American cultures.

Developing a relationship with a particular counterpart requires an attentiveness to its life and rhythms. The form of your interaction can evolve across different scripts and approaches, especially after many encounters. There is also the potential for culturally driven conflict, which you should be willing to try to resolve.

Clearly, such a relationship should be treated dynamically, whether time is measured in minutes or in months. In that light, you can continuously learn about the counterpart and the counterpart's culture *and* educate the counterpart about you and your culture. Over a long period, you may experiment with a counterpart's ways in noncritical areas (at low risk) to develop skills within and across culturally responsive strategies. In this way, you can expand the number of feasible strategies, giving both you and the counterpart more flexibility in the ways you relate to each other.

TOWARD CROSS-CULTURAL NEGOTIATING EXPERTISE

> A friend of mine, a third-generation American in Japan who was bilingual in Japanese and English, used to keep a file of items that one must know . . . to function in Japan. . . . [He] never stopped discovering new things; he added to the file almost every day.[41]

Over the years, many cross-cultural negotiators have essentially asked, "What happens when you're in Rome, but you're not Roman?" The most common advice available today was first offered 1,600 years ago: "Do as the Romans do." Yet these days, a non-Roman in Rome meets non-Romans as well as Romans and encounters Romans outside of Rome. The more we explore the variety of parties' capabilities and circumstances and the more we question the feasibility, coherence, appropriateness, and acceptability of "doing as Romans do," the more apparent the need becomes for additional culturally responsive strategies.

The range of strategies presented here provides every negotiator, including one relatively unfamiliar with a counterpart's culture, with at least two feasible options. Combinations of strategies further broaden the options.

If there is "something for everyone" here, the value of developing and sustaining cross-cultural expertise should still be clear. That includes high familiarity with a "Roman" culture—knowing the cognitive and behavioral elements of a Roman negotiating script and being able to use the script competently. The negotiator at the high familiarity level enjoys the broadest possible strategic flexibility for negotiations with Romans and the highest probability that, for a particular negotiation, one strategy will solidly meet all four selection criteria.

A negotiator can also gain a great deal from learning about more than one other culture. For lack of space I have concentrated on negotiations between two individuals, each belonging to one cultural group, but most cross-cultural negotiations involve more than two cultures: most individuals belong to more than one group; negotiations often occur between teams that have their own team cultures in addition to the members' ethnic, national, and organizational backgrounds; and multiparty, multicultural negotiations occur as well. In short, the non-Roman highly familiar with culture A still encounters cultures B, C, and D. Even though a negotiator may need to focus only on the one culture that a counterpart deems predominant at any one point in time, there are several to explore and manage across time, occasions, and people.[42]

> As soon as he was assigned to GM's Zurich headquarters in the mid-1980s, Lou Hughes, one of GM's main representatives in the GM-Toyota negotiations of the early 1980s, began taking German lessons because GM's main European plant was located in Germany. Now president of GM Europe, Hughes' effectiveness as an executive has been attributed in part to his cultural sensitivity and learning.[43]

In the process of exploring other cultures, one may discover an idea or practice useful for all of one's negotiations.

> Another American negotiator in the GM-Toyota talks was so impressed with the Toyota negotiators' template for comparing parties' proposals that he adopted it and has relied on it since for his negotiations with others.

It is in this spirit of continuous learning that this article has presented culturally responsive strategies, selection criteria, key steps in the choice process, and implementation ideas. If negotiators with a moderate amount of cross-cultural experience have the most to gain from these tools, first-time negotiators have before them a better sense of what lies ahead, and highly experienced negotiators can find some explanation for the previously unexplained and gain deeper understanding. In addition, the culture-individual considerations and ongoing challenges highlighted throughout the article will serve all cross-cultural negotiators. Perhaps we can all travel these paths more knowingly, exploring and building them as we go.

ENDNOTES

1. S. E. Weiss, "Negotiating with 'Romans'—Part 1," *Sloan Management Review*, Winter 1994, pp. 51–61. All examples that are not referenced come from personal communication or the author's experiences.

2. See J. K. Murnighan, *Bargaining Games: A New Approach to Strategic Thinking in Negotiations* (New York: William Morrow and Co., 1992), p. 22.

3. G. T. Savage, J. D. Blair, and R. L. Sorenson, "Consider Both Relationships and Substance When Negotiating Strategically," *The Executive* 3 (1989): 37–47; and S. E. Weiss, "Analysis of Complex Negotiations in International Business: The RBC Perspective," *Organization Science* 4 (1993): 269–300.

4. Attending to both culture and the individual has also been supported by S. H. Kale and J. W. Barnes, "Understanding the Domain of Cross-National Buyer-Seller Interactions," *Journal of International Business Studies* 23 (1992): 101–32.

5. To speak of an "American culture" is not to deny the existence of cultures within it that are based on ethnic, geographic, and other boundaries. In fact, the strategies described in Part 1 of this article and the five steps described here can be applied to these cross-cultural negotiations as well. These ideas deserve the attention of those, for example, who are concerned about diversity in the workplace.

6. C. Thubron, *Behind the Wall* (London: Penguin, 1987), pp. 158, 186–87.

7. See R. Keesing as quoted in W. B. Gudykunst and S. Ting-Toomey, *Culture and Interpersonal Communication* (Newbury Park, CA: Sage, 1988), p. 29.

8. H. Binnendijk, ed., *National Negotiating Styles* (Washington, DC: Foreign Service Institute, U.S. Department of State, 1987).

9. For a review of popular books, see S. Weiss-Wik, "Enhancing Negotiator's Successfulness: Self-Help Books and Related Empirical Research," *Journal of Conflict Resolution* 27 (1983): 706–39. For a recent research review, see P. J. D. Carnevale and D. G. Pruitt, "Negotiation and Mediation," *Annual Review of Psychology* 43 (1992): 531–82.

10. For self-examinations, see G. Althen, *American Ways: A Guide for Foreigners in the United States* (Yarmouth, ME: Intercultural Press, 1988): E. T. Hall and M. R. Hall, *Understanding Cultural Differences* (Yarmouth, ME: Intercultural Press, 1990): and E. C. Stewart and M. J. Bennett, *American Cultural Patterns* (Yarmouth, ME: Intercultural Press, 1991). The views of outsiders include A. de Tocqueville, *Democracy in America, 1805–1859* (New York: Knopf, 1980); L. Barzini, *The Europeans* (Middlesex, England: Penguin, 1983), pp. 219–53; and Y. Losato, "Observing Capitalists at Close Range," *World Press Review*, April 1990, pp. 38–42.

11. The original framework appeared in S. E. Weiss with W. Stripp, "Negotiating with Foreign Business Persons: An Introduction for Americans with Propositions on Six Cultures" (New York: New York University Graduate School of Business Administration, Working Paper No. 85–6, 1985).

12. Although I am not certain, my recollection is that the clients relented, and the bank team made the trip to South Africa. The point, however, is that the banker took a stand on an issue that struck values dear to him. Other examples include whether or not to make "questionable payments" and how to handle social settings in France and in Japan when one is allergic to alcohol or cigarette smoke.

On payments, see T. N. Gladwin and I. Walter, *Multinationals under Fire* (New York: John Wiley & Sons, 1980), p. 306. On smoking, see W. E. Schmidt, "Smoking Permitted: Americans in Europe Have Scant Protection," *New York Times* September 8, 1991, p. 31.

On the other hand, some customs, while different, may not be abhorrent or worth contesting. An American male unaccustomed to greeting other men with "kisses" (the translation itself projects a bias) might simply go along with an Arab counterpart who has initiated such a greeting.

13. Murnighan (1992), p. 28; and Kale and Barnes (1992), p. 122.

14. J. L. Barsoux and P. Lawrence, "The Making of a French Manager," *Harvard Business Review*, July–August 1991, p. 60.

15. For example, for each of the four categories respectively, see D. Chalvin, *L'entreprise négociatrice* (Paris: Dunod, 1984) and C. Dupont, *La négociation: conduite, théorie, applications*, 3rd ed. (Paris: Dalloz, 1990); N.C.G. Campbell et al., "Marketing Negotiations in France, Germany, the United Kingdom, and the United States," *Journal of Marketing* 52 (1988): 49–62 and G. Fisher, *International Negotiation: A Cross-Cultural Perspective* (Yarmouth, ME: Intercultural Press, 1980); L. Bellenger, *La négotiation* (Paris: Presses Universitaires de France, 1984) and A. Jolibert and M. Tixier, *La négociation commerciale* (Paris: Les éditions ESF, 1988); and Hall and Hall (1990).

16. Nonfiction writings include J. Ardagh, *France Today* (London: Penguin, 1987); L. Barzini (1983); S. Miller, *Painted in Blood: Understanding Europeans* (New York: Atheneum, 1987); and T. Zeldin, *The French* (New York: Vintage, 1983).

Fictional works include the classics by Jean-Paul Sartre and Andre Malraux and, more recently, A. Jardin, *Le Zèbre* (Paris: Gallimard, 1988).

17. I will leave to others the debate over the effectiveness of training focused on "skills" versus other types of training. Somewhat surprisingly, some research on individuals' perceived need to adjust suggests that "interpersonal" and documentary training have comparable effects. See P. C. Earley, "Intercultural Training for Managers," *Academy of Management Review* 30 (1987): 685—98.

Note also that a number of negotiation seminars offered overseas do not directly increase familiarity with negotiation customs in those countries. These seminars import and rely on essentially American concepts and practices.

18. On cultural assimilator exercises, see R. W. Brislin et al., *Intercultural Interactions: A Practical Guide* (Beverly Hills, CA: Sage, 1986).

19. J. Watson and R. Lippitt, *Learning across Cultures* (Ann Arbor, MI: University of Michigan Press 1955), as quoted in A. T. Church, "Sojourner Adjustment," *Psychological Bulletin* 91 (1982): 544.

20. See Savage, Blair, and Sorenson (1989), p.40. The following all include relationship factors (e.g., interest interdependence, relationship quality, concern for relationship) in their grids for strategic selection: R. Blake and J. S. Mouton, *The Managerial Grid* (Houston, Texas: Gulf, 1964): Gladwin and Walter (1980); and K. W. Thomas and R. H. Kilmann, *Thomas-Kilmann Conflict Mode Instrument* (Tuxedo, NY: Xicom, Inc., 1974).

21. For more extensive lists, see Weiss (1993).

22. D. G. Pruitt and J. Z. Rubin, *Social Conflict: Escalation, Stalemate, and Settlement* (New York: Random House, 1986), pp. 33–34

23. Weiss with Stripp (1985); F. Gauthey et al., *Leaders sans frontières* (Paris: McGraw-Hill, 1988), pp. 149–56, 158; and R. Moran and W. Stripp, *Dynamics of Successful International Business Negotiations* (Houston, TX: Gulf, 1991).

24. P. H. Gulliver, *Disputes and Negotiations* (New York: Academic, 1979), pp. 186–90, 200–7.

25. G. Hofstede, *Culture's Consequences* (Beverly Hills: Sage, 1984).

26. The literature on women and negotiation includes M. Gibb-Clark, " A Look at Gender and Negotiations," *The Globe and Mail,* May 24, 1993, p. B7; J. Ilich and B. S. Jones, *Successful Negotiating Skills for Women* (New York: Playboy Paperbacks, 1981); and C. Watson and B. Kasten, "Separate Strengths? How Men and Women Negotiate" (New Brunswick, NJ: Rutgers University, Center for Negotiation and Conflict Resolution, working paper).

    On gender-based communication, see D. Tannen, *You Just Don't Understand* (New York: William Morrow and Co., 1990).

27. N. J. Adler, "Pacific Basin Managers: Gajjin, Not a Woman," *Human Resource Management* 26 (1987): 169–91. This corresponds with the observation that "the different groups a person belongs to are not all equally important at a given moment." See K. Lewin, *Resolving Social Conflicts* (New York: Harper & Row, 1948), p. 46, according to Gudykunst and Ting-Toomey (1988), p. 201.

28. A. Riding, "Not Virile? The British Are Stung," *New York Times,* June 20, 1991, p. A3. See the disguises used by a female American reporter in S. Mackey, *The Saudis: Inside the Desert Kingdom* (New York: Meridian, 1987).

    On the other hand, the all-woman New York City–based firm of Kamsky and Associates has been widely recognized for their business deals in the People's Republic of China. See also C. Sims, "Mazda's Hard-driving Saleswoman," *New York Times,* August 29, 1993, Section 3, p. 6; and M. L. Rossman, *The International Business Woman* (New York: Praeger, 1987).

29. This interaction format draws on a game theoretic perspective and borrows more directly from T. A. Warschaw, *Winning by Negotiation* (New York: McGraw-Hill, 1980), p. 79.

30. T. C. Schelling, *The Strategy of Conflict* (New York: Oxford University Press, 1960), pp. 53–58. The prominence of many courses of action would seem, however, to rest on assumptions that are culturally based and thus restricted rather than universal.

31. On risk-taking propensity, see Gudykunst and Ting-Toomey (1988), pp. 153–60.

32. For discussions of similarity-attraction theory and research, see K. R. Evans and R. F. Beltramini, "A Theoretical Model of Consumer Negotiated Pricing: An Orientation Perspective," *Journal of Marketing* 51 (1987): 58–73; J.N.P. Francis, "When in Rome? The Effects of Cultural Adaptation on Intercultural Business Negotiations," *Journal of International Business Studies* 22 (1991): 403–28; and J. L. Graham and N. J. Adler, "Cross-Cultural Interaction: The International Comparison Fallacy," *Journal of International Business Studies* 20 (1989): 515–37.

33. N. Dinges, "Intercultural Competence," in *Handbook of Intercultural Training*, vol. 1., D. Landis and R. W. Brislin, eds. (New York: Pergamon, 1983), pp. 176–202.

34. Individual members do instigate change and may, over time, cause a group to change some of its values. Still, at any given point, a group holds to certain values and beliefs.

35. See Dinges (1983), pp. 184–85, 197; and D. J. Kealey, *Cross-Cultural Effectiveness: A Study of Canadian Technical Advisors Overseas* (Hull, Quebec: Canadian International Development Agency, 1990), p. 53–54. At the same time, Church cautiously concluded in his extensive review of empirical research that effects of personality, interest, and value on performance in a foreign culture had not yet demonstrated strong relationships. See Church (1982), p. 557.

36. This advice parallels the now widely supported solution for the classic negotiator's dilemma of needing to stand firm to achieve one's goals and needing to make concessions to sustain movement toward an agreement: namely, "be firm but conciliatory," firm with respect to goals, but conciliatory with respect to means. See Pruitt and Rubin (1986), p. 153.

37. Sometimes counterparts do not actually desire an agreement but some side effect. Thus their behavior may differ from that described here. See F. C. Ikle, *How Nations Negotiate* (Millwood, NY: Kraus Reprint, 1976), pp. 43–58.

38. See "Universal Look of Contempt," *New York Times*, December 22, 1986, p. C3.

39. "Going International" film series, Copeland Griggs Productions, San Francisco.

40. A. Riding, *Distant Neighbors: A Portrait of Mexicans* (New York: Vintage Books, 1984), p. 487.

41. E. T. Hall, *Beyond Culture* (Garden City, NY: Anchor Press, 1977), p. 109.

42. The assertion concerning the predominance of one culture at a time was made by Lewin (1948).

43. A. Taylor, "Why GM Leads the Pack in Europe," *Fortune*, May 17, 1993, p. 84.

Managing Difficult
Negotiation Situations:
Individual Approaches

Negotiating with Problem People

Len Leritz

In the movie *Big* Tom Hanks stars as a kid locked inside an adult body. What makes the movie funny is that it strikes a chord with viewers. "I know someone like that," they think between fistfuls of popcorn.

There are a lot of people out there who look like adults on the outside but are thinking like kids on the inside. And when it's your job to negotiate with one of them, you've got trouble. Most of these problem people fall into one of five categories: Bullies, Avoiders, Withdrawers, High Rollers, or Wad Shooters.

- *Bullies* verbally or physically attack, use threats, demand or otherwise attempt to intimidate and push others around. They say things like: "That's a stupid thing to say!" "Do you expect me to respond to that?" "If you don't, I will . . .!" "I want it, and I want it now!" "Move it!" "You can't do that!" "You better shape up!"

- *Avoiders* physically avoid or procrastinate, hide out or refuse to negotiate out of fear of losing. They say things like: "I'll do it tomorrow." "We don't have anything to talk about." "I don't have time." "That's not my problem."

- *Withdrawers* emotionally withdraw, get confused, go dumb and numb or become paralyzed with fear. You'll hear them say: "I don't understand." "That doesn't make sense." "I don't know."

- *High Rollers* attempt to shock and intimidate their opposition by making extreme demands. "You have until five o'clock to comply." "I want $50,000 for my car." "I want it all done by noon."

- *Wad Shooters* assume an all-or-nothing, take-it-or-leave-it stance. "That's my bottom line." "If you don't want it, forget it." "Either you agree to all five points or I'm leaving."

WHAT TO DO WITH THEM

The behavior of these different types of "enforcers" tends to be uncomplicated and obvious. Consequently, the following responses work effectively with most of them.

Reprinted from *Working Woman*, October 1988, pp. 35–37. Used with permission of the publisher.

1. Get Their Attention.   This step is especially important when you're up against bullies. Until you get their attention, you are wasting your time. You need to shock them out of their self-centered mindset and let them know with no uncertainty that you intend to be taken seriously. You need to make them feel your presence.

The way to get their attention is to draw a boundary. The intention is not to punish the other person but simply to let them know what you will and will not tolerate. You want to create a negative consequence that will outweigh whatever benefit they are deriving from their current behavior.

How you draw your boundary will differ in each situation. You need to ask yourself what it is that will get the other person's attention—what is important to them. You may do it by physical action, by shouting at them, by walking out, by initiating legal procedures, or by telling them in a quiet and firm voice what you will and won't accept.

The key is that you have to mean it. The other person almost always knows whether you are serious about your boundary. No one crosses your boundary when you mean it.

Here is an example of what I call the "Skillet Approach" to dealing with enforcers. I once had a client who had been physically abused by her husband for years. She had threatened to leave him many times, but he knew that she didn't really mean it.

One night she finally decided to mean it. He had pushed her around earlier in the evening. She waited until he went to sleep and then went to the kitchen and got her biggest cast-iron skillet. She woke him up while holding the skillet over his head. "If you ever hit me again, I'll kill you in your sleep," she told him.

This time she meant it, and he believed her. Though he had trouble sleeping for a while, the abuse stopped. The woman had gotten her husband's attention by creating a consequence (the skillet), and she meant it.

Ask yourself what "skillet" you need to use—and mean it when you use it. When you don't mean it you are reinforcing the behavior you don't want.

2. Call a Spade a Spade.   Identify the enforcer's behavior and invite her to do something more constructive. Explaining to a bully, for example, that she's being a bully helps her become conscious of what she's doing and will often take the power out of it. This is especially true if others are involved and the enforcer feels embarrassed.

Suggesting other options at this point will help the person save face and will keep the negotiations moving. For example, you might say something like: "Your repeated attacks are not getting us any closer to an agreement. I'd like to suggest that we each try to explain what we need, then work together to brainstorm some ways that we might both get what we need."

3. Put Their Fears to Rest.   This step is particularly important when you're dealing with Avoiders or Withdrawers. You need to help them feel safer so that their capacities expand and they can move into more cooperative behaviors.

Here are some suggestions:

- Don't be defensive. Instead, look behind their behavior to their underlying needs and interests: "Would you be more comfortable if we met in your office?" "What conditions will make you willing to stay here and talk this out?"

- Respond to the needs of the internal kid: "I can see how you feel frustrated."
- Actively listen to them so they feel understood: "What I hear you saying is . . ."
- Be aware of who their constituency is, who it is they need to impress: "I want you to be able to go back to your department and feel proud of what we accomplished," you might say.
- Don't counterattack. When dealing with aggressive enforcers, such as bullies, the usual rule is: the more aggressive, the more frightened the internal kid. Helping bullies feel safer may seem counterintuitive, but it's exactly what you need to do to get them on your level.

4. Insist on Playing by the Rules.   Bullies, High Rollers, and Wad Shooters will attempt to force you to accept unreasonable agreements. But you should refuse to be pressured. Instead, insist on fair criteria for both the process and the final settlement. You might say, "I refuse to be pressured into an agreement. I am only willing to continue the negotiation if we can agree to some fair procedures that we will both honor." Or if, for example, you feel a price the other person is asking is too high, you might say, "Let's check with some other suppliers and see what they are charging."

5. Put the Ball in Their Court.   When the other person takes extreme stands and makes unreasonable demands, ask her to explain how she arrived at her position. Point out that you need to understand her underlying needs better. You might say, "In order to understand your demands, I need to hear more from you about how you arrived at those points." Or "Your price is a little higher than I expected. I want to pay you fairly for your work. Explain to me what you will need to do to complete the job." When she answers you, demands that cannot be justified lose their power.

6. Use the Silent Treatment.   Silence can be one of your most powerful strategies, especially with Wad Shooters. When the other person is being aggressive or unreasonable, try just looking at them calmly. Silence gives them nothing to push against.

Calm silence communicates power. The other person will feel uncomfortable with the power of your silence and will probably begin to fill it in—often by backtracking and becoming more reasonable.

A variation of using silence is to walk away. "I'm willing to talk about this whenever you are willing to stop attacking me. Until then, we have nothing to talk about."

7. Do the Sidestep.   Sidestepping or ignoring a statement can be an effective response if someone is making a personal attack, an extreme demand or a take-it-or-leave-it challenge. Instead of responding directly, act as if you didn't hear what it was the person said. Change the topic and/or refocus the discussion on the underlying problem or conflict at hand.

For example, a corporate attorney says angrily to an opposing attorney: "I can't believe they pay you a professional salary." The opposing attorney might calmly respond: "I think we still have four issues we have not settled. Let's look at them one at a time." Or a film supplier says to a production manager: "The price is $10,000 per segment. Take it or leave it." The manager would answer: "How many segments did you say you had?" or "Your tone of voice sounds angry. Do you feel as if we have not been fair to you in our past dealings?"

8. Meet the Enemy Head-On.   Don't be defensive. Justifying your position or needs encourages the other party to step up their attack. If you become defensive, the other person knows that she has you on the run. Invite her to give her criticism, then refocus it as an attack on the problem at hand. Ask her to explain how her comments will help solve the problem.

For example, the account supervisor at an advertising agency says to the creative director: "If you were committed to this new ad, you would have been here last week." A defensive response from the creative director would be: "I couldn't help it. I was burned out and needed the time off." A better reply would be: "I know you are under pressure and last week was frustrating. What do we need to do so we don't get caught in that kind of last-minute bind in the future?"

9. Refuse to Be Punished.   Anyone has a right to be angry from time to time, but no one has the right to punish you. You do not deserve to be punished. You will know that you are being punished when the other person keeps repeating her attack or the person vents her anger but refuses to tell you how she wants your behavior to change in response.

Draw a boundary by asking the other person what they want from you. If their response is "I don't know," inform them that you are willing to continue the discussion when they do know. In the meantime, you're not willing to be punished.

10. Ask Questions.   Taking a stand may make the other person defensive. Instead, ask questions. Asking questions doesn't give them an object to attack; it invites them to justify their position or to vent their feelings. It gives you more information about them.

When asking your questions, ask "what" questions rather than "why" questions. "What" questions invite factual responses. "Why" questions are usually sneaky judgments that make the other party defensive. "What" questions will keep the negotiation moving. "Why" questions will tend to lead you to battle positions. For example:

- Why did you think you could do that? (attacking)
- What was your motivation for doing that? (information-seeking)
- Why did you do that? (attacking)
- What are the assumptions behind you actions? (information seeking)

11. Point Out the Consequences.   When the other person refuses to agree to a reasonable settlement, show them the ramifications of their actions. Try to present it as a statement of inevitable consequences rather than as a threat: "The reality is, if our company shows a loss again in the fourth quarter due to the strike, we will have no choice but to lay off 500 union workers."

Armed with the right approach, you can convince any Bully or Withdrawer on the block that a rational, well-negotiated settlement is in everyone's best interest.

Open Mouth—Close Career

Michael Warshaw

Quick quiz: What's worse than getting bad news? Answer: being the person who has to deliver that news.

Sooner or later, it happens: You see a disaster in the making that everyone except you seems content to ignore. Maybe that make-or-break project is going to miss its deadline; maybe the new boss is in over her head; maybe those two dueling coworkers are poisoning the team's morale. Whatever the problem, it's big, it's ugly, and it's obvious, but nobody will speak up about it—unless you do.

When you need to be the bearer of bad news, how do you deliver the message without getting killed for being the messenger?

That was the question that confronted Carol Roberts, 38, of Memphis-based International Paper. Soon after she was brought in as vice president of people development, in late 1997, Roberts realized that people weren't being developed. "We weren't giving our employees open, honest feedback," she says. "We had all kinds of processes in place to talk to our employees, but managers weren't following through. We weren't helping our people to progress, and we weren't progressing as a company."

But Roberts wasn't anxious to call attention to the problem. She was new to her job—an unknown and untested quantity in a male-dominated industry. If she spoke up and questioned IP's fundamental practices, she might get slapped down. Could she really afford to be a messenger?

"People hesitate to speak up at work, because they're afraid," says Dan Oestreich, 48, coauthor with Kathleen Ryan of *The Courageous Messenger: How to Successfully Speak Up at Work* (Jossey-Bass, 1996) and *Driving Fear Out of the Workplace: Creating the High-Trust, High Performance Organization* (Jossey-Bass, 1998). "But that fear—of being labeled as a whiner, or as someone who isn't a team player—prevents people from sharing criticisms and ideas that might ultimately benefit their companies."

We asked Oestreich to walk us through four steps toward being an effective messenger. The process starts, he says, when you decide to stop ignoring a problem and instead become part of its solution. "It takes courage to speak out effectively," he says. "Despite your good intentions, bringing up a touchy topic can blow up in your face."

That's the bad news. The good news is that you can deliver even the toughest message—if you have a strategy for doing so.

1. Deliver Your Message—to You

You need to make clear that the problem is in the message, not with the messenger. So before you say anything to anybody, make sure that you've identified the problem clearly. "When I ask people what their true message is, they often realize that they have at least four or five of them," says Oestreich. "The real challenge is to hone in on the core problem: What's the message?"

IP's Carol Roberts wrestled with that question and soon realized that she had, in fact, three messages. First, International Paper wasn't walking its talk: Managers weren't giving effective feedback to the people on the front lines. Second, this was an important issue: IP's future depended on developing its people. And her third message? That her first two messages were unselfish: She wasn't criticizing people just to get ahead.

"To get the company to commit to a new effort to develop its people, I had to win our top managers' hearts and minds," she says. "That meant forcing our senior people to think outside their comfort zones. They needed to know that I was doing this for the good of the company."

When you deliver a harsh message, people get defensive. "The first thing people will do when you deliver bad news is question why you're speaking up," says Oestreich. "If you haven't clearly explained your motivation, people are likely to assign selfish reasons to your actions. So talk about your reasons for bringing up a problem. Give people a reason to care."

Action Item—Unspeakable Bosses

Columbia University Psychology Professor Harvey Hornstein has written a book, *Brutal Bosses and Their Prey*, that's based on 200 interviews with people who tried to take on their bosses. Before you open your mouth, advises Hornstein, think about the following hard-won lessons.

- **Brutal bosses don't just survive—they thrive.** That's because they deliver exactly what *their* bosses want. Check to see whether the abusers in your company are protected—and whether those who talk back to them end up getting hammered.

- **Don't suffer in silence.** If you've spoken up and you're getting picked on for it, talk about it with a trusted coworker. "Don't pretend that you're thick-skinned," says Hornstein. "Doing so will almost invariably cause you to suffer more, not less."

- **Don't talk like a victim.** When dealing with a difficult boss, never apologize and never confess. "These bosses smell blood," says Hornstein. "Being humble invites assaults—it doesn't blunt them."

---

2. Face Your Fear—and Get over It

To deliver her message, Carol Roberts decided to bring together 33 of IP's top managers for a two-day off-site in Memphis. "I couldn't just order our senior executives to pay more attention to their people," she says. "So I booked outside consultants to discuss the way these feedback processes should really work. Instead of simply telling people that we had a problem, I tried to get them to see it for themselves."

In fact, Roberts was doing more than identifying a problem. As she soon found out, she was putting herself on the line. Just days before the meeting, she got a message from

John Dillon, IP's CEO. "He questioned my entire agenda," she recalls. "He said he couldn't see any reason for holding such a meeting, since we already had feedback processes in place. My heart sank. But then I decided to go ahead and hold the event anyway. The systems we had just weren't working, and it was important to put that information on the table. I knew it was the right thing to do."

Dillon let the event go on as planned—but not without making it clear to Roberts that he had grave reservations about the meeting. Roberts was wide-eyed the night before the off-site, as she feverishly outlined her opening talk. "There I was, new to the job, calling in the vice presidents and general managers of a $20 billion global company, and telling them that they weren't doing enough to develop their employees," she says. "If I didn't engage them properly—if my effort flopped—I was dead."

Knowing what you need to say doesn't make saying it any easier. You still have to face your fear. "Even after you think through a tough message," says Oestreich, "chances are, you'll worry about the fallout. So the next step is to be realistic about those risks of speaking up. Put a face on your dread, and ask yourself where the fear comes from. Is it based on past experience with these people, or are you catastrophizing. Maybe you're worried that the person you have to deal with will get mad. So what?

"For some people, the reward in speaking up is simply that they've quit giving life to a lie," Oestreich continues. "It's enough for them to make public the thing that everyone is talking about in private. The point is to balance the risks and the rewards, and to make a thoughtful decision on whether to be the messenger."

You might even decide to shut up instead of speak up. "If you conclude that the wise thing to do is not to go forward—because, say, you don't believe that the payoff is big enough—that's fine," Oestreich says. "The big problem comes when people let their fear of speaking up prevent them from even confronting an issue."

3. Make It Public

Everything you've done thus far has been private. Now it's time to go public, to meet face-to-face with the person who needs to hear your message. "If I was really going to effect change, I knew that I had to get right into the engine room of the company and win over the managers," says Roberts. "It helped to know that these were good people who were

---

Open Mouth, Open Career

Hollywood is notorious for letting egos run the show: People assume that any attempt to speak up will be shot down. Rob Hummel, head of international post-production at Dream Works SKG, has a different take. Here are his tips for getting people to challenge higher-ups like himself.

- **Demonstrate your concern.** "I make it crystal clear to people that they can come to me when they're angry," says Hummel. "If they're right, I'll tell them so. If they're wrong, I'll tell them why."

- **Follow through.** Hummel once promoted a brilliant but difficult employee. People complained that having more power would make this person harder to deal with. Hummel didn't renege on the promotion, but he promised to keep close tabs on the situation—and he did.

- **Be big enough to praise.** Make note of good ideas, and don't dump on someone who offers a less-than-brilliant insight. "I tell all of my people," says Hummel, "that they'll never learn anything if they aren't willing to risk being wrong."

invested in doing a better job. Why else would they have given me two days of their time on very little notice? I was counting on them to have the same epiphany that I'd had."

When you take center stage, avoid throat clearing. Get your message out. Be direct. "You can open tactfully, but don't waste time chitchatting," advises Oestreich. "Indirection creates tension. Within the first minute, you should be into your message. Make your point. And then stop."

Step back and give the listener some time to react. You've probably spent weeks thinking about this problem. But for the other person, the bomb has just been dropped. "Even if you've written a script, you can never guarantee the reaction you want," says Oestreich. "You're hitting someone with news that's hard to take. If you don't give him a chance to think it through, he's likely to close the conversation because he can't deal with it. And that's the one reaction you don't want."

The more you trust your audience, the better the chance that your message will be listened to. That's what Carol Roberts learned. "I opened by saying that no one in the room was satisfied with our efforts in developing people and that those present were the only ones who could figure out how to improve the situation—because I didn't have a solution. That was a scary thing for me to say, because I was brought in to IP to provide answers. I was really opening myself up: If I lost this audience, I'd lose my credibility.

"But they knew we had a problem, and they were able to get at the beginning of a solution on the very first day," she continues. "It amazes me, because these guys were essentially indicting their own behavior. Their attitude changed right before my eyes."

> **Listen Up!**
>
> Thomas D. Zweifel is CEO of Swiss Consulting Group Inc., a firm based in New York City that helps companies like Citibank and Novartis AG to master the fine art of listening. Before you open your mouth, says Zweifel, be sure to open up your ears.
>
> - **Think about how your message will be heard.** Anticipate the personal prejudices that people in your audience bring to the table, and shape your comments accordingly.
> - **Focus on how people are reacting to what you are saying.** If you're not connecting, you may need to toss out your script and to find a better way to state your case.
> - **Listen one minute longer than is necessary.** Sometimes that extra minute of silence on your part can be all that's needed to get the other person to come around.
> - **Listen for the gold.** Remember that it might be the *other* person who arrives at the best solution. Either way, you both win.

4. Keep the Conversation Going

When you deliver a tough message to someone, your relationship with that person will change. To make it change for the better, stay on message.

Carol Roberts knew that the off-site was just the beginning. "I had to make sure that we didn't waste this event," she says. "It was great that we learned a lot, but I knew that John Dillon would ask what we planned to do about it."

For Roberts, staying on her message meant delivering a new one: She had to convince members of IP's senior team that it was up to them to ensure that the company's culture really changed. "We could have fluffed up some report on our results, but I didn't," she says. "Instead, we boiled a report down to a few simple conclusions."

Roberts and her staff delivered their memo to IP's senior-management team. One top executive took a look at the slim document and said, "Gee, Carol, it doesn't look like you have a lot to show for that meeting."

Roberts shot back, "Well, to tell you the truth, none of the managers expect us to produce a big document. But they *are* watching for your reaction—to see how seriously you take our conclusions." It was the right message. The off-site had failed to hold its line managers accountable for maintaining a dialogue with employees. Now those same managers had spelled out some solutions—and they needed backup from the top.

Language as a Power Tool

Each time you open your mouth, you reveal something about who you are. According to Sarah McGinty, teaching supervisor at Harvard University's Graduate School of Education and author of *Language as a Power Tool,* you communicate best when you tune your conversational style to fit your audience.

- **What's the biggest misconception about how we use language?** That conversational style is based on gender. It's not—it's based on power. When you're in charge, the words you choose place you in the center of a situation. When you're not in control, you use qualifiers. You insert little flags that signal that you're not trying to run the conversation.

- **So what's the point—to be bold by speaking boldly?** Absolutely not. Sometimes you need to let other people direct the discussion. There are times when your conversational style is made more powerful by ceding power, so that other people can be heard.

Being a messenger means being willing to deal with angry reactions. "People want to have influence, they want to be involved," says Oestreich. "And getting involved means conflict. Collaboration does not occur in some happy world, where people always work in harmony. Meaningful collaboration requires relationships that can take punishment."

Carol Roberts knows that she did the right thing by speaking up. This past July, at IP's Human Issues and Management Conference, held in Silver Bay, New York, Dillon highlighted the improvements that resulted from Robert's off-site: The company adopted a new policy that requires employees to meet with their supervisors twice each year to discuss their overall performance and career development; and it appointed two "people champions"—watchdogs who will make sure that managers are developing people.

Roberts couldn't have wished for a better outcome. But she's been around long enough to know that speaking up doesn't always guarantee a happy ending. "When you try to take people in a new direction, you have to look back and see if they're still behind you. If you fail to follow through by building support for your message, you'll be known as someone who's outspoken—and who never gets results."

Negotiating with a Customer You Can't Afford to Lose

Thomas C. Keiser

"I like your product, but your price is way out of line. We're used to paying half that much!"

"Acme's going to throw in the service contract for nothing. If you can't match that, you're not even in the running."

"Frankly, I think we've worked out a pretty good deal here, but now you've got to meet my boss. If you thought I was tough. . ."

"Tell you what: If you can drop the price by 20 percent, I'll give you the business. Once you're in our division, you know, you'll have a lock on the whole company. The volume will be huge!"

"I can't even talk to you about payment schedule. Company policy is ironclad on that point."

"Look here, at *that* price, you're just wasting my time! I thought this was a serious bid! Who do you think you're talking to, some green kid?"

This wasn't supposed to happen. You've invested a lot of time earning a customer's trust and goodwill. You've done needs-satisfaction selling, relationship selling, consultative selling, customer-oriented selling; you've been persuasive and good-humored. But as you approach the close, your good friend the customer suddenly turns into Attila the Hun, demanding a better deal, eager to plunder your company's margin and ride away with the profits. You're left with a lousy choice: do the business unprofitably or don't do the business at all.

This kind of dilemma is nothing new, of course. Deals fall through every day. But businesses that depend on long-term customer relationships have a particular need to avoid win-lose situations, since backing out of a bad deal can cost a lot of future deals as well. Some buyers resort to hardball tactics even when the salesperson has done a consummate job of selling. The premise is that it costs nothing to ask for a concession. Sellers can always say no. They will still do the deal. But many sellers—especially inexperienced ones—say yes to even the most outrageous customer demands. Shrewd buyers can lure even seasoned salespeople into deals based on emotion rather than on solid business sense. So how do you protect your own interests, save the sale, and preserve the relationship when the customer is trying to eat your lunch?

Joining battle is not the solution unless you're the only source of whatever the customer needs. (And in that case you'd better be sure you never lose your monopoly.) Leaving the field is an even worse tactic, however tempting it is to walk away from a really unreasonable customer.

Surprisingly, accommodation and compromise are not the answers either. Often a 10 percent price discount will make a trivial difference in the commission, so the salesperson quickly concedes it. But besides reducing your company's margin significantly, this kind of easy accommodation encourages the customer to expect something for nothing in future negotiations.

Compromise—splitting the difference, meeting the customer halfway—may save time, but because it fails to meet the needs of either party fully it is not the proverbial win-win solution. A competitor who finds a creative way to satisfy both parties can steal the business.

The best response to aggressive but important customers is a kind of assertive pacifism. Refuse to fight, but refuse to let the customer take advantage of you. Don't cave in, just don't counterattack. Duck, dodge, parry, but hold your ground. Never close a door; keep opening new ones. Try to draw the customer into a creative partnership where the two of you work together for inventive solutions that never occurred to any of your competitors.

There are eight key strategies for moving a customer out of a hardball mentality and into a more productive frame of mind.

1. *Prepare by knowing your walkaway and by building the number of variables you can work with during the negotiation.* Everyone agrees about the walkaway. Whether you're negotiating an arms deal with the Russians, a labor agreement with the UAW, or a contract you can't afford to lose, you need to have a walkaway: a combination of price, terms, and deliverables that represents the least you will accept. Without one, you have no negotiating road map.

Increasing the number of variables is even more important. The more variables you have to work with, the more options you have to offer; the greater your options, the better your chances of closing the deal. With an important customer, your first priority is to avoid take-it-or-leave-it situations and keep the negotiation going long enough to find a workable deal. Too many salespeople think their only variable is price, but such narrow thinking can be the kiss of death. After all, price is one area where the customer's and the supplier's interests are bound to be at odds. Focusing on price can only increase animosity, reduce margin, or both.

Instead, focus on variables where the customer's interests and your own have more in common. For example, a salesperson for a consumer-goods manufacturer might talk to the retailer about more effective ways to use advertising dollars—the retailer's as well as the manufacturer's—to promote the product. By including marketing programs in the discussion, the salesperson helps to build value into the price, which will come up later in the negotiation.

The salesperson's job is to find the specific package of products and services that most effectively increases value for the customer without sacrificing the seller's profit. For example, an automotive parts supplier built up its research and development capacity, giving customers the choice of doing their own R&D in-house or farming it out to the parts supplier. Having this option enabled the supplier to redirect negotiations away from price and toward creation of value in the product-development process. Its revenues and margins improved significantly.

Even with undifferentiated products, you can increase variables by focusing on services. A commodity chemicals salesperson, for example, routinely considered payment options, quantity discounts, bundling with other purchases, even the relative costs and benefits of using the supplier's tank cars or the customer's. Regardless of industry, the more variables you have, the greater your chances of success.

2. *When under attack, listen.* Collect as much information as possible from the customer. Once customers have locked into a position, it is difficult to move them with arguments, however brilliant. Under these circumstances, persuasion is more a function of listening.

Here's an example from my own company. During a protracted negotiation for a large training and development contract, the customer kept trying to drive down the per diem price of our professional seminar leaders. He pleaded poverty, cheaper competition, and company policy. The contract was a big one, but we were already operating at near capacity, so we had little incentive to shave the per diem even slightly. However, we were also selling books to each seminar participant, and that business was at least as important to us as the services. The customer was not asking for concessions on books. He was only thinking of the per diem, and he was beginning to dig in his heels.

At this point our salesperson stopped talking, except to ask questions, and began listening. She learned a great deal—and uncovered an issue more important to the customer than price.

The customer was director of T&D for a large corporation and a man with career ambitions. To get the promotion he wanted, he needed visibility with his superiors. He was afraid that our professionals would develop their own relationships with his company's top management, leaving him out of the loop. Our salesperson decided to give him the control he wanted. Normally we would have hired freelancers to fill the gap between our own available staff and the customer's needs. But in this case she told him he could hire the freelancers himself, subject to our training and direction. The people we already employed would be billed at their full per diem. He would save money on the freelancers he paid directly, without our margin. We would still make our profit on the books and the professional services we did provide. He would maintain control.

Moreover, we were confident that the customer was underestimating the difficulty of hiring, training, and managing freelancers. We took the risk that somewhere down the road the customer would value this service and be willing to pay for it. Our judgment turned out to be accurate. Within a year we had obtained the entire professional services contract without sacrificing margin.

It was a solution no competitor could match because no competitor had listened carefully enough to the customer's underlying agenda. Even more important, the buyer's wary gamesmanship turned to trust, and that trust shaped all our subsequent negotiations.

When under attack, most people's natural response is to defend themselves or to counterattack. For a salesperson in a negotiation, either of these will fuel an upward spiral of heated disagreement. The best response, however counterintuitive, is to keep the customer talking, and for three good reasons. First, new information can increase the room for movement and the number of variables. Second, listening without defending helps to defuse any anger. Third, if you're listening, you're not making concessions.

3. *Keep track of the issues requiring discussion.* Negotiations can get confusing. Customers often get frustrated by an apparent lack of progress; they occasionally go back on agreements already made; they sometimes raise new issues at the last moment. One good way to avoid these problems is to summarize what's already been accomplished and sketch out what still needs to be discussed. Brief but frequent recaps actually help maintain momentum, and they reassure customers that you're listening to their arguments.

The best negotiators can neutralize even the most outspoken opposition by converting objections into issues that need to be addressed. The trick is to keep your cool, pay attention to the customer's words and tone, and wait patiently for a calm moment to summarize your progress.

4. *Assert your company's needs.* Effective salespeople always focus on their customers' interests—not their own. They learn to take on a customer perspective so completely that they project an uncanny understanding of the buyer's needs and wants. Too much empathy can work against salespeople, however, because sales bargaining requires a dual focus—on the customer and on the best interests of one's own company. The best negotiating stance is not a single-minded emphasis on customer satisfaction but a concentration on problem solving that seeks to satisfy both parties. Salespeople who fail to assert the needs of their own company are too likely to make unnecessary concessions.

The style of assertion is also extremely important. It must be nonprovocative. "You use our service center 50 percent more that our average customer. We've got to be paid for that. . ." will probably spark a defensive reaction from a combative customer. Instead, the salesperson should build common ground by emphasizing shared interests, avoiding inflammatory language, and encouraging discussion of disputed issues. This is a better approach: "It's clear that the service center is a critical piece of the overall package. Right now you're using it 50 percent more than our average customer, and that's driving up our costs and your price. Let's find a different way of working together to keep service costs down and still keep service quality high. To begin with, let's figure out what's behind these high service demands."

5. *Commit to a solution only after it's certain to work for both parties.* If a competitive customer senses that the salesperson is digging into a position, the chances of successfully closing the deal are dramatically reduced. A better approach is to suggest hypothetical solutions. Compare these two approaches in selling a commercial loan:

"I'll tell you what. If you give us all of the currency exchange business for your European branches, we'll cap this loan at prime plus one."

"You mentioned the currency exchange activity that comes out of your European branches. Suppose you placed that entirely with us. We may be able to give you a break in the pricing of the new loan."

The first is likely to draw a counterproposal from a competitive customer. It keeps the two of you on opposite sides of the negotiating table. The second invites the customer to help shape the proposal. Customers who participate in the search for solutions are much more likely to wind up with a deal they like.

Some salespeople make the mistake of agreeing definitively to an issue without making sure the overall deal still makes sense. This plays into the hands of an aggressive customer trying to get the whole loaf one slice at a time. It's difficult to take back a concession. Instead, wrap up issues tentatively. "We agree to do X, provided we can come up with a suitable agreement on Y and Z."

6. *Save the hardest issues for last.* When you have a lot of points to negotiate, don't start with the toughest, even though it may seem logical to begin with the deal killers. After all, why spend time on side issues without knowing whether the thorniest questions can be resolved?

There are two reasons. First, resolving relatively easy issues creates momentum. Suppose you're working with a customer who's bound and determined to skin you alive when it comes to the main event. By starting with lesser contests and finding inventive solutions, you may get the customer to see the value of exploring new approaches. Second, discussing easier issues may uncover additional variables. These will be helpful when you finally get down to the heart of the negotiation.

7. *Start high and concede slowly.* Competitive customers want to see a return on their negotiation investment. When you know that a customer wants to barter, start off with something you can afford to lose. Obviously, game playing has its price. Not only do you train your customers to ask for concessions, you also teach them never to relax their guard on money matters. Still, when the customer really wants to wheel and deal, you have little choice.

The customer too can pay a price for playing games. A classic case involves a customer who always bragged about his poker winnings, presumably to intimidate salespeople before negotiations got started. "I always leave the table a winner," he seemed to be saying. "Say your prayers." What salespeople actually did was raise their prices 10 to 15 percent before sitting down to negotiate. They'd let him win a few dollars, praise his skill, then walk away with the order at a reasonable margin.

A number of studies have shown that high expectations produce the best negotiating results and low expectations the poorest. This is why salespeople must not let themselves be intimidated by the customer who always bargains every point. Once they lower their expectations, they have made the first concession in their own minds before the negotiating gets under way. The customer then gets to take these premature concessions along with the normal allotment to follow.

A man I used to know—the CEO of a company selling software to pharmacies— always insisted on absolute candor in all customer dealings. He'd begin negotiations by showing customers his price list and saying, "Here's our standard price list. But since you're a big chain, we'll give you a discount." He broke the ice with a concession no one had asked for and got his clock cleaned nearly every time.

The key is always to get something in return for concessions and to know their economic value. Remember that any concession is likely to have a different value for buyer and seller, so begin by giving things that the customer values highly but that have little incremental cost for your company:

Control of the process.

Assurance of quality.

Convenience.

Preferred treatment in times of product scarcity.

Information on new technology (for example, sharing R&D).

Credit.

Timing of delivery.

Customization.

Service.

There's an old saying, "He who concedes first, loses." This may be true in a hardball negotiation where the customer has no other potential source of supply. But in most competitive sales situations, the salesperson has to make the first concession in order to keep the deal alive. Concede in small increments, get something in return, and know the concession's value to both sides. Taking time may seem crazy to salespeople who have learned that time is money. But in a negotiation, *not* taking time is money.

8. *Don't be trapped by emotional blackmail.* Buyers sometimes use emotion—usually anger—to rattle salespeople into making concessions they wouldn't otherwise make. Some use anger as a premeditated tactic; others are really angry. It doesn't matter whether the emotion is genuine or counterfeit. What does matter is how salespeople react. How do you deal with a customer's rage and manage your own emotions at the same time?

Here are three different techniques that salespeople find useful in handling a customer who uses anger—wittingly or unwittingly—as a manipulative tactic.

- *Withdraw.* Ask for a recess, consult with the boss, or reschedule the meeting. A change in time and place can change the entire landscape of the negotiation.

- *Listen silently while the customer rants and raves.* Don't nod your head or say "uh-huh." Maintain eye contact and a neutral expression, but do not reinforce the customer's behavior. When the tirade is over, suggest a constructive agenda.

- *React openly to the customer's anger,* say that you find it unproductive, and suggest focusing on a specific, nonemotional issue. There are two keys to this technique. The first is timing: don't rush the process or you risk backing the customer into a corner from which there is no graceful escape. The second is to insist that the use of manipulative tactics is unacceptable and then to suggest a constructive agenda. Don't be timid. The only way to pull this off is to be strong and assertive.

     For example, imagine this response to a customer throwing a fit: "This attack is not constructive. (Strong eye contact, assertive tone.) We've spent three hours working the issues and trying to arrive at a fair and reasonable solution. Now I suggest that we go back to the questions of payment terms and see if we can finalize those."

Of course, there is substantial risk in using any of these techniques. If you withdraw, you may not get a second chance. If you listen silently or react ineffectively, you may alienate the customer further. These are techniques to resort to only when the discussion is in danger of going off the deep end, but at such moments they have saved many a negotiation that looked hopeless.

The essence of negotiating effectively with aggressive customers is to sidestep their attacks and convince them that a common effort at problem solving will be more profitable and productive. Your toughest customers will stop throwing punches if they never connect. Your most difficult buyer will brighten if you can make the process interesting and rewarding. The old toe-to-toe scuffle had its points, no doubt. Trading blow for blow was a fine test of stamina and guts. But it was no test at all of imagination. In dealing with tough customers, creativity is a better way of doing business.

Two Common Mistakes

Combative buyers are hard enough to handle without provoking them further, yet many salespeople unintentionally annoy buyers to the point of complete exasperation. What's worse, the two most common mistakes crop up most frequently at times of disagreement, the very moment when poking sticks at the customer ought to be the last item on your list of priorities.

The first mistake is belaboring. Some salespeople will repeat a single point until customers begin to feel badgered or heckled. Chances are they heard you the first time. You can also belabor a customer with logic or with constant explanations that seem to suggest that the customer is none too bright.

The second mistake is rebutting every point your customer makes, which is almost certain to lead to an argument—point and counterpoint. Don't say "night" every time your customer says "day," even if you're convinced the customer is wrong.

Managing Difficult Negotiation Situations: Third-Party Approaches

When and How to Use Third-Party Help

Roy J. Lewicki

Alexander Hiam

Karen Wise Olander

It may be that in spite of your best efforts to move the negotiations back on track, the two sides are still stuck, unable to go anywhere. In that case, you should consider asking a third party to step in. A third party is someone who is not directly involved in your negotiation or dispute, but who can be helpful in resolving it. This impartial party may be a friend, in the case of a simple negotiation, or it may be a neutral person whom both parties know and invite to assist, or it might even be someone with professional credentials whose job it is to intervene in such cases.

A third party is likely to use a number of conflict resolution techniques, engaging you and the other party in activities designed to reduce tension, improve communication, change the options, adjust the number of players or issues, or help find common ground. With outside help, the disputing parties may be able to move back on track and bring the negotiation to conclusion and closure.

WHEN TO ASK A THIRD PARTY TO INTERVENE

In general, it is best to try everything you can to remedy the situation before you move to third-party intervention. However, when conflict escalates in negotiation, the parties often become suspicious of each other's motives, intentions, and behavior. One of the parties may try to use the tactics in a "partisan" way, with a bias toward achieving a specific outcome. Moreover, even when that party implements the practices in good faith, the other party doesn't see the efforts as genuine. Instead, he or she sees it as a ruse, a ploy, a tactic, or a way for the other to gain advantage. If the parties just cannot find a way to become "unstuck," then both parties should agree on the need for a third party. Although third parties can be very helpful, negotiators often resist using them because they feel they are decreasing the likelihood of achieving their preferred outcome.

Reprinted from *Think Before You Speak* (New York: John Wiley & Sons, 1996), Roy J. Lewicki, Alexander Hiam, and Karen Wise Olander, pp 177–97. Copyright ©1996 by John Wiley& Sons, Inc. Reprinted by permission of the publisher.

Sometimes, a third-party intervention will be imposed by an outside group that has the power or authority to do so, and is anxious to resolve the matter. In an intrafamily dispute, when two children are fighting, a parent may intervene. In other cases, an intervention may be imposed by a constituency, or higher level authority, or it may result from a rule or legal procedure. For example, a number of warranties and contracts now specify that if there is a question as to liability or fault, the dispute will automatically go to an arbitrator or mediator.

When two negotiating parties invite the third party to intervene, then the intervention is usually friendly and progresses smoothly. If the intervention is imposed by an outside authority, then the relationship between the disputing parties and the third party may not necessarily be friendly, and the negotiating environment may become even more hostile.

REASONS TO USE A THIRD PARTY

You may want to consider using third-party help if:[1]

- The emotional level between the parties is high, with lots of anger and frustration.
- Communication between the parties is poor or has completely broken down, or the parties appear to be talking "past" each other.
- Stereotypic views of each other's position and motives are preventing resolution.
- Behavior is negative (e.g., there is intense anger or name-calling).
- The parties have serious disagreements about what information is necessary, available, or required.
- The parties disagree on the number, order, or combination of issues.
- Differences in interests appear to be irreconcilable.
- Values differ greatly, and the parties disagree about what is fundamentally right.
- There are no established procedures for resolving the conflict, or the procedures have not been followed.
- Negotiations have completely broken down and there is an impasse.

There can be several objectives in bringing in a third party to achieve a resolution. First, the parties want to resolve the dispute; they care about the *outcome* dimension. A second reason is to smooth, repair, or improve the *relationship* between the parties—to reduce the level of conflict and the resultant damages. Finally, third parties are often used simply to stop the dispute—to get the parties to separate and not fight any more, or to make sure that they have as little future interaction as possible (e.g., when the United Nations intervenes in conflicts around the world, its first objective is often to stop warring groups from fighting). Depending on which type of objective is most important— resolving the dispute, repairing the relationship, or separating the parties—different types of third parties with different skills may be needed. The type of third party selected will focus on some or all of these objectives, and it is important to know which ones are most important and in what order they should be pursued.

Each type of third party has advantages and disadvantages, depending on the situation. Which type you choose will depend not only on the situation, but also on what services are available, who specifically is available and, if applicable, what may be required by rules and regulations that govern the conflict and its resolution (e.g., laws, contracts, documents, precedents). After we discuss the types of interventions, we will look at how to select the appropriate one for your circumstances.

The term ADR is used in the literature and elsewhere in reference to third-party resolution of disputes. ADR stands for *Alternative Dispute Resolution*. ADR procedures are alternatives to taking the conflict into the court system, hiring an attorney, and pursuing litigation. Since the early 1980s, there has been a major social movement to take *civil* disputes (where there is no criminal violation of law) out of the courts and, instead, refer them to third parties. There are a number of reasons for this: The parties have more control over what happens, the process is often quicker and less costly, and it keeps the court system from becoming hopelessly overburdened, particularly when key issues of law are not in question.

There are many people who perform ADR services, including the more formal labor arbitrators, divorce mediators, community mediators, and process consultants. Dispute resolution is also performed informally by ombudspersons, fact finders and referees, ministers, social workers, teachers, managers, or even friends of the disputing parties. There are also quasi-substitutes for formal court proceedings, such as summary jury trials and minitrials, judicial reference, court-annexed arbitration, settlement conferences, tribunals and judicial committees.

In this chapter, we will define and discuss the formal and informal processes of arbitration, mediation, and process consultation. We will discuss what these people do and how they work to resolve disputes. These methods are separate from the arena of actual litigation, which will not be discussed here, but which will be used as a point of comparison. For example, all the preceding processes are generally of shorter duration and less costly than a court trial.

ADVANTAGES AND DISADVANTAGES
OF USING A THIRD PARTY

Some of the advantages of employing a third party to assist in resolving a dispute are:

- The parties gain time to cool off as they break their conflict and describe the problem to the third party.
- Communication can be improved because the third party slows the communication down, helps people be clear, and works to improve listening.
- Parties often have to determine which issues are really important, because the third party may ask for some prioritizing.
- The emotional climate can be improved, as the parties discharge anger and hostility and return to a level of civility and trust.
- The parties can take steps to mend the relationship, particularly if this work is facilitated by the third party.
- The time frame for resolving the dispute can be established or reestablished.

FIGURE 1   Different Types of Third-Party Involvement
in Disputes

Level of Third-Party Control over Outcome

		High	Low
Level of Third-Party Control over Process	High	"Inquisition"	Mediation Process Consultation
	Low	Arbitration	Negotiation

- The escalating costs of remaining in conflict can be controlled, particularly if continuing the dispute is costing people money or opportunity (paying fees for attorneys becomes very costly).

- By watching and participating in the process, parties can learn how the third party provides assistance and in the future may be able to resolve their disputes without this help.

- Actual resolutions to the dispute and closure may be achieved.

Disadvantages of ADR include:

- The parties potentially lose face when the third party is called in, since there may be an image that the parties are somehow incompetent or incapable of resolving their own fight (this is true when those who are judging the negotiators are others who can publicly criticize them or move to have them replaced).

- There is also a loss of control of the process or the outcome or both, depending on which type of third party is called in to help. Relative to what they think they could have achieved had they "held out longer" or "fought harder," parties may be forced to accept less that 100 percent of their preferred target.

In general, when you bring a third party into the negotiations, the two contending parties will have to give up control over one or both aspects of the negotiation: the *process* and the *outcome*. The process is how the negotiation is conducted, the outcome is the result of the negotiation. As we discuss each type of third-party intervention, we will point out what the parties gain or lose in terms of process and outcome. Figure 1 depicts types of third-party involvement.

In negotiation without a third party, the opposing parties maintain control over both process and outcome. If they move to mediation, they give up control of the process but maintain control of the outcome. If they move to arbitration, they give up control of the outcome but retain control of the process. The fourth area in the diagram reflects a situation where the parties have control of neither process not outcome—and no negotiation occurs. We now consider the major types of third-party behavior individually.

ARBITRATION

Arbitration[2] is the most common form of third-party dispute resolution. When an arbitrator is called into a situation, the negotiators retain control of the process, but the arbitrator takes control of shaping and determining the outcome. Each party presents its position to the arbitrator, who then makes a ruling on either a single issue or on a package of issues.[3] This depends on the rules of the arbitration process, if any, and the request of the parties, if applicable. The arbitrator's ruling (decision) may be voluntary or binding, according to laws or a previous commitment of the parties.

The arbitrator can arrive at a recommended outcome in several ways. Usually, the arbitrator selects one side's position or the other's ("rules" in favor of one party or the other's preferred settlement). But sometimes, third parties may also offer an entirely different resolution. The arbitrator may suggest a "split" between the two parties' positions, in essence creating a compromise between their positions. In formal proceedings that are governed by law and contract agreements, such as labor and management negotiations, there is usually a very clear and strict set of policies about how arbitration rulings are to be made.

Arbitration is used in business conflicts, disputes between business and union workers, labor relations, contracts (usually in the public sector), and grievances. In the case of grievances, the arbitrator is bound to decide how the grievance should be resolved, whether consistent with the labor-management contract or current labor law.

Advantages of Arbitration

The major advantages of arbitration are:

1. A clear solution is made available to the parties (though it may not be one or both parties' choice).
2. The solution may be mandated on them (they can't choose whether to follow it or not).
3. Arbitrators are usually selected because they are wise, fair, and impartial, and therefore the solution comes from a respected and credible source.
4. The costs of prolonging the dispute are avoided. It is interesting to note that arbitrators' decisions tend to be consistent with judgments received from courts.[4] In a sense, they are "judges without robes," and their decisions are usually governed by public law or contract law.

Disadvantages of Arbitration

There are some disadvantages to arbitration.[5]

1. The parties relinquish control over shaping the outcome; thus, the proposed solution may not be one that they prefer, or are even willing to live with.

2. The parties may not like the outcome, and it may impose additional costs, sacrifices, or burdens on them.

3. If the arbitration is voluntary (they have a choice whether to follow the recommended solution or not), they may lose face if they decide not to follow the arbitrator's recommendation.

4. There is a *decision-acceptance effect*—there is less commitment to an arbitrated resolution, for at least two reasons: They did not participate in the process of shaping the outcome, and the recommended settlement may be inferior to what they preferred. If parties are less committed to an outcome, they will be less likely to implement it. (As we will see when we discuss mediation, there is better commitment to a resolution and its implementation because the parties are fully involved in making the decision.) For example, when divorce proceedings go to arbitration—particularly regarding alimony or child custody issues—the party who "loses" is often uncommitted to the settlement, refuses to follow the mandate, and the parties wind up back in court.

5. Research on arbitration has often shown that it has a *chilling effect*.[6] During negotiation, the parties may behave differently if they expect that the dispute will have to go to arbitration. During the negotiation, they may hold back on compromises so they do not lose anything in arbitration, particularly when they anticipate that the arbitrator will "split the difference." In essence, you might get a better settlement if you refuse to make any concessions, because if the arbitrator splits the difference, you can do better than if you made concessions and then the arbitrator split the difference. So negotiators may take a hard-line position. To avoid this, parties who expect to go to arbitration often use a method called "final offer arbitration." In this procedure, the arbitrator asks the parties to make their "best final offer," and then the arbitrator rules for one side or the other with no split. This in effect forces the parties to make the best deal they can during a negotiation, which reduces the distance between them as they approach arbitration. The more extreme the final offer, the less likely the arbitrator may be to rule in favor of it.

6. In the *narcotic effect*,[7] parties with a history of recurring arbitration tend to lose interest in trying to negotiate, become passive, and grow very dependent on the third party for helping them move toward resolution. Their attitude is, "We're not going to be able to agree, and a settlement is going to be imposed anyway, so why should I work hard to try to negotiate?" Thus, parties become "addicted" to arbitration and take less responsibility for themselves and resolving their own conflict. Further, a party with a strong-willed constituency may be uncompromising and unyielding during negotiation, and then blame the arbitrator for any compromises that have to be made in arbitration.

7. In the *half-life effect*,[8] the results of more and more arbitration are less and less satisfaction with the outcomes. Because the parties have become passive in the process, and have less control over the outcomes as well, arbitration frequently becomes ritualistic and simply loses its effectiveness. Eventually, the parties refuse to participate, take their case elsewhere, or remove themselves completely.

8. In the *biasing effect*, the arbitrators may be perceived not to be neutral and impartial, but to be biased. This is most likely to occur when an arbitrator makes a whole sequence of decisions that favors one side over the other. Interestingly, parties in strong conflict often try to bias the third party, and then reject the third party for being biased. (Witness the harassment that referees and umpires receive in most sporting events!) This shows how insidious and problematic destructive conflict can become. If an arbitrator is seen as biased, the parties will move toward selecting another arbitrator who will be neutral, or preferably, will favor their position.

MEDIATION

Formal mediation[9] is based on established rules and procedures. The objective of the mediator is to help the parties negotiate more effectively. The mediator does not solve the problem or impose a solution. He or she helps the disputing parties to develop the solution themselves and then to agree to it.[10] Thus, the mediator takes control of the process, but not the outcome.

A major concern for the mediator is to assist the parties in areas of communication. The intent is to improve the parties' skills so they will be able to negotiate more effectively. The assumption in mediation is twofold. First, the parties can and will come up with a better solution than one that is invented by a third party, and second, the relationship is an important one and the parties want to develop their ability to problem-solve about their conflict.

How Mediation Works[11]

There are a number of variations on the mediation process, but in general it tends to follow a reasonably common process. First, the mediator needs to be selected. The mediator can be a member of a professional mediation center or service, or can be acting informally as a mediator while in some other capacity (minister, manager, social worker, teacher, counselor, etc.).

The mediator begins by taking an active role. Usually, the mediator invites both sides to attend a meeting. The mediator sets ground rules by which the mediation will occur:

- The parties agree to follow a procedure set forth by the mediator.
- The parties agree to listen to each other and follow some rules of civility and respect toward each other.
- The role of the mediator is not to solve the parties' dispute, but to work with the parties to achieve a "negotiated" outcome.

As actual mediation starts, the mediator then takes on a more passive role. He or she meets with each party, to listen to them and learn about the dispute. In most cases, the mediator does this with the other party in the room, so that each can hear how the other sees the dispute. However, if the parties cannot be candid in front of the other, or conflict is likely to erupt, the mediator may hold these meetings with each party separately. Through active listening and questions, the mediator tries to identify and understand the issues. The mediator looks for underlying interest, priorities, and concerns, and finds areas for potential collaboration or compromise.

In the next stage, the parties agree on the agenda—the key issues to be discussed, and the order for discussion. The mediator will help them prioritize and package their proposals and counterproposals as needed.

The mediator brings the parties together and encourages exploration of possible solutions, trade-offs, or concessions. They are designed to help communication flow more freely, reduce tension, and so forth. The mediator may invent proposals, or suggest possible solutions, but will not impose any of these on the parties.

The final stage is agreement, which may be made public with an announcement of the settlement. There may be a written agreement, and it may or may not be signed. Many mediators push for some form of written agreement, to help the parties be clear about who is going to do what, and to enhance their commitment.

A long time may be involved in the mediation process, depending on the nature and degree of difficulty between the two parties. However, mediation is still less costly than going to court. The length of the stages may vary. For example, in divorce mediation, the preference is usually for both parties to begin meeting together as soon as possible, rather than having long individual meetings with the mediator. The objective is to move the parties toward communicating and working out their problems, but it will depend on the degree of cooperation of the parties and the skills of the mediator.

How Mediators Help

In addition to facilitating the negotiation process, mediators can help the parties save face when they need to make concessions. They can assist in resolving internal disagreements and help parties deal with their constituencies (e.g., by explaining the agreement to the constituency, or helping the negotiator save face with the constituency by portraying the negotiator as tough, fair, and effective). They may offer the parties incentives for agreement or concession, or offer negative incentives for noncooperation.

Mediators maintain control if the parties are unable to do so, largely by controlling the process (e.g., making sure the conflict between the parties does not escalate again, or that one side does not take undue advantage of the other). Mediators push when needed, and move into the background when the negotiators seem to be able to move forward themselves.

When Mediation Can Be Helpful

Mediation may be used in labor relations, or as a precursor to arbitration in grievance and contractual negotiations. It has also been used successfully in settling malpractice suits, tort cases, small claims, consumer complaints, liability claims, divorce,[12] civil and community disputes,[13] business disputes,[14] business and government cases involving the environment,[15] and international[16] disputes. It is increasingly being used in communities to resolve disputes between landlords and tenants or merchants and customers, and on college campuses to resolve conflicts in residence halls or between students of different genders, ethnic groups, and nationalities.

Most of these types of disputes are self-explanatory. What is interesting is to see the variety of ways that mediation can be taught and used. For example, children are being taught, as early as elementary school age, the art of mediation, and then taught how to use it to resolve conflicts in the classroom, on the playground, and in the home. While the techniques taught to children are probably not as sophisticated as they would be in a major international negotiation, the principles are exactly the same, and the dispute resolution skills children learn at an early age can carry over into their adult lives.

Factors Necessary for Success in Mediation

First, mediators *need to be seen by the disputants* as neutral, impartial, and unbiased. This is critical, because if mediators are seen by one or both disputants as "biased" toward one side or having a preferred outcome, then their actions will not be trusted. It is not enough for mediators themselves to believe they are neutral or can act in an unbiased manner—the acid test is that the *parties must see them as unbiased.*

Second, mediators may need to be expert in the field where the dispute occurs although mediation requires less expertise than arbitration. An arbitrator has to know the key laws or contract issues in the area, and usually has to make a decision that is consistent with previous rulings. In contrast, as long as a mediator is neutral and smart enough to understand the key issues and arguments of both sides, he or she can be effective. Sometimes, in fact, naive mediators have so little biases about the dispute in question that they may discover helpful approaches that experts in this area have become blind to. Expertise is especially important to industrial conflicts, where industry-specific knowledge may be important. In divorce mediation, a knowledge of marital law is helpful. (For an agreement to be legally binding, a lawyer probably has to write the document, but parties can achieve fundamental agreements in principle with almost any kind of a mediator.) It is also useful for the mediator to have experience in mediating similar disputes.

Although it is not required by law, certification of mediation training enhances the mediator's credibility. The Federal Mediation and Conciliation Service of the U.S. Department of Labor is one group that certifies mediators. There are also local mediation services and dispute settlement centers that "certify" mediators by having them participate in a mandatory training program, as well as an apprenticeship with an experienced mediator. Mediation centers can assist disputing parties in finding a mediator.

Successful mediation depends to a large degree on timing. Mediation cannot be used as a technique for dispute resolution if the parties do not agree that they need help, or are so angry and upset at each other that they cannot even civilly sit in the same room together. Mediation also depends on the willingness of the parties to make some concessions and find a compromise solution. If they are so committed to their point of view that no compromise is even possible—a problem we see in attempting to mediate value-based disputes around issues like abortion and environmental management—then mediation is doomed to fail. If the parties are not both willing to accept mediation, then it is unlikely that other techniques will work until the parties soften their views.

Success

Mediation tends to be successful in 60 to 80 percent of cases, according to statistics. Success of using mediation as an ADR technique is most likely when:[17]

- The conflict is moderate but not high.
- The conflict is not excessively emotional and polarized.
- There is a high motivation by both parties to settle.
- The parties are committed to follow the process of mediation.
- Resources are not severely limited.
- The issues do not involve a basic conflict of values.
- The power is relatively equal between the parties.
- Mediation is seen as advantageous relative to going to arbitration (or no agreement).
- The bargainers have experience and understand the process of give-and-take, and the costs of no agreement.[18]

In successful mediation, negotiators tend to be committed to the agreement that is generated.[19] Thus the implementation rate is high.

Disadvantages

Mediation is not effective or is more difficult to use when:

- The bargainers are inexperienced and assume that if they simply take a hard line, the other party will eventually give in.
- There are many issues, and the parties cannot agree on priorities.
- The parties are strongly committed to their positions (and are held to them by an uncompromising constituency).
- There is very strong emotion, passion, and intensity to the conflict.
- A party has an internal conflict, and isn't sure what to do.
- The parties differ on major social values.
- The parties differ greatly on their expectations for what is a fair and reasonable settlement.
- The parties' resistance points do not overlap—the most one party will give is still much less than the minimum the other will accept.

Mediation can be more time consuming than arbitration. The parties have to take a lot of time explaining the dispute to the third party, and then participating in the process of searching for a resolution. Also, because mediation is not binding, there is no impetus for the parties to commit to the settlement or even to settle at all. Thus there is always the potential for the dispute to reappear and continue—perhaps even for a long time. And it is always possible that the dispute will escalate.

Combining Mediation and Arbitration

Some who monitor third-party interventions have suggested that even better than mediation, in some cases, may be requiring a sequence of dispute resolution events, such as mediation followed by arbitration. This sequence seems to minimize the liabilities of each type of ADR (arbitration and mediation) and to obtain better compromises.[20] If the parties expect that they will have to progress to arbitration, they may be more willing to modify their positions in mediation to improve their chances of ruling in favor of their side. On the other hand, the expectation of arbitration may make the parties "lazy" in mediation, particularly if they think the arbitrator will ultimately rule in their favor.

Assisting the Mediator

Mediators succeed when both parties are agreeable to the mediation. Further, there are ways you can help the process.

You can help a mediator to help you negotiate by being cooperative with them and giving clear information. Tell them what is important to you, and why you want it. If you do not understand something, speak up. Express your concerns if necessary. Remember that the mediator is there to assist in the negotiation process, not to remake it. Finally, be willing to make concessions or problem-solve. The objective of mediation is to move the dispute from a competitive solution to a compromise or collaborative solution, and this requires the work of all parties. Ultimately, the success of the negotiation is your responsibility. You and the other party need to find, select, and implement a workable outcome. The mediator will assist you in this endeavor, but will not do the work for you.

PROCESS CONSULTATION

Another way of getting help with a stalled negotiation is to use a process consultant. Process consultants serve as counselors who focus on the *process* of negotiation, as their title would suggest. They assist parties in improving communication, reducing the emotionality of the proceedings, and increasing the parties' dispute resolution skills. Their objective is to enable parties to solve their own disputes in the future. Process consultants are thus useful if the relationship between the opposing parties is a long-term one.

A process consultant is somewhat like a mediator in that he or she helps with the steps in the process. But this person differs from the mediator in that there is no discussion of the specific issues or any attempt to solve them. Thus, process consultants are often more like counselors who help the parties to get along better so that they can engage in better negotiation and problem solving.

The Process

Process consultants (PCs) first interview the parties individually. Then they design a schedule of structured meetings for the parties. At these meetings, the PCs have the disputing parties discuss their past conflicts and perceptions of each other. The PCs remain neutral, guiding the parties as needed. They keep people on track, keep the emotional level from escalating, and move the parties toward problem-solving behavior. Their objective is to change the conflict management climate, improve communication, promote constructive dialogue, and create the capacity for people to act as "their own third party."

PCs have expertise in the areas of conflict and emotions. They provide emotional support to their clients. They confront and diagnose problems while remaining neutral and unbiased. They must also be authoritative to keep the process moving. They control and manage the agenda of how the parties engage each other, but not what actually happens.

Process consultation is used in marital therapy, family therapy, organizational development, and team building. It is also used in labor-management disputes and international conflict where there are ethical, political, and cultural difficulties to contend with.

Process consultation is less likely to work in the following circumstances:

- There are severe, polarized disputes over large issues.
- The relationship is short-term and the parties have no stake in improving it.
- The issues are fixed (competitive rather than collaborative negotiation).
- The party's constituency is not supportive of improving the relationship.
- One or both parties are intent on revenge or retribution.

OTHER, LESS FORMAL METHODS OF DISPUTE RESOLUTION

"Ombuds" and Others

Ombudspersons, fact finders, and referees are employed by various organizations to deal with matters before they turn into disputes. In many cases, their job is to hear and investigate conflicts between employees, or between an individual employee and "the system" (the rules, practices, and policies of the organization). At NCR,[21] as at other companies, ombuds are trained in problem solving, dispute avoidance, negotiation, and dispute resolution.

Their mission is to limit and resolve problems quickly and informally. They usually are not part of the chain of command in an organization and may report directly to the CEO rather than to a specific department. They often have links with the legal and human resources departments, so they can discuss trends in compliance or legal issues. But it is essential for ombuds to be impartial, and hence they are often unattached to the organizational hierarchy.

When an employee takes a problem to an ombud or the equivalent, the ombud engages in confidential fact-finding, then informs both sides of their rights and the opportunities for resolving the conflict. The ombud may use a combination of counseling, conciliation, negotiation, and mediation. If the complaint involves corporate policy, salary, promotion, tenure, discharge, liability, discriminatory treatment, or the like, the ombud may recommend a settlement, but usually management is involved in the final decision.

The main reason for using an ombudsperson is to make sure the process is fair and that the individual employees, with very little power, have a way to get a fair investigation and hearing about their concerns. If you are negotiating within a system or organization, an ombud can make sure you know the channels that are available to you, your rights, and what kind of outside help you may need. Ombuds can often act as "change agents," pushing an organization to change its rules and policies to deal with unfair treatments practices.

Advantages and Disadvantages of Ombuds

Using an ombud or other type of counselor can be to your advantage, if the power between the two disputing parties is out of balance. This is particularly true when a lower-level employee tries to challenge his or her employer and doesn't want to get fired simply for asking questions or raising concerns about "fairness" and "rights." As with other third-party practices, however, the final outcome may not be what you hoped for.

Some organizations specify a formal process for expressing and hearing problems and disputes in this system. They may require a staged approach, where the first step is an ombuds, the next is mediation, and the final step is arbitration.

MANAGERS AS THIRD PARTIES

Finally, we turn to managers, supervisors, and others whose jobs do not consist primarily of mediating disputes, but who nevertheless often must intervene to get work done or deal with unproductive conflicts in the workplace. It is estimated that managers spend 20 percent of their time in conflict management.[22] Their methods tend to be informal since most work environments do not have established rules or guidelines for how to mediate a dispute. Few managers have any formal training in settling disputes, and many are uncomfortable with conflict. But they need to know that some conflict is all right[23] and to seek assistance themselves if they often find themselves refereeing employee disputes.

Styles

Managers tend to solve disputes along the lines we discussed for other types of interventions—high or low process control, high or low outcome control.[24] The style used will depend on the manager's tolerance for conflict, the time frame, and, to some degree, the personalities of the parties involved.

High Control of Both Process and Outcome.   If a manager wants to maintain control of both the process and the outcome (which is the most typical scenario), the manager's style will be inquisitorial or autocratic. The manager behaves more like a judge in a European court, or like the infamous judge on the TV show, "The People's Court." The manager runs his or her own investigation, and then makes a decision. The manager will listen to both parties' stories, structure the process as he or she pleases, asking questions to learn more information, then will decide on the solution. This method tends to be the most common among managers. It is frequently used when the issues are minor, quick decisions are needed, or management needs to implement an unpopular action.[25]

High Outcome Control, Low Process.   A manager who wants to retain high control of the outcome, but low control of the process, will use passive listening and then will make a decision. This is most like the arbitration style described earlier. This is somewhat like the "high-high" method, except that the manager listens to both sides; he or she makes little effort to gather more information, ask questions, or structure the process other than to render a decision after hearing the arguments.

High Process Control, Low Outcome Control.   This approach is most like mediation. More managers are learning to use this approach, although not as much as would be hoped. In many disputes, the manager considers the outcome more important than the process, and wants to have some control over it, so this method is used less than it might be.

Low Process and Outcome Control.   If the manager does not care about controlling either process or outcome, he or she will either ignore the dispute and let the parties deal with it by themselves, or tell the disputing employees, "You solve the problem yourselves, or I will impose a solution that probably neither of you will like." This may sound like a parent acting as intervener between two arguing children.

Factors Affecting the Choice of Method

The choice of dispute resolution method will often be based on the time frame. Because outcome-control methods are believed to be quicker by the third party (hence, often ignoring a lot of the "disadvantages" of arbitration and outcome control), high outcome control methods are used when efficiency and saving time are high priorities. Other factors that affect the choice of resolution method are:

- The objectivity (neutrality) of the manager.
- The relationship of the parties (long-term or short-term).
- The effect of how this confrontation is resolved on future negotiations.
- The expected ability of the parties to resolve conflicts for themselves in the future.
- The extent of training of the manager in conflict resolution techniques.

Keys for Managers Helping Employees with Conflict

- Select a neutral site for the meeting.
- Be empathetic; listen as well as you can, and practice listening skills.
- Be assertive, particularly about setting guidelines for how the parties should deal with each other in a more productive manner.
- Ask for cooperation and be cooperative yourself.
- Ask what the parties want you to do to help solve the problem.
- When there is a resolution, if appropriate, get it in writing.
- Help the parties plan for implementation. And do not forget follow-up.

ADR'S USEFULNESS

Since 95 percent of all civil cases are settled out of court, there is room in the area of dispute resolution for ADR.[26] Alternative methods of dispute resolution can save time and money, reduce the number of cases on court dockets, and provide timely solutions to problems. In fact, about one half of state court systems now require that certain civil complaints be referred to arbitration prior to trial. Thirty-three jurisdictions require that family disputes regarding custody and visitation be brought into mediation.[27]

At the federal level, the U.S. district courts increasingly order civil cases into mandatory arbitration or refer parties to moderated settlement conferences, minitrials, and summary jury trials. The U.S. Court of Appeals for the District of Columbia and the U.S. Court of Claims are also experimenting with mediation programs.

As an example of costs, a commercial suit with a $200,000 claim will cost parties almost that much in legal fees, discovery costs, and actual trial costs. Mediation for this situation would cost about $2,500, usually shared between the two parties. So it makes sense to use third-party intervention before taking a case to court. And, as stated previously, mediation has a good track record—70 to 80 percent of all cases are successfully mediated.

Many employers now include in contracts, employment agreements, and other related documents an ADR clause that defines the dispute resolution process. It may specify:[28]

- The rules or laws that apply to the process.
- The ADR methods to use and in what order to apply them.
- The location for the ADR procedure.
- The official language of the ADR process.
- Whether the outcome will be binding.
- How the costs will be allocated among the parties.

In fact, at NCR, ADR is specified as the first, preferred method for dispute settlement.

However, ADR is not always the perfect solution. As an example, in the case of a rate-setting dispute with the Public Utilities Commission of Ohio (PUCO),[29] ADR appeared not to work well for this regulated utility, and was not a viable solution. There were several reasons. First, the intervention was not voluntary, so there was lower commitment to the process. Time constraints for public utilities prohibited the long periods of consideration that tend to be required in mediated situations. Resources were strained because the utility had to prepare for court at the same time as pursuing ADR, in case ADR failed. Statutory requirements added further constraints and costs. Utilities in dispute need to have mediators who are fully aware of industry-specific details (especially in the area of regulation) in order to be effective, and this was not true in this case.

How Some Organizations Solve Disputes

Many organizations follow a "line authority" approach to solving problems: First you go to a supervisor, then to a division supervisor, then to a panel of supervisors, and finally, to top management. If one of the parties is a union, the fourth step is binding arbitration. But there are other, more effective, more proactive ways to solve problems.

One such plan is PGR—peer group resolution[30]—which is used by Northern States Power Company. The purpose of the process is to investigate, review, and resolve disputes; employee peer groups serve on the panel and execute the process. The PGR steps are very specific:

Step 1.   The employee with a complaint completes a PGR form and submits a copy of it to the Human Resources department within 10 days of the incident. The employee gives the original form to the immediate supervisor, who completes a meeting with the employee within three working days. The supervisor writes a response to the problem on the form, and returns it to the employee within two working days. The employee then has two days to decide whether the response satisfies the complaint, or whether to progress to Step 2.

Step 2.   The employee's second-level supervisor schedules and completes a meeting with the employee within three working days of receiving the form. This person writes a response on the form, and returns it to the employee within two working days of meeting with the employee. The employee has two working days after receiving the written response to complete the appropriate section of the form, either indicating satisfaction with the response and sending it to Human Resources, or going to Step 3.

Step 3.   In this step, the employee can select from one of two options listed on the PGR form: Meet either with a third-level supervisor, or with a peer group panel. The supervisor meeting process is similar to that in Step 2. If the employee selects the peer group panel, the Human Resources department coordinates the random selection of panel members and schedules a panel review. The peer group panel consists of five employees, randomly chosen from two panelist pools. If the employee is nonsupervisory, then five panelists are selected from the nonsupervisory pool and four panelists from the supervisory pool. If the employee is supervisory, five panelists come from the supervisory pool, and four from the nonsupervisory pool. In both cases, the employee chooses two names from each pool to discard, resulting in a total of five panelists.

Within 10 working days of the employee choosing the final option, the panel meets with the employee and reviews the documentation and facts. The panel reaches a decision by majority vote to grant, modify, or deny the remedy requested by the employee. The panelists sign the form, adding explanations as appropriate. Human Resources distributes copies of the decision to the employee and supervisors. The decision reached in this manner is binding and cannot be appealed. All materials are kept confidential.

The program is successful in part because all who volunteer to be panelists receive a full day of training for this role. They practice reviewing sample cases using the role-play process.

The results of peer group resolution at Northern States Power Company have been rewarding. Many disputes have been resolved before they get to Step 3. Accountability of management has improved. Communication and problem-solving skills have improved. Concerns can be voiced and dealt with before they become major problems or disputes. The process allows all parties to deal with conflict in an organized manner. Productivity and morale are higher, because employees feel they can be heard. They also learn, as panelists, to better appreciate what goes into management decisions, and participate in a process of resolving disputes.

The company requires everyone to complete an evaluation form to assess the process, and this has provided positive feedback. In addition, each party with a grievance must be interviewed three months after settlement, to ensure that there is no retaliation.

Finding Third-Party Help

There are many organizations for mediators, arbitrators, and other third-party professionals. Among them are the Federal Mediation and Conciliation Service and the American Arbitration Association. There are private organizations which provide professional services, such as Endispute. There are also local mediation services in many communities, as well as consumer protection services available through district attorney's offices. In most communities, you can simply look up "Mediation Services" in your classified telephone directory, and find a list of individuals and organizations providing services.

If you are interviewing a potential candidate for third-party help, you may want to find out about availability, interests, and potential conflicts. Select someone who has a knowledge of the subject area that is the center of your dispute. Do not use a person who is likely to be partisan.[31]

ENDNOTES

1. C. Moore, *The Mediation Process: Practical Strategies for Resolving Conflict* (San Francisco, CA: Jossey-Bass, 1986).

2. See F. Elkouri and E. Elkouri, *How Arbitration Works,* 4th ed. (Washington, DC: BNA, 1985); P. Prasow and E. Peters, *Arbitration and Collective Bargaining: Conflict Resolution in Labor Relations,* 2nd ed. (New York: McGraw-Hill, 1983); and R. N. Corley, R. L. Black, and O. L. Reed, *The Legal Environment of Business,* 4th ed. (New York: McGraw-Hill, 1977).

3. C. Feigenbaum, "Final-Offer Arbitration: Better Theory than Practice," *Industrial Relations, 14* (1975), pp. 311–317.

4. D. Golann, "Consumer Financial Services Litigation: Major Judgments and ADR Responses," *The Business Lawyer.* Vol. 48, May 1993, pp. 1141–1149.

5. T. A. Kochan, *Collective Bargaining and Industrial Relations* (Homewood, IL: Irwin, 1980).

6. G. Long and P. Feuille, "Final Offer Arbitration: Sudden Death in Eugene," *Industrial and Labor Relations Review, 27* (1974), pp. 186–203; F. A. Starke and W. W. Notz, "Pre- and Postintervention Effects of Conventional versus Final-Offer Arbitration," *Academy of Management Journal, 24* (1981), pp. 832–850.

7. V. H. Vroom, "A New Look at Managerial Decision Making," *Organizational Dynamics, 1* (Spring 1973), pp. 66–80.

8. J. C. Anderson and T. Kochan, "Impasse Procedures in the Canadian Federal Service," *Industrial and Labor Relations Review, 30* (1977), pp. 283–301.

9. T. A. Kochan and T. Jick, "The Public Sector Mediation Process: A Theory and Empirical Examination," *Journal of Conflict Resolution, 22* (1978), pp. 209–240; T. A. Kochan, *Collective Bargaining and Industrial Relations* (Homewood, IL: Irwin, 1980).

10. P. J. D. Carnevale and D. G. Pruitt, "Negotiation and Mediation," in M. Rosenberg and L. Porter (Eds.), *Annual Review of Psychology,* Vol. 43 (Palo Alto, CA: Annual Reviews, 1992), pp. 531–582; J. A. Wall and A. Lynn, "Mediation: A Current Review," *Journal of Conflict Resolution, 37* (1993), pp. 160–194; R. J. Lewicki, S. Weiss, and D. Lewin, "Models of Conflict, Negotiation and Third Party Intervention: A Review and Synthesis," *Journal of Organizational Behavior, 13* (1992), pp. 209–252.

11. Carnevale and Pruitt, "Negotiation and Mediation."

12. See W. A. Donohue, *Communication, Marital Dispute and Divorce Mediation* (Hillsdale, NJ: Erlbaum, 1991); K. Kressel, N. Jaffe, M. Tuchman, C. Watson, and M. Deutsch, "Mediated Negotiations in Divorce and Labor Disputes: A Comparison," *Conciliation Courts Review, 15* (1977), pp. 9–12; O. J. Coogler, *Structural Mediation in Divorce Settlement: A Handbook for Marital Mediators* (Lexington, MA: Lexington Books, 1978).

13. K. Duffy, J. Grosch, and P. Olczak, *Community Mediation: A Handbook for Practitioners and Researchers* (New York: Guilford, 1991); P. Lovenheim, *Mediate, Don't Litigate: How*

to Resolve Disputes Quickly, Privately, and Inexpensively without Going to Court (New York: McGraw-Hill, 1989); L. Singer, *Settling Disputes: Conflict Resolution in Business, Families, and the Legal System* (Boulder, CO: Westview Press, 1990).

14. R. Coulson, *Business Mediation: What You Need to Know* (New York: American Arbitration Association, 1987).

15. W. Drayton, "Getting Smarter about Regulation," *Harvard Business Review, 59* (July–August 1981), pp. 38–52; R. B. Reich, "Regulation by Confrontation or Negotiation," *Harvard Business Review, 59* (May–June 1981), pp. 82–93; L. Susskind and J. Cruikshank, *Breaking the Impasse: Consensual Approaches to Resolving Public Disputes* (New York: Basic Books, 1987).

16. R. Fisher, *International Mediation: A Working Guide* (New York: International Peace Academy, 1978).

17. Carnevale and Pruitt, "Negotiation and Mediation"; K. Kressel and D. Pruitt (Eds.), *Mediation Research* (San Francisco, CA: Jossey-Bass, 1989).

18. T. A. Kochan and T. Jick, "The Public Sector Mediation Process: A Theory and Empirical Examination," *Journal of Conflict Resolution, 22* (1978), pp. 209–240.

19. C. Moore, *The Mediation Process: Practical Strategies for Resolving Conflict* (San Francisco, CA: Jossey-Bass, 1986).

20. Starke and Notz, "Pre- and Postintervention Effects"; D. W. Grigsby, *The Effects of Intermediate Mediation Step on Bargaining Behavior under Various Forms of Compulsory Arbitration,* paper presented to the Annual Meeting of the American Institute for Decision Sciences, Boston, MA, November 1981; D. W. Grigsby and W. J. Bigoness, "Effects of Mediation and Alternative Forms of Arbitration on Bargaining Behavior: A Laboratory Study," *Journal of Applied Psychology, 67* (1982), pp. 549–554.

21. T. B. Carver and A. A. Vondra, "Alternative Dispute Resolution: Why It Doesn't Work and Why It Does," *Harvard Business Review,* May–June 1994, p. 124.

22. M. A. Rahim, J. E. Garrett, and G. F. Buntzman, "Ethics of Managing Interpersonal Conflict in Organizations," *Journal of Business Ethics, 14* (1992), pp. 423–432.

23. Rahim, Garrett, and Buntzman, "Ethics of Managing Interpersonal Conflict."

24. B. H. Sheppard, "Managers as Inquisitors: Some Lessons from the Law," in M. Bazerman and R. J. Lewicki (Eds.), *Negotiating in Organizations* (Beverly Hills, CA: Sage, 1983), pp. 193–213.

25. Rahim, Garret, and Buntzman, "Ethics of Managing Interpersonal Conflict."

26. G. M. Flores, "Handling Employee Issues through Alternative Dispute Resolution," *The Bankers Magazine,* July/August 1993, pp. 47–50.

27. From American Bar Association material—Section of Dispute Resolution (1800 M Street, Washington, DC).

28. M. S. Lans, "Try an ADR and You'll Save Yourself a Court Date," *Marketing and the Law,* June 21, 1993, p. 14.

29. D. C. Bergmann, "ADR: Resolution or Complication?" *Public Utilities Fortnightly,* January 15, 1993, pp. 20–22.

30. D. B. Hoffman and N.L. Kluver, "How Peer Group Resolution Works at Northern States Power Co.," *Employment Relations Today,* Spring 1992, pp. 25–30.

31. J. Greenwald, "Resolving Disagreements: Alternative Market Finds ADR Works to Its Advantage," *Business Insurance,* June 7, 1993, p. 45.

Mediator Attitudes toward Outcomes: A Philosophical View

Kevin Gibson

Much of the work dealing with ethics in mediation has centered on the process rather than the outcome. Although there is significant convergence about mediator behavior during sessions, there is still much disagreement about how much mediators should consider the substantive settlement that parties reach or whether they should intervene to alter it. One approach, typified by Folberg and Taylor (1988) in their seminal work, *Mediation,* has at its core a belief in the primacy of client autonomy, with the consequence that mediators should be very "hands off" with regard to any potential resolution. Clients are presumed to have "the capacity, authority and responsibility to determine consensually what is best for themselves" (1988, p. 35). An associated belief is that intervention by an impartial third party is acceptable in the process but not in the substance of any settlement (Hughes, 1995; McEwen, Rogers, and Maiman, 1995). These attitudes will have a key role in determining how mediators practice their craft. "Neutral" mediators are often reluctant to monitor or intervene in a settlement that the clients have determined to be satisfactory.

In this article I maintain that client satisfaction alone is an unsatisfactory gauge of the success or legitimacy of mediation. Typically mediation operates in an atmosphere of confidentiality and without routine oversight, and hence there are few ways to judge the quality of outcomes independent of the clients' own reactions. Consequently, we cannot rely on the fact that there are high settlement rates alone to underwrite the legitimacy of mediation.

Here I outline three areas where mediation participants might be satisfied with their outcome yet intervention or review may be appropriate: (1) cases where the process may give a false perception of the settlement, (2) wider issues arising from factors external to the mediation, and (3) cases where expert review is required. I contend that mediators not only need to consider these areas in almost all cases but that they have an affirmative duty to maintain a threshold quality of settlements. I then describe the elements that would be involved in such a threshold. I conclude that mediators can never be indifferent to the nature of the outcome and that there is a case for routine review of mediated settlements. My analysis, then, has significant implications for the traditional mediator stance of neutrality and may affect present practice.

MEDIATOR PRACTICE

Many mediators refer to themselves as "neutrals." One dimension of neutrality is the belief that mediators should have no significant input or oversight with regard to the settlement. Joseph Stulberg (1981) is representative of mediators who believe that the settlement is paramount and that they should remain indifferent to its content. For example, Stulberg advises that

> A mediator must be neutral with regard to outcome. Parties negotiate because they lack the power to achieve their objectives unilaterally. . . . If the mediator is neutral and remains so, then he and his office invite a bond of trust to develop between him and the parties. (p. 96)

Thus the mediator deliberately avoids involvement in the substantive settlement in the belief that such a posture will expedite the process. Folberg and Taylor's (1988) claim is less instrumental because it derives from a fundamental belief in the primacy of client autonomy. In their words,

> Mediation . . . can be defined as the process by which the participants, together with the assistance of a neutral person or persons, systematically isolate disputed issues in order to develop options, consider alternatives, and reach a consensual settlement that will accommodate their needs. (p. 7)

Thus, the ownership of the process and the solution is squarely placed on the shoulders of the participants. It is the responsibility of the clients to make and live with their own decisions. In one sense, at least, mediation is the converse of a formal legal system that necessarily imposes solutions on disputants and "when it does interfere, the odds are that it interferes wrongly, and in the wrong place" (Mill, 1956, p. 102).

Given that mediation seeks to fulfill participant interests as a prime goal, the range of outcomes may be inventive, novel, or unusual according to orthodox formal legal remedies. I suggest, however, that whatever the nature of the settlement, it should not be outside the scope of review. An inventive settlement still needs to satisfy minimal levels of justice.

PURE JUSTICE

One objection to intervention is that any outcome will necessarily be fair by the very fact that the process itself was fair, so no independent assessment of the settlement would be appropriate. This would be akin to a notion of "pure justice": any outcome is just as long as it results from the consistent operation of specified procedures (Beauchamp, 1982). However, it is not obviously the case that if the process of mediation is fair the outcomes will be fair, too. We can imagine cases in which the mediator is impartial, follows a clear procedure, gives both parties time to air their interests and concerns, and the parties leave with a settlement they are satisfied with. Yet the outcome may not be fair, just, or appropriate in several senses: the parties may have (1) had a negative bargaining zone (that is, they would have been better off not settling), (2) based their settlement on subjective rather than objective criteria, (3) been mistaken about their preferences, (4) been information-poor, (5) shouldered the burden of the settlement onto an innocent or naive third party, or (6) violated a general policy concern in settling their immediate dispute. In all these cases, the mediation participants may express satisfaction, and yet the outcomes may be unfair or undesirable. I briefly describe some of these problems and show that client satisfaction may need to be supplemented in assessing outcomes.

ISSUES IN THE PROCESS

I now sketch several dynamics that affect mediators when they practice. Often these influences are unnoticed, and they may give an impression of professional attachment that is sometimes misleading.

The "Agreement Is Good" Bias

Max Bazerman and his colleagues have identified what they term the "agreement-is-good" bias, that is, individuals believe that an agreement is better than no agreement at almost any cost (Bazerman, Gibbons, Thompson, and Valley, 1993). In the same vein, Leigh Thompson (1990) framed a bargaining situation in which no potential for a mutually beneficial settlement existed. Despite the lack of a positive bargaining zone for both parties, she found that the vast majority (90 percent) came to an agreement. So it seems that most negotiators prefer an unprofitable settlement to an impasse.

One possible explanation for this result is that there is a "correspondence inference process" at work (Jones and Davis, 1965), that is, a psychological mechanism that links the process to the outcome so that participants who think the process itself is fair and appropriate feel compelled to reach some kind of settlement. Even though an impasse reached because of a negative bargaining zone is indeed a failure to settle, it is nevertheless a positive outcome in that both parties would leave the bargaining table no worse off. In that sense no agreement may often be better than a poor one.

Surely the main function of a mediator is to help parties come to a settlement. However, that claim needs to be qualified in that the mediator should not facilitate settlement for its own sake but rather help find an outcome only if there is a bargaining zone where settlement is beneficial. The worry that comes from the psychological findings is that mediators and their clients would not be immune from such biases and oftentimes may reach settlement when that is not appropriate. This may lead to a number of suboptimal agreements, which in itself need not be pernicious. Nevertheless, these findings cast doubt on the credibility of reports in which client satisfaction is the sole criterion of mediation success.

Problems with Objective Criteria

Fisher and Ury (1981) suggest that "objective criteria" should undergird any settlement. These criteria hold the promise of being impartial and defensible rather than arbitrary or biased. In *Getting to Yes* they say that a fair standard may be based on any of the following: "Market value; precedent; scientific judgment; professional standards; efficiency: costs; what a court would decide; moral standards; equal treatment; tradition; reciprocity; etc." (p. 87).

The "etc." is telling because it suggests that the "objective standards" that Fisher appeals to amount to any standard to which the disputants themselves will accede. This is because there are at least two ways to interpret "objective criteria." On the one hand we can think of them as denoting things that are true for all time, independent of *any* observer, and on the other as things both parties will accept as standards independent from themselves. Thus, it may be objectively true in the first sense that light travels at 186,000 miles a second—objective in that light's traveling speed is thought of as a uniform law of nature. In the second sense, though, objectivity is found in any standard that two disputants would agree to accede to. For instance, they might agree that the value of a house is what an independent appraiser says it is, or a sports statistic is correct because it is said to be so by someone both parties trust. There is an intuitive sense in which the first type of fact is grounded differently than the second. Indeed, the second may be said not to be objectively true at all but only "intersubjectively" true (Luban, 1989).

Fisher and Ury (1981) appear to invoke the second type of objectivity in their discussion of objective criteria. For example, when talking about the Law of the Sea Conference, they say

> An episode . . . illustrates the merits of using objective criteria. At one point, India, representing the Third World Block, proposed an initial fee for companies mining in the deep sea bed of $60 million per site. The United States rejected the proposal, suggesting that there be no initial fee. Both sides dug in; the matter became a matter of will. . . . Then someone discovered that the Massachusetts Institute of Technology had developed a model for the economics of deep sea bed mining. This model, gradually accepted by the parties as objective, provided a way of evaluating the impact of any fee proposal on the economics of mining. (p. 87)

Here they do not claim that the MIT model represents the correct facts, or even that it is close to the facts. Instead the model is agreed to by both parties because it has some "reasoned basis" for the figures it gives. I am not suggesting that the model they discuss is completely arbitrary, only that its qualification as an objective criterion is closer to the second type of objectivity than the first, that is, its acceptability to the negotiating parties stems from it being viewed as an impartial assessment.

The upshot of parties using objective criteria in Fisher's sense is that interest-based bargaining will not, in itself, guarantee fairness to the parties. Therefore, a mediator who takes responsibility for the outcome will need to be aware that client consent to an agreement will not automatically mean that it is fair, and for fairness to be demonstrated he or she will need to have some sort of strong external standard for comparison or established acceptable range of settlement that may be applied to any given case.

Confused Interests

Chris Moore uses a model of participant interests that says that clients need to be satisfied with three dimensions of interests: substantive, psychological, and process (Moore, 1986). Client satisfaction may easily conflate the three so that someone may report being pleased with the outcome, whereas at the moment he or she is focusing on one dimension and may come to realize that, all things considered, the outcome is less than adequate. For example, a mediation session for a divorcing couple could be far less acrimonious than dealings they are used to, and the very fact that the husband is comfortable with the setting may lead to his making substantive concessions in order to preserve the atmosphere of cordiality. In itself there is nothing wrong with doing so, and often mediation works that way. However, the risk is that clients may not fully realize what they are doing and regret their actions later—a condition that is likely to unravel any settlement.

Thus, client satisfaction may be thought of in terms of procedure that was employed as well as the subjective satisfaction derived from the attainment of a certain outcome. In any given case, then, an individual may be pleased to have had a hand in the construction of the outcome and to have been heard, and pleased as well that the mediator was useful and impartial. Yet these aspects of client satisfaction need not show that mediation was successful. Although they go some way in showing, for example, that the procedure included a fair approach and an empowerment of the parties, they only show clearly that the clients *perceived* fairness and empowerment, not that the outcome was, in fact, fair or acceptable. It is certainly possible that a fair process may lead to unfair outcomes—like the allocation of resources depending on the toss of a coin. A shrewd, disaffected mediator with a personal agenda could mislead the parties into believing the process was fair when it was not. At present we have a situation where mediation is often self-verifying: clients could reach acceptable outcomes almost accidentally from a very poor process, or they could accept substandard outcomes because the process was perceived to be fair. Independent review would be one solution to the difficulty that mediators and participants have in assessing the success of the process and its outcomes.

Mistaken Preferences: Sweet and Sour Grapes

In Aesop's fables, a fox covets some juicy grapes hanging from a vine. He tries in vain to take them. He departs, declaring that the grapes were probably sour anyway. Jon Elster (1982) describes this phenomenon as "adaptive preference formation" (p. 129).

The positive aspect of adaptive preference formation in mediation is that clients will not be disappointed if they fail to achieve unrealistic settlements, and therefore their welfare will not be diminished. For example, a parent who desires full custody and child support may be told that this is an unrealistic expectation. The parent is likely to adapt his or her preferences based on the new information. The consequence is that client satisfaction is closely related to client expectations, and these, in turn, may be shaped or colored by the mediator. The clients' perceived satisfaction with the outcome then becomes a partial function of the expectations given to them. In effect, the mediator has soured the grapes and made them less appealing.

However, there are also negative possibilities. Let us take the case of a woman who goes into small claims mediation. She has been told by a well-meaning but uninformed relative that the most she can expect is the present value of the disputed item instead of the replacement cost, which is false in her case. The effect of the poor advice will be that the woman will be very happy with an offer from the vendor of slightly more than the present value, although such a settlement might represent an unfair outcome; here the grapes are artificially sweetened, so to speak, in that what was previously unappealing is made more so.

Adaptive preference formation can work to either benefit or hurt the client in mediation, then, and the dynamic may be generated by the conduct of the mediator. Here again client satisfaction with a mediated settlement cannot be taken as the true measure of a fair outcome because satisfaction is largely a function of what clients are advised is realistic or appropriate. For example, take the case where there are two sets of disputants with identical cases except that the outcome expectations of one party in one of the pairs has been dramatically lowered by authoritative advice. It would not be surprising to find the party with lower expectations content with an outcome that is less optimal than the settlement reached by the disputant in the other case; the party may even be satisfied with an unjust outcome. However, the level of client satisfaction might be the same in both cases.

Informational Poverty

In any situation, people without adequate or complete information are not likely to make the best decisions, and poor decisions generate poor settlements. The kinds of information involved will be hard data, appropriate assessment of the data, and the ways of dealing with uncertainty (Hammond, Keeney, and Raiffa, 1998). The question then arises as to how the mediator can identify the facts and data needed and decide who will gather the information and in what form. This initially appears to be an intractable problem for "neutral" mediators.

One way out of the difficulty is to adopt the symmetric prescriptive advice (SPA) model proposed by Gibson, Thompson, and Bazerman (1996). The SPA approach recommends that a mediator actively encourage information gathering, sharing, and referrals to *all* parties. Gibson and others claim this is likely to enhance participant autonomy because participants will be better able to make informed, authentic, and efficient decisions when given access to resources and data. Because the mediator is acting symmetrically and yet still leaving the final decisions with the clients, the mediator can still be (or act) neutral. Similarly, Bush (1989) has advocated that a mediator should be "pushy" to have clients disclose and marshal all information relevant to resolving the dispute.

Choosing which information matters and how it is to be brought to the table will inevitably involve value judgments on the part of the mediator. Importantly, the authors suggest that the mediator incorporate a statement of personal values in the opening statement. I suggest that absolute value-freedom is a practical impossibility, and at least SPA announces its biases in plain terms. It values rationality, critical reflection, and creative thinking and encourages them in the mediation process.

Under SPA, the mediator would not pass on the privileged information of one party to the other but would encourage clients to be more fully aware of their bargaining zones, reservation points, and options, as well as the consequences of their decisions and their views of social justice. The SPA approach does not amount to coaching an unempowered party and may not result in fully optimal outcomes. The clients may still choose an outcome that is, all things considered, poorer than it could have been. Nevertheless, the SPA approach allows mediators to share information that could be helpful, and in many cases the outcomes would be worse if the mediator withheld the information for fear of broaching neutrality.

CONCERNS BEYOND THE PROCESS

I now turn to two classes of cases in which the clients themselves may be fully aware of the nature of their settlement but the mediator may nevertheless have a duty to intervene because of factors external to client satisfaction.

Externalities

An externality is a cost that is passed on to a third party, even though the third party may not be aware of it. For example, pollution incurs costs to those who suffer it or clean it up, and these costs are rarely borne by the producers of the pollution. Thus a generating plant may burn coal in producing electricity. The pollution that the sulphurous smoke causes generates costs, perhaps by increasing the cost of health care in the local community or by blackening buildings. The expense of providing health care or cleaning buildings is not computed in the cost of generating electricity and is left to those who are affected. Thus the real cost of energy production is understated, and the difference between the assumed cost without regard to these kinds of side effects and actual cost, all things considered, is termed an externality.

One way disputants can resolve their difficulties is to shift the burden of a decision or act onto a third party, effectively creating an externality. This strategy is clearly more effective if the third party is unaware of the extra costs or is powerless to do anything about them. Thus two neighbors arguing about paying for the removal of trash behind their houses could decide that the cheapest solution would be to haul it to a public area, and so place the burden on the community at large.

There is a moral difficulty with externalities in that they represent an easy solution to many difficulties for the disputants but may hurt uninformed third parties. Although costs may be spread among many more people and therefore may become imperceptible or slight, they are morally questionable because they are often incurred without the permission of those who will be forced to pay. In short, a high level of client satisfaction may not be a good-quality outcome if it comes at the price of the solution being passed on to the unwary or the naive, or to future generations. Mediators need to be aware that the welfare of third parties should be incorporated into the assessment of any settlement.

Policy Concerns

William Ury poses a case in which mediation runs the risk of providing a short-term solution while ignoring the underlying social problem (Ury, Brett, and Goldberg, 1988). Ury considers that a corporation operating a publicly subsidized apartment building for low-income people might favor a mediation procedure to resolve tenant complaints. Such a procedure, he believes, might resolve complaints differently from the way they would be resolved in court. For example, "if a tenant complains about rats in her apartment, mediation might result in the landlord setting rat traps rather than engaging in the full-scale extermination program that a court would require under the city housing code" (Ury, Brett, and Goldberg, p. 51).

Thus we can see the two risky elements: the tenant might not get full justice, and the policy issues of whether tenants are entitled to vermin-free housing is sidestepped. In the case of the rat-infested building, for example, the tenant is more likely to be interested in getting immediate redress than instigating a long-term legal case. Alternatively, her lawyer may have lowered her expectations, perhaps saying that the case will take time, the landlord is liable to appeal, and enforcement of a court order would be difficult. In either circumstance, it would not be surprising if the tenant settled for a number of rat traps. Repeated individual cases that are all held to be confidential may disguise an underlying problem or policy issue that needs to be addressed at a higher level. Neighborhood justice centers, environmental mediation, and public sector dispute resolution have come under criticism for this very reason. Linda Singer (1990) quotes an advocate for occupational health as saying, "The presumption of compromise may not serve the purpose of protecting public health and environment under law. . . . The goal of getting a good regulation that protects health and safety of workers and students is almost submerged by the desire to produce a regulation by consensus" (p. 149).

Moreover, although many times an individual is aware of his or her actions in creating a test case, it could be the case that someone is not aware of the larger dimensions of his or her dispute until they are pointed out by some third party (Fiss, 1984, p. 1078).

EXPERT REVIEW

As we have seen, both the clients and the mediator may approve of settlements when there are good policy reasons to reject them. Often these cases require legal expertise to assess the wider implications of the agreement. However, lawyers acting as mediators probably ought not to confuse their role by switching hats midway through the process as they analyze their own agreements. But many times mediations will involve agreements that may be strictly legal yet still questionable. By analogy, other professionals acting as mediators may not be in the best position to judge outcomes they themselves have helped to craft. In many other cases the mediator will have little proficiency in a particular area and therefore should not offer an assessment of the agreement even if inclined to do so. Thus, for example, parents with joint custody might agree to swap their child daily between cities fifty miles apart—a situation that may lead to unnecessary harm to the child. Or a nursing home may press for the use of physical restraints for an elderly man for their convenience rather than for sound medical reasons. These kinds of expedient settlements may involve potential harm or may have wider implications, and it seems that the mediator should advocate a review by professionals in the appropriate field, for instance, social workers for custody questions, lawyers for legal issues, and technical experts for environmental questions. A case like that of the commuting child would be presented, say, to a social worker or other expert in child development, and the reviewer could reject the proposal or recommend changes. In these cases, appeal to an independent outside authority appears to be the best way to maintain the integrity of mediated settlements.

WHAT STANDARDS ARE APPROPRIATE?

The problems with relying on client satisfaction support the case for external review of mediation settlements through which a reviewer has the power to reject a proposed settlement. Review of this kind would provide at least two services: (1) allow comparisons between mediated and nonmediated agreements, and (2) highlight cases in which the settlement was grossly unfair.

Robert Mnookin and L. Kornhauser (1979) have suggested that mediation operates "in the shadow of the law" (p. 997). Because most cases settle outside the court, the appropriate standard by which to judge mediation cases may not be so much the legal verdict as the settlements that are made on the courthouse steps. As mediation is still an *alternative* form of resolving disputes, it seems correct to judge its outcomes against those reached in the more conventional forums such as courts and arbitration.

Such a comparison might be thought inappropriate because people elect ADR to avoid the courts and so may be using different standards. I believe that although the comparison is not direct, it is still useful. For example, a tort case could be mediated, and the injured party might settle for much less than he would have won in court because he did not want to incur court costs and also wanted to avoid the psychological burden that going to court and testifying would place on him. Settlements may have to be discounted in order to accommodate client preferences; nevertheless, the courts do provide societal standards of remedies that can be used as a reference point. It would be incorrect to look for a direct one-to-one correlation between monetary awards in the courts and ADR; still, there should not be a huge disparity between settlements made in the formal and informal systems. For instance, in a libel case that is settled before a court appearance, it would not be surprising if the agreement mirrored on what was worked out through mediation. However, if there were a consistent trend for the awards in settled cases to be ten times as high as those in mediated cases, there would be cause for concern.

Mediation also operates under an ad hoc system of review at present. Although review is not seen as integral to the mediation process, it occurs in several ways. Court-annexed mediation has judicial oversight in that any settlement is reviewed prior to becoming a court document; that is, a judge will consider proposed settlements put forward by disputants but is not obliged to accept them. In divorce cases or small claims, for example, the settlement becomes a legal judgment. Hence there are built-in safeguards in that the chance of a judge sanctioning as unconscionable settlement is, if not remote, then at least no more probable than the judge ruling the same thing during a formal court process. Moreover, clients commonly enter mediation while simultaneously allowing an attorney to review offers and agreements.

Critical reflection or external review is therefore often incorporated into present practice, and hence it does not represent a radical departure from what already happens in many areas. Nevertheless, it does differ from present mediation theory, and some might find it objectionable.

MAJOR OBJECTIONS

Some serious objections may be raised to the issue of review. The chief problems are (1) a potential chilling effect on the mediation process, (2) an erosion of respect for client autonomy, and (3) the possibility that mediation would become more bureaucratic. Let us now review the force of these charges, although in the absence of empirical evidence claims for and against, review will necessarily be somewhat speculative.

The Chilling Effect

The argument would go, roughly, that one of the chief appeals of mediation is the ability of clients to generate their own solutions, and these may not reflect the formal resolutions of the courts (for example, being "made whole again" by monetary compensation).

Review would probably involve the shadow settlement, and hence the mediation process could effectively become an arms-length legal procedure. Clients would be discouraged from adopting novel or unusual solutions that truly fulfill their interests because the default would be the legal proceeding. Associated with these concerns is the question of whether parties in conflicts who are free to negotiate a bargain without public scrutiny of its terms should automatically be deprived of their privacy if they choose to take their dispute to mediation.

Risks to Client Autonomy

A similar but distinct claim is that one of the chief attractions of mediation is that it allows the clients to be self-determined. Oversight might mean that in mediation participants are restricted from entering into agreements that would be perfectly fine if they were privately negotiated. Under this view the role of the mediator is that of a facilitator who helps the clients achieve their own goals and is not constrained by an outsider's idea of what is correct or good.

Increased Bureaucracy

Mediation is appealing largely because it comes without the baggage of formal legal filings, representation, rulings, and potential for appeal. Inevitably, if oversight were implemented, another layer of involvement would be injected into the process; if it were more than rubber stamping, it would bring additional costs in time, money, and effort on the part of the clients. Once begun, the mediation process could become as cumbersome as the present court system.

RESPONSES

Naturally, the strength of the objections is related to the kind and extent of the review that would be implemented. Mediation comes in many varieties, and oversight need not be a Procrustean bed where all review is completely standardized. Indeed, the oversight might merely consist of a threshold standard test that the mediator refers to prior to the end of mediation.

A minimum standard might reflect the legal notion of "unconscionability." Unconscionability is found in contract law, and allows courts to refuse to enforce contracts that literally shock the conscience. The term is typically defined as "a bargain which no man in his senses, not under delusion, would make, on the one hand, and which no fair and honest man would accept, on the other" (*Hume* v. *U.S.*, 10S.Ct.133, 33LEd.393).

Unconscionability is not a strict notion though and is subject to wide interpretation in the courts. Sometimes courts have negated contracts that are thought to be grossly unfair, but there is a widespread notion that contracts freely entered into should not be annulled on the basis that they are unfavorable to one side (Dewey, 1970; Schwartz, 1974). Typically, contracts are conditional on the parties being free agents acting by informed consent, and so showing that a person was unfairly hindered or constrained might be enough to have a contract declared unenforceable. Thus legal contracts are entered into intelligently, knowingly, and voluntarily (Fort, 1978). Although lack of sophistication in bargaining or disparate bargaining power have not, in themselves, been held as grounds for unconscionability, they do flag the potential for manifest unfairness

(Fort, 1978). The fourth challenge to conscionability is if a contract goes against public policy. A contract that is contrary to public policy is called an "illegal bargain" and is defined as one where "either its formation or its performance is criminal, tortious, or otherwise opposed to public policy" (Restatement of Contracts, paragraph 512).

Thus the minimum standard may require two elements. First, the mediator needs to make sure that the clients have critically reflected on their decisions—that they truly accord with their best understanding of whether or not they further their interests, however defined. This is not a demand that outcomes be fully optimal; rather, it is an assurance that client decisions are intelligent, knowing, and voluntary. Hence in the case of a weary civil litigant in mediation who says, "Whatever; she can have all those demands as long as I never have to deal with her again," it is incumbent on the mediator to ensure that the client is fully aware of the meaning and implications of that form of words. I do not see this demand as a significant departure from standard mediation practice, and in fact such a practice would comport with and probably enhance client autonomy. It also seems that any bargain should be able to withstand examination in terms of an acceptable threshold, which would probably consist of at least bargainer informed consent, and accordance with social policy. If an outcome fails this test, then I believe it was likely to be improper anyway. Thus, the demand for privacy is not as strong as it initially appears. Scrutiny as I have described it is not necessarily open access but review by an informed agent who, in most cases, would be the mediator. If the bargain fails the threshold test, the mediator would be complicit in arranging an unconscionable settlement, which seems worse to me than maintaining bargainer privacy.

The second element is that the mediator needs to be aware of the potential for externalities and significance for social policy of settlements. There is a real risk that justice may get short-changed if all cases aspire to expedient settlement. This is not to deny that there is social utility in the efficient resolution of disputes; however, we should recognize that there is a policy trade-off between aspiring to ideal justice and rapidly resolving disputes. Still, not having review opens up mediation to severe hazards, and the alternative is to repress cases of potential societal import. Mediation is a very effective process of dispute resolution. Nevertheless, we should recognize that there is an issue about the institutionalized status of mediation in that promotion or restraint of informal dispute resolution carries the risk of bringing about injustice or the resolution of policy cases in the form of a local compromise rather than through a public airing of the issues. Ury suggests that in cases where there are risks to individual rights, there may be a duty on the part of the entity promoting mediation to make sure that all parties are educated about their legal standing prior to settlement (Ury, Brett, and Goldberg, 1988).

In dealing with biochemical engineering or genetic research the actual risks of catastrophic harm are often minimal. Still, we place great restrictions on these activities as a matter of social policy because if there were an unintended outcome it could be disastrous. Similarly, despite appeals to efficiency and to the desirability of clearing the court docket, there are significant societal risks if we unquestioningly rely on client satisfaction as the gauge of acceptability of mediated settlements. That is, we are liable to disregard legitimate claims to social justice from the underempowered or unrepresented. Therefore, I believe that we should not accept informal settlement in all areas without discussion at the policy-setting level.

Using the standard of unconscionability need not impoverish mediation. It would not mean that mediation could not have creative or innovative settlements that depart from the legal norm. Rather it suggests that mediation should not endorse agreements that would not be sanctioned by society. Additionally, the quality of outcomes should ideally be superior in mediation to those from a more formal procedure; what the threshold test means is that at least they will not be lower.

The cases that are "chilled" may not have been appropriate candidates for mediation in the first place. Moreover, the autonomy of clients is as likely to be improved as diminished by critical reflection urged by a mediator. The more significant charge is that mediation will become more bureaucratic and less efficient—claims that seem undeniable. Perhaps lowered efficiency is the price to be paid in order to ensure that mediation is not only effective in resolving disputes but also just.

CONCLUSION

The attitude of the mediator to the outcome is not necessarily a neutral one. He or she will be responsible for ensuring that settlements meet minimal standards and may require a review by another disinterested party before the settlement is sanctioned. Where issues of harm to self or others are involved, the mediator cannot be neutral in the sense of disinterested; he or she has an affirmative obligation to make sure that some kinds of settlement are questioned. However, I see no reason for the mediator to create optimal outcomes; free and informed individuals should be allowed to make any choice they wish within certain constraints; the mediator may express an opinion that the agreement is not the best, but it should remain a choice of the clients as to whether they should pursue other options.

The posture taken by the mediator about the propriety of outcomes is likely to be different depending on the kind of mediation; thus, different standards may apply to each. Often mediators must make judgment calls. This implies that mediation practice will benefit from additional ethical training for mediators. It also suggests that mediation should not be self-certifying and needs to develop standards of acceptable outcomes audited by individuals external to the mediation.

REFERENCES

Bazerman, M., Gibbons, R., Thompson, L., and Valley, K. "When and Why Do Negotiators Outperform Game Theory?" In R. N. Stern and J. Halpern (eds.), *The Role of Nonrationality in Organization Decision Making: Current Research into the Nature and Processes of the Informal Organization.* Ithaca, NY: ILR Press, 1993.

Beauchamp, T. *Philosophical Ethics.* New York: McGraw-Hill, 1982.

Bush, R. B. "Efficiency or Protection, or Empowerment and Recognition? The Mediator's Role and Ethical Standards in Mediation." *Florida Law Review,* 1989, *41* (2), 253–86.

Dewey, A. "Freedom of Contract: Is It Still Relevant?" *Ohio State Law Journal,* 1970, 31 (3), 724–68.

Elster, J. "Sour Grapes: Utilitarianism and the Genesis of Wants." In B. Williams and A. Sen (eds.), *Utilitarianism and Beyond.* New York: Cambridge University Press, 1982.

Fisher, R., and Ury, W. *Getting to Yes*. Boston: Houghton Mifflin, 1981.

Fiss, O. "Against Settlement." *Yale Law Journal,* 1984, *93* (6), 1073–90.

Folberg, J., and Taylor, A. *Mediation: A Comprehensive Guide to Resolving Conflicts without Litigation.* San Francisco: Jossey-Bass, 1988.

Fort, J. "Understanding Unconscionability: Defining the Principle." *Loyola Law Journal,* 1978, *9* (4), 765–822.

Gibson, K., Thompson, L., and Bazerman, M. "Shortcomings of Neutrality in Mediation: Solutions Based on Rationality." *Negotiation Journal,* 1996, *12* (1), 69–80.

Hammond, J., Keeney, R., and Raiffa, H. *Smart Choices: A Practical Guide to Making Better Decisions.* Cambridge: HBS Press, 1998.

Hughes, S. "Elizabeth's Story: Exploring Power Imbalances in Divorce Mediation." *Georgetown Journal of Legal Ethics,* 1995, *8* (4), 553–95.

Jones, E., and Davis, K. "From Acts to Dispositions: The Attribution Process in Person Perception." In L. Berkowitz (ed.), *Advances in Experimental Social Psychology,* 1965, *2,* 220–66.

Luban, D. "The Quality of Justice." *Denver University Law Review,* 1989, *66* (3), 381–417.

McEwen, C., Rogers, N., and Maiman, R. "Bring in the Lawyers: Challenging the Dominant Approaches to Ensuring Fairness in Divorce Mediation." *Minnesota Law Review,* 1995, *79* (4), 1317–95.

Mill, J. S. *On Liberty*. (C. Shields, ed.) New York: Bobbs-Merrill, 1956.

Mnookin, R., and Kornhauser, L. "Bargaining in the Shadow of the Law: The Case of Divorce." *Yale Law Journal,* 1979, *88* (5), 950–97.

Moore, C. *The Mediation Process*. San Francisco: Jossey-Bass, 1986.

Schwartz, A. "Seller Unequal Bargaining Power and the Judicial Process." *Indiana Law Journal,* 1974, *49* (3), 367–98.

Singer, L. *Settling Disputes: Conflict Resolution in Business, Families, and the Legal System.* Boulder, Colo.: Westview Press, 1990.

Stulberg, J. "The Theory and Practice of Mediation: A Reply to Professor Susskind." *Vermont Law Journal,* 1981, *6* (1), 85–97.

Thompson, L. "Negotiation Behavior and Outcomes: Empirical Evidence and Theoretical Issues." *Psychological Bulletin,* 1990, *108,* 515–32.

Ury, W., Brett, J., and Goldberg, S. *Getting Disputes Resolved: Designing Systems to Cut the Costs of Conflict*. San Francisco: Jossey-Bass, 1988.

The Manager as the Third Party: Deciding How to Intervene in Employee Disputes

A. R. Elangovan

Consider the following scenarios in an organization:

Two days before major contract work was to begin at an important client site, a dispute had erupted between the director of operations (DO) and controller of a small emission-testing (pollution control) company regarding hiring temporary workers. The DO argued that the extra workers were necessary to carry out the work and as per company regulations she had the authority to do whatever was needed to complete a contract. The controller disagreed saying that the company regulations allow the DO only to purchase equipment and materials and that adding employees to the payroll requires the final approval of the HR department and finance department. The dispute was brought to the attention of the president of the firm for a settlement.

The marketing manager and the production manager of a manufacturing company were at odds over the issue of design changes. The production manager was upset about the current procedures which allowed marketing to make frequent changes to product design of new products right up to the commencement of production runs in order to appease customers. Each change meant three days of work to alter the specifications of all interacting components, loss of production line time reserved earlier, and lower cost-effectiveness. The production manager wanted to limit last-minute changes by setting two weeks before production as the deadline for final design. The marketing manager argued that last-minute alterations were necessary to cope with competitors' changes, meet customer demands, and maintain market share in the tough global environment. The conflict had escalated to an extent that coordination between the groups was suffering and morale was being affected, which prompted the executive vice president to step in.

If you were the president in the first example and the vice president in the second, how would you intervene in the dispute? Would you facilitate the discussion and interaction between the two disputants but leave the final solution in their hands? Or would

Adapted from A. R. Elangovan, "Managerial Third-Party Dispute Intervention: A Prescriptive Model of Strategy Selection," *Academy of Management Review* 20 (1995), pp. 800–30. Used with author's permission.

you listen carefully to both sides, analyze the issue, and come up with a good solution? Or would you impress upon the two disputants the importance of learning to handle such disputes on their own and urge them to do so quickly? Of course, this would not be a problem if there were an intervention strategy that worked well for all disputes. Unfortunately, research has been unable to pinpoint a "magic" strategy that would be effective in all disputes. Even the highly popular and much touted approach of mediation has not lived up to its reputation under empirical scrutiny. Thus, managers are left with numerous options for intervention, and it is not always clear *how* they should intervene in a dispute between two subordinates to ensure maximum success in resolving it.

MANAGERS AS THIRD PARTIES

Conflict is an undeniable and pervasive feature of life in modern organizations. While the presence of conflict per se is not a problem, it is important that such conflict be managed properly to ensure that it is beneficial to achieving the goals of the organizations. Managed effectively, conflict can enhance performance by challenging the status quo, furthering the creation of new ideas, promoting reassessment of unit goals and activities, increasing the probability that the unit will respond to change, relieving tension, and serving as a medium for airing problems. But who is responsible for ensuring that conflict is managed successfully in organizations? At one level, it can be argued that it is every employee's responsibility to deal with daily conflict in a constructive rather than destructive manner. While an organization may aspire to this goal, the fact remains that employees or groups or departments are often unable to resolve disputes through established procedures or on their own. Often, the supervisor or manager at the next higher level intervenes in the dispute to help resolve it. Research has shown that managers frequently act as third parties in employee disputes concerning a wide range of issues such as failure to perform specified duties, usurpation of responsibility, disagreement over company policies, discrimination, and so forth.[1] Given the significance of these issues, it is important that the managers intervene in a manner that contributes to the effective functioning of the organization. But more often than not, these managers are informal third parties rather than highly trained professionals. Unlike professional mediators and arbitrators, these managers are not external to the organization or the dispute but have an ongoing relationship with the disputants. Their effort at intervening is often part of their day-to-day managing of the work unit with a history of interactions and relationships among the parties involved. This not only limits the applicability of the prescriptions from professional third-party research to managerial intervention, but it also highlights the difficulties managers have in trying to identify the most appropriate form of intervention to use when handling a dispute between subordinates. What is needed is a framework that will help managers select the right intervention strategy in a given dispute situation. In developing this framework, however, it is necessary to identify what constitutes a successful intervention, the different intervention strategies available to the manager, and the key situational factors that would influence the selection of the appropriate strategy. Linking these three components, then, would produce a framework that indicates the kind of strategy to be selected in a given situation to achieve a successful resolution.

CRITERIA FOR EVALUATING THE
SUCCESS OF AN INTERVENTION

What constitutes a successful intervention? Within the organizational context, research has identified a wide array of criteria for evaluating the quality of dispute interventions.[2] For example, it can be argued that for an intervention to be rated as successful it must address and resolve *all* the issues in the dispute. Similarly, a good case can be made for stating that a successful intervention should leave the disputants satisfied with the outcomes of the resolution. In addition, it is equally important that the intervention process be perceived as fair since that would affect the disputants' commitment to implementing the resolution. Although the criteria listed above are important, they focus on only part of the picture. For example, would an intervention that satisfies all these criteria be considered successful if it used up an inordinate amount of time and resources, and caused disruption? Probably not. In other words, the efficiency with which an intervention is undertaken also plays a role in determining the success of the intervention. Unfortunately, however, it is often extremely difficult, if not impossible, to have interventions that are concurrently high on effectiveness, efficiency, satisfaction, and fairness. Part of the problem lies with the counteracting nature of these criteria if taken together. For example, imposing a resolution on the disputants after quickly gathering information may increase efficiency but would negatively affect the satisfaction and perceived fairness criteria since disputants may not accept or feel ownership of the resolution. Similarly, spending a lot of time seeking input and facilitating discussions to arrive at a consensus may lead to increased satisfaction and perceptions of fairness but does not guarantee a high-quality decision that effectively addresses all the problems in the best interest of the organization (effectiveness). This suggests that for developing a prescriptive model of intervention strategy selection, we need to first identify the criteria that are the most critical. But which of the criteria listed above are pivotal to the success of an intervention? And whose perspective should we adopt—the disputants', the intervening manager's, or the organization's?

Given the *prescriptive* nature of this model, it can be argued that it is the *organization's* perspective that matters rather than the personal interests of the disputants or third parties. After all, the aim here is to develop a set of prescriptions that will guide managers in successfully intervening in disputes so that it benefits and enhances organizational performance. Broadly speaking, therefore, a successful intervention would be one that satisfies three criteria: *settlement effectiveness, timeliness,* and *disputant commitment. Settlement effectiveness* refers to the extent to which the issues in the dispute are fully addressed to produce a settlement congruent with the goals of the organization. *Timeliness* refers to resolving the dispute before significant costs are incurred either in the form of resources, money, and time spent in squabbling and finger-pointing before actually dealing with the dispute, or in the form of a decline in productivity due to disruptions in operations or losses incurred due to missed deadlines. *Disputant commitment* refers to the extent to which disputants are motivated or determined to implementing the agreed-upon settlement, which, in turn, is contingent on their satisfaction with the resolution and perceptions of fairness. In sum, a successful intervention is one where (*a*) the issues are fully addressed to produce a settlement consistent with organizational objectives, (*b*) the resolution is timely, and (*c*) the disputants are committed to the resolution.

FIGURE 1   Positioning of Managerial Dispute
Intervention Strategies

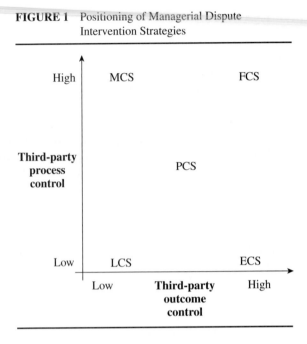

MANAGERIAL DISPUTE-INTERVENTION STRATEGIES

What are the various intervention strategies available to the manager acting as the third party? As noted in the introduction to this article, the manager has plenty of choice; the options range from imposing a settlement to encouraging the disputants to settle on their own, with numerous variations in between. Rather than compile a long, unwieldy list of the specific strategies that are available (some of which vary only by name), it is more useful and practical to identifying the major *types* or categories of strategies that are significantly different from each other. This would also help in matching the different type of strategies to different disputes for achieving a successful resolution. One popular approach to classifying and understanding intervention strategies has been to use the degree of control wielded by the intervening third parties over the process (the procedures and activities involved in arriving at a settlement) and the outcome (the actual settlement to the dispute) of the resolution as two major dimensions.[3] Figure 1 presents a two-dimensional graph with the degree of third-party process control and the degree of third-party outcome control as the two axes.

Using these two axes, different intervention strategies can be "identified" by plotting various coordinates in the graph space. While numerous combinations varying by minute degrees of outcome and process control can be devised, for the sake of parsimony and applicability, only distinctly different combinations are considered here. Figure 1 shows five such combinations that are positioned into the corners and the center of the graph: *means control strategy* (MCS), *ends control strategy* (ECS), *full control strategy* (FCS), *low control strategy* (LCS), and *part control strategy* (PCS). These five combinations

FIGURE 2   Description of Managerial Dispute Intervention Strategies

MCS	*Means control strategy:* Manager intervenes in the dispute by influencing the process of resolution (i.e., facilitates interaction, assists in communication, explains one disputant's views to another, clarifies issues, lays down rules for dealing with the dispute, maintains order during talks) but does not attempt to dictate or impose a resolution (though he or she might suggest solutions); the final decision is left to the disputants; high on process control but low on outcome control (e.g., mediation, conciliation).
ECS	*Ends control strategy:* Manager intervenes in the dispute by influencing the outcome of the resolution (i.e., takes full control of the final resolution, decides what the final decision would be, imposes the resolution on the disputants) but does not attempt to influence the process; the disputants have control over what information is presented and how it is presented; high on outcome control but low on process control (e.g., arbitration, adjudication, adversarial intervention).
LCS	*Low control strategy:* Manager does not intervene actively in resolving the dispute; either urges the parties to settle the dispute on their own or merely stays away from the dispute; low on both process and outcome control (e.g., encouraging or telling the parties to negotiate or settle the dispute by themselves, providing impetus).
FCS	*Full control strategy:* Manager intervenes in the dispute by influencing the process and outcome (i.e., decides what information is to be presented and how it should be presented and also decides on the final resolution); asks the disputants specific questions about the dispute to obtain information and imposes a resolution; manager has full control of the resolution of the dispute; high on both process and outcome control (e.g., inquisitorial intervention, autocratic intervention).
PCS	*Part control strategy:* Manager intervenes in the dispute by sharing control over the process and outcome with the disputants (i.e., manager and disputants jointly agree on the process of resolution as well as strive for a consensus on the settlement decision); works with the disputants to help them arrive at a solution by facilitating interaction, assisting in communication, discussing the issues, and so on; in addition, takes an active role in evaluating options, recommending solutions, persuading the disputants to accept them, and pushing for a settlement; moderate on managerial process and outcome control (e.g., group problem solving, med-arb).

(intervention strategies) and the activities that are contained under each of these procedures are described in Figure 2. These descriptions capture the typical intervention procedures that fit under each combination. Variations of each combination can be included as long as they fit the basic description (e.g., mediation and conciliation are listed as examples under MCS).

So a manager using FCS to intervene in a dispute would control both the process and outcome of the resolution, that is, decide what information should be presented and how, ask specific questions, decide on a settlement, and impose it. When using MCS, however, the manager would control only the process and not the outcome. He or she would explain one disputant's views to the other, clarify issues, maintain order during talks, and lay down rules for dealing with the dispute. In contrast, under ECS, the manager would let the disputants control the process (e.g., decide what information to present and how to present it), but the manager takes full control of the outcome by deciding final settlement and imposing it on the disputants. A manager using LCS would urge or tell the parties to settle the dispute on their own but would not actively intervene in the dispute. Finally, when using PCS, the manager would share control over the process and outcome with the disputants. They would jointly work toward a resolution with the manager, facilitating interaction, clarifying issues, evaluating options, recommending solutions, and persuading the disputants to accept them (e.g., group problem solving).

KEY SITUATIONAL FACTORS THAT AFFECT STRATEGY SELECTION

Given the five strategies described above, when should each strategy be used? In other words, how would the manager be able to determine that a certain dispute calls for a specific strategy to maximize intervention success? Obviously this entails assessing each dispute to identify some key characteristics or situational factors, which may, then, suggest that certain strategies are better suited for resolving that dispute than others. For example, if one of the distinguishing features of the dispute is time pressure (as in the first example in the introduction), it implies that speed is of essence and strategies that take longer to arrive at a settlement (e.g., PCS, MCS) may not be as appropriate as other strategies (e.g., FCS). Although one can focus on a plethora of factors to develop a profile of a dispute, it is both important and useful to zoom in on just the essential characteristics of the disputes that have significant bearing on the suitability and, hence, the probability of success of different intervention strategies. Described below are six factors that have been identified by prior research as being the critical ones and their implications for strategy selection:[4]

1. *Dispute importance.* How important is the dispute? A dispute is important if it is central to the survival or functioning of a group or organization. From a prescriptive standpoint, the manager should be more concerned about the dispute when the dispute importance is high than when it is low. When dispute importance is high, more care and control of outcome are needed and, therefore, the intervening manager should not select a strategy that yields full outcome control to the disputants. This will ensure some managerial influence on the outcome and, hence, will lead to an organizationally beneficial solution. At the same time, however, to ensure commitment from the disputants the manager should ensure that the process is orderly and not one-sided due to power and other differences between the disputants, and should make sure that the disputants feel that they have some influence in resolving the dispute (i.e., the manager should also retain some degree of process control).

2. *Time pressure.* Some disputes need to be settled more urgently than others. Since intervention strategies vary in how quickly they lead to a settlement, it is important to select the appropriate strategy to ensure intervention success. In general, when time pressure is high, the manager should not select a strategy that yields full control of the process and the outcome, in that order, to the disputants. Not acceding complete control of the process ensures that the manager can influence the speed at which the dispute is resolved. Not acceding complete control of the outcome ensures that the dispute will be resolved if disputants still cannot arrive at a settlement even when the process is speeded up.

3. *Nature of dispute.* Is the dispute about the interpretation, implementation, or execution of an existing rule, regulation, procedure, or operation within the existing organizational framework (dispute over "what is"), or is it about creating a new or changing the existing procedures, operations, contracts or systems (dispute over "what should be or would like it to be")? The label *dispute over privileges* (DOP) is used here to identify the "interpretive" disputes (where misunderstandings or ambiguity is at the root of the dispute), while the label *dispute over stakes* (DOS) is used to distinguish the "change" disputes (where the focus is on altering the system). For example, the dispute between a financial controller and a marketing manager regarding the interpretation of an expenses reimbursement clause is a DOP dispute. A dispute between the same individuals about increasing the maximum amount for client entertainment expenses is a DOS dispute. In a DOP dispute, the disputants are generally more open to, and might even expect, a settlement from the third party because they were unable to, on their own, agree on an interpretation or application. This implies that an intervention strategy that gives the third party some degree of outcome control will be effective for a DOP dispute and, therefore, the manager (third party) should not use strategies that limit his or her outcome control. In contrast, a DOS dispute reaches deeper to affect emotions and values, and it is imperative that disputants fully understand and accept any change in the system in order for them to be committed in the long run to the change. In such a situation, the manager should influence the process to ensure that it is orderly but leave the final settlement to the disputants; that is, for resolving a DOS dispute, the manager should not choose strategies that yield full process control but little outcome control to disputants.

4. *Nature of relations.* Are the disputants in a long-term relationship, or are they not likely to interact with each other after the dispute is resolved? This factor addresses the work-group dynamics of the two disputants and is important because different intervention strategies have different effects on the relations between disputants. Since it is in the best interests of the organization to have a normal or positive working relationship between the parties, an intervention strategy that will further this objective should be selected for any given dispute. This implies that if the disputants are involved in a long-term relationship, then in the interest of long-term commitment and cooperation, the manager should ensure that the disputants have some degree of influence or control over the dispute settlement. So the manager should not choose an intervention strategy that limits the control disputants can have over the outcome. In addition, the manager should have some influence over the process to ensure that it is orderly and fair. On the other hand, when the disputants are not likely to interact with each other in the future on a regular basis, the manager can assume more control over the outcome, since the effect of the settlement on future relations is not much of a concern.

5. *Commitment probability.* This factor refers to the probability that the disputants will be committed to a settlement if it were to be decided unilaterally by the intervening manager. This, in turn, depends on the nature of the relationship between the manager and the disputants, including the degree of power the manager

has and the subordinates' feelings of trust and loyalty. It is important to note that for long-term organizational effectiveness, it is not sufficient that the disputants merely indicate their acceptance of the settlement; they must honor the spirit of the settlement and not continue to harbor feelings of conflict or demonstrate reluctance in executing the resolution. This suggests that the manager must assess the commitment probability for imposing resolutions and select an intervention strategy accordingly. Low commitment probability implies that if the manager were to impose a settlement to a dispute then the disputants will not remain committed to it. In such cases, intervention strategies that do not accede control to disputants will be less effective than those that give disputants some control over the outcome. But if the manager perceives the commitment probability to be high, then he or she can assume more outcome control and impose a resolution whenever necessary (contingent on the status of the other attributes).

6. *Disputant orientation.* Disputant orientation addresses the question, What is the likelihood that the disputants will arrive at an organizationally appropriate settlement if given control over the resolution of the dispute (outcome control)? If disputant orientation is high, then the probability that the disputants will arrive at an organizationally compatible settlement is high; if disputant orientation is low, then the probability is low. Regarding strategy selection, if the manager views the disputants' orientation as being low, then he or she should not select intervention strategies that yield full outcome control to the disputing subordinates. This would ensure that the manager has some control and input into the final settlement and that the interests and goals of the organization are not compromised. On the other hand, if the disputant orientation is high, then the manager should select strategies that yield some degree of outcome control to the disputants to promote satisfaction and commitment.

In summary, the status of the six dispute factors discussed above have implications for the selection of strategies and help satisfy one or more of the three intervention success criteria identified earlier. Each of these factors can be represented by a question that has two response options (high/low) (see Figure 3). A manager facing a particular dispute can diagnose the main situational demands by answering the six questions. The answers to the six questions provide the basis for selecting among the five intervention strategies.

GENERATING DECISION RULES TO GUIDE STRATEGY SELECTION

Next, the recommendations for the use or avoidance of outcome and process control for each factor (discussed above) indicate when different intervention strategies should be selected for successful intervention. This logic can be captured in a set of decision rules to direct the strategy selection process. Figure 4 presents the seven rules that underlie the proposed model. These rules are a series of "if . . . then . . ." statements that indicate for a certain status (high/low) of each factor the form of control (process, outcome) that should be retained by the intervening manager or given to the disputants to ensure the success of the intervention. This, in turn, implies that certain strategies may be dropped

FIGURE 3   Key Situational Factors Influencing Strategy Selection

Question A	How important is this dispute to the effective functioning of the organization? (high/low)
Question B	How important is it to resolve the dispute as quickly as possible? (high/low)
Question C	Does the dispute concern the interpretation/application of existing rules, procedures, arrangements, and so on, or does it concern the alteration/change of existing rules, procedures, arrangements? (DOP/DOS)
Question D	What is the expected frequency of future work-related interactions between the disputants? (high/low)
Question E	If you were to impose a settlement on your subordinates (disputants), what is the probability that they would be committed to it? (high/low)
Question F	If you were to let your subordinates (disputants) settle the dispute, what is the probability that they would come to an organizationally compatible settlement? (high/low)

from the feasible full set of the five intervention strategies because of the risk they pose to a successful resolution of the dispute. For example, if the status of the commitment probability attribute is low (i.e., the likelihood that the disputants would be committed to a settlement imposed by the manager is low), then this suggests that the intervening manager should give the disputants some control over the outcome. For strategy selection purposes, this eliminates the two strategies that give the third party full outcome control (i.e., FCS and ECS) from the feasible set (Rule 5). For any given dispute, using the first six rules will lead to a feasible set of intervention strategies that would be most successful in resolving the dispute. The last rule, Priority Rule, guides the choice within the feasible set based on efficiency maximization. Each rule also contributes to protecting one or more of the three success criteria. The Dispute Importance, Nature of Dispute, and Disputant Orientation rules focus on who controls the outcome, thus ensuring *settlement effectiveness;* the Time Pressure and Priority rules focus on the need for expediency and the costs involved with delays, thus ensuring *timeliness;* and the Nature of Relations, Nature of Dispute, and Commitment Probability rules focus on ensuring acceptance and commitment of the disputants to the settlement, thus ensuring *disputant commitment.*

A DECISION TREE FOR SELECTING AN INTERVENTION STRATEGY

Figure 5 shows a decision tree developed using the five intervention strategies (Figure 2), the six questions pertaining to the situational factors of the dispute (Figure 3), and the seven rules with two status options (high/low) for each factor (Figure 4). To use the tree, a manager first identifies a dispute between subordinates that he or she has decided to help resolve. The manager starts at the extreme left of the decision tree and asks the first question. The answer, high or low, indicates the path to be taken to arrive at the next node signifying the next question. The process continues until the manager arrives at a terminal node or end point on the decision tree that indicates the optimal intervention strategy.

FIGURE 4   Rules Underlying the Model

1. The Dispute-Importance Rule—If the importance of the dispute is high, then the intervention strategy chosen should give the manager some degree of control on either or both dimensions. Accordingly, LCS is eliminated from the feasible set.

2. The Time-Pressure Rule—If the time pressure associated with settling the dispute is high, then the intervention strategy chosen should give the manager some degree of process control. Accordingly, LCS and ECS are eliminated from the feasible set.

3. The Nature of Dispute Rule—If the dispute between subordinates is a DOP dispute, then the intervention strategy chosen should give the manager some degree of outcome control. Accordingly, LCS and MCS are eliminated from the feasible set. The only exception to the rule is when time pressure is low, commitment probability is low, but disputant orientation is high (MCS is the option). If the dispute between subordinates is a DOS dispute, then the manager should allow the subordinates some degree of control on either or both dimensions (process and outcome). Accordingly, FCS is eliminated from the feasible set. The only exception to the rule is when time pressure is high, commitment probability is high, and the disputants are not likely to interact frequently in the future.

4. The Nature of Relations Rule—If the subordinates (disputants) are likely to have a high frequency of interaction in the future, then the intervention strategy chosen should give the subordinates some degree of outcome control. Accordingly, FCS and ECS are eliminated from the feasible set. The only exception to the rule is when time pressure is low, commitment probability is high, and disputant orientation is low (ECS is the option).

5. The Commitment-Probability Rule—If the probability that the subordinates (disputants) would be committed to a settlement imposed by the manager is low, then the intervention strategy chosen should give subordinates some degree of outcome control. Accordingly, FCS and ECS are eliminated from the feasible set.

6. The Disputant-Orientation Rule—If the status of the dispute based on the five rules described above suggests choosing intervention strategies that yield full outcome control to subordinates (disputants), the manager should use disputant orientation as the final criterion. If the disputant orientation is low, the intervention strategy chosen should give the manager some degree of outcome control. Accordingly, LCS and MCS are eliminated from the feasible set. If the disputant orientation is high, the intervention strategy chosen should give subordinates some degree of outcome control. Accordingly, FCS and ECS are eliminated from the feasible set.

7. The Priority Rule—If the status of the dispute based on the previous six rules suggests more than one intervention as being equally effective, the following priority conditions must be observed to select one strategy. For high-importance disputes, when time pressure is low and commitment probability is low, the manager should choose the intervention strategy that allows him or her maximum process control (so that by ensuring an orderly and fair process the commitment can be increased); when time pressure is low and commitment probability is high, the manager should select the strategy that allows him or her maximum outcome control (so that the best interests of the organization are always protected) while giving the disputants at least some control over the resolution; when time pressure is high, the manager should choose the intervention strategy that requires the least amount of time to resolve the dispute without endangering commitment. For low-importance disputes, the manager should select the strategy that requires the least amount of resources (skills, time, etc.).

FIGURE 5   A Model of Intervention Strategy Selection

DI   How important is this dispute to the effective functioning of the organization?
TP   How important is it to resolve the dispute as quickly as possible?
ND   Does the dispute concern the interpretation of existing rules, procedures, and
       arrangements or the changing of existing rules, procedures, and arrangements?
NR   What is the expected frequency of future work-related interactions between
       the disputants?
CP   If you were to impose a settlement on your subordinates (disputants), what is the
       probability that they would be committed to it?
DO   What is the orientation of the disputants? That is, if you were to let your subordinates
       (disputants) settle the dispute, what is the probability that they would come to an
       organizationally compatible settlement?

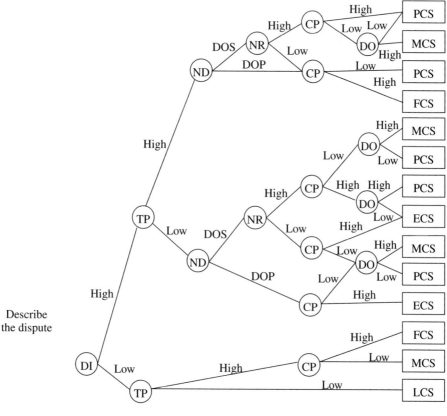

Legend:
MCS = Means control strategy
ECS = Ends control strategy
LCS = Low control strategy
FCS = Full control strategy
PCS = Part control strategy

The model uses a choice-elimination approach to arrive at the right strategy. Choices or intervention strategies that are not likely to result in a successful resolution are eliminated, thus narrowing the choice to the most appropriate intervention strategy for that specific dispute. Although six factors were identified as key dispute attributes, all of them do not become relevant for all disputes. If the status of the attribute does not make a difference to the selection of an intervention strategy with regard to the success of the resolution for a particular dispute configuration, then it is not necessary to apply that rule. For example, when the dispute importance is low and time pressure is low, the manager need not be concerned with the status of the other attributes but can directly arrive at the appropriate intervention strategy without posing any risk to the dispute resolution success. Similarly, disputant orientation becomes relevant only when the status of other attributes suggest that the manager select an intervention strategy that yields full outcome control to the disputants. However, all six attributes are important and essential for the model as a whole to be valid and useful.

CONCLUSION

Managing disputes in organizations is an important part of a manager's job. Often, the success of the manager's interventions in these disputes has significant implications for the overall morale of the employees and their productivity. This article offers some guidelines for successful intervention by highlighting the key features of a successful intervention, classifying different intervention strategies, identifying the major situational factors that ought to be considered before selecting a strategy, generating a set of rules to guide the strategy selection process, and developing a decision-tree model that can be used by practicing managers.

ENDNOTES

1. See R. I. Lissak and B. H. Sheppard, "Beyond Fairness: The Criterion Problem in Research on Conflict Intervention," *Journal of Applied Social Psychology* 13 (1983), pp. 45–65; and B. H. Sheppard, "Third-Party Conflict Intervention: A Procedural Framework," in B. M. Staw and L. L. Cummings, eds., *Research in Organizational Behavior* 6 (1984), pp. 141–90. Greenwich, CT: JAI.

2. Sheppard, "Third-Party Conflict Intervention."

3. See J. W. Thibaut and L. Walker, *Procedural Justice: A Psychological Analysis* (New York: Wiley, 1975); and R. Lewicki and B. Sheppard, "Choosing How to Intervene: Factors Affecting the Use of Process and Outcome Control in Third-Party Dispute Resolution," *Journal of Occupational Behavior* 6 (1985), pp. 49–64.

4. See Sheppard, "Third-Party Conflict Intervention,"; R. Karambayya and J. M. Brett, "Managers Handling Disputes: Third-Party Roles and Perceptions of Fairness," *Academy of Management Journal,* 32 (1989), pp. 687–704; R. Karambayya, J. Brett, and A. Lytle, "The Effects of Formal Authority and Experience on Third-Party Roles, Outcomes and Perceptions of Fairness," *Academy of Management Journal* 35 (1992), pp. 426–38; and Lewicki and Sheppard, "Choosing How to Intervene."

Applications of Negotiation

Bargaining under the Influence: The Role of Alcohol in Negotiations

Maurice E. Schweitzer

Jeffrey L. Kerr

If a client orders a glass of white wine, I'm certainly not going to order a Coke.

> *A Compuserve account executive*

We have Japanese executives coming over here. . . . It's almost expected that when you go out to dinner you have several drinks and some sake.

> *President and CEO of Saber Enterprises[1]*

Several recent trends, including the globalization of business and medical research accepting moderate alcohol consumption, have expanded the number of American managers who encounter opportunities to drink.[2] In many cultures, drinking is considered an essential element in building business relationships, and managers across a wide range of functional areas are likely to encounter opportunities and even pressure to consume alcohol with business colleagues. Generally ignored, however, is the fact that even mild amounts of alcohol can significantly influence, sometimes positively and often negatively, the process and outcomes of business interactions.

Alcohol has accompanied business transactions for centuries, and in some contexts drinking is considered by many to be a normal and natural part of organizational behavior. In fact, in some contexts alcohol is so common that managers consume or authorize the consumption of alcohol with little or no consideration of either explicit risks, such as lawsuits, or hidden costs, such as impaired professional performance. By some estimates, alcohol consumption costs American businesses over $86 billion annually in lost productivity, absenteeism, and health care costs.[3]

This article describes the advantages and disadvantages of mixing alcohol with business, and offers advice regarding the use of alcohol for managers and negotiators making decisions or setting policy. Rather than drinking out of habit or social pressure, managers should make the decision to drink carefully and rationally. We begin by identifying the role alcohol can play in building relationships. We then identify the harmful consequences

Reprinted from *Academy of Management Executive* 14, no. 2 (2000), pp. 47–57.

of mixing alcohol with business, with particular emphasis on the potential harm alcohol can cause in negotiations. We report new evidence linking alcohol to aggressive negotiator behavior and to inefficient negotiation outcomes. We then offer prescriptive advice for when it makes sense to mix or avoid mixing alcohol with business. For situations in which managers prefer to avoid or limit their alcohol consumption, we suggest methods for avoiding social pressures to drink.

ALCOHOL CAN FACILITATE RELATIONSHIP BUILDING

Alcohol has traditionally played a role in developing business relationships.[4] As one commentator remarked, "When you wanted to meet another company you invited its managers to your smoke-filled dining room and drank yourself into a partnership."[5]

Alcohol facilitates relationship building in several ways. Drinking can relieve stress and create a social routine that is comforting and familiar. In fact, the mere presence of alcohol can cue an entire set of expected social behaviors, signal commitment to the relationship, and change an atmosphere to enable participants to engage each other on a more cordial and personal level.[6] Although formal routines reassert themselves as the group returns to its primary business, lingering effects from this positive bonding experience remain.

Part of alcohol's bonding effect derives from its impairment of physical and cognitive functioning. While some of these effects are detrimental, impairment can, in some respects, facilitate relationship building. As alcohol reduces a person's ability to think and act clearly, it creates an atmosphere of shared dependency and vulnerability. Exhortations to the nondrinker to join the party may, in effect, be demands that the individual become impaired, and thereby dependent on and ultimately part of the group. In many cases group membership is defined by drinking practices. For example, one study found that longshoremen in Canada who were hardworking, young, and fit were excluded from job teams simply because they did not drink with others.[7]

Alcohol's potential relationship benefits are particularly relevant to negotiations. Building relationships is an essential element for successful negotiations,[8] and alcohol can play a role in enabling negotiators to recognize common interests. Because alcohol lowers inhibitions and encourages a sense of camaraderie, people tend to exchange information more freely.[9] In Japan, for example, information about upcoming projects and office politics is most likely to be discussed during drinking sessions.[10]

Alcohol can also help parties reach an agreement. After consuming a few drinks, negotiators may become more receptive to new ideas and more likely to make concessions. In fact, one commentator suggests, "At drinking parties, go for business concessions on your contract. If they are available, this is the setting in which you'll win them."[11]

Alcohol can also facilitate negotiations by influencing mood and affect. Although reactions to alcohol depend on the individual and the context, alcohol generally decreases anxiety and promotes a positive mood.[12] Recent research has linked affect with negotiator behavior, and found that negotiators in good moods tended to be more cooperative, creative, and effective in achieving joint gains.[13] Not surprisingly, negotiators who were angry or frustrated tended to be less cooperative, less confident, and produced less satisfactory outcomes.[14]

CROSS-CULTURAL DRINKING NORMS

Drinking norms vary widely across cultures.[15] This is true even within the United States, where substantial variation in alcohol liability laws and prosecution rates exists across regions.[16] From an international perspective, these disparities are even greater. Long-established traditions influence cultural norms concerning drinking in general and business drinking in particular. While customs dictate strict abstinence in Islamic countries such as Saudi Arabia (though not Egypt), copious drinking is common in many parts of Japan, where the refusal to drink may be interpreted as a sign of mistrust.

As commerce between regions grows, American managers will increasingly encounter the drinking norms of other cultures. These norms include expectations, etiquette, and symbolism that managers must recognize and evaluate to make an informed decision to drink or abstain with their counterparts abroad. In some cases, even the type of alcoholic beverage, such as *maotai* in China or *makkolli* in Korea, can carry deep cultural significance.[17]

U.S. managers working abroad are likely to find that alcohol is a more common aspect of business meetings than they are accustomed to in the United States. In fact, decreasing public tolerance of DWI (Driving While Intoxicated) violations, coupled with increasing corporate and personal liability, has resulted in heightened sensitivity within the United States to consumption of alcohol in business settings. Compared with American managers, foreigners are less sensitive to individual preferences for abstinence and are less concerned with corporate liability for inebriated behavior. Consequently, U.S. managers may be surprised by the drinking norms and expectations they encounter abroad.

While Western managers are generally accustomed to the idea of celebratory drinks at the conclusion of a negotiation, in Russian, Asian, and many other cultures, drinking may be used to initiate proceedings and to symbolize each party's commitment to a mutually satisfying outcome. Easterners often strive for successful business outcomes after personal relationships have been established, while Westerners develop social relationships after business interests have been addressed.

In China, business negotiations have traditionally begun with a series of toasts. Such drinking establishes relationships and serves to demarcate significant business events. The first toast of each occasion typically contains an important statement about friendship and emphasizes mutual obligations; it customarily ends in the phrase *gan bei,* meaning "dry glass" or "bottoms up." This toast is usually consumed completely, though subsequent toasts may be sipped. These drinking sessions are important because business commitments are rarely made without an existing relationship between the parties.[18] The ritual of drinking together thus provides a symbolic foundation for subsequent business dealings.

Russia has earned a reputation as an especially hard-drinking country, and alcoholic beverages are frequently present in a wide variety of settings. One particularly important example involving the combination of alcohol and negotiations is the arms control negotiations leading up to the 1979 Strategic Arms Limitation Treaty II (SALT II) between the United States and the Soviet Union. As recounted by one of the lead American negotiators, Edward Rowny, both American and Soviet generals consumed large quantities of whiskey and vodka during their negotiations.[19] Western expatriates familiar with Russian negotiations recommend that foreigners participate in the first two rounds of toasts, which are typically the most important. The first toast will customarily be to the meeting, the second to the host, and additional toasts may be made to the partnership or to cooperation in general.[20]

For centuries, Japanese business dealings of all kinds have been accompanied by drinking parties where drinking is viewed more as a ritual duty than a social pleasure.[21] These drinking sessions can occur in large groups, as they often do in China, or in groups as small as two people.[22] In Japan, important business meetings are often held after hours with the expectation that participants will become extremely intoxicated.[23] In fact, many Japanese managers believe it is impossible to truly know someone without drinking heavily with them, and may feel uncomfortable with anyone who refuses to drink at a party or celebration.[24]

The discomfort a Japanese or German businessperson might experience with a nondrinking American counterpart derives from their unequal gestures of vulnerability. In many cultures, drinking is equated with openness and candor. Thus, a refusal to drink could signal an unwillingness to let down one's guard.

Koreans have been known to take an especially aggressive approach to social drinking, and sometimes insist that reluctant guests take part in drinking and singing sessions. Refusing to drink without an obvious excuse may be considered rude and insulting. These gestures are taken a step further in drinking games and off-key singing performances. The more off-key the song, the greater the sense of openness and trust among participants. To refuse to drink and sing is to remain guarded and apart.

The symbolic candor and vulnerability associated with alcohol can also work across hierarchical levels, both in U.S. organizations and abroad, by allowing astute managers to open channels of communication with subordinates that might otherwise seem awkward. By joining subordinates for drinks, the boss sends a signal, even if the drink is untouched, that in this setting he or she is like others, dependent on the community. He or she can be approached, issues can be raised, and the strictures of protocol and hierarchy can be at least temporarily de-emphasized.

The cross-level communication effects of alcohol are perhaps most clearly seen in Japanese organizations. Hierarchical relationships and protocols are especially formal, except during *tsukiai*, when superiors are free to give candid feedback to their subordinates. These are lengthy, after-hours events typically involving large quantities of scotch. The obvious inebriation of the boss (whether actual or feigned) permits him to discuss a subordinate's performance and shortcomings without the painful loss of face such direct feedback would entail under sober conditions. Since the exchange occurred under the influence of alcohol, both parties can come to work the next day free of the embarrassment such candor would normally produce in a Japanese organization.[25] A subordinate, such as a teetotaling American manager who forgoes *tsukiai* sessions, fails to receive such performance feedback and misses an important opportunity to establish a more complete relationship with his superiors.

It is important to note that attitudes toward overt drunkenness vary across cultures almost as much as attitudes toward drinking itself. An obvious state of inebriation may elicit little or no negative reaction among Russian business associates and may even be considered a symbol of camaraderie and cohesion by Japanese or Korean hosts. In Germany, however, while alcohol consumption is high among males of all social strata, the ability to hold one's drink is considered an important aspect of masculine comportment among professional and managerial classes. Similarly, obvious signs of inebriation are considered unseemly and unacceptable in Mexico, Malaysia, Indonesia, and the Philippines.[26] There are also important cross-cultural differences with respect to accountability for the things you say while inebriated. For example, Koreans are more likely to hold you accountable for things you promise while drinking than are Japanese.[27]

Managers working abroad should also be aware of legal issues that influence drinking behavior. In Scandinavia, for example, while heavy alcohol consumption is common before and after business meetings, drunk-driving laws are extremely strict and typically require the designation of a nondrinking driver.

The usefulness of alcohol in negotiations depends on the degree to which feelings of cooperation and common interest are lacking yet necessary in the relationship. For example, in a stalled negotiation in which the parties are having difficulty understanding and accepting each other's positions, a social interlude that includes alcohol can diffuse tension and enable negotiators to recognize areas of agreement.

Of course, this same relaxation of boundaries may also produce dangerous ambiguity regarding acceptable behavior. In an era of heightened sensitivity to sexual harassment and political correctness, behavior that seems acceptable in a context containing alcohol may be deemed unacceptable upon the next day's sober reflection.

On the one hand, the symbolism and physiology of alcohol encourage the development of relationships, while on the other hand, alcohol leaves these same individuals with impaired mental faculties and less able to monitor their own behavior. The following section identifies some of the hazards of consuming alcohol, with particular emphasis on potential harm to negotiations.

HAZARDS OF CONSUMING ALCOHOL DURING NEGOTIATIONS

Drinking can harm the negotiation process in a number of important ways. The link between alcohol and aggressive behavior is well established. Prior work has documented a stable relationship between alcohol use and aggressive, and even violent, behavior.[28] While assertiveness may aid a negotiator in specific circumstances, excessive aggression can escalate a conflict. This effect apparently contributed to the confrontational approach adopted by the Allied Pilots Association during their contract negotiations with American Airlines in 1997. Even though American Airlines Chairman Robert Crandall and Allied Pilots Association President James Sovich had agreed to a tentative labor contract, dissidents within the union solidified support against the tentative accord during late-night barroom sessions in which pilots spend time sending faxes and e-mail and drinking beer.[29] This dissident movement ultimately persuaded the pilots' union to reject the proposed labor contract and agree to strike the carrier.

A recent experiment investigated the influence of a moderate amount of alcohol on the bargaining process.[30] Negotiators were randomly assigned to either a sober or an inebriated treatment condition. Inebriated negotiators consumed a moderate amount of alcohol to reach a blood alcohol level of about 0.05. This amount of alcohol is well below the legal intoxication limit for driving in all states, and translates to the consumption of about two and a half beers within an hour by a person weighing 180 pounds. Negotiations were tape recorded and independently coded for specific negotiator behaviors. Negotiated outcomes were also measured, and since the negotiation contained opportunities for joint gains, some dyads reached more efficient agreement than others.[31]

Results from this study revealed that inebriated negotiators used significantly more aggressive tactics than sober negotiators. Inebriated negotiators were more likely to insult, mislead, and threaten their negotiation partner. These tactics included insults such as, "You don't have a lot of experience," misrepresentation of facts, misrepresentation of one's interests, and threats to terminate the negotiation. In some cases these tactics can strengthen a negotiator's bargaining position, but there are costs to their use. They may escalate conflict and lead to less integrative outcomes.[32]

Alcohol also impairs cognition.[33] This impairment can harm work performance and increase the likelihood that managers will make mistakes.[34] In negotiations, alcohol's influence on cognition may contribute to less integrative outcomes as negotiators miss opportunities for realizing joint gains. Alcohol reduces the amount of information people can process, impairs short-term memory, and causes decision makers to become myopic.[35] As a result of these disadvantages, inebriated negotiators have difficulty reaching efficient solutions and tend to use simplified strategies for resolving their differences. Results from the alcohol and negotiation experiment revealed that sober dyads were able to reach significantly more efficient agreements than inebriated dyads.[36] Sober dyads were more likely to logroll (trade-off issues of different value) and realize opportunities for joint gains. Sober dyads also reached more efficient agreements than dyads where one sober negotiator was paired with an inebriated negotiator. In these cases, the inebriated negotiators were more aggressive than the sober negotiators and, as expected, the inebriated negotiators claimed a larger share of the smaller pie. That is, sober negotiators did particularly poorly when negotiating against someone who was drinking. These results suggest that managers should take particular care in bargaining with someone who has consumed even a moderate amount of alcohol.

Inebriated negotiators are also more likely to make mistakes. In the alcohol and negotiation experiment, mistakes were coded as contradictions such as, "I propose a start date of 12 weeks . . . no, 4 weeks. I'm sorry, I was confused." In this study, over 90 percent of inebriated negotiators made at least one mistake, while fewer than two-thirds of sober negotiators made a mistake.

Even moderate amounts of alcohol impair a manager's ability to handle complex situations and solve problems.[37] Inebriated negotiators are likely to perform especially poorly in situations requiring mathematical agility. One real estate investor signed a contract during a late-night dinner to sell a property she had owned for over 20 years. She awoke the next morning to realize that the property was worth double her sale price, and that, in her words, she had been "zapped by Bordeaux wine."[38] In fact, this type of mistake occurs so often that legal precedents provide some recourse for intoxicated negotiators.[39]

In some cases alcohol consumption may even impair performance the day after a night of drinking. One study documented a significant hangover effect among pilots who had drunk heavily a full 14 hours before a training exercise.[40]

Inebriated negotiators are more apt to focus on irrelevant information or to miss key components of a problem. Because drinkers must exert greater mental effort to focus on core issues, they are likely to neglect subtle aspects of a negotiation. For example, inebriated negotiators are less likely to grasp the underlying implications of an argument and thus more likely to misinterpret the key concerns of their counterparts.

A related perceptual bias is the egocentric perception of fairness. In general, negotiators tend to perceive fair agreements as those that favor themselves.[41] Alcohol is likely to exacerbate this bias by limiting a negotiator's ability to adopt different points of view and empathize with others. Ultimately, this may lead negotiators to become more confrontational and less accommodating.

Studies have also found that alcohol consumption inflates positive self-perceptions.[42] This can lead to overconfidence, especially since inebriated people frequently fail to notice nonverbal cues and negative feedback. In a quote attributed to Elizabeth Johnson, wife of the eighteenth century lexicographer and essayist Samuel Johnson, "Alcohol does not improve conversation. It only alters the mind so you are more pleased with any conversation." In a negotiation, inebriated managers may perceive that they are more convincing or more agreeable than they really are. While this may provide a boost for those lacking in self-confidence, it may also result in behavior that is overbearing or inappropriate.[43] Exaggerated self-perceptions may also explain the finding that people are willing to assume greater business risk under the influence of alcohol than they would when sober.[44] Further, the combination of overconfidence in one's ability to influence people, coupled with an exaggerated sense of camaraderie, may lead a negotiator to make overly generous commitments. This was the case in 1996 for a south Florida supplier of shoe repair products. After copious drinking at a cocktail party hosted by a wholesaler, the supplier offered to pay the $5,000 cost of the cocktail party if the wholesaler would agree to purchase his new product, something the wholesaler would have almost certainly have agreed to do anyway.[45]

In many cases, alcohol's effects on performance are likely to go unnoticed. Because inebriated negotiators perceive themselves to be more articulate, convincing, and successful than they actually are, drinkers generally underestimate the effects of alcohol on their own functioning. In the alcohol and negotiations study, most inebriated negotiators failed to recognize that alcohol had influenced their negotiation performance when, in fact, it had.[46]

Alcohol's effects are complicated. Alcohol consumption facilitates relationship building and may even be an expected part of the negotiation process, but at the same time alcohol may significantly harm the process and jeopardize the outcome. In some cases, alcohol may be used strategically by one party to gain an advantage over another. These cases merit special attention and are described in the next section.

GUARDING AGAINST THE STRATEGIC USE OF ALCOHOL BY A NEGOTIATION PARTNER

Alcohol consumption typically confers a relative advantage to one or more individuals. Obviously, not every occasion in which alcohol is present represents an attempt to gain an unfair advantage. In many cases, negotiators introduce alcohol to put others at ease, or for ritualistic or habitual reasons. For example, Russians may start a meeting with a toast and often feel compelled to finish a bottle of vodka once it is opened.[47] Similarly, many Chinese believe that they are better able to communicate and reach an understanding after a few glasses of wine. In many cases, Westerners, who are unaccustomed to these approaches to business meetings, mistakenly assume that their negotiation partners are using alcohol strategically to gain an advantage.[48]

Although alcohol is often not introduced for strategic aims, careful managers should be aware of several negotiation tactics that involve alcohol. One obvious tactic derives from differences in inebriation levels. Individual reactions to alcohol vary considerably, and differences in body weight, age, consumption history, and even genetics make one individual more susceptible than another to alcohol's effects. While many factors affect blood alcohol levels, such as time elapsed since drinking and an individual's metabolism, there is an approximate relationship between the number of drinks consumed, body weight, and blood alcohol level. For example, the blood alcohol concentration (BAC) level for a 125-pound person after a single drink is 0.03. After four drinks consumed within an hour, the BAC level for a 125-pound person rises to 0.10, the legal limit for driving in most states.[49] For a 200-pound person the corresponding BAC levels after one and four drinks are 0.01 and 0.06.

While greater alcohol consumption leads to greater impairment, managers who rarely drink and have a low body mass should be particularly aware that they are likely to be more affected by alcohol than their counterparts. In addition, managers should take precautions not to drink on an empty stomach.

Task practice will also make a difference. We know from the literature on drunk driving that the driving performance of intoxicated drivers who routinely drive under the influence of alcohol suffers less that the performance of inexperienced drunk drivers. Analogously, negotiating over drinks may confer a relative advantage to negotiators who routinely negotiate over drinks.

Returning to the example of the arms control negotiations between the United States and the Soviet Union, it was the Soviets who were more experienced at drinking while negotiating. As Edward Rowny explained, consuming alcohol during negotiations conferred a substantial advantage to the Soviets. The Soviets were able to handle their liquor, while the Americans gave away important secrets.[50] Before negotiating, you should evaluate your relative alcohol tolerance. If your negotiation partner is a regular drinker, you may be at a distinct disadvantage during negotiations.

Since drinking increases self-disclosure, an inebriated negotiator is more likely to disclose confidential business information or personal problems that provide a negotiating advantage to his or her counterpart.[51] Such revelations are more likely when a negotiator perceives his or her counterpart to be inebriated and therefore equally vulnerable. At times, actual levels of inebriation can be difficult to discern; Japanese, for example, may pretend to be more drunk than they really are. Japanese are also more comfortable with silence. The combination of alcohol, simple questions, and long periods of silence can prompt accidental disclosures by unwary Westerners. As one American executive warns, "Americans are prone to very modestly launch into lectures of valuable technical information—in some cases the very 'asset' which they are hoping to sell."[52]

In parts of Asia, negotiators sometimes intentionally schedule drinking occasions to undermine their counterpart's negotiating abilities.[53] This tactic is especially effective when coupled with other timing tricks, such as scheduling negotiations after a big dinner or before a newly arrived foreigner has had an opportunity to adjust to the time zone. A related maneuver involving two teams of negotiators has been used to fatigue business travelers negotiating abroad. The first team negotiates during the day, and the second team takes the visitors out at night for several rounds of drinks. Managers new to a culture may be unsure of the proper protocol and reluctant to risk offending their hosts by refusing to socialize. Outnumbered and on unfamiliar terrain, even self-aware managers can find the double-team tactic exhausting.

Not all negotiating tricks involving alcohol depend on physical fatigue. The psychological effects of alcohol can also lend themselves to manipulation. Under the influence of alcohol, for example, arguments based on emotional appeal may appear more convincing and salient than they would otherwise. A life insurance salesperson who makes a pitch by dwelling on worst-case scenarios may be more successful in selling policies over a few drinks than over mineral water. Similarly, appeals based on nostalgia (old times) or guilt (past favors or perceived wrongs) are likely to have greater impact when the target has been properly prepared. While alcohol's influence on physical and intellectual functioning is well known, its effect on emotional states is generally less recognized.

One context that warrants particular caution is strip clubs, where business associates are sometimes taken after work.[54] The visual stimulation and sexually charged atmosphere of the clubs are almost certain to be distracting in themselves; when combined with the effects of alcohol (lowered inhibitions, susceptibility to social pressure, and impaired cognitive functioning), targets, especially those unaccustomed to these surroundings, are less capable of focusing and functioning effectively as astute and wary customers. Besides producing sensory distractions and cognitive impairment, these meetings engender a social rather than business-like atmosphere. In keeping with the norms of social interaction, a customer in this setting may be reluctant to confront a host, to refuse the hospitality of a second or third drink, or to raise differences that might spoil the atmosphere of sociability and conviviality. Social norms of reciprocity, reinforced by the setting and the alcohol, may encourage the guest to respond in kind as the host reveals information and makes concessions.

Although alcohol is often introduced without strategic aims in mind, the fact remains that alcohol's capacity to undermine a manager's negotiating abilities provides his or her counterpart with a tempting opportunity to manipulate the context within which their business is transacted. Mangers who negotiate frequently are likely at some point to encounter a situation in which alcohol is used as a tool to obtain information or concessions. Reasonable prudence suggests that managers need to think carefully and realistically about the setting in which negotiations are to take place, the probability that alcoholic beverages will be present, and their own tolerance for drinking. Whether the effect is intentional or not, there is no doubt that alcohol can seriously interfere with a manager's ability to achieve his or her objectives.

GUIDELINES FOR ALCOHOL USE IN BUSINESS SETTINGS

The decision to introduce even low levels of alcohol into a business setting should depend on a clear sense of purpose and a thorough understanding of its effects. For example, alcohol facilitates relationship building, but harms the actual bargaining process.

Alcohol might be appropriate when the objective of an encounter is to develop a relationship or share information. Alcohol lowers inhibitions, encourages conversation, and causes individuals to feel closer to each other than they might otherwise. By encouraging disclosure, moderate use of alcohol can deepen and personalize formal business ties. And by encouraging a sense of closeness and mutual identification, it can help legitimize different points of view and reduce mistrust. It therefore might be appropriate when a primary objective is to develop a long-term relationship. Consequently, alcohol may be better suited for top decision makers structuring the general framework of an agreement than for their subordinates who need to resolve the technical details of the deal. For similar reasons alcohol may facilitate agreement in particularly contentious negotiations such as when negotiators have reached an impasse.

Decisions to consume alcohol should be made with respect to cultural norms. In many foreign cultures with strong drinking norms, alcohol may be an essential component of the negotiation process, and may even be a prerequisite for reaching a deal. In China, for example, prospective partners may be subjected to relationship tests that include extensive dining and drinking sessions. Similarly, in Korea the refusal to drink may be perceived as an insult and a signal of disrespect.

Alcohol consumption should be viewed along a continuum. Participating in a toast is quite different from spending an evening of heavy drinking, and the relative benefits and costs will change across quantity levels.

In many situations alcohol should be avoided altogether. The introduction of alcohol may create unease for those who decline a drink for personal, religious, company policy, or other reasons. Even when everyone is comfortable consuming alcohol, its introduction may create undesirable effects. For example, a manager may inadvertently reveal sensitive information, commit a serious faux pas, or escalate a conflict. In addition, alcohol should be avoided in situations that require critical judgment or creative thinking such as a technical discussion of financing arrangements. Table 1 describes some relationship and negotiation process considerations regarding alcohol consumption.

ALTERNATIVES TO DRINKING

There are many situations in which alcohol consumption should be avoided altogether. In practice, however, avoiding alcohol or declining a drink may be awkward or difficult. In this section we suggest some practical alternatives.

Choose the setting of your meeting carefully. The best approach for avoiding alcohol consumption is to choose a time and place for your meeting that minimizes the likelihood that alcohol will become an issue. By choosing lunch rather than dinner, and cafes rather than bars, managers can reduce the likelihood of being offered a drink and the potential awkwardness of declining one. In China, for example, experts have suggested that establishing relationships over meals may be as effective as establishing relationships over drinks,[55] and in many countries tea and coffee houses represent readily available alternatives to bars.[56] In Japan, heavy drinking after dinner is common, and one option for avoiding this type of alcohol consumption is to decline an invitation to join the group after dinner by citing a pressing phone call or jet lag.[57]

In Russia, steam baths represent a popular venue for building business relationships. This environment enables associates to build relationships from a sense of openness and

TABLE 1   Alcohol Consumption and the Negotiating Context

Negotiating Context	Avoid Consuming Alcohol When:	Alcohol Might Be Appropriate When:
Relationship considerations	You want to manage your impression (e.g., meeting someone of higher rank for the first time)	Social norms favor drinking and the benefits of in-group status outweigh alcohol's risks
	You want to be careful about drawing professional boundaries	The opportunities for valuable social exchange outweigh alcohol's risks
	You do not want to exert social pressure that makes others uncomfortable or forces others to drink	The value of developing a stronger bond, such as for a long-term relationship, outweigh alcohol's risks
Negotiation process considerations	The negotiation involves a large number of issues	The focus of the negotiation is the long-term relationship
	The negotiation involves calculations (e.g., financial analysis)	Appealing to emotional criteria
	You want to be careful and tactful about how you communicate	Learning information about the other party is a primary goal
	The potential to escalate interpersonal conflict is high	Your relative tolerance level is high

vulnerability. American managers hoping to avoid alcohol, however, should be wary of this environment. Vodka often plays a role in steam-bath gatherings, and the combination of alcohol and dehydration from the heat can be especially debilitating.

Develop relationships in informal settings. In general, developing and personalizing relationships can be achieved in a variety of ways and settings that do not include alcohol. These range from joining people for cultural and sporting events, rounds of golf, or any number of activities and entertainments. Note that eliminating the presence of alcohol avoids both a potentially awkward situation as well as the alcohol consumption of your counterpart. This may be particularly important during a negotiation in which your counterpart's alcohol consumption could escalate conflict or create inefficiency that could harm your outcome.

Offer brief explanations when declining a drink. When business settings do involve unwanted alcohol, managers face a difficult choice. In some cases, accepting a drink without imbibing may be practical, but in others a certain amount of drinking may be expected. In these situations declining to drink may be interpreted as impolite and aloof. Managers who decline a drink should provide a brief, clear explanation and make an effort to signal interest in the relationship in some other way. For example, in China it is acceptable to decline drinks for health reasons or to claim stomach problems.[58] In the United States, a vice president of TeleAmerica, Inc., in Evanston, Illinois, declines drinks by explaining that she has to drive some distance afterward and that drunk-driving laws in her state are quite strict.[59]

Respect the symbolic importance of alcohol across cultures. In many cultures alcohol has ritualistic and symbolic significance. If you decline a drink, take care not to offend your host. In some cases the symbolic value of alcohol consumption is more important than actual drinking. Though the appropriate course of action will vary by situation and culture, raising your glass during a toast is generally more important than actually drinking from it. In some contexts, drinking nonalcoholic versions of alcoholic beverages may also suffice.

In instances where drinking is expected, there are typically limits to these expectations. In Russia, for example, participating in the first two rounds of drinks is important, but stopping after the second round is generally acceptable.[60] In Japan, one option is to leave the glass full or half-full. This approach can tactfully signal an intention not to drink.[61]

Anticipate alcohol consumption when assembling a negotiation team. In some cases senior managers should develop negotiation teams with drinking situations in mind. For example, before American managers send groups to negotiate in Asia, they should consider the composition of the team not only in terms of technical, cultural, and language expertise, but also with respect to the potential for alcohol consumption. This strategy was employed by a senior executive from Smith Kline Beecham who routinely brought along a sales representative to participate in the evening drinking activities while she returned to her hotel room to relax and sleep.

SETTING COMPANY POLICY ON ALCOHOL USE

Develop a realistic alcohol policy. Senior managers should anticipate the role of alcohol in negotiations in setting company policy regarding alcohol consumption. Most company policies do not reflect the complex relationship between alcohol consumption and business practice. In some cases, firms ban alcohol consumption for all company-related events, both on- and offsite.[62] Such policies reflect the growing threat of corporate liability—a real concern following a 1991 ruling in which a Florida company was ordered to pay $800,000 in punitive damages after a drunken salesman caused an accident while returning home from a trade show.[63]

Prohibitionist policies, if they are actually enforced, may curtail corporate liability and may also provide employees with a ready excuse for declining an unwanted drink. However, such policies lack flexibility and may be impractical in many cross-cultural contexts. To the extent corporate alcohol policies are viewed as simplistic or unrealistic, they are likely to remain ignored and unenforced.

Articulate and enforce the company's alcohol policy. Companies should have written guidelines regarding alcohol consumption, and clearly identify job roles and cases in which alcohol consumption may be appropriate. Policies restricting the use of alcohol need to be strictly enforced and, for liability purposes, companies should keep records of how they are enforced. For example, a policy that encourages inebriated employees to take cabs might be documented with a file of used receipts from cab rides. In addition, companies should provide help for employees with drinking problems.[64]

Train managers to evaluate alcohol's hazards and benefits. Managers need to recognize the symbolic and strategic importance of alcohol in different settings. In some cases, alcohol use will engender specific benefits that outweigh its hazards. Employees in specific situations should be empowered to make informed decisions regarding their use of alcohol. They should be trained to evaluate the costs and benefits of alcohol consumption and sensitized to the serious consequences that even moderate amounts of alcohol can have on their performance and self-perception of their performance. In addition, corporations should educate their members about the serious physiological effects of alcohol as well as the symptoms of alcoholism, which are not always obvious. Alcohol abuse remains the most common form of drug abuse in the workplace, and represents a major health risk as well as a significant drain on productivity.[65]

CHOOSING WISELY

The use of alcohol introduces a complex element into business relationships with potentially important consequences for individual managers and their organizations. The decision to mix drinking with business merits careful consideration rather than the thoughtless consumption that often characterizes its use.

For centuries, alcohol has been used as a catalyst for relationship building, coalition formation, and bonding among business partners. Although it is well known that alcohol compromises cognitive and physical functioning, in many cases the costs of impaired judgment from consuming alcohol are underestimated. Used wisely, alcohol can yield relationship and strategic benefits, but these benefits must be balanced against alcohol's liabilities.

ENDNOTES

1. Wiesendanger, B. 1993. Last call. *Sales and Marketing Management*, 145: 62.

2. Mehta, S. 1996. Lunch hour is becoming happy hour again. *Wall Street Journal*, September 23: B1, B8

3. Mintcloud, B. 1991. *Supervision*. Money-saving ideas for the profit-minded supervisor. 52: 22–25. Trice, H., and Roman, P. 1972. *Spirits and demons at work: Alcohol and other drugs on the job.* New York: Hoffman Printing Company.

4. Engholm, C. 1991. *When business east meets business west.* New York: John Wiley & Sons Inc. Quanyu, H., Andrulis R., & Tong, C. 1994. *A guide to successful business relations with the Chinese.* Binghampton, NY: International Business Press.

5. *Economist,* 1995. On sin and synergy, December 23, 337: 13.

6. Tung, R. 1984. *Business negotiations with the Japanese.* Lexington, MA: D.C. Heath & Company.

7. Mars, G. 1987. Longshore drinking, economic security and union politics in Newfoundland. In M. Douglas (ed.), *Constructive drinking: Perspectives on drinking from anthropology.* 91–101. New York: Cambridge University Press.

8. Shell, G. 1991. *Bargaining for advantage.* New York: Viking.

9. Carey, K. 1995. Effects of alcohol intoxication on self-focused attention. *Journal of Studies on Alcohol,* 56: 248–52; Leaptrott, N. 1996. *Rules of the game: Global business protocol.* Cincinnati: Thomson Executive Press.

10. Brannen, C., and Wilen, T. 1993. *Doing business with Japanese men: A woman's handbook.* Berkeley, CA: Stone Bridge Press.

11. Engholm, op. cit.

12. Steptoe, A., and Wardle, J. 1999. Mood and drinking: A naturalistic diary study of alcohol, coffee and tea. *Psychopharmacology,* 141: 315–21.

13. Allred, A., Mallozzi, G., Matsui, F., and Raia, C. 1997. The influence of anger and compassion on negotiation performance. *Organizational Behavior and Human Decision Processes.* 70: 175–87.

14. Angry negotiators are also more likely to misjudge their counterparts' interests and concerns, and to misperceive hostile intentions in their counterparts' actions.

15. Heath, D. 1995. *International handbook on alcohol and culture.* Westport, CT: Greenwood Press.

16. Butler, C. 1991. The party's over. *Successful Meetings.* November: 32–49.

17. Engholm, op. cit.

18. Beamer, L. 1993. Toasts: Rhetoric and ritual in business negotiation in Confucian cultures. *Business Forum,* September: 22.

19. Rowney, E. 1992. *It takes one to tango.* Washington, DC: Brassey's (U.S.).

20. Central European Business Information Service, 1995. *Central European business guide.* The business of culture: Dos and don'ts for foreigners in Russia. April 2.

21. DeMente, B. 1994. *Japanese etiquette and ethics in business.* Lincolnwood, IL: NTC Business Books.

22. Engholm, op. cit.

23. *Economist.* 1993. Legless in Tokyo. October 16: 38.

24. Heath, op. cit.

25. Filipczak, B. 1992. Working for the Japanese. *Training,* 29: 12–23.

26. Tung, op. cit. Also, Engholm, op. cit.

27. Leaptrott, N., op. cit.

28. Scott, K., Schafer, J., and Greenfield, T. 1999. The role of alcohol in physical assault perpetration and victimization. *Journal of Studies on Alcohol,* 60: 528–36. Dougherty, D., Bjark, J., Bennett, R., and Moeller, G. 1999. The effects of a cumulative alcohol dosing procedure on laboratory aggression in women and men. *Journal of Studies on Alcohol,* 60: 322–29. Pihl, R., Zeichner, A., Niaura, R., Nagy, K., and Zacchia, C. 1981. Attribution and alcohol-mediated aggression. *Journal of Abnormal Psychology,* 90: 468–75. Zhang, L., Wieczorek, W., and Welte, J. 1997. The nexus between alcohol and violent crime. *Alcoholism, Clinical and Experimental Research,* 21: 1264–71.

29. Lyons, D. 1997. Campaign picked up steam fast. *Miami Herald.* February 12: 7B.

30. The experiment involved MBA students.

31. Efficient outcomes were defined in terms of joint gains and Pareto efficiency (the potential for negotiators to reach agreements where at least one party could improve their outcome without harming anyone else).

32. Thompson, L. 1998. *The mind and heart of the negotiator.* Upper Saddle River NJ: Prentice Hall.

33. Fillmore, M., Carscadden, J., and Vogel-Sprott, M. 1998. Alcohol, cognitive impairment and expectancies. *Journal of Studies on Alcohol,* 59(2): 174–79.

34. Price, D., and Flax, R. 1982. Alcohol, task difficulty, and incentives in drill press operation. *Human Factors*, 24(5): 573–79. Mangione, T., Howland, J., Amick, B., Cote, J., Lee, M., Bell, N., and Levine, S. 1999. Employee drinking practices and work performance. *Journal of Studies on Alcohol,* 60: 261–70.

35. Steele, C., and Southwick, L. 1985. Alcohol and social behavior: The psychology of drunken excess. *Journal of Personality and Social Psychology,* 48: 18–34.

36. Schweitzer, M. 1998. The impact of alcohol on negotiator behavior: Experimental evidence. OPIM Wharton working paper #981203, University of Pennsylvania.

37. Streufert, S., Pogash, R., Gingrich, D., Kanter, A., Lonardi, L., Severs, W., Landis, R., and Roache, J. 1993. Alcohol and complex functioning. *Journal of Applied Psychology,* 23: 847–68.

38. Schapiro, N. 1993. Before you even start negotiating. *Executive Female.* 16(2): 33.

39. Calamari, J., and Perillo, J. 1987. *The law of contracts.* St. Paul MN: West Publishing Co.

40. Yesavage, J., and Leirer, V. 1986. Hangover effects on aircraft pilots 14 hours after alcohol ingestion: A preliminary report. *American Journal of Psychiatry,* 143(12): 1546–50.

41. Babcock, L., Loewenstein, G., Issacharoff, S., and Camerer, C. 1995. Biased judgments of fairness in bargaining. *American Economic Review*, 85:1337–43. Wade-Benzoni, K., Tenbrunsel, A., and Bazerman, M. 1996. Egocentric interpretations of fairness in asymmetric, environmental social dilemmas: Explaining harvesting behavior and the role of communication. *Organizational Behavior & Human Decision Processes,* 67: 111–26.

42. Carey, K. 1995. Effects of alcohol intoxication on self-focused attention. *Journal of Studies on Alcohol,* 56: 248–52.

43. Brannen and Wilen, op. cit.

44. Jobs, S., Fiedler, F., and Lewis, C. 1990. Impact of moderate alcohol consumption on business decision making. *NIDA Research monograph 100, Drugs in the Workplace: Research and Evaluation Data.* 147–65.

45. Weinstein, S. 1996. Personal interview with M. Giordano, December 23.

46. Schweitzer, op. cit.

47. Leaptrott, op. cit.

48. Quanyu et al., op. cit.

49. The legal driving limit is 0.10 in 35 states and the District of Columbia and 0.08 in 13 states. In Massachusetts and South Carolina, driving with a 0.10 blood alcohol level is evidence of impairment, but is not illegal.

50. Rowny, op. cit.

51. Phaneuf, A. 1995. How to mix business with pleasure. *Sales and Marketing Management,* August: 96.

52. Ruzicka, M. 1995. Doing deals in Japan: Some sober advice. *Journal of Commerce,* 405: A1.

53. Kublin, M. 1995. *International negotiating: A primer for business professionals.* Binghampton NY: The Haworth Press.

54. Stossel, J. 1997. A day at the office. ABC News 20/20, Transcript #97092604-j11, September 26.

55. Cohen, A. 1996. Getting to yes, Chinese-style. *Sales and Marketing Management,* July: 44.

56. Mole, J. 1991. *When in Rome . . . A business guide to cultures and customs in 12 European nations.* New York: AMACOM; Engholm, op. cit.

57. Brannen and Wilen, op. cit.

58. Engholm, op. cit.

59. Wiesendanger, op. cit.

60. Central European Business Information Service, op. cit.

61. Engholm, op. cit.

62. Bordwin, M. 1994. Drinks are on the house: Your house. *Management Review.* 83: 35–37.

63. Ibid.

64. Trice, H., and Beyer, J. 1982. *Job-based alcoholism programs: Motivating problem drinkers to rehabilitation.* In E. Pattison and E. Kaufman (eds.), Encyclopedic handbook of alcoholism: 954–78, New York: Gardner Press. Trice, H., and Beyer, J. 1984. Work-related outcomes of the constructive-confrontation strategy in a job-based alcoholism program. *Journal of Studies on Alcohol,* 45: 393–404.

65. Scanlon, W. 1982. *Alcoholism and drug abuse in the workplace.* New York: Praeger.

She Stands on Common Ground

Jill Rosenfeld

Where there are organizations, there are people. And where there are people, there are conflicting interests. One of the most basic—and most difficult—jobs of a leader is sorting through conflicting interests to make choices and achieve common ground.

Susan Podziba, 39, has spent her career moving people to common ground. And she's developed ideas and techniques that help more people get there on their own. Podziba, a faculty associate with the Program on Negotiation at Harvard Law School, has facilitated dialogue between Israelis and Palestinians, between environmentalists and fishermen, and between prochoice and prolife activists.

What is her secret? *That there is no secret.* Her work is based on the assumption that warring factions hold the key to resolving their own conflicts. "Life isn't fair," she says. "The reality is that people everywhere have hard choices to make. My job is to challenge people to see the complexity of a situation and to encourage them to take an active part in making those hard choices."

So what, exactly, does Podziba do? First, by talking separately to each party, she untangles the issues, emotions, perceptions, and dynamics that surround a dispute. Then she decides whether mediation can help. "You don't use a hammer to tighten a screw," she says. "Mediation is a particular kind of tool that works only when appropriately applied." It won't work if one of the parties expects to achieve more through other means, such as a lawsuit. And it won't work unless everybody agrees that some resolution is better than no resolution.

Podziba's next challenge is to design a consensus process in which everyone agrees to participate. People on both sides of the dispute help develop a mission statement, as well as ground rules that will govern their deliberations: What's an achievable goal? What's the deadline? What are the roles and responsibilities of the mediators? "The ground-rules document is a tool for teaching people how to work by consensus—because it's a low-risk agreement that they create," Podziba says.

With the mission statement, Podziba is careful to explore both worst-case scenarios and the greatest aspirations of participants. "The mediator helps get these fears and outrageous hopes out of people's heads," she says. "When these issues are exposed, the group can analyze them and see what is truly realistic, and what's not."

A Life-or-Death Dispute

On a winter morning in 1994, a man walked into a Planned Parenthood clinic in Brookline, Massachusetts, shot and killed a receptionist, and wounded three other people. He then drove to a nearby clinic and killed another receptionist and injured two more people. In the aftermath of the shootings, Susan Podziba undertook one of her most sensitive facilitations: secret conversations between prolife and prochoice activists. "The emotion of the time is hard to describe now," says Podziba. "I was frightened. What if the wrong person found out that I was facilitating those meetings?"

Both camps agreed to tone down the rhetoric. "If abortion doctors are called 'murderers,' then people on the fringes of society feel there's a justification for violence," Podziba explains. "Neither side wanted that."

The participants, who met on and off for three years, also established a hot line modeled after the Cold War–era connection between the United States and the Soviet Union. In at least one instance, prolife advocates used the hot line to inform prochoice activists of a plausible threat, thereby averting potential violence. "The mediation process was life-changing for all of us," says Podziba. "The level of relationships built among people who had been 'enemies' was just mysterious."

At this point Podziba guides the details of the discussion itself. She elicits data, then frames and reframes the situation to keep the discussion moving. Participants can speak out against proposals, but they must also develop alternatives that everyone agrees on. Indeed, the group spends a significant amount of time on good communication practices. In one instance, Podziba was hired to facilitate sessions between Israeli and Palestinian health-care managers who were studying at Harvard. Podziba used a listening exercise that involved pairing people to discuss their feelings about the conflict in the Middle East.

During the sessions, each person had to repeat what the other said. Participants told stories of being stopped at military checkpoints and of Palestinian mothers who let their children throw stones at armed soldiers. "These stories are very painful to repeat," says Podziba. "When you're retelling the other side's story, you skip a lot. This exercise illustrates that people are very selective about what they hear and digest."

Finally, Podziba serves as a reality check. She helps develop what she calls a "universe of options." People brainstorm all the ways of addressing a situation that will satisfy everyone's basic needs. The exercise not only helps the group come up with inventive solutions; it also shows all sides that there are a limited number of options available.

"When the process is successful, people force themselves to think in a new way, and they reach a new level of creativity," says Podziba. "They start to work in a problem-solving mode. They understand why it's been hard to reach a resolution, and they see that they can tackle the problem together."

The Ultimate Guide to Internet Deals

Scott Kirsner

What's the deal with Internet companies these days? Deal! Lots of deals: High-priced acquisitions of fast-growing startups. Marketing alliances between old-media giants and new-media innovators. Distribution partnerships between companies that sell stuff and Web sites that attract eyeballs. It's a fact of life in the new world of business: Companies live and die by how well they do deals. And their leaders have to cut make-or-break deals at speeds that would paralyze their counterparts in slower-moving industries.

"There are two options for Internet companies," argues Kevin O'Connor, 38, cofounder and CEO of Doubleclick, the Web's advertising superpower. "Get bigger fast, or get smaller fast. If you're not one of the top three players in any category, eventually you'll be eaten—or die. That's a pretty good incentive to find partners that can help you grow."

"Everyone on the Net is scrambling to get big fast," agrees Bob Davis, 42, president and CEO of Lycos, a Web portal that recently signed a high-profile—and decidedly controversial—deal with USA Networks to create an e-commerce giant. "We did five acquisitions and three strategic investments in less than a year. There's a clear sense that speed is a necessity. This isn't just about building companies. It's about laying the foundation for an industry."

In some sense, doing business has always been about doing deals. And many of the old rules of deal making—about knowing if you can trust the folks across the table, about preparing for a negotiating session—still apply. But there are new rules as well. Internet deals get done in weeks (and sometimes even in days), and negotiations are just as likely to take place outdoors—perhaps after a game of ultimate Frisbee—as they are in a conference room. More and more negotiations take place through email rather than in person. And because so many Internet companies have neither tangible assets nor an established track record of success, the human factor looms larger than it ever has before.

If you're buying a television station, you're buying an awful lot of fixed assets and a lot of history and predictability," explains Bert Ellis, 45, chairman and CEO of iXL Enterprises, an Internet-service provider in Atlanta. Over the past few years, Ellis has been a single-minded acquirer of small Web-development agencies. Back in the early 1990s, he was a serial purchaser of television and radio stations. (He later sold his group of 15 media properties for $745 million.) And he sees a big difference between those two industries: "In the Internet business, it's much more difficult to assess value. All we're buying is people."

Of course, as more deals get done, and as those deals get done faster than ever, more suspicions get raised as well: There is a big difference between making a deal and issuing a press release. "Pressware" is to the Internet business what "vaporware" is to the software business. "We don't do 'Barney deals' here," insists Bill Nussey, 33, president of iXL. "That's what we call it when you announce a partnership that's only about 'I love you, you love me.'"

"We're looking for properties and technologies with high rates of growth," says Bob Davis, whose bookshelves are lined with baseball caps that commemorate past deals. "That's why we've acquired companies like Tripod and invested in companies like Bidder's Edge. The opportunities come at us in a fire hose, and the trick is to know what to pursue and what to decline. What's clear is that you need to make deal making a core competency."

O'Connor, Davis, Ellis, and Nussey are writing a new rule book for how deals get done, for how deal makers do their job—and for what happens after the deal. Fast Company turned to them and other elite Internet deal makers to create the ultimate guide to Internet deals. Are you ready to deal?

HOW TO BUY ON INSTINCT

From the day he came on board at Lycos, Tom Guilfoile, 34, knew that he was in for a wild ride. He had been a senior manager at Ernst & Young's entrepreneurial-services group, one of the giant accounting firm's nimblest divisions. But that was nothing compared with life at one of the Net's fastest-moving portals. Guilfoile started work as Lycos's controller in February 1996. By April, he had helped the company to navigate SEC regulations and to float an IPO. That IPO took place just 10 months after Lycos was founded, making Lycos the youngest company in NASDAQ history to go public.

And the momentum just kept increasing. "I remember calling my wife one night and telling her I had to work late," says Guilfoile, who is now vice president of finance and administration at Lycos.

> Around 11 P.M., Bob [Davis] called me and said, "I want to buy a piece of PlanetAll [an online calendar and contact-management system], and we have to get it done by tomorrow morning." There were other investors who wanted in. Bob liked the concept, could see the value, and said, "Let's do it," without much tire kicking. I got an e-mail at midnight with PlanetAll's proposal. And by 3:30 A.M., we had a letter of intent to buy 10 percent of the company. It was on Bob's desk by 9 A.M., and it had been signed by both parties by 11 A.M. I called my wife when we were done and said, "Since the last time I talked to you, we bought 10 percent of a company." (Late last year, Amazon.com snapped up all of PlanetAll for $100 million—which meant that Lycos had parlayed its investment into a $10 million gain.)

Guilfoile, a die-hard baseball fan, has a gray metal locker in his office, along with a photo of himself as a 13-year-old batboy for the Pittsburgh Pirates. To plunge into the world of Internet deals, he had to shed some of his CPA conservatism. "My inclination had always been to beat things to death, to analyze everything to the nth degree," he says. "But in this industry, you'll be swallowed up if you do that."

Guilfoile and Dennis Ciccone, 48, Lycos's vice president of mergers and acquisitions, have developed their own style of doing deals. They work quickly, and they trust their intuition. Last year, Lycos bought five companies—including Tripod, a popular Web destination for college students, and Wired Digital, the online offshoot of *Wired* magazine. As a result, the company now reaches nearly as many Internet users—49 percent—as Yahoo! does, and it has been growing at a faster rate than Yahoo!.

"With most of these deals, there's not a lot to hang your hat on in the way of financial analysis," Guilfoile says.

> There's no stable earnings growth to project into the future. You're not buying oil wells or factories. You're buying an opportunity, eyeballs, and people. That forces you to become a good reader of a company's people and its culture. You're looking for people who are committed and hard-working, who have the same vision and goals as you do. It's not going to work if you're dealing with people who are looking to check out and who see you as their ticket to retirement. The people you deal with have to be builders. Basically, we rely a lot more on instinct than on facts, because facts just aren't available in most cases.

Lycos is always on the lookout for its next acquisition, its next investment opportunity. And manning the lookout post is Dennis Ciccone's full-time job. Ciccone came to Lycos after that company acquired his company, WiseWire, in April 1998. (That acquisition, which involved a lot of office sleepovers on the part of people from both companies, was completed in just one month.) There's no shortage of work, says Ciccone: "I always have 40 to 60 business plans on my desk, and I'm on the road a few times each month, doing tours of promising young companies."

Ciccone has recently focused on e-commerce companies that are developing shopping bots, tools for building Web storefronts, or software to handle back-end transactions. He relies heavily on input from product managers and engineers at Lycos, who provide him with blueprints of their strategy and who advise him on which technologies Lycos should buy rather than build in-house. "Evaluating technology is important, and it requires a lot of input," he says. "We have to ask, 'Does it work, and will it still work when we plug it into the Lycos network and pour on the hits?'" The e-commerce tour has taken him to Toronto and Amsterdam, as well as various cities in California.

Ciccone looks tired as he leans against a credenza in Guilfoile's office. Because the expectations of Lycos's users change so quickly and because the competitive landscape shifts at an equally fantastic rate, Ciccone's universe of potential acquisitions is nearly infinite. "We're not at a stage where we're comfortable with blowing any one off," he says. "You don't want to miss an opportunity. If people e-mail me, I e-mail them back. If they call, I call them back. I can't afford not to, and usually just one phone call can clarify whether or not there's something there."

Bo Peabody, another executive from an acquired company, operates a sort of deal-making skunk works Lycos. Peabody, 27, came to Lycos in February 1998, after it acquired Tripod, the Web community that he founded in 1992. Lycos, which paid $58 million for Tripod, has given him free rein to seek out tiny, low-profile Internet companies and to shepherd them through the acquisition process. While Ciccone concentrates on big-ticket deals, Peabody finds companies that Lycos can buy for less than $10 million. Such deals are the kind that competitors tend to overlook.

"There are a lot of $5 million and $10 million companies out there that are looking to hitch their wagon to something larger, but they don't get the attention of a Yahoo! or an @Home or an Amazon," says Peabody. "Often they have a technology that leads you to say, 'We could build this in six months.' But in our world, six months is an eternity."

Working with Ethan Zuckerman, 26, a technology specialist who also came to Lycos as part of the Tripod acquisition, Peabody appeals to the founders of Internet startups in a way that Ciccone can't appeal to them. "We don't use an investment banker, and we don't come in with spreadsheets," Peabody explains. "We talk about code. We talk about products. It's deprofessionalized. It's techie-to-techie, entrepreneur-to-entrepreneur. I know what it's like to have a company with five people."

One representative acquisition involved GuestWorld, the company that created the most widely used software for putting guestbooks on personal home pages. With 800,000 registered members, GuestWorld was clearly the leader in its category, and Lycos bought the company last June for $3.9 million. (Like most of Lycos's deals, this one was an all-stock transaction.) "We did the GuestWorld acquisition inside of a week, from first contact to term sheet," crows Peabody. "Doing that kind of a deal helps us move faster. I think some of the best value that we'll get will come from those little deals—from being crafty and street-smart."

Once Lycos starts negotiating, it blocks out as much outside interference as possible. "To get the other company's undivided attention, we like to sign a letter of intent as soon as we can," says Guilfoile. "And we ask for a 30- or 60-day period in which to sit down and do our due diligence." In many cases, though, once Lycos shows an interest in a company, other portal sites declare their interest—which in turn encourages the object of Lycos's affection to start shopping around. "We're big fans of handing out offers with a fuse attached: If you don't commit within 12 hours, this deal blows up," says Peabody. "We want each deal to happen fast. We don't want to give the other company time to talk with our competitors."

HOW TO MAKE A "STANDARD" DEAL

Back in 1995—ancient history by Web standards—streaming audio was simply the latest cool idea to hit the Net. Seattle-based RealNetworks (known back then as Progressive Networks) introduced the first version of its RealPlayer, a tool that lets Internet users listen to speech and music on their computer without having to wait for a huge file to download.

From the start, though, RealNetworks understood that its undeniably nifty technology would wither if it didn't sign deals with strong content and distribution partners. When the technology was launched, the companies that supplied programming for it included National Public Radio and ABC News. Today 85 percent of Web sites that use streaming media do so via RealAudio or RealVideo. Among those content providers are more than 3,000 radio stations as well as hundreds of television broadcasters. By the end of last year, there were more than 48 million registered users of RealNetworks technology, and that technology had emerged as a de facto standard.

How do you make your technology a standard? By making lots of deals. "We're smack-dab in the middle of building the Internet into the next mass medium," says Len Jordan, 33, RealNetworks's senior vice president of media systems.

> Deal-making skills are an important commodity here. You have to partner with a lot more companies than I would ever have imagined. You have to be sharp in understanding what your company's core assets are—and what its core desires are. You have to be efficient in matching your assets and desires with those of your partners, and you can't be shy about moving aggressively to make things happen.

And on the Net, Jordan adds, you never know where your most valuable partners will turn up. "If you're DaimlerChrysler, there's not going to be another car manufacturer tomorrow that you have to know about," says Jordan.

> Because the capital requirements are so high, you'd know about any competitor years ahead of time. But on the Internet, a bunch of college kids in Illinois can come up with Mosaic, and that company can turn into Netscape in a very short time. In our industry, you can't ever say that you know who all the players are, because new players are emerging all the time.

That's why Jordan has developed an internal radar to scope out potential partners. He is a devoted user of online news services like TechWeb, Cnet, and Quicken.com, and he sifts through a half-dozen trade publications a week. When he first heard about Inktomi Corp., for example, Jordan was intrigued by the company's caching technology, which makes files more accessible to users by storing copies in several locations across the Internet. "We instantly saw that their [Inktomi's] technology could reduce the cost of streaming media, and we struck up a relationship with them. They were a young company at the time, pre-IPO, and knowing about them was just a matter of having our ears pricked up."

Companies that hope to do deals in quantity also need to send clear signals—to their own people and to the outside world—that they are an open system. "You have to immerse your employees in the notion that you win by working with other companies, not by going it alone," says Jordan.

> And people outside the company need to know that the welcome mat is out. We take meetings with a lot of little companies—outfits with just two or three people—because it wasn't that long ago that we were that size. You need to cast a wide net, because this is a big ocean. You can't count anyone out.

"Anyone" includes even Microsoft, which produces its own streaming-media player and which is RealNetworks's foremost competitor. At one point, Microsoft had invested $30 million in RealNetworks, but the software giant divested itself last year, and the two companies are now battling over technology standards. Still, in the Internet business, a company must never say never.

"MSNBC is the only major news site that doesn't use either RealAudio or RealVideo," says Mark Hall, 35, general manager of media publishing at RealNetworks. "But we would definitely be prepared to take on the MSNBC site as a content partner. It has some great programming."

Hall oversees many of RealNetworks's content partnerships. "You want to have a system that's scalable and efficient, because you're dealing with tens of thousands of sites," he says. "The simpler you keep the partnership, the faster lawyers can get through it." Indeed, the standard agreement between RealNetworks and one of its content partners is only three pages long. Under this agreement, no money changes hands: RealNetworks provides technology, offers support services, and helps distribute programming to its audience of 55 million: the partner simply agrees to provide a channel of daily content in the RealNetworks format.

"We've done deals in two or three days, and usually we do them in no more than two or three weeks," Hall boasts. Unlike the iron-clad agreements of the old economy, though, RealNetworks's content partnerships seldom remain unchanged for longer than two years—and, in fact, one year is the norm. "You don't want deals that prevent you from being flexible and nimble," says Hall. "Change is what the Net is all about."

How Steve Jurvetson Does Deals

Steve Jurvetson, 32, likes to boast that his firm, Draper Fisher Jurvetson (DFJ), has financed more Web companies in the past six years than any other independent venture-capital outfit. Many of the deals have been blockbusters. Microsoft bought Hotmail, a DFJ company, for $400 million. Yahoo! bought Four11 for $95 million. CyberMedia Inc. went public—and was then bought by Network Associates for $130 million. "We don't sit around doing lots of deep thinking," Jurvetson says. "We get a sense of what will be a billion-dollar opportunity, and we look for companies. We get to closure before others see that opportunity."

Here are Steve Jurvetson's rules for Internet deal making.

1. **Get fast or get lost.** "At most venture-capital firms, partners gather for a Monday meeting to review the business plans that they've received and to make decisions on how to proceed. We don't wait until Monday. We make decisions on an ad hoc basis, and we take iterative steps throughout the week—in person and by e-mail. We've also engineered our due-diligence process to be minimal. You've got to close deals quickly, or else you'll miss out."

2. **Bigger is better.** "The '800-pound gorilla' in a category tends to get the dominant share of business and financial partnerships. Many advertisers and media companies don't want to spend time with small properties. And that makes it tough for new entrants.

   "Hotmail, for example, was doubling in size each month, but it took six months to reach 1 million users. Until it reached that point, the company was off the industry's radar screen. By the time people came to realize that free, Web-based e-mail was indeed a hot idea, Hotmail was adding 1 million new subscribers a month."

3. **Mix work with play.** "Lots of deals happen in situations that aren't 'pure work.' We play a weekly ultimate Frisbee game with a group of entrepreneurs: We signed the term sheet for Four11's seed financing after one game. We did another deal during the 1998 NCAA Final Four tournament."

4. **Intuition is as important as analysis.** "We never use Excel spreadsheets. We don't build models. We look for entrepreneurs who want to change the world—people who are going after big opportunities. There's room for analytical error, but there's even more room for phenomenal success."

5. **Rules? There are no rules!** "On the Net, the old investment rules have been turned on their head. Investors in the software industry used to avoid low-price products like the plague. But on the Internet, free products can generate huge market value. If you let too many old rules govern your deals, you'll never be a leader."

Avoiding long-term contracts doesn't mean becoming a shortsighted company. Maria Cantwell, 40, senior vice president of the consumer and e-commerce division at RealNetworks, agrees that lengthy and exclusive contracts often work against a deal. But, she argues, nimbleness and flexibility shouldn't keep you from sharing your vision of the industry's future with your partners.

"You need to identify opportunities in which you can build alliances that involve more than just one deal," says Cantwell, who served as a member of Congress from Washington State before she joined RealNetworks.

> For example, we try to think, What are the long-term benefits if America Online and Real-Networks work together? Will a deal with AOL help us build the market for streaming media? How do we work together in the future, now that all 15 million AOL subscribers can easily gain access to RealPlayer?

Cantwell is fond of comparing deal making on the Internet to what takes place in the halls of Congress:

> In the technology world, you benefit from cutting to the chase—being up-front about your common interests. E-mail and the Web let you share information and find common ground quickly. Technology accelerates the exploratory phase. Once two companies decide that they're in sync, people here really want to do deals. In politics, though, you never know when you're going to need people again, so you focus on building coalitions, building trust, and then working out the details. You're also more fearful of a failed negotiation than you are in the Internet space. Politics is such a public arena: You're always thinking, What will the media say?

WHAT'S THE DEAL WITH TALENT?

Bert Ellis, chairman and CEO of iXL, oversaw a mind-blowing 34 acquisitions from 1996 to 1998. Bill Nussey, president of iXL, took part in about 20 of those deals. But the two men deny that they're pursuing an old-fashioned roll-up strategy (one that involves trying to dominate a decentralized industry by assembling a bunch of far-flung assets). Instead, they're simply trying to build the Web's premier design, development, and engineering firm. "This isn't a financial roll-up," Nussey claims. "This is a talent roll-up." The goal behind iXL's acquisitions, he says, is to build a big team of talented people—and to build it fast. "Our acquisitions are a way of hiring a lot of people, while reducing the risk that they won't be able to work together. We know that they can work together—they've already done it."

Because Nussey is buying not hard assets, such as a factory, or even intellectual capital, such as a patent, but rather groups of people who know how to build things on the Web, his top concern in evaluating a deal is the human dimension. "We spend at least as much time looking at the cultural fit as we spend reviewing the books," he says. "If we discover reasons why our culture and the other company's culture wouldn't mesh, we break off discussions."

When deals do go forward, iXL makes sure that all of the acquired company's stockholders have an incentive to stay on board: Selling your company to iXL is not an exit strategy. Shareholders are paid with iXL stock (which is not yet publicly traded—although iXL did recently register for an IPO). "The only people who will take our deal are those who want to be with us over the long term," says Nussey. "We hope to attract people who love their work, but who want to be part of a bigger company and have a bigger impact."

Since iXL aims with every deal to gain a fresh infusion of top-notch talent, it also works hard to make sure that rank-and-file people don't jump ship. "If you have a conquest mentality, you'll fail," says Dave Clauson, 44, iXL's executive vice president of worldwide marketing. Executives from iXL headquarters spend as long as three months working on-site with acquired companies.

> One of our objectives is to ascertain how we can add immediate value. What is this company struggling with? What is it challenged by? Maybe there are technology problems that we can help resolve, or new-client meetings that we can help with. We try to generate early momentum by fixing some things and winning new business. That eliminates a lot of anxiety.

Is This the Real Deal?

Vernon Keenan, 39, is a master decoder of deals. As president of Keenan Vision Inc., a market-research firm in San Francisco, he dedicates much of his energy to parsing press releases and news reports to find the truth about deals. Clients rely on Keenan's judgment to let them know which announcements by Microsoft, AOL, and other Internet powers are the real deal—and which are pressware. "It's like reading smoke signals from the Vatican," Keenan quips. "You mix your knowledge of the industry with common sense." We asked Keenan for his advice on getting past deal puffery.

1. **Watch your language.** "You have to deconstruct the language: Pull out all of the adjectives and adverbs. Zero in on relationships. To what extent are two companies actually sharing technology, exchanging money, or doing joint marketing? One of the things that signals a real deal is product-related activity with a date attached—something that goes beyond an 'intention to work together.'"

2. **Less can be more.** "Sometimes the tersest announcements are the ones with the biggest potential impact. When Intel bought iCat [a company that helps merchants build online stores], it put out the shortest imaginable statement—which was more interesting than a long, windy press release would have been. There was mystery in that statement. It was clearly the first step in some sort of a plan that Intel has for e-commerce, but the company isn't ready to articulate that plan. So you can't write off a short release or a tiny news item as being insignificant."

3. **More can be less.** "Lots of companies use a 'rolling thunder' strategy. They issue dozens of press releases each month, hoping to give the impression that they've got a lot of momentum—that they're doing a lot of deals. Sometimes it's a company like Microsoft, which really is doing a lot of significant deals, and sometimes it's some small-fry company that's just trying to get media attention. If you see three or four press releases about the same product or the same deal, you know that some company is desperate to seem as if it has a pulse."

4. **Money isn't everything.** "Don't discount a deal just because no money is changing hands. In the Internet space, deals are often about the exchange of value. Two companies might be agreeing to support each other's technology—which is very important. Or the two companies' sales forces might be agreeing to sell both companies' products."

5. **Beware of CEO overload.** "When you see eight or nine CEOs quoted in a press release, or eight or nine CEOs sitting on a stage at a conference, you know almost instantly that there's nothing of substance going on. It's a coalition of companies announcing their support for moving in some kind of general direction. You have to wait for real activity to emerge."

---

iXL also holds monthly summits that bring together staff from each of its 14 U.S. and 5 European offices. One summit might bring together all iXL employees who are responsible for recruitment. Another might focus on helping salespeople share selling strategies. A third might serve as a conclave for creatives. Each summit is held in a city where iXL has operations. "Most companies underinvest in knowledge transfer and in culture and emotional connection," says Clauson. "But that kind of investment is part of our battle to attract and retain the best people."

So far, iXL is winning that battle. Of the roughly 100 senior executives who came to iXL from acquired companies, only 2 have quit. "We've become a sort of magnet for people in this industry," says Nussey. "We're on the map now. Because of our reputation, we're being approached day and night, and our ability to acquire good people is increasing exponentially."

How Doubleclick Does Deals

On a December afternoon in 1995, Kevin O'Connor caught the last flight to New York out of Atlanta. A few hours later, a major snowstorm descended on the Northeast. O'Connor spent the next three days stuck in a hotel, hashing out the details of a deal that would merge his four-person Atlanta company, Internet Advertising Network, with the sales division of the interactive-ad agency Poppe Tyson.

That deal led to the creation of the Web's advertising superpower DoubleClick, which had a stellar IPO in 1997 and which now sports a market value of $1 billion. "The key," says O'Connor, DoubleClick's CEO, "was bringing together our technology expertise with Poppe Tyson's expertise in ad sales and the media business. It gave us a head start over our competitors." Here are his observations on the kind of deal making that can give rise to industry heavyweights.

1. **Get big fast.** "There are two options for Internet companies," O'Connor says. "Get bigger fast, or get smaller fast. If you're not one of the top three players in any category, eventually you'll be eaten—or die. That's a pretty good incentive to find partners that can help you grow."

2. **Show a little faith.** "There's a certain amount of intuition in every Internet deal," O'Connor admits. "What's this business going to be like in 10 years? No one knows. You're operating on faith. You're trading speed for information."

3. **Don't ignore the vision thing.** "Since there are so many intangibles involved in Internet deals, you need to make sure that you share a vision with the people across the table from you," O'Connor says. "When I met Dave Carlick [head of Poppe Tyson's sales division], we had identical visions of the way ad networks would be important to the Web—and of the way technology would be important to the delivery of dynamic ads. This was very early in the development of the market, and it was amazing that we had the same vision. It was like finding your long-lost brother on the crowded streets of Bombay."

4. **Deals are personal—they're not just business.** Rapport counts for a lot in the Internet business. "Don't do deals with people you don't like," O'Connor advises. "If people are smart and if they have the same kind of passion that you do, you're three-fourths of the way there."

DEALING YOUR WAY BACK FROM THE BRINK

Companies that live by the deal can also die by the deal. Novell Inc., the once-thriving network-software company based in Provo, Utah, almost killed itself after signing a barrage of bad deals. At its high point, Novell controlled more than 70 percent of the market for networking software, and its leaders believed that they were building a credible competitor to Microsoft. So Novell embarked on an acquisition binge, buying 17 companies (including WordPerfect) in the span of a little more than two years. But the acquired companies diluted Novell's strategy, which had focused exclusively on computer networking. Those companies also proved hard to integrate into Novell's culture.

"I can't think of a single acquisition in which the relationships really worked," admits Christopher Stone, 41, now Novell's senior vice president of corporate strategic development. "The revenues of the company shrank from $2.5 billion to $1.1 billion, and we wound up selling off most of the companies we had acquired."

For a while, Novell looked like buyout bait itself. Then it sold off WordPerfect, installed a new CEO—and changed its deal-making philosophy. Forget gobbling up

The Four Don'ts of Deals

Marc Diener argues that you don't have to master negotiating tricks or intimidation tactics to be an outstanding deal maker. "It's not about responding to the other guy's double flinch with a triple scowl, or about seeing who can stay silent the longest," says Diener, 42, an entertainment lawyer based in Los Angeles and the author of *Deal Power: Six Foolproof Steps to Making Deals of Any Size* (Henry Holt, 1998). He argues that successful deals are the result of diligent preparation, not virtuoso displays of personality.

Diener, who specializes in contract negotiations, works with such companies as 20th Century Fox, Universal Pictures, and Warner Brothers. Earlier in his career, he worked as a house counsel at CBS Records and at Orion Pictures. He has also represented individual actors and musicians. According to Diener, there are at least four reasons why negotiations go bad.

1. **You don't have enough perspective.** " 'How does this deal fit into my overall strategy? Why do I want to do it?' Those are the two most important questions to ask yourself before you sit down at the negotiating table," Diener says. "If you don't have real answers to those questions, it's easy to get wrapped up in the minutiae of a contract, and not realize that a deal has limited value or that it doesn't take you in the direction you want to go."

2. **You don't go in with a checklist.** If you enter a conference room with a complete list of what you want out of a deal—and what you don't want—it's harder for cigar chomping or chest thumping to throw you off track. How much money do you want? What's the duration of the contract? Is it an exclusive? What resources will you and the other side each commit to the deal? "Without a list of goals, there's a real good chance that you're going to overlook something," warns Diener.

3. **You don't ask for help.** Deal making isn't a solo sport. When you try to go it alone, the results can be dismal. Diener relates the story of a close friend who was seeking investors for a software startup: "Either he was too arrogant to get help, or he felt that he didn't have time to get a lawyer to review each contract." This friend, adds Diener, wound up losing control of the company. The best deal makers rely on researchers, investment bankers, lawyers, and accountants who can assist them.

4. **You don't do enough due diligence.** It's often tough to balance the need for careful analysis with the need for speed. But even with the most time-pressed deals, says Diener, an intense investigation period is indispensable: "Use the Internet, use your personal network, use any means available to make sure that the person you're dealing with isn't a crook. You don't want to have happen to you what happened to Michael Ovitz. Sure, he's one of Hollywood's most famous deal makers, but he put millions into Livent without realizing that its founders were cooking the books."

---

disparate companies and trying to become a Microsoft-sized behemoth. Novell's deals now focus on building a product line around Novell Directory Services (NDS), which Stone calls "411 for the Internet." NDS gives system administrators additional information about their corporate networks; it lets them identify and correct problems from any terminal connected to the Net; and it allows them to permit or deny users access to sensitive documents—a feature that helps to enable secure commercial transactions. For such a directory to have real value, it has to be used by all Internet-service providers, and it has to be built into the switches that control Internet traffic. "The directory has to be ubiquitous," says Stone. And making it ubiquitous means lots of deal making.

For example, Stone put together a deal with Lucent Technologies, one of the world's leading makers of switching equipment. Last October, Lucent announced that, starting this year, it would include NDS with its own software. Wall Street and the media paid attention, and a flurry of deals with other top-tier players followed: Cisco Systems, Nortel Networks, Tivoli Systems. "One of the rules of Internet deal making," says Stone, "is that if you get the big fish first, everyone else falls in line."

Sometimes it takes clever bait to land the big fish. At first, Cisco wasn't very interested in NDS, Stone says: "So we went to all of our customers who owned Cisco routers, and we asked them to help us get Cisco's attention. They set up a forum and started talking about how great it would be if Cisco's products supported NDS. We got 500 e-mails the first day, and some of them were sent to [Cisco CEO] John Chambers as well. Then he started getting phone calls too." Last November, Chambers finally gave in.

To keep its deal-making campaign moving at a fast clip, Novell used the lucent contract as a template for future deals. "Developing the Lucent contract was a nightmare," says Stone, adding that the process lasted about four months. "Everybody and his brother—every executive, every product manager, every engineer—had to have a hand in it. But having that contract as a platform made later deals much easier."

Making sure that deals are quick and simple is important to Stone, who wants Novell to regain its reputation as a company that stays ahead of the pack. That's why he does as much negotiating as possible through e-mail and the Web, and why he does his best to keep money out of the discussion. "It used to be that technology deals were all about the licensing fee that I got from you in exchange for my software," says Stone, who started and sold his own company—Object Management Group—before joining Novell.

> The problem with that model is that I didn't care how many people actually used the software; I only cared about the fees that I was collecting. In the Internet era, it's all about installed base: How many people use the product today? Besides whenever money is placed on the table, something gets screwed up.

So most of Novell's deals are joint marketing-and-sales agreements in which little or no money changes hands. That model is becoming more and more typical of Internet deal making: "These deals are about 'I'll mention you in speeches, use my Web site to distribute your product, and help you publicize the product,'" says Stone. "There are lots of things to focus on that are more important than trading dollars—like 'Will customers buy it?'"

Stone is also a fanatic about paper: He hates it. "I won't allow people to do anything on paper—except the final contract," he says, sounding as if he can't wait for the day when legal signatures can be rendered in pixels. Entrepreneurs who apply for financing from the Novell Internet Equity Fund fill out a Web-based form. Using keywords drawn from the form, a computer then forwards the applicaiton to an appropriate executive in Stone's group. Discussions about whether to do a particular deal take place largely via e-mail. Documents are edited online—which reduces the chance that an outdated copy of a contract will remain in circulation.

For Novell, doing deals digitally means identifying service providers—such as lawyers and investment bankers—who are willing to forsake paper. "It's very simple," says Stone. "You play by my rules, or I don't hire you. Working electronically is just more efficient." Many of Novell's Internet investments—which range in value from $1 million to $3 million—are wrapped up in as little as two weeks' time. The deals are templated ("all that changes are the names and the numbers," Stone says), and Novell's attorneys, along with a valuation expert from an investment company, review each contract via the Web.

Novell is also vigilant about never announcing a deal before it's finalized. Stone believes that by putting out "pressware"—instead of releasing real software—companies erode their reputation and hence the perceived value of partnering with them: "People stop listening to you because they assume that you're crying wolf."

And, Stone emphasizes, when Novell does issue a press release about a new partnership, that just marks the beginning of the deal "You'll really [tick] off your partners if you don't follow through on what you promised," he says. To enable proper follow-through, Novell assigns dedicated personnel to work with each partner. The company also holds monthly status meetings. At those meetings, Novell wants to know not only how each partnership is holding up but also how it can be expanded.

Novell treasures its relationships with partners because it knows that they hold the key to the company's future. Novell's people also acknowledge that Internet deal making—like all deal making—is social. That's why, last January, Stone and Steve Adelman, 42, vice president of corporate development, organized the first-ever Novell Global Partners Summit in Snowbird, Utah. The event attracted 400 people. "It was an opportunity to get together for a couple days to talk about how we can work together better," Adelman explains. "We want to leverage what we have as a network of companies, rather than as pairs of partners."

And lately the news about Novell has made a sharp turn for the better. The company's share price is up, and its marketplace momentum is back. "We've realized that Novell needs friends to be successful," says Stone. "Things change so fast that we can't do it all alone. In the beginning, we were nervous because of our long legacy of bad deals. But we feel that we have the formula down now. Doing smart deals is our mantra."

Exercises

The Disarmament Exercise

INTRODUCTION

The purpose of this exercise is to engage you in working together in a small group, making decisions about the nature of your relationship with another group. Your group will be paired with another group. Each group will have the opportunity to make a decision about a series of "moves." The outcome of those moves (in terms of the amount of money that your team wins or loses) will be determined by the choice that your group makes, and the choice that the other group makes. Your group cannot independently determine its outcomes in this situation. The nature of your group's choices, and how well your group performs in this exercise, will be determined by (1) your group's behavior toward the other group, (2) the other group's behavior toward your group, and (3) the communication between groups when this is permitted.

RULES FOR THE DISARMAMENT EXERCISE

The Objective

You and your team are going to engage in a disarmament exercise in which you can win or lose money. You may think of each team as a country with land mines—some land mines are armed and others are not. There are at least two rounds of play in the exercise, and each round has up to seven moves. In this exercise your objective as a team is to win as much money as you can. The team opposing yours has the identical instructions and objective.

The Task

1. Each team is given 20 cards. These are your land mines; each card represents one land mine. Each card has one side marked *X* and an unmarked side. When the marked side of the card is displayed, this indicates that the land mine is armed; conversely, when the blank side of the card is displayed, this shows the land mine to be unarmed. Each team also has an A (attack) card; this will be explained later.

Adapted by Roy J. Lewicki from an exercise developed by Norman Berkowitz and Harvey Hornstein. Reprinted from Douglas T. Hall, Donald D. Bowen, Roy J. Lewicki, and Francine Hall, *Experiences in Management and Organizational Behavior* (Chicago: St. Clair Press, 1975), pp. 85–92. Used with permission.

2. At the beginning of the exercise, each team places 10 of its 20 land mines (cards) in the armed position with the marked side up, and the remaining 10 in the unarmed position with the marked side down. All land mines will remain in your possession throughout the exercise; they must be placed so that the referee (group leader) can see them, but so that they are out of the sight of the other team.

3. During this exercise there are at least two rounds with up to seven moves each. Payoffs are calculated after each round (not after each move), and are cumulative.

    a. A move consists of a team turning two, one, or none of its land mines from armed (X) to unarmed (blank) status, or vice versa.

    b. Each team has three minutes to decide on its move and to make that move. There are 30-second periods between moves. At the end of three minutes, a team must have turned two, one, or none of its land mines from armed to unarmed status, or from unarmed to armed status. Failing to decide on a move in the allotted time means that no change can then be made in weapon status until the next move. In other words, failure to make a move by the deadline counts as a move of zero land mines.

    c. The length of the three-minute period is fixed and unalterable.

    d. The referee (instructor) will verify each move for both teams after it has been made.

4. Each new round of the exercise begins with all land mines returned to their original positions, 10 armed and 10 unarmed.

The Finances

If your referee chooses to use real money in this exercise, money will be distributed as described. If you use imaginary money, assume that each team member has made an imaginary contribution of $2.00 and that the money is also distributed as described.

Each member will contribute to the treasury. The money you have contributed will be allocated in the following manner:

1. Sixty percent will be returned to your team, to be used in the task. Your team may diminish or supplement this money depending on the outcomes during the exercise. At the end of the exercise your team's treasury will be divided among the members.

2. Forty percent will be donated to the World Bank, which is to be managed by the referee. This money will *not* be returned at the end of the exercise and should be considered as no longer yours.

3. The opposing team's money will be allocated in the same way.

The Payoffs

1. If there is an attack during a round:

    a. Each team may announce an attack on the other team (by notifying the referee) during the 30 seconds following any three-minute period used to decide upon a move (including the seventh, or final, decision period in any round). To attack, you *must* display your A (attack) card to the referee. You may not attack without an A card. The moves of both teams during the decision period immediately *before* an attack count. An attack cannot be made during negotiations (see below).

   b. If there is an attack (by one or both teams) the round ends.

   c. The team with the greater number of armed land mines wins 5 cents per member for each armed land mine it has over and above the number of armed land mines of the other team. These funds are paid directly from the treasury of the losing team to the treasury of the winning team. If both teams have the same number of armed land mines, the team that attacked pays 2 cents per member for each armed land mine to the World Bank, and the team that was attacked pays 1 cent per member for each armed land mine to the World Bank. If both teams attacked, both pay the 2-cent rate.

2. If there is no attack by the end of a round:

   a. At the end of each round (seven moves), when there has been no attack, each team's treasury receives from the World Bank 2 cents per member for each of its land mines that is at that point unarmed, and each team's treasury pays to the World Bank 2 cents per member for each of its land mines remaining armed.

   b. When a team wins funds, they are awarded by the World Bank. When a team loses funds, they are paid to the World Bank.

3. Teams may run a deficit with the World Bank. If there is a deficit at the end of three rounds, the status of the deficit will be decided by the instructor.

The Negotiations

1. Between moves each team has the opportunity to communicate with the other team through negotiators chosen by the team members for this purpose. You may *not* communicate with the other team before the first move.

2. Either team may call for negotiations (by notifying the referee) during any of the 30-second periods between decisions. A team is free to accept or reject any invitation from the other team.

3. Negotiators from both teams are *required* to meet after the third and sixth moves.

4. Negotiations can last no longer than five minutes. When the two negotiators return to their teams, the three-minute decision period for the next move begins.

5. Negotiators are bound only by (a) the five-minute time limit for negotiations and (b) required appearance after the third and sixth moves. They are otherwise free to say whatever they choose and to make an agreement that is necessary to benefit themselves or their teams. They are not required to tell the truth. Each team is similarly not bound by any agreements made by their negotiators, even when those agreements were made in good faith by the negotiators.

Reminders

1. Each move can consist of turning over two, one, or zero of your land mines to the unarmed side—or the armed side.

2. You have three minutes to decide which of the above moves you will choose.

3. If there is no attack, at the end of the round (seven moves) your team receives 2 cents per member for each unarmed land mine and loses 2 cents per member for each armed land mine.

4. If there is an attack, the team with the greater number of armed land mines wins 5 cents per member for each armed land mine it has over the number the other team has.

5. Remember that there is also a penalty if an attack is called and both teams have the same number of *X* cards displayed.

6. A team may call for negotiations after any move. Mandatory meetings of negotiators occur after moves 3 and 6.

Preparation for Round 1

1. The referee will signal that the first round begins.

2. Your team has three minutes to decide on its first move and then to actually move zero, one, or two cards.

3. When the referee returns, show him or her your move. You may also attack at this point, and/or you may call for negotiations.

4. If neither team attacks or calls for negotiations, the referee will proceed to the second move.

5. Remember that there will be mandatory negotiations after moves 3 and 6. Also remember that the game will proceed for seven moves, unless there is an attack.

6. When the round ends, the referee will state how many land mines each team had armed and whether either team attacked. Each team will calculate its financial status. Money (if used) will be transferred from one team's treasury to the other, or to/from the World Bank.

7. After accounts are settled, return the cards to their start-of-game position (10 *X*-side up and 10 *X*-side down).

Disarmament Exercise Questionnaire

For round 1, circle the appropriate number on each scale which best represents your feelings. (For subsequent rounds, use boxes or triangles or colored pencils to indicate the appropriate rating.)

1. To what extent are you satisfied with your team's current strategy?

    Highly satisfied   1   2   3   4   5   6   7   Highly dissatisfied

2. To what extent do you believe the other team is now trustworthy?

    Highly trustworthy   1   2   3   4   5   6   7   Highly untrustworthy

3. To what extent are you now satisfied with the performance of your negotiator?

    Highly dissatisfied   7   6   5   4   3   2   1   Highly satisfied

4. To what extent is there now a consensus in your team regarding its moves?

    High consensus   1   2   3   4   5   6   7   Very little consensus

5. To what extent are you now willing to trust the other people on your team?

    More than before   1   2   3   4   5   6   7   Less than before

6. Select one word to describe how you feel about your team:

7. Select one word to describe how you feel about the *other* team:

Negotiators only: Please respond to the following question:

    How did you see the other team's negotiator?

    Authentic and sincere   1   2   3   4   5   6   7   Phony and insincere

Disarmament Exercise Team Record Form

	Round 1		Round 2		Round 3		Round 4	
	Armed	*Unarmed*	*Armed*	*Unarmed*	*Armed*	*Unarmed*	*Armed*	*Unarmed*
Start	10	10	10	10	10	10	10	10
Move 1								
Move 2								
Move 3								
Negotiation								
Move 4								
Move 5								
Move 6								
Negotiation								
Move 7								
Net gain or loss in this round	My team:	Their team:	My team:	Their team:	My team:	Their team:	My team:	Their team:

At End of Round	Round 1	Round 2	Round 3	Round 4
Funds in own team treasury				
Funds in other team treasury				
Funds in World Bank				

Pemberton's Dilemma

INTRODUCTION

This exercise creates a situation in which you and the other person(s) will be making separate decisions about how to manage your firm. In this situation the outcomes (profits and losses) are determined not only by what you do, but also by a number of other factors such as the goals and motives that you and the other party have and the communication that takes place between you and them.

Read the background information for Pemberton's Dilemma that follows. In this exercise, you will represent your store in discussions with the other store about the hours that each store should open on Sundays. You and the other store will be making decisions simultaneously, and your profits will be directly affected by these decisions.

BACKGROUND INFORMATION

Pemberton is a quaint little town located in the heartland of our great country. Although it is only a 30-minute drive to a major metropolitan center, most of the town-folk prefer to do their shopping at one of the two general stores located in Pemberton. At these stores, one can buy a variety of goods, ranging from groceries to hardware equipment. Both establishments boast a soda fountain, which is quite popular among both the younger and older generations as well.

Like most small towns, Pemberton is proud of the fact that it has been able to preserve its many traditions, some of which date back to the 1890s. One of these grand traditions, which became official in 1923 when the Town Hall passed a resolution to this effect, is the cessation of all commercial activity on Sunday. Times have changed, however, and "Sunday shoppers" are becoming more and more prevalent. In fact, every Sunday there is a mass exodus to the nearby metropolitan center, where Sunday shopping has been permitted for years.

You are a member of the management team from one of the two general stores in Pemberton. Both the Country Market and the Corner Store have been consistently losing potential profit as Sunday shopping becomes more popular. Your management team, as

Written in collaboration with Gregory Leck.

well as the team from the competing general store, has recently contemplated opening the store on Sunday, in spite of the municipal resolution that prohibits this.

The ramifications of such decisions are important, since the profitability of such an action will depend on the decision made by the competing store. For instance, if neither store decides to open on Sunday, it will be business as usual, and both stores will make a profit of $20,000 in a given week.

If only one store decides to open on Sunday, that particular store would enjoy the patronage of all those Sunday shoppers and would manage to make a $40,000 profit for the week. Unfortunately, the store that decided to remain closed on that Sunday would actually incur a loss of $40,000 that week. This would be due to various reasons, most notably the preference of customers to continue to do their shopping throughout the week at the store that remained open on Sunday.

If both stores decided to stay open on Sunday, adverse consequences would be faced by both establishments. Although Town Hall may be able to turn a blind eye to one store violating the municipal resolution, two stores would be looked upon as a conspiracy against the traditionalists of Pemberton. Artemus Hampton, Pemberton's mayor and direct descendant of one of the town's founders, would no doubt pressure Town Hall into levying the highest possible fine allowable by law. In this case, the penalty would be so excessive that both stores would incur losses of $20,000 each for the week. While your lawyers have suggested that the municipal resolutions prohibiting Sunday shopping in Pemberton might be overturned in a court case, this too would be a costly option. In either case, if both stores open on Sunday, they will each incur losses of $20,000 for the week.

Keeping the above information in mind, your team is to decide each week, for the next 12 weeks, whether your store is to remain open on the Sunday of that week. The decision made for the first week must be made without prior consultation with the management team of the competing store. Subsequent decisions may be made after consulting with your competitors. Both teams shall reveal their decisions simultaneously. *Remember, the goal is to maximize profits over the next 12-week period.*

Familiarize yourself with the profit chart below. There will be 12 one-minute rounds where the stores will either open or close. Each round represents one Sunday, and every *fourth* Sunday is part of a long weekend. A three-minute planning session separates each Sunday. *There may not be any communication between the stores during the planning sessions.*

The exercise begins when representatives from the stores (one from each) meet and indicate with a card if their store will open or close on the first Sunday. Each team will record the outcome of each Sunday on their profit chart. The time periods between each Sunday are fixed, and may not be altered. Each team will complete a total of 12 moves. Profits and losses are calculated after each Sunday and are cumulative for the 12 weeks (see sample profit chart below).

		Country Market			
		Close Sunday		Open Sunday	
	Close	Corner:	+$20,000	Corner:	−$40,000
Corner	Sunday	Country:	+$20,000	Country:	+$40,000
Store	Open	Corner:	+$40,000	Corner:	−$20,000
	Sunday	Country:	−$40,000	Country:	−$20,000

Profit Chart

	Corner Store's Choice	Country Market's Choice	Profit	
			Corner Store	Country Market
First 15-Minute Planning Period				
1.				
2.				
3.				
4. **Double** profit/loss, *this round only*				
Five-Minute Negotiation Period				
5.				
6.				
7.				
8. **Triple** profit/loss, *this round only*				
Five-Minute Negotiation Period				
9.				
10.				
11.				
12. **Quadruple** profit/loss, *this round only*				

EXERCISE 3

The Commons Dilemma

INTRODUCTION

This is a simulation about the dynamics of competition and cooperation in a situation where there are multiple actors. The entire class will participate, with each individual student making a series of decisions over the course of several class periods. At each decision point, your outcomes will be determined by what everyone else does as well as by your own action. At the end of the simulation, when all decisions have been made, you will receive an overall score that can be converted into a grade for the exercise. Although the instructor will not discuss or debrief this exercise until after the final decision has been made, you and your fellow students are free to discuss it as you wish.

This version of the Commons Dilemma was developed by Michael Morris; it is based on a presentation made by Gary Throop at the 1990 Organizational Behavior Teaching Conference. Used with permission.

The Used Car

INTRODUCTION

The scenario for this role-play involves a single issue: the price of a used car that is for sale. While there is a great deal of other information that may be used to construct supporting arguments or to build in demands and requests in addition to the price, the sale price will ultimately be the indicator used to determine how well you do in comparison to other role-play groups.

BACKGROUND INFORMATION

You are about to negotiate the purchase/sale of an automobile. The seller advertised the car in the local newspaper. (*Note:* Both role-players should interpret "local" as the town in which the role-playing is occurring.) Before advertising it, the seller took the car to the local Mazda dealer, who has provided the following information:

- 1996 Mazda MX-6 two-door coupe, four-cylinder, automatic transmission, power steering, air conditioning, front-wheel drive, dual air bags, cruise control.
- Gray with black interior, power door locks, power windows, and AM/FM cassette stereo.
- Mileage: 61,300 miles; steel-belted radial tires expected to last another 30,000 miles.
- Fuel economy: 30 mpg city, 38 mpg highway; uses regular (87 octane) gasoline.
- No rust; dent on passenger door barely noticeable.
- Mechanically perfect except exhaust system, which may or may not last another 10,000 miles (costs $300 to replace).
- Blue book (2001) values: retail, $6,600; trade-in, $5,125; loan, $4,625.
- Car has been locally owned and driven (one owner).

Revised version of an original role-play that was developed by Professor Leonard Greenhalgh, Dartmouth College. Use with permission.

Statement of Agreement for Purchase of the Automobile

Price: _____

Manner of payment: _____

Special terms and conditions: _____

_____

_____

_____

_____

We agree to the terms above:

_____   _____
              Seller   Buyer

* *

Who made the first offer? _____

Initial Settlement Proposals:

Seller: _____

_____

Buyer: _____

_____

Knight Engines/Excalibur Engine Parts

INTRODUCTION

The process of negotiation combines economic transactions with verbal persuasion. A great deal of what transpires during a negotiation is the verbal persuasion—people arguing for and supporting their own preferred position, and resisting similar arguments from the other party. At the same time, underlying this layer of persuasive messages is a set of economic transactions—bids and counterbids—that are at the economic core of the negotiation process.

The purpose of this exercise is to provide some experience with combining the economic transactions and the persuasive messages to support preferred economic outcomes. You will be assigned the role of Knight Engines or Excalibur Engine Parts for this exercise. Your objective is to negotiate a deal that is most advantageous to you and your company.

Written in collaboration with Gregory Leck.

EXERCISE 6

GTechnica—AccelMedia

INTRODUCTION

The scenario for this simulation is a negotiation between a supplier of electronic components and a computer hardware maker over the price of a processor needed for the manufacture of a computer graphics accelerator adapter. The role-play information you will be given by your instructor provides details about the context of the negotiation that may help you to understand the situation, develop a bargaining strategy, and form arguments or demands to implement that strategy. Ultimately, however, how well you do in this negotiation in relation to other negotiating groups is determined by the final sale price for the part, if you are able to reach an agreement.

When you read your role information and are preparing to negotiate, keep these guidelines in mind:

- Use any plan or strategy that will help you achieve your objectives.

- If you are negotiating in a team, you may call a caucus at any time to evaluate your strategy or the opponent's strategy.

- Reach an agreement by the end of the specified time period, or conclude that you are not able to agree and that buyer and seller will explore other alternatives.

- Complete the negotiation outcome form as directed by your instructor. Be sure to write down any additional terms or conditions that were agreed to.

Universal Computer Company I

INTRODUCTION

In this exercise you will play the role of a plant manager who has to negotiate some arrangements with another plant manager. You will be in a potentially competitive situation where cooperation is clearly desirable. Your task is to find some way to cooperate, when to do so might seem to put you at a disadvantage.

Read the Universal Computer Company Background Information section (below) and the role information that the instructor has provided. Do not discuss your role with other class members. Plan how you will handle the forthcoming meeting with the other plant manager. Record your initial proposal on the Initial Settlement Proposal form. Do not show this to the other party you are negotiating with until after the negotiations are completed.

BACKGROUND INFORMATION

The Universal Computer Company is one of the nation's major producers of computers. Plants in the company tend to specialize in producing a single line of products or, at the most, a limited range of products. The company has considerable vertical integration. Parts made at one plant are assembled into components at another, which in turn are assembled into final products at still another plant. Each plant operates on a profit-center basis.

The Crawley plant produces computer chips, modules, cable harnesses, and terminal boards which in turn are shipped to other company plants. In addition to numerous computer chips, the Crawley plant makes more than 40 different modules for the Phillips plant. The two plants are about five miles apart.

The Quality Problem

Production at the Phillips plant has been plagued by poor quality. Upon examination it has been found that a considerable portion of this problem can be traced to the quality of the modules received from the Crawley plant.

The Crawley plant maintains a final inspection operation. There has been considerable dispute between the two plants as to whether the Crawley plant was to maintain

Initial Settlement Proposals

_____ Plant

How do you propose that the following expenses and repairs should be handled?

Expense of repairing all faulty modules _____

_____

Expense of repairing faulty modules other than the 12 types that fall below 95 percent level

_____

_____

Expense of repairing the faulty modules of the 12 types that fall below the 95 percent level

_____

_____

How to handle the repair of the faulty modules of the 12 types that fall below the 95 percent level

_____

_____

How to handle the repair of the modules other than the 12 types that fall below the 95 percent level

_____

_____

a 95 percent overall acceptance level for all modules shipped to the Phillips plant, or to maintain that standard for *each* of the 42 modules shipped. The Phillips plant manager has insisted that the standard had to be maintained for each of the 42 individual modules produced. The Crawley plant manager maintains that the requirements mean that the 95 percent level has to be maintained overall for the sum of modules produced. Experience at the Phillips plant shows that while some module types were consistently well above the 95 percent acceptance level, 12 types of modules had erratic quality and would often fall far below the 95 percent level. As a result, while individual types of modules might fall below standard, the quality level for all modules was at or above the 95 percent level. This raised serious problems at the Phillips plant, since the quality of its products is controlled by the quality of the poorest module.

The Interplant Dispute

The management of the Phillips plant felt that the quality problem of the modules received from the Crawley plant was causing them great difficulty. It caused problems with the customers, who complained of the improper operation of the products that contained

Final Settlement Agreement
_____

How, exactly, did you agree that the following expenses and repairs would be handled?

Expense of repairing all faulty modules _____

Expense of repairing faulty modules other than the 12 types that fall below the 95 percent level

_____

_____

Expense of repairing the faulty modules of the 12 types that fall below the 95 percent level ____

_____

_____

How to handle the repair of the faulty modules of the 12 types that fall below the 95 percent level

_____

_____

How to handle the repair of the modules other than the 12 types that fall below the 95 percent level

_____

_____

_____   _____
Representative, Phillips Plant   Representative, Crawley Plant
_____

the Crawley modules. As a result, the Phillips plant operation had earlier added secondary final inspection of its completed products. More recently it had added an incoming inspection of 12 poor-quality modules received from the Crawley plant. There were times when the number of modules rejected was large enough to slow or even temporarily stop production. At those times, to maintain production schedules, the Phillips plant had to work overtime. In addition, the Phillips plant had the expense of correcting all the faulty units received from the Crawley plant.

Ideally, the management of the Phillips plant would like to receive all modules free of defects. While this was recognized as impossible, they felt that the Crawley plant should at least accept the expense of repairs, extra inspections, and overtime required by the poor quality of the parts.

Since installing incoming inspection procedures on the 12 modules, the Phillips plant had been rejecting about $8,000 of modules a week. For the most part, these had been put into storage pending settlement of the dispute as to which plant should handle repairing them. Occasionally, when the supply of good modules had been depleted, repairs were made on some of the rejected units to keep production going. The Phillips plant had continued to make repairs on the remaining 30 types or modules as the need for repairs was discovered in assembly of final inspection.

From its perspective, the Crawley plant management felt that it was living up to its obligation by maintaining a 95 percent or better quality level on all its modules shipped to the Phillips plant. Further, they pointed out that using sampling methods on inspection meant that some below-standard units were bound to get through and that the expense of dealing with these was a normal business expense that the Phillips plant would have to accept as would any other plant. They pointed out that when buying parts from outside suppliers it was common practice in the company to absorb the expenses from handling the normal level of faulty parts.

The Phillips plant management argued that the Crawley plant management was ignoring its responsibility to the company by forcing the cost of repairs on to their plant, where only repairs could be made—rather than to have the costs borne by the Crawley plant, where corrections of faulty processes could be made.

Universal Computer Company II

INTRODUCTION

In this exercise you will play the role of a plant manager who has to negotiate the price of a new A25 computer chip. You will be in a potentially competitive situation where cooperation is clearly desirable. Your task is to find some way to cooperate, when to do so might seem to put you at a disadvantage.

Prior to negotiating, read the Background Information section (below) and the role information that the instructor has provided. Do not discuss your role with other class members. Plan how you will handle the forthcoming meeting with the other plant manager.

BACKGROUND INFORMATION

The Universal Computer Company is one of the nation's major producers of computers. Plants in the company tend to specialize in producing a single line of products or, at the most, a limited range of products. The company has considerable vertical integration. Parts made at one plant are assembled into components at another, which in turn are assembled into final products at still another plant. Each plant operates on a profit-center basis.

The Crawley plant produces computer chips, modules, cable harnesses, and terminal boards, which in turn are shipped to other company plants. In addition to numerous computer chips, the Crawley plant makes more than 40 different modules for the Phillips plant. The two plants are about five miles apart.

The A25 Computer Chip

Phillips purchases over 30 different computer chips from Crawley. Computer chip A25 represents the most advanced engineering and manufacturing technologies available at the Crawley plant, and is an important advance in multimedia hardware design for personal computers. Phillips will integrate the A25 chip into its mother boards, and in turn will sell the mother boards to Universal Computer (the parent company) and to other computer companies. Since the prices on all purchases between Phillips and Crawley have been previously negotiated, the price of the A25 chip is currently the only computer chip up for negotiation.

Twin Lakes Mining Company

INTRODUCTION

In this role-play, you will have the opportunity to negotiate a serious problem—a conflict between a mining company and the government of a small town regarding an environmental cleanup. While the issues in this scenario have been simplified somewhat for the purpose of this role-play, such conflicts between industry and governmental groups are typical throughout the country. Try to introduce as much realism into this situation as you can, based on your own personal experiences.

BACKGROUND INFORMATION

The Twin Lakes Mining Company is located in Tamarack, Minnesota, in the northern part of the state. It was established there in 1961. The town of Tamarack has a year-round population of approximately 12,000. Although there is a growing revenue that accrues to the town as a result of heavy summer tourism (summer homes, fishing, etc.) and several cottage industries, Tamarack is basically a one-industry town. Twenty-five hundred people, 60 percent of whom live within town limits, work for the Twin Lakes Mining Company; 33 percent of the town's real estate tax base of about $5 million consists of Twin Lakes Mining Company property and operations. Both in terms of direct tax revenue and indirect contribution to the economic stability of the local population, Tamarack is strongly dependent on the continued success of the Twin Lakes Mining Company.

The Twin Lakes Mining Company is an open-pit, iron ore mine. Open-pit mining consists of stripping the topsoil from the ore deposit with the use of power shovels. Train rails are then laid, and most of the ore is loaded into railroad cars for transportation to a central collecting point for rail or water shipment. As mining operations progress, rails are relaid or roads constructed to haul ore by truck. The ore is transported to a "benefication plant" located on the outskirts of Tamarack. Benefication of ore involves crushing, washing, concentration, blending, and agglomerating the ore. In the early days of ore production, such treatment was unnecessary; however, benefication is necessary today for several reasons. First, transportation costs of rejected material (gangue) are minimized. The crude ore may lose as much as one-third of its weight in grading, and, in addition, impurities are removed at a much lower cost than if removed during smelting. Second, ores of various physical and chemical properties can be purified and blended during this process. Finally, fine ore materials, which previously may have been rejected as a result of smelting problems, can now be briquetted and pelletized to increase their value. After the ore proceeds through this process of cleaning and agglomerating into larger lumps or pellets, it is shipped by railroad car to steel mills throughout the Midwest. Rejected materials are returned to "consumed" parts of the mine, and the land restored.

Twin Lakes' benefication plant is located approximately five miles outside of Tamarack. As a result of the expansion of the residential areas of the town, summer home development, and various Twin Lakes operations, the plant has become a major problem for local citizens. For years, the Tamarack Town Council has been pressing the company to clean up the most problematic operations.

While most of these discussions have been amicable, Twin Lakes has done little or nothing to remedy the major concerns. Now, as a result of more stringent environmental laws and regulations, Twin Lakes has come under pressure from both the state of Minnesota and the federal government for environmental cleanup. Both the state and the federal Environmental Protection Agency have informed Twin Lakes that the company is in major violation of water- and air-pollution quality standards, and that immediate action must be taken. Twin Lakes' estimates indicate that total compliance with the cleanup regulations will cost the company over $36 million. Because Twin Lakes is now mining reasonably low-grade ore and because foreign competition in the steel market has significantly eroded the demand for ore, environmental compliance may seriously influence the profitability of the company. Many local citizens, as individuals and through the local chapter of the United Mineworkers Union, are putting significant pressure on the Town Council to help the Twin Lakes Company in its environmental cleanup operations.

The imposition of the environmental controls on Twin Lakes, and the resulting pressure from all segments of the community, has led to renewed discussions between company officials and the Town Council. As a result of these discussions, the following environmental issues have emerged.

1. *Water quality.* The Twin Lakes plant requires large amounts of water to wash the crushed ore. In addition, much of the highest quality ore is reduced to an almost powderlike texture after washing, and is being lost in the washing operation. As a result, the company has built a series of settlement recovery ponds alongside Beaver Brook near the plant. Water that has been used for washing ore is allowed to stand in these ponds; they are periodically drained and the ore recovered. Nevertheless, granules of iron ore and other impurities continue to wash downstream from the plant. The environmental agents have insisted that the effluent from the plant and the ponds be cleaned up. Estimates for the cost of a filtration plant are $20 million. Twin Lakes claims that it cannot afford to build the plant with its own revenue. Since Tamarack has periodically talked about Beaver Brook as a secondary water source for the town (and residential development makes this a more pressing concern in two to three years), the Twin Lakes officials hope that they might interest Tamarack in a joint venture.

2. *Air quality.* The entire process of mining, transporting, and crushing ore generates large amounts of dust. This has significantly increased the levels of particulates in the air. In addition, during the dry summer months, the operation of many large trucks along dirt roads intensifies the problem considerably. Twin Lakes believes that it can control a great deal of the dust generated immediately around the plant at

a cost of approximately $8 million. The most significant debate with the town has been over a series of roads around the outskirts of town. Approximately half of the roads are town owned; the rest have been specially constructed for the transportation of ore and material. Estimates for paving all the roads are $4.8 million, with a yearly maintenance cost of $600,000; periodic oil spraying of the roads, to keep down the dust, would run approximately $800,000 annually, but an agreement to do this as a short-term measure may not satisfy the environmental agencies.

3. *Taxation of company land.* The land for the mine itself is outside of town limits. However, the plant lies within township boundaries, and current taxes on the town land are $800,000 annually. The company has always felt that this taxation rate is excessive. In addition, several of the railroad spurs used to move ore into the plant, and out to the major railway line, cross town land. The town has continued to charge a flat rate of $400,000 annually for right-of-way use. It has occasionally offered the land for sale to the company at rates varying from $2.2 million to $2.4 million. Again, the company has felt that this rate is excessive.

Both the company and the town believe that if some resolution could be obtained on these three major issues, the remaining problems could be easily resolved, and Twin Lakes would agree to keep the mine open.

EXERCISE 10

Salary Negotiations

INTRODUCTION

In this simulation, you will play the role of either a manager or subordinate in a negotiation over the subordinate's salary. Both in securing employment as well as promotions, we are frequently in a position to negotiate with our superiors over salary. Moreover, once we achieve managerial rank, we do the same with subordinates. This is one of the most common and, at the same time, most personal forms of negotiation. For many people, it is also the most difficult. Since salary can be a means of satisfying many needs—economic, recognition, status, or competitive success measure—it naturally leads to complex negotiations.

Developed from examples used by John Tarrant, *How to Negotiate a Raise* (New York: Van Nostrand Reinhold, 1976).

Job Offer Negotiation: Joe Tech and Robust Routers

INTRODUCTION

The scenario for this simulation is a negotiation over a job offer that has been extended by a technology company to an MBA student nearing graduation. The background information provided below introduces the principals involved, recaps their prior relationship, and presents a detailed summary of the terms of the offer that the firm has extended to the student. For the negotiation simulation, you will be assigned to assume the role of either the student or a representative of the hiring company. The role-play information that your instructor will then provide gives details about the specific interests and objectives of the party to which you are assigned.

In many ways, negotiation about job offers are just like any other negotiation: parties try to pursue their own interests while keeping an eye on relationship concerns and seeking areas of common ground that might allow them to bridge compatible interests. In other ways, however, job offer negotiations may be perceived as distinctive because of the stakes involved: for the job seeker, they involve the negotiation of one's personal circumstances, often with an opponent who is someone you will have to "live with" on a day-to-day basis for what could be a long time to come. As you read your role information and prepare for the encounter, think about how the pursuit of your goals—whether you are in the role of the hiring firm or the job-seeking student—may or should be affected by the unique context involved when one is negotiating about employment.

BACKGROUND INFORMATION

Joe Tech, an MBA student in the final semester before graduation, has an offer (see Offer Letter, p. 538) for permanent employment from Robust Routers (RR), and the deadline for accepting the offer is next week. Joe spent the summer before his final year in the MBA program working for RR in Mountain View, California. His boss during the

---

This simulation was developed by Jorge Ferrer, Andy Lauman, Fred Smith, and Tobey Sommer. It is adapted and used here with permission.

summer internship was Leigh Bultema, the product manager for RR's flagship product—a new terabit router. Leigh is the person at RR with whom Joe will speak to negotiate the terms of the offer.

Economic and Industry Conditions

At the time of the job offer, the U.S. economy has leveled off following a prolonged upswing. Economic growth is significantly lower than it was just a couple of years ago. The good news for MBA students, however, is that the unemployment rate remains modest, and the job market for new MBA graduates has remained strong. In recent years, "traditional" MBA employers such as investment banks have felt pressure to compete with aggressive technology companies recruiting top MBA prospects with potentially lucrative stock options. More recently, the stock market entered a period of high turbulence, dampening the outlook for smaller technology firms. Even the most promising and profitable tech companies have seen their share prices come under pressure. Companies like RR, which make Internet backbone equipment, operate with extraordinary profit margins, and yet even their shares have fallen.

Just last week, however, there was a rebound in tech share prices in large measure due to the resolution of a strike at Horizon Communications. Horizon settled its labor dispute and reaffirmed its commitment to capital spending, which Wall Street analysts had predicted would slow over the next two years. That potential slowdown would have eroded the stock valuations of network infrastructure manufacturers in general, and market leader RR in particular. Now, Horizon has reaffirmed its capital expenditure plans and announced a multiyear purchase of RR's high-end terabit routers.

Company Background

Robust Routers (RR) was started in the mid-1980s by a couple of enterprising graduate business students who had helped their university tie its computer lab machines together into a local area network. Anticipating a market for networking devices, the two borrowed money from friends and family, maxed out their credit cards, and started a company. Two years later they sold their first network router.

Originally targeting universities, RR by 1990 had expanded its marketing to include large and medium-sized corporations. As an early player with a proven track record, RR had a head start when the market for network routers took off in the early 1990s. RR's sales leapt from $1 million in 1989 to $30 million in 1992. The company went public in 1993. Since then, RR has acquired several niche players in the market and currently has a market capitalization of $70 billion, a landmark accomplishment for a company its age.

The computer hardware networking industry consists of companies designing, developing, and manufacturing products that provide connectivity solutions for multi-use computing environments, local area networks, and wide area networks. Network hardware products include PC cards, routers, hubs, remote access servers, switches, and adapters. At the time of Joe Tech's job offer, RR controls more than two-thirds of the global market and offers the industry's broadest range of products used to form information networks and power the Internet.

RR sells in approximately 75 countries through a direct sales force, distributors, value-added resellers, and system integrators. RR continues to purchase companies at a frenzied pace—it has made close to 10 acquisitions per year during the last two years. RR serves customers in three target markets: (1) enterprises—large organizations with complex networking needs, including corporations, government agencies, utilities, and educational institutions; (2) service providers—firms providing information services, including telecommunications carriers, Internet service providers, cable companies, and wireless communication providers; and (3) small/medium businesses—firms with a need for data networks of their own, as well as connection to the Internet and/or to business partners.

Joe Tech's Internship Experience at RR

Joe worked at RR during the summer between the first and second year of graduate school. He was fortunate to have secured an internship at the leading router company because they don't normally recruit from his school. He contacted an alumnus who worked for Horizon (one of RR's largest customers), who put him in touch with a friend at RR. Joe and Leigh Bultema hit it off from the initial exchange of e-mails, and after a fast-track series of telephone interviews, Joe had his internship set up for the summer.

Leigh Bultema began working at RR five years ago, when the company took the market and really began to pull away from its competition. She was in the right place at the right time. RR had proprietary technology that promised to revolutionize the telecom industry, and Leigh had drive, ambition, and brains. Leigh rose through the ranks at RR quickly, working in positions in sales, marketing, manufacturing, and business development activities. A proven performer, Leigh has been assigned to pivotal and vital roles within RR during her five-year tenure. RR has identified product management of the new terabit router as a priority function, and the CEO personally placed Leigh in this crucial role.

When he landed the summer internship, Joe expressed an interest in working in business development. However, because he did not enter RR through traditional recruiting channels from a top five MBA program, the business development internships were already filled. There were 50 MBA interns working at RR over the summer. They were spread out among marketing, strategic alliances, technical development, business development, treasury, and corporate marketing. Joe worked on product management for Leigh during the summer. The internship exposed Joe to senior management and different groups within the company, including the business development group for which Joe hoped to work after completing his MBA. Business development maintained all key business relationships at RR and was considered one of the preeminent functions within the firm. Joe received accolades from very senior executives on his internal product presentations of the terabit router.

The internship ended on a high note for the company and for Joe Tech. RR received an order from Horizon for its terabit router and Joe received an offer letter from RR. The offer came from Leigh Bultema's product management group, not the business development group Joe was targeting. However, job assignments at RR changed frequently. At the end of the summer, Leigh assured Joe that if his interest truly lay with business development, that all he had to do was perform well within product management and he could write his own ticket internally. Leigh herself had performed well in her initial job assignment within RR, and subsequently found herself courted by executives from several different internal groups who wanted her on their teams.

Although the permanent job offer was tendered back in August at the conclusion of the internship, RR told Joe that the offer would remain available until March 1. The specific terms of the offer are shown in the offer letter below. Now it is February 20, and Joe has arranged to speak with Leigh to discuss the offer before making a decision.

Offer Letter

Robust Routers, Inc.
One Robust Center
555 Silicon Way
Mountain View, CA 94201

August 25, 2000

Joe Tech
401 Owen Way
Nashville, TN 37220

Dear Joe,

On behalf of Robust Routers, Inc., I am delighted to confirm our offer to you of the position of Associate Product Manager. Your appointment will be effective June 1, 2001. The specifics of this offer are as follows:

Position: Associate Product Manager, Terabit Router Group

Salary: Starting salary will be $88,000 annually, paid monthly.

Signing bonus: You will receive a signing bonus of $10,000, paid as a lump sum within 30 days after you accept the offer in writing.

Options: You will receive 1000 stock options at a strike price equal to the share price of RR on the date of employment. Additionally, you will be eligible to receive a minimum grant of 500 incentive options after your first year of employment, and on each subsequent employment anniversary, provided your performance fully meets expectations and that you are an active employee on the subsequent grant date. The strike price for these options is set by company management and ratified by the Board of Directors annually. Options vest over a three-year period (33.3% per year).

Benefits: Robust Routers provides a comprehensive benefit plan to its employees. You will be entitled to the benefits detailed in the applicable plan document in effect at the time you join the company. Current benefits include health insurance, basic life insurance, dependent life insurance, long-term disability coverage, and immediate participation in Robust Router's matched savings plan for retirement. The Human Resources Department will send details on these benefits, along with specifics regarding paid sick leave, vacation leave, and holiday leave, under separate cover.

Relocation: You will receive a lump sum cash payment of $5,000 to help defray expenses associated with moving to Silicon Valley. Upon acceptance of our offer, you will receive a relocation handbook, which will provide detailed instructions regarding relocation benefits and information on the local area provided by several real estate firms.

Robust Routers is offering you a position with the understanding that you are not a party to a written agreement containing either a noncompete or nonsolicitation clause. Our corporation conducts routine employment checks on prospective employees. Your employment is contingent upon the successful completion and satisfactory results of these checks.

This offer remains in force until March 1, 2001. If you choose to accept the offer, please sign and return a copy of this offer letter on or before that date. Should you have any questions, the appropriate point of contact is the hiring manager, Leigh Bultema.

We are impressed with your background and experience, and we look forward to having you join the Robust Router team in June.

Sincerely,

Keith Hernandez
Managing Director
Product Management Group

xc: Leigh Bultema
       Human Resources

EXERCISE 12

The Employee Exit Interview

INTRODUCTION

This exercise involves a negotiation between the managing director of a small, privately held consulting firm and an employee who wishes to leave the firm for personal reasons. There are two main issues under discussion: (1) back pay for sick days, and (2) stocks that the employee wishes to sell back to the firm under its stock buyback plan.

This exercise was written by G. Richard Shell and is used with permission.

Newtown School Dispute

INTRODUCTION

In this simulation, you will play a member of either a school board or teachers' association bargaining team. You and the other members of your team, and the members of the other team, are negotiators representing constituencies. You will deal with a complex mix of bargaining issues; these issues have differing preference functions for each side. Finally, you will be subject to a variety of pressures during the negotiations.

BACKGROUND INFORMATION

It is now September 10, the opening day of the school year in Newtown. The contract between Newtown School District and the Newtown Teachers' Association expired on June 30. Since then, the Board of Education and representatives of the Teachers' Association have met on several occasions in an attempt to finalize a contract, but these attempts have not been successful.

Prior to June 30 and during the summer months, there was increasing talk among the membership of the Teachers' Association of the desirability of calling a strike if the contract was not finalized by opening day. However, the leadership of the Teachers' Association agreed, for the benefit of the community, to resume normal operations throughout the system (without a contract) on opening day *on a day-to-day basis*. This is in response to parent pressures to resume normal operations. Parents have been placing pressure on both teachers and the board to keep the schools operating, but voters have twice defeated referendums for increased taxes to cover unavoidable budgetary increases. Due to decreases in enrollments and income from local taxes and state and federal aid, as well as increased costs, maintenance of the school budget at par with the previous year would produce a 3.95 percent budgetary shortfall, which the board feels would begin to exhaust budgetary categories beginning in the coming April. Therefore, the board feels that programs and personnel must be cut while, at the same time, productivity (workload) of teachers must be increased if the system is to function effectively within its budgetary constraints to the end (June 30) of the current fiscal year. The district is mandated by the state law to provide 190 instructional days during the school year.

Revised version of material originally developed by Frank W. Masters. Used with permission.

The Board of Education is caught between the Teachers' Association and community pressure groups. The board believes that it must satisfy these pressure groups, while at the same time keeping the teachers on the job with a contract that is acceptable to the bargaining unit's membership. The board is concerned that if it fails to respond appropriately to community pressures for cost reductions, it may be removed. The board's primary objective, therefore, is to cut costs while retaining as many programs as possible. It hopes to do so through cutbacks in teaching personnel and increases in teacher productivity (workload). The board also wishes to eliminate certain existing agreements in order to increase productivity. In this connection, the board wants to negotiate a three-year contract that will "stabilize" the situation by creating orderly and predictable budgetary needs that will be less likely to be seen as excessive by various community groups. In contrast, the Teachers' Association wants to obtain a one-year contract to maintain flexibility.

The Teachers' Association also feels caught between community pressure groups, who want to avert a strike, and the board's apparent unwillingness to fight for increased budget allocations to run the system. The teachers feel the board has not faced up to the community's unwillingness to accept increased taxation to pay for education, and that the board is simply responding to community unwillingness by passing the burden along to teachers.

Newtown is a relatively settled and stable upper-middle-income community, with a strong interest in quality education, but is disinclined to increase its already burdensome tax rate. The Newtown School District consists of 12 schools: 9 elementary schools (K–8) and 3 senior high schools. The student population is 12,000, with 8,000 elementary and 4,000 high school students. The bargaining unit, representing 95 percent of all teachers, consists of 250 elementary teachers in all categories and 120 high school teachers in all categories.

Both sides wish to conclude an agreement to avert a strike. However, the Teachers' Association bargaining team is adamantly committed to improving the lot of its membership, and the board is just as committed to keeping its costs as low as possible. Nevertheless, each side feels it has some room to move on certain issues.

Newtown School District Teachers' Salary Schedule

Step	Amount	Last Year's Number of Teachers	Cost	This Year's Number of Teachers	Cost
1 (Entry)	$28,500	20	$ 570,000	0	$ 0
2	29,000	20	580,000	20	580,000
3	30,000	28	840,000	20	600,000
4	31,000	31	961,000	26	806,000
5	32,000	30	960,000	28	896,000
6	33,500	23	770,500	26	871,000
7	34,500	24	828,000	23	793,500
8	35,500	15	532,500	22	781,000
9	37,000	16	592,000	15	555,000
10	38,000	18	684,000	16	608,000
11	39,000	19	741,000	18	702,000
12	41,000	21	861,000	18	738,000
13	42,000	20	840,000	19	798,000
14	44,000	22	968,000	20	880,000
15	45,000	18	810,000	21	945,000
16	47,000	19	893,000	18	846,000
17	48,000	16	768,000	18	864,000
18	50,000	17	850,000	16	800,000
19	51,000	14	714,000	15	765,000
20	53,000	9	477,000	11	583,000
Totals		400	$15,240,000	370	$14,411,500

Current School Year, July 1–June 30, Projected Budget

1. Income
   1.1 Local tax (same rate as last year will continue,
       $5.85 per $1,000. No significant increase in
       property values expected.) $23,891,904
   1.2 State (formula yield per pupil will remain the
       same. Legislature may meet and possibly raise
       formula for next year.)   8,470,000
   1.3 Federal   1,369,500
       Total $33,731,404
   Note: This is a decrease of $851,716 (–2.46%) from the previous year's income.

2. Expenditures
   2.1 Administration
       2.1.1 Professional salaries $2,030,000
       2.1.2 Clerical/secretaries   497,000
       2.1.3 Other   470,000
       Total $2,997,000

Continued

Current School Year, July 1–June 30, Projected Budget *(concluded)*

2.2	Instruction		
	2.2.1	Teacher	
		Salaries	$14,411,500[a]
		Fringes	2,824,654
	2.2.2	Aides	2,047,000
	2.2.3	Materials/supplies	2,053,400[b]
		Total	$21,336,554
2.3	Plant operation/maintenance		
	2.3.1	Salaries	$2,312,400
	2.3.2	Utilities	2,023,000[c]
	2.3.3	Other	500,000[d]
		Total	$4,835,400
2.4	Fixed charges		
	2.4.1	Retirement	$2,111,200[e]
	2.4.2	Other	783,000
		Total	2,894,200
2.5	Debt service		$1,763,782[f]
2.6	Transportation		
	2.6.1	Salaries	$631,060
	2.6.2	Other	660,370[g]
		Total	$1,291,430
		Grand total	$35,118,366

Notes:
Total number of pupils = 12,000
Total number of teachers = 370
Per pupil expenditure = $2,927

[a]Thirty teachers did not return to the system due to either retirement or other reasons.
[b]Costs of materials and supplies will be up 46 percent over last year's cost based largely on the rising cost of paper.
[c]Cost of utilities is expected to increase by approximately 65 percent due to rate increases and overdue, deferred maintenance.
[d]Cost projections indicate a 13 percent increase in this category.
[e]Teacher retirement is up 5 percent due to increases mandated by the legislature to pay for new benefits. This was partially offset by attrition.
[f]Debt service is up 22 percent due to increased difficulty in floating bonds.
[g]Other transportation costs are up 31 percent due to increases in operating and maintenance costs.

Last School Year, July 1–June 30, Actual Audit

1. Income		
1.1	Local tax ($5.85 per $1,000 worth assessed real property. Assessment is at full value.)	$24,743,620
1.2	State (based on an equalization formula, improved during the last legislative session. Yielded $621.28 per pupil in administration last year.)	8,475,354
1.3	Federal	1,368,150
	Total	$34,587,124
2. Expenditures		
2.1	Administration	
	2.1.1 Professional salaries	$2,077,359
	2.1.2 Clerical/secretarial	513,529
	2.1.3 Other	454,972
	Total	$3,045,860
2.2	Instruction	
	2.2.1 Teachers	
	Salaries	$15,240,000
	Fringes	2,987,040
	2.2.2 Aides	2,277,451
	2.2.3 Materials/supplies	1,400,313
	Total	$21,904,804
2.3	Plant operations/maintenance	
	2.3.1 Salaries	$2,386,327
	2.3.2. Utilities	1,224,255
	2.3.3 Other	441,788
	Total	$4,052,370
2.4	Fixed charges	
	2.4.1 Retirement	$2,039,280
	2.4.2 Other	787,906
	Total	2,827,186
2.5	Debt service	$1,444,370
2.6	Transportation	
	2.6.1 Salaries	$729,878
	2.6.2 Other	582,656
	Total	$1,312,534
	Grand total	$34,587,124

Notes:

Total number of pupils = 12,800

Total number of teachers = 400

Per pupil expenditure = $2,702

Last year, the year of the audit on this page, there were 12,800 students in the public school system. The current year's projected enrollment is 12,000.

Initial Offer Form

Board of Education _____   Teachers' Association _____

Item	Bottom-Line Position	Desired Settlement	Opening Offer
Salary	_____	_____	_____
Reduction in staff	_____	_____	_____
Workload	_____	_____	_____
Evaluation of teachers	_____	_____	_____
Binding arbitration	_____	_____	_____
Benefits	_____	_____	_____

Final Settlement Form

Board of Education _____   Teachers' Association _____

Item	Settlement
Salary	_____
Reduction in staff	_____
Workload	_____
Evaluation of teachers	_____
Binding arbitration	_____
Benefits	_____

Bestbooks/Paige Turner

INTRODUCTION

This situation involves a negotiation between two representatives: one for an author, Paige Turner, and the other for a publishing company, Bestbooks. This is clearly a competitive situation, but some cooperation is also required. Your challenge is to get the best contract possible for your side.

Read the private material that your instructor has provided, and prepare your strategy for the negotiations. Each dyad of representatives will conduct its meeting trying to reach a new contract between Paige Turner and Bestbooks. When an agreement is reached, write down the settlement on the final settlement agreement form. Agreement must be reached on all eight issues in order for a final agreement to be struck.

Final Agreement Settlement Form

Issue	*Settlement Point*
Royalties	
Signing bonus	
Print runs	
Weeks of promotion	
Number of books	
Advance	
Countries distributed	
Book clubs	

Written in collaboration with Gregory Leck.

Elmwood Hospital Dispute

INTRODUCTION

In this exercise you will be dealing with a very complex negotiation situation. In contrast to earlier exercises, where there may have been a single opponent and one or two clearly defined issues, this simulation creates a negotiation between larger groups with less clearly defined issues—and perhaps stronger emotions. The key roles played by mediators are also introduced in this simulation.

BACKGROUND INFORMATION

The situation described below is a composite, with some data drawn from a number of similar disputes, and other information constructed specifically for this training exercise. The scenario is not to be interpreted as an account of any actual dispute. This simulation is one of several developed and tested by the Institute for Mediation and Conflict Resolution in New York, and adapted with permission by the Community Conflict Resolution Program.

Elmwood is a medium-sized, 450-bed private hospital in a southwestern city of approximately 600,000. It is well equipped for inpatient care and has an open-heart surgery team that is a matter of special pride to the board of trustees and the hospital's director. None of the trustees live in the hospital's immediate neighborhood, though some of their parents once did. Most of them are professionals or businesspeople, and one of their main functions as trustees is to help in fund-raising for the hospital.

Until 10 years ago, Elmwood was in the middle of a white, middle-class community. Now, however, it is on the eastern edge of an expanding low-income neighborhood, which has moved across the nearby expressway and is continuing to grow eastward. A good part of the low-income community is served by West Point Hospital, back on the western side of the expressway. People on the east, however, are turning to Elmwood. There are very few private physicians left in the Elmwood area, and the hospital, through its outpatient clinic, is the main source of medical care for the newer residents.

Adapted from an activity developed for the Institute of Mediation and Conflict Resolution, 1972.

These newer residents, who now make up approximately 65 percent of the service area, are a mix of relatively recent newcomers to the city, some from other parts of the United States and others from various foreign countries. Most are in low-paying service jobs. Many are on public assistance. Infant mortality is three times as high as in the rest of the city. Malnutrition is a problem, as are tuberculosis, lead poisoning, and other diseases associated with a slum environment. Most of these new residents cannot afford to be admitted to the hospital when sick and rely instead on outpatient treatment in what is now an overburdened facility at Elmwood.

Like most hospitals, Elmwood is in a financial squeeze. In addition, it has become increasingly difficult to attract new interns and residents and harder to retain present professionals. Although the hospital director is somewhat sympathetic to the medical care problems of the community, he sees his first priority as building the hospital's institutional strength by such measures as increasing intern- and resident-oriented research opportunities and adding facilities which would induce the staff to stay on rather than go elsewhere. He has apparently given some thought to sponsoring a neighborhood health center, but it has been put off by location problems. He has also heard about some heated conflicts over control of services at other hospitals in the state that took state and federal health grants. Right now, the director apparently intends to put these matters on the back burner until he gets the other things going.

Residents of the low-income community have organized a Concerned Community Coalition (CCC). The community has been asking the hospital to increase its almost nonexistent efforts in preventive medical care, improve and expand outpatient facilities, establish a satellite health center with day care facilities, and train a roving paraprofessional health team to administer diagnostic tests throughout the community. Elmwood is their neighborhood hospital and, to them, this is what a neighborhood hospital should be doing for the residents.

Two weeks ago, the CCC sent a letter to the director asking that the hospital initiate these efforts and requesting that he meet with them to discuss how the community and the hospital could work together. Although the community is deeply concerned about its medical problems and resents the fact that a city institution has not acted before this of its own volition, the letter was not unfriendly.

To date, the letter has not been answered.

Three days ago, the director and the chairman of the board announced the acquisition of a site about 15 blocks from the hospital on which it said it would build a heart research facility, a six-story nurses' residence, and a staff parking lot, with shuttle bus service to the hospital grounds.

On learning of the plans, the leaders and members of the CCC were incensed. They decided to sit in at the director's office until the hospital met their needs.

The day before yesterday, about 50 CCC supporters took over the director's office, vowing not to leave until the hospital agreed to meet the following demands:

1. Replacement of the board of trustees with a community-controlled board.
2. A 100 percent increase in outpatient facilities.
3. Establishment of a neighborhood health center and a day care facility on the newly acquired site.

4. Establishment of a preventive diagnostic mobile health team, consisting of neighborhood residents chosen by the CCC.
5. Replacement of the director by one chosen by the community.

While the hospital director indicated that he would be glad to meet with the group's leader to discuss the matters raised in its letter, he also stated quite forcefully that he considered the new demands arrogant and destructive and that, in any event, he would not meet under duress (i.e., as long as the sit-in continued).

The CCC said it would not leave until a meeting took place and the demands were accepted.

The sit-in began two days ago. This morning the hospital's lawyers moved to get an injunction against the sit-in. The CCC, aided by a legal services attorney, resisted.

The judge reserved decision, stating that to grant an injunction might only make the situation worse. He noted that both the hospital and the CCC would have to learn to live together for their own joint best interest. He therefore instructed the parties to meet to try to work out the problems between them, and has appointed a mediator to assist them. The mediator is a staff member of the city's Human Rights Commission, a unit of the municipal government.

At the judge's suggestion, the sides have agreed to meet with the mediator in the hospital library. The meeting has been scheduled for later today.

EXERCISE 16

The Power Game

INTRODUCTION

The concept of *power* is a complex, elusive, and almost paradoxical one. It is complex because there is a wide variety of definitions of what constitutes power, and how it is effectively accumulated and used. It is elusive because there seems to be very little consensus about the definitions, or the best way to describe power and talk about it in action. Finally, power is paradoxical because it doesn't always work the way it is expected to; sometimes those who seem to have the most power really have the least, while those who may appear to have the least power are most in control.

This simulation offers an opportunity to experience power in a wide variety of forms and styles. During the activity, you may become aware of your own power, and the power of others. Your objective will be to determine who has power, how power is being used, and how to use your own power in order for you to achieve your goals. This type of analysis is essential to effective negotiations when power relationships have not been well defined.

Adapted from exercise developed by Lee Bolman and Terrence Deal, Harvard Graduate School of Education, and published in *Exchange: the Organizational Behavior Teaching Journal*. Used with permission.

Coalition Bargaining

INTRODUCTION

The word *coalition* may be loosely defined as a group of individuals or subgroups who assemble to *collectively* exert influence on another group or individual. In an environment where there are many individuals, there are often many different points of view. Each individual views things differently, and each individual would like to have the "system" represent his or her views. In a dictatorship, the system usually represents the views of the dictator; but in a democratic environment, the views that are represented are usually those of a subgroup who have agreed to work together and collectively support one another's views in exchange for having a stronger impact on the system than each individual could have alone. Many of us are familiar with the work of coalitions. The patterns of influence in national politics, governments, and communities provide us with some excellent examples. Whether it be the coalitions that are formed along traditional party ties (Democrats or Republicans) or along the concerns of special interest groups (Common Cause, the Sierra Club, the AFL-CIO, the National Rifle Association, the National Organization for Women, or hundreds of others), each group is attempting to influence the direction of the larger system by effectively pooling its resources, working together as a team, and persuading those who have control of the current system.

Coalitions are a *common* phenomenon in organizations as well. The 1990s have seen a significant emergence of coalitions in the business sector. In earlier times, these may have been no more than cooperative agreements and licensing between companies, or efforts to work together to influence political and economic policy. But the demands for increased competitiveness in the 1990s have spawned a significant number of mergers, partnerships, and strategic alliances between companies, as they attempt to remain competitive in the international marketplace or move into new markets, product lines, and spin-off businesses. Organizations are a complex web of cross-pressures among various subgroups, each one striving to have its own priorities adopted as the primary

Adapted from Roy J. Lewicki and Joseph Litterer, *Negotiation: Readings, Exercises and Cases,* 1st ed., (Homewood, IL: Richard D. Irwin, 1985) and from Donald D. Bowen, Roy J. Lewicki, D. T. Hall, and F. Hall, *Experiences in Management and Organizational Behavior,* 2nd and 4th eds., (New York: John Wiley, 1996). Copyright © 1981 by John Wiley & Sons, Inc. Reprinted by permission of John Wiley & Sons, Inc.

goals of the total organization. Those who are initiating and leading these efforts must have excellent strategic skills to assess the "power dynamics" that each party brings to this game and sophisticated negotiating skills to forge and manage the relationships between the parties.

The purpose of this exercise is to help you understand the different sources and expressions of power, or *leverage,* that individuals and groups can use in multiparty decision making. In this exercise, you will see people use power and influence in a variety of different ways. See if you can determine what kind of power is being used, and how effective it is at gaining the other's compliance or cooperation. In addition, this exercise will help you explore the dynamics of trust and cooperation in a strongly competitive situation.

RULES OF THE GAME

Objective

To form a coalition with another team, in order to divide the stake. The coalition must also decide on a way of dividing the stake so as to satisfy both parties.

The Stake

Each team has *unequal* resources. In spite of the fact that you each contributed $1.00, you will receive a different stake, depending on the coalition you form. The following table should be filled in with information provided by the group leader (the individual payoffs are determined by the number of participants in the activity):

If an AB coalition forms, it will receive a stake of $_____.

If an AC coalition forms, it will receive a stake of $_____.

If a BC coalition forms, it will receive a stake of $_____.

The Strategy

Each team will meet separately to develop a strategy before the negotiations. You should also select a negotiator.

Rules for Negotiation

1. All members on a team may be present for negotiations; however, only the negotiator may speak.
2. Notes may be passed to negotiators if desired.
3. A team may change its negotiator between conversations.
4. At the termination of the game, the stake will be allocated only if a coalition has been formed.
5. Only one formal coalition is permitted.

6. A coalition will be recognized by the group leader only if (*a*) no two teams are permitted to receive the same amount of money, and (*b*) neither team in the coalition is allowed to receive zero.

7. If no coalition is reached, no funds are allocated.

8. Negotiations will be conducted in the following fixed order, and for the following fixed periods of time:

Order of Negotiation	Time for First Round of Negotiation	Time for Second and Third Rounds of Negotiation
Teams A and B	5 minutes	4 minutes
Teams A and C	5 minutes	4 minutes
Teams B and C	5 minutes	4 minutes

9. The team *not* in negotiations—that is, while the other two teams are negotiating—must leave the negotiation room. Other members of the companies who are *not* in the negotiating teams may not speak with any of the negotiators.

10. There cannot be any conversation between team members and observers at any time.

Valid Coalitions

1. A coalition will be recognized by the group leader only if (*a*) no teams are permitted to receive the same amount of money, and (*b*) neither team in the coalition is allowed to receive zero.

2. After negotiations, all three teams are given the opportunity to submit a written statement in the following form: "Team X has a coalition with Team Y, whereby Team X gets $*X.xx* and Y gets $*Y.yy*." When written statements meeting the above requirements from any two teams agree, a valid coalition has been formed.

END OF THE GAME

The group leader will ask each team to meet separately, and to submit a ballot stating the coalition that they believe was formed. A blank ballot may be distributed by the referee, or should be written on a blank sheet of paper, in the following format:

Team (your team) has a coalition with Team _____, whereby Team _____ receives _____ (dollars or points) and Team _____ receives _____ (dollars or points).

Put your own team letter (A, B, or C) on the ballot.

Each team brings its written statement to the negotiating room. The group leader will announce whether a valid coalition has been formed (two ballots agree); the money is then distributed as specified on the ballots. If a coalition has not been formed, or if the coalition that has formed does not use up all of the initial stake, a problem will arise as to what to do with the funds.

Jordan Electronics Company

INTRODUCTION

In this simulation, you will play the role of a committee member on the New Products Committee of Jordan Electronics Company. The committee oversees the development of all new products. In particular, it approves the research and design of all new products and authorizes the release from R&D to begin the manufacturing process. At the moment, the committee is faced with a decision: whether or not to authorize the manufacture of a new model of the Jordan Auto Correlator Model 36, known as the JAC 36. As a member of the committee working on this problem, you will face some of the complex and tense deliberations that often confront senior management. You will have several levels of concern on the committee: your own job and the problems you may have in getting it done, representing the members of your unit whom you supervise, and worrying about the welfare of Jordan Electronics as a whole.

BACKGROUND INFORMATION

Jordan Electronics is a manufacturing company that produces two major lines of scientific measuring instruments: instruments for use in scientific laboratories (laboratory products) and industrial instruments for use in manufacturing processes (industrial products). The management of Jordan Electronics is currently confronted with a problem in authorizing the manufacture of a redesigned model of the Jordan Auto Correlator Model 36 (JAC 36).

The original measuring instrument was designed over 20 years ago by the current president of Jordan Electronics. The original mission of the company was to manufacture the auto correlator and other scientific instruments. (An auto correlator is a device used to monitor flow processes by measuring data at different points in the process. It might measure the rate of flow of chemicals through a pipeline as well as changes in temperature of the chemical at two different points along a pipeline and then correlate that information.) At the time, the instrument revolutionized the market. The JAC 36 (so-called because it was launched on the president's 36th birthday) permitted a researcher to make correlations simultaneously on 256, 512, or 1,024 channels (monitoring levels). This device was initially picked up by physicists doing research in diffraction and gradually was adopted by scientists from other fields and by manufacturing firms using complex chemical processes. The JAC 36 became the market leader in its field and maintained that position for over 15 years.

The past few years have brought changes. First, new, faster, and more powerful microprocessors are now in existence. The use of a 16-bit microprocessor chip has been made obsolete by superior 32-bit microprocessor chips. A leading Japanese microprocessor manufacturing company has just introduced a new 64-bit chip that would certainly overshadow the speed and capacity of its predecessors. Using these components would reduce the size and weight of the completed machine and would permit greater portability. The existence of flat LCD screens would enable the manufacturing of a portable JAC 36 unit that would resemble the very popular laptop computers. Although the hardware aspect was technically quite feasible, such a unit would be successful only if a special type of software was developed that would enable the smaller units to emulate the functions of the larger ones. Changeover to this manufacturing process is costly, but once the bugs are worked out, manufacturing cost per unit could be cut significantly.

Second, although the JAC 36 holds a strong share of the market, Jordan's competitors have been nibbling away at that market share by adding a variety of new features to their instruments. One addition has been to provide voice-activated command entry that enables one to control the auto correlator using verbal commands. This frees the user to perform other manual functions during the verbal command process. A second feature was the implementation of optical coupling. Although optical devices did not enhance the capacity or speed of the units, they did reduce the amount of heat that was emitted by the auto correlator. This aspect was appreciated by those who had to use the units in strict laboratory conditions. Although it was not perceived to be a widespread problem, the erratic behavior of some microprocessors was sometimes attributed to the excess heat generated by units that did not use optical coupling. Competing products with these features sell for $3,000 to $5,000 more than the present JAC 36. Finally, as mentioned above, some competitors are rumored to be working on a laptop design that would enhance the portability of such units. While the JAC 36 typically is used as a laboratory instrument, scientists now seem to want the flexibility of a lighter machine for field experiments and mobile laboratories. Lightness and ease of movement are even more attractive in industrial applications. Although use of the new technologies requires some change in the basic circuit design, it requires extensive change in the physical design of the instrument and in the manufacturing methods.

Six months ago, the sales vice president made a very strong pitch to management to encourage the production of a JAC 36 that incorporated reduced size, voice-activated control, and optical-coupling features. Jordan's sales representatives are becoming increasingly embarrassed by customer complaints about the outdated nature of the JAC 36 and their requests for a newer version similar to the competition. The sales vice president said there should be two versions of the JAC sometime in the future, a portable machine and a stationary one, but that the portable unit was clearly the second priority because strong demand was not anticipated for several years.

In response to this request, the president requested an intensive study of the market for an updated JAC 36 and an estimate for the manufacturing costs. The market study, conducted by an independent marketing research firm, reported that there was still a very strong market for the current JAC 36. In fact, many of the companies that had purchased auto correlators from competitors—machines that included the voice-activated command features—reported that they rarely used these features. In other words, many of the newer machines on the market were "overdesigned" for their customers' actual use. Market research on the portable versus nonportable units was inconclusive: Some purchasers clearly wanted it, but the overall demand for portability was not strong.

Cost estimates for an updated JAC 36 were developed by the senior electrical engineer, the vice president of manufacturing, and an electronics designer in the R&D department. They calculated that there would be a very high cost in changeover to the more advanced microprocessors as well as the associated costs in adapting the software used on the present JACs. Adding the voice-activated control mechanism to the present manual controls was the most simple and least costly change. Manufacturing the units with optical couplers would involve considerable redesign of the cabinet and manufacturing methods and would cost considerably less than if the new machine was adapted to the new microprocessors. Moreover, there were a few nagging technical problems in the electronic design of a portable unit; the longer it took to work these problems out, the higher the R&D costs would go and the longer it would take to put the portable JAC 36 on the market.

The president reviewed all of this information and decided that in spite of these reports, Jordan needed to come out with a new JAC 36 model, if only to satisfy the need to be competitive with other machines. Since the old standard JAC 36 units were holding their market share and since the development of the portable model was plagued with problems, the president decided to proceed with a redesign of the old JAC 36 unit that would include both the voice-activated command and optical coupling features. At the meeting announcing the decision, the president stressed that the new model should maintain Jordan's reputation for providing flexible, high-quality equipment. The sales vice president commented that the new JAC 36 should be offered at about the same price as the present model. Since the revised model was not designed to be portable, weight was not a problem for the new machine. The research and development department, after reviewing the design specifications, said the development work could probably be done in three to four months.

The research and development department finished the development work in early January. Production was sent the information it needed to set production methods and to estimate costs. After talking it over with his factory superintendent, the vice president of production described the production methods and costs in detail in a memorandum to the president. These estimates were considerably higher than anticipated. The current JAC 36 sold for $16,000, but the vice president of production estimated that it would be impossible to sell the new model for less than $20,000. The president and vice president of sales were very upset by this memorandum. They asked the vice president of production to review all of the figures and distribute them to all members of the New Products Committee, who would then make the decision whether to start manufacturing the revised JAC 36. It is now early March, and the meeting of the New Products Committee is about to occur. The revised figures from the vice president of production were not substantially different from the original estimates. The basic costs are presented in Exhibit 1. The committee has a real problem on its hands. In addition, the president, who normally chairs the meeting, will not be present because of a minor surgical procedure; the vice president of finance will chair the meeting. The purpose of this meeting is to determine if the revised JAC 36 should be put into production and, if so, at what price it should be marketed. In attendance will be

Vice president of finance (chair).

Director of research and development.

Vice president of sales.

Vice president of production.

Senior electrical engineer.

EXHIBIT 1   Jordan Electronics Company Cost Structures

	Present Cost Structure JAC 36	Estimated Cost Structure Revised JAC 36
Factory price	$16,000	$20,000
Costs		
Direct labor	1,650	2,300
Raw materials	6,700	8,500
Factory overhead	3,700	5,200
Margin	3,950	4,000

	Variance Report Last Year JAC 36
Labor	
Metal shop	–2%
Electronics components	+8%
Other components	N.C.
Assembly	+5%
Test	+10%
Materials	
Metal	–3%
Electronics	+10%
Overhead	–11%

EXERCISE 19

Third-Party Conflict Resolution

INTRODUCTION

In addition to being involved in their own conflicts, managers are often called upon to intervene and to settle conflicts between other people. The two activities in this section are designed to explore how third parties may enter conflicts for the purpose of resolving them, and to practice one very effective approach to intervention. In the first activity, you will read about a manager who has a problem deciding how to intervene in a dispute, and you will discuss this case in class. Part 2 of this exercise contains a Mediation Guide, which will be useful in completing the role-playing activity in Part 3, in which some of you will attempt to resolve a managerial dispute.

PART 1

THE SEATCOR MANUFACTURING COMPANY

You are senior vice president of operations and chief operating officer of Seatcor, a major producer of office furniture. Joe Gibbons, your subordinate, is vice president and general manager of your largest desk assembly plant. Joe has been with Seatcor for 38 years and is two years away from retirement. He worked his way up through the ranks to his present position and has successfully operated his division for five years with a marginally competent staff. You are a long-standing personal friend of Joe's and respect him a great deal. However, you have always had an uneasy feeling that Joe has surrounded himself with minimally competent people by his own choice. In some ways, you think he feels threatened by talented assistants.

Last week you were having lunch with Charles Stewart, assistant vice president and Joe's second in command. Upon your questioning, it became clear that he and Joe were engaged in a debilitating feud. Charles was hired last year, largely at your insistence. You had been concerned for some time about who was going to replace Joe when he retired, especially given the lack of really capable managerial talent on Joe's staff.

Developed by Roy J. Lewicki. "The Mediation Guide" developed by Larry Ray, American Bar Association, and Robert Helm, Oklahoma State University. "The Seatcor Manufacturing Company" and "The Summer Interns" developed by Blair Sheppard, Duke Corporate Education. Used with permission.

Thus, you prodded Joe to hire your preferred candidate—Charles Stewart. Charles is relatively young, 39, extremely tenacious and bright, and a well-trained business school graduate. From all reports he is doing a good job in his new position.

Your concern centers on a topic that arose at the end of your lunch. Charles indicated that Joe Gibbons is in the process of completing a five-year plan for his plant. This plan is to serve as the basis for several major plant reinvestment and reorganization decisions that would be proposed to senior management. According to Charles, Joe Gibbons has not included Charles in the planning process at all. You had to leave lunch quickly and were unable to get much more information from Charles. However, he did admit that he was extremely disturbed by this exclusion and that his distress was influencing his work and probably his relationship with Joe.

You consider this a very serious problem. Charles will probably have to live with the results of any major decisions about the plant. More important, Joe's support is essential if Charles is to properly grow into his present and/or future job. Joe, on the other hand, runs a good ship and you do not want to upset him or undermine his authority. Moreover, you know Joe has good judgment; thus, he may have a good reason for what he is doing.

How would you proceed to handle this issue?

PART 2

THE MEDIATION GUIDE

This section presents a series of steps for effectively conducting a mediation. You may use this checklist and the flowchart depicted in Exhibit 1.

Step 1: Stabilize the Setting

Parties often bring some strong feelings of anger and frustration into mediation. These feelings can prevent them from talking productively about their dispute. You, as mediator, will try to gain their trust for you and for the mediation process. Stabilize the setting by being polite; show that you are in control and that you are neutral. This step helps the parties feel comfortable, so they can speak freely about their complaints, and safe, so they can air their feelings.

1. _____ Greet the parties.
2. _____ Indicate where each of them is to sit.
3. _____ Identify yourself and each party, by name.
4. _____ Offer water, paper and pencil, and patience.
5. _____ State the purpose of mediation.
6. _____ Confirm your neutrality.
7. _____ Get their commitment to proceed.
8. _____ Get their commitment that only one party at a time will speak.
9. _____ Get their commitment to speak directly to you.
10. _____ Use calming techniques as needed.

Step 2: Help the Parties Communicate

Once the setting is stable and the parties seem to trust you and the mediation process, you can begin to carefully build trust between them. Both must make statements about what has happened. Each will use these statements to air negative feelings. They may express anger, make accusations, and show frustration in other ways. But, with your help, this mutual ventilation lets them hear each other's side of the story, perhaps for the first time. It can help calm their emotions, and can build a basis for trust between them.

1. _____ Explain the rationale for who speaks first.
2. _____ Reassure them that both will speak without interruption, for as long as necessary.
3. _____ Ask the first speaker to tell what has happened.
   a. _____ Take notes.
   b. _____ Respond actively; restate and echo what is said.
   c. _____ Calm the parties as needed.
   d. _____ Clarify, with open or closed questions, or with restatements.
   e. _____ Focus the narration on the issues in the dispute.
   f. _____ Summarize, eliminating all disparaging references.
   g. _____ Check to see that you understand the story.
   h. _____ Thank this party for speaking, the other for listening quietly.
4. _____ Ask the second speaker to tell what has happened.
   a. _____ Take notes.
   b. _____ Respond actively; restate and echo what is said.
   c. _____ Calm the parties as needed.
   d. _____ Clarify, with open or closed questions, or with restatements.
   e. _____ Focus the narration on the issues in the dispute.
   f. _____ Summarize, eliminating all disparaging references.
   g. _____ Check to see that you understand the story.
   h. _____ Thank this party for speaking, the other for listening quietly.
5. _____ Ask each party, in turn, to help clarify the major issues to be resolved.
6. _____ Inquire into basic issues, probing to see if something instead may be at the root of the complaints.
7. _____ Define the problem by restating and summarizing.
8. _____ Conduct private meetings, if needed (explain what will happen during and after the private meetings).
9. _____ Summarize areas of agreement and disagreement.
10. _____ Help the parties set priorities on the issues and demands.

Step 3: Help the Parties Negotiate

Cooperativeness is needed for negotiations that lead to agreement. Cooperation requires a stable setting, to control disruptions, and exchanges of information, to develop mutual trust. With these conditions, the parties may be willing to cooperate, but still feel driven to compete. You can press for cooperative initiatives by patiently helping them to explore alternative solutions, and by directing attention to their progress.

1. _____ Ask each party to list alternative possibilities for a settlement.
2. _____ Restate and summarize each alternative.
3. _____ Check with each party on the workability of each alternative.
4. _____ Restate whether the alternative is workable.
5. _____ In an impasse, suggest the general form of other alternatives.
6. _____ Note the amount of progress already made, to show that success is likely.
7. _____ If the impasse continues, suggest a break or a second mediation session.
8. _____ Encourage them to select the alternative that appears to be workable.
9. _____ Increase their understanding by rephrasing the alternative.
10. _____ Help them plan a course of action to implement the alternative.

Step 4: Clarify Their Agreement

Mediation should change each party's attitude toward the other. When both have shown their commitment, through a joint declaration of agreement, each will support the agreement more strongly. For a settlement that lasts, each component of the parties' attitudes toward each other—their thinking, feeling, and acting—will have changed. Not only will they now *act* differently toward each other, but they are likely to *feel* differently, more positively, about each other and to *think* of their relationship in new ways.

1. _____ Summarize the agreement terms.
2. _____ Recheck with each party his or her understanding of the agreement.
3. _____ Ask whether other issues need to be discussed.
4. _____ Help them specify the terms of their agreement.
5. _____ State each person's role in the agreement.
6. _____ Recheck with each party on when he or she is to do certain things, where, and how.
7. _____ Explain the process of follow-up.
8. _____ Establish a time for follow-up with each party.
9. _____ Emphasize that the agreement is theirs, not yours.
10. _____ Congratulate the parties on their reasonableness and on the workability of their resolution.

EXHIBIT 1   Steps in a Mediation Process

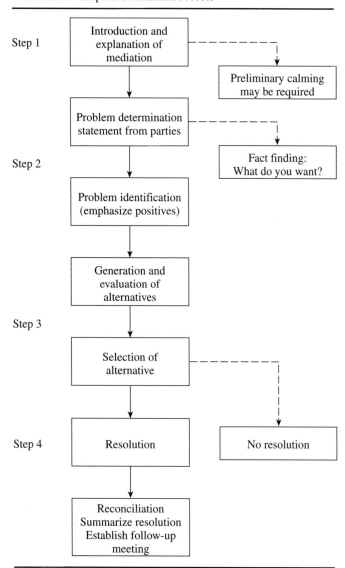

The Connecticut Valley School

INTRODUCTION

In this situation you must allocate a limited capital budget among seven competing projects. Three parties are involved in the negotiation: the headmaster, the faculty budget committee, and the board of trustees. While the issues in this exercise appear straightforward, the parties do not necessarily perceive the budget process in the same manner.

Read the Background Information section for the Connecticut Valley School (below); then read the role information that the instructor has provided for you. Participants who have been assigned to the same team (faculty budget committee, board of trustees, headmaster) will meet separately to decide how to manage the upcoming meeting.

The different parties will meet together to negotiate an agreement about the capital projects that will be funded. The chairperson of the board of trustees will chair this meeting. Participants will leave this meeting with an agreement about the priority of the capital spending projects. If no agreement is reached then each team should have a record of their final rankings and where they are willing to make further concessions.

BACKGROUND INFORMATION

The Connecticut Valley School (CVS) is a private boarding school in Massachusetts. Headmaster John Loring has just submitted his annual recommendations for capital spending to the board of trustees. Capital spending will be funded from two sources, new debt and the accumulated interest on the school's endowment. Since the school is approaching its debt capacity and trustees are committed not to draw on the principal of the endowment, the school can afford to spend only $450,000 to $500,000 on capital improvements over the next year. The seven major projects under consideration are described briefly below.

1. *Swimming Pool*

   Cost: $320,000   Expected life: 15 years

   Currently the school rents a local facility for $30,000 per year. In addition, the school pays $5,000 per year to bus students to the facility. If the school owned its own pool, it could rent out pool time to local organizations for $15,000 per year. The headmaster feels that more students would use the pool if it were located on campus.

Written by Peter Nye, University of Washington at Bothell. Used with permission.

2. *Buses*

Cost: $135,000 (3 buses)   Expected life: 6 years
Salvage value: Nil

CVS owns two campuses several miles apart. A private bus company transports students between campuses at a cost of $90,000 per year. If the school owns and operates its own buses, it will incur $40,000 in operating expenses each year.

3. *New Roof for Hockey Rink*

Cost: $30,000

A new roof is essential to prevent further damage to the rink and to the arena's infrastructure. The project could be delayed one year; but due to the additional damage that would result, total repair costs would jump to $60,000.

4. *Wood Chip Heating System*

Cost: $400,000   Expected life: 15 years

Cold New England winters and the high cost of fuel oil have been draining the school's operating funds. This new heating system could save the school between $70,000 and $80,000 per year over the next 15 years.

5. *Renovation of Fine Arts Building*

Cost: $150,000

The faculty and trustees agree that an improved fine arts program is critical to the school's liberal arts mission. The renovated fine arts building would include a photography lab, a pottery shop, and art studios, as well as a small gallery. The building would not generate any incremental revenues or cost savings. However, a wealthy benefactor (after whom the building would be named) has offered to contribute $75,000 to subsidize the project. In addition, the facility would provide some marketing benefits, as a strong arts program attracts quality students.

6. *Renovations to Women's Locker Room*

Cost: $20,000

The women's locker room has not been renovated since it was built 33 years ago for visiting men's teams. Many of the women have complained that the facility is dirty, depressing, and overcrowded. Some women refuse to use the facility. The headmaster insists that these complaints are unfounded. The renovations would generate no incremental revenues or cost savings.

7. *Upgrading the Computer Lab*

Cost: $60,000

Over the past eight years computer equipment has been purchased on a piecemeal basis with surplus operating funds. To support curricular goals, the school needs state-of-the-art computers and more workstations. The director of computing has proposed that the equipment be upgraded over three years. The first stage of this plan would require spending $60,000 on personal computers in the coming year. An additional $80,000 would be spent over the following two years.

The school uses a 12 percent annual discount rate to evaluate all cost-saving investment projects.

Since not all of these projects can be undertaken, they must be prioritized. In his report to the trustees, Headmaster Loring ranked the six projects as follows:

1. Swimming pool $320,000
2. Hockey rink roof $30,000
3. Buses $135,000
4. Heating system $400,000
5. Fine arts building $75,000
6. Women's locker room $20,000
7. Computer lab $60,000

He recommended that this year's capital funds be spent on the construction of a swimming pool, repairs to the roof of the hockey rink, and the purchase of three buses. These projects would require a total expenditure of $485,000. Loring's rankings were based on his subjective evaluation of cost/benefit trade-offs.

While the trustees must make the final decision, they have solicited advice from the faculty. The faculty is in touch with the day-to-day operations of the school and with the needs of the students. In addition, many faculty members feel that they were closed out of the decision process last year and that the ultimate allocation of funds was inconsistent with the school's objectives. In an attempt to improve the decision process, the trustees appointed a faculty budget committee to advise them on capital spending priorities. A meeting of the trustees, the budget committee, and the headmaster has been scheduled. The purpose of this meeting is to prioritize capital spending projects. It is expected to be a lively and productive session.

EXERCISE 21

Alpha–Beta

INTRODUCTION

In this situation you will negotiate a possible robot manufacturing and marketing agreement with another company. You will be a member of a team that represents either an electrical company in the nation of Alpha, or a manufacturer of electrical machinery in the nation of Beta.

BACKGROUND INFORMATION

Alpha

Alpha Inc. is a large, broadly diversified electrical company based in the nation of Alpha. The company is one of the leading makers of numerical control equipment and plans to become a leader in equipping the "factory of the future." It has recently spent hundreds of millions of dollars putting together a collection of factory automation capabilities ranging from robotics to computer-aided design and manufacturing. Alpha Inc. has been acquiring companies, investing heavily in new plants, and spending considerable sums on product development. Innovative robots, some equipped with vision, are being developed, but they have been a bit slow in making their way out of the company's R&D labs. To meet its objective of quickly becoming a major worldwide, full-service supplier of automation systems, Alpha Inc. has found it necessary to tie up, in various ways, with foreign firms that are further up the robotics learning curve.

Robotics in the Nation of Alpha

There are 30 robot manufacturers in Alpha, and big computer and auto firms have recently been entering the business. During 1980, use and production of robots in Alpha was only about 33 percent of what it was in the nation of Beta. One survey reported 4,370 robots in use in Alpha in 1980, mainly in the auto and foundry-type industries, and 1,269 produced. Robot sales in 1980 were estimated at $92 million, with a significant share accounted for by imports. The industrial automation market as a whole is growing at well over 20 percent a year, and the robotics portion of it is expected to become a $2-billion-a-year domestic market by 1990.

This exercise was first developed by Thomas N. Gladwin in 1984, and is copyrighted 1990–91 by Thomas N. Gladwin, Stephen E. Weiss, and Allen J. Zerkin. Used with permission.

Beta

Beta Inc. is the leading manufacturer of integrated electrical machinery in the nation of Beta. Run by scientists since its founding, the company is Beta's most research-oriented corporation: it employs over 9,000 researchers, and its R&D spending equals 5.9 percent of corporate sales. Beta Inc. started producing robots only in 1979 but plans within a few years to become the world's largest robot producer. To do so, it must double its manufacturing capacity and strongly push exports (to date, nearly all of its output has been sold at home). The company's deep commitment to robotics is reflected in the recent formation of a 500-man technical task force to develop a universal assembly robot with both visual and tactile sensors. Beta Inc. expects to be using the new robots for some 60 percent of its in-house assembly operations within three years.

Robotics in the Nation of Beta

Beta Inc. is only 1 of 150 companies making or selling robots in Beta, a nation with "robot fever" and a government that has declared automation a national goal. An estimated 12,000 to 14,000 programmable robots are already on the job in the nation, representing 59 percent of those in use worldwide. In 1980, Betan firms churned out nearly $400 million worth of robots (approximately 3,200 units, or 50 percent of world production). The nation exported only 2.5 percent of its production and imported less than 5 percent of its robots. Industry analysts see robot production in Beta rising to $2 billion in 1985 and to $5 billion in 1990. Over the past five months, Alpha Inc. and Beta Inc. have held preliminary negotiations over a possible robot manufacturing and marketing tie-up. The two companies have reached the following tentative agreement:

1. The tie-up over seven years will proceed in two phases: (*a*) in years 1–4, Beta will supply Alpha with fully assembled Beta Inc. robots for sale under Alpha's brand name; (*b*) in years 5–7, Alpha will begin producing these robots themselves in Alpha, using Beta technology and key components.

2. The tie-up will focus on the robots that Beta Inc. currently has on the market.

3. The agreement will be nonexclusive; that is, Beta Inc. will be allowed to enter the Alphan market directly at any time and allowed to tie up with other Alphan firms.

The two companies' negotiation teams are now scheduled to meet for discussion of remaining issues. They include the following:

1. The number of different models involved.

2. The quantity of Beta Inc. units to be imported and/or produced under license by Alpha during each year.

3. The unit price to be paid to Beta.

4. Access to Alpha's vision technology.

5. The royalty rate to be paid to Beta.

The New House Negotiation

INTRODUCTION

Many negotiations involve only two parties—a buyer and a seller. However, there are many other negotiations in which the parties are represented by agents. An agent is a person who is paid to negotiate on behalf of the buyer or seller and usually collects some fee or commission based on these services.

The purpose of this negotiation is to gain experience by negotiating through agents. The negotiation simulates the sale and purchase of a piece of real estate, a transaction which is normally conducted through agents. Some of you will play the role of agents; others will play the role of buyers and sellers. This experience should provide a simple but rich context in which to observe the ways that negotiation can very quickly become highly complex.

The House

The property in question is a three-bedroom, two-bath, one-story house. It was listed in the local real estate multiple listings service two weeks ago at $200,000. The house has the following features:

- 2,100 square feet.
- Six years old (one owner prior to current owner).
- Two-car garage.
- Contemporary styling (back wall of house is basically all glass, with sliding draperies).
- Half-acre lot (no flooding problems).
- Brick exterior.
- Built-in range, dishwasher, garbage disposal, and microwave.
- Electric cooling and gas heat.

This simulation was developed by Conrad Jackson, College of Administrative Science, the University of Alabama at Huntsville. Adapted and used with permission.

EXHIBIT 1

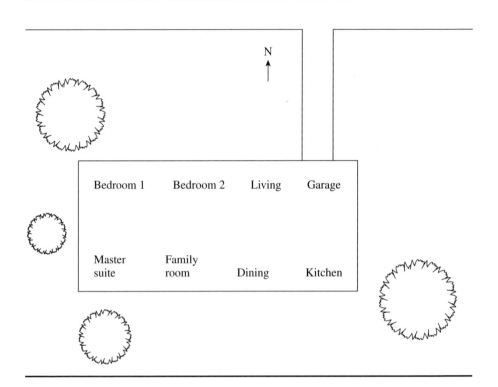

- Fireplace and ceiling fan in the family room.
- No fence.
- Assumable FHA loan.

EXERCISE 23

Eurotechnologies, Inc.

INTRODUCTION

This role-play brings three additional new features to your negotiating experience. First, the context of this negotiation is *inside* an organization. In this scenario, you will be asked to represent one of two groups: a management team or a group of scientists who are protesting against a major management decision. Second, this simulation is considerably less structured than others, in that there is a great deal more flexibility and opportunity for creative solutions. Finally, the negotiation occurs in an international context, which may provide a new experience for many of you. We hope you find this simulation an interesting negotiating opportunity.

EUROTECHNOLOGIES, INC., GENERAL INFORMATION

Eurotechnologies, Inc. (ETI), is a Munich-area firm that employs about 900 people. It is a high-technology division of Mentor, whose corporate offices are in Paris. ETI's primary product is an elaborate bioelectronic detection system developed and manufactured under contract with a consortium of European governments. This system is used for detecting various types of life forms through radar-like procedures. Because of the highly classified nature of the manufacturing process and the need for manufacturing to occur in a relatively pollution-free environment, ETI has chosen to separate its manufacturing facilities from its main offices.

The manufacturing facilities are located in a remote area near Wasserburg, Germany, and approximately 64 kilometers from downtown Munich. ETI has purchased several hundred acres of land that provide the adequate security and air quality for manufacturing and full-scale test operations. While it is a picturesque area far away from the congestion of the Munich area, it is not without its faults. Access to the plant requires travel over 16 kilometers of poor locally maintained road; manufacturing employees constantly complain of worn brakes, tire wear, and strain on their cars. The road is often rain-slicked, muddy, and treacherous in the winter. Most of the 630 workers (480 hourly, 140 staff, and 10 R&D personnel who run the test facility) employed in this plant commute from a 45–60 kilometer

---

This role play is developed by Robert Reinheimer, adapted from a scenario developed by Robert Reinheimer and Roy Lewicki. Used with permission. The case and role-play have been prepared for class discussion rather than to illustrate effective or ineffective handling of an administrative situation.

radius over this road into the plant; traffic congestion, particularly around the times of shift changes, makes travel and access a highly undesirable aspect of working for this plant.

The manufacturing facility itself is not air-conditioned and hence frequently hot in the summer and stuffy in the winter. The closest town, Wasserburg, is 16 kilometers away. The Wasserburg plant has a cafeteria, but the food is cooked elsewhere and reheated at the plant. The menu is limited and expensive.

There are two groups of support personnel at Wasserburg. One group (approximately 110 employees) is directly connected with the manufacturing operations as supervisors, shipping and receiving, plant operation and maintenance, stock and inventory, clerical, and so on. The remainder (30 employees) are professional engineers responsible for providing technical support and quality maintenance for manufacturing. Facilities for this support staff are somewhat better than for hourly employees; office space and lighting are adequate and the building is air-conditioned. There is no separate cafeteria, and no place to entertain visitors; staff alternate between bringing their lunch, occasionally purchasing the cafeteria food and taking it back to their offices to eat, or car-pooling for the 20-minute drive down to Wasserburg. Dissatisfaction and low morale among the professional staff are rampant.

The Downtown Location

The executive staff offices, the government liaison offices, and the research and development laboratory are located in suburban Munich, just north of the city center. Also, there are test facilities on a one-tenth scale for ongoing research and development programs. All administrative services are conducted from here: employment, payroll, security, data processing and system analysis, and research engineering and design. The buildings are spacious, clean and air-conditioned, and boast two cafeterias: one for hourly workers and one for research personnel and executive officers. Employees can also go out for lunch, and many good restaurants are nearby. Working hours are more flexible, and the environment is more relaxed with less visible pressure. While the normal starting time is 8:00 A.M., professional staff drift in as late as 9:30 and often leave early in the afternoon; working at home is frequent. On the other hand, when deadlines or schedules have to be met, it is not unusual to find them working 60 hours a week. The work environment is more informal and displays casualness similar to a university setting.

As the majority of the Munich-based employees are professional people, they consider themselves a cut above the manufacturing and technical service employees at Wasserburg. While they will acknowledge the value of the revenue generated by Wasserburg, they are convinced that it is really the Munich area group that carries the company. Without their high-level technical advances, ETI would not have the outside reputation it has for premium-quality products. Inside ETI, however, the rivalries between various engineering and scientific personnel led to the creation of "domains" or "kingdoms." The primary split is between Wasserburg and Munich, and over the years it has fostered extensive duplication of efforts. Each group (testing, maintenance, etc.) has been able to procure tools and equipment for itself that normally would be shared if the two locations were closer. The Munich technical divisions have even subcontracted certain testing and development operations to suppliers who are competitors of ETI, due to their basic lack of respect for in-house capabilities at Wasserburg and the red tape and expense of having to work through their own planning and scheduling staffs.

Additionally, the Munich R&D group has taken consulting contracts from other firms and has consistently failed to involve any Wasserburg personnel in those projects.

The Contract Bidding History

In recent years, ETI has put out numerous competitive bids for civilian and military contracts, but few projects have been forthcoming. Analysis of failures revealed that rejections have been due to excessive cost estimates rather than weak technical capabilities. ETI is considered to be one of the top 10 quality-based manufacturing firms of its kind on the continent. However, its overhead costs are prohibitive. The cost of operating two sites, duplication of effort, overstaffing, and a blurring of goals for corporate growth and expansion have caused the overhead rate to be 30–40 percent higher than that of competitors. For example, the United Kingdom had recently issued a request for bids on the development of a new bioelectronic system, similar to ETI's current product. The development contract alone was worth DM 24.45 million; and production of these units would be worth DM 146.700 million. ETI was positive it would get the contract. However, when the government evaluated the bids from five different companies, ETI came in first in the technical aspect of the bidding and fifth in the cost aspect; the company did not get the contract.

The Alternatives

Top management's reaction to this setback was to propose a 20 percent cost reduction plan. Many high-salaried technical and engineering personnel were destined to be laid off. The housecleaning was overdue; some deadwood and duplication of effort was eliminated. But after six months, it became a hard, cold fact that further reductions in overhead costs would be necessary in order to continue to be competitive.

ETI owned the Munich-area facility, and top management believed the most obvious way to achieve this reduction was to close it, move all of the Munich-area employees to the Wasserburg facility, and to lease out the vacated buildings. The leases would be excellent tax shelters and an additional source of revenue. This consolidation was expected to reduce much of the duplication of effort, as well as provide better coordination on existing and future projects.

In thinking through how the proposed move might be accomplished, top management considered features designed to make it as palatable as possible. First, they proposed to spread the relocations over one full year. Each employee could either accept the move or reject it and accept termination from the company. ETI management would go as far as possible with those employees who rejected the relocation. They would offer a liberal time-off policy to those involved so the employee could seek other employment, would provide a special bonus of one month's salary for relocation expenses, would notify other companies in the Munich area of the names and résumés of terminating employees, and set up employment interviews with these companies. They also would notify all placement agencies in the area and pay all placement agency fees.

It was clear to management that even with the generous plan they had outlined, the move would be hugely painful for the organization and would represent some very real costs in terms of overall effectiveness. Yet they saw no alternative but to proceed with studying the proposed consolidation.

When the details of the proposal leaked, the plan was met with a massive reaction of hostility and despair. Almost all the Munich-area professional employees felt that a transfer to Wasserburg would mean a sharp decline in status with their peers in similar industries. Most had their homes close to Munich, and the drive to Wasserburg would increase their commuting time and cause wear and tear on their automobiles. The company thus knew that a certain percentage of employees would terminate because of the relocation. It estimated that a "safe level" of termination was 22 percent; if it reached 35 percent in any occupational group, it could be considered a critical problem. Management informally surveyed employees and found that among the administrative staff, the termination rate was likely to be near 25 percent.

The strongest reaction came from the company's research and development staff. They had grown used to having their laboratory and test facilities in the Munich area and drew heavily on informal relationships with faculty at the area's most prestigious universities for ideas and information. Their view was that being forced to move to Wasserburg, in addition to being undesirable, would cripple their ability to function effectively because of their loss of contact with other professionals. Of the 11 members of the research and development staff, only two expressed a willingness to consider the move to Wasserburg. The others claimed they would avail themselves of the many other employment opportunities their specialties commanded. They formally expressed their resistance in a letter to the company president (Exhibit 1).

The letter was written by a committee of R&D personnel formed to represent the group's interests regarding the proposed move. In the letter, they outlined their concerns and volunteered to take 20 percent salary cuts to contribute to the reduction of overhead costs. This reduction would total approximately DM 366,750.

The committee members consisted of the following six employees:

- Axle Pederson, age 52. Oldest member of the group, but only one year at ETI. Previously worked with several environmental engineering firms in the Munich area. Moved to ETI because of the quality of the other people in the research group and because of interest in the projects that were being considered.

- Thomas Hoffmann, age 49. Most senior member of the ETI group (24 years), and a likely candidate to be the next vice president of research and development. Lived near Munich all his life, and currently lives a block away from Pieter Jensen, the president.

- Manfred Berkowitz, age 42. Fifteen years with ETI, and the most professionally aggressive of the group. Most active in research with high professional visibility.

- Volker Schmidt, age 47. Twenty-two years with ETI. Also very professionally active, second to Berkowitz. Schmidt has spent a number of years developing professional contacts in the Munich area and has been the most articulate in defending the richness of the professional stimulation to be derived from the area.

- Pieter van der Velden, age 36. Five years with ETI. Worked for two years at Wasserburg before being assigned to the Munich group. A definite up and comer in this group.

- Michael Blank, age 32. Four years with ETI. Strong research orientation, a close collaborator with Berkowitz on several professional papers. Berkowitz also served as a mentor to Blank while Blank was completing his PhD at Heidelberg University.

EXHIBIT 1

Mr. Pieter Jensen, President
Eurotechnologies, Inc.
300 Reinstrasse
Munich, Germany

Dear Mr. Jensen:

Our committee, representing your research and development personnel, wishes to express its serious concern about the recent events which have affected our company. We believe that ETI's survival depends on our retaining our technical excellence. We are dismayed that you and your management team seem to be contemplating actions that could cripple that capability.

We have all been shocked by our recent loss of contracts. However, it is critical for you to note that we have never been faulted for our technical expertise. It is our cost structure that prevents us from winning these bids. But an action which addresses the cost problem, while destroying our ability to compete technically, simply trades one problem for a more disastrous one. Closing the Munich facility and consolidating operations at Wasserburg creates just such a trade and that is unacceptable.

Although no formal announcement of management's response to the current situation has been provided, it is clear that consolidation is in the wind. We believe that forcing R&D to move to the Wasserburg location will ruin the professional network that is our (and the company's) treasured asset. Some alternative must be found and, if it is not, the members of our department will seek individual solutions to their personal problems.

It is time that management emerges from behind closed doors and asks vital members of the company team to become involved in this decision. If management intends to launch this consolidation effort, we believe it will have disastrous results and that it is unlikely that research and development personnel will remain with the company.

Our interest is in the company's survival. If it were necessary, the members of the committee would be willing to agree to a 20 percent salary reduction in return for being able to remain in the Munich-area network. We request an opportunity to speak with management about this vital decision which massively affects all of us.

Sincerely,
(signed by all members of the committee)

After reading the statement sent by the committee, the president of Eurotechnologies, Pieter Jensen, conferred with the vice president for research and development (and the immediate superior of the scientists) and the vice president for human resources. The three discussed the statement that they had received and agreed that the situation was serious. It was clear that the Wasserburg move created unforeseen, legitimate problems for the vital R&D personnel and that management had erred in not seeking wider input in considering their cost-reduction alternatives.

The management team debated the alternatives. They understood the frustrations of the research and development staff but were faced with having to cut almost DM 13,000,000 from annual costs in order for ETI to remain competitive. Consolidation still seemed the obvious answer, but the problems were mounting with this employee disclosure.

EXHIBIT 2

(addressed to all committee members)
Research and Development
Eurotechnologies, Inc.
300 Reinstrasse
Munich, Germany

Dear (names):

I have given my most serious consideration to the points you raised in your recent letter. We share your interest in doing what is best for ETI and welcome your interest in contributing to that goal.

It is clear that our technical expertise is one of our greatest assets and that your work in research and development is a vital contributor to that expertise. We have no wish to reduce our technical competitiveness. Nevertheless, our failure to produce cost-competitive contract bids is a problem that requires a painful solution, and we have only 18 months to produce an effective response.

We acknowledge that we have begun to examine the consolidation of our operations at the Wasserburg facility. Such a consolidation would reduce duplication of facilities, equipment, and personnel. These reductions would contribute significantly to an overall cost saving. Page two of this letter is an exhibit of the ongoing cost savings we believe would result from such a move.

At the same time, we believe that this action would be unwise if it truly has the crippling effect on your effectiveness that you forecast. Our dilemma, as the management team for ETI, is to address the need for major, fast cost reduction while providing for the continuation of our technical excellence. We also believe that any proposal must be fair to the many employees who are a part of the Eurotechnologies family.

In response to your letter, I have ordered that further evaluation of the Wasserburg alternative be halted for the time being. I ask that your committee send some of its members to a meeting with myself and other members of the management team will discuss the situation as it has evolved. We share an interest in ETI's survival if we can develop a plan that is mutually acceptable in achieving that goal. I look forward to meeting with you.

Sincerely,
(signed, Pieter Jensen)

Jensen wrote a letter to the committee acknowledging their concerns and inviting the members of that group to come to a meeting with the president, the VP of research and development, the VP of human resources, and other senior company officials. Jensen was careful to make no commitments or promises in the letter; simply, he invited them to come to a meeting (Exhibit 2).

ETI Expense Statement (in Thousands of Deutschmarks)

Overhead	Wasserburg	Munich	Totals Current	Consolidated
Manufacturing	36,071			36,071
Administrative	5,325	10,812		5,812
R&D	965	8,685		9,063
Total	42,361	19,497	61,858	50,946
R&D expenses				
Utilities	163	408		345
Computer lease		2,038		2,038
Supplies	425	897		983
Consulting		1,498		1,245
Total	588	4,841	5,429	4,611
Salaries and benefits				
Professional	3,260	4,564		7,824
Benefits	489	685		1,174
Hourly	16,274	609		16,665
Benefits	1,627	61		1,647
Relocation				1,476[*]
Total	21,650	5,919	27,569	28,786
				27,310[†]
Facilities				
Debt service	1,630	5,260		1,630
Insurance/maintenance/taxes	815	2,141		815
Total	2,445	7,401	9,846	2,445
Grand total: current versus consolidated			104,702	85,312[†]

[*]One-time expense.
[†]Ongoing total.

EXERCISE 24

The Pakistani Prunes

INTRODUCTION

In many work settings it is not possible for people to work independently as they pursue their work goals. Often we find ourselves in situations where we must obtain the cooperation of other people, even though the other people's ultimate objectives may be different from our own. Getting things done in organizations requires us to work together in cooperation, even though our ultimate objective may be only to satisfy our own needs. Your task in this exercise is to learn how to work together more productively with others.

Adapted by Roy J. Lewicki and John W. Minton.

EXERCISE 25

Planning for Negotiations

INTRODUCTION

This exercise asks you to focus on a real negotiation that will occur in your life within the next several weeks or months. In this exercise, your objective is to plan for that negotiation and perhaps to share and discuss those plans with several other people. The sharing of information in groups illustrates the broad range of negotiations in which we engage. Presenting the plans to a small group, and then to the larger class, may help people shape and refine their plans. The posted results will illustrate the structure and direction a logical planning process can bring to any negotiation.

PROCEDURE

Divide into groups. If you have been in a regular, ongoing group in the course, use this group. Otherwise, you will be given instructions as to how to form into groups.

Each person in the group will explain briefly an actual, personal negotiation he or she is facing within the next few weeks or months. After hearing all the individual examples, each group will pick one of the personal negotiations that they feel to be most interesting, instructive, and/or demanding. The "owner" of that upcoming negotiation will become the group's "client."

Draw on any readings, assignments, observations, and experiences the class has done or accomplished in the course thus far. (For example, you may consult the readings in Section 2 of this volume.) Each group must develop a comprehensive negotiation plan for its client. The instructor may (or may not) provide a supplementary planning guide. In developing the plan, you should address the following issues:

1. Understanding the issues—that is, what is to be negotiated.
2. Assembling the issues and defining the bargaining mix:
   - Which issues are most important and which issues are less important?
   - Which issues are linked to other issues, and which are separate or unconnected?
3. Defining the interests: What are the client's primary underlying interests?

Developed by Roy J. Lewicki and John W. Minton.

4. Defining limits:
   - What is our "walkaway" point on each issue—that is, what is a minimally acceptable settlement for each issue or the issues as a package?
   - If this negotiation fails, what is our best alternative settlement (BATNA)?
5. Defining targets and openings:
   - What will be our preferred settlement in each issue?
   - What will be our opening request for each issue?
   - Where are we willing to trade off issues against each other in the bargaining mix?
6. Constituencies: To whom is the client accountable for the solution—that is, to whom does he or she report to, or have to explain or defend the outcome? Does this party also have to be involved in issue definition and goal setting?
7. Opposite negotiators: Who is the other party (or parties) in the negotiation?
   - What information do we have about them?
   - What issues will they have?
   - What priorities are they likely to have for their issues?
   - What are their interests?
   - What has been my past relationship with them? What future relationship do I need to have, or would I like to have with them?
   - What is their reputation and style, and how should I take this into consideration?
8. Selecting a strategy:
   - What overall negotiation and strategy do I want to select? How important is the outcome and the relationship with the other?
   - What strategy do I expect the other will be selecting?
9. Planning the issue presentation and defense:
   - What research do I need to do on the issues so that I can argue for them convincingly and compellingly?
   - Do I have (or can I prepare) graphs, charts, and figures that will clearly communicate my preferences?
   - In what order and sequence should I present the information?
   - What arguments can I anticipate from the other party, and how am I going to counteract their arguments?
   - What tactics will I use to present my arguments or defend against the other's arguments?
   - What tactics will I use to try to move us toward agreement?
   - What roles will different people play in the negotiation?

10. Protocol:

    - Where will we negotiate? Do we wish to influence the choice of location?
    - When will we negotiate? Do we wish to influence the time and length of negotiation?
    - Who will be at the actual negotiation meeting? Do we want to bring other parties, to serve a particular purpose (e.g., an expert or an observer)?
    - Do we have an agenda? How can we help to either create the agenda or participate in its development?
    - What will we do if the negotiation fails?
    - Who will write down and confirm the agreement? Do we need to have the contract reviewed by a professional (e.g., attorney, accountant, agent)?

One member of each group should record the results of the group's work and be able to report the plan back to the group (you may wish to use large paper, overhead transparencies, or a written handout).

Sanibel Island

INTRODUCTION

In this scenario, you will negotiate a set of environmental management issues. One of you will play the role of an environmental group, while the other will play the role of a land developer. Your objective is to negotiate three issues related to the development of a hotel/resort site on a particular piece of waterfront land.

BACKGROUND INFORMATION

Sanibel Island

Sanibel Island is located off the western coast of central Florida in the Gulf of Mexico. Sanibel is known for its natural beauty and for its shape and position—many shells wash up on its beaches because it is longer east to west than north to south. It is estimated that about 400 different types of shells can be found by the knowledgeable collector. The island is dominated by private residences and is a popular vacation site.

A large portion of Sanibel Island's 11,000 acres is composed of freshwater wetlands, a unique feature in a barrier island. These are of benefit to the residents for many reasons, one of which is as a freshwater source. The island is home to the J. N. "Ding" Darling National Wildlife Refuge, a wetland system that covers 4,700 acres of habitat (about 40 percent of the island) and is home to more than 267 species of birds, including snakebirds, egrets, and numerous species of ducks, and many plant species, including the epiphyte and the mangrove. The mangrove is of particular interest to the wetlands because it begins a food chain—its leaves and roots in the water create a habitat for microorganisms that get eaten by animals higher on the food chain, leading all the way up to shrimp and waterfowl. The roots of the mangrove are also partially responsible for binding up the shore.

Due to the popularity of the island as a vacation site, a causeway was built from the mainland, allowing cars direct access to the island for the first time. Although tourism is the island's main source of income, residents began to have many concerns about the

---

This exercise was developed by Tim Poland, Craig Davis, and Roy J. Lewicki, all of Ohio State University, for classroom and research use.

effects of development and tourism on the island. Many residents rely on the waters for commercial catching of fish and scallops and were afraid of interference from increased population and traffic.

Tourists enjoy walking along the beach. Some collect the shells. This island's beaches are typical of many coastal areas in that there are cyclical periods of erosion and creation. In other words, the boundaries of the island are constantly in a state of flux—what was once dry land is now beach, and what were once coastal areas may become dry land.

Development of homes and hotels was also of concern to Sanibel's residents. In an effort to maintain Sanibel's aesthetics, a limit on building height was established. Other restrictions may include those requiring stilts and/or open first floors. This is more for safety than for any other reason. When the tide gets too high during a storm, the water can go right under the building without any hindrance, and the buildings remain intact.

The focus of this role-play will be the proposed development of a piece of Sanibel Island waterfront property into a hotel and beachfront recreation complex. The discussions will take place between the developer who wants to develop this property and representatives of an environmental group who are concerned about environmental preservation. Additional information will be provided in your private role briefing information. You should also refer to two maps: a map of the undeveloped property (Exhibit 1), and a map of the developed property as proposed by the developer (Exhibit 2).

In an effort to protect wetlands, state and federal laws have been enacted that must be followed by land developers. Simply put, these laws require "no net loss" of wetlands. Ideally, this means no loss of existing wetlands; failing that, if any wetlands are lost through development, they must be recreated elsewhere.

Local enforcement of these wetland regulations is difficult. First, a commonly accepted definition of wetland has not yet been formulated. Basically, a wetland is any type of transitional area between dry land and open water, such as swamps, bogs, fens, and marshes. This leaves broad leeway for interpretation; in fact, many wetlands are not even "wet" during certain seasons. Second, because local regulations are more strict than state and federal wetland regulations, environmental conflicts are often played out at different political levels.

The current focus of attention is a proposed hotel development on Sanibel Island (see maps) and its possible environmental consequences. A developer has purchased a beachfront property and intends to create a resort, which includes a multistoried hotel building and a nature preserve.

In order to build this resort, the builder must apply for a permit from the U.S. Army Corps of Engineers. It is the task of the Corps to ensure compliance with existing laws, and to provide a forum in which interested parties can voice their concerns. Therefore, they have suggested bringing together the developers and environmentalists to negotiate the issues surrounding this development. The Corps hopes that this process will set a precedent that will balance the conservation of natural resources against further development on the island.

EXHIBIT 1   Map of the Undeveloped Property

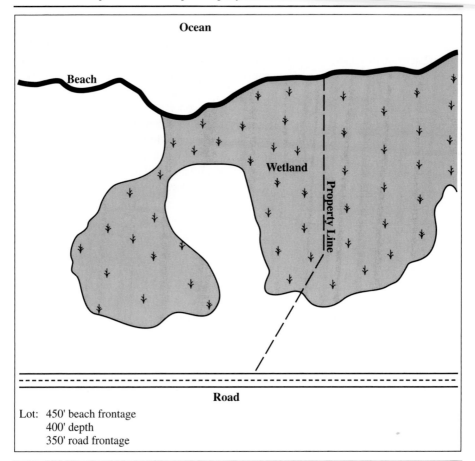

Lot: 450' beach frontage
      400' depth
      350' road frontage

EXHIBIT 2   Map of the Proposed Development

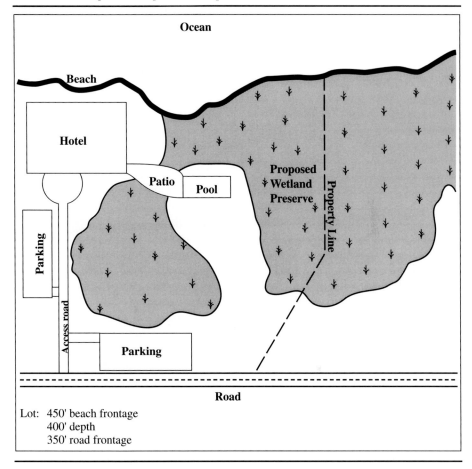

The Playground Negotiation

INTRODUCTION

This is a true-to-life case. Two elected local officials, one elected on a community involvement plank (herein referred to as the community volunteer representative) and the other elected because of a commitment to support the Parks Department (hereafter referred to as the Parks Department representative) comprise the Ithaca Special Projects Task Force. They have been charged with deciding whether to fund a playground for the community and, if so, how much of the city's limited special project funds they should spend. Other projects requesting funding will be presented to them later in the year. Both representatives share the common goal of bettering the community. However, the issue is complicated by a variety of potential intergroup conflicts that can threaten their position as elected officials, and that could jeopardize the harmony of the community that they are trying to help. Moreover, both representatives are aware that they, as well as their constituents, may have interests in both community volunteerism as well as in the well-being of the Parks Department; for example, Parks Department employees may also be community volunteers after work.

BACKGROUND INFORMATION

You were elected (as either Parks Department representative or community volunteer representative) to the city council, a position in the local Ithaca government. Recently, you were appointed to the Ithaca Special Projects Task Force (ISPTF). This committee makes recommendations to the full council for funding special projects that will benefit the Ithaca community. The council then provides one-time funding for special projects that are not included in the budgets for any other department. ISPTF does not guarantee ongoing support for the projects it funds; thus, most projects are those that can be completed within one fiscal year.

Each year the council considers three proposals. These proposals never arrive at the same time and are therefore considered independently from each other. The budget for ISPTF is fixed, and members of the task force must seriously consider the merits of each

Adapted from an exercise written by Jennifer J. Halpern and Dera L. Connelley and published in the *International Journal of Conflict Management* 7, no. 3 (1996), pp. 247–74. Used with permission of the authors and publisher.

project as it is presented. Later projects may be more worthy of funding than the current project under consideration; alternatively, the current project may be more promising than either or both of the two later projects, but the ISPTF can't possibly know this at the time of its decision.

Your Task

You and your task force partner are to consider a proposal for an expanded playground at Titus Flats. This playground will require ISPTF funds, some Parks Department sponsorship (including human resources), and volunteer effort. Titus Flats is a low- to middle-income area across a four-lane street from the enormous Tops Supermarket at the southwest corner of Ithaca. Titus Flats is inland and on the opposite shore of the middle-income Inlet development and recreation area. Currently, Titus Flats is a recreation area with four softball fields, an outdoor basketball court, and a very small playground for children containing a tiny wooden climbing structure, a slide, and a tire swing.

The neighborhood around Titus Flats is home to a culturally diverse population. Across the street from the recreation area is a large public housing facility, Landmark Square. Its residents include welfare families with children and teenagers. These families have often borne the brunt of malicious stereotyping based on their socioeconomic status and their race, predominantly African American. They would prefer not to be seen as a source of trouble. At the same time, they do not wish to see their interests and needs ignored.

Adjacent to the park is a senior citizens' housing facility, Titus Towers. The residents here are functioning members of the community, doing their shopping and socializing in the neighborhood. Because of the proximity of the "Flats" to the "Towers," residents have come to view the area as an extension of their own grounds.

The surrounding neighborhood is low- to moderate-income single-family housing. These property owners pay more taxes than any of the other members of the neighborhood and expect to have a voice in how their neighborhood is managed. They are concerned about their liability for children playing in the streets and sidewalks in front of their homes, since Ithaca laws state that sidewalks in front of private homes are the owners' responsibility, and many children live in the area.

The different members of the community all make use of the existing park. The children of Landmark Square and the single-family property owners use the small playground. In addition, seniors from the Towers occasionally bring visiting grandchildren to play. The playground gets overcrowded during peak after-school and weekend hours, and as a result, young children can often be found playing in the street. Although there has not yet been an automobile accident causing serious injury to a child, parents and City Council members are concerned about the possibility of such a tragedy in the future.

While there is support for a safe place for children to play, all parties are concerned that a larger playground could become a magnet for teenage gang activity and drug dealers. Some parents have already indicated that they keep their children away from the playground because of the "tough" teens on the basketball court. The Landmark Square teenagers and young adults use the basketball court heavily. It is rare when a game is not in progress.

Finally, impromptu ball games are sometimes organized by the residents at Landmark Square, but the fields are mainly used by citywide softball leagues and thus are unavailable throughout the season. In addition, many residents of Titus Towers complain that the playground is already too noisy and the basketball games are raucous and profane, and the residents say that they cannot enjoy sitting quietly on the benches that were provided for such use.

The Parks Department claims that it does not have enough money to build a new playground in an area where one already exists and that there are more pressing needs for its shrinking funds.

Ithaca is a town (some like to call it a small city) of about 30,000 year-round inhabitants. Students from the several colleges in the area almost double Ithaca's size during the school term, but very few of them choose to make Titus Flats their home. Ithaca also has several wealthy neighborhoods, two neighborhoods surrounding its largest colleges, and a downtown shopping area called the Commons that attracts tourists and well-to-do consumers. Each neighborhood has at least one children's playground. Two of these were built almost entirely by community volunteers, as was the Ithaca Science Center. The Commons also has a graceful wooden structure for children to play on while their parents shop or work downtown.

INSTRUCTIONS FOR EVERYONE

Playground Options

There are two options for building a playground and three options for a ground cover. These options can be implemented in a variety of ways, with costs depending on the particular elements chosen. Each option has advantages and drawbacks. You are to consider these options and negotiate with your task force partner in determining a recommendation for the City Council.

Keep in mind that you and your task force partner do not have vested interests in the options or alternatives you read about in the proposals. Also keep in mind that this playground is just one of three proposals that the city will ask you to consider funding during the year. The two representatives share a common goal: the betterment of community life in Ithaca through the wise and efficient use of ISPTF funds.

Goals

Your roles are intentionally vague. It is important for you to put yourself in the shoes of this task force member, to be creative and responsive as if you were actually in this situation. Experience has shown that role-players with detailed guidelines pay too much attention to what they should do rather than to what they could do.

The ISPTF is empowered to make recommendations about the funding of this playground only. It does not have the power to levy or even to depend on fines, fees, taxes, or large donations.

Budget Considerations

The budget for all three special projects for this year is $63,750. The first of the three projects to be proposed this year is a playground. You may choose to recommend that the City Council spend the entire $63,750 on this one playground project; not fund a playground at all; or recommend any other amount be granted, below, equal to, or above the amount requested.

Remember that the council considers three special projects a year, although at the present time you know nothing about the nature of the other two later proposals. These other projects may be more or less deserving of funding than this project. You cannot know for sure.

Money that is not used this year is returned to Ithaca's general budget and is not added to the ISPTF's budget the following year. In fact, moneys not used may be seen as superfluous, and may cause ISPTF to receive less money the next year.

You and your task force partner must make the best decision you can within these limitations, keeping in mind your responsibility to the public trust, the merits of this particular proposal, the limits of the special projects budget, and the unknown concerning other projects that will be proposed later this year. Over the past two years, the council funded special projects as follows:

Special Projects (two years ago)

Project Title	Amount Requested	Amount Granted
Inlet exercise path	$31,675	$24,900
Lighting Improvements, the Commons	$59,100	$42,850
Seed money, Science Center	$10,000	$ 9,450
Total budget for the year		$77,200

Special Projects (last year)

Project Title	Amount Requested	Amount Granted
The Commons renovation	$68,976	$57,145
Landscaping, Stewart Park	$10,000	$14,300
Bike lanes, State Street	$26,800	0
Total budget for the year		$71,445

Descriptions of Past Projects

See Figure 1 for a map of Ithaca, highlighting the locations of past projects.

Inlet Exercise Path.   The inlet area of Ithaca is a lovely greenway that sits astride a channel leading from Six Mile Creek to Lake Cayuga. It is home to two college crew teams, a community theater, a pool and skating rink, tennis courts, ball fields and picnic

FIGURE 1   Map of Ithaca, New York, Highlighting Areas Improved by the ISPTF

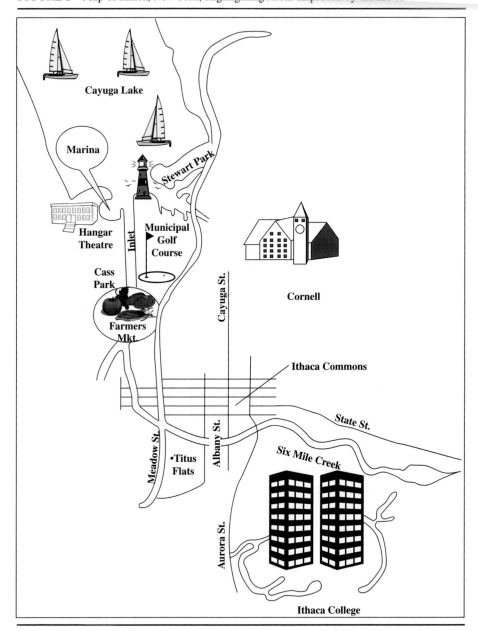

areas, a marina, and a covered outdoor market. The ISPTF provided funds for a cardio-
vascular exercise course that can also be used for bicycling, running, walking, and roller
or in-line skating. It is open to everyone, without charge. It is most easily accessible by
automobile.

Lighting Improvements and Renovations, Ithaca Commons.   The Commons is an outdoor, downtown pedestrian mall featuring upscale boutiques, specialty shops, restaurants, and bars. When business proprietors suggested that customers would stay away in the evenings because of concerns about safety, the city installed new lights on the mall through ISPTF funding. The next year the ISPTF also made available funds to renovate a play structure for children, repair benches and other seating, and commission a public work of art.

Seed Money, Science Center.   The Science Center is a highly visible organization in the Ithaca community that enjoys widespread support. After years of temporary quarters and mobile exhibits (including a regular one at a nearby covered market), the Science Center built a permanent home with seed money provided by the ISPTF. Located on the outskirts of a moderate-income area of private homes and small businesses, the building was erected with volunteer labor over several weekends.

Landscaping, Stewart Park.   Stewart Park is a large park at the south end of Cayuga Lake, adjacent to the municipal golf course. Although the park is owned by the city, it is utilized by a regional population. The park is also home to part of the Ithaca Festival, a summer celebration of music and the arts that draws several thousand people every year. ISPTF funding helped with planting bushes and renovating flower beds, as well as reworking fences and decks around the ponds and pavilions.

State Street Bike Lanes.   This project was not funded. The proposal called for bike lanes along a treacherous bus and automobile artery from Cornell University through a commercial district to the inlet exercise path. The proposal would have eliminated parking along the route, which is bordered by low-rent student apartments, inexpensive restaurants and bars, used furniture stores, and other businesses that make heavy use of on-street parking.

TITUS FLATS PLAYGROUND PROPOSAL

The proposal is summarized below. The parties proposing the playground have presented two options for equipment and three for ground covers. These options can be mixed and matched, and are presented as guidelines so that task force members will know what can be done at different levels of funding. See Figure 2 for a map of the existing park and playground.

Equipment

Option One.   Price range: $40,360–$46,100. A ready-to-assemble metal-and-vinyl playground can be purchased from a supplier in Illinois. The unit is manufactured in Korea and imported to the United States. Assembly would be accomplished easily by Ithaca Parks personnel. This unit is estimated to last for 15 years, and maintenance would include paint touch-ups to prevent rust corrosion and replacement of vinyl parts after

FIGURE 2   Map of Titus Flats Park

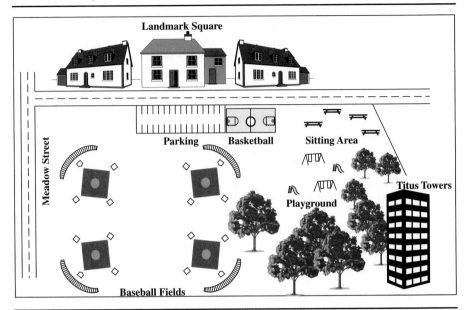

seven years. Cost of replacement is estimated to be approximately $5,000–$6,500 (above the original purchase price), although it is difficult to foresee the effects of changes in inflation and exchange rates, oil prices (affecting the cost of the vinyl), and so on. At the present time, Ithaca has no playgrounds constructed of similar materials, although many other cities the size of Ithaca use these units extensively. There is some concern that these metal units are not as attractive as the wooden units used throughout the town, and one city council member has stated his opposition to erecting structures which are not in harmony with the other parks.

The cost of the structure ranges with size. The low estimate calls for one slide, one play platform, six swings, monkey bars, a firefighter's pole, and an elevated crawl-through tunnel. The high estimate calls for two regular slides, one twisting slide, 10 swings, four platforms, monkey bars, a jungle gym, two elevated tunnels, a firefighter's pole, and a climbing rope. Units of intermediate size can be ordered by omitting different parts.

Option Two.   Price range: $34,600–$39,800. A custom-designed wood structure can be built on the spot. The plans would be drawn up by a local contractor who has designed and built several playground facilities in the city. Substantial savings could be achieved by using donated community labor. Even so, skilled carpenters would have to be hired and much of the materials purchased. Similar community efforts have been successful in renovating the playground at Belle Sherman School and building a new facility at Southside Community Center. However, each of those projects had a constituent community with a strong interest in contributing their time and efforts not only to construction activities, but also in providing food, child care for the workers, and a considerable amount of time in organizing the project and procuring labor and donated materials. You are not sure that the community surrounding Titus Flats would be as supportive as these other communities. One possibility is that a part-time coordinator may have to be hired for an additional cost of $3,000–$5,000.

Maintenance includes minor structural repair each year, easily accomplished by Parks personnel. Even so, wooden structures usually have nicked and rough boards which can inflict minor abrasions and splinters on the children. Every four to five years, major structural replacement would be required to replace rotting, loose, or broken boards and corroded or loose bolts. This maintenance could not be handled solely by Parks Department employees. Additional personnel from the community would be required for this work, involving periodic organizing of donated labor and resources. Because the extent of wear and tear on the facility cannot be anticipated, the cost of periodic maintenance cannot be estimated. The contractor calculates the life of such a unit, properly maintained, to be 20 years.

The range in cost depends on the size of the unit desired. The low estimate calls for four swings, a tire swing, a suspension bridge between two play platforms, a firefighter's pole, monkey bars, and a small toddler's slide. The high estimate includes six swings, two tire swings, three suspension bridges between four play platforms, a tower with a turret, four seesaws, one toddler's slide, one twister slide, one large slide with three bumps, a balance beam, monkey bars, a climbing wall, and two firefighter's poles. Units of intermediate size can be ordered by omitting different parts.

Ground Preparation

If you choose to recommend to the ISPTF that a playground should be constructed, you must recommend an appropriate ground cover for the area as well as the type of playground structure. Again there are several options, and you must consider such factors as additional cost, maintenance, and safety.

Option One.   Price range: $4,580–$5,150. Pea gravel (small, rounded, smoothed stones) can be used to cover the playground. Advantages to this covering include the following: it is relatively permanent, it requires little maintenance, and it is clean because dirt and debris would sift through the gravel. Many Ithaca playgrounds use this for ground cover. One disadvantage, in addition to its relatively high cost, is that children who fall on it may get abrasions. Other concerns are that small children may swallow it, and it can be dangerous when thrown.

Option Two.   Price range: $3,320–$3,700. Sand is a possible ground cover. It provides a soft medium that would reduce injuries if children fall from the structure. Sand also furnishes an additional play medium for children using toy dump trucks, shovels and buckets, and so on. Sand requires more maintenance than gravel, and additional sand would have to be spread each year. It is also not as clean as gravel, and some parents claim that cats and other animals would be attracted to the sand, thereby posing possible health and cleanliness risks.

Option Three. Price range: $850–$925. Following construction of the play structure, the ground could simply be leveled and grass could be planted. Maintenance would be minimal and could be handled by regular Parks maintenance crews. However, heavily trafficked areas would become hard-packed, and no grass would grow in those areas. Hard-packed ground would also yield more extensive injuries if a child should fall from the structure. Because of Ithaca's rainy climate, there is concern that the poor drainage qualities of this ground preparation would frequently reduce the park to a mud pit. This drawback could be dealt with by combining grass with chipped bark or shredded recycled tires in heavy traffic areas. This would result in an added cost of $1,000 initially and yearly replenishment costs. There is also a high probability that loose materials will get spread over grassy areas, creating mowing problems and giving the playground a messy appearance if not meticulously maintained.

EXERCISE 28

Collecting Nos

INTRODUCTION

In all work settings, there comes a time when we need something from someone else. It might be an approval, it might be resources, or it might be some form of assistance. Whatever it might be, it is virtually impossible for us to get our work done without the cooperation of others. And the best way to get what you want from others is to ask them for it. Yet many people would rather do it themselves than ask someone else. One reason people are hesitant to ask for things is because they do not want to get a no.

A similar problem exists in negotiations. On the one hand, inexperienced negotiators often are afraid to ask for what they want or need because they are afraid to get a no. On the other hand, those who are asked will frequently *not* say no, in spite of their strong dislike of the request or having to fulfill it. Therefore, many negotiations are incomplete because the requester did not ask for enough, or the respondent actually gave more than they wanted to. Several negotiation experts have argued that negotiation only *begins* when the other party says no; if you do not get a no, you probably have not asked for enough!

The purpose of this exercise is to give you experience in making requests and dealing with others' objections. Your task in this exercise is to collect nos.

PART A

Continue to make requests until you have collected 10 nos. Keep a verbatim written record of *each* request you make, the response you receive to each request, and what meaning or interpretation you gave to the response (what thoughts or feelings you had in reaction to the response). Create the following table:

Request I Made	Response I Received	My Reaction to the Response
1.		
2.		
3.		
etc.		

Developed by Professor Jeffrey Ford of the Fisher College of Business, the Ohio State University, for this volume. Used with permission.

PART B

Pick one of the requests for which you received a no, and make that same request of the same person a second time. If you receive another no, wait until later and make the same request yet a third time. Write down what the person says each time.

PART C

Pick at least one of the requests for which you received a no, and ask the person who said no, "What would have to happen for you to say yes to my request?" Write down what the person says.

500 English Sentences

INTRODUCTION

This exercise involves a cross-cultural negotiation where there are several tangible and intangible factors at stake. You will play the role of either a Japanese teacher who is head of the English Department that is responsible for the publication of an English text-book, or an American assistant English teacher who has been asked to work on the book.

This exercise was written by Laura Turek. Copyright 1996. Used with permission.

EXERCISE 30

Sick Leave

INTRODUCTION

This exercise involves a cross-cultural negotiation where there are several tangible and intangible factors at stake. You will play the role of either a Japanese manager responsible for the supervision of several foreign assistant English teachers, or an American assistant English teacher.

This exercise was written by Laura Turek. Copyright 1996. Used with permission.

Town of Tamarack

INTRODUCTION

In this role-play, you will have the opportunity to negotiate a serious problem—a conflict between a mining company and the government of a small town regarding an environmental cleanup. Conflicts between community, government, and industry groups are very common, particularly around environmental management issues. The issues in this simulation may be similar to environmental cleanup, development, or management problems ongoing in your own community.

BACKGROUND INFORMATION

The largest regional office of the Twin Lakes Mining Company is located in Tamarack, Minnesota, in the northern part of the state. It was established there in 1941. The town of Tamarack has a population of approximately 12,000. Although there is a growing revenue that accrues to the town as a result of heavy summer tourism (summer homes, fishing, etc.) and several cottage industries, Tamarack is basically a one-industry town. Two thousand five hundred people, 60 percent of whom live within town limits, work for the Twin Lakes Mining Company; 33 percent of the town's real estate tax base consists of Twin Lakes property and operations. Both in terms of direct tax revenue and indirect contribution to the economic stability of the local population, Tamarack is strongly dependent on the continued success of the Twin Lakes Company.

The primary activity of the Twin Lakes Mining Company consists of mining iron ore from open-pit mines. Open-pit mining consists of stripping the top soil from the ore deposit with the use of a power shovel. Train rails are then laid, and most of the ore is loaded into railroad cars for transportation to a central collecting point for rail or water shipment. As mining operations progress, rails are relaid or roads constructed to haul ore by truck. The ore is transported to a plant located on the outskirts of Tamarack, where it is crushed, washed, concentrated, blended, and agglomerated into larger lumps or pellets. After the ore proceeds through this process of cleaning and agglomerating, it is shipped by railroad car to steel mills throughout the Midwest. Rejected materials are

---

This exercise was written by Jeff Polzer. Used with permission.

returned to parts of the mine where the mining process has been completed. Mines that are no longer in use are called *consumed* mines.

Twin Lakes' plant is located approximately five miles outside of Tamarack. As a result of the expansion of the residential areas of the town, summer home development and various Twin Lakes operations, the plant has become an environmental problem for local citizens. The primary problem is that the mining operations pollute the air with dust. For years, the Tamarack Town Council has been pressing the company to clean up the most problematic operations. Although several discussions between the town and the company have occurred, Twin Lakes has done little to remedy the major concerns. Now, as a result of more stringent environmental laws and regulations, Twin Lakes has come under pressure from the state of Minnesota and the federal government for environmental cleanup. Both the state and the Federal Environmental Protection Agency have informed Twin Lakes that they are in major violation of air pollution quality standards and that immediate action must be taken. Because Twin Lakes is now mining reasonably low-grade ore and because foreign competition in the steel market has significantly eroded the demand for ore, the high cost of environmental compliance might force the company to shut down its Tamarack operations. Many local citizens, as individuals and through the local chapter of the United Mineworkers Union, are putting significant pressure on the Town Council to help the Twin Lakes Company in its environmental cleanup operations.

The imposition of the environmental controls on Twin Lakes, and the resulting pressure from all segments of the community, has led to renewed discussions between company and town officials about the future of Twin Lakes in the Tamarack area. As a result of these discussions, the following major issues, including environmental issues and others, have emerged:

Air Quality—Paving Dirt Roads.   The entire process of mining, transporting, and crushing ore generates large amounts of dust. This has significantly increased the levels of particulates in the air. During the dry summer months, the operation of many large trucks along dirt roads intensifies the problem considerably.

Twin Lakes believes that it can control a great deal of the dust generated immediately around the plant and is planning to incur this expense without help from Tamarack. The most significant debate with the town has been over a series of roads around the outskirts of town. They need to be paved to reduce the dust in the air to acceptable levels. Many of the roads are town-owned, and some have been specially constructed by the company for the transportation of ore and material. Almost all of the roads, including those constructed by the company, are used frequently by tourists. All of the roads have to be paved for Twin Lakes to comply with the environmental regulations and stay in business.

Air Quality—Road Maintenance.   The roads in question currently require a minimal amount of maintenance. They will require a much higher degree of maintenance if they are paved, however, especially because the harsh winters tend to break up paved roads. To keep the roads in an acceptable condition, the town and company will have to agree on who will maintain them.

Site of Next Mine.   Twin Lakes has been testing several locations in the Tamarack area to determine the extent of iron ore deposits. Several of the locations have enough ore to be profitable, and Twin Lakes would like to open a new mine. Although the actual mining may not begin immediately, the decision concerning the location of a new site has to be made now to allow time for both the company to plan for a new mine and the town to plan its expansion around any new mining site.

Restoration of Consumed Mines.   The consumed mines that are no longer used by the company are outside of the town limits. Some of these mines lie alongside main roads leading into the town from the most popular resort areas on local lakes. The town considers the consumed mines unsightly and is afraid that tourists may be repelled by the mines. The company has restored the land to the extent required by law, but the town would like to see further restoration.

Tax Rate on Company Land.   The land for the mine currently in operation is outside of town limits. However, the plant lies within township boundaries, and Twin Lakes pays a substantial amount of money in taxes. The company has always felt that the Tamarack taxation rate is excessive.

Both the company and the town believe that if some resolution could be obtained on these major issues, the remaining problems could be easily resolved, and Twin Lakes would agree to keep its operations in the Tamarack area in business. Toward this end, a formal negotiation has been arranged between the Town of Tamarack and the Twin Lakes Mining Company.

EXERCISE 32

Bacchus Winery[1]

INTRODUCTION

This exercise is a three-party negotiation between representatives of three cultural groups: an American, a Japanese, and a Serbian. The American firm (Bacchus) produces a variety of wines; the Japanese firm (Tokyo Saki) produces saki and rice wines; the Serbian firm (Serbian Steins & Stems) produces fine decanters, wine glasses, and accessories. The three firms will discuss the terms of a possible merger/joint venture between them.

---

[1]Adapted by Roy J. Lewicki from an exercise developed by Judi McLean Parks, Washington University. Used with permission.

Cases

CASE 1

Capital Mortgage
Insurance Corporation (A)

Frank Randall hung up the telephone, leaned across his desk, and fixed a cold stare at Jim Dolan.

> OK, Jim. They've agreed to a meeting. We've got three days to resolve this thing. The question is, what approach should we take? How do we get them to accept our offer?

Randall, president of Capital Mortgage Insurance Corporation (CMI), had called Dolan, his senior vice president and treasurer, into his office to help him plan their strategy for completing the acquisition of Corporate Transfer Services (CTS). The two men had begun informal discussions with the principal stockholders of the small employee relocation services company some four months earlier. Now, in late May 1979, they were developing the terms of a formal purchase offer and plotting their strategy for the final negotiations.

The acquisition, if consummated, would be the first in CMI's history. Furthermore, it represented a significant departure from the company's present business. Randall and Dolan knew that the acquisition could have major implications, both for themselves and for the company they had revitalized over the past several years.

Jim Dolan ignored Frank Randall's intense look and gazed out the eighth-floor window overlooking Philadelphia's Independence Square.

> That's not an easy question, Frank. We know they're still looking for a lot more money than we're thinking about. But beyond that, the four partners have their own differences, and we need to think through just what they're expecting. So I guess we'd better talk this one through pretty carefully.

COMPANY AND INDUSTRY BACKGROUND

CMI was a wholly owned subsidiary of Northwest Equipment Corporation, a major freight transporter and lessor of railcars, commercial aircraft, and other industrial

---

Capital Mortgage Insurance Company (A), 9-480-057. Copyright ©1980 by the President and Fellows of Harvard College.

This case was prepared by James P. Ware as a basis for class discussion rather than to illustrate either effective or ineffective handling of an administrative situation. Reprinted by permission of the Harvard Business School. Although this case is more than 20 years old, the editors of this volume believe that it presents valuable lessons about the negotiation process.

equipment. Northwest had acquired CMI in 1978, two years after CMI's original parent company, an investment management corporation, had gone into Chapter 11 bankruptcy proceedings. CMI had been created to sell mortgage guaranty insurance policies to residential mortgage lenders throughout the United States. Mortgage insurance provides banks, savings and loans, mortgage bankers, and other mortgage lenders with protection against financial losses when homeowners default on their mortgage loans.

Lending institutions normally protect their property loan investments by offering loans of only 70 percent to 80 percent of the appraised value of the property; the remaining 20 to 30 percent constitutes the homeowner's down payment. However, mortgage loan insurance makes it possible for lenders to offer so-called high-ratio loans of up to 95 percent of a home's appraised value. High-ratio loans are permitted only when the lender insures the loan; although the policy protects the lender, the premiums are paid by the borrower, as an addition to monthly principal and interest charges.

The principal attraction of mortgage insurance is that it makes purchasing a home possible for many more individuals. It is much easier to produce a 5 percent down payment than to save up the 20 to 30 percent traditionally required.

CMI had a mixed record of success within the private mortgage insurance industry. Frank Randall, the company's first and only president, had gotten the organization off to an aggressive beginning, attaining a 14.8 percent market share by 1972. By 1979, however, that share had fallen to just over 10 percent even though revenues had grown from $18 million in 1972 to over $30 million in 1979. Randall attributed the loss of market share primarily to the difficulties created by the bankruptcy of CMI's original parent. Thus, he had been quite relieved when Northwest Equipment acquired CMI in January 1978. Northwest provided CMI with a level of management and financial support it had never before enjoyed. Furthermore, Northwest's corporate management had made it clear to Frank Randall that he was expected to build CMI into a much larger, diversified financial services company.

Northwest's growth expectations were highly consistent with Frank Randall's own ambitions. The stability created by the acquisition, in combination with the increasing solidity of CMI's reputation with mortgage lenders, made it possible for Randall to turn his attention more and more toward external acquisitions of his own. During 1978 Randall, with Jim Dolan's help, had investigated several acquisition opportunities in related insurance industries, with the hope of broadening CMI's financial base. After several unsuccessful investigations, the two men had come to believe that their knowledge and competence was focused less on insurance per se than it was on residential real estate and related financial transactions. These experiences had led to a recognition that, in Frank Randall's words, "we are a residential real estate financial services company."

THE RESIDENTIAL REAL ESTATE INDUSTRY

Frank Randall and Jim Dolan knew from personal experience that real estate brokers, who play an obvious and important role in property transactions, usually have close ties with local banks and savings and loans. When mortgage funds are plentiful, brokers often steer prospective home buyers to particular lending institutions. When funds are scarce, the lenders would then favor prospective borrowers referred by their favorite brokers. Randall believed that these informal relationships meant that realtors could have a significant impact on the mortgage loan decision and thus on a mortgage insurance decision as well.

For this reason, CMI had for many years directed a small portion of its marketing effort toward real estate brokers. CMI's activities had consisted of offering educational programs for realtors, property developers, and potential home buyers. The company derived no direct revenues from these programs, but offered them in the interest of stimulating home sales and, more particularly, of informing both realtors and home buyers of how mortgage insurance makes it possible to purchase a home with a relatively low down payment.

Because he felt that real estate brokers could be powerful allies in encouraging lenders to use mortgage insurance, Randall had been tracking developments in the real estate industry for many years. Historically a highly fragmented collection of local, independent entrepreneurs, the industry in 1979 appeared to be on the verge of a major restructuring and consolidation. For the past several years many of the smaller brokers had been joining national franchise organizations in an effort to gain a brand image and to acquire improved management and sales skills.

More significantly, in 1979, several large national corporations were beginning to acquire prominent real estate agencies in major urban areas. The most aggressive of these appeared to be Merrill Lynch and Company, the well-known Wall Street securities trading firm. Merrill Lynch's interest in real estate brokers stemmed from several sources; perhaps most important were the rapidly rising prices on property and homes. Realtors' commissions averaged slightly over 6 percent of the sales price; *Fortune* magazine estimated that real estate brokers had been involved in home sales totaling approximately $190 billion in 1978, netting commissions in excess of $11 billion (in comparison, stockbrokers' commissions on all securities transactions in 1978 were estimated at $3.7 billion).[1] With property values growing 10 to 20 percent per year, commissions would only get larger; where 6 percent of a $30,000 home netted only $1,800, 6 percent of a $90,000 sale resulted in a commission well in excess of $5,000—for basically the same work.

There were also clear signs that the volume of real estate transactions would continue to increase. Although voluntary intercity moves appeared to be declining slightly, corporate transfers of employees were still rising. One of Merrill Lynch's earliest moves toward the real estate market had been to acquire an employee relocation company several years earlier. Working on a contract basis with corporate clients, Merrill Lynch Relocation Management (MLRM) collaborated with independent real estate brokers to arrange home sales and purchases for transferred employees. Like other relocation companies, MLRM would purchase the home at a fair market value and then handle all the legal and financial details of reselling the home on the open market. MLRM also provided relocation counseling and home search assistance for transferred employees; its income was derived primarily from service fees paid by corporate clients (and augmented somewhat by referral fees from real estate brokers, who paid MLRM a portion of the commissions they earned on home sales generated by the transferred employees).

---

[1]"Why Merrill Lynch Wants to Sell Your House," *Fortune*, January 29, 1979.

Later, in September 1978, Merrill Lynch had formally announced its intention to acquire at least 40 real estate brokerage firms within three to four years. Merrill Lynch's interest in the industry stemmed not only from the profit opportunities it saw but also from a corporate desire to become a "financial services supermarket," providing individual customers with a wide range of investment and brokerage services. In 1978 Merrill Lynch had acquired United First Mortgage Corporation (UFM), a mortgage banker. And in early 1979 Merrill Lynch was in the midst of acquiring AMIC Corporation, a small mortgage insurance company in direct competition with CMI. As *Fortune* reported:

> In combination, these diverse activities hold some striking possibilities. Merrill Lynch already packages and markets mortgages through its registered representatives. . . . If all goes according to plan, the company could later this year be vertically integrated in a unique way. Assuming the AMIC acquisition goes through, Merrill Lynch will be able to guarantee mortgages. It could then originate mortgages through its realty brokerages, process and service them through UFM, insure them with AMIC, package them as pass-through or unit trusts, and market them through its army of registered representatives. (January 29, 1979, p. 89)

It was this vision of an integrated financial services organization that also excited Frank Randall. As he and Jim Dolan reviewed their position in early 1979, they were confident that they were in a unique position to build CMI into a much bigger and more diversified company. The mortgage insurance business gave them a solid financial base, with regional offices throughout the country. Northwest Equipment stood ready to provide the capital they would need for significant growth. They already had relationships with important lending institutions across the United States, and their marketing efforts had given them a solid reputation with important real estate brokers as well.

Thus, Randall, in particular, felt that at least he had most of the ingredients to begin building that diversified "residential real estate financial services company" he had been dreaming about for so long. Furthermore, Randall's reading of the banking, thrift, and real estate industries suggested that the time was ripe. In his view, the uncertainties in the financial and housing industries created rich opportunities for taking aggressive action, and the vision of Merrill Lynch "bulling" its way into the business was scaring realtors just enough for CMI to present a comforting and familiar alternative.

THE METROPOLITAN REALTY NETWORK

Frank Randall spent most of the fall of 1978 actively searching for acquisition opportunities. As part of his effort, he contacted David Osgood, who was the executive director of the Metropolitan Realty Network, a national association of independent real estate brokers. The association, commonly known as MetroNet, had been formed primarily as a communication vehicle so its members could refer home buyers moving from one city to another to a qualified broker in the new location.

Randall discovered that Osgood was somewhat concerned about MetroNet's long-term health and viability. Though MetroNet included over 13,000 real estate agencies, it was losing some members to national franchise chains, and Osgood was feeling increasing pressures to strengthen the association by providing more services to member firms. Yet the entrepreneurial independence of MetroNet's members made Osgood's task particularly difficult. He had found it almost impossible to get them to agree on what they wanted him to do.

One service that the MetroNet brokers *were* agreed on developing was the employee relocation business. Corporate contracts to handle transferred employees were especially attractive to the brokers, because the contracts virtually guaranteed repeat business in the local area, and they also led to intercity referrals that almost always resulted in a home sale.

MetroNet brokers were also resentful of how Merrill Lynch Relocation Management and other relocation services companies were getting a larger and larger share of "their" referral fees. Osgood told Randall that he had already set up a committee of MetroNet brokers to look into how the association could develop a corporate relocation and third-party equity capability[2] of its own. Osgood mentioned that their only effort to date was an independent firm in Chicago named Corporate Transfer Services, Inc. (CTS), that had been started by Elliott Burr, a prominent Chicago broker and a MetroNet director. CTS had been formed with the intention of working with MetroNet brokers, but so far it had remained relatively small and had not met MetroNet's expectations.

As Randall explained to Osgood what kinds of activities CMI engaged in to help lenders and increase the volume of home sales, Osgood suddenly exclaimed, "That's exactly what *we're* trying to do!" The two men ended their initial meeting convinced that some kind of working relationship between CMI and MetroNet could have major benefits for both organizations. Osgood invited Randall to attend the next meeting of MetroNet's Third-Party Equity Committee, scheduled for March 1. "Let's explore what we can do for each other," said Osgood. "You're on," concluded Randall.

THE THIRD-PARTY EQUITY BUSINESS

Randall's discussion with David Osgood had opened his eyes to the third-party equity business, and he and Jim Dolan spent most of their time in preparation for the March 1 committee meeting steeped in industry studies and pro forma income statements.

They quickly discovered that the employee relocation services industry was highly competitive, though its future looked bright. Corporate transfers of key employees appeared to be an ingrained practice that showed no signs of letting up in the foreseeable future. Merrill Lynch Relocation Management was one of the two largest firms in the industry; most of the prominent relocation companies were well-funded subsidiaries of large, well-known corporations. Exhibit 1 contains Jim Dolan's tabulation of the seven major relocation firms, along with his estimates of each company's 1978 volume of home purchases.

Dolan also developed a pro forma income and expense statement for a hypothetical firm handling 2,000 home purchases annually (see Exhibit 2). His calculations showed a

---

[2]The term *third-party equity capability* derived from the fact that a relocation services company actually purchased an employee's home, freeing up the owner's equity and making it available for investment in a new home. Within the industry, the terms *third-party equity company* and *employee relocation services company* were generally used interchangeably.

EXHIBIT 1 Major Employee Relocation Services Companies

Relocation Company	Parent Organization	Estimated 1978 Home Purchases	Estimated Value of Home Purchases[*]	Estimated Gross Fee Income[†]
Merrill Lynch Relocation	Merrill Lynch	13,000	$975,000,000	$26,800,000
Homequity	Peterson, Howell, & Heather	12,000	900,000,000	24,750,000
Equitable Relocation	Equitable Life Insurance	5,000	375,000,000	10,300,000
Employee Transfer	Chicago Title and Trust	5,000	375,000,000	10,300,000
Relocation Realty Corporation	Control Data Corporation	3,000	225,000,000	6,200,000
Executrans	Sears/Coldwell Banker	3,000	225,000,000	6,200,000
Transamerica Relocation	Transamerica, Inc.	3,000	225,000,000	6,200,000

[*] Assumes average home values of $75,000.
[†] Assumes fee averaging 2.75 percent of value of homes purchased.

609

EXHIBIT 2 Hypothetical Employee Relocation Company Pro Forma Income Statement

Key assumptions

1. Annual purchase volume of 2,000 homes.
2. Assume average holding period of 120 days. Inventory turns over three times annually, for an average of 667 units in inventory at any point in time.
3. Average home value of $75,000.
4. Existing mortgages on homes average 50 percent of property value. Additional required capital will be 40 percent equity, 60 percent long-term debt.
5. Fee income from corporate clients will average 2.75 percent of value of properties purchased (based on historical industry data).
6. Operating expenses (marketing, sales, office administration) will average 1 percent of value of properties purchased (all costs associated with purchases, including debt service, are billed back to corporate clients).

Calculations

Total value of purchases	
(2,000 units at $75,000)	$150,000,000
Average inventory value	50,000,000
Capital required	
Existing mortgages	25,000,000
New long-term debt	15,000,000
Equity	10,000,000
Fee income at 2.75%	4,125,000
Operating expenses at 1%	1,500,000
Net income	$2,625,000
Tax at 50%	(1,312,500)
Profit after tax	$1,312,500
Return on equity	13.1%

potential 13.1 percent return on equity (ROE). Dolan then discovered that some compa-nies achieved a much higher ROE by using a Home Purchase Trust, a legal arrangement that made it possible to obtain enough bank financing to leverage a company's equity base by as much as 10 to 1.

Randall and Dolan were increasingly certain that they wanted to get CMI into the employee relocation services business. They saw it as a natural tie-in with CMI's mort-gage insurance operations—one that could exploit the same set of relationships that CMI already had with banks, realtors, savings and loans, and other companies involved in the development, construction, sale, and financing of residential real estate. The two men felt that real estate brokers had a critically important role in the process. Brokers were not only involved in the actual property transactions, but in addition they almost always had local contacts with corporations that could lead to the signing of employee relocation contracts. Equally important, from Randall's and Dolan's perspective, was their belief that a close relationship between CMI and the MetroNet brokers would also lead to significant sales of CMI's mortgage insurance policies.

The March 1 meeting with MetroNet's Third-Party Equity Committee turned into an exploration of how CMI and MetroNet might help each other by stimulating both home sales and high-ratio mortgage loans. After several hours of discussion, Frank Randall proposed specifically that CMI build an operating company to handle the corporate relocation business jointly with the MetroNet brokers. As a quid pro quo, Randall suggested that the brokers could market CMI mortgage insurance to both potential home buyers and lending institutions.

The committee's response to this idea was initially skeptical. Finally, however, they agreed to consider a more formal proposal at a later date. MetroNet's board of directors was scheduled to meet on April 10; the Third-Party Equity Committee could review the proposal on April 9 and, if they approved, present it to the full board on the 10th.

As the committee meeting broke up, Randall and Dolan began talking with Elliott Burr and Thomas Winder, two of the four owners of Corporate Transfer Services, Inc. (CTS). Though Burr had been the principal founder of CTS, his primary business was a large real estate brokerage firm in north suburban Chicago that he operated in partnership with William Lehman, who was also a CTS stockholder.

The four men sat back down at the meeting table, and Randall mentioned that his primary interest was to learn more about how an employee relocation business operated. Burr offered to send him copies of contracts with corporate clients, sample financial statements, and so on. At one point during their discussion Burr mentioned the possibility of an acquisition. Randall asked, somewhat rhetorically, "How do you put a value on a company like this?" Burr responded almost immediately, "Funny you should ask. We've talked to an attorney and have put together this proposal." Burr reached into his briefcase and pulled out a two-page document. He then proceeded to describe a complex set of terms involving the sale of an 80 percent interest in CTS, subject to guarantees concerning capitalization, lines of credit, data processing support, future distribution of profits and dividends, and more.

Randall backed off immediately, explaining that he needed to learn more about the nature of the business before he would seriously consider an acquisition. As Jim Dolan later recalled:

> I think they were expecting an offer right then and there. But it was very hard to understand what they really wanted; it was nothing we could actually work from. Besides that, the numbers they were thinking about were ridiculously high—over $5 million. We put the letter away and told them we didn't want to get specific until after the April 10 meeting. And that's the way we left it.

PREPARATION FOR THE APRIL 10 MEETING

During the next six weeks Randall and Dolan continued their investigations of the employee relocation industry and studied CTS much more closely.

One of their major questions was how much additional mortgage insurance the MetroNet brokers might be able to generate. Frank Randall had CMI's marketing staff conduct a telephone survey of about 25 key MetroNet brokers. The survey suggested that most brokers were aware of mortgage insurance, although few of them were actively pushing it. All of those questioned expressed an interest in using CMI's marketing programs, and were eager to learn more about CMI insurance.

By early May a fairly clear picture of CTS was emerging. The company had been founded in 1975; it had barely achieved a breakeven profit level. Annual home purchases and sales had reached a level of almost 500 properties, and CTS has worked with about

65 MetroNet brokers and 35 corporate clients. Tom Winder was the general manager; he supervised a staff of about 25 customer representatives and clerical support staff. Conversations with David Osgood and several MetroNet brokers who had worked with CTS suggested that the company had made promises to MetroNet about developing a nationwide, well-financed, fully competitive organization. To date, however, those promises were largely unfulfilled. Osgood believed that CTS's shortage of equity and, therefore, borrowing capacity, had severely limited its growth potential.

Jim Dolan obtained a copy of CTS's December 1978 balance sheet that, in his mind, confirmed Osgood's feelings (see Exhibit 3). The company had a net worth of only $420,000. Three of the four stockholders (Elliott Burr, William Lehman, and Michael Kupchak) had invested an additional $2 million in the company—$1.3 million in short-term notes and $700,000 in bank loans that they had personally guaranteed. While CTS owned homes valued at $13.4 million, it also had additional bank loans and assumed mortgages totaling $9.8 million. Furthermore, the company had a highly uncertain earnings stream; Frank Randall believed the current business could tail off to almost nothing within six months.

During late March both Randall and Dolan had a number of telephone conversations with Burr and Winder. Their discussions were wide ranging and quite open; the CTS partners struck Randall as being unusually candid. They seemed more than willing to share everything they knew about the business and their own company. On one occasion, Burr asked how much of CTS Randall wanted to buy and how Randall would feel about the present owners retaining a minority interest. Burr's question led Randall and Dolan to conclude that in fact they wanted full ownership. They planned to build up the company's equity base considerably and wanted to gain all the benefits of a larger, more profitable operation for CMI.

In early April, Randall developed the formal proposal that he intended to present to MetroNet's board of directors (see Exhibit 4). The proposal committed CMI to enter negotiations to acquire CTS and to use CTS as a base for building a third-party equity company with a capitalization sufficient to support an annual home purchase capability of at least 2,000 units. In return, the proposal asked MetroNet to begin a program of actively supporting the use of CMI's insurance on high-ratio loans.

Randall and Dolan met again with the Third-Party Equity Committee in New York on April 9 to preview the CMI proposal. The committee reacted favorably, and the next day MetroNet's board of directors unanimously accepted the proposal after discussing it for less than 15 minutes.

FORMAL NEGOTIATIONS WITH
CORPORATE TRANSFER SERVICES

On the afternoon of April 10, following the MetroNet board meeting, Randall and Dolan met again with Elliott Burr and Tom Winder. Now that CMI was formally committed to acquisition negotiations, Burr and Winder were eager to get specific and talk numbers. However, Randall and Dolan remained very cautious. When Burr expressed an interest in discussing a price, Randall replied, "We don't know what you're worth. But we'll entertain any reasonable argument you want to make for why we should pay more than your net worth." The meeting ended with a general agreement to firm things up by April 25. Later, reflecting on this session, Jim Dolan commented:

EXHIBIT 3   CTS Balance Sheet

CORPORATE TRANSFER SERVICES, INC.
Unaudited Balance Sheet
December 1978

	($ 000)
Assets	
Cash	$ 190
Homes owned	13,366
Accounts and acquisition fees receivable	665
Other (mainly escrow deposits)	143
	$14,364
Liabilities	
Client prepayments	$1,602
Notes payable to banks	4,161
Assumed mortgages payable	5,670
Loan from stockholders	700
Advance from MetroNet	300
Other liabilities	211
	$12,644
Capital	
Subordinated debenture due	
stockholder (April 1981)	1,300
Common stock	450
Deficit	(30)
	$14,364

Our letter of agreement committed us to having an operating company by July 12, so the clock was running on us. However, we know that after the April 10 board meeting they would be hard pressed not to be bought, and besides they were obviously pretty eager. But at that point in time we had not even met the other two stockholders; we suspected the high numbers were coming from them.

FURTHER ASSESSMENT OF CTS

Even though the April 10 meeting had ended with an agreement to move ahead by April 25, it quickly became evident that a complete assessment of CTS and preparation of a formal offer would take more than two weeks. Other operating responsibilities prevented both Randall and Dolan from devoting as much time as they had intended to the acquisition, and the analysis process itself required more time than they had expected.

During the first week of May, Jim Dolan made a "reconnaissance" trip to Chicago. His stated purpose was to examine CTS's books and talk with the company's local bankers. He also scrutinized the office facilities, met and talked with several office employees, observed Tom Winder interacting with customers and subordinates, and generally assessed the company's operations. Dolan spent most of his time with Winder, but he also had an opportunity to have dinner with William Lehman, another of CTS's stockholders. Dolan returned to Philadelphia with a generally favorable set of impressions about the company's operations and a much more concrete understanding of its financial situation. He reported to Randall, "They're running a responsible organization

EXHIBIT 4 Letter of Intent

Board of Directors
The Metropolitan Realty Network
New York, NY

April 9, 1979

Gentlemen:

It is our intention to enter negotiations with the principals of Corporate Transfer Services, Inc., for the acquisition of the equity ownership of this Company by Capital Mortgage Insurance Corporation.

In the event Capital Mortgage Insurance Corporation is successful in the acquisition of Corporate Transfer Services, Inc., it is our intention to capitalize this Company to the extent required for the development of a complete bank line of credit. The initial capital and bank line of credit would provide the MetroNet association members an annual equity procurement of 1,500–2,000 units. In addition, we would be prepared to expand beyond this initial capacity if the MetroNet Association volume and profitability of business dictate.

We are prepared to develop an organizational structure and support system that can provide a competitive and professional marketing and administrative approach to the corporate transfer market.

Our intentions to enter negotiations with Corporate Transfer Services, Inc., are subject to the following:

1. The endorsement of this action by you, the board of directors of MetroNet, for Capital Mortgage Insurance Corporation to acquire this organization.

2. The assurance of the MetroNet Association for the continuation of their support and use of CTS. Upon completion of the acquisition, the MetroNet Association would agree to sign a Letter of Agreement with the new owners of Corporate Transfer Services.

3. The assurance of the MetroNet Association to cooperate in the development of a close working relationship with CMI for the influence and control they may provide when seeking high-ratio conventional mortgage loans using mortgage insurance.

Capital Mortgage Insurance will need the support of expanded business by the MetroNet Association, due to the heavy capital commitment we will be required to make to CTS to make this acquisition feasible. In this regard, CMI is prepared to offer the MetroNet nationwide members a range of marketing programs and mortgage financing packages that will help earn and deserve the mortgage insurance business and expand the listings, sales, and profitability of the MetroNet members.

Upon receiving the endorsement and support outlined in this letter from the board of directors of MetroNet, we will proceed immediately with the negotiations with Corporate Transfer Services, Inc. It would be our intention to have the acquisition completed and the company fully operational by the time of the MetroNet national convention in San Francisco in July 1979.

Sincerely,

Franklin T. Randall
President and Chief Executive Officer

in a basically sensible manner." At the same time, however, Dolan also reported that CTS was under increasing pressure from its bankers to improve its financial performance.

Dolan's trip also provided him with a much richer understanding of the four men who owned CTS: Elliott Burr, William Lehman (Burr's real estate partner), Michael Kupchak (a private investor), and Tom Winder. Of these four, only Winder was actively involved in the day-to-day management of the company, although Elliott Burr stayed in very close touch with Winder and was significantly more involved than either Lehman or Kupchak. From their meetings and telephone conversations, Randall and Dolan pieced together the following pictures of the four men:

- *Elliott Burr,* in his middle 50s, had been the driving force behind Corporate Transfer Services. He was a classic real estate salesman—a warm, straightforward, friendly man who enthusiastically believed in what he was doing. An eternal optimist, he had been an early advocate of MetroNet's getting into the employee relocation business. Burr knew the relocation business extremely well; he personally called on many of the large Chicago corporations to sell CTS's services.

  Burr appeared to be very well off financially. Burr and Lehman Real Estate was one of the largest realty firms on Chicago's North Shore, and Burr was held in high regard by local bankers. One banker had told Dolan, "Burr's word is his bond."

- *William Lehman,* Burr's real estate partner, was in his mid-60s. He appeared to be much more of a financial adviser and investor than an operating manager. Lehman personally owned the shopping center where Burr and Lehman Real Estate was located, as well as the office building where CTS was leasing space.

  Dolan characterized Lehman as an "elder statesman—a true gentleman." Dolan recalled that when he had had dinner with Lehman during his visit to Chicago, Lehman had kept the conversation on a personal level, repeatedly expressing concern about Dolan's plane reservations, hotel accommodations, and so on. He had hardly mentioned CTS during the entire dinner.

- *Michael Kupchak* was the third principal stockholder. Kupchak, about 50, had been a mortgage banker in Chicago for a number of years. Recently, however, he had left the bank to manage his own investments on a full-time basis.

  Dolan met Kupchak briefly during his Chicago visit, and characterized him as a "bulldog"—an aggressive, ambitious man much more interested in financial transactions than in the nature of the business. He had apparently thought Dolan was coming to Chicago to make a firm offer and had been irritated that one had not been forthcoming. Frank Randall had not yet met Kupchak face to face, although they had talked once by telephone.

- *Thomas Winder,* 44, had spent most of his career in real estate-related businesses. At one time he had worked for a construction company, and then he had joined the mortgage bank where Michael Kupchak worked.

  Kupchak had actually brought Winder into CTS as its general manager, and the three original partners had offered him 25 percent ownership in the company as part of his compensation package.

Winder was not only CTS's general manager, but its lead salesperson as well. He called on prospective corporate clients all over the country, and he worked closely with MetroNet. That activity primarily involved appearing at association-sponsored seminars to inform member brokers about CTS and its services.

It was obvious to Jim Dolan that CTS had become an important source of real estate sales commissions for the Burr and Lehman partnership. Most of CTS's clients were in the Chicago area, and a large portion of the real estate transactions generated by CTS were being handled by Burr and Lehman Real Estate.

Dolan also inferred that the three senior partners—Burr, Lehman, and Kupchak—were close friends socially as well as professionally. The men clearly respected each other and valued each other's opinions. On one occasion Burr had told Dolan, "It's because of Bill Lehman that I have what I have today. I can always trust his word." Tom Winder was also woven into the relationship, but he was apparently not as closely involved as the other three. Randall and Dolan both sensed that Elliott Burr was the unofficial spokesman of the group. "I have the impression he can speak for all of them," commented Dolan.

In late April, Randall obtained a copy of a consultant's report on the employee relocation industry that had been commissioned by MetroNet's Third-Party Equity Committee. The report estimated that there were more than 500,000 homeowner/employees transferred annually, generating over 1 million home purchases and sales. However, fewer than 55,000 of these transfers were currently being handled by relocation services companies. Dolan's own analysis had projected a 10–15 percent annual growth rate in the use of relocation companies, leading to industry volume estimates of 60,000 in 1979, 67,000 in 1980, and 75,000 by 1981. The consultant's report stressed that success in the relocation business depended on a company's ability to provide services to its corporate clients at lower cost than the clients could do it themselves. In addition, profitability depended on a company's ability to turn over its inventory of homes quickly and at reasonable prices. Dolan's own financial projections showed a potential return on equity of over 30 percent by 1983, assuming only an 8 percent share of the market. And that return did not include any incremental profits resulting from new sales of CMI mortgage insurance policies generated by MetroNet brokers. Randall in particular was confident that the close ties between CMI and MetroNet would result in at least 5,000 new mortgage insurance policies annually—a volume that could add over $400,000 in after-tax profits to CMI's basic business.

On May 10, Randall and Dolan attended a Northwest Equipment Corporation financial review meeting in Minneapolis. Prior to their trip west Randall had prepared a detailed analysis of the CTS acquisition and the employee relocation industry. The analysis, in the form of a proposal, served as documentation for a formal request to Northwest for a capital expenditure of $9 million. Randall had decided that he was willing to pay up to $600,000 more than the $420,000 book value of CTS's net worth; the remaining $8 million would constitute the initial equity base required to build CTS into a viable company. The financial review meeting evolved into a lengthy critique of the acquisition proposal. Northwest's corporate staff was initially quite skeptical of the financial projections, but Randall and Dolan argued that the risks were relatively low (the homes could always be sold) and the potential payoffs, both economic and strategic, were enormous. Finally, after an extended debate, the request was approved.

FORMAL NEGOTIATIONS WITH CTS

When Randall and Dolan returned from Minneapolis, they felt it was finally time to proceed in earnest with the acquisition negotiations. Randall sensed that at present CTS was limping along to no one's satisfaction—including Elliott Burr's. The company was sucking up much more of Burr's time and energy than he wanted to give it, and its inability to fulfill MetroNet's expectations was beginning to be an embarrassment for Burr personally.

In spite of these problems, Randall remained interested in completing the acquisition. Buying CTS would get CMI into the relocation business quickly, would provide them with immediate licensing and other legal documentation in 38 states, and would get them an experienced operations manager in Tom Winder. More important, Randall knew that Elliott Burr was an important and respected MetroNet broker, and buying CTS would provide an effective, influential entry into the MetroNet "old boy" network. Though he couldn't put a number on the value of that network, Randall believed it was almost more important than the acquisition of CTS itself. Randall was convinced that the connection with the MetroNet brokers would enable him to run CTS at far lower cost than the established relocation companies, and he also expected to realize a significant increase in CMI's mortgage insurance business.

MAY 21, 1979

Now, as Randall and Dolan sat in Randall's office on May 21, they discussed the draft of a formal purchase offer that Dolan had prepared that morning (see Exhibit 5 for relevant excerpts). The two men had decided to make an initial offer of $400,000 more than the $420,000 book value of CTS's net worth, subject to a formal audit and adjustments depending on the final sales prices of all homes owned by CTS as of the formal purchase date. This opening bid was $200,000 below Randall's ceiling price of $600,000 for the firm's goodwill. The offer was for 100 percent of the ownership of the company. The $2 million in outstanding notes would pass through to the new company owned by Randall and Dolan. The offer also included a statement of intent to retain Tom Winder as CTS's general manager and to move the company to CMI's home office in Philadelphia.

As Randall and Dolan reviewed their plans, it was clear that they were more concerned about how to conduct the face-to-face negotiations than with the formal terms themselves. In the telephone call he had just completed, Randall had told Elliott Burr only that they wanted to meet the other stockholders and review their current thinking. At one point during the conversation Jim Dolan commented:

> I really wonder how they'll react to this offer. We've been putting them off for so long now that I'm not sure how they feel about us anymore. And our offer is so much less than they're looking for.

Randall replied:

> I know that—but I have my ceiling. It seems to me the real question now is what kind of bargaining stance we should take, and how to carry it out. What do you think they are expecting?

EXHIBIT 5   Draft of Purchase Letter

The Board of Directors and Stockholders
Corporate Transfer Services, Inc.
Chicago, IL

May 24, 1979

Gentlemen:

Capital Mortgage Insurance Corporation (the "Purchaser") hereby agrees to purchase from you (the "Stockholders"), and you, the Stockholders, hereby jointly and severally agree to sell to us, the Purchaser, 100 percent of the issued and outstanding shares of capital stock of Corporate Transfer Services (the "Company") on the following terms and conditions.

Purchase Price. Subject to any adjustment under the following paragraph, the Purchase Price of the Stock shall be the sum of $400,000.00 (four hundred thousand dollars even) and an amount equal to the Company's net worth as reflected in its audited financial statements on the closing date (the "Closing Date Net Worth").

Adjustment of Purchase Price. The Purchase Price shall be reduced or increased, as the case may be, dollar-for-dollar by the amount, if any, by which the net amount realized on the sale of homes owned as of the Closing Date is exceeded by, or exceeds, the value attributed to such homes in the Closing Date Net Worth.

Continuation of Employment. Immediately upon consummation of the transaction, the Purchaser will enter into discussion with Mr. Thomas Winder with the intent that he continue employment in a management capacity at a mutually agreeable rate of pay. Mr. Winder will relocate to Philadelphia, Pennsylvania, and will be responsible for the sale of all homes owned by the Company at the Closing Date.

Covenant-Not-to-Compete. At the closing, each Stockholder will execute and deliver a covenant-not-to-compete agreeing that he will not engage in any capacity in the business conducted by the Company for a period of two years. If the foregoing correctly states our agreement as to this transaction, please sign below.

Very truly yours,

CAPITAL MORTGAGE INSURANCE
CORPORATION

The foregoing is agreed to and accepted.   By _____
                                                          President

DISCUSSION QUESTIONS

1. Prepare, and be ready to discuss, a negotiation strategy for Randall and Dolan.

2. What should CMI be expecting from CTS?

CASE 2

Pacific Oil Company (A)

For the discussion of Pacific Oil Company, please prepare the following:

1. As background information, read the appendix to this case: "Petrochemical Supply Contracts: A Technical Note" (p. 638).
2. Read Pacific Oil Company case.
3. Prepare the following questions for class discussion:

   a. Describe the problem that Pacific Oil Company faced as it reopened negotiations with Reliant Chemical Company in early 1985.

   b. Evaluate the styles and effectiveness of Messrs. Fontaine, Gaudin, Hauptmann, and Zinnser as negotiators in this case.

   c. What should Frank Kelsey recommend to Jean Fontaine at the end of the case? Why?

THE PACIFIC OIL COMPANY

"Look, you asked for my advice, and I gave it to you," Frank Kelsey said. "If I were you, I wouldn't make any more concessions! I really don't think you ought to agree to their last demand! But you're the one who has to live with the contract, not me!"

Static on the transatlantic telephone connection obscured Jean Fontaine's reply. Kelsey asked him to repeat what he had said.

"OK, OK, calm down, Jean. I can see your point of view. I appreciate the pressures you're under. But I sure don't like the looks of it from this end. Keep in touch—I'll talk to you early next week. In the meantime, I will see what others at the office think about this turn of events."

Frank Kelsey hung up the phone. He sat pensively, staring out at the rain pounding on the window. "Poor Fontaine," he muttered to himself. "He's so anxious to please the customer, he'd feel compelled to give them the whole pie without getting his fair share of the dessert!"

Case prepared by Roy J. Lewicki.

Although this case is almost 20 years old, the editors of this volume believe that it presents valuable lessons about the negotiation process.

Kelsey cleaned and lit his pipe as he mentally reviewed the history of the negotiations. "My word," he thought to himself, "we are getting completely taken in with this Reliant deal! And I can't make Fontaine see it!"

BACKGROUND

Pacific Oil Company was founded in 1902 as the Sweetwater Oil Company of Oklahoma City, Oklahoma. The founder of Sweetwater Oil, E.M. Hutchinson, pioneered a major oil strike in north central Oklahoma that touched off the Oklahoma "black gold" rush of the early 1900s. Through growth and acquisition in the 1920s and 30s, Hutchinson expanded the company rapidly and renamed it Pacific Oil in 1932. After a period of consolidation in the 1940s and 50s, Pacific expanded again. It developed extensive oil holdings in North Africa and the Middle East, as well as significant coal beds in the western United States. Much of Pacific's oil production is sold under its own name as gasoline through service stations in the United States and Europe, but it is also distributed through several chains of independent gasoline stations. In addition, Pacific is also one of the largest and best-known worldwide producers of industrial petrochemicals.

One of Pacific's major industrial chemical lines is the production of vinyl chloride monomer (VCM). The basic components of VCM are ethylene and chlorine. Ethylene is a colorless, flammable, gaseous hydrocarbon with a disagreeable odor; it is generally obtained from natural or coal gas, or by "cracking" petroleum into smaller molecular components. As a further step in the petroleum cracking process, ethylene is combined with chlorine to produce VCM, also a colorless gas.

VCM is the primary component of a family of plastics known as the vinyl chlorides. VCM is subjected to the process of polymerization, in which smaller molecules of vinyl chloride are chemically bonded together to form larger molecular chains and networks. As the bonding occurs, polyvinyl chloride (PVC) is produced; coloring pigments may be added, as well as "plasticizer" compounds that determine the relative flexibility or hardness of the finished material. Through various forms of calendering (pressing between heavy rollers), extruding and injection molding, the plasticized polyvinyl chloride is converted to an enormous array of consumer and industrial applications: flooring, wire insulation, electrical transformers, home furnishings, piping, toys, bottles and containers, rainwear, light roofing, and a variety of protective coatings. (See Exhibit 1 for a breakdown of common PVC-based products.) In 1979, Pacific Oil established the first major contract with the Reliant Corporation for the purchase of vinyl chloride monomer. The Reliant Corporation was a major industrial manufacturer of wood and petrochemical products for the construction industry. Reliant was expanding its manufacturing operations in the production of plastic pipe and pipe fittings, particularly in Europe. The use of plastic as a substitute for iron or copper pipe was gaining rapid acceptance in the construction trades, and the European markets were significantly more progressive in adopting the plastic pipe. Reliant already had developed a small polyvinyl chloride production facility at Abbeville, France, and Pacific constructed a pipeline from its petrochemical plant at Antwerp to Abbeville.

The 1979 contract between Pacific Oil and Reliant was a fairly standard one for the industry and due to expire in December of 1982. The contract was negotiated by Reliant's purchasing managers in Europe, headquartered in Brussels, and the senior marketing

EXHIBIT 1   Polyvinyl Chloride Major Markets, 1982 (units represented in MM pounds)

Market	MM Pounds	Percent of Market Share
Apparel		
Baby pants	22	0.6
Footwear	128	3.2
Miscellaneous	60	1.5
	210	5.3
Building and construction		
Extruded foam moldings	46	1.2
Flooring	428	10.8
Lighting	10	0.3
Panels and siding	64	1.6
Pipe and conduit	720	18.5
Pipe fittings	78	2.0
Rainwater systems	28	0.7
Swimming pool liners	40	1.0
Weather stripping	36	0.9
Miscellaneous	50	1.2
	1,500	38.2
Electrical		
Wire and cable	390	9.9
Home furnishings		
Appliances	32	0.8
Miscellaneous	286	9.8
	318	10.6
Housewares	94	2.4
Packaging		
Blow molded bottles	64	1.6
Closure liners and gaskets	16	0.4
Coatings	16	0.4
Film	124	3.2
Miscellaneous	80	2.0
	300	7.6
Recreation		
Records	136	3.4
Sporting goods	46	1.2
Miscellaneous	68	1.7
	250	6.3
Transportation		
Auto mats	36	0.9
Auto tops	32	0.8
Miscellaneous	164	4.2
	232	5.9

Continued

EXHIBIT 1 *Concluded*

Market	MM Pounds	Percent of Market Share
Miscellaneous		
Agriculture (including pipe)	106	2.6
Credit cards	24	0.4
Garden hose	40	1.0
Laminates	44	1.1
Medical tubing	42	1.1
Novelties	12	0.3
Stationery supplies	32	0.8
Miscellaneous	12	0.3
	312	7.6
Export	146	3.7
Miscellaneous	98	2.5
	244	6.2
Total	3,850	100.0

managers of Pacific Oil's European offices, located in Paris. Each of these individuals reported to the vice presidents in charge of their company's European offices, who in turn reported back to their respective corporate headquarters in the States. (See Exhibits 2 and 3 for partial organization charts.)

THE 1982 CONTRACT RENEWAL

In February 1982, negotiations began to extend the four-year contract beyond the December 31, 1982, expiration date. Jean Fontaine, Pacific Oil's marketing vice president for Europe, discussed the Reliant account with his VCM marketing manager, Paul Gaudin. Fontaine had been promoted to the European vice presidency approximately 16 months earlier after having served as Pacific's ethylene marketing manager. Fontaine had been with Pacific Oil for 11 years and had a reputation as a strong up and comer in Pacific's European operations. Gaudin had been appointed as VCM marketing manager eight months earlier; this was his first job with Pacific Oil, although he had five years of previous experience in European computer sales with a large American computer manufacturing company. Fontaine and Gaudin had worked well in their short time together, establishing a strong professional and personal relationship. Fontaine and Gaudin agreed that the Reliant account had been an extremely profitable and beneficial one for Pacific and believed that Reliant had, overall, been satisfied with the quality and service under the agreement as well. They clearly wanted to work hard to obtain a favorable renegotiation of the existing agreement. Fontaine and Gaudin also reviewed the latest projections of worldwide VCM supply, which they had just received from corporate headquarters (see Exhibit 4). The data confirmed what they already knew—that there was a worldwide shortage of VCM and that demand was continuing to rise. Pacific envisioned that the current demand–supply situation would remain this way for a number of years. As a result, Pacific believed that it could justify a high favorable formula price for VCM.

EXHIBIT 2   Partial Organization Chart—Pacific Oil Coompany

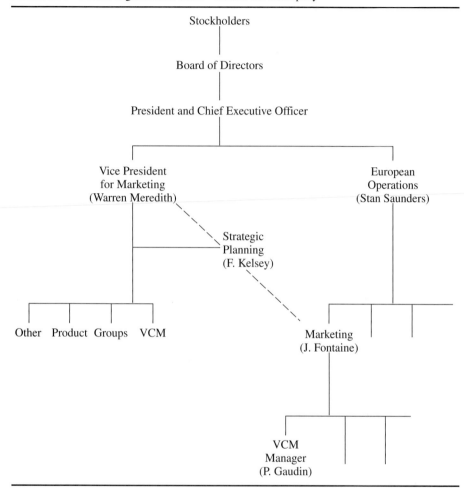

Fontaine and Gaudin decided that they would approach Reliant with an offer to renegotiate the current agreement. Their basic strategy would be to ask Reliant for their five-year demand projections on VCM and polyvinyl chloride products. Once these projections were received, Fontaine and Gaudin would frame the basic formula price that they would offer. (It would be expected that there would be no significant changes or variations in other elements of the contract, such as delivery and contract language.) In their negotiations, their strategy would be as follows:

a. To dwell on the successful long-term relationship that had already been built between Reliant and Pacific Oil, and to emphasize the value of that relationship for the success of both companies.

b. To emphasize all of the projections that predicted the worldwide shortage of VCM and the desirability for Reliant to ensure that they would have a guaranteed supplier.

EXHIBIT 3   Partial Organization Chart—Reliant Chemical Coompany

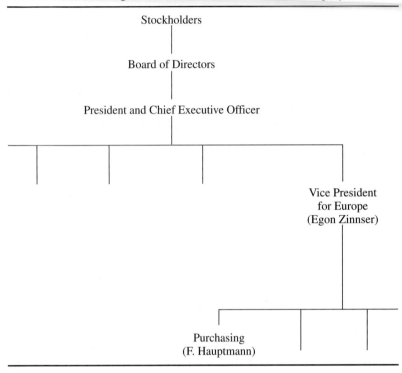

EXHIBIT 4   Memorandum, January 17, 1982

TO: All VCM Marketing Managers
FROM: F. Kelsey, Strategic Planning Division
RE: Worldwide VCM Supply/Demand Projections
DATE: January 17, 1982

CONFIDENTIAL—FOR YOUR EYES ONLY
Here are the data from 1980 and 1981, and the five-year projections that I promised you at our last meeting. As you can see, the market is tight, and is projected to get tighter. I hope you will find this useful in your marketing efforts—let me know if I can supply more detailed information.

Year	*Total Projected Demand (in MM pounds)*	*Supply Plant Capacities*	*Operating Rates to Meet Demand (percent)*
1980	4,040	5,390	75%
1981	4,336	5,390	80
1982	5,100	6,600	77
1983	5,350	6,600	81
1984	5,550	6,600	83
1985	5,650	7,300	75
1986	5,750	7,300	78

c. To point out all of the ways that Pacific had gone out of its way in the past to ensure delivery and service.

d. To use both the past and future quality of the relationship to justify what might appear to be a high formula price.

e. To point out the ways that Pacific's competitors could not offer the same kind of service.

Over the next six months, Gaudin and Fontaine, independently and together, made a number of trips to Brussels to visit Reliant executives. In addition, several members of Pacific's senior management visited Brussels and paid courtesy calls on Reliant management. The net result was a very favorable contract for Pacific Oil, signed by both parties on October 24, 1982. The basic contract, to extend from January 1983 to December 1987, is represented as Exhibit 5.

EXHIBIT 5   Agreement of Sale

This Agreement, entered into this <u>24th</u> day of <u>October, 1982</u>, between <u>Pacific Oil Company</u>, hereinafter called Seller, and <u>Reliant Chemical Company of Europe,</u> hereinafter called Buyer.

WITNESSETH:

Seller agrees to sell and deliver and Buyer agrees to purchase and receive commodity (hereinafter called "product") under the terms and conditions set forth below.

1. Product: Vinyl Chloride Monomer

2. Quality: ASTM requirements for polymer-grade product

3. Quantity: 1983: 150 million pounds
             1984: 160 million pounds
             1985: 170 million pounds
             1986: 185 million pounds
             1987: 200 million pounds

4. Period: Contract shall extend from January 1, 1983, and extend until December 31, 1987, and every year thereafter, unless terminated with 180 days' prior notification at the end of each calendar year, but not before December 31, 1987.

5. Price: See Contract formula price.

6. Payment Terms:
   a. Net 30 days.
   b. All payments shall be made in United States dollars without discount or deduction, unless otherwise noted, by wire transfer at Seller's option, to a bank account designated by Seller. Invoices not paid on due date will be subject to a delinquency finance charge of 1 percent per month.
   c. If at any time the financial responsibility of Buyer shall become impaired or unsatisfactory to Seller, cash payment on delivery or satisfactory security may be required. A failure to pay any amount may, at the option of the Seller, terminate this contract as to further deliveries. No forbearance, course of dealing, or prior payment shall affect this right of Seller.

Continued

EXHIBIT 5 *Continued*

7. Price Change:

The price specified in this Agreement may be changed by Seller on the first day of any calendar half-year by written notice sent to the Buyer not less than thirty (30) days prior to the effective date of change. Buyer gives Seller written notice of objection to such change at least ten (10) days prior to the effective date of change. Buyer's failure to serve Seller with written notice of objection thereto prior to the effective date thereof shall be considered acceptance of such change. If Buyer gives such notice of objection and Buyer and Seller fail to agree on such change prior to the effective date thereof, this Agreement and the obligations of Seller and Buyer hereunder shall terminate with respect to the unshipped portion of the Product governed by it. Seller has the option immediately to cancel this contract upon written notice to Buyer, to continue to sell hereunder at the same price and terms which were in effect at the time Seller gave notice of change, or to suspend performance under this contract while pricing is being resolved. If Seller desires to revise the price, freight allowance, or terms of payment pursuant to this agreement, but is restricted to any extent against doing so by reason of any law, governmental decree, order or regulation, or if the price, freight allowance, or terms of payment then in effect under this contract are nullified or reduced by reason of any law, governmental decree, order, or regulation. Seller shall have the right to cancel this contract upon fifteen (15) days' written notice to purchaser.

8. Measurements:

Seller's determinations, unless proven to be erroneous, shall be accepted as conclusive evidence of the quantity of Product delivered hereunder. Credit will not be allowed for shortages of 1/2 of 1 percent or less of the quantity, and overages of 1/2 of 1 percent or less of the quantity will be waived. The total amount of shortages or overages will be credited or billed when quantities are greater and such differences are substantiated. Measurements of weight and volume shall be according to procedures and criteria standard for such determinations.

9. Shipments and Delivery:

Buyer shall give Seller annual or quarterly forecasts of its expected requirements as Seller may from time to time request. Buyer shall give Seller reasonably advanced notice for each shipment which shall include date of delivery and shipping instructions. Buyer shall agree to take deliveries in approximately equal monthly quantities, except as may be otherwise provided herein. In the event that Buyer fails to take the quantity specified or the pro rata quantity in any month, Seller may, at its option, in addition to other rights and remedies, cancel such shipments or parts thereof.

10. Purchase Requirements:

    a. If during any consecutive three-month period, Buyer for any reason (but not for reasons of force majeure as set forth in Section 12) takes less than 90 percent of the average monthly quantity specified, or the prorated minimum monthly quantity then applicable to such period under Section 12, Seller may elect to charge Buyer a penalty charge for failure to take the average monthly quantity or prorated minimum monthly quantity.

    b. If, during any consecutive three-month period, Buyer, for any reason (but not, however, for reasons of force majeure as set forth in Section 12) takes Product in quantities less than that equal to at least one-half of the average monthly quantity specified or the prorated minimum monthly quantity originally applicable to such period under Section 12, Seller may elect to terminate this agreement.

    c. It is the Seller's intent not to unreasonably exercise its right under (*a*) or (*b*) in the event of adverse economic and business conditions in general.

Continued

EXHIBIT 5 *Continued*

---

    d. Notice of election by Seller under (*a*) or (*b*) shall be given within 30 days after the end of the applicable three-month period, and the effective date of termination shall be 30 days after the date of said notice.

11. Detention Policy:

Seller may, from time to time, specify free unloading time allowances for its transportation equipment. Buyer shall be liable to the Transportation Company for all demurrage charges made by the Transportation Company, for railcars, trucks, tanks, or barges held by Buyer beyond the free unloading time.

12. Force Majeure:

Neither party shall be liable to the other for failure or delay in performance hereunder to the extent that such failure or delay is due to war, fire, flood, strike, lockout, or other labor trouble, accident, breakdown of equipment or machinery, riot, act, request, or suggestion of governmental authority, act of God, or other contingencies beyond the control of the affected party which interfere with the production or transportation of the material covered by this Agreement or with the supply of any raw material (whether or not the source of supply was in existence or contemplated at the time of this Agreement) or energy source used in connection therewith, or interfere with Buyer's consumption of such material, provided that in no event shall Buyer be relieved of the obligation to pay in full for material delivered hereunder. Without limitation on the foregoing, neither party shall be required to remove any cause listed above or replace the affected source of supply or facility if it shall involve additional expense or departure from its normal practices. If any of the events specified in this paragraph shall have occurred, Seller shall have the right to allocate in a fair and reasonable manner among its customers and Seller's own requirements any supplies of material Seller has available for delivery at the time or for the duration of the event.

13. Materials and Energy Supply:

If, for reasons beyond reasonable commercial control, Seller's supply of product to be delivered hereunder shall be limited due to continued availability of necessary raw materials and energy supplies, Seller shall have the right (without liability) to allocate to the Buyer a portion of such product on such basis as Seller deems equitable. Such allocation shall normally be that percent of Seller's total internal and external commitments which are committed to Buyer as related to the total quantity available from Seller's manufacturing facilities.

14. Disclaimer:

Seller makes no warranty, express or implied, concerning the product furnished hereunder other than it shall be of the quality and specifications stated herein. Any implied warranty of FITNESS is expressly excluded and to the extent that it is contrary to the foregoing sentence; any implied warranty of MERCHANTABILITY is expressly excluded. Any recommendation made by Seller makes no warranty of results to be obtained. Buyer assumes all responsibility and liability for loss or damage resulting from the handling or use of said product. In no event shall Seller be liable for any special, indirect, or consequential damages, irrespective of whether caused or allegedly caused by negligence.

15. Taxes:

Any tax, excise fee, or other charge or increase thereof upon the production, storage, withdrawal, sale, or transportation of the product sold hereunder, or entering into the cost of such product, imposed by any proper authority becoming effective after the date hereof, shall be added to the price herein provided and shall be paid by the Buyer.

Continued

EXHIBIT 5 *Concluded*

16. Assignment and Resale:

This contract is not transferable or assignable by Buyer without the written consent of Seller. The product described hereunder, in the form and manner provided by the Seller, may not be assigned or resold without prior written consent of the Seller.

17. Acceptance:

Acceptance hereof must be without qualification, and Seller will not be bound by any different terms and conditions contained in any other communication.

18. Waiver of Breach:

No waiver by Seller or Buyer of any breach of any of the terms and conditions contained in this Agreement shall be construed as a waiver or any subsequent breach of the same or any other term or condition.

19. Termination:

If any provision of this agreement is or become violate of any law, or any rule, order, or regulation issued thereunder, Seller shall have the right, upon notice to Buyer, to terminate the Agreement in its entirety.

20. Governing Law:

The construction of this Agreement and the rights and obligations of the parties hereunder shall be governed by the laws of the State of New York.

21. Special Provisions:

BUYER:

_____

(firm)

By: _____

Title: <u>Senior Purchasing Manager</u>

Date: _____

SELLER:
PACIFIC OIL CORPORATION

By: _____

Title: <u>Marketing Vice President</u>

Date: _____

A CHANGED PERSPECTIVE

In December of 1984, Fontaine and Gaudin sat down to their traditional end-of-year review of all existing chemical contracts. As a matter of course, the Reliant VCM contract came under review. Although everything had been proceeding very smoothly, the prospects for the near and long-term future were obviously less clear, for the following reasons:

1. Both men reviewed the data that they had been receiving from corporate headquarters, as well as published projections of the supply situation for various chemicals over the next 10 years. It was clear that the basic supply–demand situation on VCM was changing (see Exhibit 6). While the market was currently tight—the favorable supply situation that had existed for Pacific when the Reliant contract was

EXHIBIT 6   Memorandum, December 9, 1984

TO: All VCM Marketing Managers
FROM: F. Kelsey, Strategic Planning Division
RE: Worldwide VCM/Supply/Demand Projections
DATE: December 9, 1984

CONFIDENTIAL—FOR YOUR EYES ONLY
This will confirm and summarize data that we discussed at the national marketing meeting last month in Atlanta. At that time, I indicated to you that the market projections we made several years ago have changed drastically. In early 1983, a number of our competitors announced their intentions to enter the VCM business over the next five years. Several facilities are now under construction, and are expected to come on line in late 1986 and early 1987. As a result, we expect a fairly significant shift in the supply/demand relationship over the next few years.

I hope you will give this appropriate consideration in your long-range planning effort. Please contact me if I can be helpful.

Year	Total Projected Demand (in MM pounds)	Supply Plant Capacities	Operating Rates to Meet Demand (percent)
1982	5,127 (actual)	6,600	78%
1983	5,321 (actual)	6,600	81
1984	5,572 (rev. 11/84)	6,600	84
1985	5,700	7,300	78
1986	5,900	8,450	70
1987	6,200	9,250	64
1988	6,500	9,650	67
1989	7,000	11,000	63

first negotiated—the supply of VCM was expected to expand rapidly over the next few years. Several of Pacific's competitors had announced plans for the construction of VCM manufacturing facilities that were expected to come on line in 20–30 months.

2. Fontaine and Gaudin knew that Reliant was probably aware of this situation as well. As a result, they would probably anticipate the change in the supply–demand situation as an opportunity to pursue a more favorable price, with the possible threat that they would be willing to change suppliers if the terms were not favorable enough. (Although rebuilding a pipeline is no simple matter, it clearly could be done, and had been, when the terms were sufficiently favorable to justify it.)

3. Fontaine was aware that in a situation where the market turned from one of high demand to excess supply, it was necessary to make extra efforts to maintain and re-sign all major current customers. A few large customers (100 million pounds a year and over) dominated the marketplace, and a single customer defection in an oversupplied market could cause major headaches for everyone. It would simply be impossible to find another customer with demands of that magnitude; a number of smaller customers would have to be found, while Pacific would also have to compete with spot market prices that would cut profits to the bone.

4. In a national product development meeting back in the States several weeks prior, Fontaine had learned of plans by Pacific to expand and diversify its own product line into VCM derivatives. There was serious talk of Pacific's manufacturing its own PVC for distribution under the Pacific name, as well as the manufacture and distribution of various PVC products. Should Pacific decide to enter these businesses, not only would they require a significant amount of the VCM now being sold on the external market, but Pacific would probably decide that, as a matter of principle, it would not want to be in the position of supplying a product competitor with the raw materials to manufacture the product line, unless the formula price were extremely favorable.

As they reviewed these factors, Gaudin and Fontaine realized that they needed to take action. They pondered the alternatives.

A NEW CONTRACT IS PROPOSED

As a result of their evaluation of the situation in December 1984, Fontaine and Gaudin decided to proceed on two fronts. First, they would approach Reliant with the intent of reopening negotiation on the current VCM contract. They would propose to renegotiate the current agreement, with an interest toward extending the contract five years from the point of agreement on contract terms. Second, they would contact those people at corporate headquarters in New York who were evaluating Pacific's alternatives for new-product development, and inform them of the nature of the situation. The sooner a determination could be made on the product development strategies, the sooner the Pacific office would know how to proceed on the Reliant contract.

Gaudin contacted Frederich Hauptmann, the senior purchasing manager for Reliant Chemicals in Europe. Hauptmann had assumed the position as purchasing manager approximately four weeks earlier, after having served in a purchasing capacity for a large German steel company. Gaudin arranged a meeting for early January in Hauptmann's office. After getting acquainted over lunch, Gaudin briefed Hauptmann on the history of Reliant's contractual relationships with Pacific Oil. Gaudin made clear that Pacific had been very pleased with the relationship that had been maintained. He said that Pacific was concerned about the future and about maintaining the relationship with Reliant for a long time to come. Hauptmann stated that he understood that the relationship had been a very productive one, too, and also hoped that the two companies could continue to work together in the future. Buoyed by Hauptmann's apparent enthusiasm and relative pleasure with the current agreement, Gaudin said that he and Jean Fontaine, his boss, had recently been reviewing all contracts. Even though the existing Pacific–Reliant VCM agreement had three years to run, Pacific felt that it was never too soon to begin thinking about the long-term future. In order to ensure that Reliant would be assured of a continued supply of VCM, under the favorable terms and working relationship that was already well established, Pacific hoped that Reliant might be willing to begin talks now for contract extension past December 31, 1987. Hauptmann said that he would be willing to consider it but needed to consult other people in the Brussels office, as well as senior executives at corporate headquarters in Chicago. Hauptmann promised to contact Gaudin when he had the answer.

By mid-February, Hauptmann cabled Gaudin that Reliant was indeed willing to begin renegotiation of the current agreement, with interest in extending it for the future. He suggested that Gaudin and Fontaine come to Brussels for a preliminary meeting in early March. Hauptmann also planned to invite Egon Zinnser, the regional vice president of Reliant's European operations and Hauptmann's immediate superior.

MARCH 10

Light snow drifted onto the runway of the Brussels airport as the plane landed. Fontaine and Gaudin had talked about the Reliant contract, and the upcoming negotiations, for most of the trip. They had decided that while they did not expect the negotiations to be a complete pushover, they expected no significant problems or stumbling points in the deliberations. They thought Reliant negotiators would routinely question some of the coefficients that were used to compute the formula price as well as to renegotiate some of the minimum quantity commitments. They felt that the other elements of the contract would be routinely discussed but that no dramatic changes should be expected.

After a pleasant lunch with Hauptmann and Zinnser, the four men sat down to review the current VCM contract. They reviewed and restated much of what Gaudin and Hauptmann had done at their January meeting. Fontaine stated that Pacific Oil was looking toward the future and hoping that it could maintain Reliant as a customer. Zinnser responded that Reliant had indeed been pleased by the contract as well but that it was also concerned about the future. They felt that Pacific's basic formula price on VCM, while fair, might not remain competitive in the long-run future. Zinnser said that he had already had discussions with two other major chemical firms that were planning new VCM manufacturing facilities and that one or both of these firms were due to come on line in the next 24–30 months. Zinnser wanted to make sure that Pacific could remain competitive with other firms in the marketplace. Fontaine responded that it was Pacific's full intention to remain completely competitive, whether it be in market price or in the formula price.

Zinnser said he was pleased by this reply and took this as an indication that Pacific would be willing to evaluate and perhaps adjust some of the factors that were now being used to determine the VCM formula price. He then presented a rather elaborate proposal for adjusting the respective coefficients of these factors. The net result of these adjustments would be to reduce the effective price of VCM by approximately 2 cents per pound. It did not take long for Fontaine and Gaudin to calculate that this would be a net reduction of approximately $4 million per year. Fontaine stated that they would have to take the proposal back to Paris for intensive study and analysis. The men shook hands, and Fontaine and Gaudin headed back to the airport.

Throughout the spring, Gaudin and Hauptmann exchanged several letters and telephone calls. They met once at the Paris airport when Hauptmann stopped over on a trip to the States and once in Zurich when both men discovered that they were going to be there on business the same day. By May 15, they had agreed on a revision of the formula price that would adjust the price downward by almost one cent per pound. Gaudin, relieved that the price had finally been established, reported back to Fontaine that significant progress was being made. Gaudin expected that the remaining issues could be closed up in a few weeks and a new contract signed.

MAY 27

Hauptmann contacted Gaudin to tell him that Reliant was now willing to talk about the remaining issues in the contract. The two men met in early June. Gaudin opened the discussion by saying that now that the formula price had been agreed upon, he hoped that Reliant would be willing to agree to extend the contract five years from the point of signing. Hauptmann replied that Reliant had serious reservations about committing the company to a five-year contract extension. He cited the rapid fluctuations in the demand, pricing structure, and competition of Reliant's various product lines, particularly in the construction industry, as well as what appeared to be a changing perspective in the overall supply of VCM. Quite frankly, Hauptmann said, Reliant didn't want to be caught in a long-term commitment to Pacific if the market price of VCM was likely to drop in the foreseeable future. As a result, Reliant wanted to make a commitment for only a two-year contract renewal.

Gaudin tried to give Hauptmann a number of assurances about the continued integrity of the market. He also said that if changing market prices were a concern for Reliant, Pacific Oil would be happy to attempt to make adjustments in other parts of the contract to ensure protection against dramatic changes in either the market price or the demand for Reliant's product lines. But Hauptmann was adamant. Gaudin said he would have to talk to Fontaine and others in Paris before he could agree to only a two-year contract.

The two men talked several times on the telephone over the next two months and met once in Paris to discuss contract length. On August 17, in a quick 45-minute meeting in Orly Airport, Gaudin and Hauptmann agreed to a three-year contract renewal. They also agreed to meet in early September to discuss remaining contract issues.

SEPTEMBER 10

Hauptmann met Gaudin and Fontaine in Pacific's Paris office. Hauptmann stressed that he and Zinnser were very pleased by the formula price and three-year contract duration that had been agreed to thus far. Fontaine echoed a similar satisfaction on behalf of Pacific and stated that they expected a long and productive relationship with Reliant. Fontaine stressed, however, that Pacific felt it was most important to them to complete the contract negotiations as quickly as possible, in order to adequately plan for product and market development in the future. Hauptmann agreed, saying that this was in Reliant's best interest as well. He felt that there were only a few minor issues that remained to be discussed before the contract could be signed.

Fontaine inquired as to what those issues were. Hauptmann said that the most important one to Reliant was the minimum quantity requirements, stipulating the minimum amount that Reliant had to purchase each year. Gaudin said that based on the projections for the growth of the PVC and fabricated PVC products over the next few years, and patterns established by past contracts, it was Pacific's assumption that Reliant would want to increase their quantity commitments by a minimum of 10 percent each year. Based on minimums stipulated in the current contract, Gaudin expected that Reliant would want to purchase at least 220 million pounds in year 1, 240 million pounds in year 2, and 265 million pounds in year 3. Hauptmann responded that Reliant's projections were very different. The same kind of uncertainty that had led to Reliant's concern about the term of the contract also contributed to a caution about significantly overextending themselves on a minimum quantity commitment. In fact, Reliant's own predictions were that they were likely to take less than the minimum in the current year ("underlifting," in the parlance of the industry) and that, if they did so, they would incur almost a $1 million debt to Pacific. Conservative projections for the following year (1987) projected a similar deficit, but Reliant hoped that business would pick up and that the minimum quantities would be lifted. As a result, Hauptmann and Zinnser felt that it would be in Reliant's best interest to freeze minimum quantity requirements for the next two years—at 200 million pounds—and increase the minimum to 210 million pounds for the third year. Of course, Reliant *expected* that, most likely, they would be continuing to purchase much more than the specified minimums. But given the uncertainty of the future, Reliant did not want to get caught if the economy and the market truly turned sour.

Fontaine and Gaudin were astonished at the conservative projections Hauptmann was making. They tried in numerous ways to convince Hauptmann that his minimums were ridiculously low and that the PVC products were bound to prosper far more than Hauptmann seemed willing to admit. But Hauptmann was adamant and left Paris saying he needed to consult Zinnser and others in Brussels and the States before he could revise his minimum quantity estimates upward. Due to the pressure of other activities and vacation schedules, Gaudin and Hauptmann did not talk again until late October. Finally, on November 19, the two men agreed to a minimum quantity purchase schedule of 205 million pounds in the first year of the contract, 210 million pounds in the second year, and 220 million pounds in the third year. Moreover, Pacific agreed to waive any previous underlifting charges that might be incurred under the current contract when the new contract was signed.

OCTOBER 24

Jean Fontaine returned to Paris from meetings in New York and a major market development meeting held by senior Pacific executives at Hilton Head. After a number of delays due to conflicting market research and changes in senior management, as well as the general uncertainty in the petroleum and chemical markets, Pacific had decided not to develop its own product lines for either PVC or fabricated products. The decision was largely based on the conclusion—more gut feel than hard fact—that entry into these new markets was unwise at a time when much greater problems faced Pacific and the petrochemicals industry in general. Fontaine had argued strenuously that the VCM market was rapidly going soft, and that failure to create its own product lines would leave Pacific Oil in an extremely poor position to market one of its basic products. Fontaine was told that his position was appreciated but that he and other chemical marketing people would simply have to develop new markets and customers for the product. Privately, Fontaine churned on the fact that it had taken senior executives almost a year to make the decision, while valuable time was being lost in developing the markets; but he wisely decided to bite his tongue and vent his frustration on 36 holes of golf. On the return flight to Paris, he read about Pacific's decision in the October 23 issue of *The Wall Street Journal* and ordered a double martini to soothe his nerves.

DECEMBER 14

Fontaine and Gaudin went to Brussels to meet with Hauptmann and Zinnser. The Pacific executives stressed that it was of the utmost importance for Pacific Oil to try to wrap up the contract as quickly as possible—almost a year had passed in deliberations, and although Pacific was not trying to place the "blame" on anyone, it was most concerned that the negotiations be settled as soon as possible.

Zinnser emphasized that he, too, was concerned about completing the negotiations quickly. Both he and Hauptmann were extremely pleased by the agreements that had been reached so far and felt that there was no question that a final contract signing was imminent. The major issues of price, minimum quantities, and contract duration had been solved. In their minds, what remained were only a few minor technical items in contract language. Some minor discussion of each of these should wrap things up in a few weeks.

Fontaine asked what the issues were. Zinnser began by stating that Reliant had become concerned by the way that the delivery pipeline was being metered. As currently set up, the pipeline fed from Pacific's production facility in Antwerp, Belgium, to Reliant's refinery. Pacific had built the line and was in charge of maintaining it. Meters had been installed at the exit flange of the pipeline, and Reliant was paying the metered amount to Pacific. Zinnser said that some spot-checking by Reliant at the manufacturing facility seemed to indicate that they may not be receiving all they were being billed for. They were not questioning the integrity of the meters or the meter readers, but felt that since the pipe was a number of years old, it may have developed leaks. Zinnser felt that it was inappropriate for Reliant to absorb the cost of VCM that was not reaching its facility. They therefore proposed that Pacific install meters directly outside of the entry flange of Reliant's manufacturing facility and that Reliant only be required to pay the meter directly outside the plant.

Fontaine was astonished. In the first place, he said, this was the first time he had heard any complaint about the pipeline or the need to recalibrate the meters. Second, if the pipeline was leaking, Pacific would want to repair it, but it would be impossible to do so until spring. Finally, while the meters themselves were not prohibitively expensive, moving them would mean some interruption of service and definitely be costly to Pacific. Fontaine said he wanted to check with the maintenance personnel at Antwerp to find out whether they could corroborate such leaks.

Fontaine was unable to contact the operating manager at Antwerp or anyone else who could confirm that leaks may have been detected. Routine inspection of the pipeline had been subcontracted to a firm that had sophisticated equipment for monitoring such things, and executives of the firm could not be reached for several days. Fontaine tried to raise other contract issues with Zinnser, but Zinnser said that this was his most important concern, and this issue needed to be resolved before the others could be finalized. Fontaine agreed to find out more about the situation and to bring the information to the next meeting. With the Christmas and New Year holidays approaching, the four men could not schedule another meeting until January 9.

JANUARY MEETINGS

The January 9 meeting was postponed until January 20, due to the death of Mr. Hauptmann's mother. The meeting was rescheduled for a time when Hauptmann needed to be in Geneva, and Gaudin agreed to meet him there.

Gaudin stated that the investigation of the pipeline had discovered no evidence of significant discharge. There were traces of *minor* leaks in the line, but they did not appear to be serious, and it was currently impossible to determine what percentage of the product may be escaping. The most generous estimate given to Gaudin had been 0.1 percent of the daily consumption. Hauptmann stated that their own spot monitoring showed it was considerably more and that Reliant would feel infinitely more comfortable if the new metering system could be installed.

Gaudin had obtained estimates for the cost of remetering before he left Paris. It was estimated that the new meters could be installed for approximately $20,000. Tracing and fixing the leaks (if they existed) could not be done until April or May and might run as much as $50,000 if leaks turned out to be located at some extremely difficult access points. After four hours of debating with Hauptmann in a small conference room off the lobby of the Geneva Hilton, Gaudin agreed that Pacific would remeter the pipeline.

Hauptmann said that as far as he was concerned, all of his issues had been settled; however, he thought Zinnser might have one or two other issues to raise. Hauptmann said that he would report back to Zinnser and contact Gaudin as soon as possible if another meeting was necessary. Gaudin, believing that Pacific was finally beginning to see the light at the end of the tunnel, left for Paris.

JANUARY 23

Hauptmann called Gaudin and said that he and Zinnser had thoroughly reviewed the contract and that there were a few small issues of contract language which Zinnser wanted to clarify. He said that he would prefer not to discuss them over the telephone and suggested that since he was going to be in Paris on February 3, they meet at the Pacific offices. Gaudin agreed.

Fontaine and Gaudin met Hauptmann on February 3. Hauptmann informed them that he felt Reliant had been an outstanding customer for Pacific in the past and that it probably was one of Pacific's biggest customers for VCM. Fontaine and Gaudin agreed, affirming the important role that Reliant was playing in Pacific's VCM market. Hauptmann said that he and Zinnser had been reviewing the contract and were concerned that the changing nature of the VCM market might significantly affect Reliant's overall position in the marketplace as a purchaser. More specifically, Reliant was concerned that the decline in market and price for VCM in the future might endanger its own position in the market, since Pacific might sign contracts with other purchasers for lower formula prices than were currently being awarded to Reliant. Since Reliant was such an outstanding customer of Pacific—and Fontaine and Gaudin had agreed to that—it seemed to Reliant that Pacific Oil had an obligation to write two additional clauses into the contract that would protect Reliant in the event of further slippage in the VCM market. The first was a "favored nations" clause, stipulating that if Pacific negotiated with another purchaser a more favorable price for VCM than Reliant was receiving now, Pacific would guarantee that Reliant would receive that price as well. The second was a "meet competition" clause, guaranteeing that Pacific would willingly meet any lower price on VCM offered by a competitor, in order to maintain the Reliant relationship. Hauptmann argued that the "favored nations" clause was protection for Reliant, since it stipulated that Pacific valued the relationship enough to offer the best possible terms to Reliant. The "meet competition" clause, he argued, was clearly advantageous for Pacific since it ensured that Reliant would have no incentive to shift suppliers as the market changed.

Fontaine and Gaudin debated the terms at length with Hauptmann, stressing the potential costliness of these agreements for Pacific. Hauptmann responded by referring to the costliness that the absence of the terms could have for Reliant and suggesting that perhaps the Pacific people were truly *not* as interested in a successful long-term relationship as they had been advocating. Fontaine said that he needed to get clearance from senior management in New York before he could agree to these terms and that he would get back to Hauptmann within a few days when the information was available.

FRANK KELSEY'S VIEW

Frank Kelsey was strategic planning manager, a staff role in the New York offices of the Pacific Oil Corporation. Kelsey had performed a number of roles for the company in his 12 years of work experience. Using the chemistry background he had achieved in college, Kelsey worked for six years in the research and development department of Pacific's Chemical Division before deciding to enter the management ranks. He transferred to the marketing area, spent three years in chemical marketing, and then assumed responsibilities in marketing planning and development. He moved to the strategic planning department four years ago.

In late 1985, Kelsey was working in a staff capacity as an adviser to the executive product vice president of the Pacific Oil Company. Pacific had developed a matrix organization. Reporting relationships were determined by business areas and by regional operating divisions within Pacific Oil. Warren Meredith, the executive vice president, had responsibility for monitoring the worldwide sale and distribution of VCM. Jean Fontaine reported to Meredith on all issues regarding the overall sale and marketing of VCM and reported to the president of Pacific Oil in Europe, Stan Saunders, on major issues regarding the management of the regional chemicals business in Europe. In general, Fontaine's primary working relationship was with Meredith; Saunders only became involved in day-to-day decisions as an arbiter of disputes or interpreter of major policy decisions.

As the negotiations with Reliant evolved, Meredith became distressed by the apparent turn that they were taking. He called in Frank Kelsey to review the situation. Kelsey knew that the VCM marketing effort for Pacific was going to face significant problems. Moreover, his dominant experience with Pacific in recent years had been in the purchasing and marketing operations, and he knew how difficult it would be for the company to maintain a strong negotiation in VCM contracts.

Meredith asked Kelsey to meet with Fontaine and Gaudin in Paris, and review the current status of negotiations on the Reliant contract. While Kelsey could act only in an advisory capacity—Fontaine and Gaudin were free to accept or reject any advice that was offered, since they were the ones who had to live with the contract—Meredith told Kelsey to offer whatever services the men would accept.

Kelsey flew to Paris shortly after New Year's Day 1986. He met with Fontaine and Gaudin, and they reviewed in detail what had happened in the Reliant contract negotiations over the past year. Kelsey listened, asked a lot of questions, and didn't say much. He felt that offering advice to the men was premature and perhaps even unwise; Fontaine and Gaudin seemed very anxious about the negotiations and felt that the new contract would be sealed within a month. Moreover, they seemed to resent Kelsey's visit and clearly didn't want to share more than the minimum amount of information. Kelsey returned to New York and briefed Meredith on the state of affairs.

When Fontaine called Meredith for clearance to give Reliant both "favored nations" and "meet competition" clauses in the new contract, Meredith immediately called Kelsey. The two of them went back through the history of events in the negotiation and realized the major advantages that Reliant had gained by its negotiation tactics.

Meredith called Fontaine back and advised against granting the clauses in the contract. Fontaine said that Hauptmann was adamant and that he was afraid the entire negotiation was going to collapse over a minor point in contract language. Meredith said he still thought it was a bad idea to make the concession. Fontaine said he thought he needed to consult Saunders, the European president of Pacific Oil, just to make sure.

Two days later, Saunders called Meredith and said that he had complete faith in Fontaine and Fontaine's ability to determine what was necessary to make a contract work. If Fontaine felt that "favored nations" and "meet competition" clauses were necessary, he trusted Fontaine's judgment that the clauses could not cause significant adverse harm to Pacific Oil over the next few years. As a result, he had given Fontaine the go-ahead to agree to these clauses in the new contract.

MARCH 11

It was a dark and stormy night, March 11, 1986. Frank Kelsey was about to go to bed when the telephone rang. It was Jean Fontaine. Kelsey had not heard from Fontaine since their meeting in Paris. Meredith had told Kelsey about the discussion with Saunders, and he had assumed that Fontaine had gone ahead and conceded on the two contract clauses that had been discussed. He thought the contract was about to be wrapped up, but he hadn't heard for sure.

The violent rainstorm outside disrupted the telephone transmission, and Kelsey had trouble hearing Fontaine. Fontaine said that he had appreciated Kelsey's visit in January. Fontaine was calling to ask Kelsey's advice. They had just come from a meeting with Hauptmann. Hauptmann and Zinnser had reported that recent news from Reliant's corporate headquarters in Chicago projected significant downturns in the sale of a number of Reliant's PVC products in the European market. While Reliant thought it could ride out the downturn, they were very concerned about their future obligations under the Pacific contract. Since Reliant and Pacific had already settled on minimum quantity amounts, Reliant wanted the contractual right to resell the product if it could not use the minimum amount.

Kelsey tried to control his emotions as he thought about this negative turn of events in the Reliant negotiations. He strongly advised against agreeing to the clause, saying that it could put Pacific in an extremely poor position. Fontaine debated the point, saying he really thought Reliant might default on the whole contract if they didn't get resale rights. "I can't see where agreeing to the right to resale is a big thing, Frank, particularly given the size of this contract and its value to me and Pacific."

Kelsey: Look, you asked for my advice, and I gave it to you. If I were you, I wouldn't make any more concessions. Agreeing to a resale clause could create a whole lot of unforeseen problems. At this point I think it's also the principle of the thing!

Fontaine: Who cares about principles at a time like this! It's my neck that's on the line if this Reliant contract goes under! I'll have over 200 million pounds of VCM a year to eat in an oversupplied market! It's my neck that's on the line, not yours! How in the world can you talk to me about "principle" at this point?

Kelsey: Calm down, Jean! I can see your point of view! I appreciate the pressures on you, but I really don't like the looks of it from this end. Keep in touch—let me ask others down at the office what they think, and I'll call you next week.

Kelsey hung up the telephone, and stared out of the windows at the rain. He could certainly empathize with Fontaine's position—the man's neck was on the block. As he mentally reviewed the two-year history of the Reliant negotiations, Kelsey wondered how they had gotten to this point and whether anyone could have done things differently. He also wondered what to do about the resale clause, which appeared to be the final sticking point in the deliberations. Would acquiescing to a resale clause for Reliant be a problem to Pacific Oil? Kelsey knew he had to take action soon.

APPENDIX Petrochemical Supply Contracts: A Technical Note

Supply contracts between chemical manufacturing/refining companies and purchasing companies are fairly standard in the industry trade. They are negotiated between supplier and purchaser in order to protect both parties against major fluctuations in supply and demand. Any purchaser wishing to obtain a limited amount of a particular product could always approach any one of a number of chemical manufacturing firms and obtain the product at *market price*. The market price is controlled by the competitive supply and demand for the particular product on any given day. But purchasers want to be assured of a long-term supply and do not want to be subject to the vagaries of price fluctuation; similarly, manufacturers want to be assured of product outlets in order to adequately plan manufacturing schedules. Long-term contracts protect both parties against these fluctuations.

A supply contract is usually a relatively standard document, often condensed to one page. The major *negotiable* elements of the contract, on the *front side* of the document, include the price, quantity, product quality, contract duration, delivery point, and credit terms (see Exhibit 1A for a sample blank contract). The remainder (*back side*) of the contract is filled with traditionally fixed legal terminology that governs the conditions under which the contract will be maintained. While the items are seldom changed, they may be altered or waived as part of the negotiated agreement.

EXHIBIT 1A   Agreement of Sale

This Agreement, entered into this _____ day of _____, _____, between Pacific Oil Company, hereinafter called Seller, and _____, hereinafter called Buyer.

WITNESSETH:

Seller agrees to sell and deliver and Buyer agrees to purchase and receive commodity (hereinafter called "product") under the terms and conditions set forth below.

1. Product:

2. Quality:

3. Quantity:

4. Period:

5. Price:

6. Payment Terms:
   a. Net _____.
   b. All payments shall be made in United States dollars without discount or deduction, unless otherwise noted, by wire transfer at Seller's option, to a bank account designated by Seller. Invoices not paid on due date will be subject to a delinquency finance charge of 1% per month.
   c. If at any time the financial responsibility of Buyer shall become impaired or unsatisfactory to Seller, cash payment on delivery or satisfactory security may be required. A failure to pay any amount may, at the option of the Seller, terminate this contract as to further deliveries. No forbearance, course of dealing, or prior payment shall affect this right of Seller.

7. Price Change:

   The price specified in this Agreement may be changed by Seller on the first day of any calendar _____ by written notice sent to the Buyer not less than thirty (30) days prior to the effective date of change. Buyer gives Seller written notice of objection to such change at least ten (10) days prior to the effective date of change. Buyer's failure to serve Seller with written notice of objection thereto prior to the effective date thereof shall be considered acceptance of such change. If Buyer gives such notice of objection and Buyer and Seller fail to agree on such change prior to the effective date thereof, this Agreement and the obligations of Seller and Buyer hereunder shall terminate with respect to the unshipped portion of the Product governed by it. Seller has the option immediately to cancel this contract upon written notice to Buyer, to continue to sell hereunder at the same price and terms which were in effect at the time Seller gave notice of change, or to suspend performance under this contract while pricing is being resolved. If Seller desires to revise the price, freight allowance, or terms of payment pursuant to this agreement, but is restricted to any extent against doing so by reason of any law, governmental decree, order, or regulation, or if the price, freight allowance, or terms of payment then in effect under this contract are nullified or reduced by reason of any law, governmental decree, order or regulation, Seller shall have the right to cancel this contract upon fifteen (15) days' written notice to purchaser.

8. Measurements:

   Seller's determinations, unless proven to be erroneous, shall be accepted as conclusive evidence of the quantity of Product delivered hereunder. Credit will not be allowed for shortages of 1/2 of 1% or less of the quantity and overages of 1/2 of 1% or less of the quantity will be waived. The total amount of shortages or overages will be credited or billed when quantities are greater and such differences are substantiated. Measurements of weight and volume shall be according to procedures and criteria standard for such determinations.

Continued

9. Shipments and Delivery:

Buyer shall give Seller annual or quarterly forecasts of its expected requirements as Seller may from time to time request. Buyer shall give Seller reasonably advanced notice for each shipment which shall include date of delivery and shipping instructions. Buyer shall agree to take deliveries in approximately equal monthly quantities, except as may be otherwise provided herein. In the event that Buyer fails to take the quantity specified or the pro rata quantity in any month, Seller may, at its option, in addition to other rights and remedies, cancel such shipments or parts thereof.

10. Purchase Requirements:

a. If during any consecutive three-month period, Buyer for any reason (but not for reasons of force majeure as set forth in Section 12) takes less than 90 percent of the average monthly quantity specified, or the prorated minimum monthly quantity then applicable to such period under Section 12, Seller may elect to charge Buyer a penalty charge for failure to take the average monthly quantity or prorated minimum monthly quantity.

b. If, during any consecutive three-month period, Buyer, for any reason (but not, however, for reasons of force majeure as set forth in Section 12) takes Product in quantities less than that equal to at least one half of the average monthly quantity specified, or the prorated minimum monthly quantity originally applicable to such period under Section 12, Seller may elect to terminate this agreement.

c. It is the Seller's intent not to unreasonably exercise its rights under (*a*) or (*b*) in the event of adverse economic and business conditions in general.

d. Notice of election by Seller under (*a*) or (*b*) shall be given within 30 days after the end of the applicable three-month period, and the effective date of termination shall be 30 days after the date of said notice.

11. Detention Policy:

Seller may, from time to time, specify free unloading time allowances for its transportation equipment. Buyer shall be liable to the Transportation Company for all demurrage charges made by the Transportation Company, for railcars, trucks, tanks, or barges held by Buyer beyond the free unloading time.

12. Force Majeure:

Neither party shall be liable to the other for failure or delay in performance hereunder to the extent that such failure or delay is due to war, fire, flood, strike, lockout, or other labor trouble, accident, breakdown of equipment or machinery, riot, act, request, or suggestion of governmental authority, act of God, or other contingencies beyond the control of the affected party which interfere with the production or transportation of the material covered by this Agreement or with the supply of any raw material (whether or not the source of supply was in existence or contemplated at the time of this Agreement) or energy source used in connection therewith, or interfere with Buyer's consumption of such material, provided that in no event shall Buyer be relieved of the obligation to pay in full for material delivered hereunder. Without limitation on the foregoing, neither party shall be required to remove any cause listed above or replace the affected source of supply or facility if it shall involve additional expense or departure from its normal practices. If any of the events specified in this paragraph shall have occurred, Seller shall have the right to allocate

Continued

EXHIBIT 1A *Continued*

in a fair and reasonable manner among its customers and Seller's own requirements any supplies of material Seller has available for delivery at the time or for the duration of the event.

13. Materials and Energy Supply:

If, for any reasons beyond reasonable commercial control, Seller's supply of product to be delivered hereunder shall be limited due to continued availability of necessary raw materials and energy supplies, Seller shall have the right (without liability) to allocate to the Buyer a portion of such product on such basis as Seller deems equitable. Such allocation shall normally be that percent of Seller's total internal and external commitments which are committed to Buyer as related to the total quantity from Seller's manufacturing facilities.

14. Disclaimer:

Seller makes no warranty, express or implied, concerning the product furnished hereunder other than it shall be of the quality and specification stated herein. Any implied warranty of FITNESS is expressly excluded and to the extent that it is contrary to the foregoing sentence: any implied warranty of MERCHANTABILITY is expressly excluded. Any recommendation made by Seller makes no warranty of results to be obtained. Buyer assumes all responsibility and liability for loss or damage resulting from the handling or use of said product. In no event shall Seller be liable for any special, indirect or consequential damages, irrespective of whether caused or allegedly caused by negligence.

15. Taxes:

Any tax, excise fee, or other charge or increase thereof upon the production, storage, withdrawal, sale, or transportation of the product sold hereunder, or entering into the cost of such product, imposed by any proper authority becoming effective after the date hereof, shall be added to the price herein provided and shall be paid by the Buyer.

16. Assignment and Resale:

This contract is not transferable or assignable by Buyer without the written consent of Seller. The product described hereunder, in the form and manner provided by the Seller, may not be assigned or resold without prior written consent of the Seller.

17. Acceptance:

Acceptance hereof must be without qualification and Seller will not be bound by any different terms and conditions contained in any other communication.

18. Waiver of Breach:

No waiver by Seller or Buyer of any breach of any of the terms and conditions contained in this Agreement shall be construed as a waiver or any subsequent breach of the same or any other term or condition.

19. Termination:

If any provision of this agreement is or becomes violate of any law, or any rule, order, or regulation issued thereunder, Seller shall have the right upon notice to Buyer, to terminate the Agreement in its entirety.

20. Governing Law:

The construction of this Agreement and the rights and obligations of the parties hereunder shall be governed by the laws of the State of _____.

Continued

EXHIBIT 1A   *Concluded*

21. Special Provisions:

BUYER: SELLER:

_____   _____
              (firm)   (firm)

By: _____   By: _____
Title: _____   Title: _____
Date: _____   Date: _____

The primary component of a long-term contract is the price. In the early years of the petrochemical industry, the raw product was metered by the supplier (either in liquid or gaseous form) and sold to the purchaser. As the industry became more competitive, as prices rose rapidly, and as the products developed from petrochemical supplies (called *feedstocks*) became more sophisticated, pricing became a significantly more complex process. Most contemporary contract prices are determined by an elaborate calculation called a *formula price,* composed of several elements:

1. *Feedstock characteristics.* Petrochemical feedstock supplies differ in the chemical composition and molecular structure of the crude oil. Differences in feedstocks will significantly affect the refining procedures and operating efficiency of the refinery that manufactures a product, as well as their relative usefulness to particular purchasers. While some chemical products may be drawn from a single feedstock, large-volume orders may necessitate the blending of several feedstocks with different structural characteristics.

2. *Fuel costs.* Fuel costs include the price and amount of energy that the manufacturing company must assume in cracking, refining, and producing a particular chemical stream.

3. *Labor costs.* Labor costs include the salaries of employees to operate the manufacturing facility for the purpose of producing a fixed unit amount of a particular product.

4. *Commodity costs.* Commodity costs include the value of the basic petrochemical base on the open marketplace. As the supply and demand for the basic commodity fluctuate on the open market, this factor is entered into the formula price.

A formula price may therefore be represented as a function of the following elements:

$$\text{Formula price} = \text{feedstock cost} + \text{energy cost} + \text{labor cost} + \text{commodity cost (per unit)}$$

If only one feedstock were used, the chemical composition of the feedstock would determine its basic cost, and the energy, labor, and commodity costs of producing it. If several feedstocks were used, the formula price would be a composite of separate calculations for each particular feedstock, or a weighted average of the feedstock components, multiplied by the cost of production of each one.

Each of the elements in the formula price is also multiplied by a weighting factor (coefficient) that specifies how much each cost will contribute to the determination of the overall formula price. The supplier generally sets a *ceiling price,* guaranteeing that the formula price will not exceed this amount. Below the ceiling price, however, the supplier endeavors to maximize profits while clearly specifying the costs of production to the purchaser, while the purchaser attempts to obtain the most favorable formula price for himself. Since basic cost data and cost fluctuations are well known, negotiations typically focus on the magnitude of the coefficients that are applied to each element in the formula. Hence, the actual formula computation may be represented as follows:

$$
\begin{aligned}
\text{Formula price} = {}& (\text{weighting coefficient} \times \text{feedstock cost}) \\
& + (\text{weighting coefficient} \times \text{energy cost}) \\
& + (\text{weighting coefficient} \times \text{labor cost}) \\
& + (\text{weighting coefficient} \times \text{commodity cost})
\end{aligned}
$$

A fairly typical ratio of the weighting coefficients in this formula would be 70 percent (0.7) for feedstock cost, 20 percent (0.2) for energy costs, 5 percent (0.05) for labor costs, and 5 percent (0.05) for commodity costs. Multiple feedstocks supplied in a particular contract would be composed of a different set of costs and weighting elements for each feedstock in the supply.

The computation of a formula price, as opposed to the determination of a market price, has a number of advantages and disadvantages. Clearly, it enables the supplier to pass costs along to the purchaser, which minimizes the risk for both parties in the event of rapid changes in cost during the duration of the contract. The purchaser can project directly how cost changes will affect his supply costs; the supplier is protected by being able to pass cost increases along to the purchaser. However, when the market demand for the product is very high, the formula price constrains the seller in the ceiling price he can charge, hence curtailing potential profit for the product compared to its value on the open marketplace. Conversely, when market demand is very low, the contract may guarantee a large market to the supplier, but at a price for the product that could be unprofitable compared to production costs.

QUANTITY

Formula prices are typically computed with major attention given to quantity. Costs will fluctuate considerably based on the efficiency with which the production plant is operated, number of labor shifts required, and so on. Hence, in order to adequately forecast demand, attain particular economies of scale in the manufacturing process, and plan production schedules, suppliers must be able to determine the quantities that a particular customer will want to acquire. (Because of the volumes involved, no significant inventory is produced.) Quantities will be specified in common units of weight (pounds, tons, etc.) or volume (gallons etc.).

Quantity specifications are typically treated as minimum purchase amounts. If a purchaser desires significantly more than the minimum amount (*overlifting*) in a given time period (e.g., a year), the amount would be sold contingent on availability and delivered at the formula price. Conceivably, *discount* prices or adjustments in the formula price could be negotiated for significant purchases over minimum quantity. Conversely, underpurchase of the minimum amount (*underlifting*) by a significant degree typically results in penalty costs to the purchaser. These are typically referred to as *liquidated damages* in the industry and may be negotiated at rates anywhere from a token fine of several thousand dollars to as much as 30 percent of the formula price for each unit underlifted. Faced with the possibility of underlifting (due to market or product demand changes that require less raw material in a given time period), purchasers typically handle underlifting in one of several ways:

a. Pay the underlifting charges (liquidated damages) to the supplier, either as stated or according to some renegotiated rate.

b. Not pay the liquidated damages, under the assumption that the supplier will not want to press legal charges against the purchaser at the expense of endangering the entire supply contract.

c. Resell the commodity to another purchaser who may be in need of supply, perhaps at a discounted price. Such action by the purchaser could cause major instability in the market price and in supply contracts held at the original manufacturer or other manufacturers. For this reason, sellers typically preclude the right of the purchaser to resell the product as part of the standard contract language.

QUALITY

The quality of the product is related to the particular feedstock from which it is drawn, as well as the type and degree of refining that is employed by the supplier. Standard descriptions for gradations of quality are common parlance for each major chemical product.

DELIVERY

Most contracts specify the method of delivery, point of delivery, and way that the quantity amounts will be measured as the product is delivered. Gases are typically metered and delivered by direct pipeline from the manufacturer to the purchaser; liquids and liquefied gases may be sold by pipeline or shipped via tank truck, railroad tank car, tank barges, and tank ships.

CONTRACT DURATION

Most typical supply contracts extend for a period from one to five years; significantly longer or shorter ones would probably only be negotiated under extreme circumstances. Negotiations for contract renewal are typically begun several months prior to contract expiration.

PAYMENT TERMS

Payment terms are determined by the credit ratings and cash flow demands of both parties. Typical contracts specify payment within 30 days of delivery, although this time period may be shortened to payment on delivery or lengthened to a period of three months between delivery and payment.

CONTRACT LANGUAGE

As can be determined from Exhibit 1A, there are a number of elements in the contract that delineate the conditions under which the parties agree to bind themselves to the contract, or to deviate from it. Terminology and agreements were typically standard, unless altered by negotiation prior to contract signing. These elements include the following:

1. *Measurements.* A mechanism for specifying how quantity amounts will be determined and how disputes over differences in delivered quantity will be resolved.

2. *Meet competition.* The seller agrees to meet competitive market prices for the product if they become substantially lower than the current negotiated formula price.

3. *Favored nations.* The supplier agrees that if he offers a better price on the product to any of the purchaser's competitors, he will offer the same price to this buyer.

4. *Purchase requirements.* The purchase requirements govern the conditions and terms under which liquidated damages may be invoked.

5. *Force majeure.* The force majeure clause exempts the parties from contract default in the event of major natural disasters, strikes, fires, explosions, or other events that could preclude the seller's ability to deliver the product or the buyer's ability to purchase.

6. *Disclaimers.* The disclaimers protect both buyer and seller against unreasonable claims about the product or its quality.

7. *Assignability.* The assignability clause limits the right of either party to assign the contract to another purchaser or supplier if they so desire.

8. *Notifications.* The notifications section specifies the lead time during which one or both parties must notify the other party of any change in the contract or its renewal.

9. *Other clauses.* Other clauses include conditions under which the product may be assured delivery, application of taxes, provisions for resale, definitions of contract breach and termination, the legal framework used to enforce the contract (in the event of cross-state or cross-national agreements), and methods of notification of one party to the other.

CONTRACT MANAGEMENT AND MAINTENANCE

While a supply contract is a legally binding document that attempts to articulate the way two companies will work together, it more commonly stands as the cornerstone of a complex long-term social relationship between buyer and seller. This relationship requires constant monitoring, evaluation, and discussion by representatives of both organizations. Thus, while similar supply contracts may exist between a particular manufacturer and three different buyers, there may be major differences in the day-to-day interactions and quality of relationships between the manufacturer and each buyer. Experienced sales representatives have defined a good seller-buyer relationship as meeting the following criteria:

- *The purchaser can be counted on to live up to the terms and conditions of the contract as negotiated.* The purchaser accepts a fair formula price in price negotiations and does not attempt to push the supplier into an artificially low price.

The purchaser lifts as much of the product per time period as he agreed to lift under the contract. The purchaser is trustworthy and follows a course of action based on sound business ethics.

- *The purchaser does not attempt to take advantage of fluctuations or aberrations in the spot market price to gain advantage.* He accepts the fact that a formula price has been negotiated and that both parties agree to live up to this price for the duration of the contract. He does not seek contract price changes as the market price may drop for some time period.

- *When there is a mutual problem between seller and purchaser, it can be openly discussed and resolved between the two parties.* Problems resulting from the continued inability of the supplier to provide the product, and/or the continued inability of the buyer to consume the product, can be openly addressed and resolved. Problems in the quality of the product, labor difficulties resulting in problems in manufacturing, loading, shipping, unloading, cleanliness of the shipping equipment, and so on can be promptly explored and resolved to mutual satisfaction. Finally, changes in the business projections of one or both parties can be shared, so that difficulties anticipated by the supplier in providing all of the product, or difficulties anticipated by the purchaser in consuming all of the product, can lead to amicable and satisfactory resolutions for both parties. Ability to resolve these problems requires mutual trust, honesty, open lines of communication, and an approach to problem solving that seeks the best solution for both sides.

CASE 3

The Ken Griffey Jr. Negotiation

BACKGROUND NOTE

This case is a journalist's account (originally published in *Sports Illustrated*) of negotiations surrounding a professional baseball player in the United States named Ken Griffey Jr. that took place during the winter of 2000. For readers unfamiliar with Griffey, the sport of baseball, or the nature of U.S. major league baseball teams, contracts, and negotiations, this introductory note will provide some basic details that will help you follow the case. You do not need to be particularly knowledgeable about baseball to understand and analyze what went on, but it does help to know a little bit about the context in which negotiations over Griffey's future took place.

Who Is Ken Griffey Jr.?

Griffey (also known as "Junior") is generally regarded as one of the premier professional baseball players in the two North American leagues collectively known as Major League Baseball. Consequently, at the time the events in the case took place, many other teams coveted his talents and would have liked to have signed him. For those who care to know the baseball-related details, he is an outfielder who has proven to be both an excellent hitter and a superb fielder over a career of several years. But despite his experience, he was at the time of the dispute only 30 years old in a game where players can be very successful into (and occasionally beyond) their late 30s.

What Was Going on at the Time of the Case?

As the negotiations opened, Griffey played for the a team called the Seattle Mariners. His contract with Seattle was to end following the 2000 season (which started in April and ended in October 2000). If Griffey stayed in Seattle for the 2000 season and let his contract run out, he could have become a free agent who could sell his talents and services to any other team in baseball, and the Seattle ballclub would get nothing if Griffey signed with another team. But if the Seattle team could trade him (at the time of the case, during the winter preceeding the season), they could get something for him. Because Griffey is a first-rate talent, a trade would presumably bring Seattle several very good players in return.

Couldn't Seattle Have Kept Griffey?

They could have tried to sign him to a new contract, either before or after his existing contract ran out. But it was widely known that Griffey was unhappy in Seattle for a variety of reasons (some of which are mentioned in the case). It also says in the case that Seattle offered Griffey a new eight-year, $138 million dollar contract in July 1999, which Griffey met "with indifference." As a result, it was in Seattle's interest to try to trade him, rather than waiting, which would have brought the risk that they would lose him with no compensation if his contract ran out at the end of the 2000 season and he became a free agent and signed with another team.

What Control Did Griffey Have over His Fate?

In most cases, a player can be traded without his consent. Teams trade players for all kinds of reasons: to get rid of an expensive player with declining skills; to attract talent at some other position; bad fit in team chemistry and so on. Griffey, however, met a league threshold—10 years playing, and the past 5 with his current team—that gives a player the right to veto any trade. Of course, even for players who do not have this veto, trading them near the end of their contract means the new team will soon have to sign them to a new contract. The player might not have the contractual right to formally veto a trade, but he can signal his preferences by indicating which teams would find him more or less cooperative in agreeing to a new contract.

Who the Mariners Got

Mike Cameron: If this deal ever is to be perceived as 'close to' an even swap, Cameron is the key. The 27-year-old is on the verge of developing into an impact player. The Reds realized last year he was miscast as a leadoff hitter despite his speed and a significant improvement in his willingness to take walks. Those walks and a leap to 21 home runs and 34 doubles make his still-high strikeout rate palatable as long as he's batting in an RBI position. Cameron is much faster than Ken Griffey Jr. and runs the bases extremely well. The Mariners will notice little drop-off defensively. How much higher Cameron can push his batting average (280–290?) and power numbers (30–35 home runs a year?), while inevitably and unfairly being compared to Griffey, will determine how much sting Seattle fans will feel.

Brett Tomko: The big right-hander has been on the trading block since early last season, from about the time the Reds concluded he doesn't pitch big. That is, for a guy who throws in the low 90s, his command has been slipping and he's become homer prone. Despite falling out of favor by May, Tomko actually pitched better during the second half of the season. And he's not much more than a year removed from being considered a future front-of-the-rotation starter. Unless the Mariners trade another pitcher in the meantime, Tomko won't be asked to slot in any higher than No.5.

Antonio Perez: His (Class A) Midwest League numbers last season are good, albeit indicative of how raw the infielder is. But when you realize he didn't turn 18 until late July, the stats are more than promising. He's fast—35 steals—but still learning to run the bases—caught 24 times. He showed pop in his bat (20 doubles and seven homers) that is good for a teenager with time to build on his 5-11, 175-pound frame. He showed outstanding strikezone judgment in the 1998 Dominican Summer League. That slipped some when he was tossed in among older players last season. His 36 errors are not uncommon for a green shortstop, but he spent half the season at second base, which could turn out to be his better position. His on-base ability has been good from the beginning so he projects as a solid candidate to eventually be at or near the top of a major league batting order.

Jake Meyer: He's the one you're least likely to see in the majors at any point. He has been close to a strikeout-an-inning man through his three minor league seasons, with a fastball scouts say is in the low- to mid-90s. Some folks around last year's Class A Rockford club claim it approached 100 mph at times. His control is the issue and it took a noticeable dive when he reached Double-A for the first time midway through last season. The 5.96 ERA in 20 games at Chattanooga muddled future-closer thoughts created by his 2.54 ERA and 16 saves at Rockford. The biggest negative is that the UCLA product just turned 25 and hasn't yet proven himself in Double-A.

Bottom line for Mariners: Wait and see. First to learn if GM Pat Gillick has enough surplus, especially in pitching, to make another deal. It made more sense to make the trade with Cincinnati then assess other possibilities rather than lock into a three-way deal. Cameron will be fine in center field but this team needs a corner outfielder who is an offensive threat. Someone who could hit in or near the middle of the order would be nice but a better fit would be someone who could keep Seattle from forcing Cameron or Brian Hunter into the leadoff spot. Anaheim's Jim Edmonds has been mentioned, as has Montreal's Rondell White. The best fit might be Johnny Damon of the Royals, who have plenty of outfielders and need pitching. Of more long-term concern is whether all of this will have any effect on free-agent-to-be No. 2, Alex Rodriquez. He's not going to sign during the season, but Gillick will have to gauge if there's any chance of luring him back next winter. If not, he needs to see if there's a reasonable trade package out there for him before August. Seattle's improved pitching thrusts it into contention. They could stay there with another deal that brings back some offense.

Bottom line for Reds: Getting a superstar without deleting anybody you need is the perfect trade. Cincinnati's biggest concern remains its starting pitching, but Tomko was nothing more than a fifth starter to them. Of course, the rest of the rotation is not without its concerns, most of them physical. Remember though, that the Reds added a 48-homer guy and the NL Central-champion Astros lost 22-game winner Mike Hampton. And the difference between the two clubs was just one game. It would appear the Reds have obliterated the gap. But have they made up the seven games between themselves and the Braves?

HOME ECONOMICS

Aloft in a $35 million Falcon 900 jet, Ken Griffey Jr. told the story of recently playing golf with Jack Nicklaus for the first time. Nicklaus, his son Mike, and Mark O'Meara, a PGA Tour pro and friend of Griffey's, smacked their drives off the first tee down the middle of the fairway. Griffey, hitting last, could feel his knees trembling as he stood over the ball. He didn't know Nicklaus well, and the golfing legend had said almost nothing to him. Griffey promptly sent an ugly slice screeching far into the rough. "So Jack walks by me," Griffey said, "and as he's walking, he says to me, 'In my sport we play the foul balls.'"

Griffey howled with laughter, as did the rest of the passengers, including his wife, Melissa; his son, Trey, 6; his daughter, Taryn, 4; and a few Reds executives and members of their families. This went on for two hours—Griffey, the life of the party, telling one funny story after another. Never had a man seemed so ebullient upon signing away the next 10 years of his career for about half his market value.

What mattered more than selling himself short was that Griffey, Cincinnati Moeller High class of '87, son of Reds coach Ken and Birdie Griffey of Cincinnati, was heading home. Reds majority owner Carl Lindner had approved the trade with the Seattle Mariners and Griffey's new contract and then had provided his jet to make the sentimental journey possible. Considering his status as one of the game's greatest players now and forever, Griffey accepted such a huge discount that commissioner Bud Selig greeted the news of his signing by yelling, "Thank you! Thank you very much!" and nearly weeping.

Griffey is guaranteed $116.5 million over the next nine years with the Reds holding an option for a tenth season. Although Griffey's salary will be $12.5 million a year (plus a $4 million buyout for the 10th year), the deal is worth only about $89 million in present-day dollars because Griffey agreed to defer $57.5 million of that total at 4 percent interest. Those payments are stretched between 2010 and 2025, when Griffey will be 56 years old.

Griffey agreed to those terms one day after the Mariners finally blinked following four months of talking and posturing about a trade with the Reds. Seattle agreed to take righthanded starter Brett Tomko, outfielder Mike Cameron, and two minor leaguers, righthander Jake Meyer and infielder Antonio Perez.

Lindner, a Cincinnati financier who has a controlling interest in Chiquita Brands International Inc. and Amtrak, among other holdings, sent his jet to Orlando, where Griffey lives, to bring him to Ohio in style for the posttrade news conference. Two thousand people greeted the Falcon 900 as it touched down. A Rolls-Royce and two limousines pulled up while two news choppers with searchlights hovered above. Lindner told Griffey to hop in the front seat of the Rolls—with the 80-year-old Lindner driving—and told Junior's wife and kids to sit in the back. The rest of the traveling party jumped into the limos. As the vehicles crawled out of the airport, fans swarmed the cars, popping the flashes of their cameras, banging on the hoods and windows, and yelling, "Welcome home!"

Lindner, in the lead car, slowly steered the Rolls free from the knot of people; the sleeves of his jacket slid back enough to reveal a pair of gold cuff links he wears every day that read ONLY IN AMERICA. As the caravan gathered speed onto Kellogg Avenue, something happened that seemed serendipitous—that is, if you hadn't known how well-connected Lindner is in Cincinnati. Every one of the traffic lights on the avenue switched to flashing yellow, affording Griffey an unimpeded trip downtown to Cinergy Field, where a burst of fireworks welcomed him.

Unimpeded? If only the trip had been so easy from the beginning. Griffey wound up in Cincinnati only after the Mariners alienated him with their curious trade tactics; only after the Reds twice pulled out of the talks, including as recently as three days before the actual trade; only after Griffey's agent illegally jump-started discussions; and only after Griffey was snubbed by his first choice, the Atlanta Braves, who wanted his teammate, shortstop Alex Rodriguez, instead. According to several insiders familiar with the deal, this is the story of how Griffey came home.

The first sign of trouble in Seattle came in July, when the Mariners offered Griffey (who was scheduled to become a free agent after the 2000 season) $138 million over eight years and were met not with a counterproposal but with indifference. Griffey, whose Mariners salary was $8.5 million, had no problem with the money—though he didn't tell Seattle that at the time—but he wasn't sure if he wanted to stay. His children were reaching school age, and that had made him ponder more often the idea of playing closer to Orlando. "We'll think about it," his agent, Brian Goldberg, told Seattle.

Later that month the Mariners opened Safeco Field, a resplendent $517 million stadium with a sliding canopy that keeps out the Northwest rain but not the chill. Between one wall of the Mariners' clubhouse and Griffey's locker the club did not install the three other lockers that would have fit there. This area was designed specifically for Griffey, who in that space could store his personal travel trunk for his bats, as well as the assortment of gadgets, boxes and other equipment he accumulates during a season.

Griffey showed his appreciation for this custom-made jewel of a park by saying nothing. The franchise player who made the team's continued existence in Seattle possible refused to comment on Safeco Field. He would explain later that he did so to avoid misleading people about his future. If he praised the place, people might thank he was staying. If he ripped it, people might think he was leaving. But the silence was ominous. His private grumblings were worse. The ball had jumped in the Kingdome, his old, indoor home stadium. Safeco was, in the words of one of his teammates before the final price was toted up, "a $450 million icebox. He knows it might cost him the home run record." Balls hit in the air died. Centerfield, in particular, was a graveyard; the Mariners couldn't hit balls out even in batting practice.

One night, after yet another of his well-struck fly balls had died in an opposing outfielder's glove, Griffey called Woody Woodward, the Seattle general manager at the time, from a dugout telephone. In front of his teammates Griffey screamed through the phone at Woodward, "Get me out of this place! Trade me right now!"

"That wasn't why he left," Goldberg said last Friday, referring to Safeco Field. "It was one piece in the puzzle. There was no one thing, no one event. I want to emphasize [that] what happened was not anyone's fault. Things just kind of went sideways."

Griffey's mood darkened on August 12. That's when his wife and children returned to Orlando in preparation for the school year. A few days later he told friends that he was leaning toward playing for the Braves or the Houston Astros, contending teams with spring training sites within minutes of his home. (The Mariners train in Arizona.) Griffey liked the idea of gaining five weeks at home with his family during the school year. "What can the Mariners offer me that nobody else can?" he said. "Nothing."

Griffey's season deteriorated. He hit just .255 after the All-Star break, including .212 in the final month, and finished at .285, albeit with 48 homers and 134 RBIs. Teammates noticed how he'd skip batting practice and stretching exercises for weeks at a time, preferring to linger in the clubhouse. The Mariners lost 83 games, failing to make the postseason for the ninth time in his 11 seasons with the club.

Woodward retired after the season, remaining true to the words he repeated to Cincinnati general manager Jim Bowden on the three or four occasions every season when Bowden would ask, "When are you going to trade me Griffey?" Woodward would say, "I'm not going to be remembered as the guy who traded Ken Griffey Jr."

That distinction would fall to 62-year-old Pat Gillick, Woodward's successor. In November, Gillick and Mariners CEO Howard Lincoln flew to Orlando to meet with Griffey. The outfielder did not want any more offers. He wanted out. He told Gillick and Lincoln he preferred to be traded rather than play the last season of his contract in Seattle. As a player with 10 years of major league service, including at least the past five with his current team, Griffey had the right to veto any trade. He gave the Mariners a list of four teams he would consider playing for. He listed them in his order of preference: Braves, Reds, Astros, and New York Mets.

Gillick made a request before leaving Orlando: Would it be OK with Griffey if he talked to teams not on his list? Gillick wanted to gain some leverage by expanding the market. Griffey gave his approval.

Over the next month that tactic blew up on Gillick. The GM seemed to Goldberg and Griffey to be spending more time talking with clubs not on the list than with those on the list. Gillick tried to cut deals with the Cleveland Indians, New York Yankees, Pittsburg Pirates, St. Louis Cardinals and Tampa Bay Devil Rays, each time asking Goldberg if Griffey would accept a trade based on what were supposed to be only diversionary talks. Gillick was also telling baseball people that Griffey had 20 teams on his approval list—every team that trains in Florida. "After a month of that, it was starting to wear on Junior," Goldberg says. The idea of coming back to Seattle for one last season became more remote.

Privately, Gillick had been told by Seattle executives that Griffey was known to change his mind easily. So Gillick didn't assume the list of four teams was written in stone. Meanwhile, that list was quickly sliced in half. The Braves told Gillick they might have interest in Griffey as a free agent, but they would not trade for him. Atlanta did, however, want to talk about a trade for Rodriguez, who will be a free agent after the 2000 season. Gillick passed, explaining that he had to resolve the Griffey matter first. The Astros also dropped out; owner Drayton McLane already had worries about his payroll, with second baseman Craig Biggio, outfielders Derek Bell and Carl Everett, and left-handed starter Mike Hampton all entering the last year of their contracts. (All but Biggio, who signed an extension, were eventually traded.)

That left the Reds and the Mets. Talks with Cincinnati got off to an awful start at the general managers' meetings on November 19. Sitting in an ocean-view suite at the Ritz Carlton in Laguna Niguel, California, Gillick made his first offer to Bowden: Griffey for four frontline players—second baseman Pokey Reese, first baseman Sean Casey, left-handed starter Denny Neagle, and righthanded closer Scott Williamson—and one player from a list of the five best prospects in the Cincinnati system. Bowden nearly fell out of his chair. His club had won 96 games last season. All his plans were aimed at building a winning team in 2003, when the Reds are scheduled to open a new ballpark. A deal like this would decimate the team and his plans. Before leaving the room, he recovered enough to tell Gillick firmly, "Casey and Reese are not going to be in this deal."

Gillick and Bowden exchanged many proposals in the ensuing weeks without getting close to a trade. One of Bowden's earliest pitches included Cameron, a speedy outfielder with a .240 career average. Gillick said he didn't want Cameron. Bowden drew up a secret list of 11 players, including prospects, that he wouldn't trade. At the top of that list was Reese, a natural shortstop and the player Gillick demanded as a hedge against Rodriguez's leaving by trade or free agency. Also, as a condition of any deal,

Bowden insisted that the Mariners pay Griffey's entire 2000 salary of $8.5 million and allow Cincinnati a window to sign him to an extension; Seattle refused on both counts.

Once, after Bowden faxed a proposal to Seattle, Gillick left a voice mail for Bowden: "Jim, you may have a problem. Someone used your letterhead and signed your name to the most ridiculous proposal for Ken Griffey Jr. that's ever been made. If I were you, I would order an investigation to find out what's going on."

Bowden called back and left his own voice mail for Gillick: "Pat, we checked with security about the faxed proposal. You're right. It is ridiculous. I would never give up that much for Ken Griffey Jr."

That was one of the few light moments between Gillick, the old-school, close-mouthed veteran, and Bowden, who at 38 still hadn't outgrown his reputation as a whiz kid with an affinity for reporters, TV cameras, and Austin Powers. Both of them knew Gillick's hand was growing weaker, and the tension between them escalated.

Bowden tried to turn up the heat on Gillick on December 9, the eve of the winter meetings in Anaheim, by publicly announcing that he was going to bring Griffey home. The next day, though, Reds managing executive John Allen told Bowden the chase was over; Lindner had decided the Reds could not afford to trade for and sign Griffey. Allen ordered Bowden to announce that the Reds were out of it.

Bowden couldn't do that . . . not yet, anyway. It would mean all the spadework of the past month had been a public sham. No, instead Bowden scheduled a meeting with Gillick for the morning of December 11 in Gillick's suite. When Gillick began the session by asking for Reese again, Bowden wasted no time. He shot up from his chair, "That's it!" he yelled. "I told you we weren't trading Pokey Reese, and you continue to insist on Pokey Reese! We have nothing more to talk about! We're finished!" He wheeled and hustled out of the room, making sure Gillick had no chance to respond. Bowden called a news conference to announce that the Reds were finished trying to get Griffey because of the Mariners' intractable demand for one player, Reese. It was a masterpiece of showmanship.

Now Bowden was worried about the Mets, especially when one New York executive told him at the winter meetings, "We're going to step up and do it." Mets general manager Steve Phillips agreed to send righthanded starter Octavio Dotel, outfielder Roger Cedeño, and one other player to Seattle for Griffey, but the two teams could not agree on the third player. Gillick wanted righthanded closer Armando Benitez, but Phillips wasn't biting. Deadlocked, the general managers decided they would see if Griffey would approve a deal to the Mets before they tried to settle on the third player.

At 11:15 P.M. EST, Mariners president and COO Chuck Armstrong, who was in Hawaii, telephoned Goldberg at his Cincinnati home and asked if Griffey would accept a trade to New York. "I'm going to dinner in 15 minutes," Armstrong said. "We need to have an answer as soon as possible, because if the answer is no, the Mets need to get on to other things as early as tomorrow morning."

Goldberg called Griffey at home with the news. Griffey talked it over with his wife and mother. By this time he was annoyed at Gillick's games of thrust and parry. Now he had to decide his future in 15 minutes? (Armstrong later explained that he did not mean to imply that the deadline was a mere 15 minutes.) Besides, even though the Mets were on Griffey's list, they were a weak fourth. He had listed them because they were a contending club that trained in Florida, and a part of him was intrigued with the idea of tweaking George Steinbrenner, the Yankees' owner, who Griffey claims once had him chased from the clubhouse when his father played for New York. Griffey's desire to play for the Reds far surpassed his vague interest in the Mets. He called Goldberg back, "I don't feel right about this," he said. "I feel cornered. Tell them no."

Now only the Reds were left—and by this time Griffey was sure he didn't want to return to the Mariners. Some fans had peppered his website with hate messages, and a letter from Seattle threatening his family had arrived at his Orlando home. The idea of playing in the town where his parents and grandmother lived looked better and better.

Bowden, sensing his strengthened bargaining position, took it upon himself to quietly reopen talks with Seattle in January. The Mariners wavered about what to do: Midway through that month Gillick decided he'd rather have his team play the season with Griffey than cave in and make a bad trade; Lincoln preferred to honor Griffey's request rather than bring back a hostile star. The talks continued to go nowhere, but Bowden couldn't stop himself from dropping hints about them in public. He held a panel discussion about the possible trade at a Reds publicity event on January 28. One fan asked him, "How about Tomko, [lefthanded reliever Dennys] Reyes, and [outfielder Dmitri] Young for Griffey?" Responded Bowden, "I like that one. I'd do that one." Then he laughed. In fact, Bowden had made that exact proposal earlier that morning.

On January 30, after two more days of no movement, Bowden presented this idea to Gillick: "Forget about the issues of the 2000 salary and the long-term contract. Let's just see if we can make a baseball trade, and we'll let Chuck Armstrong and John Allen negotiate the dollars." On February 5 Mariners vice president Roger Jongewaard called Bowden with a new proposal, this one without Reese: Seattle wanted Perez, Reyes, Tomko, and catcher Jason LaRue (one of the 11 players on Bowden's secret list and the only top young catcher in Bowden's system). Bowden couldn't part with LaRue. Perez was also on the list of 11, but with Reese, veteran shortstop Barry Larkin, and shortstop prospect Travis Dawkins in the organization, Bowden felt deep enough in the middle infield to make him expendable.

When Jongewaard ended the conversation by saying, "Where are you going to be tomorrow?" Bowden detected the scent of urgency. After he hung up the phone, Bowden said softly to himself, OK, we're Jason LaRue away from getting Griffey. I can find a way to make this deal.

Bowden dialed Allen. "John, we've agreed on three players," he said. "I feel I can make this deal tomorrow. Do I have the OK?"

"I'll call Mr. Lindner and call you back," Allen said.

Not until 6:30 the next evening, just as Bowden sat down to dinner, did Allen call back. "Jim, I've got some bad news for you," Allen said. "You're going to have to pull out. It can't work financially. I want you to release a statement tomorrow."

Bowden drove the next morning, Monday, February 7, with his wife, Amy, to the airport for a flight to Florida to prepare for two arbitration hearings, conveniently postponing work on the statement. He randomly pulled into a parking spot in the lot. He and Amy looked at each other. The car was parked in section D-30 (Griffey Sr.'s number), row 24 (Junior's Seattle number). "It's going to happen," Amy said. On Tuesday morning Armstrong telephoned Goldberg. "We heard the Reds are going to release a statement pulling out of trade talks," Armstrong said. "We're giving you permission to contact the Reds."

The Mariners had no authority to grant Goldberg such permission—that lies only with the commissioner's office—but Goldberg didn't know that. He called Allen. "Junior's willing to commit to a long-term deal with the Reds in the event of a trade," Goldberg said. "He's willing to work with terms that are very reasonable, less than market value."

(A high-ranking Major League Baseball source says that an investigation did confirm that the contact was illegal but that baseball considered it not serious enough to jeopardize the deal because the Mariners had endorsed the contact and no third team was harmed. Another source familiar with the investigation says that baseball officials are so pleased to see Griffey in Cincinnati under such reasonable contract terms that "they're willing to look the other way on this one" and may choose only to levy a small fine on each club.)

With that phone call the endgame had begun. Suddenly Griffey was affordable. Allen telephoned Lindner, who immediately gave a green light to make the deal. Allen called Bowden and said, "Mr. Lindner has had a change of heart. You have permission to go make a baseball deal. Whatever money you can get them to include in the deal will help, but Mr. Lindner is not putting any financial restrictions on you."

Bowden called Gillick. They agreed to a 4 P.M. conference call the next day, February 9. Gillick said he and Armstrong needed to be somewhere at 8 P.M. Fine, Bowden thought, a deadline. It'll be done by eight.

Bowden started the conference call where they had left off: Perez, Reyes, and Tomko, and let's talk about the fourth player. "Wait," Gillick said. "We want Pokey Reese in it. Now that you're considering Griffey long-term, the price has gone up."

Executives from the two clubs alternately argued and caucused for the next hour. The Mariners gave in. They asked for Cameron instead of Reese. Bowden coyly refused. He offered to get outfielder Jim Edmonds from the Anaheim Angels and pass him on to the Mariners. Gillick didn't want Edmonds, who could be a free agent at the end of the season and who, the Mariners already knew, would not sign a long-term deal with them.

Bowden came back with another offer: Tomko and Cameron for Griffey. Gillick insisted on Reyes and Perez, as well. "You're not getting Reyes and Perez," Bowden exclaimed. "No way. We don't want to do it, but we'll put Perez in. That's it. No more. And this deal is off the table tomorrow. Let's make it or not right now."

Said Gillick, "Are you going to let Dennys Reyes keep you from trading for Ken Griffey, and are you willing to live with that for the rest of your life?"

Bowden shot back, "Are you willing to lose Ken Griffey for nothing and live with that for the rest of your life?"

It was 7:55 P.M. The conference call ended abruptly. The Mariners hung up without so much as a goodbye. Bowden sat in silence by the phone. They hadn't said goodbye, he thought. That's a good sign. Maybe they'll call back.

His telephone rang at 8:21 P.M. One of the lower-level Mariners executives said they had to have a fourth player. What about Meyer, a relief pitcher the Reds had left unprotected in the December Rule V draft? That was it. The deal was done.

Beginning at 9 P.M. and only now with the proper blessing of Major League Baseball, the Reds had 72 hours to work out a deal with Griffey and Goldberg. "I don't want to be an albatross around anybody's neck," Griffey told Goldberg. "I don't want to take up such a huge part of somebody's payroll that they can't do other things. They should still have money to get a player at the [trading] deadline if they need one."

The contract came together quickly. "The secret to the deal working is the amount of deferred money," Allen says. "This is a return to fiscal responsibility." Actually, the deal is an anomaly. Griffey had limited his own market value by announcing he wanted to play for one team—a team with limited resources, at that. Neither he nor Goldberg, an attorney and longtime family friend who represents no other ballplayer, had a history of playing hardball at negotiating tables.

Other agents reacted with as much horror as Selig did glee. Surely, they figured, the deal must include some form of income escalation, such as a guarantee that Griffey would always be the highest-paid Red, or an attendance clause similar to what Mark McGwire has with the Cardinals. But none exists.

It took only a few hours for Griffey to begin to have the effect on Cincinnati that McGwire had on St. Louis after the slugging first baseman's trade there in July 1997. The Cinergy Field switchboard was overwhelmed with incoming calls for tickets. The only way to reach anyone in the Reds office was on a cell phone. So many people showed up to buy season tickets that they had to take numbers in the lobby and wait to be called into a room to buy them—and even then Reds employees couldn't get an open phone line to run charge cards. An advertising agency called to offer free billboard space with a picture of Griffey to hawk season tickets.

The rest of the National League celebrated, too, now that it can promote dates featuring Griffey, McGwire, and the Chicago Cubs' Sammy Sosa, probably the three greatest drawing cards in the game today. The only three players still alive to have hit more than 55 home runs in a season all play in the National League Central, which gives teams such as Selig's own cash-strapped Milwaukee Brewers 18 dates to sell the Big Three. Look for special ticket packages—the 18-game Power Pack—at a National League ballpark near you.

Remember this, though: Griffey, McGwire, and Sosa hit 176 home runs among them last year, yet all played for losing teams that finished a combined 67½ games out of first place. Beyond the glamour of the home run race, the success of the Reds, Cardinals, and Cubs will depend mostly on pitching, which none have in abundance.

Bowden will try to deal from his surplus of outfielders to find another starter to join Neagle, Pete Harnisch, Steve Parris, and Ron Villone, though Bowden's history suggests he will do so in July. (He has picked up Dave Burba, Juan Guzman, Mark Portugal, and David Wells in deadline deals.) He postponed any such thoughts, though, on the jet ride back to Florida last Thursday night. This was a time to celebrate, especially when Lindner's son Craig popped the corks on the Dom Pérignon.

It was also a time to reflect. Bowden thought about his seven years with the Reds, all but the last in the employ of the penurious Marge Schott, whom Lindner replaced as the majority owner. He thought about how Schott wouldn't provide the offices and clubhouse with bottled water. (That's why we have water fountains, she reasoned.) Now here he was sipping champagne and sinking softly into the cushioned leather upholstery of a private jet that cost nearly as much as his team's entire 1999 payroll, surrounded by fresh food, a DVD player, a big-screen television, and one of the 50 greatest players of the twentieth century. Only two others, he figured, had changed teams in their youthful primes: Babe Ruth and Rogers Hornsby.

He saw Griffey laughing with his children, and he knew the fit was right. Junior last wore a Cincinnati uniform when he was eight years old and his father was an All-Star outfielder with the Reds. The kids beat their dads 12-0 in the player–family game. Junior would relish victories by his father's teams because after them he could grab "red pop and bubble gum" from the clubhouse. He'd cry after losses because that's when children weren't allowed in. Now Trey and Taryn can scamper around the same places he did, only this time at the feet of their father *and* grandfather.

Bowden had felt a tightness in his gut ever since he'd hung up the phone at 8:30 the night before. That and a sense of decorum were all that kept him from yelping with joy as loud as he could. Yes, sir. He was flying.

Collective Bargaining at Magic Carpet Airlines: A Union Perspective (A)

HISTORY OF MAGIC CARPET AIR

Magic Carpet Air (MCA) began operations in 1961, serving 2 cities, and grew to serve 18 cities by 1987. River City Airlines (RCA) began in 1969 with service to 4 cities and grew to serve 12 cities by 1987. In January 1987, Magic Carpet Air purchased River City Airlines and merged the two operations. The joining of these two regional airlines created a small "national" airline (defined as a carrier with sales between $100 million and $1 billion) with sales of $140,265,000 in 1987. Even so, the firm competed primarily in only one region of the country and managers constantly compared it to other large regional airlines.

In May 1988, Magic Carpet Air entered into a marketing agreement with a major national carrier and became a "feeder" airline for that carrier (e.g., American Eagle is a feeder airline for American Airlines, United Express is a feeder for United Airlines). That is, MCA delivered passengers from small airports to larger ones, where passengers could make connections using that airline. Subsequently, no more reservations were given to the public as Magic Carpet Air; passengers believed that they bought tickets for the major carrier. The company also repainted all aircraft to make the public believe Magic Carpet Air was part of the major carrier.

Prior to 1989, the flight attendants at neither company were unionized. However, both MCA and RCA flight attendants worried about what they perceived as the arbitrary way that MCA management resolved personnel issues such as merging seniority lists.

This case was prepared by Peggy Briggs and William Ross of the University of Wisconsin–LaCrosse and is intended to be used as a basis for class discussion rather than to illustrate either effective or ineffective handling of the situation. The names of the firms, individuals, and locations; dates; conversation quotations; and financial information have all been disguised to preserve the firm's and union's desire for anonymity.

An earlier version of this case was presented and accepted by the refereed Midwest Society for Case Research and appeared in *Annual Advances in Case Research, 1991.* All rights reserved to the authors and the MSCR.

Copyright ©1991, 1997 by Peggy Briggs and William Ross.

Such fears led several workers to contact the League of Flight Attendants (LFA), a union whose membership consisted solely of flight attendants. Despite opposition to unionization from MCA, the LFA won a union certification election with 82 percent of the vote.

PREVIOUS CONTRACT NEGOTIATIONS

Negotiations for the first MCA–LFA contract began in November 1989, and negotiators from both sides cooperated effectively. The committee borrowed language from other airline contracts (e.g., Piedmont Airlines). The committee also incorporated the past practices and working conditions that were used at River City Airlines. These rules had not been written down but had been mutually acceptable past practices. Negotiators signed the final contract in August 1990. The contract was effective until August 1994.

Negotiations for the second contract also went smoothly. In terms of contract provisions, the second contract was basically an extension of the first, with a modest pay increase and one additional paid holiday. The agreement was effective until August 31, 1997.

What follows is a synopsis of the 1997 contract negotiations from a union negotiator's perspective.

LEAGUE OF FLIGHT ATTENDANTS (LFA) NEGOTIATING TEAM

Whenever an LFA carrier began negotiations, the National Office of LFA sent a national bargaining representative (NBR) to the scene. Dixie Lee, the NBR assigned to the MCA negotiations, met with the flight attendants' Master Executive Council (MEC) to select a negotiating team. The negotiating team prepared for negotiations and conducted the actual bargaining sessions. Once at the table, Dixie spoke for the committee. Using an NBR as the spokesperson lessened the likelihood that a flight attendant who was emotionally involved with an issue might say something inappropriate while trying to negotiate. Dixie had 14 years' experience and had also assisted with the 1994 MCA contract negotiations. Although Dixie was the spokesperson, the negotiating team was formally chaired by Ruth Boaz, LFA MEC president at Magic Carpet Air. Other members of the team included local LFA union presidents Peggy Hardy, Marie Phillips, and Jody Rogers.

DETERMINING THE UNION'S BARGAINING OBJECTIVES

The LFA negotiating committee members first identified their bargaining objectives. For the 1997 contract, the LFA negotiating committee devised an opening offer based on the average working conditions and wage rates for flight attendants offered by other, similarly sized carriers. They looked at wage, unemployment, and cost-of-living data from government sources such as the *Monthly Labor Review*. The committee members knew the financial history of MCA and kept their proposals within financial reach of the company. They also used other employee groups (e.g., pilots, mechanics) within MCA as a guide—many of the LFA proposals were items that these other unions already had in their contracts. The LFA negotiating committee hoped to bring wages and work rules in line

TABLE 1 1996–97 Regional Airline Industry Comparisons

	Starting Wage/Hour	Days off per Month	Duty Rig* as Airline (percent of time)
A	$17.00	11	60%
B	$15.00	12	62%
C	$15.00	12	none
D	$14.00	13	none
E	$14.00	10	none
F	$13.50	10	33%
Magic Carpet	$13.00	10	none

*Duty rig is a pay calculation that is a certain percentage of the period of time which a flight attendant is on duty with the company. Duty time normally begins 45 minutes prior to first scheduled trip departure time and ends 15 minutes after final arrival time at the end of the day.

with the company's financial performance and industry standards (see Table 1). Finally, they looked at past grievances and arbitration cases to determine if contract wording needed changes.

Committee members also considered the wishes of the rank-and-file members. To do this, the committee mailed a survey to the 115 LFA members asking questions regarding wages, working conditions, and issues of concern to flight attendants. They received a 75 percent response rate; results are shown in Table 2.

After tallying the responses, negotiating team members discovered that the flight attendants' major concern was wage determination. MCA currently paid flight attendants for the time they were in the aircraft with it moving under its own power—they were not paid for the time spent sitting in airports waiting for flights. Union members wanted MCA to implement "duty rigs." A duty rig paid the attendant a fixed percentage of the period of time he or she was on duty with the company.

For example, suppose an attendant worked a 15-hour day, but worked in moving aircraft for only six hours. Under the current system, MCA paid wages for six hours, plus one hour for preparation time ("duty time") at the beginning of the day. However, if the duty rig pay rate was 67 percent, MCA would pay the attendant for 10 hours of work, plus 1 hour for duty time. Thus, duty rigs would require the airline to pay a percentage of the wage for all time at work, whether flying or sitting.

Flight attendants also voiced concern over job security and working conditions. When they analyzed the job security issue, team members found that in the event of any merger or buyout of MCA, the flight attendants wanted their seniority with the carrier to be continued by any new company. Second, flight attendants sought protection from layoffs in the event of a merger or acquisition.

The survey also had a section for employee comments. The area that members most frequently relayed as a concern was their current sick leave program. Many flight attendants complained that they were not allowed to use their accrued sick time when they were sick. Others complained that they had to give management a five-day notice whenever they wanted to swap routes with other MCA attendants.

TABLE 2   Results of the Flight Attendant Survey

Questionnaires mailed: 115

Questionnaires returned: 86

Question: What was the flight attendant's top priority for the new contract?
Direct wages	40%
Job security	31%
Working conditions	26%
Other	3%

Question: How did the flight attendant want to receive her/his direct wages?
Duty rigs	47%
Hourly rate	34%
Holiday pay	15%
Other	4%

Question: How did the flight attendant want her/his job security?
Seniority protection	60%
Protection from layoffs	28%
Protection of contract	12%

From this information, union negotiating committee members identified two broad objectives: increased wages via a duty rig provision, and increased job security. They also decided that their initial package would be very close to their final objectives. The committee members proposed a duty rig clause with the same standards as the pilots, although the dollar amount was less important than just obtaining the provision itself. They also devised a "successorship clause" allowing attendants to arbitrate their seniority rights in the event someone bought MCA. In order to obtain these clauses, the union also proposed two throwaway clauses: an expensive health care package and double-time wages for working holidays.

STRATEGIES OF THE UNION

During planning sessions, the negotiating committee identified four strategies for achieving its objectives through bargaining:

1. Keeping union members informed of negotiation progress.
2. Getting union members involved.
3. Convincing the company that the union's demands were serious.
4. Settling an issue only with the unanimous consent of the negotiating committee.

Informing Union Members

The first strategy attempted to keep the union members informed. The negotiating committee mailed a short letter after each bargaining session, explaining the issues discussed and the general content of any agreed-upon sections. Members were also sent

Negotiation Update newsletters every two weeks, telling flight attendants of their progress. These newsletters did not reveal any initial proposals because committee members knew that union members would be disappointed if the union did not receive what was initially requested.

Involving Union Members

The second strategy sought to get the union members involved. The negotiating committee printed the slogan, "We make the difference and they make the money" on pens, buttons, and T-shirts. These were distributed to all members and to all passengers on selected flights. This program was loosely modeled after the United Airlines' 1996–97 Create Havoc Around Our System (CHAOS) program, where the union sought to enlist the aid of the public and employed creative tactics (e.g., intermittent strikes, informational picketing) to pressure management to resolve their contract dispute. The union also invited any member in good standing to attend any negotiation session.

Convincing the Company

The third strategy attempted to convince the company to take the LFA seriously. In a widely publicized move, negotiation team members did extensive research on both economic picketing and informational picketing, inquiring at all of their domicile cities as to what permits would be needed to picket. The union mailed their *Negotiation Update* newsletters to each manager's home address, informing managers of the LFA's preparations in the event of a future strike. Committee members hoped these actions would convince management that the LFA made serious proposals—and would strike if those proposals were not met.

Settling Issues

The fourth strategy was that the team would not proceed with an item without the entire team being in total agreement. All planning meetings, and caucuses (meetings without the company team member present) during negotiations would involve every committee member.

COMPANY NEGOTIATING TEAM

The company negotiating team consisted of the following people:

- Bill Orleans, director of labor relations.
- Ross Irving, director of human resources.
- Kristine Lamb, director of inflight services.
- Christian Andrew, executive vice president.
- Willie Sanders, senior vice president of operations.
- Tom Windham, chief executive officer (CEO) and president.

The company team was in a state of transition, and consequently seemed to suffer from much confusion. Bill Orleans had recently been demoted from director of human resources to director of labor relations—a move he resented. Ross Irving, the new director of human resources, hired from another firm, avoided the sessions; he seemed uncomfortable sitting next to his predecessor, particularly since Mr. Orleans had negotiated most of the union contracts at MCA. Finally, Mrs. Lamb, who was used to giving orders to flight attendants, acted as if the negotiations reflected a lack of loyalty on the part of the workers and interference with her job on the part of management. Tom Windham was grooming Willie Sanders to take over upon Windham's retirement.

THE NEGOTIATING PROCESS: INITIAL POSITIONS

Airlines are governed under the Railway Labor Act of 1926, as amended. This act states that labor contracts never expire, but may be amended on their amendable dates. When the amendable date comes near, a letter is mailed by the party requesting changes in the contract to the counterparty in the contract. This letter allows contract talks to begin. Dixie mailed MCA such a letter on March 31, giving a full 60 days' notice of the flight attendants' intent to open talks for amending their current contract before September 1.

Inasmuch as the company would not meet in a neutral city, LFA negotiators agreed to an MCA proposal to meet at a hotel located near corporate headquarters. MCA paid for the meeting room. The first negotiation session was scheduled for May 29, 1997.

Everyone on the LFA committee had the jitters. It was the first time in negotiations for Marie, Jody, and Peggy. Dixie gave them some last-minute instructions:

> I don't want y'all to speak or use any facial expressions at the table. Instead, I want all of y'all to silently take notes. Draw a vertical line down the middle of each note page. Write whatever the managers say on the left side of the page and write whatever I say on the right-hand side of the page. Is it OK with y'all if I do the negotiating? I've found things go best if only one person talks at the bargaining table.

As the LFA negotiators filed into the conference room, they saw it was empty. Each of the managers arrived late. Twenty minutes later, Mr. Orleans still had not come. As everyone waited, CEO Tom Windham arrived. Small talk began as Mr. Windham glanced over his notes and spoke:

> You know that as a feeder airline we do not have full control over our own destiny; the marketing agreement with the major carrier restricts our flexibility. Even so, I am willing to give your flight attendant group a modest increase. I am not looking for any concessions. Also, my philosophy is that all the groups (pilots, agents, office personnel) should be treated equally. However, your union does have a good agreement right now—say, why don't we just agree to continue the present contract for another six years? It could save a lot of time!

As everyone chuckled at Mr. Windham's joke, Mr. Orleans arrived. The union negotiators could tell by the expression on his face that he was surprised and embarrassed to see Tom Windham there. Mr. Windham stood up, wished everyone good luck, and left.

THE UNION'S INITIAL POSITION

Dixie spent the first day describing problems with the current contract. At 4:15 P.M., the union presented the company with its neatly typed contract proposal. Dixie had written "change," "new," "clarification," and so on in the margin next to each paragraph that had been changed in any way from the 1994 contract.

Orleans: This is a "wish book"! Do I look like Santa Claus?

Lee: Stop fidgeting, Mr. Orleans. Let me explain why we are insisting on these changes.

Dixie read only about one-third of the provisions in the union's contract proposal. Two additional sessions were necessary to read through the entire proposal. The major changes are summarized in Table 3.

MANAGEMENT'S INITIAL POSITION

On the fourth day, company representatives presented their initial offer to the union. Mr. Orleans handed each of the LFA committee members a book in a binder. As they leafed through the book, members were puzzled. They did not see any notations indicating changes from the current contract. Mr. Orleans talked quickly, summarizing the provisions in the contract; most of the proposed provisions included some type of union concessions, but he did not highlight these.

Lee: Is this a serious proposal? The union presented a realistic proposal using industry standards, and your opener (opening offer) is totally unreasonable.

Orleans: Don't get your panties in a wad. The party has just begun and there is lots of time to dance. Why, we didn't even list any wages in our proposal—we were hoping you would work for free, ha ha.

Mr. Orleans then gave a long, patronizing, sermon regarding MCA's poor financial health and how the company could be bankrupt at any time. However, in the history of Magic Carpet Air, the company had never shown a loss on its financial statement.

A recess was called for lunch. As the union members caucused, Peggy looked depressed. Marie sat with fists clenched.

Marie: I can't eat anything! I am furious at Mr. Orleans—he has some nerve!

Jody: The others were not much better. Did you hear their snide remarks about us when they went to lunch?

Peggy: What are we going to do? They have asked for concessions on everything! And Mr. Windham promised us just the opposite.

Dixie: Now girls, just relax. It is still the first week of negotiations. I suggest that we just work from our initial contract proposal and ignore theirs. It can't be taken seriously anyway, in my opinion.

Marie: Well, you'll have to carry on without me tomorrow; I have to work. Management won't let me rearrange my schedule to negotiate. At least I won't have to watch Mr. Orleans chain smoke!

Talks resumed after lunch break. Dixie summarized each section of the LFA proposal. Mr. Orleans fidgeted and kept saying "No." Nothing was settled that day.

TABLE 3   Changes in the Magic Carpet Air–League of Flight Attendants Contract

Contract Provision	1994–97 Contract	Union Proposal
Compensation		
Base wage	$13.00	$15.45
Wage after five years	$20.20	$25.55
Duty rig pay	None	1 hour pay per 2 hour duty (50%)
Daily guarantee	3.25 hours	4.5 hours
Holiday pay	None	8 holidays at double-time rate
Job security		
Successorship	None	Contract will still be binding
Protection of seniority rights in the event of a merger	None	Arbitrator combines MCA seniority list with that of the other airline
Working conditions		
Trip trading lead time	5 days	24 hours
Shoe allowance	None	$100/year
Winter coat	None	Total cost
Uniform maintenance	$16/month	$20/month

By noon the next day, it became obvious that not much was getting accomplished. Finally, the union moved to sections where it did not propose any changes and the managers tentatively agreed to keep those intact. It seemed like a mountain had been climbed just to get the company to agree to those "no changes." Negotiations were adjourned for the day.

Lee: When can we meet? Monday, at 8:30?

Sanders: No good for me. I have important meetings that day.

Lee: How about Tuesday?

Andrew: I can't make it. Every day next week is bad.

Orleans: The following week I will be out of town. Sorry!

Lee: OK, y'all tell us when y'all's schedules are free.

Orleans: We'll have to caucus. We'll get back to you.

Instead of caucusing and deciding when they could next meet, the managers simply went home, leaving the union negotiating team to wonder when—or if—bargaining would continue.

ROUND 2

On Wednesday, July 16, Ruth Boaz got a letter from management asking for a meeting two days later. Ruth quickly scheduled a planning session for Thursday night, where the LFA team members reviewed their objectives and the progress to date. Negotiations with MCA resumed Friday.

JULY 18: GRIEVANCES AND UNIFORMS

Mr. Irving proposed using the same language for a revised grievance procedure as that printed in the pilot's contract. The union caucused. Ruth telephoned the pilot's union and, once she was satisfied that the pilots were happy with their grievance procedure, convinced the union negotiating team to agree.

The discussion moved to the section on uniforms. After some countering back and forth on various issues, a winter coat was added as an optional item; however, who would pay the cost was still an issue. The union wanted MCA to pay the total cost.

Orleans: Unacceptable. You'll have to buy your own coats. We already give $16 per month for uniform cleaning.

Lee: But a winter coat is expensive. Surely y'all recognize that a poor little ol' flight attendant couldn't be expected to shoulder the entire cost of a new coat. Mr. Orleans, have a heart.

Orleans: I do have a heart; fortunately, it is not attached to my wallet, ha ha. OK, we will allow $40 every five years to buy a coat.

Lee: According to my research, a new cost costs $120. And it costs $10.00 per month to clean.

Orleans: How often does someone dry-clean a coat she only wears three months of the year? She doesn't clean it 12 times! *(Pause.)* OK, if you drop this silly request for free shoes, then we'll raise the combined uniform and coat maintenance allowance to $16.50 per month.

Lee: But, Mr. Orleans, shoes are a part of our uniform, too. You expect us to all wear the same type of shoes, don't you? You pay for the other parts of our uniforms, so it is only reasonable that MCA should also pay for shoes. Our research shows that two pairs of standard shoes cost, on average, $100.

Orleans: However, you can wear the shoes when you are not on duty, too. You probably wouldn't do that with other parts of your uniforms. So we're not paying for shoes you can wear other places.

Boaz: Mr. Orleans, I can assure you that we don't wear our uniform shoes when we go dancing on the weekends. (Everyone laughed.)

Orleans: If we pay $25 for shoes and $45 for a coat, then we will pay $17.50 per month for uniform maintenance.

Lee: Good, but not good enough.

(Both sides sat in silence for nearly four minutes. Mr. Orleans was obviously uncomfortable with this period of silence.)

Orleans: Let's see . . . *(fumbling with a pen and paper)* we'll split the cost of the new coat, so that is $60 and we'll pay $25 for shoes. Good enough now?

Lee: Raise the combined uniform and coat maintenance to $18 per month and you have a deal.

Lee: *(As they were writing the agreed-upon section.)* Why don't we make it one new coat for the life of the three-year contract, instead of one new coat every five years? That makes it so much easier for everyone to keep track of.

Mr. Orleans rolled his eyes and nodded in acquiescence. The meeting then adjourned for the weekend. At last the union team felt that some progress was being made.

CASE 5

Vanessa Abrams (A)

Vanessa Abrams, executive vice president of sales and marketing, after nine years with Swanton & Gardner (S&G), found herself involved unexpectedly in a tense negotiation with her boss, Jerome Bailey, president and franchise owner of S&G's New York office. Hired in 1980 as director of sales and marketing, a position then new to S&G's office, Abrams had over the years turned in consistently excellent performances for the health care consulting firm, and she had been promoted to vice president and, later, executive vice president. She had been a member of the New York office's management committee since her promotion to vice president in 1983. S&G's 42-person New York office was one of a chain of 73 offices throughout the United States, each of which was owned locally.

As executive vice president of sales and marketing, Abrams participated in setting the office's yearly revenue goal and was responsible for meeting that goal with her staff of two account managers, one administrative person, and a number of consultants who reported indirectly to her. Some of the New York office's revenues came through other S&G offices (including corporate headquarters in Boston), and some originated in New York.

Historically, Abrams had herself brought in between 30 and 40 percent of the office's revenues each year. Her compensation package consisted of base salary plus commission. The commission that she and all members of her sales group received could total to about 16 percent on any one account. Each member of the sales group (including Abrams) received a 4 percent commission on any new business brought in and a 12 percent commission on any accounts managed. In addition, Abrams received a 2 percent override commission on all new business generated by her sales team. In fiscal 1989–90, her team had exceeded the total revenue goal of $4.7 million. (S&G's fiscal year ended on August 31.) In addition to her revenue-generation responsibilities, Abrams made all management decisions regarding pricing, assigning of consultants to accounts, and workloads. Abrams oversaw training for both new and existing staff and was responsible for the New York office's public relations needs.

Vanessa Abrams, who held a master's degree in psychology, had been a therapist prior to coming to S&G. Her training in her "first career," as she put it, came through

This case was prepared by Deborah Kolb and Cinny Little for the Institute for Case Development and Research, Simmons Graduate School of Management, Boston, MA 02215. Copyright ©1992 by the President and Trustees of Simmons College. No part of this publication may be reproduced, stored in a retrieval system, or transmitted by any form or by any means, including photocopying, without the permission of the Simmons Graduate School of Management.

clearly in conversations with her. She listened attentively and well, often making notes in a small leather notebook that was always close at hand, bristling with pieces of paper. Though Abrams was persistent when pursuing a line of questioning or seeking information, she spoke in a quiet voice and frequently pushed her long hair gently back from her face as she paused for thought. An observer could not help but notice Abrams's appearance. She was very tall and strikingly slender. Her wardrobe was sophisticated, unusual, and elegant, and included bright colors and artful jewelry.

During the spring of 1990, Bailey came to Abrams and asked her to sign a nondisclosure agreement. It was very common for companies to protect themselves by having employees sign an agreement stating that they will not share company or client knowledge with other companies. Most such agreements would require that an employee not solicit former clients for business for a certain length of time after termination. It was particularly common for employees in positions with sales or bottom-line responsibilities as well as senior management to work under the terms of such an agreement. As she understood the S&G nondisclosure agreement, Abrams said, "It meant that if I ever left S&G, I couldn't work for a competitor or solicit any of my clients for a year. I couldn't solicit clients for *anything;* I mean if I had wanted, for whatever reason, to sell them recycling services or anything else, I couldn't do that. And he could do anything he wanted after I signed it."

This was not the first time that Bailey had asked her to sign the agreement, but Abrams had always refused to sign, since, she said, "I had been working for Jerry for years without a nondisclosure. He had asked me to sign it time and again, and I refused. There was absolutely no reason, in my mind, why I needed to sign it. It was the only way I had leverage over him."

But in May 1990, Bailey was insistent that this time she really had to sign the agreement. Corporate headquarters was pressuring him, he said, "and they just don't want anybody in the company without one." Somewhat confused by the sudden urgency of Bailey's request, Abrams decided to call Jim, a good friend of hers who was an attorney. Jim thought it might be a good idea for her to get someone to look over the S&G nondisclosure agreement, and he referred her to Nick, an attorney who worked in the same firm. Nick told Vanessa that S&G's nondisclosure agreement seemed to be pretty standard. But, he told her, "Jerry can't *make* you sign the agreement." He suggested to Abrams that she should get some compensation for signing. "He said," Vanessa recounted, "that I should really get tough with Jerry; if Jerry really needed me to sign this, then I should be able to get something for it."

Vanessa thought about Nick's advice to "get tough," and she considered past situations in which she had negotiated with Jerry:

> I had always negotiated with him in a very psychological way, and it's always been very successful. I'm a therapist from my first career, and a lot of it was intuitive for me. I'd play to his ego, and I'd make him feel good. I'd put myself in his shoes and try to figure out what he thinks. He would huffle and buffle and try to make me feel sorry for him. That was his negotiating style. He acts out of his emotions.

Vanessa said that what she really wanted from Jerry at this point was for him to show her how much he valued her. She also decided to take Nick's advice about getting tough and seeking compensation for signing the nondisclosure. She wrote a memo to

Jerry in early June 1990 in which she stated that in exchange for signing the nondisclosure, she wanted a contract with the following protections in place:

1. The right of first refusal should Jerry decide to sell the New York office franchise.

2. The continuation of reimbursement for all "customary and reasonable" professional expenses incurred (e.g., parking, mileage, car phone, client entertainment) and continuation of all customary S&G employee benefits.

3. A salary in the range that is equal to the compensation she had historically received, and which takes into account the revenues she had historically generated and places a value on the loss of mobility she would incur if she signed the nondisclosure.

4. A parachute clause that provides her with customary benefits in the event she is no longer employed by S&G. (*Note:* A *parachute* is an agreement that provides for payment after termination of employment.)

5. A signing bonus of 5 percent of her salary.

In the June 13 meeting they held to discuss her memo, Jerry said that he "really didn't have to do anything for" her. Vanessa said:

> Then I became much harder. Here I was the goose laying the golden eggs. I told Jerry that my attorney had advised me in this matter, and with that Jerry was just furious. He got enraged. He is a large man, on the stocky side and his broad face got redder than I have ever seen it. He said, "How did you get an attorney involved in this?" I said, "Jerry, if this were you, wouldn't you?" And he replied, "No! We've had a relationship for all these years!" I said, "But look what you're trying to do to me; you're going to take away all this." He said, "Well, look what you're doing to *me*. I got written up." "Written up" in our corporate lingo means that he was cited by corporate headquarters for having a senior member of management who is not covered by the agreement. So I understood about him having to have the agreement. I really did. But the feeling that he wasn't willing to give me a goddamn thing for signing was enraging. It was the feeling that was important to me. The one thing I had over him, in my mind, was the leverage of *not* signing the nondisclosure. The leverage was important to me, too.
>
> After the June 13 meeting, he brought a lot of pressure to bear on me. He took me off the management committee [which had been made up of Bailey, Abrams, and two others]. He told me that he couldn't let me be privy to management discussions if I didn't sign the nondisclosure. Nick was telling me that I had to be ready to walk out. But psychologically, I was not prepared to walk. I couldn't. I was making good money, and I knew that the next quarter was going to be big. Nick said, "Don't sign it, and then you can work for a competitor." And I even went so far as to speak to one of them. I flew to Baltimore and talked to them. But the money was nowhere near where it was at S&G. And the thing is, I *loved* S&G. I loved the people, loved the work.

In July 1990, Abrams decided to sign the nondisclosure agreement. She said:

> I succumbed to the pressure. Being taken off the management committee was public and it was embarrassing. So, I signed it, and I did get one consideration. I got the consideration that if he fired me, I would get one year's salary. In my mind, I didn't think this was worth a thing, but on the other hand, I figured he wouldn't fire me. After all, I was the major revenue-producer.
>
> The thing was in all of this, I had negotiated from my attorney's style rather than the style I'd used over the years with Jerry. With Jerry, I *knew* I had to cajole him and just work things out, but when I took a much stronger stand and had this and that in writing, he was furious. And I ended up giving in. Taking a hard line just didn't seem to work.

As soon as Abrams signed the nondisclosure statement, S&G New York experienced a rush of new business. Abrams said, "We had six phenomenal months, which started with July 1990 and August 1990. Fiscal 1989–90 ended up with a bang and made it a great year for us." This high-level performance continued for the first months of fiscal 1990–91, and the sales group made their numbers in the first half of the fiscal year, which was very unusual. As Abrams said, "This meant that if we held even for the rest of fiscal year, we'd have the best year ever. We were staffed up on the service delivery side, and we took more space in our building to accommodate new people . . . and then things began to slow down."

All through the spring and summer of 1991, Abrams noticed empty offices and could see that S&G was spending more and more money on office equipment and other materials. Abrams told Bailey that she thought they needed to do something about the expenses. Her feeling was that, if sales slowed down and expenses were too high, profits would be unnecessarily low. Jerry replied that he wasn't terribly concerned and that July and August were always S&G's best months. Abrams said, "But Jerry, although that's usually true, this year is unusual. The market is shifting, and I don't see an August 1991 that looks good. I feel it in my bones. I don't see anything in the pipeline."

DISCUSSION QUESTIONS

1. At the conclusion of the noncompete negotiations, Vanessa Abrams said, "I ended up giving in." Do you agree?
2. How did Abrams get herself in this position? What other choices did she have? Why didn't she pursue them?
3. Have you had similar experiences? What were they and how did you handle them?

CASE 6

500 English Sentences

Scott sat looking out the window, watching a group of boys playing baseball in the school yard. Poor kids, he thought, they are the real losers in all of this. He looked down at a copy of *500 English Sentences* and the endorsement letter on his desk. He glanced at the clock and realized that he had to have an answer for Mr. Honda within the hour. He was feeling very frustrated and stressed from the events of the past 10 days. He decided that he would go to the karate school after work, something which always made him feel better. He sighed as he thought about what he had to do next.

SCOTT

Scott was 26 years old and had been living in Japan for 18 months. He was born in Auburn, Massachusetts, and had spent most of his life in the United States. Scott's father was a successful entrepreneur who believed that hard work and good old-fashioned principles were the ingredients to success. He always taught his children to stand up for what they believed in and to never sacrifice their values in order to get ahead. Scott's mother was a housewife who took care of the family home and the children. She loved to travel and encouraged Scott's father to take the family abroad every year so that their children would have a better understanding of the world around them.

Scott was a very disciplined student. He was an English major and had been on the dean's honor role for every semester throughout his four years at college. During his senior year, Scott worked as a teaching assistant, grading papers and tutoring students.

Scott started studying karate when he was a junior in high school. He enjoyed the physical workout and the disciplinary aspect of the sport and continued to train throughout his undergraduate years. By the time he was ready to graduate, Scott had earned a third-degree black belt.

It was through karate that I first became interested in Japan. I thought it would be enlightening to experience Japanese culture and learn more about their ways of thinking. My goal was to one day go over to Japan and train in a Japanese karate dojo (school) and learn from a real

This case was written by Laura Turek. Copyright ©1996 by Laura Turek. Used with permission. This case was prepared as a basis for classroom discussion, not to illustrate either the effective or ineffective management of an administrative situation.

karate sensei. My biggest problem was to figure out how to go about doing this. I knew that I didn't have the luxury of just moving to Japan to study karate and since I didn't speak the language I figured that my chances of working for a company in Japan were about nil.

In the fall of his senior year, Scott saw a poster for the Japan Exchange and Teaching (JET) Program at school that advertised teaching jobs in Japan. He had heard of other students going over to Japan to teach English but had never given any serious thought to a career in teaching, even if only for a short time. To work as an assistant English teacher on the JET program, applicants had to have a bachelor's degree and an interest in Japan. Knowledge of Japanese language or a degree in education were not listed as requirements. This was what Scott had been hoping for, an opportunity to go over to Japan to continue his karate under a Japanese instructor as well as a chance to put his English degree to good use. He wrote the address in his notebook and sent for an application that very night.

THE JAPAN EXCHANGE AND TEACHING (JET) PROGRAM

Before the JET Program

The origins of the JET program can be traced back to 1982. In that year, the Japanese Ministry of Education (Monbusho) initiated a project known as the Monbusho English Fellows (MEF) Program, which hired Americans to work at the local boards of education in order to assist Japanese English teaching consultants who acted as advisors to the Japanese teachers of English in the public schools. The task of the MEFs was to oversee the junior and senior high school English teachers and to assist them with their training. In 1983, the British English Teachers Scheme (BETS) was inaugurated by the Ministry of Education. However, from the outset the British teachers were stationed at schools, and the goals of the program did not only concern English instruction but also sought to increase mutual understanding and improve friendly relations between the peoples of Japan and Britain. While there were some differences between the two programs, both shared a common goal: inviting native English speakers to Japan to assist in improving foreign-language instruction.

The Birth of the JET Program

The realization that Japan must open itself more fully to contact with international society began to foster an awareness of the importance of promoting internationalization and international exchange at the local level. This brought about not only expanded English instruction, but also a rapid increase in exchange programs. Taking these new circumstances into account, the Japanese Ministry of Home Affairs in 1985 released a paper entitled "Plans for International Exchange Projects" as part of its priority policy of local governments for the following year. In the paper, the Ministry of Home Affairs proposed a definite course for the internationalization of local governments, which ideally would lead to smoothly functioning cultural exchanges. All of these ideas were finally implemented in a concrete project: the Japan Exchange and Teaching (JET) Program.

The Ministry of Home Affairs abolished the two projects currently in effect (MEF and BETS) and created a new one that was entrusted simultaneously to three ministries: the Ministry of Foreign Affairs, the Ministry of Education, and the Ministry of Home Affairs. However, the concept of appointing local authorities to implement the program and act as host institutions was preserved. While discussions were held with each of the local authorities to work out the details and ensure the smooth implementation of such a massive program, the formation of a cooperative organization for all local governments was expedited.

The Creation of CLAIR

CLAIR, originally the Conference of Local Authorities for International Relations, was established in October 1986 by the *Todofuken* (the 47 prefectures of Japan) and the *Seireishiteitoshi* (the [then] 10 designated cities) as a cooperative organization responsible for implementing the JET program in conjunction with the three Japanese ministries named above.

CLAIR's Role in the JET Program

To ensure smooth implementation of the JET program, the three ministries, the local authorities, and CLAIR were all given specific functions. The functions that the conference attempted to fulfill for implementing the JET program were as follows:

1. Advice and liaison during recruitment and selection.
2. Placement of participants.
3. Participant orientation, conferences.
4. Guidance for local authority host institutions.
5. Participant welfare and counseling.
6. Travel arrangements for participants coming to Japan.
7. Liaison with related groups and institutions.
8. Publications and reference materials.
9. Publicity for the program.

The larger goal behind these functions of the conference was the promotion of international exchange at the local level. Independent of this development, the Council of Local Authorities for International Relations (a publicly endowed foundation) was inaugurated in July 1987. The council's main duty was to study and survey participating nations' local authorities overseas with the ultimate objective being to support local government programs for the promotion of internationalization. By fostering international exchange at the regional level, the council came to assume the same duties as the Conference of Local Authorities for International Relations. It was suggested that both organizations merge since they held information relevant to each other's work and shared the goals of improving work efficiency and performing their tasks more effectively. Moreover, the annual growth of the JET program led to an increased number of interrelated duties and tasks. Thus, it was necessary to strengthen the structure of the Conference of Local Authorities for International Relations.

It was decided that the operations and financial assets of the conference would be assumed by the council, and in August 1989 they were amalgamated, under the acronym of CLAIR, to form a joint organization of local public bodies in Japan to support and promote internationalization at the regional level.

SCOTT'S ACCEPTANCE

Scott reviewed the JET information he had received. There were two different positions available: (1) the coordinator for international relations (CIR) and (2) the assistant language teacher (ALT). The first position, although it sounded interesting, was out of the question since knowledge of Japanese was a requirement. Scott applied for the second position because as an English major he felt that he was qualified to assist in the teaching of English. Scott was chosen for an interview and was successful in obtaining an offer to teach English in Japan.

> The JET program and CLAIR were very good at trying to prepare the participants for their stay in Japan. I attended several workshops and orientations concerning my job in Japan as well as seminars on what to expect living in such a different culture from my own. I remember thinking some of the potential situations they were preparing us for seemed a bit unrealistic and that I would probably never encounter them, but I found out soon enough that Japan and the United States are culturally a world apart, and I was glad to have received the predeparture training. Without it, I would have thought that I had arrived in Wonderland with no idea on how to behave at the tea party.

SCOTT'S SITUATION IN JAPAN

Scott was sent to a small village on the northern island of Hokkaido, where he taught English at Naka High School. At first, Scott had some difficulties adjusting to living in such a remote place. The people were friendly, yet since they were not accustomed to seeing many foreigners, Scott always felt that he was on display, or that his every move was under scrutiny.

> It was strange being the only non-Japanese person living in the town. I was there to do my job, and study karate, but somehow ended up as the town celebrity. Everyone in town knew everything about me. They all knew where I lived, when I entertained guests. I felt like my every move was monitored. It got so bad that I even had to hang my wash inside my house because people started to tell me that they liked my colorful boxer shorts.
>
> People not only watched what I did, but how I did it. Everyone wanted to know how the American talked, walked, and how he ate. People asked me daily if I could eat with chopsticks. I made a conscious effort very quickly to blend in as much as I could. It was either that or get angry, and I don't think people were being malicious, they were just overly curious.

The biggest problem that Scott encountered from the start was feelings of incompetence and frustration. The only people in the whole village with whom he could speak without much difficulty were the Japanese English teachers at the high school. If he ran into problems at the bank or supermarket, he was forced to rely on a mixture of basic Japanese and English accompanied by an elaborate display of sign language which more often than not ended in frustration. To overcome the communication problems, Scott began studying Japanese every night at home. He also found a Japanese language teacher at the high school who agreed to tutor him.

> Until I moved to Japan, I never realized how frustrating life can be when you cannot even do the simplest tasks for yourself like read your electric bill or use an automated teller machine. I felt pretty helpless a lot of the time and no one seemed to understand what I was going through. Whenever I had a problem involving a language or cultural misunderstanding, I would go see Mr. Honda, the head of English, not only because his English was the best of all of the teachers, but also because he had lived abroad in England and Australia, and I figured that he would be able to understand what I was going through.

MR. HONDA

Mr. Honda was the head of English at Naka High School. He was 46 years old and had been teaching English at various schools in the prefecture for more than 22 years. In his youth, Mr. Honda had studied English at Oxford, and had spent two summers in Australia on homestays. His command of spoken English and his vocabulary were quite remarkable. Mr. Honda acted as a mentor to Scott. He considered Scott as his *kohai* (junior) and believed that as a good Japanese manager, it was his duty to guide the young foreigner throughout his stay in Japan. Mr. Honda showed this same kind of paternalistic concern for all of the junior English teachers and counseled them on everything from lesson planning to when they should think about marrying. None of the younger teachers in the English department made any decision without the approval of Mr. Honda. Scott thought that this was a waste of talent and initiative. He knew a couple of young teachers who were very dynamic and had some creative teaching ideas, yet were forced to use the dated teaching methods of Mr. Honda because he was their superior.

Although he never expressed it openly, Mr. Honda did not really like dealing with these young ALTs. He found it insulting to work with such young foreigners, who more often than not had no formal training as English teachers yet were hired to tell him how to do his job better. He did not share in the opinion that these foreign assistants were experts in English teaching just because they could speak the language fluently. Mr. Honda, as well as the other teachers on the staff, had trouble adjusting to the ALTs since they were hired on a yearly contract basis which was renewable only to a maximum of three years. This left the school barely enough time to get to know an ALT before he or she left and another took over. Mr. Honda also didn't like the fact that these young assistant teachers were earning nearly the same salary as he each month, despite his 22 years of experience.

In spite of his feelings for ALTs in general, Mr. Honda liked Scott. He not only felt that Scott was qualified to be doing the job but also thought that Scott was adapting very well to the Japanese style of management.

> Scott works very hard. He shows great enthusiasm for teaching English at our school. He is very pleasant to work with and is making a big effort to learn the Japanese language and ways. It is a pleasure to have such a good teacher on our staff.

ACCEPTANCE IN THE GROUP

Scott joined the local karate school and began training every night after work.

> I felt very much at ease at the karate dojo. Despite the fact that I had no idea what my karate teacher and the other men were saying to me, we seemed to get along very well because we were all there for a common goal: to study karate. I think the other members accepted me into their group because I showed them that I was serious about the sport and had a determination to learn. At first, I saw the other members only at the karate school, but after a few months, they started inviting me to dinners and other social gatherings. Sometimes we even went out drinking after practice. It was good to feel like I was a part of something. I was tired of being treated like the "funny *gaijin*" all the time.

For the first few months, Scott felt isolated at work. Excluding the English teachers, many of his co-workers did not talk to him at all, which made him feel unwelcome at the school. It wasn't until he asked a young English teacher about the situation that she told Scott how several of the teachers were afraid to speak to him because they felt that their English skills were too weak. Scott told the young teacher that it was he who should be embarrassed for not speaking Japanese. After that, Scott made an effort to speak in Japanese, even though his mistakes often made him feel ridiculous and self-conscious. The other teachers slowly began to warm up to Scott and started to converse more with him at school.

Scott went out of his way to get involved at school. He not only taught his courses but also became involved with many of the clubs after school. He ran the English-speaking club and helped coach the karate club. He was also willing to come in on weekends when there was a special event going on at the school.

> I got involved with extracurricular activities at school, not necessarily for altruistic reasons, but I guess because aside from karate, there was really not much for me to do in such a remote place where I could barely speak the language. I guess the other teachers thought that I was different from some of the other foreigners who had worked at Naka High because I was putting in extra time and work. What ever the reason, they began to treat me like one of the group.

THE MOVE

Scott had been in Japan almost a year and made the decision to renew for another. He asked to be transferred to Satsuki, the capital city of the prefecture, because his girlfriend back in the United States was thinking of coming over to Japan and there would be no work for her in such a small town as the one he was in. The teachers at Naka High were sad to see Scott leave and gave him a huge farewell party at which everyone made speeches saying how they would miss him.

> It was kind of sad to leave Naka High. Once I got to know them, the teachers at Naka were quite a down-to-earth group who treated me like I was one of the family. The problem was that life in such a small town no longer offered what I needed. My girlfriend wanted to come over to Japan and I knew that she could get a job in Satsuki. My karate sensei also told me that if I wanted to test for my fourth-degree black belt, I would get better training at one of the bigger karate dojos in the city, and this was the reason that I came to Japan in the first place.

The city was quite a change for Scott. Since many foreigners lived there—English teachers, university students, and businesspeople—he did not receive the same attention as he had in the village. Compared to the small town, it was like living back in the United States. Nishi High, the school where Scott was assigned, was not at all like Naka High. Instead, it was a large academic high school where there was a particular emphasis placed on preparing for the rigorous university entrance exam. Only students who scored in the very top percentile were admitted to the best universities in the country, and Nishi prided itself on the number of students who were accepted to Tokyo University, the best in the country.

Scott was not the only foreigner working at this school. John, a 22-year-old from Australia had just been hired to replace a Canadian woman who had spent two years teaching at the school. John had just graduated with a degree in chemistry but he had studied Japanese for about seven years before moving to Japan.

One surprise Scott encountered was that Mr. Honda had also been transferred to Nishi High to head their English department. Mr. Honda spoke very highly of Scott to the teachers at Nishi and, as a result, Scott was put in charge of the *advanced English* class, which was cramming for the university entrance exams.

The English department used a textbook entitled *500 English Sentences,* which had been written approximately 10 years before by members of Nishi's staff. The book had become a standard and was used by virtually every high school in the prefecture. The teachers who wrote it were all subsequently promoted to work as advisers at the Satsuki Board of Education. Scott had tried the book in his classes, but thought that it was an inferior text riddled with grammatical inconsistencies, spelling mistakes, and archaic usages of the English language. Although this book was part of the curriculum, Scott refused to use it and instead taught from the other texts. Scott assumed this was not a problem since none of the other teachers ever mentioned the fact that he did not use the text in his classes.

IN THE LIMELIGHT

After three months of working at Nishi, Scott found out that there was going to be a prefecturewide English teachers' convention held at the school. Scott was surprised when the English staff asked him to conduct a demonstration class for one of the seminars. He was told that, in total, about 200 teachers were expected to attend.

Despite initial misgivings and stage fright, Scott's demonstration class was a huge success and Nishi High received outstanding commendations from all the teachers who attended and from the board of education. The English teachers at Nishi praised Scott for bringing honor to their school. Scott was glad that everything had gone well, but he did not think that he deserved the only credit.

For various reasons, I was awarded much of the credit for the outstanding commendations, though I felt most of the work had been done by the regular English staff. Anyway, at this point I had built an excellent relationship with the school's staff, and found that this made the whole working situation function much easier, made getting things done possible, and kept me "part of the loop" in decisions in the English department.

Scott began to receive more and more responsibilities at work. The English staff would consult with him on problems big or small concerning the teaching of English. Although Scott and John both arrived at Nishi High at the same time, Scott was considered *sempai* (the senior). Scott attributed this to a combination of his age and the fact that he had already worked one year at another school in Japan.

> It was a bit unnerving that I was given more authority than John, I had been in Japan one year longer than he had and was a few years older, but he was able to speak their language fluently and was a capable teacher. The Japanese English teachers treated me as though I were John's superior and often put me in an awkward position by making John answer to me.

THE DILEMMA

One afternoon while Scott was sitting at his desk in the staff room, he was approached by several of the Japanese English teachers, including Mr. Honda. Mr. Honda began by inquiring after Scott's health, and complimenting him on his students' recent test scores. After several minutes of small talk, Mr. Honda cleared his throat and got to the point. He laid a copy of *500 English Sentences* on Scott's desk and smiled at him. Scott thought that Mr. Honda and the other teachers had finally come to ask him to use the text in his class. "Yes, it's a textbook, and a humdinger at that," said Scott. Scott's comment was met with confusion, nervous laughs, and several coughs. "No," replied Mr. Honda, "We were hoping that you would be so kind as to help us in repairing any errors there might be in this text for republication by the prefecture." Mr. Honda continued saying that Nishi High had been assigned the duty of editing the text and resubmitting it to the publisher for printing. He said that Scott's help would be greatly appreciated since he had been an English major at university and the Japanese teachers already knew that he was a more capable teacher. Mr. Honda also said that they desired Scott's help because he was a native English speaker and he would have an excellent grasp of both current and colloquial usage of the language, something which none of the Japanese English teachers had.

Scott agreed to help them with the project and asked Mr. Honda how soon he wanted the manuscript returned. Again Mr. Honda cleared his throat and said, "Very soon."

"How soon is very soon?" asked Scott. Mr. Honda replied that the manuscript had to be into the publisher within 10 days. Ten days seemed unreasonably short to Scott, so he asked Mr. Honda how long he had known about the project. Mr. Honda replied that the school had been asked to do the project more than six months ago. Not wanting to ask why the English teachers took so long to begin working on the manuscript, Scott took the project and promised to have it back within a few days. Mr. Honda smiled and thanked Scott. Scott went home that night and started working on the project.

> I was glad to have the opportunity to do something productive and lasting. I had hated this text since I had first seen it and had secretly ridiculed the foolish foreigner whose name and recommendation graced its inner cover. I exalted in the opportunity to finally dismember the text and replace the reams of errors with actual functional English.

Scott worked on the manuscript every night for four nights, putting in an average of eight hours of work each night. He returned the text to Mr. Honda on the fifth day, full of red ink: corrections, sample replacement sentences, and explanations as to why the changes were necessary. To Scott's surprise, Mr. Honda did not thank him for the work. Instead, he looked very uncomfortable and smiled nervously as he flipped through the marked pages of the manuscript.

Two days later, Mr. Honda returned to Scott's desk. He praised Scott for his work and reminded him of their mutual indebtedness. He talked about the weather, asked Scott how his karate training was progressing, and inquired about Scott's girlfriend's health. Eventually, Mr. Honda turned the discussion to the manuscript. Apologetically, he said, most of the corrections could not be used. Scott was confused and asked why. Mr. Honda revealed that he had given the corrected manuscript to John to look at and that John had disagreed with some of the corrections. Scott became concerned and asked to see the manuscript to see the contended corrections. Upon reviewing the manuscript, Scott noted three places where John had marked disagreement. John had also noted that the differences with these three sentences were probably due to usage in Australia compared with the United States and that since he was not an English major, like Scott, Scott was probably correct. Mr. Honda agreed that Scott's corrections were valid and went back to his desk.

Mr. Honda returned an hour later to say that despite their earlier conversation all of the corrections could not be used because it was so late in the process and that it would be very troublesome for the publisher to make so many changes.

> By now I was getting frustrated. I told Mr. Honda that he should have thought of this six months ago when he first learned about the project and then asked him which was more important to him, the publisher or the students?

That night, one of the junior members of the Japanese English staff offered Scott a ride home. They discussed various topics, including how much Scott liked living in Japan. The young teacher then told Scott a story involving a junior member of the staff who tried to be helpful by correcting a memo that his boss had written. Since the memo had already been circulated once, the subsequent recirculation with the corrections resulted in a great loss of face for the boss. This resulted in strained relations, even though no offense was intended. By the time the teacher finished his anecdote, they had already arrived at Scott's house. He thanked the teacher for the ride, then got out of the car.

The next day, Scott did not discuss the topic of the manuscript and the situation seemed to have resolved itself. He assumed that Mr. Honda would go ahead and not use his changes, but he was unsure of what he could do about it.

After a few days of silence between Scott and the English teachers, Mr. Honda and the same group of English teachers came over to Scott's desk. This time they looked extremely nervous and spoke in very polite *keigo* (extremely respectful Japanese) that Scott could barely follow. Upon reaching some sort of consensus among themselves, they presented Scott with a single sheet of paper. On it was the verbatim endorsement of the previous issue of *500 English Sentences* with a blank line and Scott's name typed under the blank. "Would you be so kind as to sign this?" asked Mr. Honda. Scott was shocked. He thought the issue was closed when he had made a fuss about the corrections.

> I looked at the group and plainly and directly said that there was no way that I would sign such a statement since I felt that the text was substandard and that my integrity as a teacher would be compromised by signing the statement.

Scott suggested that Mr. Honda ask John to sign the endorsement, but Mr. Honda replied that due to his seniority, English degree, and good association with Nishi High, the board of education had personally asked for Scott's signature. Mr. Honda then added that he needed to send it in to the publisher by 5:00 P.M. that same day.

WHAT TO DO

Mr. Honda went back to his own desk, and Scott sat thinking about what he should do. All he could think about was having his name endorsing a text that he considered to be substandard. He didn't see how he could knowingly sign his name to a project that he knew was flawed.

CASE 7

Sick Leave

Kelly tried to control her anger as she thought about her supervisor. She couldn't understand why he was being so unreasonable. Maybe to him it was only a couple days of paid leave and not worth fighting over, but to her it meant the difference between being able to go on vacation during Golden Week[1] or having to stay home. She looked at her contract and the phone number of CLAIR on her desk. She wasn't the only person in the office affected by this. She sat and thought about how she should proceed.

KELLY

Kelly was 22 years old and had been working for the past six months at the Soto Board of Education office in Japan. This was her first job after graduating from college with a degree in management, and she was really excited to finally be in the real world.

Kelly was born in Calgary and had spent most of her life in Alberta, Canada. Kelly's father was a successful lawyer in Calgary, and her mother was a high school English teacher. Kelly had an older sister, Laurel, 27, who had just passed the bar exam and was working for a corporate law firm in Edmonton.

Kelly had studied Japanese in high school and in university and spoke and wrote the language quite well. When she was 15 years old, Kelly spent four months in Japan on a school exchange. She had enjoyed the time she spent there and always planned to return one day. Upon graduating from high school, Kelly went to the University of Alberta, in Edmonton, to study management.

During her final year at the university, Kelly heard some of her friends talking about the Japan Exchange and Teaching (JET) Program. She was told that it was quite easy to get accepted—all an applicant needed was a university degree and an interest in Japan— and that it would be a great way to make money and see another part of the world. Kelly would have her degree by the end of the year and thought that having lived in Japan and knowing the language showed enough interest to have her application considered. Kelly thought that a year or two in Japan after her management degree would improve her

---

This case was written by Laura Turek. Copyright ©1996 by Laura Turek. Used with permission. This case was prepared as a basis for classroom discussion, not to illustrate either the effective or ineffective management of an administrative situation.

[1]Golden Week is the period from April 29 to May 5, in which there are four Japanese national holidays. Many Japanese employees and their families take advantage of this period to go on vacation.

Japanese and give her more of a competitive advantage when she returned to Canada to begin her career. She also thought that it would be a great way to make money and have some fun before she came home to start a real job. She asked her friend how she could apply to the program and returned home that night to work on her résumé.

THE JAPAN EXCHANGE AND TEACHING (JET) PROGRAM

Before the JET Program

The origins of the JET program can be traced back to 1982. In that year, the Japanese Ministry of Education (Monbusho) initiated a project known as the Monbusho English Fellows (MEF) Program, which hired Americans to work at the local boards of education in order to assist Japanese English teaching consultants who acted as advisors to the Japanese teachers of English in the public schools. The task of the MEFs was to oversee the junior and senior high school English teachers and to assist them with their training. In 1983, the British English Teachers Scheme (BETS) was inaugurated by the Ministry of Education. However, from the outset the British teachers were stationed at schools, and the goals of the program did not only concern English instruction but also sought to increase mutual understanding and improve friendly relations between the peoples of Japan and Britain. While there were some differences between the two programs, both shared a common goal: inviting native English speakers to Japan to assist in improving foreign-language instruction.

The Birth of the JET Program

The realization that Japan must open itself more fully to contact with international society began to foster an awareness of the importance of promoting internationalization and international exchange at the local level. This brought about not only expanded English instruction, but also a rapid increase in exchange programs. Taking these new circumstances into account, the Japanese Ministry of Home Affairs in 1985 released a paper entitled "Plans for International Exchange Projects" as part of its priority policy of local governments for the following year. In the paper, the Ministry of Home Affairs proposed a definite course for the internationalization of local governments, which ideally would lead to smoothly functioning cultural exchanges. All of these ideas were finally implemented in a concrete project: the Japan Exchange and Teaching (JET) Program.

The Ministry of Home Affairs abolished the two projects currently in effect (MEF and BETS) and created a new one that was entrusted simultaneously to three ministries: the Ministry of Foreign Affairs, the Ministry of Education, and the Ministry of Home Affairs. However, the concept of appointing local authorities to implement the program and act as host institutions was preserved. While discussions were held with each of the local authorities to work out the details and ensure the smooth implementation of such a massive program, the formation of a cooperative organization for all local government was expedited.

The Creation of CLAIR

CLAIR, originally the Conference of Local Authorities for International Relations, was established in October 1986 by the *Todofuken* (the 47 prefectures of Japan) and the

Seireishiteitoshi (the [then] 10 designated cities) as a cooperative organization responsible for implementing the JET program in conjunction with the three Japanese ministries named above.

CLAIR's Role in the JET Program

To ensure smooth implementation of the JET program, the three ministries, the local authorities, and CLAIR were all given specific functions. The functions that the conference attempted to fulfill for implementing the JET program were as follows:

1. Advice and liaison during recruitment and selection.
2. Placement of participants.
3. Participant orientation, conferences.
4. Guidance for local authority host institutions.
5. Participant welfare and counseling.
6. Travel arrangements for participants coming to Japan.
7. Liaison with related groups and institutions.
8. Publications and reference materials.
9. Publicity for the program.

The larger goal behind these functions of the conference was the promotion of international exchange at the local level. Independent of this development, the Council of Local Authorities for International Relations (a public endowed foundation) was inaugurated in July 1987. The council's main duty was to study and survey participating nations' local authorities overseas with the ultimate objective being to support local government programs for the promotion of internationalization. By fostering international exchange at the regional level, the council came to assume the same duties as the Conference of Local Authorities for International Relations. It was suggested that both organizations merge since they held information relevant to each other's work and shared the goals of improving work efficiency and performing their tasks more effectively. Moreover, the annual growth of the JET program led to an increased number of interrelated duties and tasks. Thus, it was necessary to strengthen the structure of the Conference of Local Authorities for International Relations.

It was decided that the operations and financial assets of the conference would be assumed by the council, and in August 1989 they were amalgamated, under the acronym of CLAIR, to form a joint organization of local public bodies in Japan to support and promote internationalization at the regional level.

Counseling System of JET (Figure 1)

1. *Role of the host institution.* Basically problems which JET participants faced during their stay in Japan were addressed by the host institution. If a JET had a complaint or a problem at work or in his or her private life, the JET could alert his or her supervisor, who took up the matter and attempted to solve it.

2. *Role of CLAIR.* Problems or difficulties which JET program participants faced were as a rule dealt with by host institutions. However, if the issues were

FIGURE 1   Counseling System

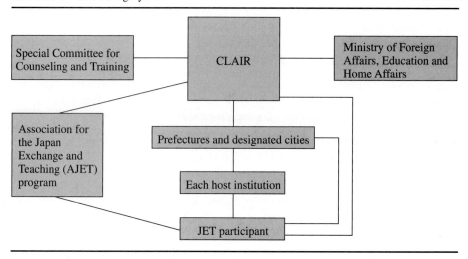

difficult to solve at this level, or if they concerned grievances between the JET participant and the host institution, CLAIR employed a number of non-Japanese program coordinators who would intervene and respond directly to participants' needs. CLAIR would then step in on behalf of the JET participant and work to solve the problems with the host institution.

3. *The Special Committee for Counseling and Training.* The Special Committee for Counseling and Training consisted of the staff members of the three ministries (Foreign Affairs, Home Affairs, and Education), embassies of the participating countries, and host institutions. It took charge of orientation, conferences, public welfare, and counseling. If necessary, it answered the questions and concerns of the JET participants.

AJET

The Association for the Japan Exchange and Teaching (AJET) Program was an independent, self-supporting organization created by JET program participants, whose elected officers were all volunteers. Membership in AJET was also voluntary. AJET provided members with information about working and living in Japan and provided a support network for members at the local, regional, and national levels. Many Japanese and JETs considered AJET to be the union of the JET program participants.

THE FIRST JOB

Kelly looked over the information she received from JET. There were two different positions available: (1) the coordinator for international relations (CIR) and (2) the Assistant Language Teacher (ALT). The first position sounded quite interesting to Kelly since applicants were required to have a functional knowledge of Japanese. ALTs, on the other hand, were not required to know any Japanese before arriving in Japan. She realized that her odds of getting accepted were greater if she applied to the second position since almost 600 ALTs were selected across Canada, compared with only 25 CIRs. Kelly was chosen for a CIR interview but in the end was offered a position as an ALT. At first she was a little disappointed, but then she reminded herself that her original goal was to perfect her Japanese, and she started to look forward to her trip to Japan.

Kelly received a lot of information about working and living in Japan from CLAIR. CLAIR also offered several predeparture training sessions and orientations about life in Japan and its potential problems, but she decided not to attend, because after four months in Japan she already knew what to expect.

THE PLACEMENT

Kelly was sent to Soto, a medium-sized city on the island of Shikoku. Kelly found the area a far cry from Osaka, where she had stayed the previous time she was in Japan. Soto was, in Kelly's opinion, "a small provincial town, stuck in the middle of nowhere." She had enjoyed the activity and night life of Osaka and, except for sports, her only entertainment options in Soto were one movie theater, several pachinko[2] parlors, and scores of karaoke bars. Kelly very quickly developed the habit of going away on the weekends to tour different parts of the island. She would also use her holidays to take advantage of visiting parts of Japan that she might never again get a chance to see. After a few months, Kelly decided that Soto was at least a good place to improve her Japanese since not many people spoke English very well, and only a few other foreigners lived there.

Kelly worked at the board of education office three days a week and visited schools the other two days to help with their English programs. There were three other JET participants who worked in the same office: Mark, 27, another Canadian; Andrea, 26, an American; and Suzanne, 25, from Britain. Like Kelly, Suzanne had been in Japan for only the past six months, while Mark and Andrea had been working there for a year and a half. Kelly was on good terms with the other JETs in the office, although she was closest with Suzanne since they had both arrived in Japan at the same time and had met at their orientation in Tokyo.

Although Kelly had lived in Japan before, this was the first time she had worked in a Japanese office. She had learned about Japanese work habits in a cross-cultural management class at the university, yet she was still surprised at how committed the Japanese were to their jobs. The workday began each morning at 8:30 with a staff meeting and officially ended each night at 5:00 P.M., yet no one left the office before 7:00 or 8:00 P.M. The Japanese also came in on Saturdays, which Kelly thought was absurd since it left the employees with only one day a week to relax or spend time with their families.

Kelly and the other JETs in the office had a standard North American contract given to them by CLAIR which stipulated hours, number of vacation days, amount of

---

[2]Pachinko is a Japanese-style game of chance that resembles a cross between pinball and a slot machine. It is a very popular pastime among certain groups and, like any form of gambling, can be quite lucrative.

sick leave, and so on (Figure 2). The contract stated that the JET participants only worked from Monday to Friday until 5:00 P.M. and did not mention working on Saturdays. Neither Kelly nor the other foreigners ever put in extra hours at the office, nor were they ever asked to do so.

FIGURE 2   Contract of English Teaching Engagement

Article 11: Paid Leave

Section 1

During the period of employment and with the approval of his/her supervisor, the JET participant may use 20 paid holidays individually or consecutively.

Section 2

When the JET participant wishes to make use of one of the above-mentioned paid holidays, he/she shall inform his/her supervisor three days in advance. Should the JET participant wish to use more than three paid holidays in succession, he/she is required to inform his/her supervisor one month in advance.

Article 12: Special Holidays

Section 1

The JET participant shall be entitled to special holidays under the following circumstances:
1. Sick leave—the period of serious illness or injury resulting in an acknowledged inability to work.
2. Bereavement—the period of 14 consecutive days, including Sundays and national holidays, immediately after the loss of father, mother, or spouse.
3. Natural disaster—the period the board of education deems necessary in the event of destruction of or serious damage to the JET participant's place of residence.
4. Transportation system failure—the period until the said problem has been resolved.

Section 2

Under the conditions of Article 12, Section 1 (1), above, the JET participant may take not more than 20 days of consecutive sick leave. Moreover, if the interval between two such periods of sick leave is less than one week, those two periods shall be regarded as continuous.

Section 3

The special holidays noted above in Article 12, Section 1, are paid holidays.

Article 17: Procedure for Taking (Sick) Leave

Section 1

When the JET participant wishes to make use of the special holidays/leave specified in Article 12, Section 1, he/she must apply and receive consent from his/her supervisor before taking the requested holidays. If circumstances prevent the JET participant from making necessary application beforehand, he/she should do so as soon as conditions permit it.

Section 2

In the event of the JET participant taking three or more consecutive days of sick leave, he/she must submit a doctor's certificate. The board of education may require the JET participant to obtain the said medical certificate from a medical practitioner specified by the board.

Kelly's supervisor was Mr. Higashi. At first Kelly thought that he was very kind and helpful because he had picked her and Suzanne up from the airport and had arranged their housing before they arrived in Japan. Mr. Higashi even took the two women shopping to help them buy necessary items like bedding and dishes so they did not have to be without, even for one night.

MR. HIGASHI

Mr. Higashi was born and had lived all of his life in Soto. He was 44 years old and had been teaching high school English in and around Soto for more than 20 years. Two years ago, Mr. Higashi was promoted to work as an adviser to all English teachers at the Soto Board of Education. This was a career-making move, and one that placed him on the track to becoming a school principal.

This new position at the board of education made Mr. Higashi the direct supervisor over the foreign JET participants in the office, as well as making him responsible for their actions. He had worked with them before when he was still teaching in the schools, but since they only came once a week to his school, he had never had the chance to get to know any of them really well.

Mr. Higashi found it very difficult to work with JETs. Since they were hired on a one-year contract basis, renewable only to a maximum of three, he had already seen several come and go. He also considered it inconvenient that Japanese was not a requirement for the JET participants because, since he was the only person in the office who could speak English, he found that he wasted a lot of his time working as an interpreter and helping the foreigners do simple everyday tasks like reading electric bills and opening a bank account. Despite this, he did his best to treat the foreign assistants as he would any other *kohai,* or subordinate, by nurturing their careers and acting as a father to them, since he knew what was best for them. Mr. Higashi was aware that his next promotion was due not only to his own performance but also to how well he interacted with his subordinates, so he worked hard to be a good mentor.

Mr. Higashi took an instant liking to Kelly because she spoke Japanese well and had already lived in Japan. Although she was the youngest of the four ALTs, he hoped that she would guide the others and assumed that she would not be the source of any problems for him.

THE ALTS' OPINION OF MR. HIGASHI

At first, Mr. Higashi seemed fine. All of the ALTs sat in two rows with their desks facing each other, as they used to do in grade school, with Mr. Higashi's desk facing Kelly's. The foreigners all agreed that Mr. Higashi acted more like a father than a boss. He continually asked Kelly and Suzanne how they were enjoying Japanese life and kept encouraging them to immerse themselves in Japanese culture. He left brochures on Kelly's desk for courses in flower arranging and tea ceremony and even one on Japanese cooking. At first Kelly found this rather amusing, but she soon tired of it and started to get fed up with this constant pressure to "sign up" for Japanese culture. What she resented the most was that Mr. Higashi kept insisting she try activities that were traditionally considered a woman's domain. Not that she had anything against flowers, but if she had been a man, she knew that Mr. Higashi would not have hassled her this much to fit in. She knew that Japanese society was a male-dominated one. On her first day at the office, Kelly had looked around and noticed that there were no Japanese women who had been promoted to such a senior level within the board of education. The only women who worked there were young and single "office ladies" or secretaries. Although they were all very sweet young women, Kelly was not about to become one of them and "retire" if and when she found a husband.

Kelly had been very active in sports back in Canada and bought herself a mountain bike when she arrived in Japan so that she could go for rides in the country. At Suzanne's encouragement, Kelly joined a local Kendo club. She had seen this Japanese style of fencing before back in Calgary, and had always been attracted to the fast movements and interesting uniforms. Kelly hoped that Mr. Higashi would be satisfied that she was finally getting involved in something traditionally Japanese and leave her alone.

On top of his chauvinistic attitudes, Kelly didn't think much of Mr. Higashi as a supervisor. If Kelly or any of the other foreigners had a problem or question concerning living in Japan, he would either ignore them or give them information that they later found out was incorrect. Andrea told Kelly that she stopped going to Mr. Higashi when she had problems and instead consulted the office lady, since she was always able to help her. Andrea had even joked that the office lady should be their supervisor because she was by far more effective than Mr. Higashi.

As far as Suzanne was concerned, Mr. Higashi was utterly exasperating. He was forever arranging projects and conferences for the ALTs to participate in, then changing his mind and canceling at the last minute without bothering to tell them. He would also volunteer the ALTs to work on special assignments over the holiday periods and then get angry when they told him that they had previous plans and were unable to go. Suzanne recalled that one week before the Christmas vacation, Mr. Higashi announced that he had arranged for her to visit a junior high school. Suzanne informed him that while she would love to go, it was impossible since she had already booked the time off and had arranged a holiday to Seoul, Korea. Mr. Higashi got angry and told her that he and the board of education would lose face if she didn't attend. Suzanne told Mr. Higashi that losing face would not have been an issue if he had told her about the visit in advance so she could have prepared for it. As a result, Suzanne lost all respect for Mr. Higashi as a manager and continually challenged his authority. Whenever a problem arose, she was quick to remind him that things were very different and much better in Britain.

Mark also had difficulties with Mr. Higashi. Mark was not much of a group player and resented Mr. Higashi's constantly telling him what to do. He preferred to withdraw and work on his own. He didn't like Mr. Higashi's paternalistic attitude. He just wanted to be treated like a normal, capable employee and given free rein to do his work. As a show of his independence, Mark refused to join in on any of the "drinking meetings" after work.

THE JAPANESE OPINION OF THE ALTS

The other Japanese employees in the office found it difficult to work with the ALTs because, as far as they were concerned, the ALTs were never there long enough to become part of the group. It seemed like just after they got to know one ALT, he or she left and was replaced by another. Another problem was that since the foreigners usually did not speak Japanese, communication with them was extremely frustrating.

The biggest problem that the employees at the board of education office had with the ALTs was that they were so young and inexperienced. All of the men in the office had worked a minimum of 20 years to reach this stage in their careers, only to find themselves working side by side with foreigners who had recently graduated from college. To make matters worse, these young foreigners were also hired to advise them how to do their jobs better. The employees were also aware that the ALTs earned practically the same salary as their supervisor each month.

The Japanese employees did not consider the ALTs to be very committed workers. They never stayed past 5:00 P.M. on weekdays, and never came to work on the weekends even though the rest of the office did. It seemed as though the ALTs were rarely at the office. The ALTs also made it very clear that they had a contract that allowed them vacation days, and they made sure that they used every single day. The Japanese employees, on the other hand, rarely ever made use of their vacation time and knew that if they took holidays as frequently as the foreigners, they could return to find that their desk had been cleared.

THE INCIDENT

Kelly woke up one Monday morning with a high fever and a sore throat. She phoned Mr. Higashi to let him know that she wouldn't be coming in that day and possibly not the next. Mr. Higashi asked if she needed anything and told her to relax and take care of herself. Before he hung up, Mr. Higashi told her that when she came back to the office, to make sure to bring in a doctor's note. Kelly was annoyed. The last thing she wanted to do was to get out of bed and go to the clinic for a simple case of the flu. As she was getting dressed she thought she was being treated like a schoolgirl by being forced to bring in a note.

Two days later, Kelly returned to the office with the note from a physician in her hand. Andrea informed her that Mark and Suzanne had also been sick and that she had been by herself in the office. She also said that Mr. Higashi was suspicious that the three of them had been sick at the same time and had commented that he knew that foreigners sometimes pretended to be sick in order to create longer weekends. Kelly was glad that she had gone to the doctor and got a note so she could prove that she was really sick. Kelly said good morning to Mr. Higashi and gave him her note. He took it from her without so much as looking at it and threw it onto a huge pile of incoming mail on his desk. He asked her if she was feeling better and then went back to his work.

At midmorning, the accountant came over to Kelly's desk and asked her to sign some papers. Kelly reached for her pen and started to sign automatically until she noticed that she was signing for two days of paid leave and not sick leave. She pointed out the error to the accountant, who told her that there had not been a mistake. Kelly told the accountant to come back later and went over to speak with Mr. Higashi. To her surprise, Mr. Higashi said that there had been no mistake and that this was standard procedure in Japan. He said that typical Japanese employees normally did not make use of their vacation time due to their great loyalty to the company. If an employee became sick, he often used his paid vacation first out of respect for his employers.

Kelly responded that this was fine for Japanese employees, but since she was not Japanese, she preferred to do things the Canadian way. Mr. Higashi replied that since she was in Japan, maybe she should start doing things the Japanese way. Kelly turned away and looked at Andrea, not believing what had just happened.

The next day, both Mark and Suzanne returned to the office only to find themselves in the same predicament as Kelly. Suzanne called Mr. Higashi a lunatic and Mark chose to stop speaking to him altogether. Kelly was furious that they were being forced to waste two of their vacation days when they were guaranteed sick leave. She threw the JET contract on Mr. Higashi's desk and pointed out the section that stipulated the number of sick days they were entitled to and demanded that he honor their contract as written.

Mr. Higashi looked extremely agitated and said that he had to go to a very important meeting and would discuss the situation later. The accountant reappeared with the papers for the three ALTs to sign, but they all refused. Suzanne started to complain about Mr. Higashi's incompetence, while Mark complained about the Japanese style of management. Suzanne said that it was a shame that none of them had bothered to join AJET, for wasn't this the kind of problem that unions were supposed to handle? Kelly stared at the contract on her desk and said that they could take it to a higher level and involve CLAIR. Andrea said that things could get ugly and people could lose face if it went that far. Kelly took her agenda out of her desk and started looking for CLAIR's phone number.

DISCUSSION QUESTIONS

1. What should Kelly and the other ALTs do now?
2. Why did conflict occur? How could it have been prevented?

Questionnaires

The Personal Bargaining Inventory

INTRODUCTION

One way for negotiators to learn more about themselves, and about others in a negotiating context, is to clarify their own personal beliefs and values about the negotiation process and their style as negotiators. The questionnaire in this section can help you clarify perceptions of yourself on several dimensions related to negotiation—winning and losing, cooperation and competition, power and deception—and your beliefs about how a person "ought" to negotiate. Your instructor is likely to ask you to share your responses with others after you complete the questionnaire.

ADVANCE PREPARATION

Complete the Personal Bargaining Inventory questionnaire in this exercise. Bring the inventory to class.

Personal Bargaining Inventory Questionnaire

The questions in this inventory are designed to measure your responses to your perceptions of human behavior in situations of bargaining and negotiation. Statements in the first group ask you about *your own behavio*r in bargaining; statements in the second group ask you to judge *people's behavior in general.*

Part I: Rating Your Own Behavior

For each statement, please indicate how much the statement is *characteristic of you* on the following scale:

1 Strongly uncharacteristic
2 Moderately uncharacteristic
3 Mildly uncharacteristic
4 Neutral, no opinion
5 Mildly characteristic
6 Moderately characteristic
7 Strongly characteristic

Adapted from an exercise developed by Bert Brown and Norman Berkowitz.

Rate each statement on the seven-point scale by writing in one number closest to your personal judgment of yourself:

Rating	Statement
_____	1. I am sincere and trustworthy at all times. I will not lie, for whatever ends.
_____	2. I would refuse to bug the room of my opponent.
_____	3. I don't particularly care what people think of me. Getting what I want is more important than making friends.
_____	4. I am uncomfortable in situations where the rules are ambiguous and there are few precedents.
_____	5. I prefer to deal with others on a one-to-one basis rather than as a group.
_____	6. I can lie effectively. I can maintain a poker face when I am not telling the truth.
_____	7. I pride myself on being highly principled. I am willing to stand by those principles no matter what the cost.
_____	8. I am a patient person. As long as an agreement is finally reached, I do not mind slow-moving arguments.
_____	9. I am a good judge of character. When I am being deceived, I can spot it quickly.
_____	10. My sense of humor is one of my biggest assets.
_____	11. I have above-average empathy for the views and feelings of others.
_____	12. I can look at emotional issues in a dispassionate way. I can argue strenuously for my point of view, but I put the dispute aside when the argument is over.
_____	13. I tend to hold grudges.
_____	14. Criticism doesn't usually bother me. Any time you take a stand, people are bound to disagree, and it's all right for them to let you know they don't like your stand.
_____	15. I like power. I want it for myself, to do with what I want. In situations where I must share power I strive to increase my power base, and lessen that of my co-power holder.
_____	16. I like to share power. It is better for two or more to have power than it is for power to be in just one person's hands. The balance of shared power is important to effective functioning of any organization because it forces participation in decision making.
_____	17. I enjoy trying to persuade others to my point of view.
_____	18. I am not effective at persuading others to my point of view when my heart isn't really in what I am trying to represent.
_____	19. I love a good old, knockdown, drag-out verbal fight. Conflict is healthy, and open conflict where everybody's opinion is aired is the best way to resolve differences of opinion.
_____	20. I hate conflict and will do anything to avoid it—including giving up power over a situation.
_____	21. In any competitive situation, I like to win. Not just win, but win by the biggest margin possible.
_____	22. In any competitive situation I like to win. I don't want to clobber my opponent, just come out a little ahead.
_____	23. The only way I could engage conscientiously in bargaining would be by dealing honestly and openly with my opponents.

Part II: Rating People's Behavior in General

For each statement, please indicate how much you agree with the statement on the following scale:

1   Strongly disagree
2   Moderately disagree
3   Mildly disagree
4   Neutral, no opinion
5   Mildly agree
6   Moderately agree
7   Strongly agree

Think about what you believe makes people effective negotiators. Rate each statement on the seven-point scale by writing in one number closest to your judgment of what makes an excellent negotiator:

Rating	*Statement*
_____	24. If you are too honest and trustworthy, most people will take advantage of you.
_____	25. Fear is a stronger persuader than trust.
_____	26. When one is easily predictable, one is easily manipulated.
_____	27. The appearance of openness in your opponent should be suspect.
_____	28. Make an early minor concession; the other side may reciprocate on something you want later on.
_____	29. Personality and the ability to judge people and persuade them to your point of view (or to an acceptable compromise) are more important than knowledge and information about the issues at hand.
_____	30. Silence is golden—it's the best reply to a totally unacceptable offer.
_____	31. Be the aggressor. You must take the initiative if you are going to accomplish your objectives.
_____	32. One should avoid frequent use of a third party.
_____	33. Honesty and openness are necessary to reach equitable agreement.
_____	34. It is important to understand one's values prior to bargaining.
_____	35. Be calm. Maintaining your cool at *all* times gives you an unquestionable advantage. Never lose your temper.
_____	36. Keep a poker face, never act pleased as terms are agreed upon.
_____	37. A good negotiator must be able to see the issues from the opponent's point of view.
_____	38. An unanswered threat will be read by your opponent as weakness.
_____	39. In bargaining, winning is the most important consideration.
_____	40. The best outcome in bargaining is one that is fair to all parties.
_____	41. Most results in bargaining can be achieved through cooperation.
_____	42. Principles are all well and good, but sometimes you have to compromise your principles to achieve your goals.
_____	43. You should never try to exploit your adversary's personal weakness.
_____	44. A member of a bargaining team is morally responsible for the strategies and tactics employed by that team.

_____ 45. Good ends justify the means. If you know you're right and your goal is worthy, you needn't be concerned too much about *how* your goal is achieved.

_____ 46. Honesty means openness, candor, telling all and not withholding pertinent information, not exaggerating emotion. One should always be honest during bargaining.

_____ 47. Imposing personal discomfort on an opponent is not too high a price to pay for success in negotiation.

_____ 48. Regardless of personal considerations, team members should accept any role assigned to them by the bargaining team.

_____ 49. There is no need to deal completely openly with your adversaries. In bargaining as in life, what they don't know won't hurt them.

_____ 50. There is nothing wrong with lying to an opponent in a bargaining situation as long as you don't get caught.

The SINS II Scale

INTRODUCTION

The purpose of the SINS II scale is to inquire about your general disposition toward ethical issues in negotiation. It will help you determine your views on a range of ethical and unethical negotiation tactics. The instructor will explain how to score and interpret this questionnaire.

ADVANCE PREPARATION

Complete the SINS II scale as specified by your instructor.

Incidents in Negotiation Questionnaire

This questionnaire is part of research study on how negotiators decide when certain strategy and tactics are ethical and appropriate in negotiations.

In completing this questionnaire, **please try to be as candid as you can about what you think is appropriate and acceptable to do.** You are being asked about tactics that are controversial; however, your responses on this questionnaire are completely anonymous, and no one will ever know your individual responses.

You will be asked to consider a list of tactics that negotiators sometimes use. You should consider these tactics in the context of a *situation in which you will be negotiating for something which is very important to you and your business.* For each tactic, you will be asked to indicate how appropriate the tactic would be to use in this situation. Then assign a rating to each tactic, evaluating how appropriate it would be to use this tactic in the context specified above, based on the following scale:

1	2	3	4	5	6	7
Not at all appropriate			Somewhat appropriate			Very appropriate

(If you have any need to explain your rating on a tactic, please do so in the margin or at the end/back of the questionnaire.

SINS stands for Self-reported Inappropriate Negotiation Strategies. Questionnaire developed by Robert Robinson, Roy J. Lewicki, and Eileen Donahue, 1998. Modified by Roy J. Lewicki, 2001, using items developed by Bruce Barry. Used with permission of the developers.

Rating

1. Promise that good things will happen to your opponent if he/she gives you what you want, even if you know that you can't (or won't) deliver these things when the other's cooperation is obtained. _____

2. Get the other party to think that I like him/her personally despite the fact that I don't really. _____

3. Intentionally misrepresent information to your opponent in order to strengthen your negotiating arguments or position. _____

4. Strategically express anger toward the other party in a situation where I am not really angry. _____

5. Attempt to get your opponent fired from his/her position so that a new person will take his/her place. _____

6. Intentionally misrepresent the nature of negotiations to your constituency in order to protect delicate discussions that have occurred. _____

7. Express sympathy with the other party's plight although in truth I don't care about their problems. _____

8. Gain information about an opponent's negotiating position by paying your friends, associates, and contacts to get this information for you. _____

9. Feign a melancholy mood in order to get the other party to think I am having a bad day. _____

10. Make an opening demand that is far greater than what you really hope to settle for. _____

11. Pretend to be disgusted at an opponent's comments. _____

12. Convey a false impression that you are in absolutely no hurry to come to a negotiated agreement, thereby trying to put time pressure on your opponent to concede quickly. _____

13. Give the other party the false impression that I am very disappointed with how things are going. _____

14. In return for concessions from your opponent now, offer to make future concessions which you know you will not follow through on. _____

15. Threaten to make your opponent look weak or foolish in front of a boss or others to whom he/she is accountable, even if you know that you won't actually carry out the threat. _____

16. Deny the validity of information which your opponent has that weakens your negotiating position, even though that information is true and valid. _____

17. Give the other party the (false) impression that I care about his/her personal welfare. _____

18. Intentionally misrepresent the progress of negotiations to your constituency in order to make your own position appear stronger. _____

19. Talk directly to the people who your opponent reports to, or is accountable to, and tell them things that will undermine their confidence in your opponent as a negotiator. _____

20. Stimulate fear on my part so that the other party will think I am tense about negotiating. _____

21. Gain information about an opponent's negotiating position by cultivating his/her friendship through expensive gifts, entertaining, or "personal favors." _____

22. Pretend to be furious at my opponent. _____

23. Make an opening demand so high/low that it seriously undermines your opponent's   ——
    confidence in his/her ability to negotiate a satisfactory settlement.

24. Guarantee that your constituency will uphold the settlement reached, although you   ——
    know that they will likely violate the agreement later.

The Influence Tactics Inventory

INTRODUCTION

The questionnaire in this exercise is designed to measure your predisposition to use different influence tactics at work. In responding to these questions, you will learn something about the influence tactics that you use, depending on whom you want to influence.

PROCEDURE

Step 1

Identify three different people whom you have needed to influence at work. One should be a superior, one a subordinate, and the other a co-worker.

Step 2

Work completely through the questionnaire for *each* of the three people you have chosen, keeping only one person in mind at a time. Use the following scale to respond to each of the statements below. Be sure to respond to all of the statements for each of the three people.

5 I usually use this tactic to influence him or her.

4 I frequently use this tactic to influence him or her.

3 I occasionally use this tactic to influence him or her.

2 I seldom use this tactic to influence him or her.

1 I never use this tactic to influence him or her.

Step 3

Your instructor will hand out a scoring key. Follow the key in order to score the questionnaire.

Adapted from David Kipnis, Stuart M. Schmidt, and Ian Wilkinson, "Intraorganizational Influence Tactics: Explorations in Getting One's Way," *Journal of Applied Psychology* 65, pp. 440–52. Used with permission.

Superior	Subordinate	Co-Worker	Statement
_____	_____	_____	1. Kept checking up on him or her.
_____	_____	_____	2. Made him or her feel important ("only you have the brains, talent to do this").
_____	_____	_____	3. Wrote a detailed plan that justified my ideas.
_____	_____	_____	4. Gave no salary increase or prevented that person from getting a raise.
_____	_____	_____	5. Offered an exchange (e.g., if you do this for me, I will do something for you).
_____	_____	_____	6. Made a formal appeal to higher levels to back up my request.
_____	_____	_____	7. Threatened to notify an outside agency if he or she did not give in to my request.
_____	_____	_____	8. Obtained the support of co-workers to back up my request.
_____	_____	_____	9. Simply ordered him or her to do what I requested.
_____	_____	_____	10. Acted very humbly to him or her while making my request.
_____	_____	_____	11. Presented him or her with information in support of my point of view.
_____	_____	_____	12. Threatened his or her job security (e.g., hint of firing or getting him or her fired).
_____	_____	_____	13. Reminded him or her of past favors that I had done for him or her.
_____	_____	_____	14. Obtained the informal support of higher-ups.
_____	_____	_____	15. Threatened to stop working with him or her until he or she gave in.
_____	_____	_____	16. Had him or her come to a formal conference at which I made my request.
_____	_____	_____	17. Demanded that he or she do what I requested.
_____	_____	_____	18. Acted in a friendly manner prior to asking for what I wanted.
_____	_____	_____	19. Explained the reasons for my request.
_____	_____	_____	20. Promised (or gave) a salary request.
_____	_____	_____	21. Offered to make a personal sacrifice if he or she would do what I wanted (e.g., work late, work harder, do his/her share of the work, etc.).
_____	_____	_____	22. Filed a report about the other person with higher-ups (e.g., my superior).
_____	_____	_____	23. Engaged in a work slowdown until he or she did what I wanted.
_____	_____	_____	24. Obtained the support of my subordinates to back up my request.

The Trust Scale

INTRODUCTION

The purpose of the Trust Scale is to inquire about your general level of trust in another person before or after a negotiation. The instructor will explain how to score and interpret this questionnaire.

ADVANCE PREPARATION

Complete the Trust Scale as specified by your instructor.

PROCEDURE

1. Complete the Trust Scale.
2. Your instructor will hand out a scoring key for the Trust Scale. Follow the key in order to score your questionnaire. A description of the questionnaire and what it measures will be provided by the instructor.
3. Be prepared to share your answers to the questions with others in a small group or class discussion.

Trust Scale

Identify a *specific other person* for whom you have some level of trust. Then rate that other person on the following five-point scale:

1	2	3	4	5
Strongly disagree		Undecided		Strongly agree

Rating

1. This person's behavior meets my expectations.   ____
2. This person wants to be known as someone who keeps promises and commitments.   ____
3. This person knows that the benefits of maintaining trust are higher than the costs of destroying it.   ____

Questionnaire developed by Roy J. Lewicki and Maura Stevenson.

Trust Scale *(concluded)*

	Rating
4. This person does what he or she says he or she will do.	____
5. I hear from others about this person's good reputation.	____
6. I have interacted with this person a lot.	____
7. I think I really know this person.	____
8. I can accurately predict what this person will do.	____
9. I think I know pretty well what this person's reactions will be.	____
10. This person's interests and mine are the same.	____
11. This person and I share the same basic values.	____
12. This person and I have the same goals.	____
13. This person and I are pursuing the same objectives.	____
14. I know that this person will do whatever I would do if I were in the same situation.	____
15. This person and I really stand for the same basic things.	____

DISCUSSION

In recent years, a great deal of research has been conducted on the nature of trust and the role it plays in critical social relationships. Trust is essential to productive social relationships with others, and can play a critical role in negotiations, particularly integrative negotiations. High trust contributes to better negotiations, and more cooperative, productive negotiations are likely to enhance trust. Conversely, low trust may contribute to less productive negotiations, and less productive negotiations are likely to decrease trust.

There are many definitions of trust, reflecting different views about trust as either a core characteristic of one's personality or a set of situation-based perceptions and expectations shaped by what we know about the other party and the situation in which that relationship occurs. In discussing it here, we will define *trust* as an individual's belief in, and willingness to act on the basis of, the words, actions, and decisions of another.

Recent research on trust suggests that there are three different types of trust—calculus-based trust, knowledge-based trust, and identification-based trust:

- *Calculus-based trust* is based on consistency of behavior—that people will do what they say they are going to do. Behavioral consistency is sustained by offering either the promise of rewards for people who do what they say they are going to do or the threat of punishment (e.g., loss of relationship) that will occur if consistency is not maintained (i.e., when people do *not* do what they say they will do). This type of trust is based on an ongoing, economic calculation of the value of the outcomes to be received by creating and sustaining the relationship relative to the costs of maintaining or severing it. Not only are these rewards and punishments given directly to the other, but we also can reward or punish the other by enhancing or destroying the other's reputation with friends, associates, and business partners if they honor or violate the trust.

- *Knowledge-based trust* is grounded in the other's predictability—knowing the other sufficiently well so that the other's behavior can be anticipated. Knowledge-based trust relies on information rather than rewards and punishments. It develops over time, largely as a function of the parties having a history of interaction that allows them to get to know the other well enough to understand how the other thinks, what is important to him or her, and how he or she is likely to behave in a variety of situations. There are several dimensions to knowledge-based trust. First, and most simply, information contributes to the predictability of the other, which contributes to trust. The better one knows the other, the more accurately one can predict what the other will do. Second, predictability enhances trust—even if the other is predictably unreliable—because we can predict the ways that the other might violate the trust. Finally, accurate prediction requires an understanding that develops over time in multidimensional relationships (similar to calculus-based trust). In knowledge-based trust, *regular communication* and *courtship* are key processes. Regular communication puts a party in constant contact with the other, exchanging information about wants, preferences, and approaches to problems. Without regular communication, we lose touch with each other—not only emotionally but in our ability to think like and predict the reactions of the other. Second, courtship is behavior that is specifically directed at relationship development, at learning more about a possible partner. Courtship permits actors to gain enough information to determine whether the parties can work together well.

- *Identification-based trust* is based on a complete empathy with or identification with the other party's desires and intentions. At this third level, trust exists because each party effectively understands, appreciates, agrees with, empathizes with, and takes on the other's values because of the emotional connection between them—and thus can act for the other. Identification-based trust thus permits one to act as an agent for the other and substitute for the other in interpersonal transactions. The other can be confident that his or her interests will be fully protected, and that no surveillance or monitoring of the actor is necessary. A true affirmation of the strength of identification-based trust between parties can be found when one party acts for the other in a manner even more zealous than the other might demonstrate; the parties not only know and identify with each other but come to understand what they must do to sustain the other's trust. One comes to learn what really matters to the other, and comes to place the same importance on those behaviors as the other does. When one watches closely knit groups work together—such as jazz quartets, basketball teams, or skilled work groups under pressure—we get to see identification-based trust in action.

In addition to proposing these three different types of trust, recent theorizing on trust suggests several additional aspects to this approach to trust:

- The three types of trust are linked sequentially; that is, in most relationships, calculus-based trust develops first, followed by knowledge-based trust and then identification-based trust.

- Not all relationships move to the identification-based trust level. Most relationships do not develop past calculus-based trust, while only the closest, most personal, and most intimate develop true identification-based trust.

- Trust probably develops slowly over time but can decline rapidly if the other side violates the trust.

- Repairing violated or broken trust is a very complex, difficult process.

Communication Competence

Generally speaking, *communication competence* can be defined as the ability to enact both appropriate and effective messages in any communication setting. Appropriate communication conforms to the expectations and rules of a situation, while effective communication allows parties in an interaction to achieve their goals. Communication competence, then, is a broad construct that refers to the ability to accurately assess situations and other people and respond to them in ways that allow you to get what you want while still complying with social rules and expectations.

The scale below is a diagnostic tool to help you determine your current level of communicative competence. Answer the questions as honestly as you can, thinking about what you actually do in most situations you encounter. Once you have completed the instrument, your instructor will help you interpret your score.

Directions
The following are statements about the communication process. Answer each as it relates to what you generally think about concerning social situations. Please indicate the degree to which each statement applies to you by placing the appropriate number (according to the scale below) in the space provided:

    5 Always true of me
    4 Often true of me
    3 Sometimes true of me
    2 Rarely true of me
    1 Never true of me

Rating	*Statement*
_____	1. Before a conversation, I think about what people might be talking about.
_____	2. When I first enter a new situation, I watch who is talking to whom.
_____	3. During a conversation, I am aware of when a topic is going nowhere.
_____	4. After a conversation, I think about what the other person thought of me.
_____	5. Generally, I think about how others might interpret what I say.
_____	6. After a conversation, I think about my performance.
_____	7. During a conversation, I am aware of when it is time to change the topic.

Adapted by Roy J. Lewicki from R.L. Duran and B.H. Spitzberg, "Toward the Development and Validation of a Measure of Cognitive Communication Competence," *Communication Quarterly* 43, (1995), pp. 259–75. Used with permission.

Rating	*Statement*
_____	8. When I first enter a new situation, I try to size up the event.
_____	9. Before a conversation, I mentally practice what I am going to say.
_____	10. After a conversation, I think about what I said.
_____	11. Generally, I think about the consequences of what I say.
_____	12. Before a conversation, I think about what I am going to say.
_____	13. Generally, I study people.
_____	14. After a conversation, I think about what I could have said.
_____	15. When I first enter a new situation, I think about what I am going to talk about.
_____	16. Generally, I think about how what I say may affect others.
_____	17. During a conversation, I pay attention to how others are reacting to what I am saying.
_____	18. Generally, I am aware of people's interests.
_____	19. During a conversation, I think about what topic to discuss next.
_____	20. After a conversation, I think about what I have said to improve for the next conversation.
_____	21. Generally, I think about the effects of my communication.
_____	22. During a conversation, I know if I have said something rude or inappropriate.

Title Index

Name Index

Names printed in **bold face** are of authors with selections in this volume, along with the appropriate page references.

A

Abel, R. L., 20n
Achen, Christopher H., 191n
Adler, Nancy J., 350, 391, 415
Agnew, J., 278
Alba, R., 206n
Alger, C. V., 393
Ali, Faizunisa, 351
Allen, Robert W., 186, 191n
Allred, A., 493n
Altany, David, 351
Althen, G., 413
Amick, B., 494n
Anand, R. P., 351
Anderson, J. C., 452n
Anderson, Terry, 122
Andrews, I. R., 39n
Andrews, J. Douglas, 352
Andrulis, R., 492n
Aoki, M., 278
Archibald, K., 140
Ardagh, J., 414
Arrow, Kenneth, 264, 278
Asbrand, Deborah, 130
Ashford, Susan E., 158
Austin, Nancy, 206n
Axelrod, R., 139

B

Babcock, L., 494n
Bacharach, S. B., 39n, 247, 253n
Bagur, J. Susanna, 351
Banks, John C., 351
Barnard, Chester I., 264, 278
Barnes, J. W., 413, 414
Barnum, Cynthia, 351
Barry, Bruce, 336, 647
Barsoux, J. L., 414
Bartholomew, S., 391
Bartolomé, F., 204n, 205n
Barzini, Luigi, 413, 414
Baskett, G. D., 285, 286
Bass, Bernard M., 191n
Bazerman, Max H., 21n, **142,** 151,
    159, 253n, 265, 278, 456, 459,
    465, 466, 494n
Beamer, L., 493n
Beauchamp, Thomas, 229, 455, 465
Beliaev, Edward, 351
Bell, N., 494n
Bell, Robert, 204, 204n
Bellenger, L., 414
Beltramini, R. F., 415
Belzer, Ellen J., 130
Bennett, J., 493n